SEW FAR ✦ SEW GOOD

The Comprehensive Sourcebook for Home and Professional Sewers, Quilters, Beaders, Needleworkers, Weavers, Knitters, and Other Creative Persons

HEATHER M. CLAUS

Oracle Publications

Edited by Grant Moser
Illustrations by Christopher Rich
Other Illustrations by Heather M. Claus
Cover and Text Design by Heather M. Claus
Illustrations Copyright ©1996 by Heather M. Claus
Text Copyright ©1996 by Oracle Publications

Oracle Publications
1226 Carroll Avenue, Ames, Iowa 50010
Phone (515) 233-6226, Fax (515) 233-6744, E-mail OraclePubl@aol.com

Printed by: Heuss Printing, Ames, Iowa

Bound by: Tallerico, Des Moines, Iowa

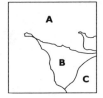

Yarns

A. Provided by Mountain Colors.
B. Provided by Bergere de France.
C. Provided by Aurora Silk.

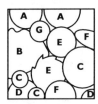

Buttons

A. Provided by Oiye Buttons.
B. Provided by P.L. Greene's Country Jumpers and Handpainted Buttons.
C. Provided by Stone Age.
D. Provided by Fresh Water Pearl Button Company.
E. Provided by Renaissance Buttons.
F. Provided by Wood Forms.
G. From the author's collection.

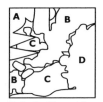

Fabric Swatches

A. Provided by Bead In Hand.
B. Provided by Soho South.
C. Provided by The Copper Coyote.
D. From the author's collection.

Fabric Swatches

A. Provided by Dimples.
B. Provided by Batiks Etcetera.
C. Provided by Sawyer Brook Distinctive Fabrics.
D. Provided by The Seraph Textile Collection.
E. Provided by Waechter's Silk Shop.
F. Provided by Super Silk.
G. Provided by Outdoor Wilderness Fabrics.
H. Provided by Fabric Gallery.

Various Metal and Metallic Threads

All ten varieties provided by Kreinik Manufacturing Co., Inc.

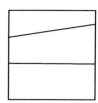

Sewing Checks

All three provided by Styles Check Company.

This book is dedicated to my mother,
who inspired and encouraged me, and to
Gerard, without whom many things
would have been impossible.

Table of Contents

Introduction

Just a note on why this book was done, how I feel about it, and how to register for your free update.

Have you ever looked in a fashion magazine and thought to yourself, "How do they make clothes that look so great? I know how to sew, but my efforts never look like that."

Or have you ever seen a beautiful knitted cashmere sweater, decided to make one for yourself, then found that your local store only carried pastel acrylics?

What about the time you were inspired to learn to weave, but couldn't find any classes or supplies?

After months of painstaking research, I am happy to present to you the book that will change the way you look at your creative choices with fibers and fabric.

This book will show you where to find your supplies, how to get instruction—in person, and by video—and even provide information on starting or running your own business.

We originally began this endeavor part-time, but it soon took over our lives. We worked long hours to gather as much information as possible to put into this first edition, and we have already begun to gather more for the second edition and update. The second edition is guaranteed to have more of everything.

We're committed to making this the best sourcebook ever, to keeping our information current, and to making sure that you will always have access to it. Your first update is free, and we'll offer subsequent update for a special discount. We want this to be your resource guide through the next decade.

We welcome any comments and suggestions on how we can make this book better, more complete, and easier to use.

There are several forms provided in the back of the book for your use. One is for the registration of this edition and your comments. For your free update, you must send the original page. <u>No photocopies will be accepted</u>.

If you own a company connected with fabric and fibers, and are interested in listing your company in the next edition of <u>Sew Far Sew Good</u>, you will find the necessary forms in the back as well. The listing is free of charge, we simply ask that you be as thorough as possible in your response, so that your potential customers are able to make an informed decision.

Thank you for your interest in <u>Sew Far Sew Good</u>. We look forward to hearing from you.

Heather M. Claus

Satisfaction Guarantee

We at Oracle Publications think that you will be completely delighted with <u>Sew Far Sew Good</u>. If you are not satisfied—for any reason—then we will refund the full cover price. Just call us to let us know why you would like to return your copy, and we will help you with your return. That's all there is to it!

How To Use This Book

Here are a few helpful hints to help you find what you are searching for.

I have been as complete as possible in cross-referencing and indexing this book, so there are several ways to get the most out of it, depending upon your needs and personality.

A good choice with any book is to just skim through it, stopping at interesting words, generally getting the feel for what it contains, and how it is laid out. Once you have done that and feel comfortable with the information it contains, start looking for your specific interests. You can look at the first page of a chapter to find out what kinds of items are in that chapter; you can browse chapters to find specific companies; or you can look in the index for a keyword and find the page you want to use.

In order for you to get the most out of this book, I'll mention a few things that you should be aware of. Some of these things you will find elsewhere as reminders, but I have collected them all here for easy reference.

Please keep in mind that in my quest for unique products and services, I have contacted quite a few businesses. Many of these businesses provided an 800 number to be used for ordering, and another number to be used for questions and information. If a company has asked that an 800 number be used only for ordering, then the 800 number is listed after their regular number. Please be courteous to the businesses and use the phone numbers appropriately.

Many businesses offer wholesale prices to qualified businesses. A qualified business is one with both a resale permit and a Federal Employer Identification Number (EIN). If you are not a business, or cannot supply one or both of these pieces of information, you will not be able to purchase wholesale, no matter how much you purchase. Also remember, reputable businesses will send a wholesale order only to an address licensed by a resale number. This is not only a good business practice, it also helps wholesale dealers avoid trouble. Once again, your courtesy in these matters is appreciated.

In the product listings, the title of video topics, audio tapes, computer software, books, and other publications are printed in bold italics. However, in the company listings, such titles are printed in regular italics.

I have set all e-mail addresses in lower case letters throughout this book. You can use all lower case letters in e-mail addresses and rest assured that your e-mail will get to the right business.

Please note that although each Compuserve address number is typed with a period (.), such as 75643.7894, when you try to contact a company from any service other than Compuserve (such as AOL, Prodigy, Genie, E-world, and others), you must replace the

How to find particular sideline information...

Each sideline will be indexed by title.

This information will give credit to the source I have received the sideline information from. If it is a company, I will let you know where to find their listing. If it is a person, I will list their name–and company, if applicable. If the source is a book, I will give the title, author, copyright date and publisher.

Hint attributions...

There are hundreds of sidelines throughout this book, and each of them contains a snippet of information, an illustration, or an interesting quote related to fibers and fabric.

Many of these sidelines have been generously provided by companies or individuals, and each has been given due credit.

Others sidelines have been taken from various books, many of which are no longer in print. Each of these is noted by the title, author, copyright date, and publisher of the book.

Many more of these tips are common sense, public domain, illustrations, or ideas directly from myself. These have not been given any attribution at all. (This will save you from having to read my name too many times.)

period with a comma and include the Compuserve addressor. So, when you are typing in an address such as the one above, it will look like this: 75643,7894@compuserve.com.

Although many of these companies accept cash as a payment option in their stores, I have chosen not to include this as an option in their company listings. I have created this book primarily as a reference for mail and phone order sources, and have provided you with options that are acceptable forms of payment through the mail and over the telephone. Also, as always, sending cash through the mail is not a good idea.

If a company does not have a store for you to visit, and they have made me aware of that, I have included that in the company's information. However, many companies without stores may not indicate that in their listings. So, if you are planning to visit one of the companies listed, please call to confirm that they have a store and their hours of operation, before you are disappointed with a post office box after a long trip.

Below is a sample listing, with explanations of the categories. There are a few categories that I have added here and there for clarification, but those shown below are the most common.

I hope this forward has offered you the information you need to make the most of the resources available to you in this book. Happy hunting!

Company Name
It will tell you here if it is wholesale or mail order only, if it is in parentheses, it is part of the company name, such as: (A Division of So & So).
The company address. If both a street and P.O. Box are included, use both when addressing your envelope.
Phone: Company phone number.
Fax: Company fax number. If the phone and fax are the same, please call before faxing to allow them time to switch to fax mode.
E-mail: Company internet address.
Web Page: Company web site.
Services/Merchandise: Products they carry and services they offer, general company description.
Payment Options: The payment they accept for mail order purchases.
Shipping Options: Which shippers they use regularly.
Minimum Order: What their minimum order is.
Membership Dues: How much it costs to join their club.
Club/Association Benefits: Benefits of being a part of their club, OR benefits they offer national guilds and associations, such as 10% discount to ASG members.
Other Information: More information about the company, including, but not limited to, company history, how many years they have been in business, more products and services, etc.
Special Discounts/Offers: Special discounts to the readers of *Sew Far Sew Good*, whether a company offers wholesale, quantity, or educational discounts.
Author's Note: A thought or two from me here and there about various companies and their products.
Catalog: How much they charge for their catalog, and whether it is refundable with a purchase.

Product Listings

Accessory Findings

Findings for purses, shoes, chatelaines, candy jars, etc.

Beaded purse straps…

When designing and stringing a beaded purse strap, remember to attach clasps at both ends.

This allows you to interchange hand-beaded straps, making your handbag more wearable.

Tip provided by:
Janene A.O. Samet
Bead Works
Page 247

Are they taking you to the cleaners?

Try cleaning sterling silver with baking soda and a little water, then rinse.

No more expensive jewelry cleaning solutions!

Tip provided by:
Boca Loca Beads
Page 251

Cufflinks...

It's easy to make cuff-flinks that match your buttons.

All you need is a little wire or two jump rings, and four shank buttons–two for each cuff-link.

Use the wire or jump rings to connect two of your buttons so that they move easily (see the picture below). Connect the other two buttons in the same way. Now you have your cuff-links.

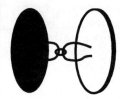

*From accessory find-
ings to quick fixes...*

*Buy some earring posts
or tie tacks to make
quick-attach buttons for
emergency situations.*

*Just glue a tie tack or
earring post to the back
of a button, and pin
through your button
placket to replace your
missing button.*

*If the earring post is too
long, and causes discom-
fort, clip it down with a
pair of wire cutters.*

*If you keep an extra tie
tack or earring post and
some glue in your purse,
you can make an emer-
gency button that match-
es your garment as soon
as the button falls off.*

Button covers

Clasps

Cones

Crimp beads

Earring findings

Eye pins

Head pins

Metal cast feathers

Key rings

Tie tack mounts

Sterling silver

The Ornamental Resources catalog has 26
pages full of findings for jewelry and
accessories.

Barrette bases

Blank button covers

Bolo tie supplies

Buckles

Earring clips

Earring hoops

Earring posts

Endless hoops/Memory Wire

Hair forks

Handbag frames

Mounting plates for collage jewelry
with buttons, beads, etc.

Scarf slides

Toggle clasps

Brooches

Porcelain boxes

Bra and slip accessories

Bra closures

Underwires

Buckles

Knapsack and backpack clips

Shoulder pads

Beads & Beading

I have tried not to repeat the word "bead" unless absolutely necessary for clarification.
You can assume that if there is no description, it is a bead.

7 Trumpets Bead Studio

Page 237

They have a full line of beads and beading supplies:

Austrian crystals

Chevron

Cinnabar

Cloisonné

Czech glass

Faux pearls

Pearls

Semi-precious

Thread

Tigertail wire

Trade

Accents Bead Shop

Page 237

Antique

Glass

Metal

Pearls

Semi-precious

Tools

ARA Imports, Inc.

Page 241

Balinese

Corals

Indian

Pearls

Precious

Precious metal findings

Semi-precious

Audlin

Page 243

Antique

Venetian

Old turquoise

Pre-Columbian

Old Roman

Bally Bead Company

Page 245

Bally Bead Company's catalog contains a huge variety of metal beads and charms. They have more than the basics of other types of beads.

African glass

African turquoise

African wood

American turquoise

Austrian crystals

Bali silver

Bone

Chinese turquoise

Cinnabar

Cloisonné

Coins

Czech seed

Ethiopian silver crosses

Faux pearls

Fetishes

Filigree enamel

Gold-plated

Heishi

Hollow blown glass beads, with the pictures painted inside the bead

Indian glass

Indian silver

Lampwork

Bead dangles...

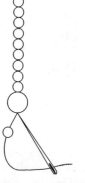

Great for trim on a scarf, the bottom of an evening bag, or on your own beaded pouch.

Couching...

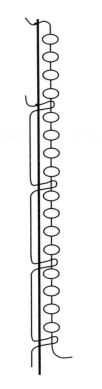

This is a very easy stitch to use while attaching a string of beads in a line, to a seam, or around the edges of a jacket.

Leather cord

Mali amber

Peruvian handpainted

Precious

Rattail cord

Semi-precious

Silver-plated

Soft Flex wire

Tigertail Wire

Trade

Barbara L. Grainger Enterprises
Page 246

BeadAcademy, a beading correspondence course

Bead in Hand
Page 247

Bead Store Café
Page 247

Bead Works, Inc.
Page 247

BeadZip
Page 248

BeadZip offers single beads, and also carries many bead and finding samplers, so you can try things out without making an expensive commitment.

Austrian crystals

Bali Silver

Bone

Chevron

Chinese carved turquoise

Chinese porcelain

Cinnabar

Cloisonné

Czech glass

Faux pearls

Filigree enamel

Gold-plated

Heishi

Indian glass

Indian silver

Leather cord

Mali amber

Mirace

Pearls

Peking glass

Peruvian

Precious

Rattail cord

Semi-precious

Silver-plated

Thai

Thread

Tigertail wire

Trade

Beadazzled, A Bead Emporium
Page 248

Beads & Beyond
Page 248

Beads & Rocks
Wholesale Only
Page 248

Beads Galore International, Inc.
Page 248

Austrian crystal

Bone

Chevron

Cinnabar

Cloisonné

Coral

Czech glass

Fetishes

Metal

Pearls

Semi-precious

Silver

Trade

Bedlam Beadworks
Page 249

Antique German glass

Beading notions

Bead boards

Czech seed

Delicas

Freshwater pearls

Semi-precious

Swarovski lead crystal

Beyond Beadery
Page 250

They specialize in seed beads.

Austrian crystals

Bone

Dichroic

Druk

Fire-polish

Seed

Blue Heron Bead Company
Page 250

Antique

Glass

Handmade

Boca Loca Beads
Page 251

Bovis Bead Co.
Wholesale Only
Page 252

French glass and metal beads

Brian's Crafts Unlimited
Page 252

Bridals International
Page 253

Buck's County Classic
Page 253

African trade

Antique silver from Thailand

Bone

Chinese carved turquoise

Cinnabar

Cloisonné

Czech lamp

Golden horn

Goldstone

Pearls

Precious metal findings

Precious

Semi-precious

Sterling rice

Sterling seed

Swarovski crystal

Taiwanese jade

Buttons & Things
Page 255

Byzantium
Page 255

African trade

Balinese

Cinnabar

Contemporary glass

Czech deco

Findings

Indian

Metal

Seed

Semi-precious

Canyon Records & Indian Arts
Page 257

Brass

Glass

Nickel

Plastic

Seed

Caravan Beads, Inc.
Page 257

Center for the Study of Beadwork
Page 259

Coastal Button and Trim
Page 260

Commercial Art Supply
Page 261

Czech glass

Czech Seed

Delica

Findings

French seed

Gemstone

Japanese seed

Trade

Copper Coyote Beads, Ltd.
Page 262

Glass drops

Glass hearts

Graph paper

2-Drop peyote

Brick

Loom

Peyote

Japanese

Seed in many unusual matte colors

Cotton Ball
Page 263

The Crowning Touch-FASTURN
Page 266

Dawn's Hide and Bead Away, Inc.
Page 268

Austrian crystal

Delica

Beads from fabric scraps...

Using a good fabric glue, a few bits of fabric or decorative paper, and a nail (or other cylindrical object), you can create your own beads.

Cut a long, triangular piece of fabric (like the one shown below), making the bottom as wide as you would like your bead to be.

Pour some glue into a small dish. Wet your fabric piece with glue, so that it is thoroughly saturated. Gently squeeze off the excess glue.

Beginning with the wide end of your triangle, wrap your fabric around the nail, making sure that you don't allow much air between the layers. When you have completed your wrapping, gently remove the nail and allow your bead to dry. Start your next bead!

This can also be done with decorative papers, threads, and ribbons.

Use a sealing varnish or polyurethane, if you would like a waterproof finish.

Be creative and explore various shapes, colors and textures.

Matte-ing beads...

To create matte beads to match others in your collection, follow these tips:

Make sure that you are not using dyed beads; the chemicals used to create a matte finish will eat the color away.

Also avoid trying to matte silver or color lined beads. With most widely available etchers, you will have to leave the beads in for some time, and this will deteriorate the lining.

Start off with a small batch and some Dip 'n Etch. This is easily found in most hobby stores, and it is easy to work with.

There are more powerful solutions available, such as Jack Frost, but they are also more toxic and require greater care.

Record the results with your test batch(es), and include information such as the beads used and length of time necessary.

Tip provided by: Gwenn Yaple Copper Coyote Beads, Ltd. Page 262

Austrian crystal

Bone

Bugle

Ceramic

Chains

Cording

Nymo

Tigertail wire

Glass

Gold-filled

Seed

Semi-precious

Sterling silver

H.E. Goldberg & Co.
Page 286

Hansa Corp.
Page 288

Handmade Venetian glass beads

Harriet's Treadle Arts
Page 289

Hedgehog Handworks
Page 289

3mm beads for embroidery

Bead Hives storage system

Bead Nabbers (helps pick up beads and hold them in a convenient position while you thread the bead)

Bead sorting trays (six tapered sections with tops, pouring spouts, and two design grooves)

Mill Hill

Heritage Looms
Page 291

Bead looms

Herrschners, Inc.
Page 291

Aurora borealis pony

Faceted

Nugget

Pendant shapes

Spacers

High Country West Needleworks
Page 291

The Hillsinger Company
Page 291

Bead carrying cases

Bead looms

Pattern designs

History International, Inc.
Page 292

Bone

Home-Sew
Page 292

Homestead Needle Arts
Page 292

Jaggerspun
Page 296

James W.M. Carroll Antiques
Page 296

Antique

Jehlor Fantasy Fabrics
Page 296

The Kirk Collection
Page 299

Variety packs for crazy quilters

L.C. Smith's
Page 300

Bugle

Crow

Czech seed

French seed

Peruvian ceramic

Seed

The Lacemaker
Page 301

Lark Books
Page 301

The Leather Factory
Page 302

Bone

Pony

Sterling silver

Leather Unlimited
Page 302

Ledgewood Studio
Page 302

M & J Trimming Co.
Page 304

All trims sold by the yard.

Beaded fringe

Beaded trim

Glass beads on tape

Pearls on tape

Satin stitch...

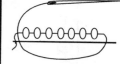

This stitch is primarily used when you would like to embroider a large area of color with beads.

Backstitch...

This is a very easy stitch to learn, and it is ideal for creating curved lines, as you can backstitch every bead, or every four beads, depending on the look you like.

Findings

Freshwater pearls

Gemstone chips

Heishi

Hare pipe

India glass

Jade

Millefiori face beads from India

Memory wire

Metal beads and fetishes

Mother of pearl beads and fetishes

Natural material

Needles

Pewter pendants and Charms

Plastic

Rattail cord

Rondells

Semi-Precious

Synthetic leather cord

Thread

Trade

Turquoise

Wood

Personal FX
Page 321

Amber

Bone

Cords

Jade

Metal

Stone

Personal Threads Boutique
Page 321

The Pin Cushion
Page 322

Planet Bead
Page 323

Prairie Edge/Sioux Trading Post
Page 323

Promenade's Le Bead Shop
Page 325

Ceylonese

Crystal

Czech

Delica

Rocaille

Semi-precious

Threads

Quest Beads & Cast, Inc.
Page 326

The Quilt Rack
Page 327

Mill Hill

Rings & Things
Wholesale Only
Page 330

Bone

Ceramic

Crystal

Gemstone

Glass

Plastic

SAX Arts & Crafts
Page 333

Shipwreck Beads
Page 336

3-cut seed

Abalone

Austrian cut lead crystal

Bells

Black Coral

Bone

Buffalo horn

Bugle

Coconut shell heishi

Cord

Cartwheel

Chevron

Craft wire

Crow

Cultura pearls

Cut lead crystal

Czech glass

Czech lamp

Czech "potato"

Czech rhinestone crosses

Czech seed

Dancing Coins

Delica

Dentillium shell

Findings

Freshwater pearls

Gemstone chips

A tip with no tip...

Beadwork is a needle-craft where you don't need a pointy needle. The holes are already in the beads.

If you take your wire cutters and snip the tip of your bead needle off, it doesn't hurt anything and:

No more piercing of threads (pierced threads are greatly weakened).

Easy mistake correction and going backwards through beads.

Fewer poked fingers.

Just snip straight across your needle tip and run the flattened end across an emery board a few times to remove burrs.

Tip provided by:
Anne Hawley
The Hillsinger
Company
Page 291

- AND -

Roni Hennen
Prodigy member, jewelry designer, beading enthusiast

Bead sizes...

2mm
3mm
4mm
5mm
6mm
7mm
8mm
9mm
10mm
12mm
14mm
16mm

Heishi
Hare Pipe
India Glass
Jade
Millefiori face beads
Memory wire
Metal beads and fetishes
Mother of pearl beads and fetishes
Natural material
Needles
Olive wood
Pewter pendants and charms
Plastic
Rattail cord
Rice
Rondell
Satina
Sequins
Snowflake obsidian
Synthetic leather cord
Thread
Trade
Turquoise
Wood

Snowgoose
Page 338

Beaded purse kits

Soho South
Page 338

14k

Bead findings

Czech crystal
Freshwater pearls
Gemstone
Glass
Gold-filled
Star
Sterling
Teardrop

Sojourner
Page 339

African
Chinese
Czech
Indian
Indonesian
Seed
Vintage

Spinning Wheel
Page 340

Stevie Didn't Do It.
Page 340
He makes beads of Fimo based on these themes:

Animals
Ankhs
Faces
Faces
Millefiori
Peace Signs
Smiles
Skeletons

Swirl
Yin/Yang

Timeless Treasures
Page 347

African
Bone
Chinese
Crystal
Czech
Enamel
Findings
German
Glass
Horn
Indian
Indonesian
Italian
Japanese
Metal
Porcelain
Semi-precious
Turkish
Vintage
Vintage findings

Universal Synergetics
Page 350
Many unique, indescribable beads. The list is just a few of the more recognizable names.

Antique seed beads
Bugle
Czech cuts

Delica

Lampworked

Pony

Pressed

Seed

Six-Sided bugle

Twisted bugle

Wakeda Trading Post

3-cut seed

Bells

Bugle

Chevron trade

Crow

Findings

Hex-cut seed

Mosaic trade

Rocaille

Seed

Tile

White hearts

Westbrook Bead Co.

The Whole Bead Show

Stem stitch...

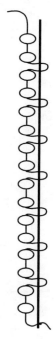

The stem stitch has a tendency to be somewhat wavy.

If you'd like to straighten your line after you've made your stitches, just bring your needle up at the beginning of your line, run it through each bead, and bring it back down through the cloth at the end of your line.

That should help smooth it out.

Blank Clothing & Fabric to Decorate

Sweatshirts, t-shirts, scarves, and many other pieces of clothing and accessories to embellish with dyes, paints, beads, embroidery, or all of the above.

5T's Embroidery Supply
Page 237

    Oxford shirts, 60% cotton/40% poly

Amazon Vinegar & Pickling Works Drygoods
Page 239

    White dyeable satin shoes

Associated Sewing Supply Co., Inc.
Page 243

Audlin
Page 243

    Silk scarves

Banasch's Fabrics
Page 245

Blueprints-Printables
Page 251

    Cotton

        Aprons

        Caftans

        Dolman tops

        Handbags

        Hapi coats

Jackets

Jumpers

Kimonos

Long skirts

Vests

    Silk

        Caftans

        Cap sleeve blouses

        Crinkled skirts

        Dolman sleeve jackets

        Dolman tops

        Finger-tip vests

        Handbags

        Hapi coats

        Jackets

        Kimonos

        Long skirts

        Long vests

        Palazzo pants

        Regular vests

        Rembrandt hats

        Ruanas

Sashes

Short sleeved blouses

Ties

Tunic blouses with belt

Viscous rayon

A-line skirts

Baggy pants

Dolman tops

Empire dresses

Fingertip vests

Jackets

Long skirts

Long vests

Palazzo pants

Regular vests

Ruanas

Sashes

Scarves

Short sleeve blouses

Split skirts

Sun dresses

Tank dresses

Scarf sizes...

Handkerchief 6" or 10" square.

Shoulder Scarf 32"–36" square.

Short Neck Scarf 10" x 20".

Long Neck Scarf 18" x 72".

Can you tell the difference?

Hemp looks and feels like its pedigreed cousin, linen. In fact, only an expert armed with a microscope can distinguish between the two fibers.

Hemp, however, is considerably more durable. In stress tests conducted by Patagonia, hemp had eight times the tensile strength and four times the durability of cotton.

Tunics

Constance Lowery

Cotton Ball

Daisy Kingdom

Dharma Trading Co.

Cotton

Aprons

Bags

Bathing suits

Bibs

Bike shorts

Boys' and girls' sailor rompers

Children's shorts

Children's T-shirts

Children's tanks

Empire bubble suits

Empire dresses for girls

Fanny packs

Gloves

Hats

Henleys

Infant A-line jumper

Infant bloomer dress

Infant jersey bubble

Infant jumpsuits

Infant onesies

Infant T-shirts

Leggings

Leotards

Light jackets

Panties (They say these look great tie-dyed!)

Playsuits

Rib knit dresses

Rib knit T-shirts

Socks

Sports bras

Sweats

T-shirt dresses

Tank tops

Thermals

Toddler A-line jumpers

Toddler dropwaist dresses

Toddler T-shirts

Toddler T-suits

Youth T-shirts

Hemp

Vests

Silk

Barrettes

Baseball caps

Bunchies for your hair

Boxer shorts

Camisoles

Earrings

Fringe shawls

Hair bows

Handkerchiefs, men's and women's

Hapi coats

Hawaiian shirts

Kimonos

Pillow covers

Pins

Ponchos

Sarongs

Scarf clips

Scarves

Skirts

Sun visors

Suspenders

T-Shirt clips

Tank tops

Ties

Earth Guild

Silk barrettes

Silk earrings

Silk scarves

The Enchanted Cottage

Exotic-Thai Silks

Scarves

Fabric Temptations

Gramma's Graphics

Grey Owl Indian Craft

Texture rubs...

Remember grade school, when you went on field trips and took rubbings of the world around you? Remember the great textures you produced?

Why not combine such an easy technique with fabric painting?

Find a prominent texture, such as brick, corrugated cardboard, etc. Lay a swatch of fabric over your texture, for a test run. Run a dry brush across the surface of the fabric, using a light touch to pick up the texture of the object underneath.

You can use more than one color, turn the fabric, or use a different texture for various effects.

Books, Magazines & Newsletters

Although most places carry more than the books listed, I couldn't list everything, so I tried to list the more interesting titles for you. We asked each company to fill out an information sheet for their books. Those listings with more information, and a general description are a result of that effort.
I think the selection here will keep you busy for quite some time!

A & B Jewels and Tools
Page 237

Accents Bead Shop
Page 237

AK Sew & Serge
Page 237

Albe Creations, Inc.
Page 238

The Alcott Press
Page 238

Complete Book of Fabric Painting
Linda Kanzinger
$32.95 postpaid
190 pages
185 illustrations

Fabric Painting Resources
Linda Kanzinger
$15.95 postpaid
64 pages

Alpel Publishing
Page 238

Catalog of Canadian Catalogs
Leila & Elie Albala
$16, postpaid

Softcover, 168 pages
Over 900 Canadian mail order sources.

Easy Halloween Costumes for Children
Leila Albala
$15.54, postpaid
Softcover, 128 pages
60 costumes for 3-12 year old children. Accessories, history, safety tips.

Easy Sewing for Adults
Leila Albala
$15.54, postpaid
Softcover, 120 pages
78 basic, timeless patterns for women and men.

Easy Sewing for Children
Leila Albala
$15.54, postpaid
Softcover, 136 pages
75 basic, timeless patterns for 3-10 year old children.

Easy Sewing for Infants
Leila Albala
$15.54, postpaid
Softcover, 120 pages
78 basic, timeless patterns for 0-24 months.

AlterYears
Page 239

Amazon Vinegar & Pickling Works Drygoods
Page 239
Amazon Vinegar & Pickling Works Drygoods carries over 1,200 books. A few of the catchier titles are listed below.

100 Traditional Bobbin Lace Patterns

A History of Costume

Authentic American Indian Beadwork

Care & Preservation of Textiles

Copy Creations

Corsets & Crinolines

Dress and Morality

Encyclopedia of Victorian Needlework

Every Lady Her Own Shoemaker

Favorite Charted Designs by Anne Orr

Hatmaking

How To Do Beadwork

Coat styles...

3/4 Trench

Knit, Net, Crochet & More of the Era of the Hoop

Natural Dyes and Home Dyeing

Old Fashioned Ribbon Art

Patterns of Fashion, Vols. I, II, & III

Renaissance Patterns for Lace, Embroidery & Needlepoint

The Ladies' Handbook of Fancy & Ornamental Work, Civil War Era

The Way to Wear'Em

American Quilt Study Group
Page 239

Uncoverings
Edited by: Sally Garoutte (1980-87), Laurel Horten (1988-93), Virginia Gunn (1995-95)
Focusing on the history of quilts, quiltmakers, quiltmaking and related topics.
$18 per volume
75-256 pages
10-50 illustrations

American Quilter's Society
Page 240

And Sew On
Page 240

Anne Powell, Ltd.
Page 241

An Illustrated History of Needlework Tools

Chatelaines

Collector's Guide to Miniature Teddy Bears

Darn It!

Toy and Miniature Sewing Machines

Victorian Brass Needlecases

Antiquity Press
Page 241

Art & Craft of Ribbonwork Vol. I

Art & Craft of Ribbonwork Vol. II

Draping & Designing With Scissors & Cloth, 1920s

Draping & Designing With Scissors & Cloth, 1930s

Ribbonry

Apparel Component Supply
Page 241

Arthur M. Rein
Page 242
(Limited supply - out of print)

How to Sew Leather, Suede, Fur
Schwebke & Krohn
$30, postpaid in U.S. (NY and CT add sales tax)
Softcover, 151 pages
250+ drawings

Associated Sewing Supply Co., Inc.
Page 243

Atlanta Puffections
Page 243

Biennial Newlsletter

Aura Registered
Page 244
Aura has hundreds of books. A few of the titles are listed below.

Aura Yarn Pattern Books

Brunswick Pattern Books

Knitting The Old Way

The Anchor Manual of Needlework

Aurora Silk
Page 244

A Silkworker's Notebook
$13.95, postpaid
Softcover, 155 pages

Hemp! For Textile Artists
$37, postpaid
Wirebound, 100 pages
All about hemp as a textile fiber. Printed on hemp paper.

Banasch's Fabrics
Page 245

Banasch's, Inc.
Page 245

Barbara L. Grainger Enterprises
Page 246

Peyote At Last!: Beginning Peyote Beadwork Technique
Barbara L. Grainger
$14.95 + $3 S&H
71 pages
Peyote at Last! is the most comprehensive peyote primer on the market today, and has received very positive reviews from *Bead & Button* and *A Beadworker's Journal.*

Peyote Design Techniques
Barbara L. Grainger
$19.95 + $3 S&H
A reference book of peyote design techniques. Although it is geared toward the intermediate to advanced

beadworker; it is also great for beginners.

Batiks Etcetera
Page 246

Bead & Button/Conterie Press
Page 247

Bead & Button
$19.95 per year (6 issues)
36-40 pages per issue
Over 100 color illustrations
Stylish beading and jewelry projects for all skill levels. An inspirational magazine to return to again and again.

Bead in Hand
Page 247

Bead Works, Inc.
Page 247

BeadZip
Page 248

20 Easy Steps to Identifying Most Beads in Most Collections
Peter Francis, Jr.
$10
Softcover, 21 pages

Advanced Beadwork
Ruth F. Poris
$14.95
Softcover, 148 pages
(I own this book and definitely recommend it. Be careful, though, you are not likley to remain a "dabbler" after this one!)

The Bead Dictionary
Peter Francis, Jr.
$11
Softcover, 47 pages

Elizabeth Ward's Step by Step Guide to Professional Bead Stringing
Elizabeth Ward
$6.75
Softcover, 24 pages

Embroidery With Beads
Angela Thompson
$32
Hardcover, 120 pages

Beadazzled, A Bead Emporium
Page 248

Beads & Beyond
Page 248

Bedlam Beadworks
Page 249

A Beadworker's Tool-Book
Pam Preslar
Graphing Tools for Beadwork
$16.95
Spiral Bound, 104 pages
A comprehensive collection of nearly 100 easy-to-copy graph papers for seven different stitches and many styles (different sizes, round beads, Delicas, etc.) A one-time investment.

Basics of Bead Stringing
Mel Anderson
$4.95
56 pages

Bead Talk
Peggy Crisman and Shirley Worley
$8.95
201 pages, illustrated

Beaded Bags
Beverly Mayfield
$6.99

11 pages

The Beading Book
Julia Jones
$29.95
Hardcover, 142 pages
Color photos

Beautiful Beads
Alexandria Kidd
50+ Bead Projects
$19.95
128 pages

Picot Lace
Sandy Forrington
$22
160 pages
A technique that combines tatting and beadwork.

Beaded Amulet Purses
Nicolette Stessin
$19.95
72 pages

The History of Beads, Concise Edition
The history of beads from 30,000 B.C. to the present.
$19.95
136 Pages

Berman Leather Co.
Page 249
They carry many books on working with leather

Blueprints-Printables
Page 251

Blueprints on Fabric: Innovative Uses for Cyanotype
Barbara Hewitt
$12.95
Softcover, 96 pages

Needle threading made easy...

Needle eyes are wider on one side than the other. If you are having trouble threading a needle, try turning it over.

Moisten the needle eye rather than the thread end. The moisture attracts the dry fibers, and the thread does not expand by soaking up your saliva.

Tailors thread needles by pinching the thread between the thumb and index finger of their dominant hand, so that only the tiniest bit of thread sticks up. They then lay the needle eye on top of the thread. With this method, you'll soon be able to thread the thinnest needle almost without looking.

Thread has grain (even filament thread). Close your eyes as you stroke the thread to feel which direction raises its nap and which smoothes it. Thread it so that it pulls through the eye in the smoothing direction.

Tip provided by: The editors at Bead & Button/ Conterie Press Page 247

Length Measurement chart for women...

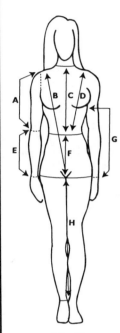

A. Arm (Shoulder to Elbow)

B. Shoulder to Crotch (Vertical Trunk)

C. Neck to Waist

D. Shoulder to Waist

E. Arm (Elbow to Wrist)

F. Crotch Depth (Waist to Crotch)

G. Arm (Underarm to Wrist)

H. Crotch to Ankle (Inseam Length)

Full-color throughout

Boca Loca Beads
Page 251

Bonfit America, Inc.
Page 251

Fashion Concepts and Design
Martin Fung
$19.95
Softcover, 144 pages
Designing fashions that will flatter your figure.

Fashion Sewing Instructions
$14.95
112 pages

Brookfield Craft Center
Page 253

Quarterly Newsletter

Retail Books

Butterick Company, Inc.
Page 254
In addition to their pattern magazines, they also carry books on sewing and knitting.

Butterick Home Catalog

Vogue Patterns Magazine

Vogue Knitting Magazine

Buttons 'n' Bows
Page 255

Byzantium
Page 255

C & T Publishing
Page 258
They have a wide variety of quilting, sewing and related crafts books. A few of their titles are listed below.

88 Leaders in the Quilt World Today

Beyond the Horizon: Small Landscape Appliqué
Valerie Hearder
$21.95
Softcover, 80 pages
96 color illustrations

Elegant Stitches: An Illustrated Stitch Guide and Sourcebook of Inspiration
$24.95
Hardcover, 176 pages
Color throughout

Faces & Places: Images in Appliqué

Hats: A Heady Affair

Heirloom Machine Quilting

Imagery on Fabric

Impressionist Quilts
Gai Perry
$24.95
Softcover, 128 pages
94 color illustrations

Mariner's Compass Quilts

Memorabilia Quilting
Jean Wells
$17.95
Softcover, 96 pages
38 color illustrations

Nifty Neckwear
Virginia Avery
$11.95
Softcover, 32 pages
Color throughout

Schoolhouse Appliqué

The Art of Silk Ribbon Embroidery

Judith Baker Montano
$21.95
Softcover, 120 pages
42 color plates

The Crazy Quilt Handbook

The Fabric Makes the Quilt

Canyon Records & Indian Arts
Page 257
They carry books on beading and American Indian crafts.

Caravan Beads, Inc.
Page 257

Carol Harris Co.
Page 257

Center for the History of American Needlework
Page 258

Center for the Study of Beadwork
Page 259
They also carry back issues of magazines with beading articles

Africa Adorned
Angela Fisher
$65
Hardcover, 304 pages
Full-color with many pages of African dress and beads.

Delica Bead Loom
Miyuki Shoji Co., Ltd.
$28
Hardcover, 72 pages
Many full-color photos of the type of beadwork being done in Japan today.

Chalet Publishing
Page 259

Quilter's Travel Companion
Audrey Anderson, Editor
$10.95
Softcover, 400 pages
A guide to quilt shops across the USA and Canada. Includes addresses, hours, descriptions and maps for over 1,000 shops.

Clearview Triangle
Page 260

Building Block Quilts
Sara Nephew
$14.95
Softcover, 64 pages
16 color plates
Includes traditional favorites like Tumbling Blocks and other contemporary designs.

Mock Appliqué
Sara Nephew
$15.95
Softcover, 72 pages
Thirteen original designs and sixteen step-by-step quilt plans.

Close to Home–The Sewing Center
Page 260

Clotilde
Page 260

Clotilde carries books on a variety of topics, including appliqué, crafts, doll and toy making, quilting, and teaching children to sew. One of their most popular titles is listed below.

Sew Smart/Woven Knits and Ultrasuede
Judy Lawrence and Clotilde
$16.80
Spiral bound, 272 pages

900+ illustrations
Sew confidently with Sew Smart and avoid that loving hands-at-home look.

Coastal Button and Trim
Page 260

Button Lover's Book
(I used this book in my research, and it is great for anyone interested in buttons.)

Collins Publications
Page 260

Books and accessories designed to help you start your own sewing business–and be successful.

The "Business" of Sewing: How to Start, Maintain, and Achieve Success
Barbara Wright Sykes
$14.95
192 pages

The "Business" of Sewing
Newsletter
$15 for one year, $25 for two years

Sew To Success
Kathleen Spike
$10.95

Commercial Art Supply
Page 261

Constance Lowery
Page 261

The Sewing Secret
Constance Lowery
$20 postpaid
Softcover
How to recycle new and used clothing.

Contemporary Quilts
Page 261

The Pillow Book
Marilyn Califf
$3.50
Softcover, 26 pages
Start learning patchwork by making simple pillows.

Copper Coyote Beads, Ltd.
Page 262

An Earful of Designs

The Bead Fun Club (Japanese)

Beaded Animals in Jewelry

Decorative Beadwork

Innovative Beaded Jewelry Techniques

Kralenwerk (Dutch)

Picture Beading

The Corner Stitch, Inc.
Page 262

The Costume Society of America
Page 262

CSA News
Features listings of exhibitions and events here and abroad, lists employment and educational opportunities. Published quarterly

Dress
CSA's annual scholarly journal contains informative articles on a broad range of dress related topics.

Cotton Ball
Page 263

Cotton Clouds
Page 263

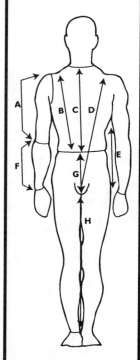

Length Measurement chart for men...

A. Arm (Shoulder to Elbow)

B. Shoulder to Crotch (Vertical Trunk)

C. Neck to Waist

D. Shoulder to Waist

E. Arm (Underarm to Wrist)

F. Arm (Elbow to Wrist)

G. Crotch Depth (Waist to Crotch)

H. Crotch to Ankle (Inseam Length)

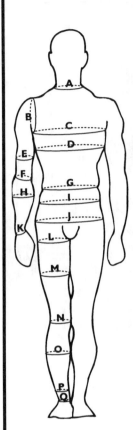

Girth/Circumference chart for men...

They have a quarterly newsletter with sales and new product information. They also carry books about knitting, crochet, spinning, weaving and other topics.

A Weaver's Book of 8-Shaft Patterns

Ashford Book of Spinning

Beadweaving

Glorious Crocheted Sweaters

Knitters Guide to Sweater Design

Learning to Weave

Sweater Design Workbook

Sweater Workshop: Teach Yourself to Knit

Tapestry Weaving

The Uncomplicated Knitting Machine

The Cotton Club
Page 263
They have a newsletter with swatch sets, new products, book reviews.

Cottons, Etc.
Page 263

Counted Thread Society of America
Page 264

Counted Thread
Counted Thread Society of America
$11 per year

Double Running
Elizabeth Stears
$5
28 pages
Gives the history of the technique, old and newer examples, and how to work the double running stitch.

Judging Counted Thread and Other Embroidery
Counted Thread Society of America
$4.95
29 pages
Contains embroidery categories for entries, sample judging forms, guidelines for judging, and definitions of embroidery techniques.

Crafter's Choice
Page 264
A Book-of-the-Month club devoted to crafting in every form, including sewing, quilting, and other fiber-related topics. They have a wide selection of books that is constantly changing.

Craftmaster Enterprises
Page 265

Craftmaster News
Marsha Reed, Editor
$30 per year
11 issues per year

Turn Your Talent Into Gold
Marsha Reed
$12.95, postpaid
60 pages

Crafts By Donna
Page 265

Baker's Dozen of Trapunto Patterns
Donna Friebertshauser
$7.95
Spiral bound, 21 pages
Full-size trapunto patterns and instructions. No previous needlework experience is required.

The Crafts Report
Page 265

The Crafts Report: The Business Journal for the Crafts Industry
$29 for a one year subscription, $52 for two years, $5 for a single copy

Creative Beginnings
Page 265

Fancy Ribbons

French Ribbons

Ribbon Basics

Ribbon Florals

Silk Ribbon Embroidery

Victorian Ribbon and Lacecraft Designs

Creative News
Page 265

Creative News-8000
For New Home 8000 enthusiasts
Eileen Roche, Editor
$20 per year
4 issues per year

Creative News-9000
For New Home 9000 enthusiasts
Eileen Roche, Editor
$20 per year
4 issues per year

Creative Quilting Magazine
Page 265

Creative Quilting Magazine
$16.97 per year
5 issues per year

The Crowning Touch-FASTURN
Page 266

Decorating With Fabric Tubes
Theresa Robinson
$6.50
12 pages

Easy Quilts With Fabric Tubes
Theresa Robinson
$6.50
12 pages

Fabric Tube Weaving Project Booklet
Theresa Robinson
$6.50
12 pages

Toobie Family
Theresa Robinson
$5.95
12 pages

Toobie Pets
Theresa Robinson
$5.95
12 pages

Crystal Palace Yarns
Wholesale Only
Page 266

Daisy Kingdom
Page 267

David Simpson, BookFinder
Page 268
He offers a search service for rare and out-of-print books.

Dawn's Hide and Bead Away, Inc.
Page 268

Decorating Digest Craft & Home Projects
Page 268

Decorating Digest Craft & Home Projects
$16.97 per year
5 issue per year

Design Originals Publications
Page 269

Design Challenges
Sigrid Sample Piroch
$24.95
160 pages
Includes fabric project, design inspiration, color, texture and historic notes on weaving presented in a workbook style.

Dharma Trading Co.
Page 269
They carry many books on fabric dyeing and painting.

All About Cotton

Colors From Nature: Growing, Collecting and Using Natural Dyes
Bobbi A. McRae
$16.16
160 pages
Drawings, charts and color photos.

Fabric Painting & Dyeing
Deborah M. Dryden
$31.45
256 pages
Color and B&W photos.

The Great T-Shirt Book

Northwest Indian Designs

Silk Painting: New Ideas & Textures
Jill Kennedy and Jane Varrall
$11.66
127 pages
Many color photos

Donna McFadden
Page 270

Quilting Through the Life of Christ
Dave and Donna McFadden
$25
Teacher's guide for lap quilting bible study.

Donna Salyers' Fabulous Furs
Page 270
Books about using synthetic furs and leathers to make clothing and accessories.

Fabulous-Furs Goes Creative
Donna Salyers
$6.95

The Great Pretenders
Donna Salyers
$6.95

Luxury Accessories
Donna Salyers
$6.95

Sewing The Fabulous Fakes
Donna Salyers
$6.95

Sewing With Fabu-Leather
Donna Salyers
$6.95

Dover Publications Inc.
Page 271

Favorite Irish Crochet Designs
Rita Weiss
$3.50
48 pages

Left-Handed Sewing
Sally Cowan
$2.95
64 pages

A. Neck Base

B. Armscye

C. Chest at Base of Armscye

D. Chest

E. Upper Arm (Bicep)

F. Elbow

G. Waist

H. Forearm

I. Abdomen

J. Hips

K. Wrist

L. Maximum Thigh

M. Midway Thigh

N. Knee

O. Maximum Calf

P. Minimum Leg

Q. Ankle

Having a hard time coordinating?

D'Leas Fabric and Button Studio offers any silk with a lining dyed to match in 95 colors. The best part of this deal is that there is only a five yard minimum.

Tip provided by: D'Leas Fabric and Button Studio Page 266

Eagle's View Publishing

Page 272

They have over 2,000 books. A few of the titles are listed below.

A Beadwork Companion: A Step by Step Illustrated Workbook for Beaded Projects
Jean Heinbuch
$10.95
Softcover, 112 pages

A Quillwork Companion: An Illustrated Guide to Techniques of Porcupine Quill Embroidery
Jean Heinbuch
$15.95 Hardcover
$9.95 Softcover
92 pages

The Techniques of North American Beadworks
Monte Smith
$15.95 Hardcover
$10.95 Softcover
106 pages

Earth Guild

Page 272

An Introduction to Multishaft Weaving

The Dyer's Companion

Creating Color–A Dyer's Handbook

Dover Pictorial Archive

Glamour Earrings For Beginners

Illustrated Dictionary of Knitting

Inspirational Silk Painting From Nature

Introduction To Batik

The Key To Weaving

Knitting Techniques Book

Lichens for Vegetable Dyeing

Marbling Paper & Fabric

New Adventures In Beaded Earrings

Sectional Warping Made Easy

The Sweater Workshop

The Tap-Dancing Lizard: 337 pictorial charted designs for the adventurous knitter.

The Embroiderers Guild of America

Page 274

They have a lending library available to their members.

Needle Arts Magazine

The Enchanted Cottage

Page 274

They carry books in a variety of topics, including crochet, embroidery, hardanger, lacemaking, ribbon embroidery, smocking and tatting.

Enterprise Art

Page 274

Eric's Press & Design & Sew Patterns

Page 274
Books by Lois Ericson:

Design & Sew It Yourself!: A Workbook for Creative Clothing
Co-author and Illustrator, Diane Ericson
$15
120 pages

Fabrics... Reconstructed: Surface techniques explored.
$14
175 pages
80 B&W photos

The Great Put On: Sew Something Smashing!
$20
208 pages
Illustrations and photos

What Goes Around
$21.95
144 pages
Illustrations and black and white photos

A Newsletter from Eric's Press:

Good News Rag
Lois Ericson and Margaret Scovil, Editors
$8 per year
6 issues per year

F & W Publications

Page 275

Creative Bedroom Decorating

Make Costumes

Teddy Bear Sourcebook

The Fabric Carr

Page 275

Creative Pattern Skills for Fashion Design

Fiberworks Sourcebook

Fitting and Pattern Alterations

Great Sewn Clothes

Fabric Gallery

Page 276

Fabric Temptations
Page 276

Carries many books related to sewing, couture, quilting, and fabric crafts. They will special order most books.

Fancywork
Page 277

Over 10,000 counted cross-stitch pattern books, and a bimonthly newsletter.

Fancywork and Fashion
Page 278

They have pattern books for doll making, and a quarterly newsletter.

Feathered Star Productions
Page 278

100 pieced Patterns for 8" Quilt Blocks

Feathered Star Quilts

Feathered Star Sampler

Guide to Rotary Cutting

Make Your Own Outdoor Flags and Banners

Pieced Borders: The Complete Resource

The Feedsack Club
Page 278

Switches and Swatches
Jane Clark Staple and Ann Eelman, Editors
$12 per year ($15 international)
6 issues per year
Newsletter devoted to feedsacks of the early 1900s.

Fiber Fantasy Knitting Products
Page 279

The Uncomplicated Knitting Machine
Leslye Soloman
$27.95+$3.50 s/h

The Fiber Studio
Page 279

Fiberfest Magazine
Page 279

Fiberfest Magazine
$20 per year in the U.S.
$30 per year in Canada
$42 per year in other countries
4 issues per year

Fire Mountain Gems
Page 280

Beadeaving: New Needlework Techniques & Original Designs
Ann Benson
$24.94
Hard cover, 144 pages
How to create beautiful beaded jewelry using one or two simple techniques.

Bead Embroidery
Valerie Campbell-Harding and Pamela Watts
$37.95
Hard cover, 128 Pages
The authors explore traditional and new ways of applying beads in embroidery.

Fiskars, Inc.
Wholesale Only
Page 280

Four Seasons Knitting Products
Page 281

Designs For Knitting Kilt Hose & Kickerbocker Stockings
Veronica Gainford
$17.50
Collected by Lady Gainford—who has spent most of her life collecting these patterns—this book is a piece of knitting history.

Photographing Your Craftwork
Steve Meltzer
$18.25
Good photos are essential for work for sale, catalogs and good records.

Shetland Lace
Gladys Amedro
$39.95
Includes dozens of patterns for cobweb and lace weight yarn, gorgeous color photos and row-by-row instructions, stitch patterns, hints, and more.

G Street Fabrics
Page 282

They stock over 4,000 titles related to sewing, crafts, quilting, decorating, etc.

Gaelic College Craft Shop
Page 282

Ghee's
Page 282

More…Texture With Textiles: More techniques for fabric embellishment.
Linda McGehee
$14.95
52 pages
Techniques include: appliqué, spiraling, lattice piecing, fuzzies, tassles.

Texture With Textiles: Manipulation and embellishment

Here's what the designers do with hemp…

Calvin Klein…

Mr. Klein had hemp in his fall '95 home line, including duvet covers, pillows, pillow shams made from a 50-50 hemp/linen blend.

"I believe that hemp is going to be the fiber choice in both the home furnishings and fashion industries, and I wanted to be one of the first designers to use this fabric in an innovative way….I love the fabric. The plan for us is to eventually introduce 100 percent hemp products."

Ralph Lauren…

For more than a decade, he has secretly used hemp fabric in his clothing lines starting with his safari-inspired fall '84 collections.

"I've always loved the look of natural, rustic fabrics….I especially like the contrast of the rugged and refined—the mix of hemp against silk—it's very romantic."

European fit...

For a better fit, cut
European patterns two
sizes smaller from the
armhole to the shoulder.

Tip quoted from:
*Power Sewing by
Sandra Betzina
Power Sewing
Page 323*

of fabric.
Linda McGehee
$13.95
40 pages
Techniques include: crinkling fabric,
couching, pintucking, corded piping,
and others.

Ginger's Needleworks
Page 283

GLP International
Page 283
All magazines include many patterns,
instructions, etc.

Anna Knitting & Needlecrafts
$40 per year
12 issues per year

Burda
$60 per year
12 issues per year

Burda Baby Boutique
$15 per year
2 issues per year

Burda Baby Knits
$15 per year
2 issues per year

Burda Blouses/Skirts/Trousers
$15 per year
2 issues per year

Burda Bonnie
$15 per year
2 issues per year

Burda Boys and Girls, Age 7-14
$15 per year
2 issues per year

Burda Bridal Fashions
$9 per year
Annual

Burda Christmas Issue
$9 per year
Annual

Burda Crochet Lace
$9 per year
Annual

Burda Crochet Projects
$9 per year
Annual

Burda Cross Stitch
$9per year
Annual

Burda Doilies
$9 per year
Annual

Burda Festive Fashions
$9 per year
Annual

Burda Filet Crochet (large format)
$15 per year
2 issues per year

Burda Filet Crochet (small format)
$10 per year
2 issues per year

Burda Home Designs
$15 per year
2 issues per year

Burda International
$40per year
4 issues per year

Burda Maternity Wear
$9 per year
Annual

Burda Men's Fashions
$9 per year
Annual

Burda Petite Fashions

$15 per year
2 issues per year

**Burda Plus Fashions for Fuller
Figures**
$30 per year
4 issues per year

Burda Quilting/Patchwork
$9 per year
Annual

Burda Sewing Made Easy
$30 per year
4 issues per year

Burda Silk Painting
$9 per year
Annual

Burda Stenciling
$9 per year
Annual

Burda Toddlers, age 2-6
$15per year
2 issues per year

Sandra Fashion Hits (knitting)
$6 per year
Annual

Sandra Knits for Large Sizes
$6 per year
Annual

Sandra Knits for Tots & Toddlers
$6 per year
Annual

Sandra Men's Knits
$6 per year
Annual

Sandra Trend Knitting
$40 per year
12 issues per year

Verena Knits for Children

$15 per year
2 issues per year

Verena Knits for Men
$9 per year
Annual

Gossamer Threads & More
Page 284

Granny's Quilts
Page 285

Great Divide Weaving School
Page 285

Great Northern Weaving
Page 295

Grey Owl Indian Craft
Page 286

The Gypsy's Bead Shoppe
Page 286

Halcyon Yarn
Page 286
Halcyon has over 900 books. A few are listed below.

> *Dye Painting*
>
> *Flavor Quilts for Kids to Make*
>
> *Miniature Crocheting and Knitting for Dollhouses*
>
> *Practical Tatting*
>
> *Reupholstering At Home*

Handweaver's Guild of America, Inc.
Page 287

Handy Hands, Inc.
Page 288

Helping Hands Newsletter
Barbara Foster, Editor
$5 per year
3 issues per year
A Newsletter For Tatters.

Needle Tatting: Books 1 & 2
Barbara Foster
$16.80 for the set
Step-by-step instructions.

Hard-to-Find Needlework Books
Page 288
They have over 10,000 books. Two recent titles are listed below.

> **China's Silk Pattern Through The Ages**
> Miao Liangyun
> $125
> 268 pages
> 401 illustrations, 239 photos
> Features the silk patterns of various stages in the Chinese history ranging from Shang Dynasty to Quing Dynasty.
>
> **Creative Hardanger**
> Sally Miller
> $12.95
> 61 pages
> Twenty pretty projects from simple bookmark or sampler to more ambitious christening gowns.

Harpagon/Sideline Design
Page 288

> **"I Do" Veils–So Can You!**
> Claudia Lynch
> $19.95
> Softcover, 140 pages
> Bridal veils, hats, and various headpieces

Harper House
Page 288
Here is a short selection of the books available from Harper House:

> **The History of Underclothes**
>
> **Late Georgian Costume: The Tailor's Friendly Instructor & The Art of Tying the Cravat (two books in one!)**
>
> **Men's Garments 1830-1900: A Guide to Pattern Cutting and Tailoring**
>
> **Period Costume for Stage and Screen, Vols 1 & 2**
>
> **Tambour Work**
>
> **The Workwoman Guide**

Harriet's Treadle Arts
Page 289

> **Heirloom Machine Quilting**
> Harriet Hargrave
> $27.95
> 176 pages
> Many color photos
>
> **Mastering Machine Appliqué**
> Harriet Hargrave
> $21.95
> 144 pages
> A comprehensive guide to machine appliqué techniques.

Harris Publications
Page 289

Hedgehog Handworks
Page 289
Hedgehog Handworks carries over 300 books. A few titles are listed below

> **20,000 Years of Costume**
>
> **ABC: Costume and Textiles from the Los Angeles County Museum of**

Salt and dyeing...

When creating dyed effects with salt, make sure that your fabric is a little more than damp, but not dripping or soaked.

Always use salt that has been stored in an airtight container, to assure that it has not picked up too much moisture from the air. You are counting on the dryness of the salt to attract the moisture, creating the starburst patterns unique to this technique.

In addition, try using resin-based paints; the effects will be more noticeable.

Inches to Millimeters to Centimeters...		
Inches	MM	CM
1/8	3	
1/4	6	
3/8	10	1
1/2	13	1.3
5/8	15	1.5
3/4	20	2
7/8	22	2.2
1	25	2.5
1 1/4	32	3.2
1 1/2	38	3.8
1 3/4	45	4.5
2	50	5
2 1/2	65	6.5
3	75	7.5
3 1/2	90	9
4	100	10
4 1/2		11.5
5		12.5
5 1/2		14
6		15
7		17.5
8		20
9		22.5
10		25
19		48.5
20		51
21		53.5
22		56
23		58.5
24		61

Art

After a Fashion: How to Reproduce, Restore & Wear Vintage Styles

Antique Sewing Tools & Tales

Art of Arabian Costume

Assisu Embroidery: Old Italian Cross Stitch Designs

Beadweaving: New Needle Techniques & Original Designs

DMC Encyclopedia

Dress Accessories: Medieval Find from Excavations in London, c. 1150–1450

Hat Book: Creating Hats for Every Occasion

Historic Textile Patterns in Full-color

Lessons in Bobbin Lacemaking

Millinery: A Complete Course

Needlework of Mary Queen of Scots

Queen Elizabeth's Wardrobe Unlocked

Ribbon Embroidery Alphabets with Iron-on Transfers

Sewing and Collecting Vintage Fashions

Heirloom Knitted Lace
Page 289
(All books are $12.70)

The Art of Lace Knitting: The Complete Works of Rachel Schnelling With Over 35 Projects

Knitted Heirloom Lace II: Beautiful

Old Lace Patterns

Knitted Heirloom Lace III: Over 20 Old Heirloom Centerpieces

Knitted Lace In Miniature: 35 Tiny Lace Doilies From 1-5 inches

Heirlooms Forever
Page 290

Helyn's Hoops
Page 290

Herrschners, Inc.
Page 291

Historic Needlework Guild
Page 292

House of White Birches
Page 293

Quick & Easy Quilting Magazine
$14.97 per year
6 issues per year

Quilt World Magazine
$14.97 per year
6 issues per year

In Cahoots
Page 293

In Cahoots Guide to Needles and Threads
Debbie L. Garbers and Janet F. O'Brien
$15
90 pages
Learn to select the correct needle and thread for your project, and why this combination will be successful.

International Fabric Collection
Page 294

Australian Themes in Machine Embroidery

Embroidered Countryside

Gardening Ribbons

Jacket Jazz

Patches of Australia

International Old Lacers, Inc.
Page 294

Interweave Press
Page 295
Magazines:

Handwoven

Spin-Off

Piecework

Interweave Knits

Interweave Beadworks

Books:

In Sheep's Clothing: A Handspinner's Guide to Wool
Nola and Jane Fournier
$24.95
Hardbound, 240 pages
Looks at 100 breeds of sheep, with special attention to the characteristics of the wool of each.

A Dyer's Garden
Rita Buchanan
$9.95
Paperbound, 112 pages
Color photos throughout
With a simple kitchen alchemy, marigold blossoms create bright golds and greens, cosmos flowers give soft corals and rust, and false indigo results in a range of blues.

Islander Sewing Systems
Page 295

Pants Etc!
Margaret Islander
$14.95
66 pages
Learn to draw your own pants pattern for a perfect fit.

Ivy Imports, Inc.
Page 295

The Complete Book of Silk Painting
Diane Tuckman and Jan Janas
$26.99
A comprehensive manual that describes the unique methods of silk painting on all fabrics.

Creative Silk Painting
Diane Tuckman and Jan Janas
$26.99
Traditional silk painting techniques are put to innovative uses.

The Silkworm Newsletter
Anne Sendgikoski, Editor
$15 per year
6 issues per year

Jehlor Fantasy Fabrics
Page 296

Be-Dazzling: Hand-Beading Techniques for Clothing and Costume
Tahia Alibek
$12.95
32 pages

Judy's Heirloom Sewing
Page 297

Elegant Stockings: Knit and

Crocheted Stockings for Dolls
Nancy Longley
$21.50+$2.50 S&H
43 pages

Thumbelina Collection: Crochet Thread Dresses for Small Dolls
Nancy Longley
$21.50
82 pages

K & K Quilteds
Page 297

Quilt Restoration: A Practical Guide
Camille Cognac
$29.95
128 pages
Information and resources for quilt restoration.

Kasuri Dyeworks
Page 298

Kay Guiles Designs
Page 298

New Ideas For Heirloom Sewing
Kay Guiles
$20
44 pages
Many illustrations
Features innovative heirloom techniques including: stitchless smocking, smocked appliqué, and shaped puffing. Patterns included.

The Creative Yoke Dress, Book I
Kay Guiles
Heirloom Sewing and Smocking
$20
44 pages
Many illustrations
A collection of patterns for girls dresses; sized 3 months to size 10.

Heirloom techniques are fully covered.

KC Publishing
Page 298

Heirloom Quilts
$24.95
150 pages
Color illustrations
Full-size templates of pattern pieces are provided, along with step-by-step instructions for assembling blocks and borders. A brief history of each quilt is also included.

Keepsake Quilting
Page 298

The Kirk Collection
Page 299
They carry many books on quilting and textiles. I've listed some of the titles that really stand out.

Encylopedia of Pieced Quilt Patterns
Barbara Brackman
$34.95

Clues in the Calico: A Guide to Identifying and Dating Antique Quilts
$39.95

North American Dye Plants
Bliss
$8.95

Old and New Quilt Patterns in the Southern Tradition
Bets Ramsey
$9.95

Repiecing the Past
Sarah Rhodes Dillow
$19.95

Inches	CM
25	63.5
26	66
27	68.5
28	71
29	73.5
30	76
31	79
32	81.5
33	84
34	86.5
35	89
36	91.5
37	94
38	96.5
39	99
40	101.5
45	115
48	120
50	127
56	140
60	150
70	175
72	180

What is millefiori?

Millefiori is literally a thousand flowers. It is also the name of a type of glass bead made of many very small pieces of glass rods, heated and pressed together to create a pattern.

Textile Designs, Two Hundred Years of European and American Patterns for Printed Fabrics Organized by Motif, Style, Color, Layout, and Period [whew, a title as long as mine!]
Susan Meller and Joost Elffers
$75 (and they say its definitely worth it!)

Kite Studio
Page 299

Kites for Everyone
Margaret Gregor
$12.95
136 pages

One Hour Kites
Jim Rolands
$14.95
95 pages

Stunt Kites to Make and Fly
Servaas van der Horst and Nop Velthuizen
$21.95
96 pages

Kreinik Mfg. Co., Inc.
Wholesale Only
Page 299

L.C. Smith's
Page 300

The Best Little Beading Book

Chinese Knotting

You Can Make Glass Beads Using a Propane Torch

Labours of Love Heirloom Sewing Supplies, Inc.
Page 300

Lace Heaven, Inc.
Page 301

Kwik-Sew™ Books
Kirstin Martin

Appliqué

Beautiful Lingerie

Sewing for Baby

Sewing for Children

Sweatshirts Unlimited

Swim and Action Wear

The Lace Merchant
Page 301

The Old Lace and Linen Merchant
A newsletter for the buyers and sellers of antique lace, linens, pre-Edwardian clothing, and textiles.
$8 per year
4 issues per year

The Secrets of Real Lace
Elizabeth M. Kurella
$16.95
70 pages
Over 100 illustrations
How to tell handmade from machine lace, and what it means to the value.

The Lacemaker
Page 301
The Lacemaker carries books about lacemaking, needlework, kumi himo, and many other thread arts. Here are just a few.

Art of Tassel Making
Sue Dickens
$39.95
Hardcover

Carickmacross Lace

Nellie O'Cleirigh
$13.95
64 pages

Creative Ribbon Embroidery
Salli Van Rensburg
$23.95

Kumi Himo, Japanese Silk Braiding Technique
Catherine Martin
$14.95

Making Fabulous Pincushions
Jo Packham
$24.95
144 pages

Needlelace
Pat Earnshaw
$23
Color illustrations

Pulled Thread Embroidery
M. McNeill
$6.95

Lacis
Page 301
Lacis has over 3,000 titles relating to textiles and costume in the subjects listed below.

Accessories

Bead embroidery

Beadwork

Blackwork

Bobbin lace

    Patterns

    Techniques

Costume, fashion

Crochet

Cross stitch

Cut work

Design

Dimensional embroidery

Discontinued titles

Dolls

Filet crochet

Filet lace/netting

Hardanger

Historical

Home decoration

Huck embroidery

Irish crochet

Knitted lace

Knitting

Kumi himo

Lace history/identification

Machine embroidery

Machine knitting

Medieval

Metal thread embroidery

Monograms

Needlelace patterns

Needlelaces/Battenberg

Needlepoint

Needlework/lace techniques

Needlework magazines

Patterns, drafting

Quilting

Ribbon embroidery

Ribbon work

Sewing

Shadow work

Smocking/French hand sewing

Special order

Tatting

Textiles/reference

Victoriana, novelty

Weaving

Lark Books
Page 301
Lark has a wide range of books on various topics. Here are a few of their titles.

Button Craft Book

The Complete Book of Silk Painting

The Costume Maker's Art

Creative Bead Jewelry

Fiberarts

Hands On Spinning

Home Decorating with Fabric

Kumihimo

Sewing the New Classics

Splendid Samplers to Cross-Stitch

Textured Embroidery

The Leather Factory
Page 302

Basic Leatherwork

Encyclopedia of Rawhide & Leather Braiding

The Leatherworking Handbook

Leather Unlimited
Page 302

Live Guides, Inc.

Page 302
Live Guides has workbooks and companion booklets for their videos.

Logan Kits
Page 303

Londa's Sewing, Etc.
Page 303

Magic Cabin Dolls
Page 304

The Dolls' Dressmaker

Feltcraft, Making Dolls, Gifts & Toys

Toymaking with Children

Mallery Press
Page 305
Mallery has several books by Ami Simms.

Classic Quilts: Patchwork Designs from Ancient Rome

Creating Scrapbook Quilts

Every Trick In The Book

How <u>Not</u> To Make A Prize-Winning Quilt

How To Improve Your Quilting Stitch

Invisible Appliqué

The Mannings Handweaving School & Supply Center
Page 305

Manny's Millinery Supply Center
Page 305

Jacket contours…

Cut interfacing for a jacket on the bias, so the jacket conforms better to the body.

Tip provided by: Power Sewing by Sandra Betzina Power Sewing Page 323

Shoe styles...

Mimi Boot

Mule

T-Strap

Pump

Marinda Stewart
Page 306

Marine Sewing
Page 306

Mary Ellen & Co.
Page 306

Here are just a few of Mary Ellen's historical books.

Civil War Ladies

Edwardian Hats

History of Underclothes

Who Wore What

Mary Jane's Cross 'N Stitch
Page 307

Mary Roehr Books & Video
Page 307

Sewing As A Home Business: How to start and operate a sewing business in your home.
Mary Roehr
$14.95
Softcover, 144 pages

Altering Women's Ready-to-Wear
Mary Roehr
$19.95
Softcover, 200 pages
300+ illustrations

Altering Men's Ready-to-Wear
Mary Roehr
$17.95
Softcover, 150 pages

Speed Tailoring
Mary Roehr
$14.95
Softcover, 45 pages

Sew Hilarious
Mary Roehr
$9.95
Softcover, 64 pages
Sewing's first cartoon book.

Mary Wales Loomis
Page 307

Make Your Own Shoes
Mary Wales Loomis
$19.95 + $3.50 S&H
Softcover, 87 pages
Full of illustrations

Mary's Productions
Page 307

Country Style Appliqués
Mary Mulari
$7.95
42 pages
Over 100 country motif appliques and 10 sewing projects to trim with appliques.

Travel Gear and Gifts to Make
Mary Mulari
$12.95
88 pages
Instructions and patterns for over 50 travel accessories and gift items, along with travel tips and a travel resource section.

Master Designer
Page 308

Master Designer has books on designing, tailoring and pattern making. Here are their titles.

Designing Men's & Boy's Garments
$29.95

Designing Women's & Children's Garments
$29.95

How to Draft and Grade the Conventional Sport Shirt
$14.95

Shirt Drafting and Grading Book
$14.95

Tailoring and Repairing
$29.95

Mimi's Books & Patterns for the Serious Dollmaker
Page 309

Mimi's Bertie: A Seventeenth Century Barmaid

Mimi's Blossom: The Universal Folk Dancer

Mimi's Dollmaker's Source-Book

Mimi's Father Christmas

Mimi's Mr. & Mrs.

Mimi's New Clays for Dollmaking: Everything you always wanted to know about the new cellulose and polymer clays

Mimi's Universal Toddler

Let's Talk About Dollmaking
$14.95 per year
Irregular arrival, sometimes twice per year, sometimes more.

Mimi's Fabrications
Page 309

Australian Sewing and Embroidery Books

Crazy Quilting and Embellishment

Embroidery Patterns

Fine Handsewing

"Mimi's" Machine Heirloom

Ribbon Embroidery

Victorian Crafts

Minifest

Page 309

This is a new annual publication with instructions for winning Minifest competitions and illustrations of favorite miniature quilts from past Minifest seminars.

Minifest Memories
Janet Wickell
$23 (estimated)
Softcover (approximately 96 pages)

Miss Maureen's Fabrics and Fancies
Page 309

Morning Light Emporium
Page 310

Morning Light Emporium offers many books on beading.

Morning Star Indian Gallery
Page 310

American Indian Needlepoint Designs
Epstein
$18
Thirty-seven authentic designs adapted for modern needlepoint projects.

Beading With Seed Beads, Gem Stones, & Cabochons
Starr
$24.95
256 pages
A how-to book with more than 60 patterns.

Quillwork Companion
Heinbuch
$9.95
Quillwork techniques explained and illustrated.

mRAYO's Fiberworks
Page 311

Machine Embroidery: Stitches & Techniques Workbook
Mary Ray Osmus
$19.95 + $3 S&H
122 pages
Free-motion embroidery on the sewing machine. There are 70 machine embroidery stitches and/or techniques in the book. Also, detailed "how-to" instructions plus designs for each side.

Nancy's Notions
Page 311

Nancy's Notions carries quite a few books on sewing, quilting, etc., as well as several books by Nancy Zieman, who stars in *Sewing With Nancy* on public television. A few titles are listed below.

Appliquilt Couture Sewing Techniques

Easy Machine Paper Piecing

Ester's Silk Ribbon Embroidery Book & Video

Exactly to the Point

Fabric Origami

French Hand Sewing by Machine

French Sewing by Serger

Fun with Fat Quarters

Grandmother's Hope Chest Book, plus Pattern Supplement

Heirloom Machine Quilting

Jacket Jazz

Make it Your Own

Peppering

Sashiko Made Simple: Japanese Quilting by Machine

Sewing Machine Fun–Sewing for Kids

Quilting Concepts in Sulky

Wardrobe Quick-Fixes

Books by Nancy Zeiman:

Let's Sew
Teens and pre-teens learn to sew.

10•20•30 Minutes to Sew

The Best of Sewing With Nancy

Sewing Express

Fitting Finesse

National Thread & Supply
Page 312

National Thread & Supply offers thee Master Designers System books. These are a few titles.

Designing Men's and Boys Garments

Designing Women's and Children's Garments

Modern Custom Tailoring for Men: Tailoring and Repairing

The Natural Fibre Club of Canada
Page 312

Shoe styles...

Spectator

Derby

Demi-Boot

Loafer

Second Impressions™

Now you can transfer photos or prints to fabric with the Second Impressions technique and Stitchless Glue. Take your photo and make either a color or black-and-white copy of it. You can also transfer prints from magazines but the glossy ones don't work as well as others. You may want to experiment before you begin.

Practice Hints:

Work on a hard, rigid surface, both for making the transfer and removing the paper backing. Cover your working surface with waxed paper for easy clean up. Remember that your copy or print will be reversed (or a mirror image) after you make the transfer. If you want to transfer words or letters, make a reverse copy of your letters by making a copy made with acetate (made especially for copiers). Then turn the acetate copy over and re-copy on regular copier paper so the letters are reversed and a mirror image of the original.

Advance Preparation:

Prewash garment or fabric before applying the print. Do not use softeners. When dry, iron to remove wrinkles.

Cont.

Needleart Guild
Page 312

The Needlecraft Shop
Page 312

The American Needlecrafter
The official newspaper of The American Needlecraft Association.
$15 per year
24 pages
A newspaper that covers the exciting people, ideas, and trends in the world of needlecraft. Subscribe and automatically become a member on the American Needlecraft Association.

Magazines:

Hooked on Crochet
$2.95 U.S./3.95 CAN per issue
$14.95 U.S./23.95 CAN per year
6 issues per year
48 pages
20 color illustrations
Designs for afghans, doiles, baby items, toys, and decorating ideas.

Crochet Home
$2.95 U.S./3.95 CAN per issue
$14.95 U.S./23.95 CAN per year
6 issues per year
48 pages
20 color illustrations
Crochet designs for every room in the house.

Plastic Canvas!
$2.95 U.S./4.25 CAN per issue
$14.95 U.S./23.95 CAN per year
6 issues per year
32 pages
15 color illustrations

Quick & Easy Plastic Canvas
$2.95 U.S./4.25 CAN per issue
$14.95 U.S./23.95 CAN per year
6 issues per year
32 pages
15 color illustrations

Cross-Stitch
$2.95 U.S./4.25 CAN per issue
$14.95 U.S./23.95 CAN per year
6 issues per year
32 pages
15 color illustrations

Simply Cross-Stitch
$2.95 U.S./4.25 CAN per issue
$14.95 U.S./23.95 CAN per year
6 issues per year
32 pages
15 color illustrations

Neighbors and Friends
Page 312

Arts & Crafts Market Guide
Show listings, supply listings, craft malls.
$21 per year, or only $18 with the mention of *Sew Far Sew Good*.
12 issues per year
Business articles for the professional crafter, show opportunities, lists of wholesale suppliers, craft malls and more.

Nimble Thimbles
Page 313
Books by Tammie Bowser:

How to Make Lazy Lucy
A cute, cuddly doll to make from rags.
$15 postpaid
27 pages

T-Shirt Masterpiece
How to make 10 cute, comfortable, and flattering outfits out of ordinary T-shirts.
$34 postpaid
80 pages

Pants, Pants, Pants: How to Make Them Fit!
$28 postpaid
65 pages

Nordic Fiber Arts
Page 313

Fancy Feet
Fisherman's Sweaters
Folk Socks
Knitting Ganseys
Knitting in the Nordic Tradition
The Mitten Book
More Sweaters
Nordic Knitting
Sweaters
Swedish Sweaters
Twined Knitting

Norton House
Page 314
Norton House has many quilting books.

Old Style Trading Company
Page 314

American Indian Beadwork
Beads to Buckskin, Vols. 1–8
Bugle Beading
Loom Beading
W. Ben Hunt : The Complete

"How-to" Book of Indian Crafts

Open Chain Publishing, Inc.
Page 314

Creative Machine Newsletter
4 issues/year
$16 per year or $36 for two years
48 pages

The Complete Book of Machine Quilting

Sewing Machine Blue Book

Sewing Machine/Serger Survey

Optional Extras, Inc.
Page 315

Oracle Publications
Page 315

Oregon Street Press
Page 316

Polychromatic Screen Printing
Joy Stocksdale
$12.95
128 pages
28 photos

Oregon Worsted Company/Mill End Store
Page 316

Original Sewing & Craft Expo
Page 316

Original Sewing & Craft Expo Sourcebook
$18.95 at expo, $26.95 after expo
Tips, techniques, projects and instructions. Specific topics vary by show.

Ornament
Page 317

Collectible Beads
Robert K. Liu
$49.95
256 pages
300+ color illustrations

Ornament Magazine: The Art of Personal Adornment
Robert K. Liu and Carolyn L.E. Benesh, Co-Editors
$23 per year
4 issues per year

Palmer/Pletsch Publishing
Page 318
Palmer Pletsch has a grand array of books on sewing and serging. Here are a few titles.

The Business of Teaching Sewing
Marcy Miller and Pati Palmer
$29.95
128 pages

Couture-The Art of Fine Sewing
Roberta Carr
$29.95
208 pages

Decorating with Fabric: An Idea Book
Judy Lindahl
$6.95
128 pages
(I checked this book out of my library and was very reluctant to give it back.)

Dream Sewing Spaces: Design & Organization for Spaces Large and Small
Lynnette Ranney Black
$19.95
128 pages

Sensational Silk: A Handbook of

Sewing Silk and Silk-Like Fabrics
Gail Brown
$6.95
128 pages

The Serger Idea Book: A Collection of Inspiring Ideas from Palmer/Pletsch
$19.95
160 pages

Park Bench Pattern Company
Page 318
Park Bench's sampler booklet is designed to teach sewers to identify fabric by "feel and weight", so they can make wise fabric choices. The booklet contains 24 fabrics, categorized by feel and weight, along with suggestions for matching the right fabric with the right pattern.

Park Bench Fabric "Feelie" Sampler
Mary Lou Rankin
$14.95

Patternworks
Page 320
Patternworks offers many unique, inspiring books about knitting and other yarn arts, here is a sampling of their titles:

Cottage Creations Presents an Eclectic Collection

Great Crocheted Sweaters in a Weekend

Knitted Animals

Knitted Historical Figures

Knitting and Design for Mohair

Knitting with Dog Hair

Minnowknits: Uncommon Clothes for Kids

Materials Needed:

Second Impressions Kit or kit contents:

Stitchless Fabric Glue

Brayer or roller

Applicator sponge

Color or black-and-white copies of photos or prints

Prewashed fabric or garment

Waxed paper

Scissors

Iron and ironing board

Instructions:

Trim off white borders of copy or prints. Working on waxed paper, apply generous amounts of Stitchless to the image side of the copy or print using a sponge or your fingers. Glue should be 1/8" thick or thick enough to barely see the image through glue. Coat all edges and corners well.

Place copy Stitchless-side down onto the prewashed fabric. Use roller or brayer to press the copy to the fabric. As glue is pushed out around the edges, immediately wipe away with sponge. Let dry naturally—at least six hours or overnight.

Heat set glue by pressing each side of copy/fabric ten seconds with dry iron set on highest heat setting safe for fabric. This will

Cont.

improve the transfer bond. Let cool.

To remove paper backing, flood paper with water. Let sit 5 minutes. Gently rub away the paper with sponge or your fingers. As you work, layers of paper will roll away until all paper is removed. If small area of transfer lifts and tears, work more carefully in that area to keep tear small. You can repair it with Stitchless later. Clean and clear off the rolled paper often and re-moisten as you work. Print will be slightly cloudy. Gently move fingers over transfer area to find places where paper hasn't been removed. Continue to roll away bits of paper until surface feels completely smooth. Rinse transfer in cold water to remove final paper particles.

DO NOT WRING DRY. Line dry.

Thin a small amount of Stitchless with an equal part of water. Sponge or brush-on to coat the transfer. This will help clear the cloudiness. Allow to dry. The transfer image will never be as intense as the original.

For fabric care, wash in cool water on gentle cycle or hand wash. Use soap, not detergent!

Cont.

The Principals of Knitting

The Scrap Vest Pattern

Small Knit Purses

Where Did You Get That Hat: Twenty Absolutely Fabulous Designs to Knit and Crochet

Peddler's Wagon
Page 320
Peddler's offers older and out-of-print needlework books. Here is a sampling of their titles.

97 Needlepoint Alphabets

Bargello: An Explosion in Color

The Beatrix Potter Needlepoint Book

Girlhood Embroidery, American Samplers & Needlework Pictures

Historic Textile Fabrics

Pulled work on Canvas & Linen

Reversible Blackwork

Scandinavian Embroidery

Personal Threads Boutique
Page 321

Picking Up The Pieces Quilt Shop
Page 322

The Pin Cushion
Page 322

Pioneer Quilts
Page 322

PJS Publications
Page 323

Sew News

$23.98 per year (discount to ASG members)
12 issues per year

Serger Update
$29.95 per year (discount to ASG members)
12 issues per year

Sewing Update
$19.50 per year
6 issues per year

Planet Bead
Page 323

Power Sewing
Page 323
Power Sewing offers books by Sandra Betzina:

Power Sewing
$29.95

More Power Sewing
$29.95

Fear of Sewing
$5.95

Prairie Edge/Sioux Trading Post
Page 323

Prairieland Quilts
Page 324

Notes from The Prairie
A newsletter on quilts, with humor, tips, recipes, and classes.
John and Suzanne Brun
$5 per year
8 pages

Promenade's Le Bead Shop
Page 325

French Beaded Flowers
Helen McCall
$14.95
32 pages
18 color photos
Directions for 17 different flowers: iris, poppy, baby's breath, calla lily, miniature tea rose, daisy, and more.

Beaded Dreamcatchers
Mary R. Musgrove
$3.95

American Indian Beadwork
$6.95

Beaded Clothing Technique
$6

Contemporary Loomed Beadwork
$6.95

Qualin International
Page 326

Color Changing Hue

Fit to Be Tied!

Silk Painting: The Artist's Guide to Gutta and Wax Resist Techniques

Queen Ann's Lace
Page 326

Quilt in a Day
Page 326
This publisher/retail store specializes in easy-to-follow instruction for quilting. They have published over 50 books in the past 16 years, and are going strong.

An Amish Quilt in a Day

Appliqué in a Day

Creating With Color

From Blocks to Quilt

Irish Chain in a Day

Quilt in a Day–Christmas Quilts & Crafts
Eleanor Burns
$24.95
Softcover, 127 pages
Full-color throughout

Star Log Cabin Quilt
Eleanor Burns
$14.95
Softcover, 92 pages

The Quilt Rack
Page 327

The Quilting Bee
Page 328

Quilting Books Unlimited
Page 328

Quilting From The Heartland
Page 328
Over 20 books devoted to your favorite quilt patterns, as featured on the show *Quilting From The Heartland*.

Quilts and Other Comforts
Page 328

Gather Round the Table
Margaret Hanon and Judy McKinney
$19.95
100 pages
55 Sew easy projects that will make your dining room look special every month of the year.

How To Make a Quilt
Bonnie Leman and Louise Townsend
$7.95
How to make patchwork and appliqué quilts.

Log Cabin Quilts
Bonnie Leman and Judy Martin
$14.95
40 pages
Includes Magic Number System to help you figure yardage.

Quilter's Newsletter Magazine
$19.95 + $1.97 S&H per year
10 issues per year
Quilt patterns, lessons, designs and inspiration.

Quiltmaker Magazine
$17.95 + $1.97 S&H per year
6 issues per year
Quilting patterns, instructions and illustrations.

Quilts & Other Comforts Catalog: The Catalog for Quilt Lovers
Free

Scrap Quilts
Judy Martin
$14.95
96 pages
250 photos and illustrations
90 patterns included

Taking the Math out of Patchwork Quilts
Bonnie Leman and Judy Martin
$6.95
36 pages
Quilt sizes for any bed size or block size and 36 yardage charts.

Quilts By the Oz
Page 329

Ranita Corporation
Page 329

Wrapped in Fabriqué™
Glenda D. Sparling

$24.95
182 pages

Renaissance Buttons
Page 330
Renaissance has books related to buttons.

Revelli
Page 330
Custom color and design books for your own personalized style.

Baby & You
Clare Revelli
$10
Discover your baby's own style.

Color & You
Clare Revelli
$10

The Colors of Your Life
Clare Revelli
$12

Design & You
Clare Revelli
$10

Style & You
Clare Revelli
$10

Ribbons & Roses
Page 330

Australian Smocking and Embroidery

Classic Cushions

Embroider A Garden

Floral Embellishments: 23 Embroidery Projects for Your Wardrobe

Gardening with Ribbons

Inspirations

DO NOT DRY IN DRYER! DO NOT DRY CLEAN! LINE DRY!

Iron if necessary following these instructions.

Place image face down over waxed paper and use press cloth to cover back and press. If press cloth sticks to the transfer, let cool completely and then remove press cloth. (Heating the glue softens it.)

Decorating Tips

Line edges of transfer with Delta Dimensional Fabric Paint to cover areas where glue extends over photo images and to add decorative color and interest to your transfer.

Give your black and white photos an old-fashioned look by tinting the final coating (see Step 5) with a drop or two of Fabric Color. Apply with small brush to color the transfer as desired.

Transfer may be made as an appliqué and applied to decorative pieces, purses, bags, or right onto your garment with Stitchless Fabric Glue.

Project provided by: Delta Technical Coatings, Inc. Page 268

Ribbon Basics

Victorian Embroidery

Wool Embroidery and Design

Robin's Bobbins & Other Things
Page 331

Robin's Bobbins carries over 300 books on tatting, lacemaking, and lace history. Here is one by the owner of the company.

101 Torchon Patterns
Robin Lewis-Wild
$19.95 Softcover
$40 Hardcover
Pattern book for Torchon Lace in visual diagrams.

Rupert, Gibbon & Spider
Page 331

Rupert, Gibbon & Spider carries books on fabric dyeing and painting, including:

A Complete Guide to Silk Painting

Creating Color

Silk Painting: The Artist's Guide to Gutta & Wax Resist Techniques

Sandeen's Scandinavian Art, Gifts & Needlecraft
Page 332

Sawyer Brook Distinctive Fabrics
Page 332

SAX Arts & Crafts
Page 333

The Scarlet Letter
Page 333

Schoolhouse Press
Page 333
Schoolhouse has over 150 knitting titles.

A few titles are listed below.

Handknitting With Meg Swanson
$15.95
Softcover

Knitter's Almanac
Elizabeth Zimmerman
$4.95
Softcover

Knitting Without Tears
Elizabeth Zimmerman
$14.95
Softcover
In continuous print since 1971.

Seattle Fabrics, Inc.
Page 334

The Seraph Textile Collection
Page 334

Bedchamber to Buttery
Alexandra Pifer
$3
How to use homespun fabrics.

Sew-Pro Workshop
Page 334

Tailoring Ladies' Jackets
Mary Ellen Flury
$18.95 + $3 s/h US, $5 s/h Canada
96 pages, 233 illustrations
Step-by-step instructions on how to tailor a lady's suit jacket.

SewBaby!
Page 334

Easy to Make Cloth Dolls and All the Trimmings
Jodie Davis
$13.95
220 pages

Easy to Make Endangered Species to Stitch and Stuff
Jodie Davis
$13.95
192 pages

Easy to Make Fairy Tale Dolls and All the Trimmings
Jodie Davis
$13.95
155 pages

For Boys Only: Appliqué Book
Mary Meyer
$9.95
47 pages, 20 patterns

Sewing Emporium/Sew-Easy Products
Page 335

Get It All Done and Still Be Human

Jane Asher's Costume Book

Machine-Quilted Jackets, Vests, and Coats

Learn Bearmaking

The Quilter's Guide to Rotary Cutting

Sewing Sampler Productions, Inc.
Page 335

Sewing Supplies, Inc.
Page 335

SewStorm Publishing
Page 335

Sew up a Storm: All the Way to the Bank!
Karen Maslowski
$19.95
213 pages

Sewing for profit.

Sew up a Storm: The Newsletter for Sewing Entrepreneurs
Karen L. Maslowski, Editor
$20 per year
4 issues per year
12 pages
Business information–no how-to-sew articles. Resources are provided, and it answers tax and other business questions.

Workroom Design: Space Solutions for Sewing Workrooms
Karen L. Maslowski
$7
24 pages
Aimed at those with sewing business-es, with hints on adapting space to various specialties (bridal, upholstery, etc.), but very useful for those who sew for pleasure as well.

SewSweet Dolls from Carolee Creations
Page 336

The SewSweet Dolls Cloth Doll Book
Carolee Luppino
$14
54 pages
36 illustrations
Cloth doll-making techniques and variations. Written in a conversational style that makes it very easy to use. Chapters are clearly marked so doll-makers can find help immediately, while making a doll.

SewSweet Hair Style Book
Carolee Luppino
$6

30 pages
75 illustrations
Includes 15 hair-yarn hairstyles and variations, boys' and girls' styles included.

Shuttle-Craft Books
Page 336
Shuttle Craft has over 40 books and monographs related to weaving and feltmaking, including:

Color and Dyeing

The Complete Book of Drafting

Contemporary Tapestry

Doup Leno

Extended Manifold Twill Weaves

Fundamentals of Feltmaking

Handweaver's Instruction Manual

Handwoven Clothing, Felted to Wear

Multiple Tabby Weaves

Point Twill with Color-and-Weave

The Shuttle-Craft Book of American Handweaving

Surface Interest: Textiles of Today

Weft Twining

Sievers School of Fiber Arts
Page 336

The Smocking Horse Collection
Page 337

Snowgoose
Page 338

Burda #E294

Classic Knitted Cotton Edgings

First Book of Modern Lace-Knitting

Knitted Lace-Japanese

Shetland Lace

Software Directory for Fibre Artists
Page 328

Software Directory for Fibre Artists
Lois Larson
$30 + $5 S&H U.S.
#35 +$5 S&H Canada
246 pages, 146 illustrations
Directory of software available for weaving, knitting, needlework, quilting, and sewing.

Soho South
Page 338

Tie-Dye to Die For & Batik You Can't Resist
Otten. Feltus and Niemiec
$5.95
Paperback
28 pages

Solo Slide Fasteners, Inc.
Page 339

SouthStar Supply Company
Page 339

The Methods of Sewing
Watson M. Hannon of the Singer Sewing Co.
$18.45
85 pages
Contains the following chapters: Methods Breakdown, Method Improvement, Sewing Machine Maintenance, Glossary of Sewing and

Cuff styles...

Band

Gauntlet

Fitted

French

Deep Cowl

Halter

Sweetheart

Manufacturing Terms.

How to Make Raincoats and Weatherproofs
$18.45
64 pages
A thorough presentation covering cloth and plastic raincoats. Includes the following chapters: Drafts, Designs and Patterns; Glossaries of Fabric, Manufacturing, and Sewing Terms; Sequential Processes in Cloth and Plastic Garment Manufacturing.

Speigelhoff Stretch & Sew/Great Copy Patterns
Page 340

Polarfleece Pizazz
Ruthann Speigelhoff & Judy Laube
$19.99
Illustrations and patterns.

Spinning Wheel
Page 340

Stone Mountain & Daughter Fabrics
Page 341

Straw Into Gold
Page 342

Sunshine Artist Magazine
Page 342

Sunshine Artist
$29.95 per year
12 issues per year
America's premier show and festival publication for crafters

Surface Design Association
Page 343

Surface Design Journal/SDA Newsletter
Patricia Malarcher, Editor
$7 for a single issue
$45 for a Membership Subscription
50 pages
50-60 color illustrations
Surface designer interviews, show reviews, and technical information.

Suzanne Cooper, Inc.
Page 343

Dancing Light
Suzanne Cooper
Beaded Amulet Purse Necklaces
$19.95 + $2.50 S&H
32 pages
30 color photos, 84 color illustrations, pattern graphs

Torch Beads: Glass Beadmaking Simplified
Suzanne Cooper
$10.95

Suzanne Roddy, Handweaver
Page 343
Many books on spinning, weaving and other crafts. A few titles are listed below.

Beads and Threads

Color and Fiber

Completely Angora

Creating Original Handknit Lace

Eight Shafts: A Place to Begin

Geometric Designs in Weaving

Growing Herbs and Plants for Dyeing

Lace and Lacey Weaves

Putting on the Dog

The Whole Craft of Spinning

Sweet Child of Mine
Page 343

An Encyclopedia of Embroidery Flowers
Evelyn O'Neil
$19.50
Softcover, 64 pages
Color throughout

Aspire

Australian Smocking and Embroidery

Dolls, Bears & Collectibles

Embroiderer's Book of Designs
Lee Lockheed
$21.95
Softcover, 95 pages
Color photos

Embroidery & Cross-Stitch

Inspirations

Silk Ribbon Embroidery
Mary Jo Hiney
$5.95
Softcover, 23 pages
Color throughout

Smocking for Pleasure
Madeline Bird and Margie Prestedge
$22.95

Taunton Press
Page 344

Threads Magazine

Fitting Your Figure
$15.95
Softcover, 96 pages
173 photos
Discover easy ways to take accurate

body measurements, make your own dress form, and adjust your sewing patterns so the clothes you make will fit beautifully.

Techniques for Casual Clothes
$15.95
Softcover, 96 pages
173 photos and drawings
A variety of techniques for vests, shirts, skirts, jackets, coats—even jeans and stretchy activewear.

Taylor's Cutaways & Stuff

Easy-to-Make Dolls with 19th Century Costumes

Hatmaking for Dolls

Quick-Quilting on Sewing Machines

Tess' Designer Yarns

Knit Like Crazy!
Poochie Meyers
$19.95
62 pages
Creative inspiration and patterns for knitting and crochet.

Textile Reproductions

Things Japanese

All About Silk: A Fabric Dictionary and Swatchbook
Julie Parker
$29.95
A comprehensive guide to silk fabrics.

The Thrifty Needle
Books about working with knitted fabrics.

Timeless Treasures

TLC Yarns

Wool Tips Newsletter
Bruce Mackey, Caroline Blatner and Lynn Mackey, Editors
Free to customers or $8 per year
Supporting and promoting a natural fiber artist's network.

Trendsetter Yarns/Ornashi Filati
Wholesale Only

UltraScraps by D.M. Design

Unicorn Books and Crafts, Inc./Glimåkra Looms 'n Yarns/Frederick J. Fawcett, Inc.
They have approximately 2,000 textile craft books. A few are listed below.

About Buttons–A Collectors Guide: 150 A.D. to the Present

Armenian Needlelace and Embroidery

Banners for Beginners

Beading and Bonding in Ribbon Embroidery

Blackwork Embroidery: Design and Technique

Color and Cloth: The Quiltmaker's Ultimate Workbook

Pieced Clothing: Patterns For Simple Clothing Construction

Metric Quiltmaking

Putting on the Glitz: Unusual Fabrics and Threads for Quilting & Sewing

Sew Chiffon and Other Sheers: Exciting Ways to Sew Beautiful Woven Sheers.

Shirley Adam's Belt Bazaar: Dozens of Fabric Belts to Make for Every Outfit and Every Occasion

Short Kutz: The Fabulous New Sewing System That Quickly Transforms Old Clothes Into Stylish Wearables For Children

The Unique Spool

Unique Techniques

The Ins and Outs of Interfacings: A Complete Guide to Their Selection and Use

Mitered Vent

Mitered Welt Pocket

Timeless Tailoring

Universal Synergetics

Bead Directory
Linda Benmour
$18.95

Designs for Beadwork, Appliqué and Embroidery, Vols 1-4

Those Bad Bad Beads
Virginia Blakelock
$15

Neckline styles...

Drawstring

Off-the-Shoulder

Funnel

Neckline styles...

Scalloped

Wide V, or Decolleté

Crew

Softcover, 110 pages
B&W, illustrations

Vale Cottage Studio
Page 350

New Stitches: Original Quilting Designs, III, IV, V, VI
Dianna Vale
$7.50 + $2.50 S&H
Spiral bound, approximately 24 pages each
B&W, illustrations

Virginia West
Page 351

A Cut Above
Virginia West
$15, postpaid
43 pages
26 patterns

Designer Diagonals
Virginia West
$12, postpaid
44 pages
22 patterns

The Weaving Works
Page 352
Weaving Works has over 1,800 current titles in stock.

Wendy Schoen Design
Page 352

Westbrook Bead Co.
Page 352

Whetstone Hill Publications
Page 353

Michael James Studio Quilts
Patricia Harris, David Lyon, and

Patricia Malarcher
$75
120 pages
63 color illustrations, 22 B&W
Deluxe, clothbound monograph, over-sized, printed in Switzerland on acid-free paper.

The Quiltmaker's Handbook

The Second Quiltmaker's Handbook

The Whole Bead Show
Page 353

Wonderful World of Hats
Page 353

Designer Custom Shoe Covering

Hat Lovers Dictionary

Vintage Hair Styles Booklet

The Woolery
Page 354

XRX, Inc.
Page 354

Knitters Magazine

Weavers Magazine

Yarn Barn
Page 354

Yarns International
Page 354

Business Planning & Resources

The businesses listed here offer information about starting and running a successful business. Once again, I have tried not to overlap books, so a particular title will likely be listed only once.

Alpel Publishing
Page 238

Amazon Vinegar & Pickling Works Drygoods
Page 239

Do-It-Yourself Advertising

Do-It-Yourself Marketing

Do-It-Yourself Publicity

Homemade Money

In Business For Yourself

Scams, Swindles and Rip-Offs

The Popcorn Report
(I have read this book and consider it to be "right on the money", if you are planning a business decision–ANY business decision–read this book first!)

Associated Sewing Supply Co., Inc.
Page 243

Atkinson Fabrics, Inc.
Page 243

Home-based distributorship opportunities for fabrics and curtains.

BeadZip
Page 248

The Bead Business

Caravan Beads, Inc.
Page 257

Consulting and training available for those interested in starting their own bead store.

Center for the Study of Beadwork
Page 259

List of bead suppliers

Bead cabinet plans

Christopher Rich
Page 259

He is available on a freelance basis to illustrate anything you need–at reasonable prices.

Collins Publications
Page 260
Books and accessories designed to help you start your own sewing business and be successful.

The "Business" of Sewing: How to Start, Maintain, and Achieve Success, (audio tape)

The "Business" of Sewing: How to Start, Maintain, and Achieve Success covers business plans, financial planning, how to attract clients, and more.

The "Business" of Sewing (newsletter) Business and tax tips, new product reviews, and announcements of sewing events.

A Complete Set of Forms, includes contracts, measurement charts, price sheets, and more. They are also available on disk.

Marketing Your Sewing Business (audio tape)

Sew To Success
Kathleen Spike
$10.95
Includes sample forms and pricing methods.

Taking The Fear Out of Pricing (audio tape)

Craftmaster Enterprises
Page 265

Craftmaster News, Magazine

Turn Your Talent Into Gold

What are you worth?

Remember, once you begin to accept money for your sewing and fiber works, it is no longer just a hobby, you are in business.

If you undercharge, you are not just hurting yourself, but others in your profession who have to make a living off their craft.

It also hurts you in the end, because people often feel that if something is inexpensive, it is cheap, while if they pay what it is truly worth, though it may seem a lot to you, they will be proud of their deal.

If you find yourself fitting custom-made suits for $150, ask yourself how much that suit would cost in a store, then remember, yours will last longer and fit better than any suit from a store.

What else do your customers get?

Do you remember to create a detailed, itemized bill for each transaction? This is particularly important for custom clothiers and contracted pieces.

An itemized receipt is much easier for a client to understand and will help you make a case if they accuse you of overcharging. If you are able to show what each dollar is for, that you are professional and competent, and that you care about their satisfaction, you are more likely to win a loyal customer for life.

Fabric Temptations
Page 276

Fancy Threads/Fancy Threads Custom
Page 277

Grant Moser
Page 285

Grant Moser writes, edits, and designs books, manuals and other materials.

Greenberg & Hammer, Inc.
Page 286

Greenberg and Hammer contributes samples and information to authors working on research for articles relating to sewing. Please contact Frank Piazza for more information.

Notions and dressmaker's supplies

Halcyon Yarn
Page 286

The Basic Guide to Selling Arts & Crafts

The Kirk Collection
Page 299

Business Forms: Contracts In Plain English for Craftspeople

Photographing Your Craftwork

Lark Books
Page 301

Crafting as a Business

Lifetime Career Schools
Page 302

They offer accredited courses in these careers:

  Doll Repair

  Sewing/Dressmaking

  Small Business Management

Londa's Sewing, Etc.
Page 303

Magic Fit Patterns
Page 304

They are looking for enthusiastic people to retail their custom-fit pattern systems.

Mother Nurture
Page 310

Mother Nurture sometimes commissions the development of prototype designs, patterns, and instructions. Readers who might want such an assignment are encouraged to inquire.

They are eager to offer and distribute new entries in the maternity field. They can provide an effective marketing conduit for the producer. Interested parties should contact their executive director.

Mother Nurture is seeking a skilled seamstress to update the existing *Sewers Guide* and adapt it for use by those who speak Spanish or Japanese. Any qualified person interested should contact the executive director.

Mother nurture is also seeking a skilled seamstress to author a new *Sewers Guide: To modify clothes you already own and adapt conventional patterns for pregnancy*. Any qualified person interested should contact the executive director.

Neighbors and Friends
Page 312

Arts & Crafts Market Guide
Show listings, supply listings, craft malls.
Regularly $21 per year, only $18 with the mention of *Sew Far Sew Good*.
12 issues per year.
Business articles for the professional crafter, show opportunities, lists of wholesale suppliers, craft malls and more.

Oracle Publications
Page 315

They offer personal consulting for small businesses interested in expanding their customer base through a combination of innovative marketing techniques, professional business consulting and design. They specialize in design, research, marketing, and publishing. They are for businesses seeking to get the most out of their budget.

Patria Gardens Video
Page 319

Practical Applied Logic, Inc.
Page 323

Custom software for businesses

Professional Association of Custom Clothiers
Page 325

Revelli

Page 330

They offer the Complete Professional Color Kit, which will train you to become a color consultant.

SewStorm Publishing

Page 335

Sew Up a Storm: All the Way to the Bank!
Karen Maslowski
$19.95
213 pages
Sewing for profit.

Sew Up a Storm: The Newsletter for Sewing Entrepreneurs
Karen L. Maslowski, Editor
4 issues per year
$20 per year
12 pages
Business information, no how-to-sew articles. Resources are provided, and it includes tax and other business questions.

Workroom Design: Space Solutions for Sewing Workrooms
Karen L. Maslowski
$7
24 pages
Aimed at those with sewing businesses, with hints on adapting space to various specialties (bridal, upholstery, etc.), but very useful for those who sew for pleasure as well.

Sunshine Artist Magazine

Page 342

The Whole Bead Show

Page 353

How do you present your business to others?

This is an important question to ask yourself at least once a year.

What's in a name? Plenty, if it's your business. Embroidery Boutique might be limiting the perception of your store or business. Why not try Embroidery and More? Remember, if you plan to stay in business for years, you will likely expand your products and services beyond the specialty you originally choose.

Are your flyers handwritten? Handwriting your notices is not always a bad idea, IF you have good handwriting, and IF your business is trying to project a homey, handmade look. But most of the time it just looks sloppy. The cost of computers is coming down fast, they are easier to use than ever, and they can create any look from high-tech to high country. If you are not up to the computer challenge, visit your local print center for a tour and some price information. Many will design a flyer for $15 or less that will knock your socks off.

Creating your business image is like buying fabric. Buy the best you can afford; it will save you grief in the long run.

Business Suppliers & Wholesale Dealers

Here are a few sources of unique products for you to offer to your customers.

Please keep in mind that wholesale dealers require a Federal Employer Identification Number (EIN) and/or your state resale number. These are the only proofs acceptable to any business for true wholesale distribution. Also, many dealers will not ship to an address that is not listed on your resale certificate.

Each of the companies listed here works hard for you and your small business, so please call with serious inquiries only.

How to get wholesale...

When a listing has a minimum, but does not say "Wholesale Only", that usually means that you have to order a certain amount to get the best price.

A great way to meet the quota is to get a bunch of friends to order a small amount, and place them all in one order. Many people do this with their on-line friends, and everyone wins!

Just remember, no matter how much you spend for true wholesale, you MUST be a legitimate company.

Quick and easy mending...

Each time you finish a project, re-thread your sewing machine with clear thread.

This allows you to make quick repairs on any garment without hunting for the right color of thread.

Tip provided by: Jerry Parser AOL member, sewing enthusiast

Bedlam Beadworks
Page 249

Beggars' Lace
Page 249

Blueprints-Printables
Page 251

Boca Loca Beads
Page 215

Body-Rite, Inc.
Page 251

　　Posture aid

Bonfit America, Inc.
Page 251

　　Multi-sized patterner

BottomLine Designs
Page 252

Bovis Bead Co.
Page 252

Bramwell Yarns, USA
Page 252

By Jupiter!
Page 255

California Stitchery
Page 256

　　Judaic needlework supplies

Caravan Beads, Inc.
Page 257

　　Beads

Carolin Lowy Customized Designs and Graphs
Page 257

Chalet Publishing
Page 259

　　Quilter's Travel Companion

Chilton Book Company
Page 259

　　Books

Cinema Leathers, Inc.
　　Wholesale Only
Page 259

　　English domestic cow hide

　　Halian nappa

　　Lamb suede

　　Pig suede

Clearview Triangle
Page 260

Collins Publications
Page 260

　　Books and accessories designed to help people start their own sewing businesses—and be successful.

Continuity...
Page 262

Copper Coyote Beads, Ltd.
Page 262

　　Beads

Cotton Ball
Page 263

Cotton Clouds
Page 263

　　Cotton and cotton blend yarns

Cottons, Etc.
Page 263

Counted Thread Society of America
Page 264

Crafts By Donna
Page 265

Creative Beginnings
Page 265

　　Brass charms

　　Embellishment POP displays

　　Silk ribbon embroidery supplies

Crystal Palace Yarns
　　Wholesale Only
Page 266

　　Ashford products for spinning and weaving

　　Fibers for spinning or doll hair

　　Knitting yarns

D'Anton Leather
Page 266

　　Leathers

　　Suedes

Danforth Pewterers
Page 267

　　Button covers

　　Buttons

Dawn's Hide and Bead Away, Inc.
Page 268

Delta Technical Coatings, Inc.
　　Wholesale Only
Page 268

The Fur Product Labeling Act...

The Fur Product Labeling Act became effective in 1952. The stipulations of this act are as follows:

Purchasers must be informed by labels, invoices, and in advertisements of:

The true English name of the animal from which the fur is taken (for example, rabbit–not lapin).

The country of origin.

Whether the product is composed of used, damaged, scrap fur, or fur that has been dyed or bleached.

The act also requires that the name of the animal as stated must be based on a list developed and added to the law by amendment in 1967. The act prohibits the use of fictitious names in labeling and advertising.

The important definitions for this act are:

FUR PRODUCTS: Any article of wearing apparel made in whole or in part of fur or used fur; exceptions provide that the term shall not include any articles exempted by the Federal Trade Commission (FTC) due to relatively small quantities or low value of fur or used fur in the product.

Cont.

FUR: Any animal skin or part thereof with hair, fleece, or fur fibers attached thereto; either in the raw or processed state. It does not include skins that are to be processed into leather.

USED FUR: Any fur that has been previously used or worn by a consumer.

WASTE FUR: Scrap pieces and ears and throats that have been severed from the pelt.

Fiber-Etch® Tip

Remember, a little FiberEtch® goes a long way.

First embroider (or apply fabric paint) around a design shape.

Just within the outline, apply a small amount of FiberEtch® and "scratch" with the bottle tip into the fabric, leaving a thin (not raised) layer.

Apply to both sides of thicker fabrics.

Dry area with a hairdryer, iron until the applied area is brittle, and simply rinse the fabric away.

Tip provided by:
Michelle Hester
Silkpaint Corporation
Page 337

Vest styles...

Long Vest

Buttons

Button, button. Who's got the button?
These companies carry just about any button imaginable.

A Fabric Place
Page 237

AK Sew & Serge
Page 237

Albe Creations, Inc.
Page 238

    Covers

    Designer fashion

    Handmade porcelain

    Holiday themes

    Children's

Amazon Vinegar & Pickling Works Drygoods
Page 239

    Military reproduction buttons in brass or pewter

And Sew On
Page 240

Aura Registered
Page 244

    Leather-look

    Metal

    Pewter

    Wood

Baer Fabrics
Page 245

    Over 10,000 styles

Banasch's Fabrics
Page 245

Banasch's, Inc.
Page 245

Banksville Designer Fabrics
Page 245

Bead in Hand
Page 247

Bead Works, Inc.
Page 247

Beads & Beyond
Page 248

Beads & Rocks
   Wholesale Only
Page 248

Blue Heron Bead Company
Page 250

Blueprints-Printables
Page 251

    Buttons to dye or paint

Brian's Crafts Unlimited
Page 252

Bridals International
Page 253

Button Factory
Page 254

    Cotton

    Metal

    Plastic

    Rubber

    Wood

The Button Shoppe
Page 254

    Abalone

    Antler

    Beaded

    Bone

Button Tassels

Try embellishing your clothing with button tassels. They are easy to make and fun.

Use yarn or leather thong to attach the button to your garment. Instead of starting from the back and going to the front, start in the front and go to the back, then back to the front—with two or more ties. Tie both at the front, and clip to even them out. Your button tassel should look like the one shown below.

Tired of buttonholes?

Try using cording or picot loops to attach buttons as shown below.

Cording

Picot Loops

Cameo

Carved mother of pearl

Ceramic

Crystal

Enameled

Fimo

Fused glass

Glass

Horn

Metal

Paperweight glass

Passementarie

Plastic

Rhinestone

Shell and pearl

Sterling silver

Wood

Button Treasures
Page 254

Cameo

Carved mother of pearl

Ceramic

Casein

Corozo (also known as vegetable ivory or tagua nut)

Coconut Shell

Enameled

Glass

Handpainted silk

Horn

Leather

Metal

Nylon

Passementarie

Plastic

Polyester

Rhinestone

Shell and pearl

Sterling silver

Wood

Buttons & Things
Page 255

Buttons 'n' Bows
Page 255

Buttons Unlimited
Page 255

Acrylic

Antler

Bone

Dichroic

Nickel-silver

Novelty

Porcelain

Carol Harris Co.
Page 257

Antique

Carolina Mills Factory Outlet
Page 257

Coastal Button and Trim
Page 260

Variety packs

The Corner Stitch, Inc.
Page 262

The Costume Shop
Page 262

Button covers

Nickel

Red Brass

Sterling silver

Cotton Ball
Page 263

Cottons, Etc.
Page 263

CR's Crafts
Page 264

D'Leas Fabric and Button Studio
Page 266

Daisy Kingdom
Page 267

Danforth Pewterers
Page 267

Button covers

Button collections (four buttons on a card)

High-quality pewter buttons

Winnie the Pooh sets

Dimples
Page 269

Doering Designs
Page 270

Pewter buttons

The button factor...

When using large decorative buttons on a blouse or shirt, determine beforehand whether you would like to wear it tucked in or loose.

If you are going to wear your shirt tucked, use standard shirt buttons below the waist, to avoid a lumpy appearance, as shown below.

If you'd like to keep your options open, use one of the temporary button attachment suggestions given throughout this book for the buttons below your waist line.

Button Sizes...

10 ligne = 1/4" = 6mm

14 ligne = 5/16" = 9mm

16 ligne = 3/8" = 10mm

18 ligne = 7/16" = 11mm

20 ligne = 1/2" = 13mm

24 ligne = 5/8" = 16mm

30 ligne = 3/4" = 19mm

36 ligne = 7/8" = 22mm

Cont.

Agate

Balinese

Batik Bone

Beaded

Beatrix Potter®

Bridal

Cameo

Carved mother of pearl

Ceramic

Casein

Children's

Cloisonne

Corozo (also known as vegetable ivory or tagua nut)

Coconut shell

Doll

Enameled

Glass

Handpainted

Horn

Leather

Metal

Paddington Bear

Passementarie

Peruvian

Plastic

Polyester

Porcelain

Recycled

Rhinestone

Shell and pearl

Sterling silver

Terra cotta

Wood

K & K Quilteds
Page 297

Keepsake Quilting
Page 298

    Ceramic

    Porcelain

    Tiny-sized

The Kirk Collection
Page 299

    Victorian

Lace Heaven, Inc.
Page 301

The Lacemaker
Page 301

    Antique shoe buttons

    Paperweight buttons

Lacis
Page 301

The Leather Factory
Page 301

Leather Unlimited
Page 302

Ledgewood Studio
Page 302

Londa's Sewing, Etc.
Page 303

M & J Trimming Co.
Page 304

Marilyn's Button Sales
Wholesale Only
Page 306

    Antique

    Collectible

    Fine porcelain

    Fused glass

    Nickel

    Pewter

    Silver

Meredith Stained Glass Center, Inc.
Page 308

    Supplies for hot glass button making

Mimi's Fabrications
Page 309

Miss Maureen's Fabrics and Fancies
Page 309

Morning Star Indian Gallery
Page 310

    Abalone

    Antler

    Buffalo nickel

    Button covers

    Indian head nickel

    Pink conch

National Thread & Supply
Page 312

    Army

Blue jeans and coverall tack

Fish eye

Metal

Suit

Suspender and fly

Uniform

Nimble Thimbles

Pewter buttons and clasps

Nina Designs

Sterling silver

Nolting Mfg., Inc.

Norton House

Oiye Buttons

Handmade porcelain buttons

Oregon Buttonworks

Hand-cut semi-precious buttons

Oregon Tailor Supply Co.

Oregon Worsted Company/Mill End Store

P.L. Greene's Country Jumpers & Handpainted Ceramic Buttons

Patternworks
They carry unique buttons and clasps to complement their yarns.

Bone

Ceramic

Glass

Horn

Leather

Metal

Nut

Plastic

Shell

Stone

Wood

Personal FX

Personal Threads Boutique

Pieces

The Pin Cushion

Pioneer Quilts

Prairieland Quilts

Queen Ann's Lace

Quest Beads & Cast, Inc.

Custom buttons

The Quilt Rack

Quilts & Other Comforts

Quilts By the Oz

Renaissance Buttons

Glass

Horn

Metal

Mother of pearl

Plastic

Tagua nut

Vintage

Sawyer Brook Distinctive Fabrics

SAX Arts & Crafts

Schoolhouse Press

Deer antler

Handmade porcelain

Norwegian pewter buttons and clasps

Russian olive wood

Sealed With A Kiss, Inc.

Buttons to match their sweater patterns

40 ligne = 1″ = 25mm

45 ligne = 1/8″ = 29mm

60 ligne = 1 1/2″ = 38mm

75 ligne = 1 7/8″ = 51mm

Buttonholes...

Bartack

Round End

Round End with Bartack

Keyhole

Classes & Instruction

Here are opportunities for learning and exploring new techniques in the needlearts. This chapter is organized by state and city, so you can find education where you want it.

ALABAMA

Double Springs
Picking Up The Pieces Quilt Shop
Page 322

History of Quilting

Quilting Techniques

Mobile
Miss Maureen's Fabrics and Fancies
Page 309

ALASKA

Anchorage
University of Alaska Anchorage
53211 Providence Drive, 99508
(907) 786-1480, (907) 786-4888

Offers area of study in Textile Arts.

ARIZONA

Flagstaff
High Country West Needleworks
Page 291

Tucson
University of Arizona
Art Building, Room 108, 85721
(602) 621-7570, (602) 621-2955

Offers area of study in Textile Arts.

ARKANSAS

Fordyce
Spinning Wheel
Page 340

Crocheting

Knitting

Needlepoint

Silk ribbon embroidery

Tatting

CALIFORNIA

Arcata
Fabric Temptations
Page 276

Berkeley
Lacis
Page 301

Downey
Craftmaster Enterprises
Page 265

Seminars on Finding Profits in Crafting

Fullerton
California State University, Fullerton
Department of Art, 92634
(714) 773-3471

Offers area of study in Fashion Design.

Los Angeles
Otis College of Art and Design
Admissions
2401 Wilshire Boulevard, 90057
(213) 251-0505, (213) 480-0059 fax

Offers area of study in Fashion Design.

Morro Bay
Cotton Ball
Page 263

Mountain View
The Quilting Bee
Page 328

Oakland
California College of Arts & Crafts
5212 Broadway, 94618
(510) 653-8118

Offers area of study in Textiles.

Knot another knot!

Do you know how to keep your knot from slipping through fabric? Try this:

Double thread your needle. Insert needle into fabric. Pull the needle all the way through the fabric. Now slip the needle back through the double thread before the knot. This is a great idea when gathering!

Tip provided by: Atlanta Puffections Page 243

San Diego

Park Bench Pattern Company
Page 318

San Francisco

Academy of Art College
79 New Montgomery Street, 94105
(415) 274-2222

Offers area of study in Fashion Design.

Louise Salinger Academy of Fashion
Admissions, 101 Jessie Street, 94105
(415) 974-6666

Offers areas of study in Fashion Design and Technology, and Textiles and Clothing.

San Jose

The Fabric Carr
Page 275
Sew Week topics:

Art-To-Wear With a Couture Attitude

The Best of Couture

Beyond The Book - A Perfectionist's Paradise

Chanel

Drafting Patterns

Pants—And What Goes On Top

Silk-Sleeves-Blouses-Dresses

Skirting The Issue

Tailoring

San Jose State University
One Washington Square, 95192-0089
(408) 924-2080

Offers area of study in Textile Arts.

San Marcos

Quilt in a Day
Page 326

Quilting

Valencia

California Institute of the Arts
24700 McBean Parkway, 91355
(805) 253-7863

Offers area of study in Costume Design.

COLORADO

Boulder

Promenade's Le Bead Shop
Page 325

Colorado Springs

The Enchanted Cottage
Page 274

Denver

D'Leas Fabric and Button Studio
Page 266

Divide

Great Divide Weaving School
Page 285
Tapestry weaving classes in one and two week sessions.

Durango

Gossamer Threads & More
Page 284

Lace knitting

Rangely

Old Style Trading Company
Page 314
Beading classes by appointment.

Wheat Ridge

Harriet's Treadle Arts
Page 289

CONNECTICUT

Brookfield

Brookfield Craft Center
Page 253

Everything About Beads

Feltmaking

Fiber Jewelry

Needlepoint Magic

Glastonbury

Close to Home—The Sewing Center
Page 260

DELAWARE

Newark

University of Delaware
103 Recitation Hall, 19716
(302) 831-2244, (302) 831-8000 fax
martha.carothers@mus.udel.edu

Offers area of study in Fibers.

FLORIDA

Kissimmee

Queen Ann's Lace
Page 326

Orlando

University of Central Florida
4000 Central Florida Boulevard, 32816
(407) 823-3000

Offers area of study in Fibers.

Tallahassee

Florida State University

328 Fine Arts Building, 32306-2008
(904) 644-7234, (904) 644-7246 fax

Offers area of study in Costume Design.

Tampa

E & W Imports, Inc./The Bead Shop
Page 272

Bead and Pearl Stringing

Wire Wrapping

Consumer Gemology

International Academy of Merchandising & Design, Ltd.
Admissions, Memorial Highway, 33634
(813) 881-0007

Offers area of study in Fashion Design.

Winter Haven

AK Sew & Serge
Page 237

All sewing topics

Silk ribbon embroidery

Smocking

Winter Park

Fabric Collections
Page 276

GEORGIA

Athens

University of Georgia
114 Academic Building, 30602
(706) 542-2112, (706) 542-1466 fax

Offers area of study in Fabric Styling.

Marietta

In Cahoots
Page 293

Classes on wearable art, embellishment and machine embroidery.

Mineral Bluff

Robin's Bobbins & Other Things
Page 331
Classes for the beginner to the advanced lacemaker, focusing on bobbin lace.

Savannah

Savannah College of Art and Design
P.O. Box 3146, 31402-3146
(912) 238-2483, (912) 238-2456 fax

Offers areas of study in Fashion Design and Technology, and Textile Arts.

HAWAII

Honolulu

University of Honolulu at Manoa
2535 The Mall, 96822
(808) 956-8251, (808) 956-9043 fax

Offers area of study in Fibers.

IDAHO

Coeur d'Alene

7 Trumpets Bead Studio
Page 237

Bead stringing

Bead weaving

Beading incorporated into kumi himo

Beading incorporated into weaving

ILLINOIS

Carbondale

Southern Illinois University at Carbondale

Southern Illinois University at Carbondale, 62901-4301
(618) 453-4315, (618) 453-7710 fax
ge1085@siucvmb.edu

Offers area of study in Fibers.

Champaign

Londa's Sewing, Etc.
Page 303

University of Illinois at Urbana-Champaign
10 Henry Administration Building, 506 South Wright, 61801
(217) 333-0302

Offers area of study in Costume Design.

Chicago

DePaul University
2135 North Kenmore, 60614
(312) 362-8374, (312) 362-5453 fax

Offers area of study in Costume Design.

International Academy of Merchandising & Design, Ltd.
Admissions, One North State Street, 60602-9736
(312) 541-3900

Offers area of study in Fashion Design.

Cissna Park

Prairieland Quilts
Page 324

De Kalb

Northern Illinois University
Admissions, Williston Hall, Room 101, 60115
(815) 753-0446

Spiderweb roses in ribbon embroidery...

Step 1

Step 2

Step 3

Step 4

Step 5

Finished Stitch

Tip provided by Prym-Dritz Corporation Page 325

Post-It buttonholes...

To correctly repeat the length of a button hole and its position from the garment edge, use a 3M Post-It Note and draw the length and position on the paper with the sticky section running along the garment edge. Make a test buttonhole through the Post-It Note on a sample of the garment fabric with the same interfacing used. The needle will perforate the paper. Remove the paper, and test button in hole of fabric sample. Re-use the Post-It Note for remaining button holes, stitching the perfect size every time.

Tip provided by: Fancy Threads/Fancy Threads Custom Page 277

Offers areas of study in Crafts and Textile Arts.

Edwardsville
Southern Illinois University at Edwardsville
Campus Box 1774, 62026
(618) 692-3071, (618) 692-3096 fax

Offers area of study in Textile Arts.

Ray College of Design
401 North Wabash Avenue, 60611
(312) 280-3500, (312) 280-3528

Offers areas of study in Fashion Design and Technology, Fashion Merchandising, and Textiles and Clothing.

School of the Art Institute of Chicago
37 South Wabash Avenue, 60603
(312) 263-0141

Offers areas of study in Fashion Design and Technology and Textile Arts.

Evanston
Beadazzzled, A Bead Emporium
Page 248

McHenry
Granny's Quilts
Page 285

Moline
Quilts By the Oz
Page 329

Normal
Illinois State University
Art Department, Department Code 5620, 61761
(309) 438-5623

Offers area of study in Fibers.

Oak Park
Bead in Hand
Page 247

Basic Beading For Adults

Basic Necklace Beading For 4-6 Year Olds

Basic Necklace Beading For Ages 7 And Up

Beaded Embellishments

Beaded Watchbands

Blinking Bracelet

Earrings In An Instant

Fittings, Findings, and Fasteners

Needlewoven Jewelry

Polymer Clay Face Beads

Polymer Clay Flower Beads

Polymer Clay For Kids

Quadruple Helix

Rectangular Bugle Bead Earrings

Right Angle Weave

Wire Wrapping Stones

INDIANA

Bloomington
Indiana University Bloomington
Hope School of Fine Arts
Fine Arts 123, 47405
(812) 855-0188
mhostetl@indiana.edu

Offers area of study in Textile Arts.

Fort Wayne
Indiana University–Purdue University at Fort Wayne
2101 Coliseum Boulevard East, 46805
(219) 481-6705

Offers area of study in Crafts.

Richmond
Past Patterns
Page 319

IOWA

Ames
Iowa State University of Science and Technology
Admissions, 100 Alumni Hall, 50011-3092
(515) 294-6724
mchinn@iastate.edu

Offers areas of study in Craft Design, and Textiles and Clothing.

Iowa City
Dawn's Hide and Bead Away
Page 268

Earring Making

Glass Bead Making

Jewelry Design

Necklace Making

Seed Bead Making

KANSAS

Garden City
The Quilt Rack
Page 327

Hardanger

Needlepoint

Silk ribbon embroidery

Smocking

Lawrence
Yarn Barn
Page 354

KENTUCKY

Louisville

Embroiderers' Guild of America, Inc.
Page 274

> Appliqué
>
> Blackwork
>
> Embroidery
>
> Embellishment
>
> Hand sewing
>
> Lacework
>
> Patchwork
>
> Quilting
>
> Smocking
>
> Surface stitchery

University of Louisiana
104 Schneider Hall, 40292
(502) 852-6794, (502) 852-6791 fax
mhland@ulkyvm.louisville.edu

> Offers area of study in Textile Arts.

LOUISIANA

Shreveport

Ghee's
Page 282

> Hands-On Workshop: Prestige
> Handbag Collection
>
> Going Beyond...Texture With Textiles

MARYLAND

Baltimore

Bridal Sewing School
Page 253
Learn the fine art of couture sewing for bridal and evening wear from couturièr Susan Khalje. For advanced sewers and professionals.

Maryland Institute, College of Art
Admissions, 1300 Mt. Royal Avenue, 21217
(410) 225-2222

> Offers area of study in Fibers.

Bethesda

Accents Bead Shop
Page 237

> Beaded Jewelry and Repair

Yarns International
Page 354

Rockville

G Street Fabrics
Page 282

Meredith Stained Glass Center, Inc.
Page 308

> Hot Glass Bead and Button Making

MASSACHUSETTS

Boston

Boston University
Theatre Arts Department, 855 Commonwealth Avenue, Room 470, 02215
(617) 353-3390, (617) 353-4363 fax

> Offers areas of study in Costume Design and Costume Production.

Massachusetts College of Art
621 Huntington Avenue, 02115-5882
(617) 232-1555

> Offers areas of study in Fashion Design and Technology, Textile Arts, and Textiles and Clothing.

Lowell

New England Quilt Museum,
Page 312

Shelburne

Becky's Väv Stuga
Page 249

MICHIGAN

Adrian

Adrian College
110 South MAdison Street, 49221
(800) 877-2246

> Offers area of study in Fashion Design.

Ann Arbor

University of Michigan
2000 Bonisteel, 48109-2069
(313) 763-5249, (313) 936-0469 fax
eugene_pijanowski@um.cc.umich.edu

> Offers areas of study in Crafts and Textile Arts.

Detroit

Center for Creative Studies–College of Art & Design
201 East Kirby Street, 48202
(313) 872-3118

> Offers area of study in Textile Arts.

Wayne State University
150 Art Building, 48202
(313) 577-2980, (313) 577-3491 fax

Topstitching guide...

Whenever you need straight stitching, quilting lines, or topstitching, try using masking tape as your guide. It comes in many widths, it is inexpensive and reusable, and will pull off your fabric easily, leaving no residue.

Garment ease for women...

For the arm...

Upper arm:	*3–4"*
Elbow:	*1"*
Forearm:	*3/4"*
Wrist:	*1/2"*
Inside Seam:	*1/2"*
Outside Length:	*1/2"*

For the upper body...

Neck:	*1/4–1/2"*
Chest:	*1/2"*
Bust	*2 1/2"*
Front:	*1 1/4"*
Back:	*1 1/2"*
Waist	*1"*
Front:	*3/8"–1/2"*
Back:	*1/2"–5/8"*
Shoulder Blade:	*1/2"–1"*
Neck to Waist:	*1/2"–1"*
Shoulder to Waist:	*1/2"*
Shoulder to Crotch:	*1"–2"*

For the lower body...

Waist:	*1"*
Front:	*3/8"–1/2"*
Back:	*1/2"–5/8"*
Abdomen:	*1 1/4"*
Hips:	*1 1/2"–2"*
Crotch Depth:	*1 1/2"–3"*

Offers area of study in Textile Arts.

Ferndale

Bedlam Beadworks
Page 249

> Bead Stringing
>
> Earrings
>
> Loom Weaving
>
> Off-Loom Weaving

Grand Blanc

Homestead Needle Arts
Page 292

> Needlepoint
>
> Hardanger
>
> Samplers

Mount Pleasant

Central Michigan University
Art Department, 132 Wightman Hall, 48859
(517) 774-3025

> Offers area of study in Fibers.

MINNESOTA

Minneapolis/St. Paul

Associated Sewing Supply Co., Inc.
Page 243

Stillwater

And Sew On
Page 240

MISSISSIPPI

Meridian

The Corner Stitch, Inc.
Page 262

> Basic sewing

> Heirloom sewing
>
> Smocking
>
> Hand quilting
>
> Machine quilting
>
> Embroidering

Petal

Kay Guiles Designs
Page 298

> Heirloom sewing and smocking

Tupelo

Heirlooms Forever
Page 290

MISSOURI

Columbia

Columbia College
1001 Rogers Street, 65216
(314) 875-7352

> Offers area of study in Fashion Design.

Stephens College
Box 2012, 65215
(314) 876-7251, (314) 786-7248 fax

> Offers area of study in Fashion Design and Technology.

Kansas City

Kansas City Art Institute
Admissions, 4415 Warwick Boulevard, 64111
(800) 522-5224

> Offers areas of study in Fashion Design, Fibers and Textile Arts.

Kirksville

Northeast Missouri State University

Baldwin Hall #118, 63501
(816) 785-4417
nemomus@academic.nemostate.edu

> Offers area of study in Textile Arts.

Springfield

Southwest Missouri State University
901 South National, 65804
(417) 836-5110

> Offers area of study in Fibers.

St. Louis

Fashion Fabrics Club/Natural Fiber Fabrics Direct
Page 278

Treasures of the Past by Annie B. Wells
Page 348
Annie will travel to your shop to teach. Shop owners may request a teaching packet.

> Fine embroidery
>
> Heirloom sewing
>
> Pattern drafting
>
> Sewing for boys
>
> Sewing for girls
>
> Sewing for ladies
>
> Silk ribbon embroidery

Washington University
Admissions, Campus Box 1089, Brookings Drive, 63130
(314) 935-6000

> Offers area of study in Fashion Design.

Webster University
470 Lockwood Avenue, 63119-3194

(314) 968-7000

Offers areas of study in Costume Design and Costume Management.

NEBRASKA

Omaha
The Kirk Collection
Page 299
Call for details on lectures, workshops, and trunk shows.

NEW HAMPSHIRE

Hanniker
The Fiber Studio
Page 279

Newton
Fancy Threads/Fancy Threads Custom
Page 277

Altering Ready-to-Wear

Creating Neckties for All

Gee, I've Never Heard of Them (effective advertising)

Starting Your Own Sewing Business

Yes, You Are Worth It! (correctly pricing yourself and your services)

Randolph
Grand View Country Store
Page 284

Knitting at all levels

NEW JERSEY

Point Pleasant
Mimi's Books & Patterns for the Serious Dollmaker
Page 309

Upper Montclair
Montclair State University
Fine Arts Department, 1 Normal Avenue, 07043
(201) 655-4320

Offers area of study in Fibers.

NEW MEXICO

Thoreau
Zuni Mountain Lodge
Page 355

Navajo Rug Weaving

NEW YORK

Amherst
Daemen College
4380 Main Street, 14226
(716)-839-8225

Offers area of study in Apparel Design.

Brooklyn
Pratt Institute
Admissions, 200 Willoughby Avenue, 11205
(718) 636-3669, (718) 636-3670

Offers area of study in Fashion Design and Technology

Buffalo
Accents Bead Shop
Page 237

Beaded Jewelry and Repair

Hillsdale
K & K Quilteds
Page 297

New York City
Fashion Institute of Technology
Admissions, Seventh Avenue at 27th Street, 10001
(212) 760-7675

Offers areas of study in Fabric Styling, Fashion Design and Technology, and Textile Surface Design.

Parsons School of Design, New School for Social Research
Admissions
66 5th Avenue, 10011
(212) 229-8910, (212) 229-8975 fax

Offers areas of study in Fashion Design and Technology and Textile Arts.

Tisch School of the Arts
22 Washington Square, 10003
(212) 998-1918, (212) 995-4060

Offers area of study in Costume Design.

Oneida
Cottons, Etc.
Page 263
Over 50 classes available.

Syracuse
Syracuse University
202P Crouse College, 13244-1010
(315) 443-2769, (315) 443-1935
jsl@law.syr.edu

Offers area of study in Fibers.

West Fulton
Patria Gardens Video
Page 319

Slipcovering

What is décolletage?

Décolletage (DAY-col-let-TAJ) is the low cut of a dress, revealing the neck and shoulders.

Too bright, not quite right?

If a new flower or element print is introduced and it looks too bright, don't immediately discard it; flip the fabric over to the reverse side and try it again.

Tip quoted from: Impressionist Quilts by Gai Perry, published by C & T Publishing Page 258

Pillows/Cushions

NORTH CAROLINA

Asheville
Earth Guild
Page 272

Waechter's Silk Shop
Page 351
Classes with Sandra Betzina, Shermane Fouche, Carol Britt, Ginny Ann, Laura Sims, and others at least six times per year

Charlotte
Peas & Carrots
Page 335

> Doll Clothing

> Children's Clothing

University of North Carolina at Charlotte
Reese Administration Building, 1st Floor, 28223
(704) 547-2213, (704) 547-3340 fax

> Offers areas of study in Fibers and Textile Arts.

Clyde
Haywood Community College
Page 289

> Dyeing

> Weaving

> Woven clothing construction

Greenville
East Carolina University
Jenkins Fine Arts Center, East Fifth Street, 27858-4353
(919) 757-6563

> Offers areas of study in Fabric Styling, Textile Arts, Weaving, and Surface Design.

Waynesville
The Glass Giraffe
Page 283
Classes in Hot Glass Bead Making. They will travel to teach for your organization. Please call for more information.

Mimi's Fabrications
Page 309

OHIO

Cincinnati
University of Cincinnati
Mail Location 0016, 45221
(513) 556-2962

> Offers area of study in Fibers.

Xavier University
3800 Victory Parkway, 45207-5311
(513) 745-3811, (513) 745-4301

> Offers area of study in Textile Arts.

Cleveland
The Smocking Horse Collection
Page 337

> Brazilian embroidery

> Heirloom sewing

> Lacemaking

> Sewing (beginner to advanced)

> Silk ribbon embroidery

> Smocking

> Stretch and sew

Columbus
Byzantium
Page 255
Classes in bead stringing, bead weaving, and polymer bead making. Call for details.

Columbus College
107 North Ninth Street, 43215
(614) 224-9101

> Offers area of study in Fashion Design and Technology.

Picking up the Pieces Quilt Shop
Page 322

> Quilting Techniques

Kent
Kent State University
School of Art, 211 Art Building, 44242-1001
(216) 672-4729

> Offers area of study in Textile Arts.

Rocky River
Harpagon/Sideline Design
Page 288

> Bridal headpieces

OREGON

Ashland
Southern Oregon State College
1250 Siskiyou Boulevard, 97520
9503) 552-6411, (503) 552-6329 fax

> Offers area of study in Textile Arts.

Grants Pass
Islander Sewing Systems
Page 295

> 7-Day Intensive Drafting Course, the same method taught to professional designers. You will learn to develop a personal pattern (sloper) and from

there proceed with designing and making your own patterns.

Couture Techniques

Lectures

Pattern Drafting

Seminars

Medford

The Crowning Touch-FASTURN
Page 266

    Classes on using their products

Oregon City

Palmer/Pletsch Publishing
Page 318
Palmer/Pletsch International School of Sewing Arts & Teacher Training Institute

Classes:

    Basic Pant and Trouser Pattern Fit

    Beginning Quilting

    Beginning Sewing

    Beyond the Basics

    Block of the Week

    Blouse-In-A-Day I & II

    Bow Tie Wallhanging

    Busy Bag

    Contemporary Tailoring

    Couture—The Art of Fine Sewing

    Creative Jacket In-A-Day

    Fabric Batiking

    Fashion Pattern Re-Designing

    FASTURN Reversible Tube Vest

    Fine Art of Upholstery

    Fit and Sew

    Fuzzy Lamb Baby Quilt

    Half Square Triangles

    Kaleidoscope Quilt

    Pant and Trouser Sewing

    Paper Piecing Wallhanging

    Pro Tips and More Pro Tips

    Polar Fleece Jackets for The Whole Family

    Quilt-In-A-Day

    Sewing With Burda Patterns

    Skirt-In-A-Day I & II

    Serger Workshop, Advanced Serger Workshop

    Stencil Styles 1 & 2

    Super Beginner on the Serger

    Swimwear and Leotards

Workshops:

    Creative Serging I & II

    Fit I, II & III

    Pant I, II & III

    Tailoring I, II & III

    Teacher Training Program Level I & II

    Ultrasuede

Portland

Bassist College
2000 Southwest Fifth Avenue, 97201
(503) 228-6528

    Offers areas of study in Apparel Design and Textiles and Clothing.

Bridal Sewing School
Page 253
Learn the fine art of couture sewing for bridal and evening wear from couturièr Susan Khalje. For advanced sewers and professionals.

Oregon Worsted Company/Mill End Store
Page 316

Salem

Eric's Press & Design & Sew Patterns
Page 274

Vale Cottage Studio
Page 350
Their lecture and demonstration series includes the topics Heirlooms to Honor, Tricks in Transferring, Quilt Clinic, and God's Gifts: Developing Our Talents.

PENNSYLVANIA

Clarion

Clarion University of Pennsylvania
Art Department, Marwick-Boyd, 16214
(814) 226-2291
Catheryn Joslyn can be contacted at: joslyn@vaxb.clarion.edu

    Offers area of study in Fiber and Fabric.

East Berlin

The Mannings Handweaving School & Supply Center
Page 305

    A Beginners Guide to Weaving Rag Rugs

    A Little Taste of the Southwest

    A Little Taste of Weaving

    Beginning Spinning Day

    Beginning Weaving

    Cardweaving

The Rules of Couture

Sew with your head.

Maintain accuracy.

Let grain be paramount is all decisions.

Talk to the fabric, and listen to the fabric talking to you.

Reduce bulk wherever possible.

Understand that couture requires judgement.

Know that your hands are your best sewing tools.

Accept the fact that pressing and sewing are synonymous.

Anticipate that the final garment will show "evidence of effort".

Enjoy the process as well as the results.

Tip provided by:
Robbie Carr
The Fabric Carr
Page 275

An easy wrap-around scarf...

Hold your scarf in front of you. Wrap each end around the back of your neck to the opposite side, creating a "collar" around your neck.

This is an easy way to wear any long scarf.

Designer Scarves (with your left over yarns)

Double Weave Blanket

Finishes

Flax Seed to Linen Thread

Intermediate Spinning

Overshot Workshop

Spindle Spinning

Spinning in the Old Way

Tatting

Warp and Weave

Weft Face Boundweave

Greensburg

Seton Hill College
Admissions, Seton Hill College, 15601
(412) 834-2200, ext. 4255

Offers area of study in Fashion Design and Technology.

Pittsburgh

The Feedsack Club
Page 278

Quilt and Feedsack Lectures

Insomac

Historic Needlework Guild
Page 292

Latrobe

Saint Vincent College
300 Fraser Purchase Road, 15601

Offers area of study in Fashion Design and Technology.

Philadelphia

Moore College of Art and Design
Admissions, 20th and The Parkway, 19103-1179
(215) 568-4515

Offers areas of study in Fashion Design and Technology, Fashion Illustration, Textile Arts, and Textiles and Clothing.

Tyler School of Art
Beech and Penrose Avnues, Elkins Park, 19027
(215) 782-2875, (215) 782-2711 fax

Offers areas of study in Fibers/Fabric Design and Textile Arts.

University Park

Pennsylvania State University–University Parks Campus
103 Arts Building, 16802
(814) 865-7586, (814) 865-7140

Offers area of study in Costume.

RHODE ISLAND

Providence

Rhode Island School of Design
2 College Street, 02903
(401) 454-6300, (401) 454-6309 fax

Offers areas of study in Apparel Design and Textiles.

SOUTH CAROLINA

Columbia

University of South Carolina
Art Department, 29208
(803) 777-4236

Offers area of study in Fibers.

SOUTH DAKOTA

Rapid City

Pioneer Quilts
Page 322

Spearfish Canyon Quilter's Spree

TENNESSEE

Dyersburg

Carol Harris Co.
Page 257

Johnson City

East Tennessee State University
Art Department, P.O. Box 7078, 37614-0708
(615) 929-4247

Offers area of study in Fibers.

Memphis

Memphis College of Arts
Admissions, 1930 Poplar Avenue, 38104
(901) 726-4085, ext. 30

Offers areas of study in Fiber and Surface Design and Textile Arts.

Nashville

Treasures of the Past by Annie B. Wells
Page 348

TEXAS

Alpine

Sul Ross State University
Box C-2, 79832
(915) 837-8050

Offers area of study in Textile Arts.

Baytown

The Pin Cushion
Page 322

Basic sewing

Crafts

Embroidery

Machine embroidery

Quilting

Denton

University of North Texas
School of Visual Arts, P.O. Box 5098,
76203
(817) 565-4004, (817) 565-4717 fax

Offers areas of study in Fashion
Design and Technology, Fibers and
Textile Arts.

Houston

Buttons 'n' Bows
Page 255
Classes in Smocking, Heirloom Sewing,
and Silk Ribbon Embroidery.

Lubbock

Texas Tech University
Mailstop 5005, 79409-1030
(806) 742-1482

Offers area of study in Textile Arts.

San Antonio

Southwest Craft Center
Page 340

VERMONT

Wilmington

Norton House
Page 314
Quilting

VIRGINA

Herndon

Ribbons & Roses
Page 330

Norfolk

Old Dominion University
Visual Arts Building, 49th Street, 23529
(804) 683-4047

Offers area of study in Fibers.

Radford

Radford University
Art Department, Box 6965, 24142
(703) 831-5475, (703) 831-6313

Offers area of study in Fibers.

Richmond

Virginia Commonwealth University
School of the Arts, 325 North Harrison
Street, 23284-2519
(804) 828-2787, (804) 828-6469 fax

Offers areas of study in Crafts Fashion
Design and Technology, Textile Arts,
and Textiles and Clothing.

WASHINGTON

Bellevue

Beads & Beyond
Page 248

Coupeville

Coupeville Arts Center
Page 269

The Weaver's School
Page 352

Seattle

Cornish College of the Arts

710 East Roy Street, 98102
(206) 323-1400, ext. 218

Offers area of study in Costume
Design.

The Weaving Works
Page 352

Dyeing

Handspinning

Knitting

Weaving

Jehlor Fantasy Fabrics
Page 296

University of Washington
Admissions, PC-30 98195
(206) 543-9686

Offers area of study in Textile Arts.

Snohomish

Clearview Triangle
Page 260

Spokane

Jill McIntire Designs
Page 297

Machine Embroidery

WASHINGTON, D.C.

Ivy Imports, Inc.
Page 295
Workshops focusing on:

FabricARTS Liquid "All Fabric" Paints

FabricARTS Silk Dyes (steam set)

Kimono Workshop

Visionart Instant Set Silk Dyes

---

*Garment ease for
men...*

For the arm...

Upper arm:	3-3 1/2"
Elbow:	3 1/2"
Forearm:	1"–1/2"
Wrist:	1"
Inside Seam:	1/2"
Outside Length:	1/2"

For the upper body...

Neck:	1/4"
Chest:	2"
Bust:	2"
Waist:	1/2"
Shoulder Blade:	1/2"
Shoulder to Waist:	1/4"
Shoulder to Crotch:	1 1/2–3"

For the lower body...

Waist:	1/2"
Abdomen:	1/2"
Hips:	3/4–1 1/2"
Crotch Depth:	1 1/2"

When working basketweave in needlepoint...

Always stitch on the grain. This gives agreement to the ground fabric and thread you are working, and produces perfect seating for your stitches. Off-grain needlepoint looks uneven, has ridges, and is rather lumpy in appearance.

Tip provided by:
High Country West Needleworks
Page 291

WEST VIRGINIA

Huntington
Marshall University
Department of Art, 400 Hal Greer Boulevard, 25755
(304) 696-6760
dfa003@marshall.wvnet.edu

Offers area of study in Textile Arts.

WISCONSIN

Eau Claire
University of Wisconsin-Eau Claire
Admissions, P.O. Box 4004, 54702-4004
(715) 836-5415, (715) 836-2380 fax

Offers area of study in Fibers.

Milwaukee
University of Wisconsin-Milwaukee
Art Department, P.O. Box 413, 2400 East Kenwood Boulevard, 53201
(414) 229-6054

Offers area of study in Fibers.

Washington Island
Sievers School of Fiber Arts
Page 336

8-Harness Weaving

Advanced Quilting

Basic Quilting

Beaded Victorian Net Bag

Beginning Feltmaking

Beginning Knitting

Batik Ancient and Modern

Color and Weave

Combing for Multi-Colored Yarns

Computer Drafting

Creativity Camp

Designing and Weaving in Wearable Art

Fancy Twined Pouch

From Fabric to Fashion

Intermediate Knitting

Intermediate Spinning

Introduction to Tapestry Weaving

Marbling on Fabric

Pin Weaving Techniques

Polymer Clay Buttons and Beads

Personalize Your Art to Wear

Silk Painting

Spinning Novelty Yarns

Vested Interest

Weave, Cut and Sew: Second Step Weaving

Weaving on a 4-Harness Floor Loom

CANADA

Halifax, Nova Scotia
Nova Scotia College of Art and Design
5163 Duke Street, B3J 3J6
(902) 422-7381, ext.188

Offers areas of study in Crafts and Textile Arts.

INTERNATIONAL

The Art Institute in La Antigua Guatemala
Page 241

Beading

Jewelry Making

Weaving

WILL TRAVEL TO YOU & CORRESPONDANCE COURSES

American Needlepoint Guild
Page 239

Atelier Plateau Collection Menzwear
Page 243
Lenora Elkin will travel on request to give classes on menswear construction, embellishment, and various other topics. Call for more information.

Barbara L. Grainger Enterprises
Page 243
BeadAcademy. Beading correspondance courses on a variety of techniques for the beginner to advanced levels. Barbara L. Grainger is a beadwork instructor and author of several peyote beading books. The courses include instruction sheets, kits, and upon completion of the course, an official certificate of completion.

Blueprints-Printables
Pag 251

Blueprinting Techniques and Inspiration

Buck's County Classic
Page 253
Five-step bead stringing course with free phone support.

Color Me Patterns
Page 261
Shirley Stevenson is a nationally known teacher and lecturer on wearable art and quilt making. Teaching brochure sent upon request.

Afghani Piecing

Appliqué

Art to Wear

Patriotic Quilts

Craftmaster Enterprises
Page 265

Seminars on Finding Profits in Crafting

Current Events Productions
Page 266
In Stitches Sewing, Needlework and Craft Shows has many different classes.

Eric's Press & Design & Sew Patterns
Page 274
Lois Ericson travels to many shows and shops around the country offering classes. Her itinerary is listed in the *Good News Rag*, or write for more information.

Fiber Statements
Page 279
Pat Rodgers will tailor-make a class with you to provide what you and your group want to learn in two hours, or five days, or anytime in between. Call or write for more details. Classes include:

Machine embroidery

Machine quilting and appliqué

The Glass Giraffe
Page 283
Classes in hot glass bead making. They will travel to teach for your organization. Please call for more information.

Handweaver's Guild of America, Inc.
Page 287

Certification courses

Islander Sewing Systems
Page 295

Couture Techniques

Lectures

Pattern Drafting

Seminars

Ivy Imports, Inc.
Page 295
Workshops:

Basics of Silk Painting

Designer Original (shirt painting)

Instant Success with Instant Set Dyes

Intensive 5-day Class In Traditional and Contemporary Silk Painting Techniques

Kid Stuff

Landscape

Silk Painting Demo

Silk Scarf (floral)

Silk Scarf (shells/fish)

Silk Tie

Lifetime Career Schools
Page 302
They offer accredited courses in these hobby/careers:

Doll Repair

Sewing/Dressmaking

Small Business Management

Mallery Press
Page 305
Ami Simms will travel to your location to offer any of these lectures and workshops.

Lectures

Don't Make the Same Mistakes I Did

Classic Quilts: Patchwork Designs from Ancient Rome

Creating Scrapbook Quilts

Humorous Quilts and Their Makers

The Old Order Amish

The World's Worst Quilts

Workshops

A New Way To Piece: Appliqué

Creating Scrapbook Quilts

Feathers That Fit

Geometric Patchwork Pattern Drafting

How To Improve Your Quilting Stitch

Invisible Appliqué

Pictorial Quilts

String Quilting

Michael James/Studio Quilts
Page 308

Color: Concepts and Investigations

Color Dynamics and Expression

Pattern: Exploring Two Dimensions

Visual Dynamics: Studies in Line, Space, Texture, and Pattern

Mimi's Books & Patterns for the Serious Dollmaker
Page 309
Available for travel to shops and doll clubs.

Cloth Dollmaking

Making Dolls With Paperclay

Patience is a virtue—and a seam saver...

When winding bobbins with polyester threads, wind slowly. The polyester thread will stretch if wound fast, causing puckered seams when sewn.

Tip provided by:
In Cahoots
Page 293

A few quilt squares...

Nine Patch

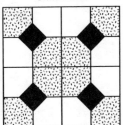

True Lover's Knot

Crimson Rambler

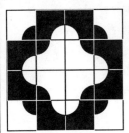

Cleopatra's Puzzle

Making Dolls With Polymer Clay

National Academy of Needlearts
Page 311

Park Bench Pattern Company
Page 318
Mary Lou Rankin offers trunk shows, lectures, and classes for stores, clubs and shows. Call or write for more information.

Pepper Cory
Page 321

The 19th Century Pineapple Block

The Art of Real Scrap Quilting

Happy Trails Rides Again (Drunkard's Path)

How to Become a More Creative Quiltmaker

Little Crazy Houses (a funny 6″ square house that is designed to delight)

Mastering Quilt Marking

The Revival of the Signature Quilt

Sarah's Star

Seeing Stars - The Starry Night Sampler from the Oxmoor House 1997 Calendar

Signature Quilts 101

The Signature Reel Block

Waste Not, Want Not

Smocking Arts Guild of America
Page 337

Sonya Lee Barrington
Page 339

Stitches Great Fiber Getaways
Page 341
Seminars and hands-on workshops available across the country, upon request.

Unique Techniques
Page 349
Judy Barlup offers several classes and seminars.

Burda Patterns

Interfacings

Sergers

Tailoring

Wonderful World of Hats
Page 353

Secrets of Hatmaking (a home study course)

Clubs, Guilds & Associations

These are groups that gather on a regular basis to discuss the methods of their interests. If you don't see one near you, contact the national headquarters to inquire about starting a regional branch in your community.

NATIONAL ASSOCIATIONS

American Needlepoint Guild
Page 239

American Quilt Study Group
Page 239

American Quilter's Society
Page 240

American Sewing Guild
Page 240

Begere de France Yarn Club, From Bergere de France
Page 249

Center for the History of American Needlework
Page 258

The Costume Society of America
Page 262

The Cotton Club
Page 263

Counted Thread Society of America
Page 264

The Crazy Quilt Support Group, From The Kirk Collection
Page 299

   ...because you should never have to face this form of addiction alone.

Handweaver's Guild of America, Inc.
Page 287

Historic Needlework Guild
Page 292

International Old Lacers, Inc.
Page294

The Knitting Guild of America
Page 299

Professional Association of Custom Clothiers
Page 325

Quilt Restoration Society
Page 297

Textile Arts Forum
Page 345

Thimble Collector's International
Page 346

ALABAMA

Birmingham
American Sewing Guild
Page 240
Mary Alice Smith, (205) 836-6161

Huntsville
American Sewing Guild
Page 240
Theresa Smith, (205) 882-9221

ARIZONA

Thimble Collector's International
Page 346
Arizona Thimblers

Phoenix
American Sewing Guild
Page 240
Joanne Woodfill, (602) 253-5125

Professional Association of Custom Clothiers
Page 325
Joanne Woodfill, (602) 253-5125

Prescott
American Sewing Guild
Page 240
Nancy Owens, (602) 772-6457

Skirt styles...

Full Skirt

Fitting historically...

When fitting historical costumes, it's important to make a muslin mock-up first and adjust that to your figure while wearing the proper underpinnings. (Historical fit is often quite different than modern.) Then use the mock-up as your personalized pattern to cut your expensive fashion fabric.

Tip provided by: Janet Wilson Anderson AlterYears Page 239

Tucson
American Sewing Guild
Page 240
Connie Curtis, (602) 751-0735

Silk Painting Guild
Deborah McDonnell
2555 East Water Street, 85716
(602) 327-1457

Tucson Bead Society
Page 348

Yuma
American Sewing Guild
Page 240
Wanda Hinkhouse, (602) 342-5719

CALIFORNIA

Thimble Collector's International
Page 346
Bay Area Thimble Society
Southern California Thimble Collectors
Thimble Collectors, San Diego

Chatsworth
Silk Painting Guild
9950 Topango Canyon Boulevard, #85, 91311
(818) 882-7422

Monterey Bay
American Sewing Guild
Page 240
Betty Bloomer, (408) 633-3602

Oakland
Surface Design Association
Page 343

Orange County, Southern Calif.
American Sewing Guild
Page 240

Rosemary Poor, (714) 968-7545

Pasadena
Silk Painting Guild
883 South Oakland Avenue, 91106
(818) 795-0845

Port Hueneme
Silk Painting Guild
421 Reed Way, 93041
(805) 984-2840

Sacramento
American Sewing Guild
Page 240
Jeane White, (916) 362-7030

San Diego
American Sewing Guild
Page 240
Patricia Dickenson, (619) 480-0704

San Jose/South Bay
American Sewing Guild
Page 240
Janet Caudle, (408) 445-8424

San Francisco
Professional Association of Custom Clothiers
Page 325
Cathy Beck, (707) 875-9613

Silk Painting Guild
172 Precita Street, 94110
(415) 826-8248

San Jose
Silk Painting Guild
7241 Scarsdale Place, 95120
(408) 997-2370

Santa Rosa
American Sewing Guild
Page 240

Kitty Kerrigan, (707) 795-0531

Vacaville
The Unique Spool
Page 349

Walnut Creek
American Sewing Guild
Page 240
Kim Nunes, (510) 825-4384

COLORADO

Thimble Collector's International
Page 346
Rocky Mountain Thimblers (CO, WY)

Colorado Springs
The Enchanted Cottage
Page 274

Denver
American Sewing Guild
Page 240
Terry (303) 423-8791

Professional Association of Custom Clothiers
Page 325
(303) 795-5404

Ft.Collins
American Sewing Guild
Page 240
Beverly J. Veazie, (303) 490-1486

Greeley
American Sewing Guild
Page 240
Billie Lou Baxter, (303) 330-4497

Golden
Quilts & Other Comforts
Page 328

CONNECTICUT

Thimble Collector's International
Page 346
The Priscilla Nutmeggers (CT, MA, RI)

Brookfield
Brookfield Craft Center
Page 253

Danbury
American Sewing Guild
Page 240
Karen M. Frank, (203) 748-7191

Professional Association of Custom Clothiers
Page 325
Norma Bucko, (203) 748-6506

Roxbury
Silk Painting Guild
21 Carriage Lane, 06783
(203) 354-4222

Glastonbury
Northeast Quilters Association
Page 313
Ron, (860) 633-0721

DISTRICT OF COLUMBIA

Thimble Collector's International
Page 346
Capitol Area Thimble Society (DC, MD, VA)

FLORIDA

Thimble Collector's International
Page 346
Dorcas Thimblers (West Coast FL)
Gold Coast Thimbles (East Coast FL)

Thimblers of Tampa Bay (Northwest FL)
Tropical Thimblers (Southwest FL)

Ft. Lauderdale
American Sewing Guild
Page 240
Rita Moore, (305) 452-9943

Ft. Meyers
American Sewing Guild
Page 240
Barbara Hayes, (941) 768-9590

Jacksonville
American Sewing Guild
Page 240
Brenda Adair, (904) 642-5812

Miami
American Sewing Guild
Page 240
Jeane Sheldon, (305) 238-1873

Orlando
American Sewing Guild
Page 240
Marilyn Gordon, (407) 277-7864

Tampa
American Sewing Guild
Page 240
Pat Chester, (813) 595-2042

GEORGIA

Atlanta
American Sewing Guild
Page 240
Cliff Trussell, (404) 662-6012

Macon
American Sewing Guild
Page 240

Jacqueline Peacock, (912) 929-9319

HAWAII

Honolulu
American Sewing Guild
Page 240
Mary Ann Duff, (808) 623-5265

ILLINOIS

Thimble Collector's International
Page 346
Southern Illinois Thimble Collectors Auxilliary
Thimble Fools of Northern Illinois

Chicago
American Sewing Guild
Page 240
Joni Bock, (708) 415-2740

Deerfield
Silk Painting Guild
859 Westcliff Lane, 60015
(708) 945-0872

Peoria/Central Illinois
American Sewing Guild
Page 240
Ruth Blackford, (309) 245-2047

Springfield
American Sewing Guild
Page 240
Linda Schlouski, (217) 245-9167

INDIANA

Thimble Collector's International
Page 346
Michigan-Indiana Thimble Society
Ohio Valley Thimblers (OH, KY, IN)

French knots in ribbon embroidery....

Step 1

Step 2

Finished Stitch

Tip provided by Prym-Dritz Corporation Page...

Bloomington
American Sewing Guild
Page 240
Mary Lou Walker, (812) 659-1473

Evansville
American Sewing Guild
Page 240
Jan Gallo, (812) 985-2877

Ft. Wayne
American Sewing Guild
Page 240
Mary Scott, (219) 747-4717

Indianapolis
American Sewing Guild
Page 240
Helen Harbin, (317) 291-1922

Kokomo
American Sewing Guild
Page 240
Vickey Weir, (317) 457-2828

Marion
American Sewing Guild
Page 240
Kathy D. Dively, (317) 395-5038

Richmond
American Sewing Guild
Page 240
Carla Metzger, (317) 935-7168

South Bend
American Sewing Guild
Page 240
Sondra Kalwitz, (219) 291-1222

IOWA

Thimble Collector's International

Page 240
Hawkeye Thimblers
Tiny Thimble Treasures of Iowa

Ames
American Sewing Guild
Page 240
Pat Wood, (515) 232-0605

Cedar Rapids
American Sewing Guild
Page 240
Vicki L. Thompson, (319) 849-2418

Council Bluffs
American Sewing Guild
Page 240
Carol Brockman, (712) 323-4643

Waterloo
American Sewing Guild
Page 240
Pat McKinney, (319) 478-2194

KANSAS

Flint Hills
American Sewing Guild
Page 240
Velma Walker, (316) 342-4091

Hutchinson
American Sewing Guild
Page 240
Delia Harder, (316) 665-8028

Leavenworth
Silk Painting Guild
1023 South 2nd Street, 66048
(913) 682-2218

Pittsburg
American Sewing Guild

Page 240
Jean Jack, (316) 724-8336

Yates Center
American Sewing Guild
Page 240
Terri Kretzmeier, (316) 365-5756

KENTUCKY

Thimble Collector's International
Page 346
Ohio Thimble Seekers
Ohio Valley Thimblers (OH, KY, IN)

Louisville
Embroiderers' Guild of America, Inc.
Page 274

Professional Association of Custom Clothiers
Page 325
Saundra L. Palmer, (502) 267-5057

LOUISIANA

Baton Rouge
Baton Rouge Bead Society
Page 246

MAINE

Bangor
American Sewing Guild
Page 240
Louise Kirkland, (207) 942-7396

Scarborough
Silk Painting Guild
Marion Jordan Road, 04074
(207) 883-2379

MARYLAND

Thimble Collector's International
Page 346
Capitol Area Thimble Society (DC, MD, VA)

Baltimore
Professional Association of Custom Clothiers
Page 325
Christine Ryan, (410) 360-2104

Bowie
American Sewing Guild
Page 240
Gail Hartung, (301) 262-8310

Chesapeake
Professional Association of Custom Clothiers
Page 325
Eva Motta, (301) 434-5231

Laurel
Silk Painting Guild
14921 Cherrywood Drive, 20707
(301) 490-6405

Rockville
G Street Fabrics
Page 282

MASSACHUSETTS

Thimble Collector's International
Page 346
The Priscilla Nutmeggers (CT, MA, RI)

Boston
American Sewing Guild
Page 240

Joan Hanlon, (617) 484-7737

Franklin
Professional Association of Custom Clothiers
Page 325
Jo Frongillo, (508) 528-2348

Springfield/Western Mass.
American Sewing Guild
Page 240
Doris Zeleznok, (413) 547-6483

MICHIGAN

Thimble Collector's International
Page 346
Great Lakes Thimblers
Michigan-Indiana Thimble Society

Detroit
American Sewing Guild
Page 240
Bonnie Push, (313) 386-6508

Kalamazoo
American Sewing Guild
Page 240
Becky Larner, (616) 342-0315

Lansing
American Sewing Guild
Page 240
(517) 321-6342

MINNESOTA

Duluth/Superior
American Sewing Guild
Page 240
Norma Pavola, (218) 722-5107

Minneapolis/St. Paul
American Sewing Guild
Page 240

Ruth Lucas, (612) 339-5568

Associated Sewing Supply Co., Inc.
Page 243

Thimble Collectors International
Page 346
Lady Slipper Thimblers (Twin Cities)

MISSISSIPPI

Hattiesburg
Professional Association of Custom Clothiers
Page 325
Mary Ross, (601) 544-1830

MISSOURI

Kansas City
American Sewing Guild
Page 240
Regina Kraus, (816) 524-2191

Professional Association of Custom Clothiers
Page 325
Brenda Coulter, (816) 836-8558

St. Louis
American Sewing Guild
Page 240
Kay Curry, (314) 837-6914

NEBRASKA

Omaha
American Sewing Guild
Page 240
Bonita Klinger, (402) 331-2027

Professional Association of Custom Clothiers
Page 325

Hemming a pair of pants...

Have the owner of the pants wear them with the shoes they are most likely to wear with the pants often.

The proper length is just hitting the top of the foot, so that the front crease is "broken" slightly. Mark that length.

Rip out the original hemming stitches. Press out the creases. Add the depth of the cuff to the length (usually 1 1/2"- 1 3/4"), and mark that length.

At that mark, fold the pant leg to the inside and press a crease. Stitch near the edge of the hem (the cuffs will hide the stitching when they are turned up). Fold the cuff back up to the outside at the right length and press.

Tack the cuffs to the pant leg at the outseam and inseam.

Knitting with cotton...

Since the cotton fiber is less elastic than other fibers, special steps should be taken to assure that the finished piece will keep its shape.

Knit tightly to prevent your sweater from stretching out of shape. A thin cotton, knit on size 3 or 4 needles will help to hold your sweater's shape.

Tightly knit the ribbing on smaller size needles. Cast on with a wider needle than called for. Immediately, on the first row, switch to needles three to four sizes smaller than those indicated for the body of the sweater. The number of ribbing stitches should be 10%-15% fewer than the body.

Knit into the backs of all your rib stitches. Insert the needle through the back, instead of the front of the loop.

For extra elasticity, try a rib with a right-over-left crossed knit stitch, a cable rib, or a reverse cross-stitch rib.

Use a translucent elastic thread (Magic Yarn) tacked inside the ribbing. After you have finished the sweater, sew

Cont.

Mary Bahl, (402) 496-1150

NEVADA

Las Vegas
American Sewing Guild
Page 240
Melinda Mata, (702) 565-6435

NEW HAMPSHIRE

Portsmouth
Silk Painting Guild
27 Elm Court, 03801
(603) 436-4389

NEW JERSEY

Thimble Collector's International
Page 346
Garden State Thimblers

Princetown/South Jersey
American Sewing Guild
Page 240
Alice Kopinitz, (609) 239-8547

Rutherford
Professional Association of Custom Clothiers
Page 240
Maria Guzman, (201) 933-4233

Somerset/Union
American Sewing Guild
Page 240
Sarah Ann Megletti, (201) 729-2774

NEW MEXICO

Albuquerque
American Sewing Guild
Page 240

Ann Jacobi, (505) 877-5253

NEW YORK

Thimble Collector's International
Page 346
Empire State Thimble Collectors

Canandaigua
Silk Painting Guild
3690 Woolhouse Road, 14424
(716) 394-7177

Rochester
American Sewing Guild
Page 240
Pat Miller, (716) 377-2419

Syracuse
American Sewing Guild
Page 240
June B. Weber, (315) 458-7244

West Danby
Silk Painting Guild
311 Tupper Road, 14896
(607) 564-7178

Younkers
Silk Painting Guild
205 Devoe Avenue, 10705
(914) 968-0573

NORTH CAROLINA

Charlotte
American Sewing Guild
Page 240
Gina McKenzie, (704) 596-3514

Gastonia
Audlin
Page 243

Raleigh
American Sewing Guild
Page 240
Nina Johnson, (919) 846-3785

NORTH DAKOTA

Bismarck/Mandan
American Sewing Guild
Page 240
Dawna Twist, (701) 255-0518

OHIO

Thimble Collector's International
Page 346
Ohio Thimble Seekers
Ohio Valley Thimblers (OH, KY, IN)

Akron/Canton
American Sewing Guild
Page 240
Lois Cunningham, (216) 494-5913

Cincinnati
American Sewing Guild
Page 240
JoAnn McKinley, (513) 984-5658

Cleveland
American Sewing Guild
Page 240
Brenda Jackson, (216) 439-0220

Columbus
American Sewing Guild
Page 240
Dee Dee Ptaszek, (614) 793-7122

Dayton
American Sewing Guild
Page 240
Betty Sherrill, (513) 426-5441

Niles
American Sewing Guild
Page 240
Thelma Schmid, (216) 755-5561

OKLAHOMA

Thimble Collector's International
Page 346
Thimblers of Oklahoma

Oklahoma City
American Sewing Guild
Page 240
Marilyn Highley, (405) 721-4846

Tulsa
American Sewing Guild
Page 240
Patti Pafford, (918) 245-4677

Professional Association of Custom Clothiers
Page 325
Suzanne Adamson, (918) 495-1544

OREGON

Thimble Collector's International
Page 346
Oregon-Southern Washington Thimble Collectors (OR, WA)

Medford
American Sewing Guild
Page 240
Pat Van Auken, (503) 474-7392

Portland
American Sewing Guild
Page 240
Lynn Derbyshire, (503) 236-4983

Portland Bead Society
Page 323

Professional Association of Custom Clothiers
Page 325
Marsha McClintock, (503) 760-3614

Salem
American Sewing Guild
Page 240
Sylvis Brown, (503) 362-9977

PENNSYLVANIA

Thimble Collector's International
Page 346
The Philadelphia Thimble Society
Three Rivers Thimblers (Western PA)

Altoona
American Sewing Guild
Page 240
Janice Kennedy, (814) 234-2215

Erie
American Sewing Guild
Page 240
Dorothy Cooney, (814) 838-1725

Mohnton
Silk Painting Guild
Route 1, Box 1290, 19540
(610) 856-7529

Philadelphia
American Sewing Guild
Page 240
Chris Hofmann, (610) 277-1557

Pittsburgh
American Sewing Guild
Page 240
Rebecca Bell, (304) 527-0572

Scranton
American Sewing Guild
Page 240
Theresa Kowatch, (717) 378-3243

Wescosville
Kite Studio
Page 299

York
Silk Painting Guild
1800 Barrington Drive, 17404
(717) 767-4644

RHODE ISLAND

Thimble Collector's International
Page 346
The Priscilla Nutmeggers (CT, MA, RI)

SOUTH CAROLINA

Greenville
American Sewing Guild
Page 240
Alicea Smith, (803) 271-4190

SOUTH DAKOTA

Rapid City
Pioneer Quilts
Page 322

TENNESSEE

Thimble Collector's International
Page 346
Tennessee Valley Thimble Collectors

TEXAS

Thimble Collector's International
Page 346
Houston Thimble Society

---

the Magic Yarn on by picking up each stitch of the top, middle, and bottom row of the ribbing all the way around the garment.

Add body to your cotton knitting by using either a garter, seed, or plaited stockinette stitch. You can also knit into the back of the purl stitches or a simple stockinette stitch. On circular needles, knit into the back of stitches on alternate rounds only.

Allow for a greater than usual reduction of stitches at points of body contact and control (at the underarms and wrists). The length of the underarm decrease for a set-in sleeve should always be a half-inch greater for cotton than for wool.

Always knit a test swatch before beginning your project. This is the single most important step you can take in assuring an accurate fit for your completed cotton garment. Machine-wash and dry before making final calculations.

***Tip provided by:
Cotton Clouds
Page 263***

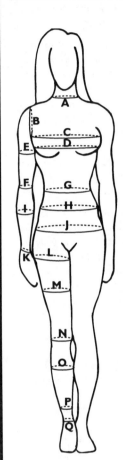

Girth and circumference chart for women...

Thimblers Are Us
Page 346
(Nothwest, Central, East TX)

Austin
Professional Association of Custom Clothiers
Page 325
Karen Roath, (512) 450-0277

Baytown
The Pin Cushion
Page 322

Dallas/Ft.Worth
American Sewing Guild
Page 240
Susan Fergus, (817) 468-5311

Houston
American Sewing Guild
Page 240
Margo Martin, (713) 867-9186

UTAH

Salt Lake City
American Sewing Guild
Page 240
Kelley Palmer, (801) 943-4077

VERMONT

Thimble Collector's International
Page 346
Vermont Stitch-In-Timers

Burlington
American Sewing Guild
Page 240
Joanne Latrell, (802) 244-8373

VIRGINA

Thimble Collector's International
Page 346
Capitol Area Thimble Society (DC, MD, VA)

Hampton Roads (Southeast VA)
American Sewing Guild
Page 240
Carole Aitken, (804) 474-1822

McLean
Silk Painting Guild
7020 Hector Road, 22101
(703) 893-5246

Radford/NRV
American Sewing Guild
Page 240
Dr. Edith Carter, (703) 639-1263

Richmond
American Sewing Guild
Page 240
Anita C. Lightfoot, (804) 378-3379

Roanoke
American Sewing Guild
Page 240
Nancy Farris, (703) 362-9598

WASHINGTON

Thimble Collector's International
Page 346
Nimble Fingers Thimble Club
Oregon-Southern Washington Thimble Collectors (OR, WA)
The Seattle Thimble Society

Puget Sound
Professional Association of Custom Clothiers
Page 325
Julie Engel, (206) 868-1925

WEST VIRGINIA

Camas
Silk Painting Guild
32903 Northeast 94th Street, 98607
(360) 834-1504

WISCONSIN

Milwaukee
American Sewing Guild
Page 240
Linda Doran, (414) 423-1529

Professional Association of Custom Clothiers
Page 325
Judith Ann Pagenkopf, (414) 964-4720

WYOMING

Laramie
American Sewing Guild
Page 240
Maletsa Mangan, (307) 742-3370

CANADA

Winnepeg, Manitoba
Professional Association of Custom Clothiers
Page 325
Anne Baetsen, (204) 255-4453

INTERNATIONAL CHAPTERS

Thimble Collector's International
Page 346
Dorset Thimble Society (England)

Freunde des Fingerhuts (Germany)
Needlework Tool Collectors' Society of Australia
Thimble Collectors' Guild (Scotland)
Thimble Collectors of South Africa
Thimble Society of London

A. Neck Base

B. Armscye

C. Chest at Base of Armscye

D. Bust

E. Upper Arm (Bicep)

F. Elbow

G. Waist

H. Abdominal Girth

I. Hips

J. Forearm

K. Wrist

L. Maximum Thigh

M. Midway Thigh

N. Knee

O. Maximum Calf

P. Minimum Leg

Q. Ankle

Collectibles & Novelties

Here are businesses that offer antique and reproduction items, note pads, collector's buttons, and more.

Accents Bead Shop
Page 237

    Antique beads and jewelry

Amazon Vinegar & Pickling Works Drygoods
Page 239

    24k gold-plated thimbles

    Chatelaine pins

    Embroidery scissors

    Needle case, seam ripper, needle threader, and stiletto set

    Selected sterling silver needlework tools

    Solid walnut knitting needles and crochet hooks

Anne Powell, Ltd.
Page 241

    Antique sewing and needlework tools

    Charms

    Chatelaines

    Sewing related figurines

    Sterling silver Thimbles

    Thimbles

Arise, Inc.
Page 241

    Historic textiles

    Ethnic textiles

Audlin
Page 243

BeadZip
Page 248

    Beads

Blue Heron Bead Company
Page 250

    Antique beads

Buttons & Things
Page 255

    Collector thimbles

Buttons Unlimited
Page 255

    Antique buttons

C & T Publishing
Page 258

    Notecards

    T-shirts

    Posters

Cotton Ball
Page 263

Daisy Kingdom
Page 267

Danforth Pewterers
Page 267
All items made from high-quality pewter.

    Quilt square buttons

    Quilt square charms

    Quilt square keyrings

    Quilt square picture frames

    Quilt square pins

Eagle Feather Trading Post
Page 272

Fabric Temptations
Page 276

G Street Fabrics
Page 282

    Antique buttons

Hansa Corp.
Page 288

Did you know...

Many vintage fabrics are as strong, or even stronger than contemporary fabrics. Many were made with higher quality greige goods (pronounced "gray goods," which is the basic cloth that is dyed and printed) than are used by manufacturers today. One measure of quality is thread count—the number of threads in the warp and the weft of the weave (length and cross threads). Count could be 68 square (68 threads in each direction in one square inch), or 74 by 62, or 200 square. The more threads, generally the better quality the cloth.

Tip provided by:
The Kirk Collection
Page 299

Antique German cases and boxes for sewing goods

Handmade Venetian glass beads

Harper House
Page 288

Chatelaine pins

Needle cases

Quilt Mate

Seam rippers

Sewing birds

Stilettos

Harriet's Treadle Arts
Page 289

Hedgehog Handworks
Page 289

Chatelaine pins

Fine needlework scissors

Needle cases

Quilt Mate

Stilettos

Thimble cases

Herrschners, Inc.
Page 291

Infiknit
Page 294

Notecards with knitting motifs

James W.M. Carroll Antiques
Page 296

Antique beads

Antique buttons

Antique fabrics

Antique quilts

JHB International
Page 296

Sewing-themed charms, buttons, and jewelry.

K & K Quilteds
Page 297

Vintage Fabrics

Quilts

The Kirk Collection
Page 299

Antique fabrics

Calling card/needle cases

Cigarette silks

Notecards

Quilt Pins

Victorian buttons

The Lacemaker
Page 301

Charms

Chatelaines

Earrings (to mount your lace in)

Jewelry

Pewter pincushions

Lacis
Page 301

Antique needle cases

Needle cases

Thimble cases and holders

Marilyn's Button Sales
Wholesale Only
Page 306

Antique and collectible buttons

Mary Ellen & Co.
Page 306

Nancy's Notions
Page 311

Calendars

Oiye Buttons
Page 314

Handmade porcelain buttons

Oregon Worsted Company/Mill End Store
Page 316

The Pin Cushion
Page 322

Pioneer Quilts
Page 322

Prairie Edge/Sioux Trading Post
Page 323

Prairieland Quilts
Page 324

Queen Ann's Lace
Page 326

Quilting Books Unlimited
Page 328

Quilts & Other Comforts
Page 328

Renaissance Buttons
Page 330

Antique buttons

Did you know...

Cigarette companies gave out printed silk pictures as premiums with cigarette packages from the turn of the century through the 20s. This was done to increase brand loyalty. The silks featured popular actresses of the day, historic queens, kings, presidents, Indians, flowers, birds, butterflies, animals, flags, and more. Most were done in a series, so one could collect all the butterflies, farm animals, etc. The companies even sent out instructions for making pillow tops and quilts from the silks, suggesting layouts similar to today's quilting pattern books. Today silks are used by quilters in crazy quilts. Often, people will include flowers, birds or flags of states or countries where they have lived. Others will choose images, such as cows, horses, or dogs which have special meaning to them.

Tip provided by:
The Kirk Collection
Page 299

Contests & Shows

Here are some consumer markets, judged competitions, and annual events. Events are broken down into national and specific state events.

NATIONAL SHOWS & CONTEST OPPORTUNITIES

American Needlepoint Guild
Page 239

Blue Heron Bead Company
Page 250

The Costume Society of America
Page 262

> Annual meeting and symposium

Current Events Productions
Page 266
In Stitches sewing, needlework and craft shows

> Spring - San Jose; Arlington, TX, Philadelphia; Atlanta

> Fall - Boston, Cleveland, Toledo, Chicago

Fancy Threads/Fancy Threads Custom
Page 277

Monthly Necktie Contest.

Send photo of your work. It must contain one or more of the ties that you have constructed from Fancy Threads Patterns,

the pattern envelope from your Fancy Threads Necktie Pattern, and your name and address on the back of the photo (photos will not be returned, and become the property of Fancy Threads). All ties must be constructed with Fancy Threads pattern and interfacing.

On a 3"x 5" note or post card, write your name, address, phone, where you purchased your pattern and interfacing, and any comments you have about the products (good or bad). To this card attach a 2"x 2" scrap of each fabric and Fancy Threads interfacing.

You may enter as often as you like–and be sure to send a card for each of the ties pictured (they draw the winners from the cards).

Each month's winner will win one pack of interfacing, or a $5 gift certificate. On December 1st each year, they will award a grand prize to someone randomly chosen from all previous months, then start again.

Keepsake Quilting
Page 298
Two quilt challenges each year, each based on a special theme. The entry quilt size is 30"x 30". Write to Keepsake Quilting Customer Service for more information.

The Knitting Guild of America
Page 299

> Annual conference

Mallery Press
Page 305
The Worst Quilt In The World Contest. Call or write for more information.

Nimble Thimbles
Page 313
Monthly Pattern Contest. If your idea for a custom pattern is chosen, it will be drawn to your measurements for free.

Original Sewing & Craft Expo
Page 316

> Traveling consumer show

CALIFORNIA

American Quilt Study Group Conference
Page 240

David M. & Peter J. Mancuso, Inc.
Page 261

Speaking their mind...

"Being a good craftsman will in no way prevent you from having genius."

Renoir

How to tie a bow in a scarf...

Cont.

Pacific International Quilt Festival

Quilt Contest

Wearable Art Contest

Arcata
Fabric Temptations
Page 276

Bay Area
Quilici Fay Productions
Page 326
Fall Colors...Fashion, Fabric, Fiber & Fun is held each October. Call for more information.

Oakland
Surface Design Association
Page 343
For those interested in textiles, techniques, artists' studios, and the textile industry.

San Francisco
Celebration of Craftswomen
Page 258

COLORADO

Denver
D'Leas Fabric and Button Studio
Page 266

Rangely
Old Style Trading Company
Page 314

CONNECTICUT

Glastonbury
Northeast Quilters Association
Page 313
Quilt festival each July. Call for more information.

FLORIDA

Jacksonville
Handweaver's Guild of America, Inc./Small Expressions
Page 288

Largo
Enterprise Art
Page 274

Winter Haven
AK Sew & Serge
Page 237
Sewing experts from across the country. Last week of Oct. and the first two weeks of Nov., $200-$250

LOUISIANA

Shreveport
Ghee's
Page 282

Ghee's 1996 Fiber Art Challenge Entry deadline: June 30, 1996

Entry fee: $8

All entries must incorporate some type of Mettler thread (machine embroidery, topstitching, or all-purpose).

Ghee's Sewing Escapes 1996
May 8-12 and September 25-29, 1996

4-4½ Days of Creative Sewing Registration Fee: $4.50

Held at Ghee's Studio and includes five noon and four evening meals.

MARYLAND

Earleville
The Costume Society of America
Page 262

22nd Annual Meeting and Symposium Celebrating the Seasons: Dressing for Life's Rites of Passage

May 29th to June 1, 1996 Sheraton Colony Square Hotel, Atlanta, GA

How nature and the seasons affect dress and how we dress to celebrate the changing "nature" and "seasons" of our lives.

Rockville
G Street Fabrics
Page 282

MASSACHUSETTS

Cambridge
Cambridge Artists Cooperative
Page 256
Art To Wear annual show each fall.

West Springfield
Eastern States Exposition/ CraftAdventure
Page 272

Crochet

Lace

Tatting

Weaving

Spinning

Basketry

Needlework

Rugging

MINNESOTA

Minneapolis
Associated Sewing Supply Co., Inc.
Page 243

NORTH CAROLINA

Asheville
Earth Guild
Page 272

Cedar Mountain
Minifest
Page 309

Gastonia
Audlin
Page 243

PENNSYLVANIA

Philadelphia
David M. & Peter J. Mancuso, Inc.
Page 267

    Pennsylvania National Quilt
Extravaganza

       Quilt Contest

       Wearable Art Contest

Pro Show, Inc.
Page 325

SOUTH DAKOTA

Sioux Falls
XRX, Inc.
Page 354

    Stitches Knitter's Fair

TEXAS

Baytown
**The Pin Cushion/The Art of Sewing
Extravaganza**
Page 322

Dallas
Bramwell Yarns, USA
Page 252

    Third British-American Machine
Knitting Expo

VIRGINA

Williamsburg
David M. & Peter J. Mancuso, Inc.
Page 267

    Williamsburg Festival Week

       Mid-Atlantic Quilt Festival and
Quilt Contest

       Mid-Atlantic Wearable Art
Festival and Wearable Art Contest

       Williamsburg Vintage Fashion and
Accessories Show

WASHINGTON

Bellevue
Beads & Beyond
Page 248
Juried show open to Northwestern artists,
juried in late September every year.

WASHINGTON, D.C.

Ivy Imports, Inc.
Page 295
First World Silk Painting Congress, 1997.
For continuous updates, subscribe to *The*

Silkworm.

    Lectures and workshops

    Educational displays and juried shows

    Forum for interaction

WISCONSIN

Steven's Point
Herrschners, Inc.
Page 291

    Afghan Contest
July 15th deadline. Call for more
information.

Costuming Supplies & Services

The companies listed here offer patterns, fabrics, and accessories for costumes for all occasions.

Accents Bead Shop
Page 237

Alpel Publishing
Page 238

  Easy Halloween Costumes for Children

AlterYears
Page 239

Amazon Vinegar & Pickling Works Drygoods
Page 239

Banasch's Fabrics
Page 245

Banasch's, Inc.
Page 245

Banksville Designer Fabrics
Page 245

Beyond Beadery
Page 250

Eagle Feather Trading Post
Page 272

  Traditional Native American and frontier patterns

G Street Fabrics
Page 282

Gaelic College Craft Shop
Page 282

  Scottish tartans

Greenberg & Hammer, Inc.
Page 286

  Boning

  Padding

  Shoulder pads

Harper House
Page 288

  Hundreds of historically correct patterns

Harriet's TCS/Harriet's Patterns
Page 288

  Period patterns, circa 1600-1945

Hedgehog Handworks
Page 289

  Corset busks

  Corset laces

  Corset stays

  Hook and Eye tapes

  Hoop wire

  Pewter buttons

  Pewter clasps

  Pewter lacers

  U-tips

Lacis
Page 301

Ledgewood Studio
Page 302

M & M Trims
Page 304

Manny's Millinery Supply Center
Page 305

Margola Corporation
  Wholesale Only
Page 306

Mary Ellen & Co.
Page 306

  Corset kits

Fitting hint for a full-skirted dress worn over hoops or petticoats...

Adjust the back bodice measurements so they are slightly shorter, as they did in the 1800s.

The added fullness at the waist can push the waistband up and cause horizontal wrinkles across the bodice.

Boning the seams is also helpful.

Tip provided by:
Janet Burgess
Amazon Vinegar & Pickling Works Drygoods
Page 239

Never underestimate the importance of underpinnings...

When making most historical costumes, the proper underpinnings are the key to the correct line and look.

Build your outfit from the skin out.

Tip provided by:
Janet Wilson
Anderson
Alter Years
Page...

Gone With the Wind

Hoop boning

Past Patterns

Patterns of History

Mediaeval Miscellanea
Page 308

Morning Star Indian Gallery
Page 310

Native American costuming

Optional Extras, Inc.
Page 315

Paperdolls' Design
Page 318

Fabrics and costume design for roller and ice skaters

Patchworks
Page 319

Patterns of History
Page 319

1870s - 1900s period patterns

Pegee of Williamsburg Patterns from Historie
Page 320

Historical patterns

Pennywise Fabrics
Page 320

Promenade's Le Bead Shop
Page 325

Richard the Thread
Page 330

Corset supplies

Shoulder pads

Sewing Emporium/Sew-Easy Products
Page 335

Stone Age
Page 341

Custom gemstone buttons and button covers, including tuxedo sets and cufflinks.

SouthStar Supply Company
Page 339

Textile Reproductions
Page 345

Trendsetter Yarns/Ornashi Filati
Wholesale Only
Page 348

Fantasy fibers for knitting, weaving, etc.

The Unique Spool
Page 349

Custom Materials & Services

The businesses listed here offer customized patterns, labels, swatching services, and more.

Apparel Component Supply
Page 241
They offer a custom coordinated color card to match zippers, thread, seambinding, snaps, velcro, cordings and cord locks.

Arthur M. Rein
Page 242
He will find your requested fur, or create your custom fur clothing and accessories.

Atkinson Fabrics, Inc.
Page 243

Aurora Silk
Page 244

  Custom natural dyeing

B & J Fabrics, Inc.
Page 244

  Swatch-matching service

Banksville Designer Fabrics
Page 245

  Custom swatch service

Beadazzled, A Bead Emporium
Page 248

  Beading birthday parties

BeadZip
Page 248
They offer a Personal Shopping service for finding the beads you need.

Blond Woven Labels
Page 250

  Custom woven labels

Blueprints-Printables
Page 251

  Custom sewing in quantities

  Fabric-covered earring blanks

Boca Loca Beads
Page 251

Butterick Company, Inc.
Page 254

  Custom labels

The Button Shoppe
Page 254
They will match buttons to your fabric or yarn swatches.

Buttons 'n' Bows
Page 254

Carol Harris Co.
Page 257

  Custom embroidery

Carolin Lowy Customized Designs and Graphs
Page 257

Carolina Mills Factory Outlet
Page 258

The Corner Stitch, Inc.
Page 262

  Custom clothing design

  Custom sewing of heirloom clothing

D'Anton Leather
Page 266

David Simpson, BookFinder
Page 268

  They offer a search service for out-of-print books.

Dawn's Hide and Bead Away, Inc.
Page 268

  Jewelry

Identify your child...

If you have young children, instead of purchasing labels with your name, try purchasing labels with each child's name and your phone number.

If your child is ever lost, it could aid greatly in identifying them for a safe and quick return.

Length measurement chart for women, back view...

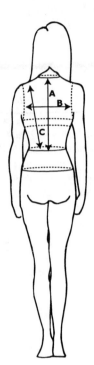

A. *Neck to Waist*

B. *Shoulder Blade Width*

C. *Shoulder to Waist Length*

Elegance Unlimited, Inc.
Page 273

Swatch-matching service

Enterprise Art
Page 274

Fabric Gallery
Page 276

Belt and button covering

Seamstress referral

Special order bridal

Swatch service

Fancy Threads/Fancy Threads Custom
Page 277

Interfacing counseling

Invisible zipper matching

Thread matching

Fireside Fiberarts
Page 280

Custom looms and weaving supplies

G Street Fabrics
Page 282

Fabric covered belts

Fabric covered buttons

Labels

Monogrammed buttons

Gaelic College Craft Shop
Page 282

Hemming and pressing of kilts

Greenberg & Hammer, Inc.
Page 286

Clothing labels

Monogram buttons

Hancock's
Page 287
They will laminate any fabric purchased from them for a fee.

Handweaver's Guild of America, Inc.
Page 287
A beginner's Help Line is available to members.

Harriet's TCS/Harriet's Patterns
Page 288
They do consulting for accurate accessorizing of historic costumes, creating the total look.

Harriet's Treadle Arts
Page 289

Heirloom Knitted Lace
Page 289
They do troubleshooting for knitted lace patterns and techniques.

Heirloom Woven Labels
Page 290

Custom labels

Heritage Looms
Page 291

Weaving equipment

High Country West Needleworks
Page 291

Custom needlework finishing

The Hillsinger Company
Page 291

Beadwork pattern design

Ident-ify Label Corp.
Page 293

Custom labels

Jehlor Fantasy Fabrics
Page 296

Swatching service

Jill McIntire Designs
Page 296

Design editing for machine embroidery

Scanning service

K & K Quilteds
Page 296

Quilt restoration

The Kirk Collection
Page 299
If you specify the age and amount of fabric you are interested in, they will send you a surprise box of fabrics each month that meet your criteria. Some clubs: Chicken Fabric Club, Feedsack Club, all Novelty Prints Club, and others.

Quilt restoration

Restoration scraps by decade

Kite Studio
Page 299
They will give suggestions on kite building and banner making.

Kreinik Mfg. Co., Inc.
Wholesale Only

Page 299

Custom threads and decorative trims

The Leather Factory
Page 302

Magic Fit Patterns
Page 304

Custom-fit patterns

Marine Sewing
Page 306

Advice is free with any purchase.

Mimi's Fabrications
Page 309

National Thread & Supply
Page 312

Nimble Thimbles
Page 313

They offer custom patterns created to fit your body. They can make a pattern from a magazine photo, a catalog picture, or your drawing.

Northwest Tag & Label, Inc.
Page 314

Care/content labels

Custom logo labels

Hang tags

Iron-on label material

Printed size labels

Size stickers

Woven labels

Picking Up The Pieces Quilt Shop
Page 322

Quilt repair and restoration

Referrals to quilters for hire

Prairieland Quilts
Page 324

Quest Beads & Cast, Inc.
Page 326

Custom beads and buttons

Quilts & Other Comforts
Page 328

Quilts By the Oz
Page 329

Custom quilting

Free advice

Revelli
Page 330

They have custom color and design kits for your own personalized style.

Running Stitch Studio
Page 331

They will quilt your unfinished masterpieces (and who doesn't have a few of those laying around—now be honest).

The Scarlet Letter
Page 333

Archival Mounting of Needlework

Custom period-style frames for needlework made from tiger maple, birdseye maple, flame birch, Carpathian elm, or walnut burls.

Seattle Fabrics, Inc.
Page 334

Silkpaint Corporation
Page 337

Something Pretty
Page 339

Custom and handpainted ceramic buttons

Spinning Wheel
Page 340

Stitches Great Fiber Getaways
Page 341

They have seminars and hands-on workshops available across the country, upon request.

Stone Age
Page 341

Custom gemstone buttons and button covers, tuxedo sets, and cufflinks

Taylor's Cutaways & Stuff
Page 344

Custom labels that say... "If I misplace my clothes, phone:"

Craft suppliers finder service - $1 per title/subject.

Textile Reproductions
Page 345

Custom vegetable dyeing for authentic period color

Fabric searches for institutions

Thimbles by T.J. Lane/Integrity Patterns by T.J. Lane
Page 345

Custom thimbles

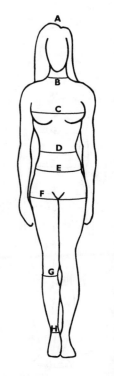

Height measurement chart for women...

A. Stature

B. Neck

C. Bust

D. Waist

E. Hips

F. Crotch

G. Knees

H. Ankle

Height measurement chart for men...

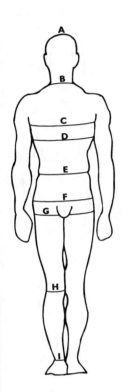

A. *Stature*

B. *Neck*

C. *Chest at Armscye*

D. *Chest*

E. *Waist*

F. *Hips*

G. *Crotch*

H. *Knee*

I. *Ankle*

Things Japanese
Page 346

They offer advice on the use of their silk products, based on many years of experience with silk.

Treadle Yard Goods
Page 349

　　Custom swatching service

Unique Patterns Design
Page 350

　　Custom-fit patterns

Vale Cottage Studio
Page 350

　　Quilt appraisals

　　Quilt restoration and conservation

Waechter's Silk Shop
Page 351

　　Personal shopping services. Call for information

The Whole Bead Show
Page 353

Doll & Soft Toy Making Supplies

The businesses listed here have everything you need to create stuffed friends and pets for the young (and young-at-heart) in your life.

AK Sew & Serge
Page 237

Ashland Bay Trading Company, Inc.
   Wholesale Only
Page 242

   Fibers for doll hair and Santa beards

Atlanta Puffections
Page 243

   Doll patterns

   Animal

   Christmas

   Dishtowel

   Doorstop

   Family

   Mice

Banasch's Fabrics
Page 245

Banasch's, Inc.
Page 245

Brian's Crafts Unlimited
Page 252

   Craft fur

   Muslin animals

   Muslin dolls

Buffalo Batt & Felt
Page 254

   Polyester stuffing

Buttons 'n' Bows
Page 255

   Apple Valley Doll Kits

Carolina Mills Factory Outlet
Page 258

Color Me Patterns
Page 261

Cotton Ball
Page 263

   Patterns

CR's Crafts
Page 264

   Accessories

   Armatures

   Bear and animal patterns and books

   Books and patterns for all kinds of dolls

   Buttons and appliques

   Cloth bodies

   Clothing patterns and books

   CR's original patterns and kits

   Designer clothing

   Eyes, noses and joints

   Fur fabrics (including mohair)

   Glorfix doll supplies

   Hats

   Jewelry

   Mauerhan doll supplies

   Music boxes, growlers and criers

   Painted designer porcelain

   Papier maché doll parts

   Porcelain head sets of all sizes

   Shoes

   Socks, tights, and underwear

   Stuffings

   Wigs and hair

Crystal Palace Yarns
   Wholesale Only
Page 266

   Fibers for doll hair

Washable handmade toys…

Whenever a doll or toy pattern calls for cardboard, try substituting washable buckram or plastic.

Bodice styles...

French Dart

Surplice

Bodice styles...

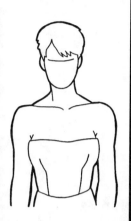

Strapless

Princess Seamed

Dyes & Fabric Paints

Are you sick and tired of feeling limited to static fabric designs?
Try your own surface design; it's fun, easy, creative—and great for everything from clothing to quilts.

AK Sew & Serge
Page 237

Aurora Silk
Page 244

Berman Leather Co.
Page 249

Paints and dyes for leather

Commercial Art Supply
Page 261

Airbrushes

Batik

Dyes

Marbling

Silkscreen

Cotton Ball
Page 263

CR's Crafts
Page 264

Daisy Kingdom
Page 267

Delta Technical Coatings, Inc.
Wholesale Only
Page 268

Delta Fabric Colors

Delta Brush-on Fabric Color Fabric Dye

Delta Dazzlers

Delta Shimmering Fabric Color Starlight Dye

Glitter Liner

Shiny Liner

Dharma Trading Co.
Page 269

Alum

Brushes

Carrageenan

Casolene Oil® HSA

Color remover

Deka Iron-on Transfer Paint

Deka Permanent

Fluorescent

Metallic

Opaque

Deka Print for Silkscreening

Deka-Sil Flowable Fabric Paint

Deka Silk Resist

Black

Clear

Gold

Silver

Discharge Paste

Dye-na-Flow

Dyes

Acid Dyes

Deka Series L Dyes

Dr. Ph. Martin's Spectralized

Dupont French dyes

Jacquard Silk Colors

Jacquard Textile Colors

Methcel

Milsoft

Natural dyes

Orient Express by Pebeo

Pebeo Soie

Peintex

Procion Liquid H Series Concentrates

Procion MX

Discharge dyeing demystified...

Begin by pre-washing fabric, then mix a solution of one part bleach to five parts water. Test a swatch of fabric in the bleach mixture to determine how long you will need to leave in your fabric.

When submerging your fabric, agitate it gently every minute or so with a wooden spoon, or with your hands, while wearing protective rubber gloves.

When the color is the shade you would like, remove your fabric from the mixture and submerge it in a solution of one part vinegar to two parts water for at least a half an hour..

Wash and dry your fabric.

Be flexible...

Don't limit yourself to using a certain kind of fabric paint only on the identified fabric.

For example, silk paints straight out of the bottle, used on cotton fabrics, produce a lovely soft watercolor effect.

Tip provided by:
Linda Kanziger
The Alcott Press
Page 238

Retayne

Setacolor

Fabric pens and markers

Gutta

    American

    Black

    Clear

    French

    Gold

    Silver

Glauber's salt

Glow in the dark paint

Jones Tones Stretch Fabric Paint

Lumiere

Make-Your-Own-Markers

Mordants

Neopaque

No-Flo Primer for Silk

Oxgall

Pre-stretched silk panels

ReDuRan–special hand cleaning cream

Silkpaint Air Pen

Silk steamers

Soda ash fixer

Sodium alginate thickener

Super Tinfix

Tinfix

Urea

Versatex A.B.I.

Versatex Print for Silkscreening

Visionart - Instant Setting for Silk and

Wool

Water softener

Waxes

    Batik wax

    Beeswax

    Paraffin

    Sticky wax

    Synthrapol® SP

Earth Guild
Page 272

    Batiking supplies

    Blueprinting supplies

    Deka Permanent Fabric Paints

    Deka Print Inks

    Deka Series L

    Deka Silk Paints

    Fabric Arts Liquid Dyes

    Fabricolor pens

    Lanaset Wool Dyes

    Marbling supplies

    Mordants

    Natural dyes

    Procion Reactive Dyes

    Resists

Enterprise Art
Page 274

    Brushes

    Paints

    Transfers

The Fiber Studio
Page 279

Fiskars, Inc.
Wholesale Only
Page 280

G Street Fabrics
Page 282

Gramma's Graphics
Page 284

Greenberg & Hammer, Inc.
Page 286

    Shoe and leather dyes

    Tintex

Halcyon Yarn
Page 286

    Procion Dye

    Wash Fast Acid Dye

Herrschners, Inc.
Page 291

Ivy Imports, Inc.
Page 295

Kasuri Dyeworks
Page 298

    Brushes

    Ganryo

    German Pure-K

    Japanese Indigo

    Special orders from Japan

Kite Studio
Page 299

    Design Master Paints (works on ripstop nylons)

When you have just the right colors...

Use a hairdryer to "freeze" colors as you want them, when they have mixed and produced the desired effect.

Remember, keep your hair dryer on low, so that it does not blow your dye everywhere.

Embroidery & Needlework Supplies

These companies have supplies for hand and machine embroidery and counted needlework.

5T's Embroidery Supply
Page 237

  Backings

    Cut-away

    Iron-on

    Peel-off

    Soluble

  Embroidery nippers

  Embroidery scissors

  Needles

  Mundial Scissors

AK Sew & Serge
Page 237

Amazon Vinegar & Pickling Works Drygoods
Page 239

Associated Sewing Supply Co., Inc.
Page 243

Aura Registered
Page 244

Aurora Silk
Page 244

  Natural dyed silk yarns of various thickness

Beacon Fabric & Notions
Page 247

  Machine embroidery thread and supplies

Bead in Hand
Page 247

Buttons 'n' Bows
Page 255

By Jupiter!
Page 255

  Antiqued silver charms

  Brass charms

California Stitchery
Page 256

  Judaic needlework supplies

Carol Harris Co.
Page 257

Carolin Lowy Customized Designs and Graphs
Page 257

Center for the History of American Needlework
Page 258

  Historic patterns

Continuity...
Page 262

The Corner Stitch, Inc.
Page 262

Cotton Clouds
Page 263

  Over 1,500 colors of cotton and cotton blend yarns

Crafts By Donna
Page 265

Creative Beginnings
Page 265

Downie Enterprises
Page 271

  Dazor Magnifier Lamps

  Pre-worked needlepoint

When working with eyelet stitch...

Always plunge into the center hole—never come up in it. This basically follows the clean hole/dirty hole principle. Come up in a clean hole and plunge into a dirty (already occupied) one.

The center void of these eyelet stitches is very much a part of the beauty of them, and disturbed stitches—which would produce "fuzzies" —would adversely affect the appearance of a lovely stitch.

Tip provided by: High Country West Needleworks Page 291

Transferring...

To transfer an embroidery pattern on washable fabric without using an iron-on transfer (that does not always come out), use a piece of water-soluble film.

Any black pen can be used to put the design on the smooth side of the film. Baste the film smooth side up and proceed to embroider and/or bead the design. When the work is completed, place the entire piece in cold water. The film and lines will disappear.

Note:

Since everything disappears, you do not have to embroider a drawn line if you change your mind after starting.

Tip provided by: Donna Freibertshauser Crafts by Donna Page 265

The Enchanted Cottage
Page 274

    Anchor

    Artsilk

    Brazilian embroidery kits

    Brazilian threads

    DMC

    Frames

    Glissen Gloss

    Marlitt

    Needle Necessities Fibers

    Needles

    Notions

    Rainbow Gallery Fibers

    Trebizond

    Wool embroidery threads

Enterprise Art
Page 274

Fabric Temptations
Page 276

Fancywork
Page 277

    Evenweave fabrics

    Floss

    Metallics

G Street Fabrics
Page 282

Granny's Quilts
Page 285

Great Northern Weaving
Page 285

Harriet's Treadle Arts
Page 289

Hedgehog Handworks
Page 289

    Antique stitching paper

    Balger Metallic

    Beads

    Broider Wul

    Bullions

    Caron Collection

        Watercolours

        Waterlilies

        Wildflowers

    Charts for cross-stitch

    DMC

    Evenweave fabrics

        Linen—19, 25, 28, 32, 36, 40 count

        Silk gauze—32, 40 count

        Waste canvas—10, 12, 14, 16, 18, 20 count

    Hoop and Stitch (wooden embroidery hoop permanently mounted on a base; bases allow the hoops to stand about 6″ above any surface)

    Irish linen handkerchiefs

    Japan gold and silver threads

    Lead Crystal boxes

    Madeira Metallics

    Marlitt

    Needlework frames

        Lap

        Floor

    Trebizond Twisted Silk

    Pendant frames

    Porcelain boxes

    Soie Critale

    Soie d'Alger

    Stitcher's Pocket Inventory

    Tambour hooks

    Tambour needle set

    Tassel silk

Heirlooms Forever
Page 290

Herrschners, Inc.
Page 291

HH Designs
Page 291

    Candlewicking kits

High Country West Needleworks
Page 291

Historic Needlework Guild
Page 292

Homestead Needle Arts
Page 292

    Handpainted needlepoint canvases

In Cahoots
Page 293

Jill McIntire Designs
Page 297

    Blank embroidery cards

Judy's Heirloom Sewing
Page 297

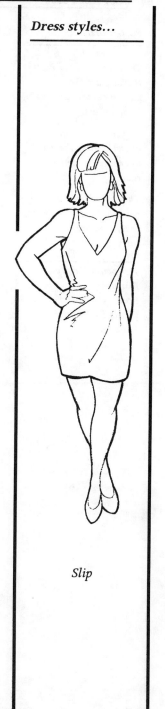

Dress styles...

Slip

Post-It markers...

The ever-so-handy Post-It Notes are excellent markers when stitching from a chart.

As you complete a row of work, move the note to another section of the chart.

They are inexpensive, do not leave residue on your chart, and are easy to carry around.

Tip provided by:
Donna Freibertshauser
Crafts by Donna
Page 265

Rachelette

Soie Crystale

Watercolors

Waterlilies

Wildflowers

DMC

Evenweave fabrics, 10–36 count

Marlitt

Needlepoint mesh

Rainbow Gallery

Backgrounds

Cresta D'oro

Flair

Fleur de Paris

Frosty Rays

Goldfingering

Gold Rush 14

Neon Rays

Madras

Overdyed Medici

Overture

Pearl 8 Overdyed

Pebbly Pearl

Rainbow Lines

Santa's Beard and Suit

Ultrasuede

Velour

Whisper

Ranita Corporation
Page 329

Ribbons & Roses
Page 330

SAX Arts & Crafts
Page 333

The Scarlet Letter
Page 333

Counted thread and silkscreen sampler kits, reproductions from 1625-1840

Flax linens

Silk threads

Sewing Emporium/Sew-Easy Products
Page 335

Silkpaint Corporation
Page 337

Fiber Etch™ fabric remover

The Smocking Horse Collection
Page 337

SouthStar Supply Company
Page 339

Spinning Wheel
Page 340

Suzanne Roddy, Handweaver
Page 343

Needlework yarns

Cotton

Linen

Silk

Wool

Sweet Child of Mine
Page 343

Minnamurra threads

Porcelain boxes

Rajmahal Art Silk

Silver-Plated boxes

Silver-Plated brooches

Silver-Plated clothes brush

Silver-Plated comb-brush-mirror set

Textile Reproductions
Page 345

Things Japanese
Page 346

Tinsel Trading Co.
Page 347

Antique and contemporary metallic threads

Filé

Lamé

Plate

Pluie

Twists

Unicorn Books and Crafts, Inc./Glimåkra Looms 'n Yarns/Frederick J. Fawcett, Inc.
Page 349

Fabrics

The Whole Bead Show
Page 353

Fabrics

These businesses offer every type of fabric imaginable. To help you find the kind of fabric you want, the fabrics are listed according to fiber content.

ACRYLIC

Art Max Fabrics
Page 242

Atkinson Fabrics, Inc.
Page 243

Baer Fabrics
Page 245

Banasch's Fabrics
Page 245

Clearbrook Woolen Shop
Page 259

Cottons, Etc.
Page 263

Daisy Kingdom
Page 267

Fabric Gallery
Page 276

Fashion Fabrics Club/Natural Fiber Fabrics Direct
Page 278

Fishmans Fabrics
Page 280

   20 colors

G Street Fabrics
Page 282

Hancock's
Page 287

   Synthetic fur

   Heathered felt

   Moire, cotton blend

   Rainbow felt

Herrschners, Inc.
Page 291

Joyce's Fabrics
Page 297

Londa's Sewing, Etc.
Page 303

M's Fabric Gallery
Page 304

   Drapery

   Upholstery

Oregon Worsted Company/Mill End Store
Page 310

The Smocking Horse Collection
Page 337

Stone Mountain & Daughter Fabrics
Page 341

TestFabrics, Inc.
Page 345
All fabrics are untreated and prepared for printing or dyeing.

The Thrifty Needle
Page 347

   Knitted sweater material

Vogue Fabrics/Vogue Fabrics By Mail
Page 351

CASHMERE

A Fabric Place
Page 237

Art Max Fabrics
Page 242

Make a habit of it...

Make it a habit to pre-wash and press all fabric as soon as it comes home from the store. It's much more efficient than stopping in the middle of something to do it, especially once the creative juices have started to flow.

Tip quoted from:
Every Trick In The Book
by Ami Simms
Mallery Press
Page 305

COTTON

Yards	Meters
3 5/8	3.35
3 3/4	3.45
3 7/8	3.55
4	3.7
4 1/8	3.8
4 1/4	3.9
4 3/8	4
4 1/2	4.15
4 5/8	4.25
4 3/4	4.35
4 7/8	4.5
5	4.6
5 1/8	4.7
5 1/4	4.8
5 3/8	4.95
5 1/2	5.05
5 5/8	5.15
5 3/4	5.3
5 7/8	5.4
6	5.5
6 1/8	5.6
6 1/4	5.75
6 3/8	5.85
6 1/2	5.95
6 5/8	6.1
6 3/4	6.2
6 7/8	6.3
7	6.4
7 1/8	6.55
7 1/4	6.65
7 3/8	6.75
7 1/2	6.9

Cont.

Yards	Meters
7 5/8	7
7 3/4	7.1
7 7/8	7.2
8	7.35
8 1/8	7.45
8 1/4	7.55
8 3/8	7.7
8 1/2	7.8
8 5/8	7.9
8 3/4	8
8 7/8	8.15
9	8.25
9 1/8	8.35
9 1/4	8.5
9 3/8	8.6
9 1/2	8.7
9 5/8	8.8
9 3/4	8.95
9 7/8	9.05
10	9.15

Batiks
 African
 Balinese
 Indian
 Javanese
Batiste
Brazilian
British
Calicos
Central American
Chinese
Damask
Egyptian
European
Ikats
 Balinese
 Guatemalan
 Indian
 Thai
Indian
Indonesian
Jacquard
Japanese
Korean
Lawn
Pima
Sateen
Sea Island
Silkscreened

Fabrics Unlimited
Page 276

Fashion Fabrics Club/Natural Fiber Fabrics Direct
Page 278

Fishmans Fabrics
Page 280

Batiste
Crinoline
Denim
Gauze
Lawn
Muslin
Organdy
Pique
Sateen
Twill
Velour

Frostline Kits
Page 282

G Street Fabrics
Page 282

Ginger's Needleworks
Page 283

Gramma's Graphics
Page 284

Granny's Quilts
Page 285

Great Northern Weaving
Page 285

Narrow cut rolls

Grey Owl Indian Craft
Page 286

Hancock's
Page 287

Alexander Henry
Ametex
Anju Woodridge
Bernatex
Bloomcraft
Braemore
Canvas
Concord Fabrics
Cute As A Button for South Seas
Debbie Mumm for South Seas
Fabriquilt
Flannel
Hoffman
Homespun
Kravet
Kona cotton broadcloth
Marcus Brothers
Mill Creek/Swavelle
Muslin
Nancy Crow for John Kaldor
Onasburg
P/Kaufman
Quilted muslin, poly batting
Richloom
Robert Kaufman
Spring's Cotton Belle broadcloth
Springs Mills

What is bias?

Of course, you have the grainline and across the grain.

Bias is any diagonal on a piece of fabric. True bias is a 45° angle.

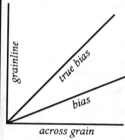

Interfacing for lace...

Bridal tulle makes excellent interfacing for collars, facings, and under buttonholes on lace garments. Tulle gives soft stability without interfering with the transparency of lace.

Tip quoted from:
More Power Sewing
by Sandra Betzina
Power Sewing
Page 323

Fitting in...

Every floral fabric that is introduced to a design should be repeated in at least two other squares.

Using just one square from a fabric will make it stand out; it will look out of place.

*Tip quoted from:
Impressionist Quilts
by Gai Perry,
published by C & T
Publishing
Page 258*

Banishing wrinkles from linen...

If you love linen but hate wrinkles, underline the entire garment with fusible knitted tricot interfacing.

Underlining white linen pants accomplishes two things: it cuts down on wrinkles and prevents "see through."

Tip quoted from: More Power Sewing by Sandra Betzina Power Sewing Page 323

Gaelic College Craft Shop
Page 282

Hemp BC
Page 290

    Basketweave

    Denim twill

    Herringbone

    Summercloth

    Twill, cotton blend

Hemp Textiles International Corp.
Page 290

Kasuri Dyeworks
Page 298

Oregon Worsted Company/Mill End Store
Page 316

Rupert, Gibbon & Spider
Page 331
All fabrics are untreated and prepared for printing or dyeing.

    Light and Heavy Weights.

LINEN

A Fabric Place
Page 237

AK Sew & Serge
Page 237

Art Max Fabrics
Page 242

Associated Sewing Supply Co., Inc.
Page 243

B & J Fabrics, Inc.
Page 244

Baer Fabrics
Page 245

Banasch's Fabrics
Page 245

Banksville Designer Fabrics
Page 245

Bridals International
Page 253

Buttons 'n' Bows
Page 255

    Bearlin (48% cotton)

    Handkerchief

Carol Harris Co.
Page 257

Carolina Mills Factory Outlet
Page 257

Clearbrook Woolen Shop
Page 259

The Corner Stitch, Inc.
Page 262

Cotton Ball
Page 263

Cottons, Etc.
Page 263

D'Leas Fabric and Button Studio
Page 266

Daisy Kingdom
Page 267

Elegance Unlimited, Inc.
Page 273

The Enchanted Cottage
Page 274

Fabric Collections
Page 276

Fabric Complements, Inc.
Page 276

    Handkerchief

    Suitings

Fabric Gallery
Page 276

Fabric Temptations
Page 276

    Cotton blends

    Rayon blends

    Silk blends

    Wool blends

Fabrics Unlimited
Page 276

Fancywork
Page 277

    Evenweave

Fashion Fabrics Club/Natural Fiber Fabrics Direct
Page 278

Fishmans Fabrics
Page 280

G Street Fabrics
Page 282

Full of hot air? Great!

When sewing with tissue lamé, the lightweight, shiny, tough-to-sew fabric, try this tip:

Plug a blow dryer in next to your sewing machine. Just before you sew an area, blow hot air from the hair dryer over the seam line, then stitch, using a fine, pointed sewing machine needle.

The hot air softens the coating on the lamé fabric, and there will be less snagging and pulling.

Tip provided by:
Jehlor Fantasy Fabrics
Page 296

Brocade

Chiffon

Cracked Ice

Lamé

Metallic sheer

Organza

Satin

Sequined

Stretch nude sheer

Super stretch spandex

Velvet

Joyce's Fabrics
Page 297

2-way stretch

Blanket bunting fleece

Cuddleskin

Lingerie

Pajama knits

Quilted

Rib knits

Sweatshirt knits

K & K Quilteds
Page 297

Vintage Fabrics

The Kirk Collection
Page 299

Antique fabrics

Brocades

Satins

Taffetas

Velvets

Kite Studio
Page 299

200 and 420 denier nylon

Dacron

Norlam Gold

Orcon

Ripstop nylon

Ripstop polyester

UV resistant film

Ledgewood Studio
Page 302

Logan Kits
Page 302

Lingerie fabrics

Lycra

Neck and arm ribbing

Londa's Sewing, Etc.
Page 303

Marine Sewing
Page 306

Fabrics for outdoor use

Miss Maureen's Fabrics and Fancies
Page 309

Nancy's Notions
Page 311

Polarfleece

Ultraleather

Ultrasuede

Ultrasuede Light

Oregon Worsted Company/Mill End Store
Page 316

Outdoor Wilderness Fabrics
Page 317

Canvas

Chamois

Cool wicking fabrics

Gore-Tex

Hunter's blaze

Lycra

Mylar

Neoprene

Netting

New fleece

Nylon ballistics

Nylon cordura, coated and uncoated

Nylon oxford

Nylon taffeta

Packcloth

Polartec, 100, 200, 300, 1000, 2000

Poplin

Quilted insulation

Ripstop

Seltech

Supplex

Tactel

Thinsulate

Tuff grip

Twill

Ultrex

Vinyl coated polyester

Cotton broadcloth has a fine cross wise rib and a lustrous finish.

BROCADE: A decorative fabric which has a raised pattern woven in relief against a background. It is made of a variety of fibers and often has metallic threads forming the raised or embossed pattern. Depending on its weight, it may be used for clothing or upholstery.

Anitque-ing fabric...

To make fabric look antique, dip in a solution of 1 cup of coffe and 2 tbsp. of vinegar.

Repeat as needed.

Iron dry for a "streaky" antiqued appearane.

Tip provided by: Debra Justice Labours of Love Heirloom Sewing Supplies, Inc. Page 300

Do not dry clean...

Never dry clean your cottons. The chemicals will yellow the yarn, make them feel stiff, and add an unpleasant odor to the cotton fabric.

Tip provided by:
Cotton Clouds
Page 263

Oregon Worsted Company/Mill End Store
Page 316

Pieces
Page 322

The Pin Cushion
Page 322

Pioneer Quilts
Page 322

Quilts & Other Comforts
Page 328

Sew Natural-Fabrics by Mail
Page 334

SewBaby!
Page...

    Children's

Sewing Sampler Productions, Inc.
Page 335

Vogue Fabrics/Vogue Fabrics By Mail
Page 351

Waechter's Silk Shop
Page 351

    Children's

    Chili peppers

    Various

Zoodads - Simply Kidz Fabrics
Page 355

POLYESTER

A Fabric Place
Page 237

AK Sew & Serge
Page 237

Art Max Fabrics
Page 242

Atkinson Fabrics, Inc.
Page 243

Baer Fabrics
Page 245

Banasch's Fabrics
Page 245

Banasch's, Inc.
Page 245

Banksville Designer Fabrics
Page245

Carolina Mills Factory Outlet
Page 237

Clearbrook Woolen Shop
Page 259

The Corner Stitch, Inc.
Page 262

Daisy Kingdom
Page 267

Elegance Unlimited, Inc.
Page 273

Fabric Complements, Inc.
Page 276

Fabric Temptations
Page 276

    Fleece

Fashion Fabrics Club/Natural Fiber Fabrics Direct
Page 278

Fishmans Fabrics
Page 280

    4-ply

    Chiffon

    Crepe

    Gabardine

    Iridescent

    Lining

    Organza

    Quilted

    Satin

G Street Fabrics
Page 282

Hancock's
Page 287

    Baby cord, cotton blend

    Broadcloth, cotton mix

    Crepe

    Dupioni suiting

    Gabardine

    Gingham, cotton blend

    Interlock knit, cotton blend

    Plush felt

    Pongee crepe

    Poplin, cotton blend

    Satin

Suit lining

Tablecloth material

Tulle

Herrschners, Inc.
Page 291

Joyce's Fabrics
Page 297

Lace Heaven, Inc.
Page 301

Logan Kits
Page 303

Londa's Sewing, Etc.
Page 303

Oregon Worsted Company/Mill End Store
Page 316

Pieces
Page 322

The Pin Cushion
Page 322

The Smocking Horse Collection
Page 337

Speigelhoff Stretch & Sew/Great Copy Patterns
Page 340

Stone Mountain & Daughter Fabrics
Page 341

Taylor's Cutaways & Stuff
Page 344

Remnants and variety packs

TestFabrics, Inc.
Page 345
All fabrics are untreated and prepared for printing or dyeing.

Vogue Fabrics/Vogue Fabrics By Mail
Page 351

Chiffon

Crepe de chine

Knit

Print

Solid

Woven

Zoodads - Simply Kidz Fabrics
Page 355

RAYON

A Fabric Place
Page 237

AK Sew & Serge
Page 237

And Sew On
Page 240

Art Max Fabrics
Page 242

B & J Fabrics, Inc.
Page 244

Baer Fabrics
Page 245

Banasch's Fabrics
Page 245

Banasch's, Inc.
Page 245

Banksville Designer Fabrics
Page 245

Batiks Etcetera
Page 246

Blueprints-Printables
Page 251
All fabrics are untreated and prepared for printing or dyeing.

Viscous challis

Viscous georgette

Carol Harris Co.
Page 257

Carolina Mills Factory Outlet
Page 257

Clearbrook Woolen Shop
Page 259

Cottons, Etc.
Page 263

D'Leas Fabric and Button Studio
Page 266

Daisy Kingdom
Page 267

Dharma Trading Co.
Page 269
All fabrics are untreated and prepared for printing or dyeing.

Viscose challis

Skirt styles...

Knife Pleated

Hate wrinkles? Learn to love them!

To make crinkled fabric, use this method:

Cut a length of fabric on the crosswise grain. Soak it in lukewarm water until wet, then gently squeeze out excess water. Fold the fabric in half lengthwise (two people are best for these maneuvers), then start twisting each end in opposite directions until the fabric is so tightly wound it curls into a ball.

Wrap the ball with string or rubber bands, and place into a leg of old pantyhose. Dry in a clothes dryer, until the middle is completely dry. You now have your crinkled fabric.

T-shirts, skirts, and simple shifts are the best items to make from this fabric. When it is next washed, treat the garment as you did the fabric at the beginning. When dry, store it in the twisted ball, until you are ready to wear it.

SILK

Blueprints-Printables
Page 251
All fabrics are untreated and prepared for printing or dyeing.

Charmeuse

Crepe

Raw

Bridals International
Page 253

Buttons 'n' Bows
Page 255

Batiste

Dupioni

Carol Harris Co.
Page 257

Carolina Mills Factory Outlet
Page 257

Clearbrook Woolen Shop
Page 259

The Corner Stitch, Inc.
Page 262

Cottons, Etc.
Page 263

D'Leas Fabric and Button Studio
Page 266

Raw

Daisy Kingdom
Page 267

Dharma Trading Co.
Page 267
All fabrics are untreated and prepared for

printing or dyeing.

Charmeuse, 19.5mm

Chiffon, 8mm

Crepe de chine, 16mm

Dupioni, 19mm

Gauze, 3mm

Habotai, 5mm, 8mm, 10mm

Noil/raw

Satin, 12mm

Elegance Unlimited, Inc.
Page 273

The Enchanted Cottage
Page 274

Exotic-Thai Silks
Page 275

Burn-out velvet

Bridal

Charmeuse

Chiffon

Crepe

Dupioni

Habotai

Handpainted

Jacquard

Organza

Shantung

Velvet

Fabric Collections
Page 276

Fabric Complements, Inc.
Page 276

Fabric Gallery
Page 276

Fabric Temptations
Page 276

Broadcloth

Charmeuse

Chiffon

Crepe

Dupioni

Embroidered

Handpainted

Lawn

Noil

Novelty

Organza

Taffeta

Thai

Fabrics Unlimited
Page 276

Fashion Fabrics Club/Natural Fiber Fabrics Direct
Page 278

Fishmans Fabrics
Page 280

4-ply

Charmeuse

Chiffon

China

Crepe de chine

Iridescent

Organza

Which fabrics crinkle the best?

All lightweight silks, including charmeuse, organza, chiffon, and china silks.

Some cotton shirtings will wrinkle, but the wrinkles will fall out after long wear.

While most wools are too heavy, crepes will wrinkle wonderfully.

Linen, of course, wrinkles even when we don't want it to, but will also pick up new wrinkles from your movements.

Vädmal

Vädmal is the Swedish word for felted wool, and while it may not be easy to say, it is certainly easy to make, if you follow these tips:

Use 100% wool, not blends.

Always try a swatch and record your methods; some fabrics will shrink more than others.

Bold patterns, they will be compacted and toned down by felting, but will add color variation and interest.

Once you have tested your swatch, determine the shrinkage by dividing the felted length by the length before felting. I would suggest using an even number for your swatch, such as one foot.

Next, use your pattern yardage requirements to figure the total fabric needed before felting to create your entire felted garment.

If you have a serger, serge the raw edges of your wool to prevent unravelling. If you do not have a serger, you could seal the edges with fray check, or leave them alone. If you do not finish the edges at all, there may be some uneven shrinkage at the ends, or ruffling.

Sandwashed charmeuse

Satin

Taffeta

G Street Fabrics
Page 282

Harriet's TCS/Harriet's Patterns
Page 288

Heirlooms Forever
Page 290

Jehlor Fantasy Fabrics
Page 296

Dupioni

Taffeta

Judy's Heirloom Sewing
Page 297

Dupioni

Kasuri Dyeworks
Page 298

Crepe

Habotai

Ikat

Jacquard

Sha

The Kirk Collection
Page 299

Cigarette silks

Labours of Love Heirloom Sewing Supplies, Inc.
Page 300

Lace Heaven, Inc.
Page 301

Ledgewood Studio
Page 302

The Linen Fabric World
Page 303

Londa's Sewing, Etc.
Page 303

M's Fabric Gallery
Page 304

Drapery

Upholstery

Mimi's Fabrications
Page 309

Miss Maureen's Fabrics and Fancies
Page 309

Oregon Worsted Company/Mill End Store
Page 316

Oriental Silk Company
Page 316

Boucle

Charmeuse

Chein shun

Chiffon georgette

China

Crepe de chine, 16mm

Corduroy

Cut velvet

Dupioni

Habotai

Heavy crepe, 4 Ply

Honan

Indian tussah

Jacquard charmeuse

Jacquard crepe

Jacquard crepe de chine

Knit jersey

Metallic stripe chiffon

Organza

Palace brocade

Pearl crepe jacquard

Peau de soie

Pongee

Raw

Satin

Satin stripe chiffon

Shantung

Spun

Thai

Tissue taffeta

Velvet

Ya Kiang tussah

The Pin Cushion
Page 322

Qualin International
Page 326
All fabrics are untreated and prepared for printing or dyeing.

Crepe de chine, 10, 14, and 16mm

Crepe georgette

Charmeuse

Flat crepe

Habotai, 8 and 10 mm

Heavy dupioni, 24 mm

Jacquard

Noil

Ribbon (georgette and satin stripes)

Satin

Rupert, Gibbon & Spider
Page 331
All fabrics are untreated and prepared for printing or dyeing.

Broadcloth

Chamois

Charmeuse

Chiffon - georgette

Crepe de chine

Gauze

Habotai

Jacquards (various)

Knit

Lycra blend

Matka

Noil

Organza

Rayon blend velvet

Satin

Satin twill

Shantung

Taffeta

Tussahs

Sawyer Brook Distinctive Fabrics
Page 332

The Scarlet Letter
Page 333

Silkpaint Corporation
Page 337

The Smocking Horse Collection
Page 337

Stone Mountain & Daughter Fabrics
Page 341

Super Silk, Inc.
Page 342

Charmeuse

Chiffon

Crepe de chine

Dupioni

Habotai

Matka

Noil

Metallic

Organza

Taffeta

Tussah

Taylor's Cutaways & Stuff
Page 344

Tess' Designer Yarns
Page 344

TestFabrics, Inc.
Page 345
All fabrics are untreated and prepared for printing or dyeing.

Textile Reproductions
Page 345

Things Japanese
Page 346

Treadle Yard Goods
Page 348

Charmeuse

Chiffon

China

Crepe de chine

Double crepe

Dupioni

Jacquards

Matka, solid and tweeds

Noil

Organza

Peau de soie

Sandwashed charmeuse

Shantung

Vogue Fabrics/Vogue Fabrics By Mail
Page 351

Charmeuse

Chiffon

China

Crepe de chine

Prints

Pleated

Raw

Solids

Begin your felting by soaking your wool in hot (110°–125°) water with mild detergent.

Place the fabric into a washer filled with hot water. Wrap the wet fabric loosely around the machine's agitator. If necessary, add a piece of fabric to balance the load.

Check your fabric every five to seven minutes, carefully wringing the water from a section to determine the felt texture. Stop washing when it has reached the desired thickness.

It is better to take it out too soon than to leave it in too long. You can always re-felt, but you cannot go back once the cloth is too thick.

Shirt styles...

Peasant

Cossack

Sueded

Thai

Waechter's Silk Shop
Page 351

WOOL

A Fabric Place
Page 237

Amazon Vinegar & Pickling Works Drygoods
Page 239

Art Max Fabrics
Page 242

Atkinson Fabrics, Inc.
Page 243

B & J Fabrics, Inc.
Page 244

Baer Fabrics
Page 245

Banasch's Fabrics
Page 245

Banksville Designer Fabrics
Page 245

Canyon Records & Indian Arts
Page 257

Carol Harris Co.
Page 257

Carolina Mills Factory Outlet
Page 257

Clearbrook Woolen Shop
Page 259

Cottons, Etc.
Page 263

D'Leas Fabric and Button Studio
Page 266

Daisy Kingdom
Page 267

Elegance Unlimited, Inc.
Page 273

Fabric Collections
Page 276

Fabric Complements, Inc.
Page 276

Fabric Gallery
Page 276

Fabric Temptations
Page 276

Blanket

Designer

Flannel

Tartan

Fabrics Unlimited
Page 276

Fashion Fabrics Club/Natural Fiber Fabrics Direct
Page 278

Fishmans Fabrics
Page 280

Crepe

Faille

Gabardine

Heavy gabardine

G Street Fabrics
Page 282

Gaelic College Craft Shop
Page 282

Grey Owl Indian Craft
Page 286

Harriet's TCS/Harriet's Patterns
Page 288

Joyce's Fabrics
Page 297

Suitings

Ledgewood Studio
Page 302

The Linen Fabric World
Page 303

Londa's Sewing, Etc.
Page 303

M's Fabric Gallery
Page 304

Drapery

Upholstery

Miss Maureen's Fabrics and Fancies
Page 309

Morning Star Indian Gallery
Page 310

Oregon Worsted Company/Mill End Store
Page 316

Taos Mountain Wool Works
Page 344

Breathable lining...

Ambiance lining breathes and does not cling. It is very silk-like.

Tip provided by: D'Leas Fabric and Button Studio Page 266

Refer to Sew Saavy in the Company Appendix for more information on purchasing quality linings.

Feathers

These companies offer feathers for a fun and fanciful addition to your special projects.

Amazon Vinegar & Pickling Works Drygoods
Page 239

    Ostrich

    Ostrich plume banding

    Peacock

Beyond Beadery
Page 250

Bitterroot Leather Company
Page 250

    Barred turkey

    Guinea

    Imitation eagle

    Imitation hawk

    White pheasant

Brian's Crafts Unlimited
Page 252

Canyon Records & Indian Arts
Page 257

    Dyed

    Natural

Eagle Feather Trading Post
Page 272

    Handpainted

    Imitation eagle

    Pheasant

    Turkey

Earth Guild
Page 272

    Guinea

    Male pheasant

    Rooster saddle hackles

    Turkey, white or dark

Enterprise Art
Page 274

Fabric Gallery
Page 276

Fabric Temptations
Page 276

Fire Mountain Gems
Page 280

    Natural feathers for beading

G Street Fabrics
Page 282

Gettinger Feather Corp.
Page 282

Grey Owl Indian Craft
Page 286

The Gypsy's Bead Shoppe
Page 286

Jehlor Fantasy Fabrics
Page 296

    Boas

    Chandelle

    Coque

    Hackle

    Marabou

    Ostrich

    Peacock

    Turkey

Judy's Heirloom Sewing
Page 297

Lacis
Page 301

Easy glamour...

The easiest way to apply feathers to your outfit is with a good fabric glue.

Feathers should be treated with care, as they are fragile. If you use glue instead of trying to sew each feather, you will be able to replace any patch that is damaged in just a few minutes.

Hatmaking Supplies

Look to these companies for the products and services you need to make headlines.

Fit your hat to your face shape…

Oval

Round

Square

Lace & Lacemaking

All listings refer to finished laces, unless they specify otherwise.

The 1752 Company - Beautiful Things
Wholesale Only
Page 237

    American lace

    Antique English lace

    Antique French lace

    Cluny

    English lace

    Entredeux

    French lace

    Swiss embroideries

A Fabric Place
Page 237

AK Sew & Serge
Page 237

Amazon Vinegar & Pickling Works Drygoods
Page 239

And Sew On
Page 240

Art Max Fabrics
Page 242

Associated Sewing Supply Co., Inc.
Page 243

Atkinson Fabrics, Inc.
Page 243

B & J Fabrics, Inc.
Page 244

Baer Fabrics
Page 245

Banasch's Fabrics
Page 245

Banksville Designer Fabrics
Page 245

Beggars' Lace
Page 249

    Lacemaking supplies

Brian's Crafts Unlimited
Page 252

    Grab bags

Bridals International
Page 253

Buttons 'n' Bows
Page 255

Carol Harris Co.
Page 257

Carolina Mills Factory Outlet
Page 257

The Corner Stitch, Inc.
Page 262

Cotton Ball
Page 263

Cottons, Etc.
Page 263

CR's Crafts
Page 264

Crafts By Donna
Page 265

    Battenberg tapes

D'Leas Fabric and Button Studio
Page 266

Daisy Kingdom
Page 267

Custom trim—it's so easy...

Sew your favorite lace on both sides of a ribbon, or any other type of trim.

This would also work with fringe instead of lace. Try beaded or leather.

What is tatting?

Tatting is a method of knotwork and lacemaking in which the stitches are made over the thread. The thread is wound over a shuttle small enough to allow its being passed backwards and forwards, over and under the thread it is forming the stitches on.

The English name of tatting, taken from the word tatters, indicates the fragile piece-meal nature of the work, as does the French name of frivolité; but, however fragile and lace-like in appearance, it is exceedingly strong and capable of bearing much rough usage.

Unlike crochet and knitting, where each stitch is slightly dependent on its neighbor, and one becoming unfastened endangers the rest, the stitches of tatting are isolated as far as their strength goes. Being composed of knots, tatting is very difficult to undo once formed.

The work consists of so few stitches that it is extremely simple and requires neither thought nor fixed attention once the nature of the stitch has been mastered. A glance, or the feel of it passing through the fingers is sufficient for an experienced tatter.

Cont.

Earth Guild
Page 272

The Enchanted Cottage
Page 274

Enterprise Art
Page 274

Fabric Gallery
Page 276

Fabric Temptations
Page 276

Antique cottons

Entredeux

Eyelets

Italian

Silk

Swiss eyelets

Fabrics Unlimited
Page 276

G Street Fabrics
Page 282

Halcyon Yarn
Page 286

Tatting needles

Tatting shuttles

Wrist yarn ball holder

Handy Hands, Inc.
Page 288

Tatting needles

Tatting shuttles

Hedgehog Handworks
Page 289

DMC tatting cord

Tatting needles

Tatting shuttles

Tatting starter kits

Heirloom Knitted Lace
Page 289

Knitted lace help line

Knitted lace patterns

Knitted lace supplies

Heirlooms Forever
Page 290

Herrschners, Inc.
Page 291

High Country West Needleworks
Page 291

Jehlor Fantasy Fabrics
Page 296

Specialty

Stretch

Joyce's Fabrics
Page 297

Judy's Heirloom Sewing
Page 297

Cotton lace

Tatting supplies

The Kirk Collection
Page 299

Crocheted

Handmade

Knitted

Machine-made

Scraps

Kreinik Mfg. Co., Inc.
Wholesale Only
Page 299

Tatting supplies

Labours of Love Heirloom Sewing Supplies, Inc.
Page 300

Lace Heaven, Inc.
Page 301

The Lacemaker
Page 301

Battenberg lace

Bobbin lace patterns

Bobbins

Lap pillows

Magnifiers

Needles

Ring gauge

Tatting shuttles and accessories

Pattern drafting supplies

Pattern prickers

Pillow stand

Pinlifters

Princess tape

Winders

Lacis
Page 301

Battenberg lace

Bobbin lace patterns

Bobbins

Cluny lace

Filet lace supplies

Lap pillows

Magnifiers

Needles

Tatting shuttles and accessories

Pattern prickers

Pinlifters

Pin pushers

Princess tape

Teneriffe lace kit

Winders

Lark Books

Kits

Ledgewood Studio

Logan Kits

Londa's Sewing, Etc.

M & J Trimming Co.

M's Fabric Gallery

Mimi's Fabrications

English and French cotton

English and French beaded

French Maline

Tatting supplies

Miss Maureen's Fabrics and Fancies

Tatting supplies

Nancy's Notions

Oregon Worsted Company/Mill End Store

Tatting supplies

Personal Threads Boutique

DMC

Finca

Kreinik Balger

Shuttles

Picking Up The Pieces Quilt Shop

The Pin Cushion

Lace

Tatting supplies

Pioneer Quilts

Prairieland Quilts

Richard the Thread

Robin's Bobbins & Other Things

They only carry lacemaking supplies.

Bobbins

Crochet hooks

Metal pin vise

Pin pullers

Pins

Pattern prickers

Tatting shuttles

Winders

SAX Arts & Crafts

Sew Sassy Lingerie

The Smocking Horse Collection

English laces

French laces

Swiss laces

Tatting supplies

Snowgoose

Armenian knotted lace

Battenberg lace kits and supplies

Bobbin lace kits and supplies

Carrickmacross lace kits and supplies

Needle lace kits and supplies

Netted lace kits and supplies

It also has the advantage of being very portable. It can be worked at for a few minutes and put down again without becoming disarranged, which is an impossibility with many other kinds of lace.

Information taken from:
The Dictionary of Needlework
©1972
Arno Press, Inc.

Which way is up?

The right side of lace is the rough side. Think of flowers being sprinkled on a trellis.

Since this is difficult to see on lace, close your eyes and feel for the rough side.

Tip provided by:
Debra Justice
Labours of Love
Heirloom Sewing
Supplies, Inc.
Page 300

Knitted lace kits and supplies

Tambour needles

Tatted lace kits and supplies

Teneriffe wheel

Spinning Wheel
Page 340

Tatting supplies

Stone Mountain & Daughter Fabrics
Page 341

Straw Into Gold
Page 342

Tatting supplies

Sweet Child of Mine
Page 343

Lace for heirloom sewing

Threads for lace making

Taylor's Cutaways & Stuff
Page 344

Lace assortments

Unicorn Books and Crafts, Inc./Glimåkra Looms 'n Yarns/Frederick J. Fawcett, Inc.
Page 349

Vogue Fabrics/Vogue Fabrics By Mail
Page 351

Waechter's Silk Shop
Page 351

Lace and linen handkerchiefs

Spoke handkerchiefs for tatting and

lacemaking

Trims (no bridal)

Yarn Barn
Page 354

Leathers, Suedes & Furs

These businesses offer everything in leather, suedes, and furs. Furs are labeled with name only, others are marked accordingly, and synthetics are noted.

A Fabric Place
Page 237

    Synthetics

AK Sew & Serge
Page 237

Art Max Fabrics
Page 242

    Synthetic leathers and furs

Arthur M. Rein
Page 242
He will supply practically anything available in genuine furs, and offers a free quotation service with no obligation. See company listing for more details.

Atkinson Fabrics, Inc.
Page 242

Banasch's Fabrics
Page 245

Banksville Designer Fabrics
Page 245

Berman Leather Co.
Page 249

    Chap leather

Garment leather

    Chamois

    Cowhide

    Deerskin

    Shearling

    Sueded pigskin

Latigo

Leather sides

Rabbit

Upholstery

Bitterroot Leather Company
Page 250

    Arctic fox

    Buffalo robes

    Buckskin

    Coyote

    Deer

    Elkskin

    Ermine

    Lynx

    Marten

    Mink

    Moose

    Skunk

    Red fox

    Wolf

Canyon Records & Indian Arts
Page 257

Cinema Leathers, Inc.
   Wholesale Only
Page 259

    English domestic cow hide

    Halian nappa

    Lamb suede

    Pig suede

Cotton Ball
Page 263

CR's Crafts
Page 264

D'Anton Leather
Page 266

    Leather

    Suede

Chinchilla fur…

Of this animal there are two varieties, both of South America. That producing the best fur is a native of Buenos Aires and Africa, and is of a silver grey, the darkest and best in color coming from the latter place.

Those from Lima are short in the fur and inferior in quality.

Chinchilla fur is extremely soft and delicate, and lies as readily in one direction as another. The skins measure 6" x 8".

Information taken from:
The Dictionary of Needlework
©1972 Arno Press, Inc.

Donna Salyers' Fabulous Furs
Page 270

Synthetic furs of all types

Ultraleather

Ultrasuede

Eagle Feather Trading Post
Page 272

Angora

Deer and elk rawhide

Ermine

Latigo

Rabbit

Earth Guild
Page 272

Leather scraps

Leatherworking tools

Enterprise Art
Page 274

The Fiber Studio
Page 279

G Street Fabrics
Page 282

Grey Owl Indian Craft
Page 286

The Gypsy's Bead Shoppe
Page 286

H.E. Goldberg & Co.
Page 286

American raccoon

Badger

Beaver

Calfskins

Canadian fisher

Coyote

Deerskin

Elkskin

Ermine

Finnish raccoon

Foxes

Arctic

Black

Blue

Cross

Gray

Red

Silver

Garment cowside

Icelandic sheepskins

Long hair

Sheared

Land otter

Marten

Mink

Moose hides

Mouton lambskins

Muskrat

Nutria

Rabbit

Reindeer

Shearling (unsueded)

Skunk

Spanish curly lamb

Timberwolf

Toscana lambskins

Wolverine

High Country West Needleworks
Page 291

Jehlor Fantasy Fabrics
Page 296

Synthetic Fur

Kreinik Mfg. Co., Inc.
Wholesale Only
Page 299

The Leather Factory
Page 302

Chap (23 colors)

Cobra skin

Deer suede

Deerskin (4 colors)

Elkskin (gold and white)

Embossed leathers

Haircalf skins

Latigo

Leatherworking tools

Nappa tanned cowhide

Python skin

Rabbit

Saddleskirting

Shearling

Sueded splits (8 colors)

Velvet suede (38 colors)

Leather Unlimited
Page 302

Ledgewood Studio
Page 302

Synthetic fur

Morning Star Indian Gallery
Page 310

Badger

Beaver

Bobcat

Coyote

Deer hide

Elk hide

Ermine

Fox

Latigo strips

Rabbit

Raccoon

Old Style Trading Company
Page 314

Black bear

Buffalo hide

Cow hide

Deer hide

Elk hide

Fox tail

Moose hide

Otter tail

Rabbit

Oregon Worsted Company/Mill End Store
Page 316

SAX Arts & Crafts
Page 333

UltraScraps by D.M. Design
Page 349

Fabulous fur scraps

Ultraleather

Ultrasuede

Ultrasuede light

Waechter's Silk Shop
Page 351

Suede

Wakeda Trading Post
Page 352

Badger

Beaver

Buckskin

Coyote

Deer hides with fur

Elk hide

Ermine

Icelandic sheep

River otter

Rabbit

Red fox

Skunk

When attaching buttons to leather...

Remember to use a needle designed for leather.

Leather and suede tear easily, and buttons should be backed with a stay button, a bit of fusing, felt, or a small scrap of suede.

Miscellaneous

This chapter contains any product or service I could not fit somewhere else, and items that did not have enough resources for chapters.

CONSERVATION MATERIALS

Lacis
Page 301

- Acid-free boxes
- Acid-free tissue
- Alligator forceps
- Crepoline
- Conservator's gloves
- Drying plates
- Hemostat
- Mini vacuums
- Orvis Wa Paste
- Scalpels
- Tweezers

DISPLAY MATERIALS

Bally Bead Company
Page 245

- Black plastic display trays
- Button cover display cards
- Zip-lock plastic bags

Banasch's, Inc.
Page 245

Ornamental Resources
Page 315

- Earring strips
- Jewelry trays
- Necklace displays
- Travel cases

JEWELRY SUPPLIES

A & B Jewels and Tools
Page 237

Beads & Rocks
Wholesale Only
Page 248

Eagle Feather Trading Post
Page 272

Fire Mountain Gems
Page 280

- Cubic zirconia
- Diamonds
- Faceted imitation birthstones
- Genuine faceted gems

L.C. Smith's
Page 300
Just about everything to start yourself off right in creating your own jewelry.

- Craft metals
- Power tools
- Settings

JUST FOR KIDS

Clotilde
Page 360

Teaching Kids to Sew

Earth Guild
Page 272

- Cottage looms
- Harrisville friendly belt looms
- Potholder loom and loopers

Halcyon Yarn
Page 286

- Arts & Crafts Series books

  Batik and Tie-Dye

  Knitting and Crochet

  Needlecraft

Jacket styles...

Hapi

Vest styles...

Single Breasted

Double Breasted

Papermaking

Weaving

Baked Beads and Beyond: Making Magic with Oven Bake Clay

Bead It!: A Complete Jewelry Kit

Bead jewelry workstation

Boys Don't Knit

No Dragons on My Quilt

Project kits

Traditions Around the World: Costumes

Ivy Imports, Inc.
Page 295
They have kid's silk painting videos. All videos are 30 minutes long and cost $12.95.

Fun With Faces

Funky Ties

Starburst Scarf

Lark Books
Page 301

Inch-worm, cord knitting kit

Loom and loops kit

Magic Cabin Dolls
Page 304

Child's craft basket

Child's handwork sampler

Child's weaving kit

Felt ball kit

Nancy's Notions
Page 311

Let's Sew!

More Sewing Machine Fun® (activity kit)

Sewing Machine Fun® (activity kit)

Step Into Patchwork® (activity kit)

Palmer/Pletsch Publishing
Page 318
They offer the Winky Cherry System of teaching young children to sew. All books are 40 pages and cost $12.95. They also have teaching manuals, videos, and classroom supplies.

Mi Primer Libro de Costura (Spanish translation, Level I)

My First Sewing Book–Hand Sewing, Level I

My First Embroidery Book, Level II

My First Doll Book, Level III

My First Machine Sewing Book, Level IV

Original Roo
(A children's story about a purple kangaroo's adventures and how she saves the day with her sewing talents.)

Classes for young children and teens

Children's machine sewing (ages 9-12)

Kids sewing camp I & II

Teen sewing (ages 13 and up)

Young children's hand sewing (ages 5-8)

Patternworks
Page 320

Sunny's Mittens
Robin Hansen

$12.95
A delightful learn-to-knit book especially for girls 9-12.

Kid Knits: Fun and Easy Patterns for Beginners
$5.95

Derek the Knitting Dinosaur
$5.95

Suzanne Roddy, Handweaver
Page 343

All About Wool

Boy's Don't Knit

Emma's Lamb

Goat In The Rug

The Purple Coat

Harrisville lap loom kits

Bag

Navajo

Mini-purse

Sheep

Drop spindle spinning kit

Knitting unspun silk kit

KIMONOS

Arise, Inc.
Page 241

Vintage kimonos

Obis

Kasuris

Yakutas

Kasuri Dyeworks
Page 298

Texuba
Page 345

KUMI HIMO SUPPLIES

Halcyon Yarn
Page 301

The Lacemaker
Page 301

Lacis
Page 301

    Bobbins

    Silk threads

    Stands

MISCELLANEOUS STUFF

AK Sew & Serge
Page 237

Amazon Vinegar & Pickling Works Drygoods
Page 239

    Fringe for flappers or lampshades

Banasch's, Inc.
Page 245

    Business signs

    Hangers

Bead in Hand
Page 247

BeadZip
Page 248

    Earring cards

    Gift boxes

    Multi-purpose adhesives

    Plastic storage boxes

    String tags

    Zip closure baggies

Berman Leather Co.
Page 249

    Metal accessories for buckles, lead chains, and saddles

    Tools for leatherworking and sewing leather

Blueprints-Printables
Page 251

    Silk bias, (5 widths)

Boca Loca Beads
Page 251

Body-Rite, Inc.
Page 251

    Posture aid

Cotton Ball
Page 263

Danforth Pewterers
Page 267
All items are made from high-quality pewter.

    Charms

    Pendants

Delta Technical Coatings, Inc.
    Wholesale Only
Page 268

    Delta Color Accents

    Designer Style Iron-On Transfers

    Jewel Glue

    Sobo

    Stencil Magic Stencil Designs

    Stitchless glue

Eagle Feather Trading Post
Page 272

Fabric Gallery
Page 276

Fiskars, Inc.
    Wholesale Only
Page 280

Frostline Kits
Page 282

    Hot Prints (transfer dye patterns to your fabric permanently)

Greenberg & Hammer, Inc.
Page 286

Herrschners, Inc.
Page 291

Jehlor Fantasy Fabrics
Page 296

    Fringe

Kite Studio
Page 299

    Accessories for kite making

Londa's Sewing, Etc.
Page 303

M's Fabric Gallery
Page 304

    Drapery hardware and poles

    Finials

    Wimpoles

Kimonos... by the bale?

Most kimono distributors offer kimonos singly or per bale.

A standard European bale weighs 100 kilos, or 220 pounds. Japanese bales weigh 133.33 pounds, as do Shanghai bales. Cantonese bales average 106.67 pounds.

Kimonos are not only wonderful for housewear, but many people also use the silks for wearable art, crazy quilting, and other decorative arts.

Waistline styles...

Pointed

Empire

Mary Ellen & Co.
Page 306

Mimi's Fabrications
Page 309

Ornamental Resources
Page 317

Cabochons

Cameos

Double stick shapes for pins, etc.

Friendly Plastic

Glass drops and pendants

Lockets

Multipurpose cement

Polishing cloths

Pronged metal appliqués

Personal FX
Page 321

Hand-carved netsuke

The Pin Cushion
Page 322

Quest Outfitters
Page 326

Metal and acetal fasteners for outdoor equipment

Quilts & Other Comforts
Page 328

Quilted wearables

Gifts

Stationary and notecards

Embellishments and charms

The Rain Shed, Inc.
Page 329

Reflective tape

RolyKit
Page 331

SAX Arts & Crafts
Page 333

SewBaby!
Page 334

Size labels

Squeakers

Sojourner
Page 339

Vintage and ethnic textiles

Solo Slide Fasteners, Inc.
Page 339

Alteration tags

Button shields

Fabric, craft, and leather glues

Fuzz busters

Garment bags

Knit cuffs, collars, and waistbands

Lingerie strap guards

Tagging guns

Tags

Pill removers

Pocketing

Signs

Skirt clips (for cleaning, etc.)

Stone Mountain & Daughter Fabrics
Page 341

The Whole Bead Show
Page 353

PACKAGING MATERIALS

Banasch's, Inc.
Page 245

Storage boxes

Fancy Threads/Fancy Threads Custom
Page 277

Necktie gift boxes

Ornamental Resources
Page 317

Clear plastic earring cards

Clear plastic storage boxes

Utility boxes

PHOTO TRANSFER SERVICES

Your original photos and drawings will NOT be damaged and will be returned to you.

Extra Special Products Corp.
Page 275

Imagination Station
Page 293

Lacis
Page 301

Photo Textiles
Page 321

POLYMER CLAY/MODELING COMPOUNDS

Commercial Art Supply

Earth Guild

RHINESTONES & GLASS STONES FOR SETTING

Banasch's Fabrics

Greenberg & Hammer, Inc.

Jehlor Fantasy Fabrics

Hot sets

Sew-ons

Ledgewood Studio

M & M Trims

Mirrors

Nailheads

Rhinstones

Margola Corporation
Wholesale Only

Ornamental Resources

Glass stones for setting

Setting tools

Sew-ons

Rhinestone chains

Rhinestone settings

Rhinestones

Wired rhinestones

Promenade's Le Bead Shop

Richard the Thread

Flat-back rhinestones

Lochraosen

Sew-ons

Timeless Treasures

Swarovski

SEQUINS

Amazon Vinegar & Pickling Works Drygoods

1" sequin banding

Banasch's Fabrics

Brian's Crafts Unlimited

Enterprise Art

Greenberg & Hammer, Inc.

Jehlor Fantasy Fabrics

Sequin banding

Sequined appliqués

Sequins

M & M Trims

Sequined trims

Ornamental Resources

Sequins

Sequined appliqués

Promenade's Le Bead Shop

The Thrifty Needle

Sequined appliqués

Waistline styles...

Dropped

Midriff Yoke

Outdoor Gear Kits & Supplies

These companies have everything for the do-it-yourself tentmaker, backpacker, or outdoor enthusiast.

Campmor
Page 256

- Heavy duty zippers
- Mosquito netting
- Repair kits
- Velcro yardage

Cottons, Etc.
Page 263

Fabric Temptations
Page 276

Frostline Kits
Page 282

All of the following are complete kits.

- Attaché cases
- Baby carriers
- Backpacks
- Banners
- Bathrobes
- Bicycle gear
  - Front panniers
  - Handlebar bag
  - Rear panniers
- Seat bag
- Bicycle cover
- Comforters
- Dog packs
- Down jackets
- Down shirts
- Duffle tote
- Expandable carry-on bag
- Frame packs
- Garment bags
- Insulated pants
- Jackets
- Lineman/welder's jacket
- Mesh reflective vests
- Parkas
- Pet bed
- Pillows
- Quick-change baby bag
- Quilter's/craft bag
- Rain gear
- Sleeping bags
- Slippers
- Stuff sacks
- Umbrellas
- Wallets

G Street Fabrics
Page 282

The Green Pepper
Page 285

- Bag patterns
- Outerwear patterns

Joyce's Fabrics
Page 297

Marine Sewing
Page 306

Outdoor Wilderness Fabrics
Page 317

- Fasteners for outdoor gear
- Patterns
  - Backpacks
  - Boot and skate tote
  - Canopies
  - Gloves

Polartec tips...

Since polartec will not ravel, sewing is incredibly easy with this fabric. Just keep a few things in mind:

Use 1/4" - 3/8" seams, large seam allowances will be too bulky.

Although polartec seems sturdy, always use a stabilizer when making buttonholes.

Wash your polartec garments in cold water, and avoid high drying temperatures–they will cause shrinkage.

Outerwear styles...

Ski Jacket

Horse blankets

Mittens

Outerwear

Rifle tote

Sleeping bags

Tennis tote

Tents

Seam sealer

Webbing

Quest Outfitters
Page 326

Clothing

Drawcord

Gear

Patterns

    Backpacks

    Dog packs

    Fanny packs

    Gloves

    Mittens

    Outerwear

    Sleeping bags

Webbing

The Rain Shed, Inc.
Page 329

Fasteners

Patterns

Seattle Fabrics, Inc.
Page 334

Clothing

Drawcord

Gear

Patterns

    Backpacks

    Dog packs

    Fanny packs

    Gloves

    Mittens

    Outerwear

    Sleeping bags

Seam sealer

Waterproofing for leather

Webbing

Patterns

Here are all the patterns you will ever need. I've organized them by pattern type, so you can more easily find what you're looking for.

What is a pinafore?

Literally, pinned afore (in the front), as in a piece of fabric pinned to the bodice of a child's dress in the front to protect it from stains.

What is a muslin?

In the couture houses in France, a muslin is called a toile and is made by draping fabric on a form (such as a dressmaker's form or an actual body).

A toile is useful in many ways and is used in every step of the designing process. With a toile, you can assure that the grain lines are right, adjust darts, re-shape the garment, etc. Each change is marked and basted into the fabric on the form.

All of the grain lines are marked, as well as stitching and adjustments.

Once the shape of the garment is right, the toiles are taken apart and used as the pattern.

These are generally kept for only a few seasons, then thrown out.

Why use a muslin?

I don't know of even one professional seamstress who would not recommend that you make a muslin for every pattern you make.

When you make a muslin, you are saving yourself a lot of grief by using a very inexpensive fabric (I never spend more than $3 per yard, as a rule) to make all the adjustments that will be necessary to fit the pattern to your body. If a mistake is made on a muslin, it makes very little difference. If you make a mistake on your $40 per yard silk brocade, it could be very discouraging, not to mention downright expensive.

It also helps to assure yourself that the pattern will truly fit you, not just the model on the package.

Once you have your pattern adjusted to your liking, you can use your muslin as a cloth pattern for as long as you need.

If you prefer less flexible patterns...

To stiffen your patterns, try using wax freezer paper. Just place the freezer paper wax side down onto the pattern, and iron on low heat to bond the paper to the pattern. Cut the pattern out, and it is now easier to handle.

COSTUME

FULL FIGURE/BIG & TALL

Another way to save your patterns...

Trace them onto inexpensive cloth such as muslin or interfacing. You can mark your pattern lines with a permanent pen, and your pattern will last for years.

Rather than tracing...

Press your patterns directly onto fusible interfacing. This allows them to be folded and manipulated, but they will not tear easily and will last longer.

MEN'S

An easy crib sheet pattern...

You will need:

Cotton fabric 69"x 45"

4-12" pieces of 1/4" elastic

Cut 8" square from each corner of your fabric, then stitch the cut seams together to form a box. Press a 3/8" hem all around the bottom edge of the sheet.

Insert elastic in each hem at corner, stretching as far as you can, then zig zag stitch the hem, securing elastic at each corner.

Handbag styles...

Box

Envelope

Shoulder

Clutch

PROJECT PATTERNS

Temporary pattern adjustments...

If you need to make pattern adjustments, but don't need them to be permanent, just use your pattern weights to hold each fold or split in place.

Outerwear styles...

Sweater

Cardigan

WOMEN'S

Another gathering technique...

To gather rows, try this easy method:

Row 1: stitch 3/8 inch from edge.

Row 2: stitch 1/8 inch from edge.

Anchor the beginning of your stitching by back-stitching and using a small length stitch, then switch to basting length. Pull top threads to distribute your gathers until it is the size you need.

Tip provided by: Londa's Sewing Etc. Page 303

Reversible buttons...

When making a reversible jacket, rather than putting buttons on both sides of one edge, try putting buttonholes on both sides of the front.

Make a 1 1/2" wide piece of fabric, as long as you will need for your reversible garment. Sew shank buttons onto the fabric strip. Now you can just button through the left side button holes (whichever way the garment is turned), and they will be ready to close.

Jehlor Fantasy Fabrics
Page 296

> Special occasion

Joyce's Fabrics
Page 297

Lace Heaven, Inc.
Page 301

Lacis
Page 301

The Leather Factory
Page 302

Leather Unlimited
Page 302

Logan Kits
Page 303

> Activewear
>
> Lingerie
>
> Swimwear

Londa's Sewing, Etc.
Page 303

Magic Fit Patterns
Page 304

> Custom-fit patterns

Marinda Stewart
Page 306

Mimi's Fabrications
Page 309

Miss Maureen's Fabrics and Fancies
Page 309

Morning Star Indian Gallery
Page 310

Nancy's Notions
Page 311

Needleart Guild
Page 312

Nimble Thimbles
Page 313

> Custom patterns

Norton House
Page 314

O.F.A.
Page 314

> Traditional African patterns

Oregon Worsted Company/Mill End Store
Page 316

Outdoor Wilderness Fabrics
Page 317

> Outerwear
>
> Sports wear

Park Bench Pattern Company
Page 318
Fun, contemporary clothing patterns with plenty of built in ease and thousands of possibilities for embellishment

Past Patterns
Page 319

> 1829-1950 period patterns

Patterns of History
Page 319

Patternworks
Page 320

> Knitting patterns

Pegee of Williamsburg Patterns from Historie
Page 320

Pieces
Page 322

The Pin Cushion
Page 322

Pioneer Quilts
Page 322

Quest Outfitters
Page 326

> Outerwear

The Rain Shed, Inc.
Page 329

> Outerwear
>
> Activewear

Ranita Corporation
Page 329

> Sure-Fit Pattern System

Ribbons & Roses
Page 330

Saf-T-Pockets
Page 332

> Patterns for travel clothing

Sealed With A Kiss, Inc.
Page 333

> Unique patterns for knitted sweaters

Outerwear styles...

Shawl

Stole

Project Kits

These kits should contain everything (or nearly everything) you need to get started on the special project of your choice.

Alpaca Sajama
Page 238

Knitting kits with 100% alpaca yarns

Amazon Vinegar & Pickling Works Drygoods
Page 239

Anne Powell, Ltd.
Page 241

Counted cross-stitch

Various samplers

Aura Registered
Page 244

Bead in Hand
Page 247

Beading

Beads & Beyond
Page 248

Blueprints-Printables
Page 251

Photo-sensitive fabric kits

Fabrics by the yard

Quilt squares

Sweat shirts

T-shirts

BottomLine Designs
Page 252

Investment Patterns include appliqué fabrics and vest pattern plus appliqué motifs.

Buck's County Classic
Page 253

Beading

C & T Publishing
Page 256

Silk ribbon embroidery

California Stitchery
Page 256

Judaic needlework

Center for the Study of Beadwork
Page 259

Continuity...
Page 262

Embroidery

Cotton Ball
Page 263

Cotton Clouds
Page 263

Casual summer top (knitting)

Chenille scarf (weaving)

Cotton lover's special sweater (knitting)

Cotton scarf (weaving)

Learn to weave (weaving)

Prism sweater (knitting)

Sampler sweater (weaving)

Simple country towels (weaving)

Taste of cotton sweater (knitting)

CR's Crafts
Page 264

Doll and toy kits

Crafts By Donna
Page 265

Brazilian embroidery

Silk ribbon embroidery

Trapunto

A few quilt squares...

Counterpane

Interlocked Squares

Starlight

Hat styles...

Scottish

Jockey

Tam-o-Shanter

Turban

Creative Beginnings
Page 265

> Silk ribbon embroidery

Daisy Kingdom
Page 267

Dharma Trading Co.
Page 269

> Design and print quilt squares
>
> Jacquard silk painting scarf
>
> Jacquard silk starter set
>
> Kid's silk painting
>
> Print a tie
>
> Tie-dye

Eagle Feather Trading Post
Page 269

> Leather Pouches
>
> Beaded Pouches

Enterprise Art
Page 274

> Beading
>
> Dream catchers
>
> Jewelry

Fiesta Yarns
Page 280

Fire Mountain Gems
Page 280

Four Seasons Knitting Products
Page 281

Frostline Kits
Page 282

> Attaché cases
>
> Baby carriers
>
> Backpacks
>
> Banners
>
> Bathrobes
>
> Bicycle Gear
>
>> Front panniers
>>
>> Handlebar bag
>>
>> Rear panniers
>>
>> Seat bag
>
> Bicycle cover
>
> Comforters
>
> Dog packs
>
> Down jackets
>
> Down shirts
>
> Duffle tote
>
> Expandable carry-on bag
>
> Frame packs
>
> Garment bags
>
> Insulated pants
>
> Jackets
>
> Lineman/welder's jacket
>
> Mesh reflective vests
>
> Parkas
>
> Pet bed
>
> Pillows
>
> Quick-change baby bag
>
> Quilter's/craft bag
>
> Rain gear

> Sleeping bags
>
> Slippers
>
> Stuff sacks
>
> Umbrellas
>
> Wallets

G Street Fabrics
Page 282

Good Wood
Page 284

> Weaving starter

Gramma's Graphics
Page 284

> Fabric sun printing kits

Grey Owl Indian Craft
Page 286

The Gypsy's Bead Shoppe
Page 286

> Jewelry

Halcyon Yarn
Page 286

> Belt loom
>
> Card weaving
>
> Crocheting
>
> Doll
>
> Dyeing
>
> Felting
>
> Knitting
>
> Lopi restart quick-knit package
>
> "Money-Wise" quick knit package
>
> Pom-pom makers

Potholders

Quick-4 floor loom weaving package

Quick-dye cotton package

Quick-dye wool package

Quick-punch rug package

Quick-spin spinning package

Quick-tapestry weaving package

Quick-weave rigid heddle weaving package

Harriet's TCS/Harriet's Patterns

Hedgehog Handworks

Silk ribbon embroidery

Tatting starter sets

Herrschners, Inc.

HH Designs

Candlewicking kits

Historic Needlework Guild

Infiknit

Knitted teacups

KC Publishing

Keepsake Quilting

Doll

Quilting

Stuffed animals

The Kirk Collection

Kite Studio

Kite building

Kite building class pack

Koigu Wool Designs

Knitting

Kreinik Mfg. Co., Inc.
Wholesale Only

The Lacemaker

Battenberg lace

Bobbin lace

Felt making

Princess lace

Silk ribbon

Tatting

Visionart dye

Lacis

Battenberg lace

Bobbin lace

Netting/Filet lace

Lark Books

Card weaving

Drop-spindle spinning

Elegant beaded bags

Exotic bead jewelry

Gorgeous glass bead jewelry

Jigg's boot, cross-stitch

Natural dyeing

Penny rug-hooking

Silk ribbon embroidery

Silk vest painting

Studio in a box (polymer clay jewelry)

The complete tatting kit

You can make glass beads!

The Leather Factory

Leatherworking

Logan Kits

Lingerie

Londa's Sewing, Etc.

Magic Cabin Dolls

Ethnically diverse dolls

Mary Jane's Cross 'N Stitch

Counted cross-stitch

Mimi's Fabrications

Morning Star Indian Gallery

Native American bead loom

Rough hands?

To remove roughness from your hands before stitching with silk ribbons or working with fine fabrics, use a mixture of equal parts cooking oil and granulated sugar. Rinse with cold water. Your fingers will be smooth and no longer snag the ribbon/fabric.

Tip provided by: Donna Freibertshauser Crafts by Donna Page 265

Mountain Colors
Page 310

    Crochet

    Knitting

    Weaving

Nancy's Notions
Page 311

    Decorator fabric (to cover frames, boxes, etc.)

    Roman stripe quilt

    Silk ribbon embroidery

The Needlecraft Shop
Page 312

    Crochet

New England Quilt Museum
Page 312

Nimble Thimbles
Page 313

    Knitting

Old Style Trading Company
Page 314

Optional Extras, Inc.
Page 314

Patternworks
Page 320

    Knitting Kits

        Children's clothes

        Dog sweaters

        "Fur" coats

        Hats

        Jackets

        Pillows

        Scarves

        Shawls

        Socks

        Suits

        Sweaters

        Twin sets

        Vests

Picking Up The Pieces Quilt Shop
Page 322

The Pin Cushion
Page 322

Prairieland Quilts
Page 324

Preemie-Yums
Page 324

    Kits for clothes that fit low birthweight babies, 4-6 pounds

Promenade's Le Bead Shop
Page 325

    Beading

Quilt in a Day
Page 326

Quilts & Other Comforts
Page 328

The Rain Shed, Inc.
Page 329

    Outerwear

Ree's Creative Ideas
Page 329

    Pre-cut and pre-fused appliqué kits

Ribbons & Roses
Page 230

    Embroidery

    Silk ribbon embroidery

Rings & Things
Wholesale Only
Page 330

    Beaded chain necklaces

Rupert, Gibbon & Spider
Page 331

    Print a tie

    Scarf painting

    Silk painting class pack

    Silk painting

    Tie-dye class pack

    Tie-dye

SAX Arts & Crafts
Page 333

Schoolhouse Press
Page 333
Kits for handknitters.

    Bavarian peplum jacket

    Cardigan details

    Catnip mouse

    Dubbelmössa (traditional Swedish cap)

    Faroe Islands sweater

    Mananita (lace shawl)

    Mary Allen's gloves

Möbius ring

Puzzle pillow

Russian prime

Shawl collared vest

Turkish/Icelandic pullover

Sealed With A Kiss, Inc.
Page 333

Unique pattern kits for knitted sweaters

Silkpaint Corporation
Page 337

Spinning Wheel
Page 340

Cross-stitch

Sweet Child of Mine
Page 343

Tea Cakes and Mud Pies
Page 344

Dust Bunnies

Hand-Me-Down Hankies

Hair-Dos—unfinished doll heads

Textile Reproductions
Page 345

Things Japanese
Page 346

Dyeing in a Teacup

Metallic Paint Sampler

Silk Dye Sampler

Stencil Styles

Steps to Stamping

The Bias Connection

Timeless Impressions
Page 347

Cool Band Patterns

Cool Crystals

Trendsetter Yarns/Ornashi Filati
Wholesale Only
Page 348

The Unique Spool
Page 349

The Weaving Works
Page 352

The Whole Bead Show
Page 353

The Woolery
Page 354

Afghan (knitting)

Hat (knitting)

Learn To Spin

Mittens (knitting)

Sock (knitting)

Stocking (knitting)

Sweater (knitting)

Coat styles...

Trench

Quilting & Patchwork Supplies

This section is not meant for a meeting at Quilter's Anonymous—it's designed to keep you hooked (or get you hooked).

What is a fat quarter?

A fat quarter is a 1/4 yard piece of fabric that measures 18"x 22" instead of 9"x 44".

Don't risk indecent exposure...

If you are making a quilt or composite of Sun Prints, make sure to expose all at the same time to ensure consistent color.

Tip provided by: Gramma's Graphics Page 284

Cottons, Etc.
Page 263

Creative Beginnings
Page 265

Charms

Daisy Kingdom
Page 267

EasiSew
Page 272

Extra Special Products Corp.
Page 275

Fabric Temptations
Page 276

Fairfield Processing Corporation
Wholesale Only
Page 277

Feathered Star Productions
Page 278

Mystery Quilt Singles
Judy Hopkins
Intriguing entertainment for the individual quilter. Step by suspenseful step to terrific traditional quilts, quick-cut, and speed pieced. Available in several themes:

A New Twist

Down On the Farm

Scrap Happy

Take Your Pick

Fiskars, Inc.
Wholesale Only
Page 280

Friends Patterns
Page 282

Quilt patterns

G Street Fabrics
Page 282

Ginger's Needleworks
Page 283

Gramma's Graphics
Page 284

Granny's Quilts
Page 285

Great Northern Weaving
Page 285

Hancock's
Page 287

Bag balm

Batting samples

Basting gun

Cotton batting

Curved needles

Dritz Quiltery rulers

Gingher scissors

Glue sticks

Needle threaders

Olfa products

Omnigrid rulers

Platinum-plated quilting needles

Polyester Batting

Quiltak

Quilter's beeswax

Quilter's fine line markers

Quilter's pins

Quilting frames

Quilting threads

Sulky products

Template plastic

Wool Batting

Harriet's Treadle Arts
Page 289

Heirlooms Forever
Page 290

Helyn's Hoops
Page 290

Herrschners, Inc.
Page 291

Hinterberg Design, Inc.
Page 292

"Easy Build" quilting frame kit

Floor standing quilting hoops

Quilting frames

Hobbs Bonded Fibers
Wholesale Only
Page 292

Batting

Fiberfill

House of White Birches
Page 293

Quilt Pattern Club (like a book or record club)

International Fabric Collection
Page 294

James W.M. Carroll Antiques
Page 296

    Antique fabric

    Antique quilts

Kasuri Dyeworks
Page 298

    Sashiko supplies

Keepsake Quilting
Page 298

Keepsake Quilting has too many quilting products and supplies for me to ever do them justice. Here is just a sampling.

    6,000+ bolts of cotton quilting fabrics

    Batting

    Cutting mats

    Fabric medley packs

    Frames

    Notions

    Project carrying cases

    Quilting kits

    Quilting patterns

    Rotary cutters

    Templates

Ken Quilt
Page 298

    Quilting machines

The Kirk Collection
Page 299

    19th Century cottons (new and used)

    19th Century scrap bag

    100% Cotton batting

    Acid-free storage box

    Acid-free tissue

    American Folk and Fabric

    Beads for crazy quilting

    Charm squares

    Crazy quilt scrap bag

    Crepelen stabilization packet

    Double-headed needle threader

    Ear polypus (for restoration)

    Fat quarters

    Feedsack charms

    Lace for crazy quilting

    Ladies' hankies

    Harriet Hargrave

    Needles

    Orphan block (adopt one today)

    Orvus Quilt Wash

    Quilter's Request batting

    Scrap bags of vintage cottons with various themes

    Soft Touch batting

    Three Cats

    Three Leopards

    Wool charms

Kreinik Mfg. Co., Inc.
    Wholesale Only
Page 299

Logan Kits
Page 303

Londa's Sewing, Etc.
Page 303

Mallery Press
Page 305

MHC
Page 308

    Hangers

    Lazy Sharyn rotary tables with cutting mats

    Patterns

Mimi's Fabrications
Page 309

Mountain Mist/The Stearns Technical Textiles Company
Page 310

    Cotton batting

    Mountain Mist Historic Quilting Stencils

    Polyester batting

Nancy's Notions
Page 311

    Basting gun

    Circle wedge ruler

    Clips

    Cutting mats

    Fabric value filter

    Frames

    Needles

    Olfa® Rotary Cutting System

    Orvus Quilt Wash

    Pins

    Scissors

    Templar

    Thread

Storage saavy...

When you make the hanging sleeve for your quilt, line it with the fabrics you used in the quilt top.

If a piece is needed to repair the quilt at a later time, the fabric is with the quilt and will have been washed and faded like the top itself.

Tip provided by: Harriet's Treadle Arts Page 289

Feeling the drag?

When marking fabric with a pencil, angle the pencil as close as possible to the fabric to create less drag.

Accuracy is key...

With any quiltmaking project, accurate templates and precise cutting are important. Trace template patterns onto see-through plastic with a fine point permanent black pen. Cut them out using a blade or paper scissors. Remember to trace the seam allowance onto the templates. This will enable you to see exactly what the squares and triangles will look like after they are sewn.

Tip quoted from: Impressionist Quilts by Gai Perry, published by C & T Publishing Page 256

Sewing Machines, Etcetera

These companies offer you sewing machines, sergers, and embroidery machines. Some also offer supplies, parts, and other elated items.

AK Sew & Serge
Page 237

All Brand Sew-Knit-Serge & Embroidery
Page 238

> Bernina
>
> Elna
>
> New Home
>
> Pfaff
>
> Viking
>
> White

And Sew On
Page 240

Associated Sewing Supply Co., Inc.
Page 243

Baer Fabrics
Page 245

> Babylock
>
> Bernina

Banasch's, Inc.
Page 245

Buttons 'n' Bows
Page 254

Close to Home–The Sewing Center
Page 260

Clotilde
Page 260

> Sewing machine accessories
>
>> Invisible zipper foot
>>
>> Pearls and piping
>>
>> Satin edge/topstitch
>>
>> Teflon foot

The Corner Stitch, Inc.
Page 262

Cottons, Etc.
Page 263

> Viking

Daisy Kingdom
Page 267

Fabric Collections
Page 276

> Viking/White

G Street Fabrics
Page 282

Goldblatt Industrial Sewing Machine Company
Page 283

> Blindstitchers, new and used
>
> Household presses
>
> Industrial cutters
>
> Industrial steam irons
>
> Sergers, new and used
>
> Sewing machines, new and used

Granny's Quilts
Page 285

> Pfaff
>
> Viking

Harriet's Treadle Arts
Page 289

Heirlooms Forever
Page 290

> Bernina
>
> Pfaff
>
> Viking
>
> White

Saving time while sewing...

Before sewing, pin everything that will be sewn in your session, for example, hems, cuffs, seams, collars, etc.

During your sewing session, don't bother to cut the threads between each piece, just sew the next item with 1/4" to 1/2" between it and the preceding item. This is often referred to as chain sewing by those in the industry.

To clean hard-to-reach areas of your sewing machine…

Try using an empty sample-size bottle of liquid dish soap. They are easy to use, small to store, easily obtainable, inexpensive, and there is no moisture residue like canned air.

Simply wash out the bottle, dry well, replace the cap, and store with cap open.

To use, apply a quick, solid squeeze to the bottle.

The best thing about this method is that you never run out of air.

Tip provided by: Fancy Threads/Fancy Threads Custom Page 277

Herrschners, Inc.
Page 291

Ken Quilt
Page 298

Quilting machines

Londa's Sewing, Etc.
Page 303

Elna

Pfaff

Mimi's Fabrications
Page 309

Nancy's Notions
Page 311

Irons

Pressers

Puff Irons

National Thread & Supply
Page 312

Brother

Juki

Pfaff

Singer

Patchogue Sewing Machine Center, Inc.
Page 319

The Pin Cushion
Page 322

Viking

Prairieland Quilts
Page 324

Queen Ann's Lace
Page 326

The Quilting Bee
Page 328

Bernina

Euro-Pro

Viking

White

Quilts By the Oz
Page 329

SAX Arts & Crafts
Page 333

Sewing Emporium/Sew-Easy Products
Page 335
They have the largest selection of sewing machine accessories and parts I have seen in one catalog, including parts for commercial machines and old/antique machines. They also rebuild motors, controls, and circuit boards.

Blindstitch

Buttonholers

Embroidery

Rufflers

Sergers

Sewing machine accessories

Feet

Parts

Sewing Supplies, Inc.
Page 335

Hard-to-find parts and accessories for sewing machines

Solo Slide Fasteners, Inc.
Page 339

Blindstitchers

Industrial machines

Portable machines

Vogue Fabrics/Vogue Fabrics By Mail
Page 351

Waechter's Silk Shop
Page 351

Bernina

Sewing Notions & Accessories

These companies offer those handy gadgets we just can't live without: dressforms, hams, point turners, and many more notions and accessories.

Did you know...

Hand sewing needles get smaller as the size number gets larger. The secret to small quilting stitches is to use a short needle and very thin batting.

Those amazing quilts with 12 to 20 stitches per inch are made with the thinnest batting and a size 12 needle.

Most beginning quilters and hand-sewers will feel more comfortable with a size 10 to start.

Tip provided by:
The Kirk Collection
Page 299

Hairspray is a notion?

Try using hairspray to:

Hold seam allowances together while sewing.

Hold paper down on fabric while cutting.

Make thread stiff for needle-threading.

Remove ball-point pen ink stains.

Spray on cone or tube to keep thread from falling down.

Hold appliqué in place while sewing.

Tip provided by: Sewing Emporium/Sew Easy Products Page 335

Daisy Kingdom
Page 267

Dress Rite Forms
Page 271

> Dress Rite Half Scale Forms
>
> Dress Rite Full Body Forms
>
> Dress Rite Gold Body Forms
>
> Dress Rite Industrial Forms
>
> Dress Rite Tailoring Forms (for men and women)

EasiSew
Page 272

Elegance Unlimited, Inc.
Page 273

Fabric Collections
Page 276

Fabric Gallery
Page 276

Fabrics Unlimited
Page 276

Fabulous Fit
Page 277

> Fabulous Fit foam pads for customizing dress forms to realistic shapes

Fiskars, Inc.
> *Wholesale Only*

Page 280

Four Seasons Knitting Products
Page 281

> Knitting needles

G Street Fabrics
Page 282

Granny's Quilts
Page 285

Greenberg & Hammer, Inc.
Page 286

> Belting
>
> Chalk
>
> Clothing tags
>
> Dressforms
>
> Hangers
>
> Marking pens and pencils
>
> Pattern paper
>
> Pins
>
> Pressing equipment
>
> Rulers
>
> Scissors

Hancock's
Page 287

> Bag Balm
>
> Basting gun
>
> Beeswax
>
> Collins thread palette
>
> Curved needles
>
> Dritz Quiltery rulers
>
> Fine line markers
>
> Gingher scissors
>
> Glue sticks
>
> Hand needles
>
> Irons
>
> Machine needles

> Needle threaders
>
> Olfa products
>
> Omnigrid rulers
>
> Pins
>
> Platinum plated quilting needles
>
> Quiltak
>
> Quilting frames
>
> Seam guides
>
> Seams Great
>
> Sulky products
>
> Tape measures
>
> Template plastic

Harriet's Treadle Arts
Page 288

Heirlooms Forever
Page 290

Herrschners, Inc.
Page 291

> Magnifiers
>
> Hoops

Jiffy Steamer Company
Page 297

> Steamers for home and professional use

Keepsake Quilting
Page 298

Kreinik Mfg. Co., Inc.
> *Wholesale Only*

Page 299

Lacis
Page 301

Bias tape maker

Bodkins

Egg darners

Frame clamps

Magnifiers

Quilt clamps

Ribbon pleaters

Sewing bird

Londa's Sewing, Etc.
Page 303

MagEye's-MFD Enterprises
Page 304

Mary Ellen & Co.
Page 306

Morning Star Indian Gallery
Page 310

Nancy's Notions
Page 311

Nancy's has too many notions for me to list them all, so I'll have a go at the more unusual and interesting ones.

Adjustable top stitch and seam guide

Basting gun

Bias tape makers

Button Ons™ (turns buttons into fashion jewelry)

Clappers

Creative Feet™

Double Eye Needle

Elastics

Fabric markers

Fabric pattern transfer kit

Fiber Etch™

Hams

Interfacings

Iron-on flexible vinyl

Liquid Pins

Olfa® Cutting Systems

Pattern boxes

Pattern Life™

Perfect Pleater®

Scissors

Sewing furniture

Sew Steady portable table

Simflex Gauge (to measure equal distances, such as button positioning)

Soapstone fabric marker

Specialty presser feet

Stabilizers

Suspender Clips

Teflon-coated fabric

Templar

National Thread & Supply
Page 312

Cutting tools and machines

Drapery supplies

Scissors

Needleart Guild
Page 312

Oregon Rule Company
Page 315

Self-adhesive rulers

Oregon Tailor Supply Co.
Page 316

Oregon Worsted Company/Mill End Store
Page 316

Palmer/Pletsch Publishing
Page 318

24k gold embroidery scissors from Italy

The Classy Catcher

Educational serger posters

Perfect Sew liquid wash-away fabric stabilizer

Perfect Sew needle threader

The Pin Cushion
Page 322

Pioneer Quilts
Page 322

Prairieland Quilts
Page 324

Prym-Dritz Corporation
Wholesale Only
Page 325

Adhesives

Cutting boards

Dressforms

Elastic guides

Machine accessories

Marking equipment

Measuring tools

Ezy-Hem gauge

See-Thru dressmaker's ruler

Skirt markers

Between what?

Betweens describe needles shorter than those called ground downs, and longer than blunts. They are longer and thicker than ordinary sewing needles, such as sharps.

Hint paraphrased from:
The Dictionary of Needlework
©1972
Arno Press, Inc.

What is pin money?

Pin money originally meant enough money for a woman to purchase pins for sewing, which were quite expensive.

In widespread usage, it now more commonly means an allowance or stipend.

Silk Ribbon Embroidery

Although the technique refers to silk ribbon, you can use any type of ribbon you please. Those listed here range from silk to polyester to metallic.

5T's Embroidery Supply
Page 237

AK Sew & Serge
Page 237

Associated Sewing Supply Co., Inc.
Page 243

Banasch's Fabrics
Page 245

Buttons 'n' Bows
Page 255

   Framecraft porcelain boxes

   Silk ribbon

C & T Publishing
Page 256

Carol Harris Co.
Page 257

The Corner Stitch, Inc.
Page 262

Cotton Ball
Page 263

Cottons, Etc.
Page 263

CR's Crafts
Page 264

Crafts By Donna
Page 265

Creative Beginnings
Page 265

   Iron-ons

   Silk ribbon

   Silk ribbon kits

Daisy Kingdom
Page 267

Dharma Trading Co.
Page 269

   White blank silk ribbon and dyes

Elsie's Exquisites
Page 273

   Silk ribbon

The Enchanted Cottage
Page 274

   Ribbon floss

   Silk ribbon

Enterprise Art
Page 274

Fabric Temptations
Page 276

   Handpainted silk ribbon

   YLI

Fancywork
Page 277

G Street Fabrics
Page 282

Ginger's Needleworks
Page 283

Granny's Quilts
Page 285

Harriet's Treadle Arts
Page 289

Hedgehog Handworks
Page289

   Lead crystal boxes

   Porcelain boxes

   Silk ribbon

Embellishment without too much color...

If you like the look of ribbon embroidery, but don't normally wear a lot of color, try this tip:

Use one color of ribbon on a matching fabric. For instance, create your favorite silk ribbon motif entirely in black on a black blazer.

Another look would be to use slightly different shades, but to keep a monochrome motif, such as all silver grey on black, or a muted tan on ivory.

There are many variations on this theme—be creative!

Avoid rust spots...

Never leave a needle in your embroidery. In a short time it may rust and become impossible to remove (especially in moist climates). If you are lucky enough to remove it, there may be a permanent rust spot in the fabric.

Instead, stitch about six cross-stitches, about 1/4" high, in the top margin of your fabric. These XXXXX's create an excellent "garage" in which to "park" your needle. The needle is always with the work but will not rust onto it.

Tip provided by:
Donna Freibertshauser
Crafts by Donna
Page 265

Silver-plated brooches

Silver-plated clothes brush

Silver-plated comb-brush-mirror set

Things Japanese
Page 346

Ribasilk ribbon

Instant set silk dye

Waechter's Silk Shop
Page 351

Fabric distortion...

Never leave an embroidery hoop on a piece of work when you stop working. The hoop will distort the fabric, which may never be flat again.

Tip provided by:
Donna Freibertshauser
Crafts by Donna
Page 265

Smocking & Heirloom Sewing

These businesses offer products for the project that will be handed down through the generations—or for one that just looks like it was.

An easy way to gather...

Try zig zag stitching over kite string or any kind of heavy thread.

When you are ready, just pull on the string to create your gathers.

This tip provided by:
Bigfig1
AOL Sewing Board

Snaps, Zippers & Other Closures

When buttons just won't do.

Can't find a zipper that's the right length?

Buy one that is slightly longer than you need and shorten it.

To do this, simply pull the slider down and mark the zipper at the desired length.

Cut off both sides an inch above the mark.

If the teeth are metal or molded plastic, remove the teeth above your mark with pliers. For coil zippers, use scissors and carefully snip through the coils and pull out the fragments. Immediately install a top stop above the remaining teeth.

Tip provided by:
Jacquart Fabric Products, Inc.
Page 296

Snaps

Velcro

Zippers

Heirlooms Forever
Page 289

Jacquart Fabric Products, Inc.
Page 296

Jehlor Fantasy Fabrics
Page 296

Kite Studio
Page 299

Lace Heaven, Inc.
Page 201

The Leather Factory
Page 302

Grommets

Snaps

Leather Unlimited
Page 302

Logan Kits
Page 303

Londa's Sewing, Etc.
Page 303

M & J Trimming Co.
Page 304

Frogs (a wide variety)

Marine Sewing
Page 306

For outdoor gear

Nancy's Notions
Page 311

National Thread & Supply
Page 312

Norton House
Page 314

Oregon Tailor Supply Co.
Page 316

Oregon Worsted Company/Mill End Store
Page 316

Outdoor Wilderness Fabrics
Page 317

Buckles

Grommets

Snaps

Zippers

The Pin Cushion
Page 322

Prairieland Quilts
Page 324

Prym-Dritz Corporation
Wholesale Only
Page 325

Quest Outfitters
Page 326

Grommets

Snaps

Zippers

The Rain Shed, Inc.
Page 329

Grommets

Sliders

Snaps

Swivel snaphooks (like those found on dog leashes)

Zippers

Richard the Thread
Page 330

Buckles

Fasteners

Snaps

Zippers

Seattle Fabrics, Inc.
Page 334

Buckles

Grommets

Snaps

Zippers

SewBaby!
Page 334

Snap Source snaps in 15 colors and two sizes

Sewing Sampler Productions, Inc.
Page 335

The Smocking Horse Collection
Page 337

The Snap Source, Inc.
Page 338

Snap attachment tools

Snaps

Capped

Jewel inset (pearl)

Open

Solo Slide Fasteners, Inc.
Page 339

Adjustable hooks and eyes

Eyelets

Grommets

Hooks and Eyes (also heavy-duty)

No-Sew snaps

Sew-On snaps

Trouser closures

Zippers

Boot

Bottom Stops

Enameled metal

Invisible

Jean

Metal

Non-separating

Parts

Separating

Skirt, slack and dress

Skiwear jacket

Tent and sleeping bag

Top Stops

Trousers

Stone Mountain & Daughter Fabrics
Page 341

Vogue Fabrics/Vogue Fabrics By Mail
Page 351

Waechter's Silk Shop
Page 351

Pants styles...

Hip-hugger Jeans

Software & Internet Addresses

These companies have programs and information for those of you who enjoy using your computer, in addition to your fabric and fiber.

All Brand Sew-Knit-Serge & Embroidery
Page 238

sewserg@aol.com

AlterYears
Page 239

72437.674@compuserve.com

America Online
(800) 827-6364

American Needlepoint Guild
Page 239

cathfelten@aol.com

Anne Powell, Ltd.
Page 241

Counted Cross-Stitch Software

The Art Institute in La Antigua Guatemala
Page 241

artguat@aol.com

Atelier Plateau Collection Menzwear
Page 243

women@the.link.ca

Atlanta Puffections
Page 243

puffector@aol.com

Barbara L. Grainger Enterprises
Page 246
Barbara Grainger can be easily reached for advice and talks on the Prodigy Beading bulletin board.

wmat@prodigy.com

Bead Store Café
Page 247

jm66@cornell.edu

Beggars' Lace
Page 249

lacelady@rmii.com

Brookfield Craft Center
Page 253

brkfldcrft@aol.com

http://www.craftweb.com/org/brookfl d.brookfld.shtml

Bucks County Classic
Page 253

bccjane@aol.com

Button Treasures
Page 254

You can reach Terry Meinrath of Button Treasures at:

100520.3323@compuserve.com

C & T Publishing
Page 256

You can browse their books on their WWW home page, or contact them at their e-mail address.

ctinfo@ctpub.com

http://www.ctpub.com/~ctpub

Campmor
Page 256

info@campmor.com

http://www.campmor.com

Canyon Art Company/WeaveIt
Page 256

WeaveIt - Weaving program for Windows
Sally Breckenridge
$95 full version, $15 demo

Outerwear styles...

Short Cape

Caravan Beads, Inc.
Page 257

caravan@mainelink.net

http://www.mainelink.net/caravan

Cathedral Window
Page 258

74554.2465@compuserve.com, Janet Befort

Block Base
$62.95
PC

Electric Quilt
$105
PC

Fittingly Sew
$139.95
PC/Mac

Personal Patterns

Quilt-Pro
$87.95
PC/Mac

Quilt-Soft
$89.95
PC/Mac

X-Stitch Designer Gold

Cochenille Design Studio
Page 260

76702.1664@compuserve.com

Collins Publications
Page 260

Dress Shop 2.0, Pattern Drafting Software

Compuserve
(800) 888-8990

Copper Coyote Beads, Ltd.
Page 262

emeraldy@aol.com

gwennyaple@prodigy.com

The Cotton Club
Page 263

102416.300@compuserve.com

cotton@micron.net

Coupeville Arts Center
Page 264

cac@whidbey.net

The Crafts Report
Page 265

tcrmag@aol.com

Crystal Palace Yarns
Wholesale Only
Page 266

cpy@straw.com

http://www.straw.com

David Simpson, Bookfinder
Page 268

des209p@bevinet

Design Originals Publications
Page 269

74200.3031@compuserve.com

Dimples
Page 269

dimplesfab@aol.com

Double Joy Beads
Page 270

hkxb59a@prodigy.com

Dundas Loom Company
Page 271

jsdweaver@aol.com

E & W Imports, Inc./The Bead Shop
Page 272

ruby@intnet.net

EasiSew
Page 272

royecrs@aol.com

The Embroiderers Guild of America, Inc.
Page 274

egahq@aol.com

Fiber Statements
Page 279
Ask Pat about her classes at:

parodgers@aol.com

Fiesta Yarns
Page 280

laboheme@rt66.com

Fiskars, Inc.
Wholesale Only
Page 280

http://www.fiskars.com

Fittingly Sew (Bartley Software)
Page 281

72133.3102@compuserve.com

Fittingly Sew® - Pattern making software for Macintosh
$149+$20 S/H U.S.
$189+$10 S/H Canada
System 6, 7 or later, 15 MB free disk space, 2MB RAM

Fittingly Sew® - Pattern making
software for Windows
$149+$20 S/H U.S.
$189+$10 S/H Canada
80386 or higher processor, Microsoft
Windows 3.1 or later, 2MB Ram,
Mouse, 1.5 MB free disk pace, 3.5"
high density floppy drive

Fresh Water Pearl Button Company
Page 281

> 73562.1377@compuserve.com

Frostline Kits
Page 282

> frostline@qli.backboard.com

> http://www.backboard.com/~frostline

G Street Fabrics
Page 282

The Glass Giraffe
Page 283

The Glass Giraffe offers specials on their
home page, or you can reach them on
Prodigy.

> nxub32a@prodigy.com

> http://www.crescendoweb.com/
> glassgiraf/index.html

Gramma's Graphics
Page 284

> 70671.321@compuserve.com

Grey Owl Indian Craft
Page 286

> tkc315@aol.com

Halcyon Yarn
Page 286

> squombus@eworld.com

> Software for Knitters

> > *Sweater 101, 2.0 for IBM*

> > *Sweater Workshop for Windows*

> > *Yarn Calc. for IBM*

> Software for Weavers

> > *Light Weave for IBM*

> > *SwiftWeave (AVL) for Mac*

> > *Weave Point (AVL) for IBM*

> > *Weave Simulator for IBM*

Hancock's
Page 287

> dsingbear@aol.com

Handweaver's Guild of America, Inc.
Page 287

> 73744.202@compuserve.com

Hard-to-Find Needlework Books
Page 288

> needlewk@tiac.net

> http://www.ambook.org/bookstore/ne
> edlework.

> http://www.tiac.net/users/needlewk

Hemp BC
Page 290

> memery@hembc.com

> http://www.hempbc.com

Hemp Textiles International Corp.
Page 290

> hti@hemptex.com

> http://www.hemptex.com~html

Heritage Looms
Page 291

> 76151.3705@compuserve.com

The Hillsinger Compaany
Page 291

> hillsinger@northwest.com

Hinterberg Design, Inc.
Page 292

> hinterbera@hnet.west-bend.wi.us

History International, Inc.
Page 292

> history@citynet.com

Infiknit
Page 294

> ctomy@interlog.com

Jill McIntire Designs
Page 297

K & K Quilteds
Page 297

> e.qrs@taconic.net

The Kirk Collection
Page 299

> kirkcoll@aol.com

They also sell these programs:

> *Block Base*

> *The Electric Quilt*

Speaking their mind...

*"Wear things you love
and love the world."*

Darbury Stenderu

Length measurement chart for men...

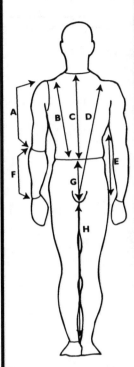

A. *Arm (Shoulder to Elbow)*

B. *Shoulder to Waist*

C. *Neck to Waist*

D. *Shoulder to Crotch*

E. *Underarm to Wrist*

F. *Arm (Elbow to Wrist)*

G. *Waist to crotch*

H. *Crotch to Ankle (inseam)*

Kite Studio
Page 299

kbi.ferrell@microserve.com

They also sell the computer program:

Kite 2.0 Kiteflght & Plotter - Prints out patterns for stunt kites

Labours of Love Heirloom Sewing Supplies, Inc.
Page 300

heirloom@direct.ca

The Lacemaker
Page 301

102254.314@compuserve.com

Londa's Sewing, Etc.
Page 303

Mag-Eyes–MFD Enterprises
Page 304

amigo@hi/conet.com

Mallery Press
Page 305

amisimms@aol.com

http://quilt.com/amisimms

Maple Hill Software
Page 305

Pattern Light Weave 2.02

Patternland Pattern Grapher 2.15

Patternland Weave Publisher 2.1

Patternland Weave Simulator 5.1

Mary Ellen & Co.
Page 306

71562.2136@compuserve.com

Mindsun
Page 309

Mindweave - Weaving software $95

Morning Light Emporium
Page 310

mle@wic.net

Mother Nurture
Page 310

sgustafs@maui.netwave.net

Neighbors and Friends
Page 312

http://www.craft.com/nbr_frnd

Nina Designs
Page 313

nina@nets.com

Norton House
Page 314

Oracle Publications
Page 315

ljbc20a@prodigy.com

oraclepubl@aol.com

Oregon Buttonworks
Page 315

buttonups@aol.com

Original Sewing & Craft Expo
Page 316

sewncraft@aol.com

Oxford Craft Software
Page 317

X-Stitch Designer

X-Stitch Designer Gold

Patchworks
Page 328

patchwrks@apinet,net

http://www.alpinet.net/~patchwrks/

Patternworks
Page 320

knit@patternworks

http://ww.patternworks.com

Photo Textiles
Page 321

phototex@aol.com

The Pin Cushion
Page 322

Portland Bead Society
Page 323

beadport@hevanet.com

Practical Applied Logic, Inc.
Page 323

Bead Pattern Design Software

Primrose Lane
Page 324

primlane@aol.com

Pro Show, Inc.
Page 325

creatvinsp@aol.com

Prodigy
(800) PRODIGY

Queen Ann's Lace
Page 326

Quilting designs

The Quilt Restoration Society
Page 327

e-qrs@taconic.net

The Quilting Bee
Page 328

quiltbee@iwe.com

http://www.iwe.com/quiltbee

Quilting Books Unlimited
Page 328

Quilts & Other Comforts
Page 328

QuiltSoft
Page 329

quiltsoft@aol.com

Rings & Things
Wholesale Only
Page 330

pollarue@aol.com

Salt Spring Island Fibre Studios
Page 332

susanb@islandnet.com

SewBaby!
Page 334

sewbaby@prairienet.org

http://www.prairienet.org/sewbaby/homepage

SewStorm Publishing
Page 335

sewstorm@aol.com

Shuttle-Craft Books
Page 336

scb@whidbey.net

Software Directory for Fibre Artists
Page 338

swp@ecinet.ab.ca

http://www.islandnet.com/~arogers/directory.html

Software Directory for Fibre Artists
Lois Larson
$30 + $5 S&H U.S.
$35 + $5 S&H Canada
246 pages, 146 illustrations B&W and color
Directory of sotfware available for weaving, knitting, needlework, quilting, and sewing.

Soho South
Page 338

sohosout@village.ios.com

SouthStar Supply Company
Page 339

jfreb@aol.com

Southwest Craft Center
Page 340

swcc@dcci.com

Stitches Great Fiber Getaways
Page 341

stitchsinc@aol.com

Stone Mountain & Daughter Fabrics
Page 341

zan3@aol.com

Straw Into Gold
Page 342

straw@straw.com

http://www.straw.com

Success Publishing
Page 342
S.O.S for Windows

Software for quick and easy reference to sewing items and to print listings of inventory.

Suzanne Cooper, Inc.
Page 343

suzycoop@aol.com

Tess' Designer Yarns
Page 344

tessyarns@mcimail.com

Textile Arts Forum
Page 345

drudings@delphi.com

See their full listing for information on a free trial period and connecting to Delphi.

Trendsetter Yarns/Ornashi Filati
Page 348

trndstr@aol.com

Unique Patterns Design
Page 349

tstrans@fox.nstn.ca

Universal Synergetics
Page 350

virginia@beadcats.com

carol@beadcats.com

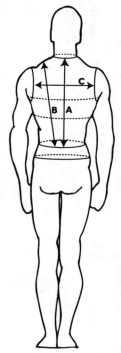

Length measurement chart for men, back view...

A. Neck to Waist

B. Shoulder to Waist

C. Shoulder Blade Width

Dress styles...

Cheongsam

Water Fountain Software, Inc.
Page 352

Personal Patterns–women's and children's basic patterns

Personal Patterns–women's basic patterns

Personal Patterns–women's designer jackets and suits

Wheeler Arts
Page 353

wheelers@aol.com

Sewing and craft clip art collection

Yarns International
Page 354

yarns2u@aol.com

Spinning & Raw Fibers

These businesses have fibers for spinning and felting, and supplies to help you.

Alpaca Sajama
Page 238

Alpaca fiber

Ashland Bay Trading Company, Inc.
Wholesale Only
Page 242

Fibers

Mohair

Silk

Wool

Bovidae Farm
Page 252

Corriedale fleece

Castlegate Farm
Page 258

Romney sheep wool

Cotton Clouds
Page 263

Ashford spinning wheels

Cotton carders

Drum carders

Fibers

Acala Cotton

Brown Cotton

Pima Cotton

Sliver Cotton

Spindle starter kit

Spindles

Spinning wheel starter kit

Crystal Palace Yarns
Wholesale Only
Page 266

Ashford spinning wheels

Fibers

Dundas Loom Company
Page 271

Shetland Style

Cherry wood

Maple wood

The Fiber Studio
Page 279

Fibers

Alpaca

Camel hair

Cotton

Flax

Silk

Wool

Frank Williams' Hemp Co.
Page 281

Hemp spinning fiber in natural, and 24 organically dyed colors

Hemp Textiles International Corp.
Page 290

Hunt Valley Cashmere
Page 291

Cashmere Fiber

The Lacemaker
Page 301

Majacraft Spinning Wheels

The Mannings Handweaving School & Supply Center
Page 305

Did you know?

All sheep produce wool and most can be slaughtered for meat.

Many producers have used the same sheep to meet the demands of both markets. The fact is that most sheep are bred primarily to meet the demands of the food industry, instead of being bred for the quality of the wool. The result has been commercial wools that are harsh, scratchy, and of unsuitable color for natural knits.

Tip provided by:
Maie Landra
Koigu Wool Designs
Page 299

Spinning dog hair...

Dog hair needs a little oil added to it before it can be spun and carded.

Many of the longer hairs will work, while Poodle and Samoyed produce especially beautiful yarns.

Luckily for those enterprising spinners who first experimented with spinning dog hair, the smell of wet dog disappears completely after the first wash.

Threads

Threads for anything and everything are represented here. Let your imagination roam wild.

5T's Embroidery Supply
Page 237

    Cording and looping

    Cotton

    Metallic

    Polyester

    Rayon

    Wool

AK Sew & Serge
Page 237

And Sew On
Page 240

    Sulky Candlelight

Apparel Component Supply
Page 247

Associated Sewing Supply Co., Inc.
Page 243

Atkinson Fabrics, Inc.
Page 243

Aurora Silk
Page 244

    Naturally dyed silk threads

Banasch's Fabrics
Page 245

Banasch's, Inc.
Page 245

    Basting

    Blindstitch

    Button

    Coats & Clark

    Gold Seal

    Gütermann

    Jean Thread

    Molnlycke

    Nymo

    Redi-Wound Bobbins

    Silcora

    Serger

    Soft Nylon

    Transparent Monofilament

    Utica Silk

Banksville Designer Fabrics
Page 245

Batiks Etcetera
Page 246

Berman Leather Co.
Page 249

    Leather sewing threads

Blueprints-Printables
Page 251

    Silk Cones

Bridals International
Page 253

Buttons 'n' Bows
Page 255

Canyon Records & Indian Arts
Page 257

    American Indian craft threads

Carol Harris Co.
Page 257

Carolina Mills Factory Outlet
Page 257

Clotilde
Page 260

Threading troubles?

Try using a bit of spray starch on the end of your thread; it will stiffen a bit, and go through the eye much easier.

Tip paraphrased from:
Mary Ellen's Giant Book of Helpful Hints by Mary Ellen Pinkham
© 1976, 1981, 1980 Random House

Sulky Sliver metallic tips...

Use a needle specifically made for metallic thread.

Set top tension at 0-1.

Use rayon thread in a matching color in the bobbin.

Stabilize your fabric with a water-soluble or heat-away stabilizer.

Use lubricant on both Sliver and bobbin threads.

Use felt or a bit of cloth under the thread spool to keep it from slipping.

Sliver thread should always come of the spool vertically.

The Corner Stitch, Inc.
Page 262

Cotton Ball
Page 263

Cottons, Etc.
Page 263

Crafts By Donna
Page 265

　　Brazilian

　　Rayon

D'Leas Fabric and Button Studio
Page 266

Daisy Kingdom
Page 267

Dharma Trading Co.
Page 299

　　100% cotton

　　100% silk

Dimples
Page 269

Eagle Feather Trading Post
Page 272

　　Nymo

The Enchanted Cottage
Page 274

Enterprise Art
Page 274

Fabric Collections
Page 276

　　Mettler 100% cotton

　　Silk

　　Sulky

Fabric Gallery
Page 276

Fabric Temptations
Page 276

Fabrics Unlimited
Page 276

Frank Williams' Hemp Co.
Page 276

　　Hemp threads available in natural, and 24 organically dyed colors. These are soft–not itchy twines.

G Street Fabrics
Page 282

Ginger's Needleworks
Page 283

Granny's Quilts
Page 285

Greenberg & Hammer, Inc.
Page 286

　　Cotton

　　Elastic

　　Embroidery

　　Fusible

　　Glace

　　Metallics

　　Nylon

　　Polyester

　　Silk

　　Woolly Nylon

Grey Owl Indian Craft
Page 286

Hancock's
Page 287

　　Gütermann cotton quilting

　　Invisible nylon

　　Mettler all-cotton machine quilting

　　Sulky embroidery

　　Sulky metallic embroidery

　　Sulky metallic Sliver

　　Sulky premium invisible

Handy Hands, Inc.
Page 288

　　DMC

　　　　Cebelia

　　　　Pearl Cotton

　　Opera

　　Metallic

　　Silk

Harriet's Treadle Arts
Page 289

Hedgehog Handworks
Page 289

　　Balger metallic

　　Broider Wul

　　Bullions

　　Caron Collection

　　DMC

　　Japan gold and silver

　　Madeira metallics

　　Marlitt

Soie d'Alger

Trebizond twisted silk

Heirlooms Forever
Page 290

Herrschners, Inc.
Page 291

High Country West Needleworks
Page 292

Homestead Needle Arts
Page 292

Cotton

Metallic

Rayon

Silk

Wool

International Fabric Collection
Page 294

Jacquart Fabric Products, Inc.
Page 296

Jehlor Fantasy Fabrics
Page 296

Judy's Heirloom Sewing
Page 296

DMC

The Kirk Collection
Page 299

Appliqué

Quilting

Kite Studio
Page 299

Nylon bonded

Kreinik Mfg. Co., Inc.
Wholesale Only
Page 299

Metallic

Blending filament

Braids

Cable

Cord

Japan threads

Ombre

Ribbons

Silk

D'Alger

Gobelin

Mori

Noppee

Perlee

Ping Ling

Platte

Serica

Lace Heaven, Inc.
Page 301

The Lacemaker
Page 301

Anchor

Appleton Crewel Wool

Appleton Tapestry Wool

Au Ver a Soie

Balger Metallics

Caron Collection

Watercolors

Wildflowers

Cordonnet

Coton a'Broder

DMC

Floss

Flower Thread

Medici

Metallic

Pearl Cotton (sizes 5, 8, 12)

Tatting Cotton

Madeira

Silk n' Colors

Silk Serica

Ledgewood Studio
Page 302

Logan Kits
Page 303

Cone

Londa's Sewing, Etc.
Page 303

M's Fabric Gallery
Page 304

Marine Sewing
Page 306

Rot-resistant

Mimi's Fabrications
Page 309

Miss Maureen's Fabrics and Fancies
Page 309

Using metallic threads...

To successfully stitch with metallic threads, keep the following in mind: any thread, metallic or not, is most vulnerable when passing through the fabric. Friction between the thread and fabric may damage the thread. To reduce friction, stitch more slowly and follow these helpful hints:

Use short lengths of thread—about 18"— to avoid excessive abrasion when pulling the thread through the fabric.

Use a needle large enough to open the hole in the fabric sufficiently. This permits the thread to go through more easily.

Stitch using the "stab" method; work your stitches in two movements—up vertically, then down vertically through the fabric. Let your needle hang frequently so the thread can untwist.

When combining blending filament with cotton floss in one needle, you must first knot the metallic thread onto the needle.

Tips provided by: Kreinik Mfg. Co., Inc.
Page 299

Do you have too many threads?

If you have more threads than can fit on your racks, try this solution.

Buy a pack of plastic drinking straws. Cut them in half, and place each half over one of the wooden dowels on your rack.

This quick and easy technique allows you to store two spools on each holder.

Fray Check tip...

After sewing on a button by hand or machine, apply a small amount of Fray Check to the sewing thread on the inside of your garment. This will help to secure the thread ends and keep them from becoming undone.

This is also a great idea for making sure that buttons last longer on your ready-to-wear clothing. Just use the same technique as soon as you bring your purchases home from the store.

Tip provided by: Prym-Dritz Corporation Page 325

At the end of your rope?

If you have problems with your bobbin thread running out in the middle of important projects, try this tip:

When winding the bobbin, hold a washable marker against the thread for two or three feet. While you are sewing, the colored thread will remind you to change the bobbin before it causes a problem.

Travel, Tours & Retreats

These businesses offer you ways to visit exotic places, meet new friends, learn a lot, and shop!

Art Institute in La Antigua Guatemala
Page 241

> Beading
>
> Jewelry Making
>
> Weaving

Beads & Beyond
Page 248

Chalet Publishing
Page 259

> ***Quilter's Travel Companion***
> A guide to quilt shops across the USA and Canada. Includes addresses, hours, descriptions, and maps for over 1,000 shops.

Craft World Tours
Page 264

Daisy Kingdom
Page 267

Eric's Press & Design & Sew Patterns
Page 274

Annual Spring Design and Sew Retreat, occurs in May. Write for more information, or subscribe to the *Good News Rag.*

G Street Fabrics
Page 282

Tours of G Street Fabrics available seven days a week.

Labours of Love Heirloom Sewing Retreat
Page 300

Mallery Press
Page 305

> Quilting Tours

The Mannings Handweaving School & Supply Center
Page 305

> Classes in Handweaving and Spinning

PJS Publications
Page 323

> Sew 'N' Go Tours
>
> > 4 times per year
> >
> > Destinations vary; recent locations have included:
>
> Northwest

New England

Seattle and Vancouver, BC

London

Hong Kong

San Francisco

New York

Saf-T-Pockets
Page 332

> Patterns for Travel Clothing

Schoolhouse Press
Page 333

They offer a knitters camp annually. Summer of 1996 will be their 23rd year.

Stitches Great Fiber Getaways
Page 341

Here's a sample of the tours they have lined up for 1996, and in 1997, they have a trip to London with Claire Shaeffer as the guide.

> Sewing Slumber Party - February
>
> Paris in the Spring Getaway - May
>
> Sew 'Til You Drop! Macphee Workshop - June

Travel accessories...

Use the fabric from a worn, favorite piece of clothing to make small travel bags that will have special meaning.

I made a shoe bag from my husband's old flannel shirt. The fabric was soft, suitable for the shoe bag project, and it gained new life as a travel accessory.

Tip provided by:
Mary Mulari
Mary's Productions
Page 307

Coat styles...

Cape

Toronto Getaway - August

San Francisco Getaway - October

Bangkok/Hong Kong Adventure - October to November

Surface Design Association
Page 343

Trims, Cords & Tassels

These companies offer decorative trims and braids for upholstery, costuming, and anything else that needs a pick-me-up.

Decorative trims...

You can use decorative trims in many ways besides home decoration. Try these ideas:

Decorate your hat.

Create a glamorous evening bag.

Make a velvet scarf with decorative cording sewn into the seams.

Make the same scarf with bullion fringe at each end.

Glue a small tassels to shoe clips, and spice up you footwear options.

Use a tie-back as a "scarf", under your coat collar.

Use decorative cording to trim your pockets and sleeves.

Create a garment with insets of tapestry ribbons.

Creating your own fabric...

To create your own designer fabric look, try using decorative trims, ribbons, and fabrics in complementary colors.

There are numerous possibilities available. For a simple effect, use various ribbons. Sew them together on a 45° angle, and then just cut as you would a regular fabric.

For other ideas, try using old ties, tapestry fabrics, fabrics from clothing that is special to you (but that is out of style, outgrown, what have you), or any scraps that you have laying around.

To keep it easy to piece, cut everything in rectangular shapes, and lay out your design before sewing or serging.

This is great for unique vests, handbags, and gifts.

Frogs

Gimp braid

Midi braid

Military braid

Pearls

Ric Rac

Sequined

Tassel fringe

Tassels

Grey Owl Indian Craft
Page 286

The Gypsy's Bead Shoppe
Page 286

Hancock's
Page 287

Braids

Brush fringes

Bullion fringes

Cords with tassels

Cords with knitted lips

Swag tassels

Tassel fringes

Harriet's Treadle Arts
Page 289

Herrschners, Inc.
Page 291

High Country West Needleworks
Page 291

Jehlor Fantasy Fabrics
Page 296

Appliqués

Beaded appliqués

Beaded fringe

Beaded trims

Fringe

Metallic cording

Sequined trims

Tassels

Judy's Heirloom Sewing
Page 297

The Kirk Collection
Page 299

Antique

Kreinik Mfg. Co., Inc.
Wholesale Only
Page 299

Metallic

Silk

Lace Heaven, Inc.
Page 301

The Leather Factory
Page 302

Suede fringe

Londa's Sewing, Etc.
Page 303

M & J Trimming Co.
Page 304
Contemporary trims and accessories

Beaded fringe

Beaded ric rac

Cords

Metallic braid

Ribbon trims

Tapestry ribbons

Tassel fringe

Tassels

Margola Corporation
Wholesale Only
Page 306

Embroidered trim

Marlene's Decorator Fabrics
Page 306

Mimi's Fabrications
Page 309

Miss Maureen's Fabrics and Fancies
Page 309

National Thread & Supply
Page 312

Nimble Thimbles
Page 313

Oregon Worsted Company/Mill End Store
Page 316

The Pin Cushion
Page 322

Planet Bead
Page 323

Prym-Dritz Corporation
Wholesale Only
Page 325

Braiding

Bouclé loop fringe

Brush fringe

Bullion fringe

Cotton ball fringe

Covered welting

Decorative cording

French twist knot fringe

Lampshade fringe

Metallic trims

Tassel fringe

Tassels

Ties

SAX Arts & Crafts

Spinning Wheel

Stone Mountain & Daughter Fabrics

Straw Into Gold

Taylor's Cutaways & Stuff

Assortment and variety packs

Textile Reproductions

Tinsel Trading Co.

Antique and contemporary trims

Cords

Fringes

Metallic braids

Tassels

Trendsetter Yarns/Ornashi Filati
Wholesale Only

Waechter's Silk Shop

Make your own tassels...

Cut a piece of cardboard the length you would like your finished tassel to be, and 3"- 4" wide.

Wind your thread around the form lengthwise. Remember, the best tassels are full and opulent, so don't hesitate to use a lot of thread.

Insert a matching thread under the wrapped threads at the end you would like to use as the top. Tie a knot, and this will become the hanging cord.

Cut the threads free at the bottom of your tassel.

Wrap another piece of matching thread around the threads close to the top of your tassel.

Even up the ends of your tassel if necessary, and fluff them out to create a bell effect at the bottom.

Experiment with different techniques and materials. Try using ribbon instead of threads, beading some of your threads, adding charms, etc.

Upholstery Fabrics

These businesses offer upholstery fabrics you can use to make your home your own style.

Atkinson Fabrics, Inc.
Page 243

B & J Fabrics, Inc.
Page 244

Banasch's Fabrics
Page 245

Banksville Designer Fabrics
Page 245

Carolina Mills Factory Outlet
Page 257

Cotton Ball
Page 263

Daisy Kingdom
Page 267

Exotic-Thai Silks
Page 275

The Fabric Center
Page 275
This is just a small sample of the brands and types of upholstery fabrics that are available through The Fabric Center.

    Allusions

Ashley

Beaujolais

Botanica

Brookhaven

Cabot

Carmen

Carroll

Cheques

Chintz

Concord

Cottage Ivy

Country Squire

Devonshire

Eden

Epiphany

Fantasia

Francesca

Grand Prix

Guinevere

Hanover II

Imperial

Jardiniere

Kelsey

Leanne

Lineage

Moire

Newman

Prestige

Regency Stripe

Regina

Royale

Spotlight

Terrazzo

Velvet

Vintage

Fabric Temptations
Page 276

G Street Fabrics
Page 282

Hancock's
Page 287

    Ametex

    Anju Woodridge

    Bloomcraft

To find ideas for decorating with fabric, try these resources…

Handcraft Magazine (see bibliography)

Decorating with Fabric, by Judy Lindahl. (see bibliography)

Sew Decor (magazine)

Sewing Slipcovers by Patria Gardens Video

Using upholstery samples...

Although many people love the look of uphol-stery fabric samples, and they are cheap to come by (usually free, if you ask), they often have a paper backing or are glued to cardboard.

To remove the paper, try using a damp sponge to soak it off.

To remove the glue, visit your local hardware or home improvement store, and pick up some Goo Gone or Goof Off. These should remove the residue easily.

Try it out on an incon-spicuous corner, to test for colorfastness.

Tip provide by:
Steve
Stelar Designs
AOL member

Braemore

Kravet

Mill Creek/Swavelle

P/Kaufman

Richloom

Waverly

Western Textiles

Leather Unlimited
Page 302

Upholstery Leather

M's Fabric Gallery
Page 304

Marine Sewing
Page 306

Marlene's Decorator Fabrics
Page 306

Upholstery Fabrics

Oregon Worsted Company/Mill End Store
Page 316

The Seraph Textile Collection
Page 334

Homespun

Stone Mountain & Daughter Fabrics
Page 314

Textile Reproductions
Page 345

Videos & Other Media

These companies offer you videos, audio tapes, films, and slides for rent or sale.

All Brand Sew-Knit-Serge & Embroidery
Page 238

Sewing and knitting machine videos

Associated Sewing Supply Co., Inc.
Page 243

Bead in Hand
Page 247

BottomLine Designs
Page 252

Brookfield Craft Center
Page 253

Butterick Company, Inc.
Page 254

Knitting videos

Carol Harris Co.
Page 257

Cathedral Window
Page 258

Center for the History of American Needlework
Page 258
They have slides, tapes, and other media

for sale or rental to individuals or groups.

Clotilde
Page 260

Clotilde's seminar videos

Collins Publications
Page 260

Copper Coyote Beads, Ltd.
Page 262

Cotton Ball
Page 262

Cotton Clouds
Page 263
Video titles:

Basic Knitting

Bead Woven Necklaces

Beginning Four Harness Weaving

Comprehensive Bead Stringing (3 vols.)

Improving Your Handspinning

Intermediate Knitting

Rigid Heddle

Spinning Cotton, Silk & Flax

Tapestry Weaving, Level I or II

Cottons, Etc.
Page 263

Creative Beginnings
Page 265

The ABC's of Ribbon Embroidery with Mary Jo Hiney
$10

The Crowning Touch-FASTURN
Page 266

Donna Salyers' Fabulous Furs
Page 270

See How It's Done: Sewing the Fabulous Furs
Donna Salyers
$29.95
40 minutes

Dos De Tejas Patterns
Page 270

A Sweater Again
Featuring L. Karen Odam
$24.95
60 minutes
A video for recycling sweaters into a sweater jacket. How to plan, cut sweaters apart and then re-sew them into a lined sweater jacket.

Eye-of-the-Needle...

Fold your scarf in half. Wrap it around the back of your neck, and put one hand through the loop. Use that hand to grab the loose ends, and pull them through the loop. Adjust your look by tightening or loosening the scarf.

Short sleeve styles...

Bell

Lapped

Ruffled

Appliquick
Featuring L. Karen Odam
$24.95
60 minutes
A technique for appliqué video. How to plan and achieve depth and distance in appliqué.

Eagle Feather Trading Post
Page 272

Embroiderers' Guild of America, Inc.
Page 274

Eric's Press & Design & Sew Patterns
Page 274

Expressions
Lois Ericson
$42
1 hour, 15 minutes
How to turn ordinary fabrics into extraordinary creations.

Fiber Fantasy Knitting Products
Page 279

Machine Knitters Uh-Oh Video
$34.95 + 3.50 S&H
1 hour

Sweater Finishing for Hand and Machine Knitters
$34.95 + $3.50 S&H
2 hours

Fiber Statements
Page 279

Cutwork and Needlelace
Patricia Rodgers and Iris Lee
$39.95

Free Motion Machine Embroidery and Beading By Machine
Patricia Rodgers
$39.95
1 hour, 43 minutes

Four Seasons Knitting Products
Page 281

Videos for handknitters

G Street Fabrics
Page 282

Great Northern Weaving
Page 285

The Gypsy's Bead Shoppe
Page 286

Handweaver's Guild of America, Inc.
Page 287

Video rentals

Heirlooms Forever
Page 290

I.T.C./Italian Trading Company
Page 293
Alterations videos

Part I–Trousers Alterations

Part II–Hems on Slacks & Skirts

Infiknit
Page 294

Islander Sewing Systems
Page 295

A Galaxy of Sewing Techniques, Vols I, II, III & IV
Margaret Islander
$34.95 each
90 minutes each

Industrial Shortcuts for Home Sewing
Margaret Islander
$59.95
2 hours

Pants Etc!
Margaret Islander
$34.95
Draw your own pants pattern for a perfect fit

Shirts, Etc!, Parts I & II
Margaret Islander
$39.95

Ivy Imports, Inc.
Page 295
Silk painting videos:

Fashion Accessories
$19.95
30 minutes

Fish Banner
$15.95
30 minutes

Floral Camisole
$15.95
30 minutes

Geisha
$19.95
30 minutes

Natural Treasures
$19.95
30 minutes

Tropical Fish Banner
$15.95
30 minutes

Silk Painting Workshop
$49
30 minutes

Kaye Wood Publishing Company, Inc.
Page 298

Kite Studio
Page 299

    KBI Video: Kite Workshop #1
    $23
    1 hour
    An introduction to the sewing of kite
    ripstop and banner nylon

Labours of Love Heirloom Sewing Supplies, Inc.
Page 300

    Precious Petticoats: An Introduction to Heirloom Sewing
    Debra Justice
    $29.95 US, $34.95 Canadian
    Heirloom sewing basics by machine.

    Sew...You Want To Get Fancy
    Debra Justice
    $29.95 US, $34.95 Canadian
    Introduction to specialty techniques
    by machine

Live Guides, Inc.
Page 303
They have instructional video tapes that give you sewing help at your point of need in the convenience of your own home.

    A New kind of Creativity: Omnistitching
    $29.50
    50 minutes

    Breaking the Rules of Sewing I-V
    $29.50 each

    Generic Serger Video I
    $49.50
    2 hours

    Generic Serger Video II Update
    $29.50
    1 hour

    Serger Lingerie
    $29.50
    1 hour

    Solving the Mystery of Tension
    $29.50
    1 hour

    The Ultimate Decorative Threads
    $29.50
    1 hour

Logan Kits
Page 303

Londa's Sewing, Etc.
Page 303

Mary Roehr Books & Video
Page 307

    Pressing to Perfection
    The companion video to *Speed Tailoring*
    Mary Roehr
    $24.95
    1 hour

Mimi's Fabrications
Page 309

New England Quilt Museum
Page 312

Nancy's Notions
Page 311
Nancy's Notions carries videos to go along with most of the sewing books by Nancy Zieman.

    Islander videos

Old Style Trading Company
Page 314

    How to Bead, Vol. I

    Native American Men's and Women's Dance Styles

Oregon Worsted Company/Mill End Store
Page 316

Outdoor Wilderness Fabrics
Page 317

    Durfee's Coat Craze Patterns
    from the Learn By Video Library
    $39.93, Rent for 1 week $5
    2 hours

Palmer/Pletsch Publishing
Page 318
All listed videos are $29.95.

    2-Hour Trousers
    Kathleen Spike
    1 hour, 40 minutes

    Creative Home Decorating Ideas: Sewing Projects for the Home
    Lynnette Ranney Black
    69 minutes

    Creative Serging–I & II
    Marta Alto and Pati Palmer
    1 hour each

    Sewing To Success
    Kathleen Spike
    45 minutes

    Sewing Today the Time Saving Way
    Lynn Raasch, Karen Dillon
    45 minutes

Accessories for your clothes...

To make unrelated clothes into an "outfit", try these ideas:

Use leftover fabric from a coordination blouse to create a matching scarf.

Or a removable collar.

Or a hat band.

Or covered earrings.

Or removable cuffs.

Or a sash belt.

All the sheep in Jacob's flock were black...

Let me pass through all your flock today, removing from it every speckled and spotted sheep and every black lamb,...and such shall be my wages.

Jacob to Laban, Genesis XXX:32

Sewing Ultrasuede Brand Fabrics–Ultrasuede, Ultrasuede Light, Caress, Ultraleather
Marta Alto, Pati Palmer
1 hour

Sewing With Sergers, Basics and Advanced
Marta alto, Pati Palmer
1 hour each

Patria Gardens Video
Page 319

Learn to Make Slipcovers, The Removable Upholstery

Learn to Make Throw Pillows and Cushions

The Pin Cushion
Page 322

Power Sewing
Page 323
All videos are by Sandra Betzina, and are $24.95 each:

Commercial Pattern Refinement

Construction Difficulties

Easy Linings

Embellishment

Fear of Sewing

Fearless Serging

Fitting Solutions

Foolproof Pants Fitting

Handwoven & Quilted Garments

Hassle Free Designer Jackets

Marketing What You Make

Pattern Sizing & Alteration

Prairie Edge/Sioux Trading Post
Page 323

Prairieland Quilts
Page 324

Quilt in a Day
Page 326

Companion videos are available for some of their most popular books.

Quilting Books Unlimited
Page 328

Quilting From The Heartland
Page 328
Quilting From The Heartland carries over 35 videos devoted to your favorite quilt patterns, from the show *Quilting From The Heartland.*

Quilts & Other Comforts
Page 328

Revelli
Page 330

Color & You
Clare Revelli
$25
45 minutes
Tips on makeup, scarves, accessories and more.

Decorate like a Pro
Clare Revelli, Hosted by Nancy Zieman
$16.95
30 minutes
Five personal Design styles for decorating.

SAX Arts & Crafts
Page 333

Schoolhouse Press
Page 333
Schoolhouse Press has 15 knitting videos available in their catalog.

Sew-Pro Workshop
Page 334
The three videos listed give step-by-step instructions, showing every detail. The entire garment is made on the video. Please note: there are no instructions on fitting.

They are available in VHS or PAL.

Shipping charges are: 1 video $3 US, $5 Canada, $10 international. 2-3 videos $5 US, $7 Canada, $15 international.

Men's Pants and Vest
Mary Ellen Flury
$34.95

Tailoring Ladies' Jackets
Mary Ellen Flury
$34.95

Tailoring Men's Suit/Sport Coat
Mary Ellen Flury
$39.95

Sewing Emporium/Sew-Easy Products
Page 335

The Smocking Horse Collection
Page 337

Silk Ribbon Smocking
Janice A. Balliett
$38.95
2 hours
How to use silk ribbon in smocking instead of floss.

SouthStar Supply Company

Consew 206RB: Troubleshooting & Repairs

Upholstery Training

Upholstery Secrets

Stone Mountain & Daughter Fabrics

Straw Into Gold

Suzanne Roddy, Handweaver

Basic Knitting Techniques

Battenberg Lacemaking - Beginner's Primer

Feltmaking By Hand - The Basic Process

Handwoven Fabric - Structure and Pattern

Introduction to Silk Ribbon Embroidery

Japanese Textile Dyeing

Spinning Cotton, Silk and Flax

Tips, Tricks and Problem Solvers for the Handweaver

Weaving Four Selvedge Textiles

Taunton Press

Thimble Collector's International
Slides of private and museum thimble and sewing tool collections are available to members for a nominal rental fee.

Unicorn Books and Crafts, Inc./Glimåkra Looms 'n Yarns/Frederick J. Fawcett, Inc.

Unique Techniques

Fearless Pressing

Japanese Tailoring

Universal Synergetics
UniSyn includes a supply list, drawn from their beads and supplies with every video.

Bead Knitting Video
Alice Korach
$39.95
1 hour, 15 minutes

Bead Woven Necklaces
Virginia Blakelock
$39.95
1 hour, 30 minutes

Peyote Stitch Video
Carol Perrenoud
$39.95
1 hour, 30 minutes

Victorian Video Production
They offer a selection of videos on the following subjects.

Appliqué

Basketmaking

Beads

Fabric painting

Needlework

Quilting and patchwork

Sewing

Silk ribbon embroidery

Spinning

Surface design and stenciling

Lacemaking and tatting

Weaving and handlooming

Waechter's Silk Shop

Wonderful World of Hats

Secrets of Hatmaking, Home Study Course

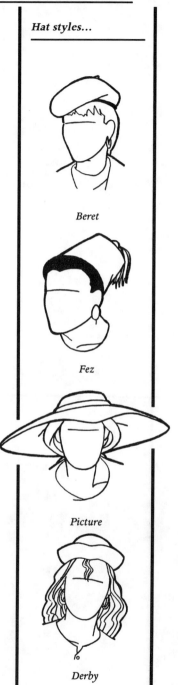

Hat styles...

Beret

Fez

Picture

Derby

Weaving Supplies

This chapter includes looms, yarns, weaving accessories, and kits.

All Brand Sew-Knit-Serge & Embroidery
Page 238

Looms

Alpaca Sajama
Page 238

100% Alpaca yarn (19 colors)

Andrea's Yarn Barn
Page 240

Ashland Bay Trading Company, Inc.
Wholesale Only
Page 242

Aura Registered
Page 244

Aurora Silk
Page 244

Naturally dyed silk yarns of various thicknesses

Banasch's, Inc.
Page 245

Bartlettyarns, Inc
Page 246

Yarns

Bulky weight wool

Heavy weight wool

Rug weight wool

Sport weight wool

Worsted weight wool

Bead in Hand
Page 247

Becky's Väv Stuga
Page 245

Bovidae Farms
Page 252

Bramwell Yarns, USA
Page 252

Castlegate Farm
Page 258

Wool yarns, no dyes

Cotton Clouds
Page 263

Learn to weave kits

Raddles

Scarf kits

Shuttles

Sweater kits

Table Settings kits

Towel kits

Looms

Floor

Rigid

Tapestry

Yarn

Baby weight cotton

Fingering weight cotton

Mercerized cotton

Sport weight cotton

Worsted weight cotton

Crystal Palace Yarns
Wholesale Only
Page 266

Ashford products

Yarns

Recycle your yarn...

When you have an old sweater that has lived past it's prime, but the fibers are still strong, try this hint:

Unravel the yarn, then wrap it loosely around a form to hold it together. Dip the whole thing in water and let it dry.

The yarn will be straightened and ready for you to wind and use.

Environmental safe tip for wool safety...

Periodically, put your wool in a freezer for 24 hours. This will kill all insects and insect eggs, thereby protecting your heritage quality project. This is an inexpensive and effective process that does not pollute the environment.

For additional protection, always store woolens in tight confinement with the presence of natural aromatic cedar.

Cared for woolens last a lifetime.

Tip provided by:
TLC Yarns
Page 348

Design Originals Publications
Page 269

The Duhesa Company
Page 271

Yarns

Acrylic

Alpaca/silk

Cotton

Mohair

Velvet chenille

Wool

Dundas Loom Company
Page 271

Looms

Small End Table

Earth Guild
Page 272

Combs

Heddles

Looms

Floor

Rigid-heddle

Table

Tapestry

Raddles

Reeds

Shuttles

Temples

Warping boards

Warping mills

Winders

Wolf traps

Edgemont Yarn Service, Inc.
Page 273

Fiber Designs
Page 279

100% wool rug yarns

The Fiber Studio
Page 279

Fiesta Yarns
Page 280

Hand-dyed yarns

Fireside Fiberarts
Page 280

Custom looms and weaving supplies

Frank Williams' Hemp Co.
Page 281

Hemp yarns available in natural, and 24 organically dyed colors. These are soft—not itchy twines.

The Gleaners Yarn Barn
Page 283

Good Wood
Page 284

Looms small enough to travel, and with a "Magic Heddle", to make it easy to weave.

Great Northern Weaving
Page 285

Halcyon Yarn
Page 286

Balancers

Ball winders

Bobbin winders

Bobbins

Cone winders

Heddles

Hooks

Looms

Inkle

Floor

Rigid

Table

Tapestry

Paddles

Pick-up sticks

Raddles

Reeds

Sectional warping equipment

Shuttles

Swifts

Tapestry

Temples

Tie-up cord and pegs

Yarn

Handweaver's Guild of America, Inc.
Page 287

Hemp Textiles International Corp.
Page 290

Hemp Yarns

Hemp/wool blend yarns

Heritage Looms
Page 291

Herrschners, Inc.
Page 291

Hunt Valley Cashmere
Page293

Cashmere yarns, 2-ply and 4-ply

In Cahoots
Page 293

Jaggerspun
Page 296

Yarns

50% wool/50% silk

Heather

Superfine Merino wool

Lacis
Page 301

Bow looms

Table looms

Shuttles

Leesburg Looms, Inc.
Page 302

Floor and table looms

Loompal
Page 303

Loom dust covers

The Mannings Handweaving School & Supply Center
Page 305

Maple Hill Software
Page305

Mindsun
Page 309

Mindweave (Weaving Software)
$95

Mountain Colors
Page 310

Handpainted Yarns

Alpaca

Mohair

Wool

The Musk Ox Company
Page 311

Norwood Looms, Inc.
Page 314

Handcrafted weaving looms

Personal Threads Boutique
Page 321

Looms

Harrisville

Schacht

Yarn

Alpaca

Angora

Cashmere

Cotton

Metallic

Mohair

Silk

Wool

Sievers School of Fiber Arts
Page 336

Loom benches

Loom accessory shelves

Looms

Inkle

Floor

Table

Shuttles

Swifts

Warping boards

Straw Into Gold
Page 342

Suzanne Roddy, Handweaver
Page 343

Looms

AVL

Cranbrook

Glimåkra

Harrisville

Heritage

Loüet

Norwood

Schacht

Yarn

Cotton

Linen

Mohair

Rayon

Silk

Wool

Tess' Designer Yarns
Page 344

Handpainted yarns...

When knitting or weaving with handpainted yarns, work alternately from two skeins to avoid striping or minor color differences between skeins.

Tip provided by:
Mountain Colors
Page 310

Specialty yarns...

Slub yarn.

Yarn, Crochet & Knitting Supplies

These companies offer you yarns of every fiber, color, and texture, and the supplies you need to use them.

All Brand Sew-Knit-Serge & Embroidery
Page 238
- Machines
  - Brother-Knitting
  - Studio-Singer

Alpaca Sajama
Page 238
- 100% Alpaca yarn (19 colors)

Andrea's Yarn Barn
Page 240
- Yarn (over 200 colors)

Ashland Bay Trading Company, Inc.
Wholesale Only
Page 242

Associated Sewing Supply Co., Inc.
Page 243
- Knitting machines
- Yarn

Aura Registered
Page 244
- Cotton
- Wool

Aurora Silk
Page 244
- Naturally dyed silk yarns of various thicknesses

Bartlettyarns, Inc.
Page 246
- Yarn
  - Bulky weight
  - Heavy weight
  - Rug weight
  - Sport weight
  - Worsted weight

Bergere de France
Page 249
- Knitting patterns
- Yarn
  - Acrylic
  - Alpaca
  - Angora

- Cashmere
- Cotton
- Mohair
- Wool

Black Sheep Wools/Hub Mills Factory Store
Page 250
- Yarns
  - Closeouts
  - Mill ends
  - Natural fibers

Bovidae Farm
Page 252
- 100% Wool Yarns
  - Bulky weight
  - Sports weight
  - Worsted weight
- Mohair/Wool Blend Yarns

Bramwell Yarns, USA
Page 252
- Yarns
  - Acrylic
  - Cotton

For a unique effect...

Knit a garment using two strands of yarn simultaneously: a wool yarn and a blend of mohair.

This results in a soft, lustrous surface. Interesting combinations of colors of the two yarns produce beautiful, novel garments.

Tip provided by:
Bovidae Farm
Page 252

Nylon

Polyester

Wool

Castlegate Farm

Undyed wool yarns

Cotton Clouds

BOND - The Incredible Sweater Machine

Sweater Kits

Yarn

Baby weight

Fingering weight

Mercerized

Sport weight

Worsted weight

Crystal Palace Yarns
Wholesale Only

Bamboo knitting needles

Yarn

The Duhesa Company

INOX Knitting Needles

Yarn

Acrylic

Alpaca/silk blend

Chenille

Cotton

Mohair

Velvet

Wool

Earth Guild

Knitting needles

Yarns

Cotton

Linen

Metallic

Rayon blends

Wool

Fiber Designs

100% wool rug yarns

Fiber Fantasy Knitting Products

Blockers kit

Fold-a-way blocking board

The Fiber Studio

Yarns

Chenille

Cotton

Handpainted

Mohair

Rayon

Wools

Fiesta Yarns

Hand-dyed yarns

Four Seasons Knitting Products

Frank Williams' Hemp Co.

Hemp yarns available in natural, and 24 organically dyed colors. These are soft–not itchy twines.

Ginger's Needleworks

The Gleaners Yarn Barn

Good Wood

3, 4 and 5 pin InchWorms to make knitted cord

Gossamer Threads & More

Grand View Country Store

Great Northern Weaving

Halcyon Yarn

Blocking aids

Cable and stitch holders

Circular needles

Counters and markers

Crochet hooks

Double pointed needles

Flex needles

Gauge aids

Single point needles

Tapered needles

Yarn

    2-ply wool

    Chenille

    Cotton

    Icelandic wool

    Linen

    Mohair

    Rug wool

    Silk noil

    Silk tussah

    Silk/wool blend

    Superfine Merino wool

    Tapestry wool

    Tweed wool

Hedgehog Handworks
Page 289

They have knitting needles and crochet hooks in the Renaissance style, made of black walnut.

Heirloom Knitted Lace
Page 289

Knitted lace patterns

Knitted lace supplies

Hemp Textiles International Corp.
Page 290

Hemp yarns

Hemp/wool blend yarns

Herrschners, Inc.
Page 291

Hunt Valley Cashmere
Page 293

    2-ply and 4-ply cashmere yarns

Infiknit
Page 294

    Foxfibre

Jaggerspun
Page 296

    50% wool/50% silk yarn

    Heather yarn

    Superfine Merino wool yarn

    Wool yarn

Judy's Heirloom Sewing
Page 297

Koigu Wool Designs
Page 299

    Yarn

        100% wool in 150 hand-dyed colors

        Mohair

        Wool/Silk blends

Kreinik Mfg. Co., Inc.
Wholesale Only
Page 299

Lacis
Page 301

    Braid knitting machine

    Crochet hooks

    Knitting mushrooms

    Knitting needles

    Mohair brushes

Point protectors

Tension thimble

Ledgewood Studio
Page 302

    Wool yarns

The Mannings Handweaving School & Supply Center
Page 305

Mountain Colors
Page 310

    Handpainted Yarns

        Alpaca

        Mohair

        Wool

The Natural Fibre Club of Canada
Page 312

Nordic Fiber Arts
Page 313

    Knitting kits

    Knitting needles

    Yarns

        Rauma Yarns From Norway

Oregon Worsted Company/Mill End Store
Page 316

Patternworks
Page 320

    Blocking tools

    Counters

    Hand Eze therapeutic gloves

---

cal seed hairs that grow on the outer skin of the cotton seed. Wild and cultivated species of cotton have been placed in the genus Gossypium. They belong to the mallow family, as do hibiscus and okra.

COTTON YARN NUMBER: Cotton yarn is measured in terms of length per unit weight. No. 1 cotton has 840 yards per pound. No. 10 has 8400 yards per pound (single ply). The count is inversely proportionate to the size of the yarn, therefore No. 100 yarn is 10 times finer than No. 10.

EGYPTIAN: One of the world's most important cottons, grown mainly in the Nile Valley. A fine, lustrous. long-staple cotton, usually of a creamy color, averaging 1 2/5" in length.

EXTRA LONG STAPLE: Cotton whose individual fibers are 1 3/8" and longer, such as Sea Island or an American-Egyptian variety such as Supima. It is distinguished by its extra strength and luster.

GASSING: The process of burning off protruding fibers from cotton yarns and cloth by passing it over a flame or heated copper plate. This gives the yarn or fabric a smooth surface.

Cont.

MERCERIZING: Named after its originator, John Mercer, this finish is extensively used for treating cotton yarn to increase luster and improve strength and dye affinity. The treatment consists of impregnating the yarn with a cold concentrated sodium hydroxide solution.

PIMA COTTON: A cross between Sea Island and Egyptian, grown in Arizona. A fine, strong cotton, creamy in color, averaging 1 3/8" to 1 5/8" in length. Used for quality high-fashion garments, airplane and balloon cloths, as well as for fine fabrics.

SEA ISLAND COTTON: Finest cotton in the world. A white, silky fiber averaging 1 3/5" staple length, which is spun into yarns as fine as 300s for lace yarns. Originally grown on small islands off the coast of the Carolinas and in the southern lowlands along the coast.

SUPIMA COTTON: Trademark for a superior type of extra-long staple fiber 1 3/8" and longer. This is an exceptionally high-quality American-Egyptian cotton grown in the Southwest United States.

Definitions provided by:
Cotton Clouds
Page 263

Knitting kits

Needles

Reuseable design grids proportioned for knitting

Stitch and row calculators

Travel cases

Yarn

    Acrylic

    Alpaca

    Angora

    Blends

    Bulky weight

    Cashmere

    Cotton

    DK weight

    Fingering weight

    Heavy worsted

    Lace weight

    Linen

    Microfiber

    Merino wool

    Metallic

    Nylon

    Shetland wool

    Silk

    Sport weight

    Super bulky weight

    Worsted weight

Yarn inventory cards

Personal Threads Boutique
Page 321

Yarn

    Alpaca

    Angora

    Cashmere

    Cotton

    Metallic

    Mohair

    Silk

    Wool

Pieces
Page 322

The Quilting B
Page 327

    Yarns

Salt Spring Island Fibre Studios
Page 332

    Alpaca yarn

    Custom-spun yarn

    Dyed kid mohair yarn

    Fine mohair yarn

SAX Arts & Crafts
Page 333

Schoolhouse Press
Page 333

    Center-pull ball winder

    Circular needles

    Coilless pins

    Double Pointed Needles

    Knitter's graph paper

    Knitting belt

    Knitting thimble

    Large-eyed wool needles

    Magnetic row finder

    Meadows wool wash

    Patterns

    Umbrella swift

    Yarn

        Guernsey wool

        Highland wool

        Homespun wool

        Québécoise wool

        Rangeley wool

        Sheepswool

        Shetland Cobweb

        Shetland Jumper-Weight

        Shetland Lace-Weight

        Spun Icelandic Lace-Weight

        Unspun Icelandic

    Yarn keeper bracelet

Sealed With A Kiss, Inc.
Page 333

    Unique patterns for knitted sweaters

Sievers School of Fiber Arts
Page 336

The Silk Tree
Page 337

    Silk Yarns

Snowgoose
Page 338

Spinning Wheel
Page340

Do you know the difference between worsted and woolen?

There are two basic spinning systems for wool—the woolen system and the worsted system. Woolen yarns generally have a softer twist and more loft than worsted yarns.

Worsted

Woolen

Company Listings

Company Listings

To ensure the accuracy of *Sew Far, Sew Good*, Oracle Publications contacted each of the listed companies within the past six months. I asked that they fill out a questionnaire to provide us with relevant information for our readers. The listings provided in this section are the result of a joint partnership between Oracle Publications and the specific companies shown. When reading the listings, keep in mind that I have encouraged each company to be as detailed as possible in giving me information that they want their potential customers to know, so please forgive me if any listing seems incomplete or unfinished. I have printed all of the information that I have been able to completely verify.

The only information that I provide is the information in the "Author's Note" portions. These are my comments about the companies and the products and/or services they offer. This information is not intended to provide hard facts—just a little insight into the nature of the company as I have come to see it during the research for this book. Many companies were very professional, polite, and prompt in sending an appropriate amount of information. But if I did not have a chance to work with a company, and develop a sense of its personality, or if the company was thorough in its reply, then I did not include my own note.

What I have tried to accomplish with this section is an opportunity for each company to speak directly (more or less) to you, so that you will be able to make informed inquiries.

It is very important to note that if a company has its toll-free number listed after its local number, you should use the toll-free number for orders only, and the local number for inquiries or sample requests. Many of these businesses are small, and you would be doing them a great favor by helping them keep their operating costs down so that they can pass the savings on to you. Enjoy.

5T's Embroidery Supply

180 Huckleberry Road, Farmington, NY 14425
Phone: (315) 986-8434, (800) 466-7945
Fax: (315) 986-8436
Services/Merchandise: They have embroidery supplies for commercial and machine embroiderers.
Payment Options: Check, Money Order, MC, Visa, COD
Shipping Options: UPS
Minimum Order: No minimum order.

7 Trumpets Bead Studio

P.O. Box 514, Coeur d'Alene, ID 83816
Phone: (208) 765-0755
Services/Merchandise: They have beads and the following classes: Bead Stringing, Bead Weaving, Incorporating Beads Into Weaving, and Incorporating Beads in *Kumi Himo*–a form of Japanese braiding.
Payment Options: MC, Visa
Author's Note: The owner of 7 Trumpets is very personable, and she is always interested in experimenting with beads and techniques for using beads.

The 1752 Company–Beautiful Things

Wholesale Only
1752 Dauphin Street, Mobile, AL 36604
Phone: (334) 478-4680
Services/Merchandise: They have a catalog, a price list, and a newsletter. Small quantity orders are accepted; credit account available with approval. They also have antique lace by the piece or yard, wedding accessories and lace wedding veils, plain cotton nets for lacemaking–Lace Base Insertions, point desprit, and Swiss Embroideries/Entredeaux.
Payment Options: Prepaid, COD, 30-day accounts
Shipping Options: UPS, U.S. Postal Service
Other Information: They send out semi-annual special price newsletters. They offer same day shipping and free samples upon request.
Author's Note: Their lace samples are beautiful. The lace they sell ranges from a robust lace that is suitable for everyday wear to a lace so delicate, you can only wonder if it was spun by spiders. Their selection is astounding.
Catalog: $4

A & B Jewels and Tools

350 West Grand River, Williamston, MI 48895

Phone: (517) 655-4664
Fax: (517) 655-4665
Services/Merchandise: They have the supplies necessary for beading, jewelry making, and display items.
Payment Options: Check, Money Order, MC, Visa, Discover
Shipping Options: UPS, U.S. Postal Service
Minimum Order: $25
Catalog: $2

A Fabric Place

6324 Falls Road, Baltimore, MD 21209
Phone: (410) 828-6777
Services/Merchandise: They have better dress goods and silk, wool, velvet, lamé, lace, Ultrasuede, bridal fabric, and buttons.
Payment Options: Check, MC, Visa
Shipping Options: UPS
Minimum Order: No minimum order.

Accents Bead Shop

513 Elmwood Avenue, Buffalo, NY 14222
Phone: (716) 884-4689
Fax: (716) 884-4689
- or -
4930 Hampden Lane, Bethesda, MD 20814
Phone: (301) 656-7307
Fax: (301) 657-8305
Services/Merchandise: They offer classes in bead restringing and repair. They have a large selection of beads in all shapes and sizes: semi-precious, metal, glass, and pearl. They also have unusual centerpieces, beading supplies, tools, and books. Finished jewelry and sterling from Nepal is also available.
Payment Options: Check, Money Order, MC, Visa
Shipping Options: UPS, U.S. Postal Service
Minimum Order: No minimum order.

AK Sew & Serge

1602 6th Street Southeast, Winter Haven, FL 33080
Phone: (941) 299-3080
Services/Merchandise: They have sewing and quilting supplies and machines.
Payment Options: Check, Money Order, MC, Visa, Amex, Discover
Shipping Options: UPS
Membership Dues: $35 per year.
Membership Benefits: 15% discount on regularly priced merchandise.

Pants styles...

Jodphurs

Avoid oil stains...

After oiling your sewing machine, remember to sew on a scrap piece of fabric first, to catch any extra oil, and to avoid damaging your garment fabrics.

Other Information: They hold a show during the last weeks of October and the first two weeks of November, when they bring in sewing experts from around the country.

Albe Creations, Inc.

2920 Century Square, Winston Salem, NC 27106
Phone: (910) 924-2911
Fax: (910) 924-2911
Services/Merchandise: They have handcrafted porcelain buttons, jewelry and scarf slides to match. Their buttons come in over 600 different designs, including country buttons, buttons for every holiday, many professions, nautical, wild animals, hearts, flowers, stars, fruit, lighthouses, toys, and the list goes on and on.
Payment Options: MC, Visa, COD for wholesale only
Shipping Options: UPS
Minimum Order: $15 retail. $40 wholesale.
Other Information: They offer special designs for needleart designers, clothing manufacturers, etc.

The Alcott Press

6325 Northeast 7th Avenue, Portland, OR 97211
Phone: (503) 287-3140
Services/Merchandise: They offer the books *The Complete Book of Fabric Painting*, and *Fabric Painting Resources*, both by Linda Kanzinger.
Payment Options: Check, Money Order
Other Information: Both of these books have been carefully researched. Linda Kanzinger tested and experimented with each paint and dye she covers in *The Complete Book of Fabric Painting*.
Special Discounts/Offers: Try one book with a 10% discount with the mention of *Sew Far Sew Good*. Purchase both books for the cover price of *The Complete Book of Fabric Painting*, $32.95 plus shipping and handling with the mention of *Sew Far Sew Good*. Wholesale to qualified businesses.
Author's Note: Linda sent me both of her books, and the careful research that she has done and her enthusiasm for fabric painting really shows.

All Brand Sew-Knit-Serge & Embroidery

9879 Florida Boulevard, Baton Rouge, LA 70815
Phone: (800) SEW SERG
Fax: (800) 866-1261
E-mail: sewserg@aol.com
Services/Merchandise: They carry sewing machines, sergers, knitting machines, pressing equipment and other products by the following manufacturers: Juki/White, Superlock, Elna, Baby Lock, Viking, Singer, Ultralock, Merritlock, Quantum, Omni-stitch, Pfaff, Nelco, Bernina, Euro-Pro, Baby Knit, Pullen, Stanley, Toyota, Simplicity, and others.
Payment Options: Check, Money Order, MC, Visa, Amex, Discover, COD
Shipping Options: UPS, U.S. Postal Service, FedEx
Minimum Order: No minimum order.
Other Information: The owners of All Brand are not just good business owners with a large company, but they also care a great deal for the world they live in. They have donated sewing machines and sergers to gun buyback programs and to small businesses in the former Soviet Republic.
Catalog: Price lists and brochures are available upon request.

Alpaca Sajama

P.O. Box 1209, Ashland, OR 97520
Phone: (800) 736-0949
Fax: (541) 488-3949
Services/Merchandise: They have knitting and weaving supplies, and 100% alpaca yarn in 19 colors in skeins and on cones. They also have spinning fiber, and alpaca knitting kits for sweaters and shawls.
Minimum Order: No minimum order for retail.
Other Information: They specialize in non-toxically produced yarns.
Special Discounts/Offers: Wholesale to qualified businesses.

Alpel Publishing

P.O. Box 203 (OP), Chambly, PQ J3L 4B3 CANADA
Phone: (514) 658-6205
Fax: (514) 658-3514
Services/Merchandise: They have the following pattern books: *Easy Sewing for Infants*, *Easy Sewing for Children*, *Easy Sewing for Adults*, and *Easy Halloween Costumes for Children*. They also publish *The Original Catalog of Canadian Catalogs* mail order directory.
Payment Options: MC, Visa
Shipping Options: U.S. Postal Service
Minimum Order: No minimum order.
Other Information: Each pattern book has over 60 patterns for you to enlarge and sew.
Special Discounts/Offers: 40% discount on orders of 10 or more books.
Author's Note: Every one of their pattern books has gotten rave reviews from consumers and magazines alike.
"I am a total amateur at sewing but can follow your patterns so easily."–from M. Marth.
A *Hands Magazine* writer said, "Without doubt the best self-published books I have ever encountered, and just as good as any of the

professional sewing books on the market."

After looking through each of the books, I can honestly say I have never seen such a straightforward approach to easy patterns–with hundreds of possibilities.

Catalog: $2 for a brochure and the booklet *Patterns for Pennies*, which includes 20 sample patterns for babies, children and adults.

AlterYears (formerly Raiments)

3749 East Colorado Boulevard, Pasadena, CA 91107
Phone: (818) 585-2994
Fax: (818) 432-4530
E-mail: 72437.674@compuserve.com
Services/Merchandise: They have over 1,400 historical, ethnic, and specialty patterns for men, women, and children from the Middle Ages to the 1950s, and also equestrienne, dance, handicapped, and millinery patterns. They also have over 1,000 costume reference books on clothing, techniques, textiles, and costume supplies. They offer complete corsetry materials and kits, some millinery, points, clasps, grommets, specialized fabrics, and more. Accessories include hoop skirts, panniers, bustles, gloves, snoods, cotton stockings, spats, suspenders, and more.
Payment Options: Check, Money Order, MC, Visa, Amex, Discover
Shipping Options: UPS, U.S. Postal Service
Minimum Order: No minimum order.
Other Information: The company is run by specialists in both re-enactment and theatrical costuming, with knowledgeable professionals on staff to help serve your costuming needs.
Catalog: In the U.S. - $5, 4th class book rate or $8 priority mail. To Canada - $6 U.S. To other countries - $9.75 U.S. via surface mail, $20 U.S. via airmail.

Amazon Vinegar & Pickling Works Drygoods
Mail Order Only

2218 East 11th Street, Davenport, IA 52803-3760
Phone: (319) 322-6800
Fax: (319) 322-4003
Services/Merchandise: They have vintage patterns and accessories, chatelaines, over 1,295 books, fabrics, millinery supplies, and interesting collectibles and novelties.
Payment Options: Check, Money Order, MC, Visa, Discover
Shipping Options: UPS, FedEx, RPS, Airborne Express
Minimum Order: No minimum order.
Author's Note: It's difficult to describe the wide range of materials and services Amazon Drygoods offers, but I'll tell you that it's a great idea to order the catalogs. Then you can marvel at the array of wonderful clothes, patterns, and books from bygone eras. A must-have for history buffs and the terminally curious.
Catalog: Pattern Catalog - $7, General Catalog - $3, Shoe Catalog - $5, Wholesale Book Catalog - Free to those who request it on business letterhead. For Canadian Orders - The prices are the same, but Amazon can only accept payment by postal money order in U.S. dollars, or by credit card. They can mail all three catalogs to other parts of the world for $20 U.S., paid by postal money order or credit card.

American Needlepoint Guild

P.O. Box 241208, Memphis, TN 38124-1208
E-mail: cathfelten@aol.com–Cathy Felten, Secretary
Services/Merchandise: They have correspondence courses, as well as teacher and judging certification programs.
Membership Dues: $23 per year USA and Canada, $33 International
Membership Benefits: Members receive *Needle Pointers* magazine, and can attend national seminar and exhibits.
Other Information: The American Needlepoint Guild is an educational, non-profit organization whose main purpose is educational and cultural development through participation in and encouragement of the art of needlepoint.

ANG defines needlepoint as any counted or free stitchery worked by hand with a threaded needle on a readily countable woven ground.

American Quilt Study Group

660 Mission Street, Suite 400, San Francisco, CA 94105-4005
Phone: (415) 495-0163
Fax: (415) 495-3516
Services/Merchandise: They offer *Uncoverings*, the journal for the American Quilt Study Group, and other publications.
Payment Options: Check, Money Order, MC, Visa (Foreign orders: MC or Visa only)
Shipping Options: UPS, U.S. Postal Service
Membership Dues: $35 per year (seniors or full-time students–$25 per year); add $1.50 for Canada and $15 for other countries.
Membership Benefits: Members receive quarterly newsletter, networking roster, other mailings, and invitations.
Other Information: The American Quilt Study Group strives to foster understanding, appreciation, and preservation of quilts as significant markers of both women's history and American material culture through the establishment of a well-respected, accessible body of research in quilt studies.
Special Discounts/Offers: 10% off first order with the mention of *Sew Far Sew Good*; offer good until December 31, 1996.
Catalog: Free membership flyer and list of publications.

Buttons that don't button...

If you have delicate buttons that you would like to use on a garment that is permanently closed, such as a jumper or sundress that slips over your head, try this technique:

Measure and mark button placement.

Stitch the garment together where you have marked, creating tacks where each button should be placed.

Use button pins or the tie tack technique to place the buttons for easy removal.

Tip provided by: Albe Creations, Inc. Page 238

Long sleeve styles...

Peasant

Leg-o-Mutton

American Quilt Study Group Conference

660 Mission Street, Suite 400, San Francisco, CA 94105-4005
Phone: (415) 495-0163
Fax: (415) 495-3516
Event Information: The American Quilt Study Group Conference is for anyone who loves quilts! It is considered the most significant conference in the field of quilt history. Everyone is welcome. There are study centers, workshops, tours, keynote address, auction of quilt collectibles, show-and-tell, and quilt history/research presentations. Most attendees are quilters, authors, collectors, curators, dealers, folklorists, historians, and students of Women's Studies.
Payment Options: Check, Money Order, MC, Visa (International orders: MC or Visa only)
How Many Years: Since 1980.
Time of Year/Month: The conference is in the fall of each year, usually October.
Approximate Costs: Registration fee is usually $275.

American Quilter's Society

501 Kentucky Dam Road, P.O. Box 3290, Paducah, KY 42002-3290
Phone: (502) 898-7903
Fax: (502) 898-8890
Services/Merchandise: They have books, AQS show memorabilia, pins, T-shirts, bags, puzzles, and calendars.
Payment Options: MC, Visa, Check, Money Order
Shipping Options: UPS, U.S. Postal Service
Membership Dues: $18 per year, $33 for years, $49 for 3 years (add $5 Canada, $10 International)
Membership Benefits: Members receive a newsletter, a quarterly magazine, quilting book discounts, and an AQS pin. 20% off books with membership, 30% with five or more books. Discount admission into annual show.

American Sewing Guild

National Headquarters
P.O. Box 8476, Medford, OR 97504-0476
Phone: (503) 772-4059
Payment Options: Check, Money Order, MC, Visa
Membership Dues: $25 first year, $20 per year after.
Membership Information, Contact:
   Jean Fristensky, ASG, P.O. Box 8476, Medford, OR 97504-0476
   Or, contact your local chapter.
Membership Benefits: Members receive a chapter newsletter, chapter events featuring local and national speakers, member fashion shows and workshops featuring a wide range of sewing, craft, and fashion topics. There are local neighborhood groups providing hands-on sewing experiences in a smaller, more social atmosphere for members only. Special member discounts to all ASG activities, free manufacturers samples at some events and new product information from the sewing industry. Discounts to guild members from many companies and retailers, contacts with sewing professionals; information on sewing related events and sewing classes offered by local retailers. They also offer access to an extensive library of sewing related books and videos.
Other Information: The American Sewing Guild is an organization for people who think sewing is a creative and rewarding activity, and that sharing the benefits and joys of sewing is almost as much fun as sewing itself. The Guild provides up-to-date sewing information and a friendly support system for all levels of sewers–from beginning to advanced. An annual national convention provides an exciting time to meet sewing enthusiasts from all over the country and to share in seminars and sewing-related special events.

And Sew On

1672 South Greeley, Stillwater, MN 55082
Phone: (612) 430-9441
Fax: (612) 430-9441
Services/Merchandise: They carry better cottons and knits, quilting supplies, many threads–all colors of sulky, candlelight, decor 6, etc., and Viking and White sewing machines and sergers. Their clubs include Serger/Pictogram and Heirloom Sewing.
Payment Options: Check, MC, Visa, Discover

Andrea's Yarn Barn

70 Potomac Lane, Sayville, NY 11782
Phone: (516) 567-2032
Services/Merchandise: They are a mail order and by-appointment Yarn Barn. Yarn at wholesale prices, with over 200 colors to choose from. Also acrylic 2/24, lurex, and various cotton and fancy yarns.
Payment Options: Check, Money Order, COD
Shipping Options: UPS, U.S. Postal Service, FedEx
Minimum Order: No minimum order.
Other Information: They take pride in supplying all of their customers with personalized service, whether choosing a color or passing along some valuable tips and ideas. Whether you're a hand or machine knitter, Andrea's can supply custom-made orders, in any amount or weight, at everyday warehouse prices.

   Every day specials: 12 pounds of acrylic 2/24 in assorted colors for only $30. Afghan special: 3 pounds of yarn in your choice of up to any three colors for only $10 plus shipping and handling.

   You can give them a call, or if you are ever in the neighborhood, set up an appointment to stop by and see Nelly, Evelyn or Andrea herself.

Special Discounts/Offers: 10% discount on first order with the mention of *Sew Far Sew Good*. Large orders of 50 pounds and over are given additional discounts.
Catalog: For a color card, send $2 and a SASE. This fee is refundable upon order.

Anne Powell, Ltd.
P.O. Box 3060, Stuart, FL 34995-3060
Phone: (407) 287-3007, (800) 622-2646
Fax: (407) 287-3007
Services/Merchandise: They carry fine needlework supplies and related gifts. Traditional counted cross-stitch patterns, kits, and the finest even-weave linen available: Glenshee from Scotland. They also have antique sewing tools and books about them, Solingen scissors, sterling silver needle tools, solid gold tapestry needles, sewing music boxes, and Christmas ornaments by Enesco.
Payment Options: Check, Money Order
Shipping Options: UPS, U.S. Postal Service Priority
Minimum Order: No minimum order.
Other Information: Anne Powell, Ltd. believes in quality. When stitching for an heirloom of the future, they suggest you use the best materials you can find. Your work deserves the best.
Catalog: $5

Antiquity Press
1734 Scott Street, St. Helena, CA 94574
Phone: (707) 967-9162
Services/Merchandise: They carry reprinted antique books. Current titles include *Art and Craft of Ribbon Work* (Vols. 1 and 2), *Ribbonology*, *Draping & Designing With Scissors And Cloth- 1920s*, and *Draping & Designing With Scissors And Cloth- 1930s*.
Payment Options: Check, Money Order, MC, Visa
Shipping Options: UPS, U.S. Postal Service
Minimum Order: No minimum for retail. Six copies of one title for wholesale.
Other Information: Antiquity Press reprints antique books in the home arts and crafts field. They'll also purchase books for reprinting.
Special Discounts/Offers: Orders of six copies of one title receive a 40% discount.
Catalog: Free brochure upon request.

Apparel Component Supply (A.C.S.)
447 West 36th Street, New York, NY 10018
Phone: (212) 239-0414
Fax: (212) 947-9281

Services/Merchandise: They have sewing notions, trims, cording, patternmaking supplies, linings, interlinings, marking and cutting tools, measuring tools, and instructional books. Also, a custom-coordinated color card to match zippers, thread, seambinding, snaps, Velcro, cording, and cord locks.
Payment Options: Check, Money Order, MC, Visa
Minimum Order: $20 minimum with credit card orders.
Other Information: A.C.S. has a wholesale division: Champion Zipper Corp.
Special Discounts/Offers: Free shipping on orders over $100.
Catalog: $5, which is refundable with purchase.

ARA Imports, Inc.
P.O. Box 41054, Brecksville, OH 44141
Phone: (216) 838-1372
Fax: (216) 838-1367
Services/Merchandise: They have a wide range of semi-precious and precious beads, precious metal findings, pearls, coral, Balinese and Indian beads.
Payment Options: Check, Money Order, MC, Visa
Minimum Order: $50
Other Information: ARA Imports is a family-owned business that has been run by Kiron and Saroj (a husband and wife team) for the last 10 years. They specialize in catering to designers, carry more than 1,500 varieties of beads, and are always striving to get unique items. Full satisfaction is guaranteed.

Arise, Inc.
6925 Willow Street Northwest, Washington, DC 20012
Phone: (202) 291-0770
Fax: (202) 291-2073
Services/Merchandise: They offer vintage Japanese silk kimonos, bale prices or hand-picked. They also have thousands of other Japanese textiles: Obi, Kasuri, Yukata, etc.
Payment Options: Check, Money Order, MC, Visa, COD
Shipping Options: UPS, FedEx
Minimum Order: No minimum retail. $200 wholesale.
Special Discounts/Offers: Wholesale to qualified businesses.
Catalog: Send a SASE.

The Art Institute in La Antigua Guatemala
4758 Lyndale Avenue South, Minneapolis, MN 55409-2304
Phone: (612) 825-0747
Fax: (612) 825-6637
E-mail: artguat@aol.com

Long sleeve styles...

Fitted

Lantern

Black sheep, black sheep...

Black fleece is not necessarily black. It is any fleece that is not white, including grey, tans, brown, and black.

The fleece of black sheep is highly prized by hand-spinners, but very difficult to find, as many black sheep are culled from herds so that they do not bring down the wool harvester's prices.

Services/Merchandise: The Institute offers 10-day workshops in the arts for sojourners, travelers, searchers, teachers and students. It's located in Antigua, a really gorgeous, arty town surrounded by volcanoes, and it's warm in the winter. Classes from earlier this year include:

Loom Beading - Students warp a frame loom and complete projects such as necklaces, belts, purses, or appliqué for clothing.

Beaded Jewelry - Create fascinating jewelry, learn knotting techniques using knotted threads, vintage beads, silver, jade, and other stones.

Weaver's Tour

Natural Dye for Cotton and Hard Fibers

Payment Options: Check, Money Order

Tuition Cost: Total cost, including airfare from most U.S. cities, lodging in a great little hotel, tuition, group transportation, and some meals is approximately $1,575.

Catalog: Free upon request.

Art Max Fabrics

250 West 40th Street, New York, NY 10018

Phone: (212) 398-0755

Fax: (212) 768-3927

Services/Merchandise: Art Max has three floors of merchandise. From materials for bridal gowns to the perfect fabric for your first skirt, they have a huge selection of fabrics, both imported and domestic.

Payment Options: Check, Money Order, MC, Visa, Amex, Discover

Shipping Options: UPS

Minimum Order: One yard

Other Information: Next time you are in New York, stop by and browse. Let fifty years of expertise help you with your fabric purchase.

Author's Note: The owners are very friendly, and their store is a marvel. I visited the store when I lived in NYC, and I'm still amazed that I walked out with my bank account intact (well, mostly).

Arthur M. Rein

Mail Order Only

32-SF New York Avenue, Freeport, NY 11520-2017

Phone: (516) 379-6421

Services/Merchandise: This place can supply practically anything available in genuine furs for home sewing and craft projects: pelts, tails, black-dyed fox pieces (sewn into approximately 45"x 80" plates)–ideal for making stuffed animals, costuming dolls, various trimmings, etc. They also have used, obsolete style mink garments to cut up for similar purposes. And there are a few copies left of *How to Sew Leather, Suede*

& Fur–now out of print.

Payment Options: Check, Money Order

Shipping Options: UPS, U.S. Postal Service

Minimum Order: $50 plus shipping, handling, insurance, and NY and CT sales tax

Other Information: Arthur M. Rein does not carry leathers, shearling, hides, or imitations. Whatever your fur requirements, please give full details for a free quotation–no obligation. Give the kind and color of fur, dimensions, quantity, etc.

Mr. Rein will also custom-make new fur garments, comforters, bed throws, and accessories, such as: hats, muffs, scarves, boas, vests, flings, eyeglasses cases, and 9½″ full pelt mink teddy bears. You can send in a pattern for the collar or cuffs you would like for your garment. They can also restyle your old fur. Please send appropriate information on fur type, approximate price range, height, weight, bust/chest, dress/suit size, hips, along with a clipping or sketch of the desired style. They will guarantee a proper fit, even when the whole transaction is handled by mail.

Their fur factory is in New York City, near Penn Station. Mr. Rein and his associate Walter Brotman have over 75 years of fur manufacturing experience. They enjoy a no-complaints record at Better Business Bureaus, State Consumer Affairs Departments, and the U.S. Postal Service.

Special Discounts/Offers: Send a SASE for sample black-dyed fox pieces, cut from plate.

Author's Note: When I contacted Mr. Rein about a listing for this book, I was somewhat nervous to be calling a furrier. After all, I don't have the money to say that I am very familiar with furs, or the business. I was surprised to have reached a very interesting and affable man, ready to share his knowledge of furs and his profession with a girl from Iowa. If you are intimidated by furs and furriers, give him a call and ask him some questions. I'm sure you won't be disappointed; he is a wonderful man.

Ashland Bay Trading Company, Inc.

Wholesale Only

P.O. Box 2613, Gig Harbor, WA 98335

Phone: (206) 265-6100

Fax: (206) 265-3422

Services/Merchandise: They carry spinning fibers, weaving and knitting yarns.

Payment Options: Credit terms

Shipping Options: UPS, U.S. Postal Service, FedEx

Minimum Order: No minimum order required to qualified shops and businesses.

Catalog: Their catalog, price list, and credit application are free to qualified businesses.

Associated Sewing Supply Co., Inc.

690 North Snelling, St. Paul, MN 55104
Phone: (612) 645-9449
Fax: (612) 641-0391
Services/Merchandise: They have Pfaff and Singer sewing machines, industrial sewing machines, Passap and Singer knitting machines, specialty threads, yarn, books, classes, seminars, and sewing clinics. They are silk ribbon, quilting, and machine embroidery specialists.
Payment Options: Check, Money Order, MC, Visa, Discover
Shipping Options: UPS
Other Information: With five locations in the twin cities, ASSC, Inc. has been serving the community since 1957. All sewing machines come with extended warranty, free user classes, expert sewing advice, and competitive prices.
Special Discounts/Offers: 10% discount on first order with the mention of *Sew Far Sew Good*, and 10% off regular prices to guild members.

Atelier Plateau Collection Menzwear

616 10th Street East, Saskatoon, SAS S7N 0G9, Canada
Phone: (306) 664-6624, (800) 269-1566
Fax: (306) 477-7175
E-mail: women@the.link.ca
Services/Merchandise: They have a collection of menswear patterns for hobby sewers, custom sewers, and small manufacturing operations.
Payment Options: Check, Money Order, MC
Other Information: The patterns are printed on heavier paper–not tissue–in order to extend the life of the pattern and facilitate easy use. They also have a fabric swatching service for shirting, suitings, and other high quality items.

In the near future, anyone who calls will receive their upcoming *STRICTLY MENZ* newsletter. Articles will include menswear sewing construction and embellishment techniques and ideas, wardrobe planning, and other information.
Author's Note: Lenora (the designer) wrote an article on making intelligent fabric purchases for *Sew Far Sew Good*. You will find it in the Company Appendix.

Lenora also sent a sample of one of her pattern instruction sheets. It is amazingly detailed and easy to follow.

I have found the staff at Atelier Plateau to be helpful, friendly, and upbeat, and their clothes are classic and contemporary.

Atkinson Fabrics, Inc.

2006 Princess Place Drive, Wilmington, NC 28405
Phone: (800) 336-0416
Fax: (910) 762-0592

Services/Merchandise: They have quilting and craft supplies, including trims, laces, flannel, nylon, fleece, wallcovering, pillow forms, placemats, bedspreads, curtain patterns, close-outs on cotton prints, workroom supplies, silks, and satins.
Payment Options: Check, Money Order, MC, Visa, Amex, Discover
Shipping Options: UPS, Freight
Minimum Order: None on in-stock items.
Other Information: They offer wholesale prices on many fabrics you will see in retail stores for much more. Call them for any need.
Special Discounts/Offers: 10% off all orders of Waverly stocking fabrics with the mention of *Sew Far Sew Good*. A list is available.
Catalog: Complimentary samples are free.

Atlanta Puffections

P.O. Box 13524, Atlanta, GA 30324-0524
Phone: (404) 262-7437
Fax: (404) 262-7437
E-mail: puffector@aol.com
Services/Merchandise: They have patterns designed with the bazaar crafter in mind. The patterns are easy to make but look like they might be difficult. If a design looks easy, the purchaser may change his/her mind when deciding to buy at craft shows. Their patterns are designed to be made without using a bunch of expensive craft materials. Leftover fabrics and laces in small pieces may be used.
Payment Options: Check, Money Order
Shipping Options: UPS, U.S. Postal Service First Class
Other Information: They have been in business since 1982. Their money-back guarantee is for those who feel they were unable to complete a project because of the pattern. Puff is the registered trademark of their designs. Look for other designs by Kay in *Craft N' Things*, *Better Homes and Gardens*, *Floral and Nature Crafts*, and *Hot Off The Press* craft booklets.
Special Discounts/Offers: 10% discount on first order with the mention of *Sew Far Sew Good*. A two-year newsletter subscription is $4 for four issues (half-off the regular price.)
Catalog: $1.50 for a 16-page newsletter with patterns.

Audlin

Dixie Village Shopping Center, Gastonia, NC 28052
Phone: (704) 866-8776
Services/Merchandise: They have a large supply of beads, including: antique Venetian, old Roman, ancient beads from Syria, and old turquoise. They carry beads from all around the world, specializing in the old and ancient, including pre-Columbian. They also have blank silk scarves for painting.
Payment Options: Check, Money Order, MC, Visa, Amex, Discover

---

What does sans-culotte mean?

During the late 1700s, it was fashionable for men to wear knee breeches, both in America and European countries. When the French Revolution came about, the rebels looked for a definitive way of dress that would set them apart from their adversaries, the aristocracy.

Since the rebels largely consisted of labor-class workers, they agreed to abandon knee breeches in favor of full-length trousers. Thus, the ruling class sneeringly bestowed upon them the title of sans-culotte (sahn COO-lot), literally, "without breeches". It now applies to any ragamuffin or "rabble".

Another great pairing of tie tacks and buttons...

For your special and delicate buttons, a tie tack base is a great way to facilitate removal for laundering.

You have the options of glueing or sewing the buttons to the tie tacks.

To sew the button to the tie tack, punch holes into the plastic disk at the top with a hot needle. Line these holes up with those on your button, and use a heavy thread to attach the button.

Tip provided by:
Albe Creations, Inc.
Page 238

Minimum Order: $50 retail. $200 wholesale.
Other Information: Open by appointment only. Audlin is at all the bead shows: East Coast, Chicago, Texas, and New Mexico.

Aura Registered

Box 602, Derby Line, VT 05830-0602
Phone: (819) 876-2998
Fax: (819) 876-5979
Services/Merchandise: They have craft books, knitting books, buttons, embroidery and needlework supplies, wool yarns, Norwegian wool, Shetland wool from Scotland, mohair, cotton, patterns, project kits (sweater kits), needlecraft kits, quilting books, notions, weaving yarn on cones, and yarn/knitting supplies.
Payment Options: Check, Money Order, MC, Visa
Shipping Options: Mail order, flat fee of $3.95 per order
Other Information: They provide full service for Canada with a Canadian catalog available, and take oversees orders. They have been in business for over twelve years. They also have over 24 different original Nordic bulky-weight patterns.

   Their other company, Vapor Trail Graphics, does desk-top publishing and catalog assistance, using Macintosh hardware, software, and graphics.
Special Discounts/Offers: Various discounts for volume orders.
Catalog: $2, which is refundable with an order.

Aurora Silk

5806 North Vancouver, Portland, OR 97217
Phone: (503) 286-4149
Services/Merchandise: They have silk yarns, threads, spinning fibers, and fabrics—all naturally dyed by hand. They also do custom-dyeing, and sell natural dyes. They sell books, including *Hemp! For Textile Artists* and *A Silkworker's Notebook*. They have four sizes of silk yarn in 150 colors, including a fine 3-ply that's great for sewing.
Payment Options: Check, Money Order, MC, Visa
Shipping Options: UPS, U.S. Postal Service
Minimum Order: No minimum order.
Other Information: Their naturally dyed yarns are completely unique and totally beautiful.
Special Discounts/Offers: Wholesale to qualified businesses.
Author's Note: The silk yarn samples sent with the brochure are gorgeous. They range from a 2-ply cord to a very fine yarn that will run through most sewing machines. The natural colors are even, and add a beautiful luster to the yarns.
Catalog: Free brochure.

B & B's Blueprints

P.O. Box 710612, Houston, TX 77271-0612
Phone: (713) 726-0406
Services/Merchandise: They have versatile patterns for children and ladies, with a new flair on classic designs. These patterns allow for a variety of embellishments, including: smocking, cross-stitch, silk ribbon embroidery, shadow work, and appliqués.
Payment Options: Check, Money Order, MC, Visa
Shipping Options: UPS, U.S. Postal Service
Minimum Order: No minimum order for retail. Low minimum for wholesale.
Other Information: Most of their patterns include the following features:

- All sizes are in one pattern.
- There are suggestions for variations of the pattern to allow for smocking, cross-stitch, shadow work, appliqué, silk ribbon embroidery, piping, lace trim, etc.
- The patterns for bubbles, gowns, and christening ensembles are designed for both boys and girls.
- Each pattern has style variations, such as variations in collars, sleeve length, pant length, cuffs or bibs.
- If a garment style requires a shirt or blouse, that pattern is included.
- The sizing is ample for the fit children prefer today.
- Each pattern has color photos and pattern fronts.

They also offer six mother/daughter patterns, with both children's and ladies' sizes included in one pattern.

   Most orders are shipped within 24 hours. Trunk shows of the pattern line are available. Call or write for more information.
Special Discounts/Offers: 10% discount on first order with the mention of *Sew Far Sew Good* for retail customers. Wholesale to qualified businesses, plus free shipping to your store with an order of over $100 and the mention of *Sew Far Sew Good*.
Author's Note: The patterns I received as samples are adorable. B & B's sent me patterns for a baby sailor bubble and a girl's smocked jumper. I don't have children yet, but I am definitely going to start the sailor's bubble as soon as I can. Very cute, very classic!
Catalog: Free with a SASE. Please include state sales tax number for a wholesale catalog.

B & J Fabrics, Inc.

263 West 40th Street, New York, NY 10018
Phone: (212) 354-8150
Fax: (212) 764-3355
Services/Merchandise: They have beautiful current fashion apparel, mostly in European fabrics and natural fibers. They get new fabrics daily, and you can send them a photo or sample of fabrics you're trying

to match. They will ship specific swatch requests to you at no charge.
Payment Options: Check, Money Order, MC, Visa, Amex, Discover
Shipping Options: UPS, FedEx
Catalog: Call for a catalog.

Baer Fabrics

515 East Market Street, Louisville, KY 40202
Phone: (800) 769-7776
Fax: (502) 582-2331
Services/Merchandise: They have everything from designer fabrics to basic materials in natural and synthetic fibers. Fabric prices range from 99¢ to $250 per yard. They also stock laces, trims, patterns, buttons, notions, Bernina sewing machines and sergers, and Baby Lock sergers.
Payment Options: MC, Visa, Amex
Shipping Options: UPS, FedEx
Minimum Order: No minimum order.
Other Information: Over 90 years ago, Nathan Baer, a cutter in a clothing factory, opened a store specializing in men's tailoring supplies, fabrics, and buttons. His son Abe, who joined the company in the 1930s, recognized several areas of expansion, especially women's fabrics, dry cleaning supplies, costuming materials, dance wear, and trims. Under Abe's son-in-law, Stuart Goldberg, who joined the firm in 1976, Baer's has expanded from a regional to a national supplier of fabrics and related products.

Baer's boasts over 1,000,000 yards of fabric and trims, and over 10,000 styles of buttons in the 85,000 square feet of its store.

Bally Bead Company

2304 Ridge Road, Rockwall, TX 75087-5101
Phone: (214) 771-4515, (800) 543-0280
Fax: (214) 722-1979
Services/Merchandise: They have unique beads from around the world including semi-precious gemstone beads, ethnic and African trade beads, amber, turquoise, and crystal beads. They also have 14k gold-filled, sterling silver, and plated jewelry findings, cast metal charms and stampings, tools, beading supplies, angel components, and more.
Payment Options: Check, Money Order, MC, Visa, COD
Shipping Options: UPS
Minimum Order: $25. All orders under $50 are charged a $5 service charge.
Special Discounts/Offers: Discounts are built into volume buying for orders by dozens, grosses, hundreds, and thousands.
Author's Note: Bally Bead Company has a new beading wire that is supposedly seven times as strong as Tiger Tail. I can say that it is strong (I'm not sure about seven times; I'm no scientist), and it is flexible. It takes a good deal of effort to put a kink in this wire. If you use wire for

beading, you will want to try this out.
Catalog: $4.95, which is refundable on first order, upon request.

Banasch's Fabrics

2692 Madison Road, Rookwood Pavillion, Suite C-1, Cincinnati, OH 45208
Phone: (513) 731-5757
Services/Merchandise: They specialize in fine fabrics, laces, bridal, and special occasion fabrics. They also have an entire wall of buttons, home decorating fabrics, and imported fabrics and laces.
Payment Options: Check, Money Order, MC, Visa, Amex, Discover, COD
Shipping Options: UPS, U.S. Postal Service, FedEx

Banasch's, Inc.

2810 Highland Avenue, Cincinnati, OH 45212
Phone: (800) 543-0355
Fax: (513) 731-2090
Services/Merchandise: They have tailoring, alteration, and dressmaker's supplies.
Payment Options: Check, Money Order, MC, Visa, Amex, Discover
Shipping Options: UPS, U.S. Postal Service, FedEx
Minimum Order: $25 to avoid handling fee.
Other Information: Banasch's was started in 1910.
Special Discounts/Offers: 10% discount on first order with the mention of *Sew Far Sew Good*.
Catalog: Free upon request.

Banksville Designer Fabrics

115 New Canaan Avenue, Norwalk, CT 06850
Phone: (203) 846-1333
Services/Merchandise: They have high-end designer fabrics purchased directly from top designers and sold to you at wholesale prices or below. Prices range from $\frac{1}{3}$ to $\frac{1}{2}$ less than those in fabric stores in NYC selling designer fabrics. The selection of fabric is extensive, with approximately a quarter of a million yards of fabric to choose from. They have a varied supply of all fabrics: cashmere, mohair, alpaca, wools, rare and hard to find silks, linens, rayons, cottons, and others.
Payment Options: Check, Money Order, MC, Visa
Shipping Options: UPS
Minimum Order: No minimum order.
Other Information: All of their salespeople have college degrees in design or textiles. They offer a personalized swatching services based on the customer's personal needs. $10 for up to 36 swatches. Your 36 swatches can be used one at a time, or all at once, and are based solely upon your requests.

Using leftovers from silk ribbon embroidery...

Those short pieces of silk ribbon left after completing a silk ribbon embroidery project are perfect for embellishing a garment for a child.

A small flower of group of several flowers on the corner of a collar adds a nice touch and can bring out the colors in the fabric, especially small calico prints.

Embroidery touches can also be added to the cuffs of long or short sleeves, and between the buttons on blouses or baby gowns. You are only limited by your imagination.

Tip provided by:
B & B Blueprints
Page 244

What is a mule?

The principle of the mule is to duplicate the motion of a handspinner. In hand spinning, the spinner's hand moves to and from the tip of a spinning bobbin. Raw wool fibers are snagged onto the end of the bobbin and are drawn and spun between the tip of the bobbin and the spinner's fingertips.

In mule spinning, a carriage containing a row of bobbins moves back and forth, simultaneously drawing and spinning a six-foot length of carded roving attached to each bobbin.

The yarn that is spun by a mule resembles the classic woolen yarns used in a wide range of garments, from Aran sweaters to Harris tweed jackets.

The mule revolutionized yarn spinning when it was invented nearly 200 years ago. In the U.S., the mule is nearly extinct. However, in many parts of Europe and Asia, it is still used exclusively.

Tip provided by: Bartlettyarns, Inc. This page.

Barbara L. Grainger Enterprises

P.O. Box 5264, Oregon City, OR 97045
Phone: (503) 652-8519
E-mail: wmat@prodigy.com
Services/Merchandise: Barbara is the author of several books on beadwork, including: *Peyote At Last* and *Peyote Design Techniques*. She also offers BeadAcademy, a beading correspondence course.
Payment Options: Check, Money Order
Shipping Options: UPS, U.S. Postal Service
Minimum Order: One book retail. 10 books wholesale.
Special Discounts/Offers: 40% discount on wholesale orders of 10 books or more.
Author's Note: Barbara has contributed many ideas to <u>Sew Far Sew Good</u>, and is frequently caught being very helpful on the Prodigy Beading Bulletin Board.

Bartlettyarns, Inc.

P.O. Box 36 SF, Harmony, ME 04942-0036
Phone: (207) 683-2251
Services/Merchandise: They offer 100% wool knitting yarns, in heathers, solids, tweeds, marls, and pure all-natural colors in thrifty, "full-measure" 4-ounce skeins. Worsted, bulky, heavyweight, sport, and rug weight yarns are also available in over 77 colors. They also offer weaving warps and 100% wool rovings.
Shipping Options: UPS, U.S. Postal Service
Minimum Order: No minimum order.
Other Information: Bartlettyarns' historic mill celebrates its 175th birthday in 1996!
     Open 8:30 - 4, Mon. - Fri.
Author's Note: Bartlettyarns is still doing business much as they have for 175 years; they take in wool from local farmers, and return it spun into yarn. They then take some yarn in trade to offer to their customers.
     Although the U.S. yarn industry relies primarily on spinning frames, Bartlettyarns uses the method still preferred in Europe and Asia—The Mule.
Catalog: Call or write for free samples and dealer names.

Bartley Software, Inc.
See Fittingly Sew, *Page...*

Batiks Etcetera

411 Pine Street, Fort Mill, SC 29715
Phone: (803) 547-4299, (800) BATIKS ETC
Services/Merchandise: Batiks Etcetera specializes in batik fabrics.

They offer batik and handpainted fabrics from around the world, including batiks from Indonesia, West Africa, and India, and Dutch Java prints from Holland. They also offer the complete collection of currently available Bali Handpaints from the Hoffman Fabric collection. In addition to their batik collection, Batiks Etcetera offers handwoven fabrics, including stripes, plaids and ikats. Australian Aboriginal design fabrics and other interesting fabrics are a part of their inventory, if available.
Payment Options: Check, Money Order, MC, Visa
Shipping Options: UPS, U.S. Postal Service
Minimum Order: ½ yard cut of one fabric.
Membership Dues: For $20 a year, Batiks Etcetera will send you swatches of their currently available fabrics. Batiks' swatch subscription service includes at least five mailings per year. Their Stripe/Plaid subscription service includes at least four mailings per year for $15.
Membership Benefits: By subscribing to Batiks' swatch services, customers are assured of receiving swatches of the newest fabrics shortly after the shipments arrive at the store. These customers will be the first to have the opportunity to order the newest batik fabrics from the comfort of their home.
Other Information: Batiks Etcetera has a wonderful collection of buttons that they offer by mail. They deal with each customer on a one-to-one basis to determine which fabrics will have coordinating buttons. They offer the same service for coordinating rayon and metallic threads.
     One of the most fun services they offer is their custom vest packs. Choose any combination of three fabrics from your swatch card, and they will send you the fabrics (two yards total), a vest pattern, two or three buttons (depending on button size) that compliment your fabric choices, a coordinating rayon or metallic thread for machine quilting, appliqué, buttonholes and/or topstitching, and some ideas to get you started. Even if you have never sewn a garment before, this pattern (sizes S-M-L included) will take you step-by-step through the process. If you are a seasoned seamstress, this pattern has a wonderful fit, and it's great for using as a base pattern for embellishing to your needle's content. All you provide is the vest lining (this can be made from the fabric in the kit if you plan ahead), a filler layer (if you want one), and sewing thread. If you can't decide which three fabrics you want, just tell them what colors you like to wear and they'll surprise you. Vest packs are just $37.95 plus $4 for shipping and handling.
Author's Note: The swatches that were sent with the company information for Batiks Etcetera were astonishing in their array of color possibilities. These are not your mother's (or your own—if you lived through the Sixties) plain old blue or brown batiks. These batiks come in colors like currant, coffee, moss, and, of course, indigo.

Baton Rouge Bead Society
919 Bromley Drive, Baton Rouge, LA 70808

Phone: (504) 767-3094

Services/Merchandise: BRBS is a non-profit organization. Its purpose is to help people learn about beads, their uses and composition, how they are made, and their importance in history all the way back to ancient times. BRBS also tells you how to use beads in jewelry.

Membership Dues: $20 per year.

Other Information: Meetings are open to the public, free of charge.

Beacon Fabric & Notions

6801 Gulfport Boulevard South, Suite 10, South Pasadena, FL 33707

Phone: (813) 345-6994, (800) 713-8157

Fax: (813) 347-1424

Services/Merchandise: Beacon Fabric & Notions offers machine embroidery thread and supplies.

Payment Options: MC, Visa, American Express, Discover

Shipping Options: UPS, U.S. Postal Service

Other Information: They have been in business for six years.

Special Discounts/Offers: Wholesale to qualified businesses.

Catalog: Free upon request

Bead & Button Magazine/Conterie Press, Inc.

P.O. Box 4520, Seattle, WA 98104

Phone: (206) 287-0071

Fax: (206) 287-9963

Services/Merchandise: *Bead & Button Magazine* is dedicated to helping its readers tap into their own creativity. Project and technique articles for making beautiful jewelry and accessories give detailed step-by-step instructions and are illustrated with color photos and drawings. All projects have been completely tested to ensure good results. Artist profiles, book and product reviews, readers' own work, and historical articles supply even more information and inspiration. The subscription price is $19.95 per year for six issues.

Payment Options: Check, Money Order

Shipping Options: UPS, U.S. Postal Service

Other Information: Conterie Press offers back issues of *Bead & Button* for $3.95 each, plus $2 shipping and handling for the first issue and $1 for each additional issue. Issue 6 is unavailable, and there are limited quantities of issues 1,2,3, and 4.

Bead in Hand

145 Harrison Street, Oak Park, IL 60304

Phone: (708) 848-1761

Services/Merchandise: Bead in Hand has a tremendous array of beads from all over the world, plus all the supplies needed to make jewelry and other beaded items. They carry a large assortment of findings (silver, gold, and basemetal earwire, chains, clasps, jump rings, pins, spacers, etc.), and antique, contemporary, and ethnic beads in a wide variety of materials, including: glass, crystal, wood, stone, ceramic, bone, shell, plastic, and polymer clay. They also carry embroidery floss and other kinds of stringing materials. Want more? This store has round and Delica seed beads from Japan and the Czech Republic in tubes and on hanks. They carry over 40 titles of books on beading, and they have video rentals. They also have tools specific to beading projects, such as roundnose, chainnose, and flatnose pliers, cutters and crimpers, and other tools for metalsmithing. They have Sculpey and Fimo polymer clay. In addition to supplies, they've got finished pieces of jewelry (both imported and made by local artists), African baskets and wall hangings, woven purses, and other gift items.

Payment Options: Check, MC, Visa

Other Information: Bead in Hand has a variety of classes in beadwork, and they host birthday parties for children and adults in their store.

Special Discounts/Offers: 10% discount on first order with the mention of *Sew Far Sew Good*. Purchase $100 in merchandise and receive $10 off your next purchase.

Author's Note: Bead In Hand sent me a wonderful little beading travel case (a bottle and the scissors from the case can be seen in the bead square on the back cover of this book). It's very handy, with needles, scissors, a leather work area, and eight bottles to hold your beads separately. Now all it needs is a strap–and I'm going to work on a beaded strap soon.

Bead Store Café

116 Center Ithaca, Ithaca, NY 14850

Phone: (607) 277-1729

E-mail: jm66@cornell.edu

Services/Merchandise: They have beads, and do custom design, and restringing. They will also locate beads and hard-to-find items.

Payment Options: Check, Money Order, MC, Visa, Amex, Discover

Shipping Options: UPS, U.S. Postal Service

Minimum Order: No minimum order.

Bead Works, Inc.

32751 Franklin Road, Franklin, MI 48025

Phone: (810) 855-5230

Services/Merchandise: They have a wide variety of beads from all over the world, jewelry making supplies, and accessories. They also restring beads and repair jewelry.

Payment Options: Check, MC, Visa, Discover

Other information: Customers at Bead Works can, with the help of the creative staff, design their own necklaces, purse-straps, bracelets, ear

---

Button accents...

With plastic buttons and a little imagination, you can create an unforgettable outfit.

With some Stichless fabrics glue and some fabrics scraps or decorative paper, you can decoupage your buttons.

Put some glue into a small container. Lay a piece of your fabric or paper into the glue and cover well. Use your fingers to remove the excess glue, and press onto your button. Don't worry about excess material right now, you can cut that off later.

Cover each button as you would like, then let dry on some wax paper or another protected surface.

When the glue is dry and completely clear, trim of the excess fabric or paper. Use a stiletto or X-acto knife to remove the fabric covering the holes in each button. With a shank button, you just need to remove the excess material.

Using a paintbrush, coat your button thoroughly once more to seal it, so that it will be washable.

Hat styles...

Sailor

Homburg

Straw

Service

rings, and stick pins. Customers can string their own beads, or have them perfectly strung by the staff.

Bead Works is open Tues. - Sat., 10 - 5, and Thurs, 10 - 7.

Beadazzled, A Bead Emporium

2002 Central Street, Evanston, IL 60201
Phone: (708) 864-9494
Services/Merchandise: They have glass beads, books related to beading, magazines related to beading, classes related to beading, beading birthday parties, and adult beading parties.
Payment Options: Check, Money Order, MC, Visa

Beads & Beyond

25 102nd Avenue Northeast, Bellevue, WA 98004
Phone: (206) 462-8992
Fax: (206) 453-9116
Services/Merchandise: Beads & Beyond is a full service bead store featuring over 6,000 beads, buttons, books, and supplies. A full complement of beading classes is offered through a quarterly newsletter. They also offer their own line of kits. The "Beyond" refers to craft/bead tours to a variety of countries starting in 1997. Write for more information.
Payment Options: Check, MC, Visa
Minimum Order: No minimum order.
Other Information: Beads & Beyond has been told by customers from all over the country that it's the best bead store they have ever visited. They invite you to visit them if you are in the Seattle area.

They also feature a juried show every December. It is open to Northwestern artists and is juried in late September every year.
Special Discounts/Offers: 10% discount offered on class supplies and items purchased during classes.

Beads & Rocks

Wholesale Only
335 Virginia Beach Boulevard, Virginia Beach, VA 23451
Phone: (804) 428-9824
Fax: (804) 428-5671
Services/Merchandise: They have glass, semi-precious, wood, metal, plastic, and ceramic beads. They also have antique glass stones and buttons, cameos, metal stampings, findings, bead stringing supplies, gem-quality minerals, rough minerals, crystals, bookends, decorative pieces, and tumbled stones. A variety of bead and jewelry related books are available for purchase at the retail store only. Also available are current issues of *Bead & Button* and *Jewelry Crafts* magazines.

Payment Options: Check, MC, Visa, Discover
Minimum Order: $30
Other Information: Beads & Rocks travels extensively to bead, rock, gem, and trunk shows. Wholesale visits are available by appointment. Wholesalers can call and add their names to the mailing list. Beads & Rocks will contact a wholesaler when they travel to the wholesaler's area. Bulk and poundage prices are available on close-out buys.
Special Discounts/Offers: 10% off to selected organizations, quantity discounts, wholesale to retailers.

Beads Galore International, Inc.

2123 South Priest #210, Tempe, AZ 85282
Phone: (602) 921-3949
Fax: (602) 921-7549
Services/Merchandise: They have beads, findings, and ethnic jewelry components.
Payment Options: MC, Visa, COD
Shipping Options: UPS, U.S. Postal Service
Minimum Order: $30
Other Information: They consider their selection of beads to be one of the largest in the U.S.
Special Discounts/Offers: Wholesale to qualified businesses.
Catalog: Free upon request, except in Arizona.

Beads to the Knees

321 9th Avenue North, Jacksonville Beach, FL 32250
Phone: (904) 356-6010

BeadZip

2316 Sarah Lane, Falls Church, VA 22043
Phone: (703) 849-8463
Fax: (703) 573-9032
Services/Merchandise: They have beads, findings, supplies, tools, and books.
Payment Options: Check, Money Order, MC, Visa
Minimum Order: No minimum order.
Special Discounts/Offers: They have money-saving packages that offer up to 30% discounts, and bulk-packaged beads and findings at a discount. Satisfaction is guaranteed.
Author's Note: The catalog is more than just a catalog; it's an information source with loads of tips and design ideas. It also has full-color inserts and descriptive illustrations.
Catalog: $5, which is refundable with purchase.

Becky's Väv Stuga

47 Bassett Road, Shelburne, MA 01370
Phone: (413) 625-6057
Services/Merchandise: Becky's Väv Stuga offers Swedish weaving equipment. Personal appointments are encouraged for purchasing weaving equipment, fabrics, and books.
Payment Options: Check, MC, Visa
Shipping Options: UPS, U.S. Postal Service
Other Information: You can learn to weave on Glimåkra-type looms during one-week intensive classes for beginning or intermediate level participants.

Bedlam Beadworks

263 West Nine Mile Road, Ferndale, MI 48220
Phone: (810)541-8827
Services/Merchandise: An in-store design team lets you pick out your own beads and then strings the beads for you. They can special order just about anything: books, beads, findings. A restringing service is also available. Special restrictions do apply. An in-store glass-and-ceramic beadmaking studio is in the works. They will be giving classes in ceramic beadmaking and daily demos in glass beadmaking.
Payment Options: Check, MC, Visa
Shipping Options: Mail order available by Fall 1996.
Minimum Order: No minimum order for retail. $50 for wholesale
Other Information: Their emphasis is on variety rather than quantity, so they have in stock a few of everything. Also, their philosophy is, "The more you buy, the more we have–and the more you have to buy!" What this means is that nearly every penny they make is spent on product, which is what happens when bead addicts own the store.
Special Discounts/Offers: 10% off your first order of $10 or more with the mention of _Sew Far Sew Good_. Wholesale to qualified businesses.

Beggars' Lace

P.O. Box 481223, Denver, CO 80248
Phone: (303) 233-2600
Fax: (303) 235-0356
E-mail: lacelady@rmii.com
Services/Merchandise: Beggars' Lace offers complete lacemaking supplies for bobbin lace, tatting, needle lace, etc.
Payment Options: Check, Money Order, MC, Visa, Discover
Special Discounts/Offers: Wholesale to qualified businesses.

Bergere de France

Mail Order Only
8238 Northwest 16th Street, Coral Springs, FL 33071
Phone: (800) 236-6140
Fax: (954) 753-3106
Services/Merchandise: They have over 120 French designer knitting patterns for men, women, and children. They also offer European designer yarns.
Payment Options: Check, MC, Visa
Minimum Order: No minimum order.
Membership Dues: You can join the Bergere de France Club for $15 annually, but you don't have to be a member to buy patterns or yarns.
Membership Benefits: You get an annual catalog with approximately 120 French designer patterns and knitting instructions for all 120 patterns. You also get a $15 redeemable coupon and special discounts.
Other Information: Bergere de France is France's oldest and largest spinner of handknitting yarns, which it sells exclusively by mail order catalogs. Bergere de France sells 25% of all handknitting yarns sold in France.
Special Discounts/Offers: Second-year club membership is free with the mention of _Sew Far Sew Good_. Call for special knitting club discounts.
Author's Note: The Bergere de France catalog is full of beautiful yarns and knitting patterns for clothes that look like they would really wear well. There is no hiding of certain problem areas in the photographs, and the variety of yarns is amazing. The catalog has yarn samples bound into the back pages for you to look at and touch.
Catalog: $6.95 which is refundable with a $25 purchase. Joining the Club is the most economical way to buy.

Berman Leather Co.

25 Melcher Street, Boston Center, MA 02210
Phone: (617) 426-0870
Fax: (617) 357-8564
Services/Merchandise: Berman Leather Company offers garment cowhide in different thicknesses and finishes, many colors of garment pigskins, chamois, deerskin, and a warehouse full of one-of-a-kind skins, plus all supplies needed for sewing leather.
Payment Options: Check, Money Order, MC, Visa, COD
Shipping Options: UPS, U.S. Postal Service
Minimum Order: $15
Other Information: The only leather-by-mail firm to offer sample cards of their stock leathers.
Special Discounts/Offers: Quantity discounts.

No two skins...

Always fit garment patterns to skins of garment leather, as no two skins are exactly alike and what fit on your skin last time, may not this time.

Tip provided by:
The Leather Factory
Page 302

A beading box to make...

Many cigar shops will sell you their wooden cigar boxes (for a reasonable price). Buy a nice, sturdy one, with a latch, if possible.

Cover the floor of the box with a scrap of ultrasuede or felt. Several strips of magnetic tape applied to the inside top of the box will keep your needles and snippers handy.

Vials of beads can be attached with velcro to the top and sides. It is also handy to attach a small (6") ruler in the same manner. Instead of carrying a large spool of thread, pre-cut a few lengths and store them in a zip-lock bag for your use.

Your project can then lay on the padded bottom, and you can spill out beads as you need them.

Tip provided by: Sylvia Harrow Prodigy member, beading enthusiast.

Beyond Beadery

54 Tinker Street, Woodstock, NY 12498
Phone: (914) 679-5548, (800) 840-5548
Fax: (914) 679-5894
Services/Merchandise: They carry thousands and thousands of beads in hundreds of colors and styles. Their specialty is seed beads, ranging in sizes from 6/0 to 15/0. They carry Czech and Japanese glass beads, including matte, silver-lined, color-lined, ghost, iris, 3-cuts, charlotte cuts, bronze, opaque and transparent. They also have over 200 colors of the exquisitely perfect Delicas from Japan, the latest rage in beadweaving. They have Swarovski Austrian crystals in every color, Dichroic art glass, Venetian and furnace glass beads, sterling silver charms and pendants, crow beads, bone beads, Druk beads and fire-polish beads, semi-precious stones, and much, much more. In addition to every kind of bead available, they also carry looms, findings, threads, cords, needles, buckskin hides, feathers, beaded curtains, handmade deerskin purses, and (of course) beautiful beaded jewelry and amulet purses.
Payment Options: Check, MC, Visa, Amex
Shipping Options: UPS, U.S. Postal Service
Minimum Order: No minimum order.
Other Information: They pride themselves on being one of the best-stocked bead stores in the Northeast, and their staff is friendly and knowledgeable. They are open daily from 11 - 6, and are located just 10 minutes off the New York State Thruway, in the middle of Woodstock. They have a mail order catalog, a toll-free number, and most orders are shipped within 24 hours of receipt.
Special Discounts/Offers: 10% discount on first order with the mention of *Sew Far Sew Good*. Bulk pricing available. 10% off orders over $100.
Catalog: Free upon request.

Big Sky Fiber Arts Festival

P.O. Box 1525, Hamilton, MT 59804
Phone: (406) 961-4846
Event Information: This festival includes fiber arts workshops, fashion shows, demonstrations, a skein contest, commercial booths, a wool and mohair fleece show, a sheep show, and a goat show.
How Many Years: Six years
Time of Year/Month: June 11-12
Approximate Costs: Free to the public.
Other Information: This is Montana's only fiber arts gathering, and it tries to offer a lot of interesting public events (herding, weaving, shearing, spinning, workshops, etc.) while keeping the hometown feeling alive.

Bitterroot Leather Company

1010 North First, Hamilton, MT 59840
Phone: (406) 363-2525
Services/Merchandise: Bitterroot offers elkskin and buckskin in a variety of colors. They also have cowhide, calfhide, beef rawhide, deer rawhide, and buffalo robes. They also have pelts/hides from lynx, arctic fox, red fox, minks, martens, wolves, coyotes, raccoons, skunks, ermine, and moose. They have imitation sinew and deer thong in many colors. Their feather offerings include guinea, barred turkey, pheasant, and handpainted eagle and hawk feathers.
Payment Options: Check, Money Order, MC, Visa, Discover
Shipping Options: UPS, U.S. Postal Service
Catalog: $2 for a packet of leather samples and price lists.

Black Sheep Wools/Hub Mills Factory Store

12 Perkins Street, Lowell, MA 01854
Phone: (508) 937-0320
Fax: (508) 452-3085
Services/Merchandise: They offer natural fiber yarns, mill ends, and close-outs at discount prices. Samples are $3.
Payment Options: Check, Money Order, MC, Visa
Shipping Options: UPS
Special Discounts/Offers: Quantity discounts.

Blond Woven Labels

20735 Darnestown Road, P.O. Box 26, Dickerson, MD 20842
Phone: (301) 428-8334
Fax: (202) 334-0001
Services/Merchandise: They offer woven garment labels, care labels, and size labels.
Payment Options: Check, Money Order
Shipping Options: UPS, U.S. Postal Service
Minimum Order: 1,000 labels.
Other Information: Their labels are available in woven polyester taffeta weave and polyester satin.
Catalog: Free mailing and samples.

Blue Heron Bead Company

3424 Silverado Trail, St. Helena, CA 94574
Phone: (707) 963-2554
Fax: (707) 963-1178
Services/Merchandise: They are importers of vintage and antique glass beads from Germany and Austria, and have beads in every size, shape, and color.
Payment Options: Check, Money Order, MC, Visa, Amex, Discover

Shipping Options: UPS
Other Information: You can see their beads at The Whole Bead Show and other shows around the country.
Catalog: Call to get on their mailing list for show information.

Blueprints-Printables
1504 Industrial Way, No. 7, Belmont, CA 94002
Phone: (800) 356-0445
Fax: (415) 594-0936
Services/Merchandise: They offer their exclusive Design & Print Blueprint Products, such as T-Shirts, Circle T® kits, sweat shirts, quilt squares, fabric by the yard, sun-fun squares, and nature paper print products.

They also carry clothing to decorate in silk charmeuse, crepe, raw silk, china silk, cotton sheeting, knits, viscous rayon challis, and georgette. The also have earrings, scarf clips, findings, hair clips, scarves, sashes, ties, hats, and handbags, ready for you to embellish.
Payment Options: Check, Money Order, MC, Visa, Discover
Shipping Options: UPS, U.S. Postal Service
Minimum Order: No minimum order.
Other Information: Blueprints-Printables designs and makes their own patterns. Products are cut and sewn in the San Francisco area (only silk scarves and limited jewelry findings are imported or purchased for resale). All blueprint materials are processed in their studio.

Blueprints-Printables has been in business since 1983, but has been involved in art shows and production blueprinting since 1974, and has been wholesale marketing their blueprint treated fabrics, kits, and book since 1987.

Blueprints-Printables is a member of the National Art Materials Trade Association, American Association of Craft Industries, Hobby Industries of America, Surface Design Association, and International Quilt Market.
Special Discounts/Offers: Blueprint Design & Print Kits are available at wholesale to qualified businesses.
Catalog: $3, which includes fabric samples.

Boca Loca Beads
124 N. Walnut Street, Bloomington, IN 47404
Phone: (812) 333-8767
Fax: (812) 333-8767
Services/Merchandise: In-store, they offer beads (wholesale and retail) of every description, including gemstones, glass, metal, and more. They also have supplies, books, tools, findings, and finished jewelry. They are a direct importer of the highest quality Peruvian ceramic beads and pendants in original and trendy designs. They also carry a fine selection of imported handicrafts and textiles.

Payment Options: Check, Money Order, MC, Visa, Amex, Discover
Shipping Options: UPS, U.S. Postal Service, COD
Minimum Order: $50
Other Information: Their experienced staff will help you create unique earrings, necklaces, bracelets, keychains, and more. They finish all jewelry in their store—you go home with a finished product that you've designed personally. Their low minimum wholesale requirement is perfect for the independent bead artist.
Special Discounts/Offers: 10% discount on first order with the mention of *Sew Far Sew Good*. Wholesale to qualified businesses.
Catalog: Their mail order catalog is free if you send a 9" x 12" SASE.

Body-Rite, Inc.
P.O. Box 599, Belton, TX 76513
Phone: (800) 490-7483
Fax: (817) 933-2820
Services/Merchandise: The Body-Rite Posture Pleaser is designed to encourage good posture, and to ease back strain caused either by repetitive movements, or by long periods spent with your arms out in front of you.
Payment Options: Check, Money Order, MC, Visa, Amex, Discover
Shipping Options: UPS, FedEx, COD
Minimum Order: One Body-Rite Posture Pleaser.
Other Information: The founder of Body-Rite, Inc., who is also the inventor of the Body-Rite Posture Pleaser, has a long history in invention and physical training. He originally developed the product for his wife, who sat for hours in front of a computer and experienced back pain.

The Body-Rite is perfect for sewers, quilters, stitchers, computer workers, and anyone else who works in the same position for long periods.
Special Discounts/Offers: 10% discount on first order with the mention of *Sew Far Sew Good*. Wholesale to qualified businesses.
Author's Note: Since receiving the Body-Rite Posture Pleaser in the mail, I have had to fight with Gerard for my chance to wear it. I feel more relaxed after wearing it while I work at the computer. I'm sure that I will be ordering a second one—before this one is torn apart from our tug-of-war.
Catalog: Free brochure upon request.

Bonfit America, Inc.
10920 Willshire Boulevard, #330, Los Angeles, CA 90024
Phone: (310) 824-6355
Fax: (310) 824-6357
Services/Merchandise: Bonfit offers their patterners for skirts, pants, and bodices, as well as books and new products launched via catalog.

Control your tension...

When a knitting pattern contains the instruction to "cast off loosely", try switching to needles 2-3 sizes larger, instead of loosening your tension.

This method will result in less hassle and fewer uneven stitches.

Payment Options: Check, Money Order, MC, Visa, Amex, Discover
Shipping Options: UPS, U.S. Postal Service, FedEx
Minimum Order: Consumers: one unit. Retailers: one case.
Special Discounts/Offers: 5% discount on first order with the mention of *Sew Far Sew Good*. Wholesale to qualified businesses.
Author's Note: I made a simple pair of pants quickly, and they fit perfectly. You do not need any previous experience with patternmaking and adjustments, and just the sewing basics to start. I recommend this for anyone who wants an all-inclusive pants pattern, or those with hard-to-fit bodies.
Catalog: Free upon request.

BottomLine Designs

Department OP, 4217 Hildring Drive West, Fort Worth, TX 76109-4725
Phone: (817) 926-4863
Fax: (817) 738-3752
Services/Merchandise: They offer hemline appliqué patterns and fabric kits.
Payment Options: Check, Money Order, MC, Visa
Shipping Options: UPS, U.S. Postal Service
Minimum Order: One pattern retail. 12 patterns—no fewer than 3 of any one pattern—wholesale.
Other Information: Her hemline patterns can be applied to skirts, shirts, and vests.
Special Discounts/Offers: 50% off to qualified businesses that place a minimum wholesale order.
Author's Note: The patterns she sent are whimsical and unique. Her many styles give you plenty of chances to show everyone your favorite hobby or profession.
Catalog: $2 for a color catalog if you send a 9" x 12" SASE.

Bovidae Farm

163 Jarvis Branch Road, Mars Hill, NC 28754
Phone: (704) 689-9931
Services/Merchandise: They offer knitting and weaving yarns, and specialize in 100% wool worsted, sport weight, and bulky weights. The yarn comes in over 60 colors in heathers, marls, tweeds, and Shetlands. They also offer mohair/wool yarns, buttons, clasps, patterns, needles for knitting, Ashford spinning wheels and parts, and Corriedale spinning fleece. Their merchandise is sold in a yarn shop located on their sheep farm and by mail order. Shop hours are Wed. - Sat., 9 - 5, and by appointment.
Payment Options: Money Order, Cash, MC, Visa
Shipping Options: UPS
Other Information: Their woolen yarn is spun by a mill that uses an antique machine dating back to the 1800s. The yarn is relaxed and soft, similar to handspun. The farm is a working farm, with registered Corriedale and Merino sheep. Visitors enjoy the Western North Carolina mountain scenery from their hillside log house and can pet lambs and friendly sheep. They are located in the heart of beautiful country, approximately 30 miles from Asheville, NC, noted for its attraction to tourists and retirees.
Catalog: Yarn samples are available for $3, which is refundable with your first order.

Bovis Bead Co.

Wholesale Only
P.O. Box 13345 , Tucson, AZ 85732
Phone: (520) 318-9512
Fax: (520) 318-0023
Services/Merchandise: They offer French glass beads.
Payment Options: Money Order
Minimum Order: $100
Other Information: Bovis Bead Co. has been in business for thirty years.
Catalog: $5

Bramwell Yarns, USA

2101 South Loop 250 West, Midland, TX 79703
Phone: (915) 345-2591, (800) 345-2591
Services/Merchandise: They carry yarns and books.
Payment Options: MC, Visa, COD
Shipping Options: UPS
Other Information: Bramwell Yarns also sponsors the British-American Machine Knitting Expo, with classes and instruction. Door prizes are awarded to attendees wearing their own knit creations.
Special Discounts/Offers: Receive a shade card packet for only $5. Wholesale to qualified businesses.

Brian's Crafts Unlimited

1421 South Dixie Freeway, Department SF, New Smyrna, FL 32168
Phone: (904) 672-2726
Fax: (904) 426-0350
Services/Merchandise: Their items for the sewer/fiber artist include button grab bags, designer-button grab bags, doilies, lace grab bags, muslin dolls and animals, rhinestones, Battenburg collar/insets, washable ribbon roses, sequins, pearls, ribbon, fabric glues, craft fur, and feathers.
Payment Options: MC, Visa, Discover
Shipping Options: UPS, U.S. Postal Service
Minimum Order: No minimum order.

Other Information: They specialize in orders for hard-to-find items, in larger quantities.
Catalog: $1, which is refundable with purchase.

Bridal Sewing School

4600 Breidenbaugh Lane, Glenarm, MD 21057
Phone: (410) 592-5711
Fax: (410) 592-6913
Services/Merchandise: The Bridal Sewing School offers an intensive six-day course for advanced and professional sewers. Couture techniques for wedding gowns and evening wear are covered in depth, while each student works on his or her own project. Courses are offered in Baltimore, MD, in the spring and fall, and in Portland, OR, in the summer. Classes are limited to ten students.
Payment Options: Check, Money Order, MC, Visa
Tuition Cost: $850 for the six-day course.
Author's Note: I wanted to add a choice quote about this course, because it sounds so juicy.
   "A week with Susan Khalje will teach you how a combination of underlining, boning and waist stays provides the skeleton upon which a couture dress is built. Combine this with a knowledge of fabric manipulation and linings and your garment's category moves from well-made to exceptional."
   -Sandra Betzina, author of *Power Sewing*.
Catalog: A free brochure with all pertinent information is available.

Bridals International

45 Albany Street, Cazenovia, NY 13035
Phone: (800) 752-1171
Services/Merchandise: They offer fashion fabrics, special occasion fabrics, bridal fabrics and laces, headpieces, ribbon, sequin fabrics, trim and appliqués, threads, patterns, and notions.
Payment Options: Check, Money Order, MC, Visa
Shipping Options: UPS, U.S. Postal Service
Minimum Order: No minimum order.
Other Information: Bridals International, the mail order division of Cazenovia Fabrics, Inc., has been owned and operated by a mother/daughter team for over 26 years. Their catalog shows the extensive array of fabrics and laces available at the store and through mail order. They have an extensive inventory of Alençon Lace, both beaded and unbeaded, organza trims and appliqués, along with satins, organzas, chiffons, velvets, silks, shantungs, and much more. All are available to the bride who wishes to create her own original gown and dresses for the entire wedding party.
Catalog: $9.50, which is refundable with a purchase of $50 or more.

Britex-By-Mail

153 Maiden Lane, San Francisco, CA 94108
Phone: (415) 392-2910

Brookfield Craft Center

P.O. Box 122, Route 25, Brookfield, CT 06804
Phone: (203) 775-4526
Fax: (203) 740-7815
E-mail: brkfldcrft@aol.com
WWW: http://www.craftweb.com/org/brookfld/brookfld.shtml
Services/Merchandise: They offer classes, workshops, a gallery, books, and videos.
Payment Options: Check, MC, Visa, Amex
Shipping Options: UPS
Membership Dues: From $35
Membership Benefits: They have discounts on merchandise and special events.
Other Information: Founded in 1954, Brookfield Craft Center has been promoting and preserving the skills and values of fine craftsmanship for more than four decades.
   For those who cannot visit their facilities, the Brookfield Video Library provides top-quality instructional tapes for home study and reference. To support high-quality arts and crafts education that is accessible to everyone, the Center offers extensive scholarship programs, plus an innovative hour-for-hour work study program. The Center is supported primarily by tuitions and retail sales, with supplemental income coming from federal, state, and private sources.
Special Discounts/Offers: 10% discount on purchases and class tuition with the mention of *Sew Far Sew Good*.
Catalog: Free 32-page catalog.

Buck's County Classic

73 Coventry Lane, Langhorne, PA 19047
Phone: (215) 757-8185
Fax: (800) 942-4367
E-mail: bccjane@aol.com
Services/Merchandise: They offer a five-step beading training course with free phone support. They sell beads, findings, precious metals, many handmade beads, and design elements.
Payment Options: Check, Money Order, MC, Visa, Amex
Shipping Options: U.S. Postal Service, First Class, Insured
Minimum Order: $10
Other Information: They sell only fine quality items.
Catalog: $2

What is a la Parisienne?

In the Parisian style.

Buffalo Batt & Felt

3307 Walden Avenue, Depew, NY 14043
Phone: (716) 683-4100
Fax: (716) 683-8928
Services/Merchandise: They offer 100% pure polyester fiberfill products for the craft world.
Payment Options: Check, MC, Visa
Shipping Options: UPS, FedEx
Minimum Order: Two cases.
Special Discounts/Offers: Sales are featured on a calendar that is provided monthly. Quantity discounts are available.
Catalog: $1 for a brochure, which is refundable with purchase.

Butterick Company, Inc.

161 Avenue of the Americas, New York, NY 10013
Phone: (800) 766-3619
Services/Merchandise: Butterick offers sewing patterns under the following names: Vogue, Butterick, and See & Sew. They also have the following sewing magazines: *Vogue Patterns Magazine*, *Butterick Home Catalog*, *Vogue Knitting Magazine*, and *Family Circle Knitting*. They also have knitting books and videos.
Payment Options: Check, Money Order, MC, Visa
Shipping Options: U.S. Postal Service

Button Factory

469 King Street West, Toronto, Canada M5V 1K4
Phone: (416) 504-4743
Fax: (416) 979-8676
Services/Merchandise: They offer all types of buttons, including metal, plastic, wood, rubber, and cotton. They also offer buckles and rings in metal and plastic, buttons covered from yard goods, and buttons dyed to match hard-to-find colors.
Payment Options: Visa
Shipping Options: UPS, U.S. Postal Service
Minimum Order: $50 U.S.
Other Information: They started doing business in 1939, and are celebrating 67 years in business
Special Discounts/Offers: 10% discount on orders over $500.
Catalog: Free upon request.

The Button Shoppe

4744 Oakfield Circle, Carmichael, CA 95608
Phone: (916) 488-5350
Fax: (916) 488-5350
Services/Merchandise: They offer retail buttons and buckles. The Button Shoppe only carries unique buttons not available in fabric stores.
Payment Options: Check, Money Order, COD
Minimum Order: $5 plus $1.50 for shipping and handling
Other Information: Fabric and yarn swatches can be sent for matching.
Author's Note: Once again, I am impressed. The Button Shoppe carries a beautiful array of buttons, ready for that particular look you have been searching for. These buttons are not inexpensive, but they're made for the most discriminating of seamstresses. The stuff dreams are made of.
Catalog: $5, which is refundable with purchase.

Button Treasures

Magna Road, South Wigston, Leicester LE18 4ZH, England
Phone: (01144) 116 278 0800
Fax: (01144) 116 278 0888
E-mail: 100520.3323@compuserve.com
Services/Merchandise: Their unique buttons, buckles, and clips for garment fastening are mostly high-fashion, European styles.
Payment Options: MC, Visa, International Money Order (in English £s)
Minimum Order: £5 (about $7.75 U.S.).
Other Information: Button Treasures is a family firm owned and run by the Meinrath family. They have been manufacturing and trading in buttons for more than 120 years. In fact, they were in the button business when buttons were only made from natural materials or metal. Today, most of their buttons never appear in shops, because they are only produced in limited quantities. The Couture Collection is available only through Button Treasures. Many of the buttons are made by craftspeople and are from natural materials, so that although colors, shapes, and sizes are consistent, each button is unique. The buttons are from the major European fashion centers: Paris, Milan, and London, as well as from more exotic locations like the Seyschelles. Wherever they come from, the buttons you will find in this collection all have three things in common:

- They are all buttons which you are unlikely to find in sewing shops.
- They are chosen to coordinate with current fashion styles and colors.
- They are all chosen for the home sewer who wants to add that special finishing touch to her garments.

The catalog shows over 840 different buttons in full color and actual size, so you can see exactly what each button looks like. Full satisfaction is guaranteed.
Author's Note: I contacted Button Treasures through e-mail, and since then have received nothing but wonderful service, and good old fashioned helpfulness. Their buttons are not cheap, running about $2 each. The catalog is an absolute delight and full of the stuff wish lists are

made of. They compare their buttons to costume jewelry. If you'll pay $15 for a pair of faux earrings, then you'll pay the same for a set of gorgeous buttons. Definitely worth the inquiry.
Catalog: £3, about $4.80 U.S., which is refundable with purchase. Mail or fax credit card number with expiration date, actual name on card, and address.

Buttons & Things
24 Main Street, Freeport, ME 04032
Phone: (207) 865-4480
Fax: (207) 865-1706
Services/Merchandise: They offer buttons, beads, buckles, and collector's thimbles.
Payment Options: Check, Money Order, MC, Visa
Minimum Order: No minimum order.
Other Information: The staff at Buttons & Things considers their button selection to be the largest anywhere in the world. They carry buttons made of all types of materials, including wood, leather, mother of pearl, horn, and glass, as well as novelty buttons of all types.
Special Discounts/Offers: Free gift with the mention of *Sew Far Sew Good*.
Catalog: Free with a 9" x 12" SASE.

Buttons 'n' Bows
14086 Memorial Drive, Houston, TX 77079
Phone: (713) 496-0170, (800) 769-3251
Services/Merchandise: They have fine fabrics and laces for smocking and heirloom sewing. Classes are offered in smocking, heirloom sewing and silk ribbon embroidery. They also have books, magazines, porcelain boxes, silk ribbon, *Inspirations*, and *Aspire*. They also carry ready-to-smock garments.
Payment Options: Check, Money Order, MC, Visa
Shipping Options: UPS, U.S. Postal Service
Minimum Order: No minimum order.
Special Discounts/Offers: 10% discount on first order with the mention of *Sew Far Sew Good*, and free shipping on orders of $40 or more.
Catalog: $2, which is refundable with purchase.

Buttons Unlimited
205 East Casino Road, Suite B20-28, Everett, WA 98204
Phone: (206) 290-3661
Services/Merchandise: They have hundreds of original buttons, antiques and collectibles, and artisan buttons. They also have glass, acrylic, dichroic, silver, nickel-silver, bone, shed antler, novelty, and porcelain buttons.

Payment Options: MC, Visa
Minimum Order: $20
Other Information: They also distribute special teas in beautiful combination packages. Contact them for more information.
Catalog: Full-size color catalog sheets are available for $1. The complete catalog, including shipping, is $17.50.

By Jupiter!
7146 North 58th Drive, Glendale, AZ 85301
Phone: (602) 931-2658, (800) 242-2574
Fax: (602) 931-2704
Services/Merchandise: They carry brass and antiqued silver-plated charms and findings in over 1150 styles. They can be purchased as single items, also some special packages (sewing-related, Noah's Ark, gardening, cats, etc.).

They also sell Picture to Fabric transfer gel (which they developed) and Fabric Fading Kits (which they also developed). This product makes new fabric appear vintage—great for repairing antique quilts or making "vintage" items. Their Fabric Fading Kit only attacks the dyes—not the fibers—so the fabric is not harmed.
Payment Options: Check, Money Order, MC, Visa, Amex
Shipping Options: UPS, U.S. Postal Service
Minimum Order: No minimum order for retail. $25 for wholesale.
Special Discounts/Offers: 10% discount on first order with the mention of *Sew Far Sew Good*. Wholesale to qualified businesses.
Catalog: $5, which is refundable with a $50 purchase.

Byzantium
245 King Avenue, Columbus, OH 43201
Phone: (614) 291-3130
Fax: (614) 291-3401
Services/Merchandise: Byzantium considers itself to have the largest and most extensive bead selection in Ohio, possibly in the Midwest. They mostly cater to jewelry makers, but carry many seed beads, charms, etc., for sewing and art quilting. They have an extensive selection of books and magazines.
Payment Options: Check, Money Order, MC, Visa, Amex, Discover
Other Information: They also have wonderful gifts, jewelry, ethnic art and textiles, African printed cotton fabrics by the yard, and classes.

As capital of the Byzantine empire, the original Byzantium was a center for trade in the ancient world, presenting wonderful items from all parts of the globe. So it is with the modern Byzantium—a huge selection of beads, many of them vintage, antique, and ancient. Also available are a large variety of books, findings, finished jewelry by their talented employees, ethnic jewelry and art, and sterling silver jewelry to die for. Their staff is available for beading technique consultation.

Stabilizing your appliqué…

A water soluble stabilizer, cut in a 1' wide strip, and placed on top of the appliqué motif will eliminate any drawing up of the fabric with a tight satin stitch.

After stitching through the stabilizer and fabric the residue can be easily peeled away.

This is a good technique because the water soluble does not leave a visible residue.

By placing a 1" strip on top and stitching through it, it is easier to keep track of it—as opposed to a paper stabilizer placed under the item being appliquéd.

Tip provided by: Jackie Boroff BottomLine Designs Page 252

Don't toss those fusible scraps!

Scraps of fusible can be used to stabilize button-holes, zipper seams, clipped seams, fraying seam allowances, etc.

All this in a beautiful setting which will set your creative urges aflame. Plan to spend some time exploring the store and the Byzantium Bead Museum and Library in the tented back room.

Author's Note: On the postcard Byzantium sent, there's a picture of the inside of the store. It looks like a bead-dreamer's heaven.

Byzantium was given a very favorable review in *Beadesigner International* by Miss Dirlie, and Kiki put in a note that said it was one of the best bead stores on this planet—or any other. Sounds like a winner to me.

Catalog: No catalog is currently available, but please send your name to be placed on their mailing list.

C & T Publishing

5021 Blum Road, #1, Martinez, CA 94553-1576
Phone: (800) 284-1114, (510) 370-9600 for international inquiries
Fax: (510) 370-1576
E-mail: ctinfo@ctpub.com
WWW: http://www.ctpub.com/~ctpub
Services/Merchandise: They have books on quilting, fabric painting, appliqué, and embroidery. They also have quilting notecards, ribbon embroidery kits, and dyes and paints.
Payment Options: Check, Money Order, MC, Visa

California Stitchery

6015 Sunnyslope Avenue, Van Nuys, CA 91401-3020
Phone: (800) 345-3332
Services/Merchandise: They have embroidery supplies and kits, and specialize in Judaic and secular stitchery. They offer supplies for needlepoint, counted cross-stitch, stamped cross-stitch, latch hook, crewel, and longstitch.
Payment Options: Check, Money Order, MC, Visa, Amex, Discover
Shipping Options: UPS, U.S. Postal Service
Minimum Order: No minimum order for retail. $50 for wholesale.
Other Information: The owner of California Stitchery has been selling Judaic needlework for more than 20 years.
Special Discounts/Offers: 10% discount on first order with the mention of *Sew Far Sew Good*. Wholesale to qualified businesses.
Author's Note: The catalog I received is in full-color and has 40 pages.
Catalog: $2, which is refundable with purchase.

Cambridge Artists Cooperative/Art To Wear Clothing Show

59A Church Street, Cambridge, MA 02138
Phone: (617) 868-4434
Event Information: They are a craft gallery located in Harvard Square.

They have an annual clothing show that features local and national artists who work with all materials. The show features one-of-a-kind and limited edition clothing, and "Art To Wear" accessories.
Payment Options: Check, MC, Visa, Amex, Discover
How Many Years: 6
Time of Year/Month: Fall (end of September through October)
Other Information: Write or call for more information on entering or attending the show.

Campmor

P.O. Box 700, Upper Saddle River, NJ 07458-0700
Phone: (800) 230-2151
Fax: (800) 230-2153
E-mail: info@campmor.com
WWW: http://www.campmor.com
Services/Merchandise: They offer rugged yard goods of nylon, Cordura®, canvas, and mosquito netting. They also have aluminum and nylon heavy duty zippers, sewing awls, grommet kits, shock cord by the yard, buckles, zipper pulls, sliders, D-rings, Velcro yardage and other Velcro accessories, and repair kits for do-it-yourselfers.
Payment Options: Check, Money Order, MC, Visa, Amex, Discover
Shipping Options: UPS, U.S. Postal Service
Other Information: Campmor's catalog includes everything you and your family will need for outdoor adventures. In addition to a wide variety of equipment and clothing for camping, backpacking, paddling, and climbing, the catalog features an extensive selection of supplies for making or repairing your own camping gear. You can send your damaged gear to their service department for expert repair at reasonable prices.
Minimum Order: No minimum order.
Catalog: Free upon request.

Canyon Art Company/WeaveIt

1519 Oak Canyon Drive, San Jose, CA 95120
Phone: (408) 323-8308
Services/Merchandise: *WeaveIt* is a weaving program designed for the weaver who would rather be weaving than struggling with a computer.
Payment Options: Check, Money Order, MC, Visa
Minimum Order: No minimum order.
Other Information: *WeaveIt* offers on-line help and an extensive glossary of weaving terms. You can chart up to 32 harnesses and 32 treadles, and view multiple patterns side-by-side.

WeaveIt will calculate yardage requirements for warp and weft, and if you give it your loom dimensions, it will compute the finished fabric dimensions.
Special Discounts/Offers: The *WeaveIt* demo is $15, which can be

applied to your later purchase of the full version of *WeaveIt*.
Catalog: Call or write for brochure.

Canyon Records & Indian Arts
4143 North 16th Street, Phoenix, AZ 85016
Phone: (602) 266-4823
Services/Merchandise: They offer craft supplies, including seed beads in sizes 10/0 to 16/0 (all colors), larger beads, including glass, plastic, brass, and nickel. They have hair pipe in bone, horn, and plastic, as well as a large variety of feathers and buckskins. They also offer beading and Indian craft books, Pendleton blankets and broadcloth, findings, and American Indian dance supplies, pre-recorded cassettes, CDs, and videos.
Payment Options: Check, Money Order, MC, Visa, Amex
Shipping Options: UPS, U.S. Postal Service
Minimum Order: $5
Other Information: The retail store is open 9:30 - 5:30 MST and is closed Sunday. Mail orders are taken by phone or mail. When ordering a catalog, please request the craft catalog.

Caravan Beads, Inc.
449 Forest Avenue, Portland, ME 04101
Phone: (207) 761-2503
Fax: (207) 874-2664
E-mail: caravan@mainelink.net
WWW: http://www. mainelink.net/caravan
Services/Merchandise: They have a wide variety of beads, beading supplies, and books. Beads include Japanese seed beads, Delicas, semi-precious beads, glass beads, and more.
Payment Options: MC, Visa, American Express, Discover
Shipping Options: UPS, U.S. Postal Service
Minimum Order: $50
Other Information: They also provide consulting and training for bead store start-ups.
Special Discounts/Offers: Wholesale to qualified businesses.
Catalog: They will send you a free Delica/DMC reference chart if you send a SASE. The chart tells which Delica beads correspond to DMC colors. Free mail order price lists are available.

Carol Harris Co.
206 B East Court Street, Dyersburg, TN 38024
Phone: (901) 285-9419
Fax: (901) 836-7609
Services/Merchandise: They offer a wide variety of fabrics, custom embellishment materials, couture supplies, sewing notions, antique but-

tons, and laces.
Payment Options: Check, Money Order, MC, Visa, Amex
Shipping Options: UPS
Minimum Order: No minimum order.

Carolin Lowy Customized Designs and Graphs
630 Sun Meadows Drive, Kernersville, NC 27284
Phone: (910) 784-7576
Services/Merchandise: Carolin Lowy offers hand-drawn customized color-coded graphs. Most graphs are drawn on paper 10 squares = 1 inch, and are color-coded to D.M.C., J.P. Coats, or Paternayan Persian Yarn. Stitch count and fabric requirements are provided.
Payment Options: Check, Money Order
Shipping Options: UPS, U.S. Postal Service, FedEx
Other Information: Send colored photograph, post card, decal, book or other descriptive material of subject to be graded. It will be returned along with the completed order. For all buildings, a full front view is preferable. Cost $15 to $50, depending upon complexity of the subject. Large graphs over 11 x 17 are $50 and up. Free estimates are gladly given. A $20 deposit is required with all orders. The remainder is due upon completion of the assignment. Please allow 4-12 weeks for an order to be completed. Any special instructions regarding finished size are preferred, as is count of the fabric to be used. For duplicate stitch and knitting patterns, gauge information is needed, including number of rows to the inch and number of stitches to the inch.
   Various ideas for graphs:
   Churches (a good fund raiser) - church kneelers and banners.
   Homes - your own, your family's or friends'.
   China and wall paper patterns - use in table linens, pictures, or chair seats.
   Business cards and company logos - use in paperweights.
   Large and small pictures of pets, cars, trucks, airplanes or boats.
   Wedding invitations and graduation notices.
   Thumbnail autobiography of Carolin Lowy: Born in England. Educated in England, France and Switzerland, emphasis on art and embroidery. Currently employed in the needlework field.
   Carolin Lowy will also assist you in locating previously printed charts.
Catalog: Free

Carolina Mills Factory Outlet
Box V, Highway 76, Branson, MO 65615
Phone: (417) 334-2291
Fax: (417) 334-8884
Services/Merchandise: They offer merchandise at 20 to 80% off man-

---

How to clean metal buttons...

Painted surfaces: Wipe with a damp cloth.

Steels: Wipe with the lead end of a lead pencil then wipe with a dry cloth.

Pewter: Use a metal polish, also try an outer leaf from a head of cabbage.

Other: Use metal polish.

Try using a soft tooth-brush to clean buttons with textured surfaces.

Cutting individual flowers on point...

Move a 2 1/4"-square template over your fabric until you can see an individual flower nicely framed within the seam allowance. Mark the fabric with a charco-line®, pencil, or pen and cut the square using fabric scissors (or a rotary cutter and board). Since all the squares will be sewn on point, it is necessary to position the flower so when it is cut, it looks as if it is "growing" toward one of the four points.

Tip quoted from: Impressionist Quilts by Gai Perry, published by C & T Publishing Page 256

ufacturer's regular retail prices, including fabrics, handstitched quilts, linens, and doilies.
Payment Options: Check, Money Order, MC, Visa, Discover
Shipping Options: UPS
Minimum Order: No minimum order.
Other Information: They also have housewares, giftwares, ladies' wear, men's wear, western wear, T-shirts, souvenirs, and a year-round Christmas shop.
Special Discounts/Offers: 10% discount on first order with the mention of *Sew Far Sew Good*.

Castlegate Farm

424 Kingwood Locktown Road, Flemington, NJ 08822
Phone: (908) 996-6152
Services/Merchandise: Their home-bred Romney sheep provide fiber for handspinners, handspun and millspun knitting yarns, and the Sweaters with a Pedigree collection of handmade wool sweaters. Handspun yarn, made to order, is creamy white—the natural color of the flock. The farm shop is open Wed. - Sat., 11- 4. Sheepskins are also available.
Payment Options: Check, Money Order, MC, Visa
Shipping Options: UPS
Other Information: Castlegate Farm is a working sheep farm breeding high-quality, registered, white Romney sheep for their longstapled lustrous wool. All the wool sold at the farm is homebred and undyed. Visitors are welcome during published hours, and mail orders are welcome as well. Handspinning fleeces are carefully skirted, and handwashed fleece is available. They specialize in "sweaters with legs"; a good sweater begins with a good sheep.
Catalog: $2.50 with yarn and spinning samples, sweater price list, catalog size chart, and order form.

Cathedral Window®

4016 North Wilder Road, Plant City, FL 33565
Phone: (813) 752-8090, (800) 997-8458
E-mail: 74554.2465@compuserve.com
Services/Merchandise: They offer the complete line of Dazor lamps, Hinterberg quilting frames, Jasmine quilting frames, ELNA presses, and Euro-Pro ironing systems. They also have computer software, including *Quilters Design Studio* for PC/MAC, *QuiltPro* for PC/MAC, *Electric Quilt* for PC, and *Block Base* for PC.
Payment Options: Check, Money Order, MC, Visa, Amex, Discover
Shipping Options: UPS, U.S. Postal Service, RPS
Minimum Order: No minimum order.
Membership Benefits: Cathedral Window offers the Marie Project, which is a very special program for volunteer organizations that make and donate articles to special projects.

With a letter from any agency, on letterhead, stating that you donate to their organization, Cathedral Window will provide you with polyfill, batting, scissors, thread, etc., at wholesale plus 10% (to cover accounting and handling expenses). They will ship the products to you at the actual cost of shipping. Call or write for more information.
Other Information: Janet Befort has over 30 years of quilting experience, and has had designs and patterns printed in several quilting magazines.
Special Discounts/Offers: Discount prices on merchandise at all times.
Catalog: Brochures available for each product.

Celebration of Craftswomen

3543 18th Street, San Francisco, CA 94110
Phone: (415) 821-6480
Fax: (415) 821-6415
Show Information: This is an all-women, juried show, geared toward female artists who represent the broad spectrum of racial and cultural diversity, particularly those who are new to selling their craft at retail shows.
Payment Options: Check, Money Order
How Many Years: 17
Time of Year/Month: First two weekends in December
Approximate Costs: $12 application fee, $175-$450 booth fees.
Other Information: This event is an annual fund raiser, presented by and supporting the San Francisco Women's Centers.

They also offer the Business of Crafts Workshops which provide an overview for women new to crafts marketing, including retailing/wholesaling, promotion, photography, display, record keeping/taxes, and public relations.

Center for the History of American Needlework

P.O. Box 359, Valencia, PA 16059
Services/Merchandise: C.H.A.N. is a national, non-profit, educational institution founded in 1974 to develop and encourage public recognition of the value and significance of the needle and textile arts in the United States. C.H.A.N. provides a number of research, referral, and information services to its members and the general public.
Payment Options: Check, Money Order
Minimum Order: No minimum order.
Membership Dues: $15 per year, $25/2 years, $125/lifetime membership.
Membership Benefits: You get a quarterly newsletter and a membership packet that includes needlework bibliographies, free patterns, and reference materials. You also get discounts on C.H.A.N. publications, and reproductions of library materials (photocopies, slides, and photographs).

Center for the Study of Beadwork

P.O. Box 13718-OP, Portland, OR 97213-0719
Phone: (503) 248-1848
Fax: (503) 248-1011
Services/Merchandise: They have books on beadwork, resource lists, and a networking newsletter for beadworkers.
Payment Options: Check, Money Order, MC, Visa
Shipping Options: UPS, U.S. Postal Service
Membership Dues: $20 per year.
Membership Benefits: You get 5% off purchases, access to their study collection, and four issues of the newsletter, which is filled with class listings, news about bead-related organizations around the world, and other articles of interest.
Other Information: The purpose of the Center for the Study of Beadwork is to gather and disseminate information on beadwork. CSB maintains a study collection, library, articles file, and a slide bank, and furthers programs of value to the advancement of beadwork. The CSB's study collection (over 400 pieces) includes works from around the world, dating back to the early 1800s.

The CSB, philosophically, is a not-for-profit entity. It is supported by the sale of books, slide kits, postcards, memberships, occasional grants, and fees for curating, writing, and speaking.
Catalog: $1

Chalet Publishing

32 Grand Avenue, Manitou Springs, CO 80829
Phone: (719) 685-5041, (800) 959-4587
Services/Merchandise: They offer the *Quilters Travel Companion* (North America Edition 1996-98). It is a guide to the quilt shops across the USA and Canada, and includes addresses, hours, descriptions, and maps for over 1,000 shops. It is soft cover and retails for $10.95.
Payment Options: Check, Money Order, MC, Visa
Shipping Options: U.S. Postal Service
Minimum Order: 1 retail. 6 wholesale.
Special Discounts/Offers: 10% off first order with the mention of *Sew Far Sew Good*. Wholesale to qualified businesses.
Author's Note: This book is the quintessential quilter's travel necessity. The maps are clear, and the listings are very descriptive. I will never leave mine at home.

Chilton Book Company

201 King of Prussia Road, Radnor, PA 19809
Phone: (610) 964-4000
Services/Merchandise: Chilton is a publisher of instructional, project, and reference books and booklets on sewing, serging, quilting, and crafting topics.

Minimum Order: Retailers please inquire.
Special Discounts/Offers: Wholesale to qualified businesses.

Christopher Rich

1502 Douglas Avenue, Ames, Iowa 50010
Phone: (515) 233-4355
Services/Merchandise: Christopher Rich is a professional illustrator whose style is ideally suited for books, newsletters, and promotional packaging. He specializes in line art, but is able to adapt his style to serve many functions.
Payment Options: Check, Money Order
Shipping Options: UPS
Minimum Order: No minimum order.
Other Information: Christopher Rich has helped to form Wednesday Studio with local artists to create art and illustration work of any kind.
Author's Note: You can view samples of Christopher's artwork throughout this book. It should be noted that Chris managed to finish the 600+ drawings for this book in less than three months. I have known him personally for years, and give him the highest recommendations.

Cinema Leathers, Inc.

Wholesale Only

1663 Blake Avenue, Los Angeles, CA 90031
Phone: (213) 222-0073
Fax: (213) 222-8221
Services/Merchandise: They have leather skins and hides, including pig suede, lamb suede, halian nappa, and English domestic cowhide.
Payment Options: Check, Money Order, COD
Shipping Options: UPS
Minimum Order: No minimum order.
Other Information: Cinema Leathers, Inc., was founded in 1928.
Catalog: Complete set of swatches for $25, which is refundable with a $100 purchase.

Clearbrook Woolen Shop

P.O. Box 8, Clearbrook, VA 22624
Phone: (800) 546-4045
Services/Merchandise: They have all types of fabrics, including silks, cottons, and wools.
Payment Options: Visa, MC, American Express
Minimum Order: No minimum order.
Catalog: If you are on their mailing list, you get free samples several times per year.

What is an Arbiter Elegantiae?

An Arbiter Elegantiae (AR-bit-er el-e-GANT-i-ai) is a director of fashion, or an arbiter in matters of taste.

Pants and shorts lengths...

Hot Pants

Boy Pants

Jamaica

Clearview Triangle

8311 180th Street Southeast, Snohomish, WA 98290
Phone: (360) 668-4151
Fax: (360) 668-6338
Services/Merchandise: They have the following books: *Building Block Quilts*, *Mock Appliqué*, *Building Block Quilts 2*, *Easy and Elegant Appliqué,* and *Stars and Flowers: 3-sided Patchwork*, by Sarah Nephew. They also have triangle templates to help with perfect piecing, graph paper, and quilting notecards.

Also, Sara Nephew will send information on classes if requested by a guild, shop, conference, or retreat.
Payment Options: Check, Money Order, MC, Visa, COD
Shipping Options: UPS, U.S. Postal Service, FedEx
Other Information: All designs and tools are based on the equilateral (60°) triangle.
Special Discounts/Offers: 10% discount on first order with the mention of *Sew Far Sew Good*. Wholesale to qualified businesses.
Author's Note: Sarah sent me copies of *Building Block Quilts* and *Mock Appliqué*. Both books are very good and include clear instructions. I particularly enjoyed *Building Block Quilts*, which has beautiful, inspiring pictures and ideas for creating quilts unlike any building block quilts ever seen before.

Her triangle templates are made of very thick plastic, and will last for years and years of hard use (which I'm sure you will give them).

Close to Home-The Sewing Center

2717 Main Street, Glastonbury, CT 06033
Phone: (860) 633-0721
Services/Merchandise: They offer all brands of sewing machines, as well as quilting books, fabrics, and classes. They are the home of the Northeast Quilters Association.
Payment Options: Check, MC, Visa

The Cloth Doll Magazine

P.O. Box 2167, Lake Oswego, OR 57035

Cloth of Gold, Inc.

1220 Spartanburg Highway, Hendersonville, NC 28792
Phone: (800) 316-0947
Fax: (704) 697-7651
Services/Merchandise: They offer 100% cotton fabrics for quilters and crafters.
Payment Options: Check, Money Order, MC, Visa
Shipping Options: UPS, U.S. Postal Service
Minimum Order: ½ yard

Special Discounts/Offers: 10% discount on first order with the mention of *Sew Far Sew Good*.
Catalog: $3 for over 300 sample swatches.

Clotilde

4301 N. Federal Highway, Fort Lauderdale, FL 33308
Phone: (954) 491-2889
Fax: (954) 493-8950
Services/Merchandise: They offer notions, quilting supplies, threads, books, videos, silk ribbon, embroidery supplies, serging supplies, irons, patterns, sewing machine accessories, buttons, and beads.
Payment Options: MC, Visa, Discover
Minimum Order: No minimum order.
Other Information: Clotilde will travel to your store, show, or guild to present a seminar. She is internationally known as an accomplished speaker.

She also travels worldwide to gather interesting, useful, and unusual sewing supplies for her customers.
Special Discounts/Offers: Always a 20% discount.
Catalog: Free upon request.

Coastal Button and Trim

P.O. Box 114, Damascus, MD 20872
Phone: (301) 829-0201
Services/Merchandise: They have buttons by the pound in terrific color/style combinations. They also have bows, charms, appliqués, books, patterns, beads, and even gift wrapping. Wonderful prices and wonderful service, and they ship within one day. Your satisfaction is guaranteed.
Payment Options: Check, Money Order, MC, Visa
Shipping Options: UPS, U.S. Postal Service, COD
Special Discounts/Offers: 10% discount on first order with the mention of *Sew Far Sew Good*. Discounts for large quantities.
Catalog: Free upon request.

Cochenille Design Studio

P.O. Box 4276, Encinitas, CA 92023
Phone: (619) 259-1698
E-Mail: 76702.1664@compuserve.com

Collins Publications

3233 Grand Avenue, Suite N-294, Chino Hills, CA 91709
Phone: (909) 590-2471

Fax: (909) 464-0078

Services/Merchandise: They have the book *The "Business" of Sewing*, and the audio tapes by the author. They also offer a complete set of sewing business forms, forms on disk, *The "Business" of Sewing Newsletter*, *Sew to Success*, and *Dress Shop* software.

Payment Options: Check, Money Order, MC, Visa, Amex

Minimum Order: No minimum order.

Other Information: The author of *The "Business" of Sewing*, Barbara Wright Sykes, is a business consultant, sewing instructor, speaker, and she owns a custom tailoring business.

Special Discounts/Offers: Wholesale to qualified businesses.

Color Me Patterns

1617 Bear Creek Road, Kerrville, TX 78028

Phone: (210) 367-2514

Fax: (210) 367-4203

Services/Merchandise: They offer patterns for wearable art, quilt, and soft-sculpture dolls. They also offer one-of-a-kind handpainted, silk screened, marbled, and air brushed fabrics done in small pieces (most common size 18" x 22"). Also available are the following instruction and lectures: Art To Wear, Pictorial Appliqué, Architectural Appliqué, Raw-Edge Reverse Appliqué, Machine Appliqué, Cats Galore, Peaceable Kingdom, Patriotic Quilts, Pieced Animal Quilts, Afghani Piecing, and more.

Payment Options: Check, Money Order, MC, Visa

Shipping Options: UPS, U.S. Postal Service

Minimum Order: No minimum retail. $24 and at least three patterns per title wholesale.

Other Information: Shirley Stevenson, designer and owner of Color Me Patterns, started publishing her designs in 1990. The wearable art patterns incorporate piecing, appliqué, and/or quilting techniques for the creative fashion sewer who wants to make a unique fashion statement. The quilt patterns are original designs of children, cats, farm animals, wild animals, frogs, and buildings. The soft-sculpture doll patterns all feature cats.

Any customer's questions during the construction phase of any pattern will be personally answered by Shirley via telephone. Shirley is a nationally known teacher and lecturer on wearable art and quiltmaking. A teaching brochure will be sent upon request.

Special Discounts/Offers: 10% discount on first order of two or more items with the mention of *Sew Far Sew Good*.

Catalog: $2, which is refundable with first order.

Commercial Art Supply

935 Erie Boulevard East, Syracuse, NY 13210

Phone: (315) 474-1000, (800) 669-2787

Fax: (315) 474-5311

Services/Merchandise: They have surface pattern design supplies and equipment for screen printing, marbling, faux finish, gold leaf, airbrushing, batik, silk painting, and fabric dyeing. They also have French, Japanese (including Delica), and Czech seed beads, Czech glass, trade beads, gemstone beads, findings, modeling supplies (Fimo and Sculpey), papermaking kits, an international paper selection, and vaban ribbon.

Payment Options: Check, MC, Visa, Amex, Discover

Shipping Options: UPS, U.S. Postal Service, FedEx

Minimum Order: $20

Author's Note: They sent a copy of one of their most popular books, *Beaded Amulet Purses*, and a tube of purple iris Delicas. Both of the people I worked with at their company were pleasant and helpful.

Catalog: No catalog is available at this time, but call or stop by when you are in Syracuse.

Constance Lowery

5523 Southeast Flavel Street, Portland, OR 97206

Phone: (503) 788-3082

Services/Merchandise: *The Sewing Secret* book gives step-by-step instructions on how to buy second-hand clothes. There are instructions on how to take several pieces apart to make something new, how to add to existing clothing to cover up stains or repair a manufacturer's defect, and how to add something to improve the look of the clothing and make it your own design.

Payment Options: Check, Money Order

Shipping Options: U.S. Postal Service

Minimum Order: One book.

Special Discounts/Offers: 10% discount for 2-10 copies, 20% for 11 or more copies.

Author's Note: Constance sent me a copy of her book, *The Sewing Secret*, and it has some good ideas for recycling clothing. Although tastes will always differ, the techniques remain the same, and this book is handy for anyone who has not had experience with recycling clothing, or who needs a few ideas to get the creative juices flowing.

Contemporary Quilts

5305 Denwood Avenue, Memphis, TN 38120

Phone: (901) 683-8654

Services/Merchandise: They offer quilting frame kits, quilt patterns, and *The Pillow Book*, which teaches you to quilt by making quilted and patchwork pillows.

Payment Options: Check, Money Order

Other Information: They've been in business since 1969.

Special Discounts/Offers: 10% discount on first order with the men-

Bermuda

Deck Pants

Clam Diggers

Toreador

Capri

Full-Length

tion of *Sew Far Sew Good*; larger discounts for quantity orders. Please write for information.

Author's Note: *The Pillow Book* is easy to read and follow. Great for the enthusiastic sewer who wants to try quilting in a small way.

Catalog: $2.50

Continuity...

P.O. Box 978, Portland, ME 04104

Phone: (207) 828-8682

Services/Merchandise: They offer surface embroidery kits based on historic designs and the world around us.

Payment Options: Check, Money Order

Shipping Options: U.S. Postal Service Priority Mail

Minimum Order: No minimum order, except for wholesale accounts.

Special Discounts/Offers: Wholesale to qualified businesses.

Author's Note: These are not your average embroidery patterns. They range from traditional to modern. The kits come complete with DMC floss, and the design is silkscreened onto the fabric, ready to stitch.

Catalog: Free upon request.

Copper Coyote Beads, Ltd.

9430 East Golf Links, #286, Tucson, AZ 85730

Phone: (520) 722-8440

Fax: (520) 886-5214

E-mail: emeraldy@aol.com, gwennyaple@prodigy.com

Services/Merchandise: They have imported 11/0 Japanese seed beads in over 180 colors, plus Japanese looms and books. They sell their custom designed graph paper in loom, brick, peyote, and two-drop peyote. They currently stock over 75 book and video titles, as well as Czech pressed glass drops (see bead picture on back cover), 14/0 Japanese seed beads, looms, thread, needles, plastic tubes, etc.

Payment Options: Check, Money Order, MC, Visa

Shipping Options: UPS, U.S. Postal Service

Other Information: In addition to the excellent quality of their beads, including many unusual matte colors, they have fast, friendly, and personalized service. They are happy to give suggestions, answer questions, and send samples. They are beaders who also sell beads and enjoy interacting with other beaders.

Special Discounts/Offers: 10% discount on first purchase with the mention of *Sew Far Sew Good*. Wholesale to qualified businesses.

Author's Note: Gwenn Yaple is frequently found being helpful on the Prodigy Beading Bulletin Board. This is where I met her, and I have enjoyed her offbeat sense of humor and her frequent insights on beading. Oh, and her bead selection is wonderful.

Catalog: Free price lists (please specify retail or wholesale).

The Corner Stitch, Inc.

1820 23rd Avenue, Meridian, MS 39301

Phone: (601) 693-2739

Fax: (601) 693-2166

Services/Merchandise: They offer specialty fabrics for heirloom sewing, smocking, and quilting. They also have imported laces, ribbons and trims, notions, patterns, Viking sewing machines, embroidery supplies, silk ribbon, books, magazines, and classes. They will do custom design and sewing.

Payment Options: Check, MC, Visa, Amex, Discover

Shipping Options: UPS, FedEx

The Costume Shop

P.O. Box 803, Corrales, NM 87048

Services/Merchandise: They offer buttons and button covers, in sterling silver, nickel-silver, or red brass, in a Southwestern design. They will consider doing custom designs of buttons, buckles, and collar tips. Although Southwestern designs are the current specialty, new styles—and new materials—are planned for the future.

Payment Options: Check, Money Order, MC, Visa, COD

Shipping Options: UPS, U.S. Postal Service

Minimum Order: No minimum order.

Other Information: The owner's background includes extensive sewing experience from costuming to leather and sheepskin garments, and she is currently studying jewelry making.

Special Discounts/Offers: 10% discount on first order with the mention of *Sew Far Sew Good*. 25% off with $150 retail order. 50% off with $300 retail order.

Catalog: $1, which is refundable with order.

The Costume Society of America

55 Edgewater Drive, P.O. Box 73, Earleville, MD 21919

Phone: (410) 275-2329, (800) CSA-9447

Fax: (410) 275-8936

Services/Merchandise: CSA advances the global understanding of all aspects of dress and appearance. It provides access to a national network of individuals and institutions interested in studying, collecting, preserving, and creating costumes.

Payment Options: Check, Money Order

Membership Dues: Individual $55, Student $35, Sustaining $80 ($25 tax-deductible), Patron $1,000 ($945 tax-deductible).

Membership Benefits: Regional benefits include lectures, exclusive tours, practical demonstrations, newsletters, and opportunities to meet others with costume interests. National benefits include the annual symposium, *CSA News*, *Dress* (CSA's annual scholarly journal), the national membership directory, discounts on selected publications,

international study tours, voting privileges for members, and awards.
Other Information: When you join the Costume Society of America, you receive both national and regional membership. CSA is composed of seven regions in the U.S. and Canada, with an eighth for international members. Your member discount applies to events in any region.

Cotton Ball

475 Morro Bay Boulevard, Morro Bay, CA 93442
Phone: (805) 772-2646
Fax: (805) 772-6357
Services/Merchandise: They offer classes and instructions in most needlecrafts, quilting supplies, notions, ribbons, gifts, buttons, home decorating fabrics, home and body decor craft supplies, accessories, beads, doll making patterns, dyes, laces, videos, patterns, kits, smocking supplies, tatting supplies, threads, trims, and more.
Payment Options: Check, Money Order, MC, Visa
Shipping Options: UPS, Post-Paid
Minimum Order: No minimum order.
Other Information: Named by *Better Homes and Gardens "Quilt Sampler"* as one of the Top Ten Stores in North America in July 1995, they have been in business since 1969.

Class schedules are printed every four months, with 70+ classes each session. The topics range from quilting, silk ribbon embroidery, and sewing to specialty classes like smocking and shadow embroidery.
Special Discounts/Offers: 10% discount on first order with the mention of *Sew Far Sew Good*. Wholesale to qualified businesses.
Catalog: $2 per year for the newsletter with class schedules.

Cotton Clouds

5176 South 14th Avenue, Suite SF102, Safford, AZ 85546
Phone: (800) 322-7888
Services/Merchandise: Cotton Clouds specializes in cotton and cotton blend yarns for hand and machine knitting, crocheting, and weaving. Yarns come on cones or skeins, with over 1,500 colors to choose from. They also carry related books, patterns, videos, kits, BOND knitting machines, Ashford spinning wheels, and Schacht looms.
Payment Options: Check, Money Order, MC, Visa
Shipping Options: UPS, U.S. Postal Service
Minimum Order: No minimum order.
Other Information: Their catalog describes 21 different kinds of yarns in a variety of sizes, textures, and weights.

They have been in business for 17 years and are available to serve all of your needs. They are sure that you will love their quick delivery and friendly service.

Give them a call to view their award winning catalog.

Special Discounts/Offers: Wholesale to qualified businesses. Bulk discounts and introductory offers also.
Author's Note: Cotton Clouds offers a Full-Color Yarn Chart© based on their updated, newly designed color system. You just choose a color you like, then check to see which yarns they carry in that color, or find a yarn you would like to work with, then look at the color table to get an idea of the colors available. Yarn color picking made easy.
Catalog: $6.50 for catalog and yarn samples.

The Cotton Club

P.O. Box 2263, Boise, ID 83701
Phone: (208) 345-5567
Fax: (208) 345-1217
E-mail: 102416.300@compuserve.com or cotton@micron.net
Services/Merchandise: They have cotton fabrics for quilting and books. They also have three different swatch clubs:
* The Cotton Club has monthly mailings, featuring no less than eight 4" samples.
* The Hoffman Fabric Club features Hoffman fabrics only. There are six mailings of no less than sixteen 4" samples, plus a Hoffman Christmas Collection mailing in the summer.
* Famous Faces Club features fabrics designed by noteworthy quilter/fabric artists, including Nancy Crow, Gerry Kimball, Debbie Mumm, and others. There are six mailings of no less than sixteen 4" samples.

Payment Options: Check, Money Order, MC, Visa
Shipping Options: UPS, U.S. Postal Service
Minimum Order: No minimum order.
Membership Dues: For the U.S. and Canada, each club costs $12 for bulk mail or $18 for first class mail per year. For other international orders, the cost is $28 per year for each club.
Membership Benefits: Along with the swatch sets, you will receive discounts, sales information, and a newsletter.
Special Discounts/Offers: Free sample set from The (original) Cotton Club to new customers who mention *Sew Far Sew Good*.

Cottons, Etc.

228 Genesee Sreet, Oneida, NY 113421-2709
Phone: (315) 363-6834
Fax: (315) 363-9507
Services/Merchandise: They have fashion, bridal and quilting fabrics, patterns from Kwik-Sew, Burda, Folkwear, and Stretch & Sew, books, Viking sewing machines and sergers, and classes.
Payment Options: Check, Money Order, MC, Visa

Recycling bargains...

When shopping for bargains on fabrics, furs, and buttons, don't forget garage sales and your local thrift stores.

Instead of looking for clothing to wear, try looking for ways to use a piece of fabric.

For instance, a $2 silk shirt could provide enough fabric for a silk scarf.

A $1.50 blouse can provide you with some beautiful buttons.

For $25, you could purchase an out-of-date fox coat, and make a removable collar and cuffs for your favorite jacket.

The possibilities are endless, if you do not limit yourself.

Skirt styles...

Circular

Shipping Options: UPS, U.S. Postal Service
Minimum Order: No minimum order.
Other Information: Although they are small, they're mighty! They try to carry unusual fabrics that you won't find in chains and other mainstream fabric sources. Their staff is knowledgeable, pleasant, and accessible.

Their swatch packets are all different and they try to offer something for everyone–at affordable prices.
Special Discounts/Offers: Free shipping on first order with the mention of *Sew Far Sew Good*. Wholesale to qualified businesses.
Author's Note: The sample swatches they sent are varied and truly have something for everyone. There are whimsical prints alongside classic silk. I'm sure Cottons, Etc. won't stay small for long!
Catalog: $10 entitles you to a year's worth of 30+ swatches arriving every 6-8 weeks.

Counted Thread Society of America

1165 South Dale Court, Denver, CO 80219-4129
Phone: (303) 733-0196
Services/Merchandise: They have *Counted Thread Magazine* as well as unusual books related to counted embroidery.
Payment Options: Check, Money Order
Shipping Options: UPS, U.S. Postal Service
Minimum Order: No minimum order.
Membership Dues: $11 per year, $20/2 years
Membership Benefits: You receive *Counted Thread Magazine*, and the chance to purchase unusual books.
Other Information: They began publishing their magazine in 1974, when counted thread materials were difficult to find in the U.S. Things changed for the better, and so they changed their emphasis from recommending places for buying supplies overseas to writing about ethnic counted embroidery. They put a lot of research into each article they print about embroidery from other countries. Articles are accompanied by charts for embroidering. They have display advertising, and review books and counted thread booklets to aid their readers in learning about other publications they may not be aware of. Send $2.50 for a sample issue.
Special Discounts/Offers: Wholesale to qualified businesses.
Author's Note: The sample magazine they sent was full of interesting and unusual information about ethnic embroidery, books available, and the history of sewing tools.

Coupeville Arts Center

P.O. Box 171, Coupeville, WA 98239
Phone: (360) 678-3396
Fax: (360) 678-7420

E-mail: cac@whidbey.net
Services/Merchandise: The Coupeville Arts Center is a non-profit visual arts organization, founded in 1987, that sponsors workshops in painting, photography, fiber arts, and carving, taught by nationally and internationally recognized faculty on Whidbey Island in Puget Sound.
Payment Options: MC, Visa
Membership Dues: $25 and up
Membership Benefits: Discounts and free admission to their conventions.
Catalog: Free catalog of workshops upon request.

CR's Crafts

P.O. Box 8-6OP, 109 5th Avenue West, Leland, IA 50453
Phone: (515) 567-3652
Fax: (515) 567-3071
Services/Merchandise: They have supplies for doll and stuffed animal making.
Payment Options: Check, Money Order, MC, Visa, Discover
Shipping Options: UPS, U.S. Postal Service
Minimum Order: No minimum order.
Catalog: $2 U.S., $4 Canada, $7 other countries.

Craft World Tours

6776 Warboys Road, Byron, NY 14422
Phone: (716) 548-2667
Fax: (716) 548-2821
Event Information: They offer craft and folkart tours for persons interested in or appreciative of handcrafts, folk art, and village life.
Payment Options: Check
How Many Years: 12 years
Time of Year/Month: Various departure dates throughout the year.
Approximate Costs: $3,000 - $5,500 for 2-3 weeks, depending on destination.
Catalog: Free brochure upon request.

Crafter's Choice

(A Division of Book-of-the-Month Club)
1225 South Market Street, Mechanicsburg, PA 17055
Services/Merchandise: They offer a discount book club, with a collection of the world's best–and hard-to-find crafts books.
Membership Dues: To find out how to begin your membership with three books for $1 each, plus shipping and handling, please write to the above address.
Membership Benefits: Money saving Bonus Point Program.

Craftmaster Enterprises

P.O. Box 39429, Downey, CA 90239-0429
Phone: (310) 869-5882
Fax: (310) 904-0546
Services/Merchandise: They offer the book *Turn Your Talent Into Gold* by Marsha Reed, *Craftmaster News* magazine, fire retardant table covers, and seminars on finding profits in crafting.
Payment Options: MC, Visa
Author's Note: *Craftmaster News* is full of information on craft shows across the country. If you are a professional crafter, this is a great resource for you. *Turn Your Talent Into Gold* has a good checklist for making sure you take care of the essentials while becoming a professional crafter.

Crafts By Donna

P.O. Box 1456, Costa Mesa, CA 92628-1456
Phone: (714) 545-8567
Fax: (714) 545-8567
Services/Merchandise: They offer embroidery kits and supplies.
Payment Options: Check, Money Order
Shipping Options: U.S. Postal Service
Minimum Order: No minimum order.
Other Information: Donna also writes for magazines, and she teaches all forms of needlework across the country.
Special Discounts/Offers: Free merchandise coupon with catalog and orders. Wholesale to qualified businesses.
Catalog: $2

The Crafts Report

300 Water Street, Wilmington, DE 19801
Phone: (302) 656-2209, (800) 777-7098
Fax: (302) 656-4894
E-mail: tcrmag@aol.com
Services/Merchandise: They publish *The Crafts Report*, the business journal for the crafts industry, which is distributed nationally each month. It covers the business of creating and selling crafts, and is geared towards artists, gallery owners, retail buyers, and show promoters. It lists shows and fairs nationally and has retail, wholesale, and supply advertisers.
Payment Options: MC, Visa, Amex
Other Information: The Crafts Report also has a book club with about 15 titles devoted to business and crafts.

Creative Beginnings

P.O. Box 1330, Morro Bay, CA 93443
Phone: (800) 992-0276
Fax: (800) 2-CHARMS
Services/Merchandise: Creative Beginnings offers a unique selection of over 2,000 brass charms, ornaments, jewelry kits, charm packs, idea books, videos, and more. All charms are 100% raw brass and made in the U.S.A.

They also offer a line silk ribbon embroidery products, including: kits, iron-on transfers, silk ribbon packs, idea books, and instructional videos. Their silk ribbon kits feature 100% silk ribbons and include all the materials you need to complete the project.
Payment Options: Check, Money Order, MC, Visa, Discover
Shipping Options: UPS, U.S. Postal Service, RPS
Minimum Order: No minimum order.
Other Information: Creative Beginnings has been designing and manufacturing innovative crafts products since 1985. They are proud to be a family-owned company that strives for excellence in both their service and their products.

Look for Creative Beginnings products in your local crafts store.
Special Discounts/Offers: Wholesale to qualified businesses.
Author's Note: I have used their products since I began silk ribbon embroidery. My very first project was one of their kits. The instructions were easy to follow, and I made a beautiful barrette.
Catalog: Call or write for a free catalog.

Creative News

Department O, 225 Fairhill Road, Morton, PA 19070
Services/Merchandise: Creative News publishes two quarterly newsletters for owners of the New Home Memory Craft 8000 and 9000. Each issue contains three original projects, designed solely for each specific machine. The magazines have color photos, and the projects are presented with clear, concise instructions. Projects include everything from fashion accessories to quilt blocks.

Creative News–8000 is devoted to the New Home Memory Craft 8000.

Creative News–9000 focuses on the New Home Memory Craft 9000.

Subscriptions are $1 per year. Please specify which magazine you are interested in when placing an order. Send $4 for a sample issue.

Creative Quilting Magazine

P.O. Box 7074, Red Oak, IA 51591-0074
Services/Merchandise: This is a magazine for the true quiltmaker. Each issue features 15-20 sought after quilting patterns for quilters of all levels. You'll find projects of all sizes, using traditional and modern techniques with step-by-step instructions. Also included are tips to improve quilting skills, reviews on the latest quilt books, a buyer's guide, and a listing of quilt shows throughout the country.

Coat styles...

Pea Coat

When did the follow-
ing clothing fads have
their heyday?

a. Bra burning

b. Bikini

c. Spandex

d. Raccoon coats

e. Nehru jackets

f. Circle skirts

g. The chemise

h. The tent dress

i. The miniskirt

Crochet Guild of America

4500 Pride Court, Rolling Meadows, IL 60008

The Crowning Touch–FASTURN

2410 Glory C Road, Medford, OR 97501
Phone: (541) 772-8430
Fax: (541) 772-5106
Services/Merchandise: They offer FASTURN turning tools, FASTUBE foot for sewing accurate tubes, and sewing machine adapters for hi-to-low shank on New Home Memory Craft 8000 and 9000 machines. They also offer booklets and patterns for projects using fabric tubes–the possibilities are endless for vests, jackets, accessories, decorator items, quilts, fabric weaving, and dolls. They encourage the use of computerized sewing machines.
Payment Options: Check, Money Order, MC, Visa
Shipping Options: UPS, U.S. Postal Service
Minimum Order: 1 unit retail. 3 each wholesale, plus a minimum of $50 on the first order.
Other Information: FASTURN is shown on many TV sewing shows, including *Sewing with Nancy*, *America Sews With Sue Housman*, *Quilting in the '90s with Kaye Wood*, and *Sewing Connection*.

Crystal Palace Yarns

Wholesale Only

3006 San Pablo Avenue, Berkeley, CA 94702
Phone: (510) 548-9988
E-mail: cpy@straw.com
WWW: http://www.straw.com
Services/Merchandise: Crystal Palace Yarns is a U.S. distributor for Ashford Handicrafts of New Zealand. They have spinning wheels, looms, equipment, and wools. They also have fiber of all types for spinning and doll hair, knitting yarns in balls and cones, and Crystal Palace bamboo knitting needles.
Payment Options: Check, Money Order, MC, Visa, Discover
Other Information: They specialize in selling to shops, designers, and producers of knits, machine knits and woven textiles.
Catalog: Potential customers can write to them on business letterhead.

Current Events Productions

P.O. Box 8014-42, Blaine, WA 98231-8014
Phone: (800) GO-TO-SEW
Fax: (604) 538-3203
Event Information: They offer consumer needlework craft shows and seminars, including the In Stitches Conference & Show and the Craftin'

Like Crazy Expo. The focus is on education and the introduction of new sewing, stitchery, and craft products. Each show offers fifty different educational lectures and seminars, and is attended by vendors from retail, mail order companies, and major craft manufacturers. Shows travel nationally.
Payment Options: MC, Visa, Discover
Time of Year/Month: Throughout the year.
Special Discounts/Offers: $5 off Priority Seminar Pass, $10 off Super Sewers Seminar Pass. Send photocopy of this listing with order.

D'Anton Leather

5530 Vincent Avenue Northeast, West Branch, IA 52358
Phone: (319) 643-2568
Services/Merchandise: D'Anton Leather offers a large selection of garment and accessory leathers perfect for your every need. Leathers are available in an exciting array of colors, finishes, and types.
Payment Options: Check, Money Order
Shipping Options: UPS, U.S. Postal Service
Minimum Order: One full skin.
Other Information: D'Anton has been in the leather industry nearly 20 years. Their printed material provides accurate, up-to-date information on the types and colors of leather available, as well as prices. They are as close as your phone, and they can help you make choices about which leather to buy and which sewing techniques to use.
Special Discounts/Offers: Wholesale to qualified businesses.
Catalog: $2

D'Leas Fabric and Button Studio

2719 East 3rd Avenue, Denver, CO 80206
Phone: (303) 388-5665
Fax: (303) 388-5346
Services/Merchandise: D'Leas Studio is a specialty retail shop in the heart of Denver's Cherry Creek North district of art galleries, restaurants, fine clothing boutiques, and gift shops. D'Leas offers the finest fabrics for fashion sewing and a fabulous selection of artful and couture buttons. D'Leas also designs and offers a private collection of fashion patterns, derived from best-selling designers and boutique shop clothing. Not just a typical fabric store, D'Leas always offers a fabulous visual display of terrific clothes and unique ideas to make your wardrobe more individual and creative.

The shop is on the second floor of an old building that used to be a business with living quarters above. Now there is an art gallery below and D'Leas occupies the rooms above. There is an entire room of buttons, a bridal room, and several rooms of fine fabrics. In the near future, rooms will be devoted to gallery space to exhibit fine crafts and art with a fiber and fashion theme. European style windows and doorways enhance the creative spirit of the shop.

Also unique to D'Leas is the expert staff and service. All their consultants have extensive backgrounds in sewing, design, pattern drafting, and textiles. Servicing the customer to achieve the desired look is their favorite thing to do!

Exclusive products available at D'Leas include fine European wools, cottons, and linens, wonderful raw silk suitings and prints, contemporary rayon crepe prints from Germany, sandwashed silk looks in several fine rayon qualities (including the new tencel), batiks and handwoven fabrics, and much more. D'Leas also shows the entire color selection of Ambiance Bemberg rayon lining–the best lining on the market. You can order any of 20 different silks in a choice of 95 colors, with a minimum of only 5 yards. (This includes silk chiffon, georgette, shantung, and 4-ply crepe, just to name a few of the most popular choices. You can also order lining dyed to match your choice.) Buttons come from all over the world, and special trunk shows from fine craftsmen happen throughout the year. Thousands of available styles make sewing–or changing the buttons on ready-to-wear–much more creative and individualistic. Fine classes are available in fashion construction and artistic pursuits such as beading, pinweaving, embellishment, ribbon embroidery, and needleweaving.
Payment Options: MC, Visa, Discover, American Express
Shipping Options: UPS
Other Information: Throughout the year, exhibits at D'Leas display the works of students and customers that are simply breathtaking. The famous Cherry Creek Arts Festival on July 4th weekend is a great time to come see the displays. D'Leas encourages mail order by simply requesting the customer to bring in or send a photograph of the desired project, favorite colors, and personal style. Swatches of fabrics and photocopies of buttons can be mailed out to the customer. Traveling to Denver in beautiful Colorado is an even better idea. Cherry Creek is a terrific experience!

Daisy Kingdom

134 Northwest 8th Avenue, Portland, OR 97209
Phone: (503) 222-9033
Services/Merchandise: Daisy Kingdom is a fabric store that offers full-service decoration, as well as bridal, quilting, craft, pattern, fine dress goods, and notions departments.
Payment Options: Check, MC, Visa
Minimum Order: No minimum order.
Other Information: Their creative designers allow them to provide an ever-changing line of new fabrics, crafts, and home decorating items for novice and expert seamstresses. They also provide their customers with an innovative merchandising approach by offering numerous displays and on-going demonstrations that help stimulate new ways of thinking and sewing.

They will begin a mail order service in June 1996.
Special Discounts/Offers: 10% discount on first order with the mention of *Sew Far Sew Good*.

Danforth Pewterers

P.O. Box 828, Middlebury, VT 05753
Phone: (802) 388-8666
Services/Merchandise: They offer fine handcrafted pewter buttons, buttons covers, charms, keyrings, and many other items. They are licensed with Disney for Winnie the Pooh designs, and also licensed for Beatrix Potter designs and several museums' designs, including Smithsonian Institute, Museum of American Folk Art, Library of Congress, and the Shelburne Museum.
Payment Options: MC, Visa, Discover
Shipping Options: UPS, U.S. Postal Service
Minimum Order: No minimum order for retail sales. Wholesale orders require $100 to open a wholesale account and $50 to re-order.
Special Discounts/Offers: Wholesale to qualified businesses.
Author's Note: Their catalogs are awe inspiring. The buttons and sewing novelties are wonderful, and the non-sewing related gift items are beautiful as well. The Winnie the Pooh buttons are great for making a sweater for a young (or young-at-heart) loved one.

David M. & Peter J. Mancuso, Inc./Pacific International Quilt Festival

P.O. Box 667, New Hope, PA 18938
Phone: (215) 862-5828
Fax: (215) 862-9753
Event Information: The Pacific International Quilt Festival features a quilt contest, wearable art contest, quilters, fabric artists, home sewers, and much more. Festival includes vendors, special exhibitions, juried and judged competitions, workshops, lectures, and a fashion show.
Payment Options: Check, Money Order, MC, Visa
How Many Years: 5 years
Time of Year/Month: October
Special Discounts/Offers: Admission discounts for groups.

David M. & Peter J. Mancuso, Inc./Pennsylvania National Quilt Extravaganza

P.O. Box 667, New Hope, PA 18938
Phone: (215) 862-5828
Fax: (215) 862-9753
Event Information: The Pennsylvania National Quilt Extravaganza features a quilt contest, wearable art contest, quilters, fabric artists,

Answers

How many did you know?

i. 1960s

h. 1960s

g. 1920s, revised in 1950s

f. 1950s

e. 1960s

d. 1920s

c. 1980s

b. 1950s

a. 1970s

Pants styles...

Jodphurs

home sewers, and much more. Festival includes vendors, special exhibitions, juried and judged competitions, workshops, lectures, and a fashion show.
Payment Options: Check, Money Order, MC, Visa
How Many Years: 3 years
Time of Year/Month: September
Special Discounts/Offers: Admission discounts for groups.

David M. & Peter J. Mancuso, Inc./Williamsburg Festival Week

P.O. Box 667, New Hope, PA 18938
Phone: (215) 862-5828
Fax: (215) 862-9753
Event Information: The Williamsburg Festival Week features a quilt contest, wearable art contest, quilters, fabric artists, home sewers, and much more. Festival includes vendors, special exhibitions, juried and judged competitions, workshops, lectures, and a fashion show.
Payment Options: Check, Money Order, MC, Visa
How Many Years: 7 years
Time of Year/Month: Last weekend in February
Special Discounts/Offers: Admission discounts for groups.

David Simpson, Book Finder™

209 Piedmont Street, Blacksburg, VA 24060
Phone: (800) 846-4231
Fax: (540) 951-4231
E-mail: des209p@bevinet
Services/Merchandise: They are a search service for out-of-print books. They search for books in all subjects, any title or author. To have them find a book for you, all they need is the title and the author–if you know who the author is.
Payment Options: Check, Money Order, MC, Visa
Shipping Options: U.S. Postal Service

Dawn's Hide and Bead Away, Inc.

203 North Linn Street, Iowa City, IA 52245
Phone: (319) 338-1566
Fax: (319) 338-3509
Services/Merchandise: They have seed beads sizes 6 to 18 in lots of colors, Delica beads, bugle beads, Czech glass, Austrian lead crystal, gemstones, sterling silver and gold-filled beads, African trade beads, vintage Austrian crystal, German, and Czech beads. They also offer silver and gold-filled necklace and earring findings, needles, threads, pliers, and wire.
Payment Options: Check, Money Order, MC, Visa

Shipping Options: UPS, U.S. Postal Service
Minimum Order: $25 retail. $500 wholesale.
Other Information: They carry unusual, one-of-a-kind, handmade beads. They also specialize in custom jewelry. They offer classes in jewelry design, necklace and earring making, seed bead weaving, and glass bead making.
Special Discounts/Offers: 15% discount on retail sales of $150 or more. Wholesale to qualified businesses.

Decorating Digest Craft & Home Projects

P.O. Box 7582, Red Oak, IA 51591-0582
Services/Merchandise: This is a magazine for homeowners who like to create their own decorations. Each issue is filled with how-to's and projects with step-by-step instructions. Topics include crocheting, quilting, needlepoint, appliqué, sewing, woodworking, painting, and more.

Delta Technical Coatings, Inc.

Wholesale Only
2550 Pellisier Place, Whittier, CA 90601-1505
Phone: (213) 686-0678, (800) 423-4135
Fax: (310) 695-5157
Services/Merchandise: They offer a number of products for fabric surfaces, including:
Delta Designer Style Iron-on Transfers, available in 40 designs.
Delta Color Accents are available in 40 shades of easy-to use, spritz-on color. Accents are available in Color Mist, Delta Glitter Mist, and Delta Highlighter. Color Mist is permanent and washable on fabrics, and all are ideal for use with stencils.
Stencil Magic Stencil Designs come in 33 designs.
Delta Craft Glues come in Sobo, Stitchless, and Jewel. Sobo is good for most crafts that do no need to be washed. Stitchless glue is washable, and it dries clear, soft, and flexible. Jewel Glue is specifically formatted to apply jewels, sequins, and other embellishments to fabric, and it stays flexible after washing.
Delta Fabric Colors come in Delta Shimmering Fabric Color Starlight Dye, Delta Brush-on Fabric Color Fabric Dye, Delta Dazzlers, Shiny Liner, and Glitter Liner. All of the colors are nontoxic, water-based, and washable. Delta Shimmering Fabric Color Starlight Dye is great for pearlized color. Delta Brush-on Fabric Color Fabric Dye provides rich, intense color for one-coat coverage. Delta Dazzlers are transparent fabric paints filled with glitter and sparkling shapes, like hearts, holographic stars, and confetti. Shiny Liner and Glitter Liner are both dimensional fabric paints.
Other Information: For retail customers, Delta's Customer Service Department can direct you to a store near you that carries their line of products.

Design Originals Publications

RD 4, Box 234, Meadville, PA 16335-8240
Phone: (814) 336-5250
Fax: (814) 337-3671
E-mail: 74200.3031@compuserve.com
Services/Merchandise: They offer the book *Design Challenges*, with designer stamps, 178 black and white photos, 13 color photos, 53 illustrations/plates/line drawings, 5 yarn charts, 47 designer notes, 24 tables, and 65 weaving drafts. An optional disk of weaving drafts is also available.
Payment Options: Check, Money Order
Shipping Options: UPS, U.S. Postal Service
Minimum Order: No minimum order.
Other Information: Optional disk includes all drafts in book–runs with *Fiberworks PCW* software program.
Special Discounts/Offers: 10% on orders of 4-5 books, 30% on 6-7 books, 35% on 8-11 books, 40% on 12-33, and 55% on 24 or more books.

Dharma Trading Co.

P.O. Box 150916, San Rafael, CA 94915
Phone: (800) 542-5227
Fax: (415) 456-8747
Services/Merchandise: They have tools and materials for fabric and wearable arts, including dyes, paints, resists, fabrics, clothing and accessory blanks, books, etc. They have over 100 colors of Procion fiber reactive cold water dyes for tie-dyeing, batiking, Ikat vat dyeing or handpainting of natural fibers like cotton, rayon, viscose, wool, silk, and even wood or paper. They also have Deka L dyes, acid dyes, silkscreen and airbrush inks, printing paint, and many brands of fabric paints, silk paints, and dyes. They have tools and chemicals necessary for dyeing, painting, marbling, batiking, etc. Their catalog features three pages of white cotton and silk fabrics, as well as 44 pages of blank white clothing and accessories that are ready for dyeing and painting. Dharma Trading Co. also carries many how-to and design books.
Payment Options: Check, Money Order
Shipping Options: UPS, U.S. Postal Service
Minimum Order: No minimum order.
Other Information: Call Mon. - Fri., 8 - 5 PST.
Special Discounts/Offers: Bulk quantities and deep discounts.
Author's Note: Dharma Trading Co.'s catalog is inspiring, and their prices are realistic. I thought that was against the law. Definitely worth drooling over! They also include a gift certificate for a free something with your first order from their catalog.
Catalog: A free mail order catalog has color charts for most of their fabric dyes and paints. Printed on recycled paper with soy ink. It includes many detailed process definitions, application techniques and tips, as well as all products, prices, and ordering and shipping information.

Dimples

Mail Order Children's Fabrics

914 Southwind Court, Collinsville, IL 62234
Phone: (618) 345-3326
Fax: (618) 345-3326
E-mail: dimplesfab@aol.com
Services/Merchandise: They have children's fabrics, both knits and wovens, primarily in cotton and cotton blends. They offer fabrics from well-known children's wear manufacturers, as well as from small, exclusive children's wear designers. They also carry select items from the Hoffman and Alexander Henry Collections. They have solid knit coordinates in interlock, jersey, rib, fleece, and French terry. Coordinating buttons, Kwik-Sew patterns, snaps, elastics, and books are also available.
Payment Options: Check, Money Order, MC, Visa
Shipping Options: UPS, U.S. Postal Service
Minimum Order: No minimum order.
Other Information: They try to carry a wide selection of knits and wovens for boys and girls, from infants to pre-teen.
Special Discounts/Offers: Free sample catalog and swatch mailing with the mention of *Sew Far Sew Good*.
Author's Note: You can see a swatch of Dimples' fabric on the back cover of this book. Their selection is fun and frolicsome–you'll be able to find something for every kid in your life.
Catalog: $5 per year for 4-6 mailings, which is refundable with your first purchase.

Djenne Beads & Art/African Imports

508 Monroe Street, Suite 317 , Detroit, MI 48226
Phone: (313) 965-6620
Fax: (313) 965-0066
Services/Merchandise: They have hundreds of African trade beads, amber, Amazonite stone, and beaded work from the Yoruba, Kuba, and Masai tribes. They have antique and new baskets, with or without cowrie shells, drums, and stools. They have asante ewe kente, asoke clothes, abada clothes, and Kuba cloth made in Raphia. They also have Lhausa men's wear, with embroidery on indigo mud cloth.
Payment Options: Check, Money Order, MC, Visa, Discover
Shipping Options: UPS, U.S. Postal Service
Minimum Order: $50
Special Discounts/Offers: 10% discount on first order with the mention of *Sew Far Sew Good*. Wholesale to qualified businesses.
Catalog: $3, which is refundable with first order.

Add a special touch...

When finishing a garment, add a special touch with beads-around the collar, on the pocket, or on the sleeves.

When you are looking for the perfect button, consider beads.

Tip provided by:
Bead in Hand
Page 247

Gathering with elastic thread...

A good way to gather is to use elastic thread in the bobbin. You have to hand wind the bobbin, then baste with long stitches just above and just below the seam line on the piece being gathered. This "overgathers" the material, so you can stretch it to fit the smaller piece and make sure the gathers are even. Also, the same tip helps ease the sleeve caps to the shoulder of a garment or other project. After you stitch, just pull the elastic out.

Doering Designs

68935 233 Street, Dassel, MN 55325
Phone: (612) 275-3828
Services/Merchandise: You can sew Scandinavian costumes for men, women, children, and dolls with their illustrated, multi-sized patterns. They also carry a full line of imported pewter findings, wool braid, and cotton ribbons.
Catalog: $2

Dogwood Lane

Main Street, P.O. Box 145, Dugger, IN 47848
Phone: (800) 648-2213
Fax: (812) 648-2212
Services/Merchandise: They offer handcrafted porcelain buttons, and ladies' and girls' dress patterns.
Payment Options: Check, Money Order, MC, Visa
Other Information: Founded in 1981, Dogwood Lane is a premier maker of handcrafted porcelain buttons and jewelry. Their products are handcrafted in Dugger, Indiana, and shipped throughout the United States.
Catalog: $2.50, printed twice yearly.

Doll's Delight

P.O. Box 3226, Alexandria, VA 22302-0226
Phone: (703) 519-8845
Fax: (703) 519-8847
Services/Merchandise: They carry small clothing and accessories (shoes, boots, skates, socks, tights, and jewelry) for 18" American Girls Collection® dolls.
Payment Options: Check, Money Order, MC, Visa
Shipping Options: UPS, U.S. Postal Service
Minimum Order: No minimum order.
Other Information: They have been in business for five years.
Special Discounts/Offers: 10% discount on first order with the mention of *Sew Far Sew Good*.
Catalog: $2 brochure

Donna McFadden

115 Stephanie, Kerrville, TX 78028
Phone: (210) 895-1894
Services/Merchandise: They have the book *Quilting Through The Life of Christ* by Dave and Donna McFadden, a teacher's guide for a lap quilting bible study.

Donna Salyers' Fabulous Furs

700 Madison Avenue, Covington, KY 41011
Phone: (606) 291-3300
Fax: (606) 291-9687
Services/Merchandise: Specializing in man-made furs, leather, fleece, and related books and patterns.
Payment Options: Check, Money Order, MC, Visa, Discover
Shipping Options: UPS, U.S. Postal Service
Minimum Order: $10 minimum for credit card orders.
Special Discounts/Offers: 25% discount coupon with swatch order.
Catalog: Free upon request.

Dos De Tejas Patterns

P.O. Box 1636, Sherman, TX 75091
Phone: (903) 893-0064, (800) 8-TEJAS-8 (Orders Only)
Fax: (903) 893-0064
Services/Merchandise: Dos De Tejas has a line of 34 patterns, two instructional videos, kits, and related notions. They carry fashion and craft patterns, and instructions for recycling sweaters.
Payment Options: Check, Money Order, MC, Visa
Shipping Options: UPS, U.S. Postal Service, FedEx, COD
Minimum Order: $10 retail. $50 wholesale. Wholesalers must order at least 12 patterns, with at least 3 of each type.
Catalog: $2

Double Joy Beads

7121 East Sahuaro Drive, Scottsdale, AZ 85252
Phone: (602) 998-4495
Fax: (602) 443-9540
E-Mail: hkxb59a@prodigy.com
Services/Merchandise: Double Joy Beads has one of the largest collections of faceted beads, old and new, in Arizona. They have a catalog of brass beads, and also a huge collection of vintage glass beads, seed beads, Delicas, and regular Japanese seed beads. They have all the findings you might want, and if they don't have it, they'll find it. They sell books relating to beads, and have an extensive library for use in the store.
Payment Options: Check, Money Order, MC, Visa, Amex, Discover
Shipping Options: UPS, U.S. Postal Service
Minimum Order: $50
Other Information: They hope that their customers love beads as much as they do.
Catalog: $1

Dover Publications Inc.

31 East 2nd Street, Mineola, NY 11501
Phone: (516) 294-7000
Services/Merchandise: They publish sewing and needlecraft books.
Payment Options: Check, Money Order, MC, Visa, Amex, Discover
Minimum Order: No minimum order.
Catalog: Free upon request. Please specify the needlecraft catalog.

Downie Enterprises

P.O. Box 9526, 1929 Tippah Avenue, Charlotte, NC 28299
Phone: (800) 256-4882
Fax: (704) 375-5095
Services/Merchandise: They sell all models of Dazor Magnifier Lamps produced by Dazor, Inc., for needlework or reading magnification. They also sell the Alweiss line of pre-worked needlepoint, #10 double mesh canvas, and kits with Brunswick or DMC yarn. They have a huge selection of over 700 different pieces from Medeira.
Payment Options: MC, Visa, Check
Shipping Options: They ship free by UPS to the 48 contiguous states only.
Minimum Order: No minimum order.
Special Discounts/Offers: 4% discount on prepaid orders.
Catalog: Free brochure about Dazor Lamps. $10 charge for pre-worked needlepoint catalog, which is refundable with a $50 order for needlepoint.

Dress Rite Forms

3817 North Pulaski, Chicago, IL 60641
Phone: (312) 588-5761
Fax: (312) 588-4456
Services/Merchandise: They have tailoring forms in all shapes and sizes, male and female. They make custom forms on request. Forms come in two models: industrial and professional. 1996 prices range from $165 for the professional model to $465 for the industrial model.
Payment Options: Check, Money Order
Shipping Options: UPS
Other Information: Vivian and William Rankin purchased the 50-year old Rite Dress Form Co. in 1990 and renamed it Dress Rite Forms. Since then, they have upgraded their product and are now producing one of the finest tailoring forms available. The January, 1996, issue of *Sew News* features their Gold body form, which duplicates the shape of the mature woman. Forms carry a lifetime warranty.
Special Discounts/Offers: Special educational price with a five form minimum.
Catalog: Free upon request.

Dress Shop/Livingsoft

P.O. Box 819, Susanville, CA 96130
Phone: (800) 626-1262

The Duhesa Company

Mail Order Only
423 State Highway 11, Laramie, WY 82070
Phone: (307) 745-8543, (800) 438-4372
Services/Merchandise: They offer quality knitting and weaving yarns from the Brown Sheep Company. The yarns are wool, cotton, and sock yarns, ranging from fingering to a super-bulky weight, and are available in skeins or cones. The Duhesa Company also supplies yarn from Swedish Yarn Imports, which has a variety of cotton, wool, acrylic, and fiber blends, including their popular PeerGynt and Smart Wool yarns. Dyed in The Wool yarns are wonderful hand-dyed fibers, including an alpaca/silk blend, velvet chenille, mohair, and cotton or wool homespun. The quality yarns from The Duhesa Company cover a wide range of prices to fit almost anybody's budget. Knitting patterns from the Brown Sheep Company and Swedish Yarn Imports are available as well. The Brown Sheep Company patterns have a variety of styles, while Swedish Yarn Imports feature the Norwegian style of knitting. Fun felted patterns are available, too. A large selection of Norwegian style pewter buttons, clasps, and belt buckles are available, as well as the INOX line of knitting needles. All calls are returned.
Payment Options: Check, Money Orders, MC, Visa
Shipping Options: UPS, U.S. Postal Service
Minimum Order: No minimum order.
Other Information: Business hours are from 7:30 a.m. to 7:30 p.m. MST (keeping in mind that an answering machine is used occasionally).
Catalog: Free upon request.

Dundas Loom Company

1605 Stephens, Missoula, MT 59801
Phone: (406) 728-3050
Fax: (406) 728-4695
E-mail: jsdweaver@aol.com
Services/Merchandise: They make a full line of small looms, including table looms convertible to floor looms. They manufacture a full line of weaving accessories. They also make a Shetland style spinning wheel in cherry or maple with purple heart highlights.
Payment Options: MC, Visa, Discover
Shipping Options: UPS
Other Information: Dundas Loom Company has been in business since 1972.
Special Discounts/Offers: 10% off retail to educational institutions.
Catalog: $2.50, which is refundable with order.

Coat styles...

Tuxedo

Skirt top styles...

Banded

Bandless

Yoke

E & W Imports, Inc./The Bead Shop

4023 West Waters Avenue, Tampa, FL 33614
Phone: (813) 885-1138
Fax: (813) 885-1138
E-mail: ruby@intnet.net
Services/Merchandise: They have top-of-the-line gemstone beads, gold-filled and sterling wire (round, square, ½ round), findings, earrings, and chains. They also have Austrian crystal beads, Czech glass beads, cloisonne beads, gemstone carvings (for necklaces), and stringing supplies.
Payment Options: MC, Visa, Amex, Discover
Shipping Options: UPS, U.S. Postal Service
Minimum Order: $50
Other Information: E&W is Tampa's oldest bead shop, with twenty-one years in the same location. They have a graduate gemologist on staff. Hours are Mon. - Fri., 9:30 - 4, and Sat., 10 - 2. Classes are available in bead and pearl stringing, wire wrapping, and consumer gemology.
Special Discounts/Offers: Wholesale to qualified businesses.
Catalog: $2

Eagle Feather Trading Post/Eagle's View Publishing

168 West 12th Street, Ogden, UT 84404
Phone: (801) 393-3991
Fax: (801) 745-0903
Services/Merchandise: They specialize in Native American and Mountain Man arts and crafts, including beads of all types and beading supplies. They carry frontier clothing patterns and an extensive book selection. They also have finished beadwork, pottery, mandellas, dreamcatchers, moccasins, warbonnets, headdress kits, and blankets.
Payment Options: Check, Money Order, MC, Visa, Amex, Discover, Bank Americard
Shipping Options: UPS, U.S. Postal Service
Minimum Order: No minimum order.
Other Information: Open Mon. - Sat., 9 - 6 MST.
Special Discounts/Offers: Wholesale catalog available to dealers.
Catalog: Complete large-format catalog: $3.50. Book catalog: $2

Earth Guild

33 Haywood Street, Asheville, NC 28801
Phone: (704) 255-7818, (800) 327-8448
Fax: (704) 255-8593
Services/Merchandise: They have books, tools and materials for handcrafts, including dyes, yarns, spinning fibers and equipment, weaving equipment, world-wide folkwear patterns, knitting supplies, leatherworking tools, beading supplies, beading looms, and looms for kids.

Payment Options: Check, Money Order, MC, Visa, Amex, Discover
Shipping Options: UPS, U.S. Postal Service
Other Information: 25 years of service to crafts people at all levels, novice to professional–fast. They are reliable, and informed.
Special Discounts/Offers: Quantity discounts.
Catalog: Their complete catalog $3. Their starter catalog is free upon request.

EasiSew

3250-C Peachtree Corners Circle, Norcross, GA 30092
Phone: (800) 327-2677
Fax: (800) 650-3277
E-mail: royecrs@aol.com
Services/Merchandise: They have the tools, machines, and supplies for cutting, pattern designing and samplemaking, sewing, and finishing.
Payment Options: Check, Money Order, MC, Visa
Shipping Options: UPS, U.S. Postal Service, FedEx
Other Information: EasiSew is a division of Eastman Machine Co., a manufacturer of machinery used in sewn products industries like apparel and upholstered furniture. EasiSew features Eastman products of interest to smaller users—home sewers, crafts-makers, alteration shops, etc.
Catalog: Free upon request.

Eastern States Exposition/CraftAdventure

1305 Memorial Avenue, West Springfield, MA 01089
Phone: (413) 787-0158
Fax: (413) 787-0125
Event Information: CraftAdventure is for anyone interested in fabric and fiber arts. For craftspeople who wish to compete, there are competitions in quilting, weaving, knitting, spinning, crocheting, basketry, lacemaking, needlework of all types, tatting, and rugging of all types. Entries are judged in three divisions: Instructor/Professional, Non-Instructors, and Junior (16 and under). Ribbons, cash, and special awards are offered. Prize-winning entries are held for display during a 17-day fair in September. Brochures with entry forms are mailed in June to those who request them. Entry forms are due in August.

CraftAdventure is open to the public for its 3-day show, which runs Aug. 23-25, 1996. The show features a grand display of all competition entries, a judge's showcase, special exhibits, lecturers, demonstrations, and vendors.

During the 3-day show, fabric and fiber oriented guilds are given a free space to promote membership and skills. Guilds may present small displays, demonstrations, etc.

Vendors may rent space during the 3-day show to sell fabric- and fiber-related products. Rates and other information are available upon

request.
Payment Options: Check, Money Order
How Many Years: 23
Time of Year/Month: Late August
Approximate Costs: The competition entry fee is $1.50 per item. Admission to the show is $3.50. Vendors' sales booths are $100 (3-day rate). Booths are 10' x 10'
Other Information: Craftadventure is an educational program of the Eastern States Exposition, New England's Great State Fair. Their purpose is to promote and preserve the traditions of creative handarts, a goal they are proud to sustain. The inclusive scope of fabric/fiber art categories has been the focus of Craftadventure since it was initiated in 1974. The program, sponsored and funded by the Exposition, has also gained the support of many leading manufacturers and businesses, who provide many special awards.
Special Discounts/Offers: 50% reduction in admission for groups of 50 or more.

Edgemont Yarn Service, Inc.

P.O. Box 205, Washington, KY 41096
Phone: (606) 759-7614, (800) 446-5977
Services/Merchandise: They have Maysville and oriental carpet warp, Maysville rug filler, 4/4 heavy warp, mercerized pearl cotton, wools, rags, loopers, jazz strings, closeouts, looms, loom parts, and videos.
Shipping Options: UPS, COD
Minimum Order: Five pounds
Other Information: Edgemont Yarn has been serving weavers for over 40 years with quality products at low prices. They purchased the Oriental Rug Co. of Lima, Ohio, in 1991, and now carry Orco Looms.
Special Discounts/Offers: Monthly specials.

Elegance Unlimited, Inc.

Mail Order Only

45 Park Place South, Suite 176, Morristown, NJ 07960
Phone: (201) 984-8075, (800) 4321-SEW
Fax: (201) 984-8075
Services/Merchandise: They have unique, high-end fashion fabrics, linings, and hard-to-find interfacings for custom clothiers and home sewers.
Payment Options: Check, Money Order, MC, Visa
Shipping Options: UPS, U.S. Postal Service
Minimum Order: No minimum order.
Other Information: Elegance Unlimited is the successor to Jan Marie Fashion Fabrics, and they are carrying on the traditions of quality and service begun by Jan Marie years ago. Their catalog sample box contains almost 300 fabrics, and about 20 new ones are added every six weeks. Some custom clothiers borrow the sample box to show their clients. There is a small charge for this service. Elegance Unlimited enjoys looking for that special fabric you can't find locally, and they encourage you to call if you need to match fabric, or have a special need that perhaps they could supply.

Elizabeth Lee Designs

P.O. Box 696, Bluebell, UT 84007
Phone: (801) 454-3350
Fax: (801) 454-3450
Services/Merchandise: They have a wide variety of sewing patterns for nursing mothers, nursing bras in sizes up to 46H, and a few children's patterns. Their nursing patterns are wonderful for making clothes that allow discreet, easy nursing. They include easy to follow sewing guides with lots of tips and fashion suggestions. Patterns are easy to sew and include a wide range of sizes.
Payment Options: Check, Money Order, MC, Visa, Amex
Shipping Options: U.S. Postal Service
Other Information: This business was born because, as a first time mom, Elizabeth Lee found how hard it was to wear normal clothes to nurse a baby. She needed to support herself after the death of her first husband, and, as a teacher and seamstress, she made the decision to place her main emphasis on patterns for the breastfeeding mother.

Elizabeth provides personal, friendly service. Her phone hours are Mon. - Fri., 9:00 - 11:30 a.m.—otherwise please leave a message.
Special Discounts/Offers: 10% discount on first order with the mention of *Sew Far Sew Good*.
Author's Note: When I think of nursing patterns, I think of out-of-date, seventies-style clothes, or clothes obviously meant for something other than fashion and fit. Boy, have I got it wrong. These patterns are fashionable enough to wear even after your babe has grown.
Catalog: Free upon request.

Elsie's Exquisites

208 State Street, St. Joseph, MI 49085
Phone: (616) 982-0449
Fax: (616) 982-0963
Services/Merchandise: They offer silk ribbons and silk ribbon roses, as well as antique, vintage, and reproduction trims and ribbons for embellishment.
Payment Options: Check, Money Order, MC, Visa, Amex, Discover
Shipping Options: UPS, U.S. Postal Service, FedEx
Minimum Order: No minimum order for retail. $100, to avoid processing fee, for wholesale.
Special Discount/Offers: Wholesale to qualified businesses.
Catalog: Free price lists for retail buyers. $5 for a wholesale catalog.

Skirt top styles...

Hip Hugger

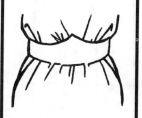

Pointed

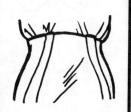

High Waited

Pants styles...

Slacks

The Embroiderers Guild of America, Inc.

335 West Broadway, Suite 100, Louisville, KY 40202
Phone: (502) 589-6956
Fax: (502) 584-7900
E-mail: egahq@aol.com
Services/Merchandise: The Embroiderers Guild of America, Inc., is open to ALL stitchers, beginner, intermediate, and advanced. They are a non-profit, educational organization founded in 1958 to foster high standards of design, color, and workmanship in embroidery, and to teach and preserve embroidery art. EGA offers its members access to a large inventory of needlework and needlework related books through its lending library. The library is housed at the EGA Headquarters. Book lists are available by subject, by title, and by author for $3 per list. Only members may borrow books; however, non-members may do research at the library.
Payment Options: Check, Money Order, MC, Visa, AmEx
Membership Dues: $24 per year
Membership Benefits: Members get *Needle Arts* magazine, numerous educational programs, seminars, exhibits, certification programs, and more.

The Enchanted Cottage

112 East Cheyenne Road, Colorado Springs, CO 80906
Phone: (719) 475-9244
Fax: c/o Pats Deli (719) 442-6457
Services/Merchandise: They carry embroidery supplies, including Mill Hill beads, Trigger fabric for Brazilian embroidery, Brazilian (rayon) embroidery thread, such as: Lola, Nova, Iris, Boricle, Glory, and Ciré. They also have Marlitt rayon floss, Artsilk, Charleston, Appletons tapestry wool, Royal Stitch embroidery Wool, DMC Cebelia #10-20-30, DMC Cordonet #10-20-30-40-50-60-70-80-90-100 in white or ecru, DMC tatting cotton #80 in colors, Anchor and DMC pearl cotton #5, #8, #12 Frebizard silk, Kanagawa silk buttonhole twist, Soie d'Alger silk floss, Madeira silk floss, ribbon floss rayon and metallics, and Anchor embroidery Floss.

They carry French wired ribbons, spark organdy ribbon, Mokuba ribbons, YLI silk ribbons 2mm-4mm-7mm-13mm, and Sweet Child Of Mine overdyed silk ribbons.

They have fabrics, such as silk batiste, Pima cotton batiste, Wistful batiste, Nelona, Super Sheen Nelo, cotton tulle, and net darning canvas.

They carry *Inspirations and Sew Beautiful, Australian Smocking and Embroiders*, and *Anne's Glory Box* magazines.

They have supplies for tatting and smocking, books, and classes on a variety of topics.

Brazilian or Dimensional Embroidery International Guild (BDEIG) member. For $5 per year, you can join the Colorado Dimensional Embroidery (CODE) club. CODE meets once a month for new stitches

and ideas in Brazilian embroidery.
Payment Options: Money Order, MC, Visa, Discover
Shipping Options: U.S. Postal Service
Minimum Order: $5
Other Information: They try to get any orders out in the next drop mail.
Special Discounts/Offers: 10% discount on first order with the mention of *Sew Far Sew Good*.
Catalog: $2, which is refundable with first order.

Enterprise Art

P.O. Box 2918, Largo, FL 34649
Phone: (813) 536-1492
Fax: (813) 536-3509
Services/Merchandise: They have beads, crafts, jewelry making supplies, wearable art supplies, doll parts, kits, needlework supplies, paints, books, and general craft supplies.
Payment Options: Check, Money Order, MC, Visa, Discover
Shipping Options: UPS, U.S. Postal Service
Other Information: Enterprise Art considers their company the U.S. leader in quality costume jewelry and craft supplies. They have a large research and development staff who constantly keep up with trends, then create new project ideas and kits to meet the demand. They manufacture and package their own products and pass the savings on to their customers. Their motto is "Quality Product At A Great Price".

They are holding a 1996 sweepstakes; call for more information.
Author's Note: Enterprise Art sent some samples from their various product lines. They sent jewelry making supplies, a bow maker, and some Indian crafts supplies.

My partner, Gerard, was very enthusiastic about their American Indian craft kits. He said they are very easy to use, the instructions are clear, and it took very little time for him to create an interesting piece of artwork. He originally created it for a friend, but now he's not sure he wants to part with it.
Catalog: Free upon request.

Eric's Press & Design & Sew Patterns

P.O. Box 5222, Salem, OR 97304
Phone: (503) 364-6285 (Wholesale orders only. For retail information, please write.)
Fax: (503) 391-1639
Services/Merchandise: They have workshops, patterns, books, a newsletter, and videos. Their service is excellent; each order is shipped the day after receipt.
Payment Options: Check, Money Order

Shipping Options: UPS, U.S. Postal Service
Minimum Order: No minimum order.
Other Information: They are committed to sharing their enthusiasm for exploring innovative techniques in fabrics and clothing in their Design & Sew Pattern line. They promise you fresh, timeless styles and easy construction with detailed directions and illustrations that are beyond the direction sheets of most other patterns. They give the sewer room to be creative, to get involved and make choices for unique garments. As you sew each pattern, notice the imaginative options and ideas for using the same pattern to create other designs.

They also have a bi-monthly newsletter, *The Good News Rag*, for $8 annually.
Special Discounts/Offers: 10% discount on first order with the mention of *Sew Far Sew Good*.
Author's Note: Their patterns provide very clean, easy designs with a contemporary flair and plenty of room for embellishment!

Exotic-Thai Silks

252 State Street, Los Altos, CA 94022
Phone: (415) 948-8611
Fax: (415) 948-3426
Services/Merchandise: They have silk fabrics, including habotai, crepe, charmeuse, dupioni, bridal satin, chiffon, Thai, velvet, shantung, handpainted, and more. They also have a fabric club, which offer four mailings per year.
Payment Options: Check, Money Order, MC, Visa, Amex
Minimum Order: ½ yard
Membership Dues: $20 Fabric Club (4 mailings per year)
Membership Benefits: Members have first access to closeout sales and new arrivals.
Other Information: They have been serving the home sewer and dressmaker for 30 years.
Special Discounts/Offers: 10% discount on first order with the mention of *Sew Far Sew Good*. Discounts to dressmakers and artists. Wholesale to qualified businesses.
Catalog: Free brochure upon request.

Extra Special Products Corp.

125 12th Street, Greenville, OH 45331
Phone: (513) 548-9388, (800) 648-5945
Fax: (513) 548-9580
Services/Merchandise: They have quilting notions and tools, copper sheets and shapes, jewelry findings, transfers with foil, stencil templates, Ultrasuede shapes, flex-o-mirro, and razzles.

Payment Options: Check, Money Order, COD
Shipping Options: UPS, U.S. Postal Service, FedEx
Minimum Order: Wholesale $50.
Other Information: They ship orders within 24 hours of receipt of order.
Special Discounts/Offers: 10% discount on first order with the mention of *Sew Far Sew Good*. Free freight net $100.
Catalog: Free upon request.

F & W Publications

1507 Dana Avenue, Cinicinnati, OH 45207
Phone: (513) 531-2690, ext. 593
Services/Merchandise: They carry the books *Creative Bedroom Decorating*, *Make Costumes*, and *Teddy Bear Sourcebook*.
Payment Options: Check, Money Order, MC, Visa
Shipping Options: UPS

The Fabric Carr

P.O. Box 32120, San Jose, CA 95152
Phone: (408) 929-1651
Services/Merchandise: They carry videos, books, fine sewing notions, and *The Fabric Carr* newsletter.
Payment Options: MC, Visa
Shipping Options: UPS, U.S. Postal Service
Minimum Order: No minimum order.
Other Information: The Fabric Carr also offers Sew Weeks with Bobbie Carr throughout the year. The topics cover most aspects of couture sewing and pattern creation.

The Fabric Center

485 Electric Avenue, Fitchburg, MA 01420
Phone: (508) 343-4402
Fax: (508) 343-8139
Services/Merchandise: They have hundreds of upholstery fabrics and trims.
Payment Options: Check, Money Order, MC, Visa
Shipping Options: UPS
Minimum Order: One yard.
Author's Note: For $2, you will receive a 160+ page, full-color catalog with hundreds of fabrics and trims. If you like to decorate your home, or just love the look of upholstery fabric for couture effects, this is the catalog for you.
Catalog: $2

Accurate yardages...

If you regularly need more or less fabric than a pattern recommends, due to a dowager's hump, protruding tummy, or because you are petite or tall, keep track of your fabric needs by marking each patterns envelope with the correct yardage for future reference.

Fabric Collections

919 Orange Avenue, Suite 100, Winter Park, FL 32789

Phone: (407) 740-7737

Services/Merchandise: They have designer fashion fabrics from New York and Europe, silk and rayon Bemberg linings, industry shoulder pads, industry interfacings, Burda patterns, and beautiful buttons. They have a large selection of silk in a variety of weights and designer prints, linens, lightweight wools from Chanel and Armani, and companion rayons for extended wardrobes.

Other Information: They have nationally known guest speakers several times a year. They also offer classes and private sales.

Special Discounts/Offers: ASG members receive 10% off regular purchases.

Fabric Complements, Inc.

7689 Lakeville Highway, Petaluma, CA 94954

Phone: (800) 828-6561

Fax: (707) 778-1729

Services/Merchandise: They have the finest quality fabrics, linings, and interfacings, and provide very personalized and fast service. Large swatches are provided every six weeks to their club members. Their *Insights* newsletter provides pertinent fashion information quarterly.

Payment Options: MC, Visa

Shipping Options: UPS, U.S. Postal Service

Minimum Order: No minimum order.

Membership Dues: $50 per year or $25 for six months.

Membership Benefits: Members receive swatches of fine quality fabrics with great coordinates.

Other Information: Fabric Complements, Inc., has been in business for six years and provides a jewel box collection of the finest fabrics for the woman who wants quality.

Special Discounts/Offers: 20% discount to professional dressmakers with a resale number.

Fabric Gallery

146 West Grand River Avenue, Williamston, MI 48895

Phone: (517) 655-4573

Services/Merchandise: They have very fine lines of imported and domestic silks, wools, cottons, blends, and synthetics. They offer over 2,500 styles of designer buttons, bridal fabrics and laces, beaded and sequined appliqués, designer buckles, and trims. Fine cotton shirtings are a specialty. They also have a wide selection of books on garment construction, fashion history, dyeing, surface design, and other topics.

Payment Options: Check, Money Order, MC, Visa, Discover

Shipping Options: UPS, U.S. Postal Service

Minimum Order: One yard.

Other Information: Fabric Gallery offers a specialty swatch service, and they will send one or two swatches of specific fabrics you request. They also offer swatch sets of silks, wool gabardines, and cotton shirtings. Each set is $3, or you can get all three for $10.

They also offer seamstress referrals, a knowledgeable staff, folkwear patterns, button and belt coverings, fabric coatings, and many fabrics from around the world.

Author's Note: Upon receiving the three swatch sets from Fabric Gallery, I was very pleased with their selection. The silk set had beautiful colors in varied weaves and weights, all of high quality. The wool gabardines also had several weaves and a good variety of solid colors. The cotton shirtings were also very impressive, once again with a wide variety of colors, and good quality. I would love to visit their retail store.

Fabric Mart

511 Penn Avenue, Sinking Spring, PA 19608

Phone: (800) 242-3695

Fabric Temptations

942 G Street, Arcata, CA 95521 (in the Northeast corner of the plaza)

Phone: (707) 822-7782

Services/Merchandise: They concentrate on natural fibers from around the world and carry cotton, silk, rayon, wool, linen, and many blends in their 1,900 square foot store.

Payment Options: Check, Money Order, MC, Visa

Shipping Options: UPS, U.S. Postal Service

Minimum Order: No minimum order.

Special Discounts/Offers: 10% discount on first order with the mention of *Sew Far Sew Good*.

Author's Note: Fabric Temptations sent me four handwritten pages, packed with information that you will find in the product listings section of this book. The owner is very interested in her business and willing to work with all customers to ensure that they are satisfied with their selection. She offers washing instructions, information on changes in fabrics when they are washed, and she makes unique products available for her customers.

They also have a bead store and a yarn shop within a block of their store.

Catalog: $4 for a generous swatch pack tailored to your request. For example, you can ask for all Liberty of London, Guatemalan ikats, or wool flannels.

Fabrics Unlimited

5015 Columbia Pike, Arlington, VA 22204

Phone: (703) 671-0324

Fax: (703) 671-0324

Services/Merchandise: They specialize in better dress fabrics and have many current season selections from European designer cutting rooms and U.S. designers. They carry many unusual prints, mostly in natural fibers, including Swiss, Italian, French, Abraham, Bucol, and more. All fibers are carried year round. Mail orders are handled on a per request basis. Customer service is their specialty, and they can process group orders by mail (i.e., bridal parties, choral groups, etc.). They have great buttons, French laces, and Ultrasuede for $37.99 per yard!

Payment Options: Check, Money Order, MC, Visa, Amex, Discover

Shipping Options: UPS, U.S. Postal Service

Membership Benefits: 10% discount to any valid club.

Other Information: They have been doing business for 35 years in the same location. If you request swatches of specific materials for a mail order, they will send them to you at no charge. Ultrasuede sample cards are available for $5 each, which is refunded if you order from Fabrics Unlimited.

Special Discounts/Offers: 10% discount on first order with the mention of _Sew Far Sew Good_. Student discounts (design and sewing majors) and professional discounts.

Fabulous Fit

P.O. Box 29326, San Francisco, CA 94129

Phone: (415) 441-9066

Fax: (415) 441-0994

Services/Merchandise: Fabulous Fit (pat. pend.) is a series of 15 contoured foam pads and a lycra bodysuit that work with any dressform to duplicate many realistic body shapes on the same form. They also offer a dressform that is manufactured with a very sturdy cast iron base and a pinnable body. Their kit is $65 plus $9.95 for shipping and handling. The dressform and kit are $235 plus $18.95 for shipping and handling.

Payment Options: Check, Money Order, MC, Visa

Shipping Options: UPS, U.S. Postal Service

Fairfield Processing Corporation
Wholesale Only

88 Rose Hill Avenue, P.O. Box 1130, Danbury, CT 06813-1130

Services/Merchandise: Fairfield is the manufacturer of Poly-fil® brand top-quality polyester products. Their long list of products includes: Poly-fil® polyester fiberfill, Poly-fil® Supreme fiberfill, poly-Pellets®, Soft Touch® pillow inserts, and Pop-in-Pillow® forms. They are also the manufacturers of a wide variety of quilt battings, beginning with their needlepunched line of battings: Poly-fil® Traditional® 100% polyester, Poly-fil Ultra Loft® 100% polyester, and their newest batting, Soft Touch® 100% Cotton Batting. They also have bonded battings, including Poly-fil® Low Loft® 100% polyester, Poly-fil® Extra Loft® 100% polyester, Poly-fil® High Loft®, and Poly-fil® Cotton Classic® 80% Cotton, 20% polyester.

Other Information: Fairfield Processing Corporation is a manufacturer whose products are sold by retail stores throughout the country.

Fait Accompli

10700 Sun Tree Cove, Austin, TX 78730

Phone: (800) 340-0115

Famous Labels Fabrics Outlet

P.O. Box 8128, Tacoma, WA 97030

Phone: (503) 666-3187

Fancy Threads/Fancy Threads Custom

57B South Main Street, Newton, NH 03858

Phone: (603) 382-3989

Fax: (603) 382-7608

Services/Merchandise: They have necktie patterns for children and men, classes, and lectures. They also carry a wide variety of interfacing, and they offer counseling on which interfacing to use for your project.

Payment Options: Check, Money Order, MC, Visa

Shipping Options: UPS, U.S. Postal Service, FedEx

Minimum Order: No minimum order.

Membership Benefits: ASG members receive a 10% discount.

Special Discounts/Offers: Free shipping on first order with the mention of _Sew Far Sew Good_. Wholesale to qualified businesses.

Catalog: $1

Fancywork

P.O. Box 130, 2708 Slaterville Road, Slaterville Springs, NY 14881

Phone: (607) 539-6610

Services/Merchandise: They have over 10,000 counted cross-stitch books and patterns, hundreds of evenweave fabrics, floss, metallic threads, and beads.

Payment Options: Check, Money Order, MC, Visa

Shipping Options: U.S. Postal Service

Minimum Order: $10 minimum on credit card orders.

Other Information: Their bi-monthly newsletter is $4 a year, and it includes listings of new books available, new fabrics and accessories, and photos of thousands of books and of the owner's grandchildren

You will receive a "buy 12, get 1 free" book card with your newsletter subscription.

Special Discounts/Offers: There are coupons in the bi-monthly

Skirt styles...

Kilt

newsletter.

Catalog: $2, add $4 for a one-year subscription.

Fancywork and Fashion

4728 Dodge Street, Duluth, MN 55804

Phone: (218) 525-5811, (800) 365-5257

Fax: (218) 525-5811

Services/Merchandise: They have four books with clothing and acces-sory patterns designed for 18" vinyl dolls. The titles are *Best Doll Clothes Book*, *Best Storybook Costumes Book*, *Best Smocking Designs for Dolls*, and *Time Machine: The Modern Girls* (this one also fits porcelain and vinyl doll bodies 16"-23").

Payment Options: Check, Money Order, MC, Visa

Shipping Options: UPS, U.S. Postal Service

Minimum Order: One book or pattern.

Other Information: They also carry a matching cape-patterns set for girls and 18" dolls. Their quarterly newsletter is $10 per year, and it has seasonal clothing and accessory ideas, sewing tips, and more.

Catalog: Send a 9" x 12" SASE with 55¢ postage for a sample newslet-ter and catalog.

Fashion Blueprints

2191 Blossom Valley Drive, San Jose, CA 95124

Phone: (408) 356-5291

Services/Merchandise: They carry patterns that have ethnic styling, and are simple to sew, and come with easy-to-follow directions. Many have craft notes for special techniques that apply to the style. Most styles lend themselves to embellishment techniques by fiber artists. Patterns are multi-sized and easily adjustable for larger sizes. Women's, men's, and children's patterns are in the line, and more will be added within the year. The various style influences are Japanese, Chinese, Mexican, Central American, African, Turkish, Korean, Moroccan, Indian, and more.

Payment Options: Check, Money Order

Shipping Options: UPS, U.S. Postal Service

Minimum Order: No minimum order.

Author's Note: Fashion Blueprints' patterns are simple and have a very stylish look.

Catalog: $2

Fashion Fabrics Club/Natural Fiber Fabrics Direct

10490 Baur Boulevard, St. Louis, MO 63132

Phone: (314) 993-4919, (800) 468-0602

Services/Merchandise: They have fabric from the lines of top designers such as Liz Claiborne, Jones NY, and Polo (Ralph Lauren).

They have silks, linens, cottons, wools, rayons, and blends at a fraction of comparative retail. They also have a swatch club.

Payment Options: Check, Money Order, MC, Visa,

Shipping Options: UPS, U.S. Postal Service

Minimum Order: No minimum order. $5.95 shipping on any order.

Membership Dues: $5 per year for swatch mailings of your requested fabrics.

Membership Benefits: Club members receive nine to twelve swatch mailings per year.

Other Information: Their warehouse outlet is open to the public and contains mail order offerings and sample cuts of many more designer fabrics.

Feathered Star Productions

2151 7th Avenue West, Seattle, WA 98119

Phone: (206) 283-5214

Fax: (206) 283-5214

Services/Merchandise: They are the publisher and distributor of quilting and craft books by Marsha McCloskey, and *Mystery Quilt Singles Patterns* by Judy Hopkins.

Payment Options: Check, Money Order, MC, Visa

Shipping Options: UPS, U.S. Postal Service

Minimum Order: No minimum order for retail. Four items for whole-sale.

Special Discounts/Offers: Discounts are offered seasonally.

Catalog: Free price list upon request.

The Feedsack Club

P.O. Box 4168, Pittsburgh, PA 15202

Phone: (412) 766-3996

Services/Merchandise: They are a club devoted to buying, selling, and collecting early 1900s printed feedsacks and feedsack items such as clothing. They also carry quilts, quilt tops, underwear, toys, feedsacks with logos, floral feedsack, children's clothing, antique and new book-lets and pamphlets, and linens.

Payment Options: Check, Money Order

Shipping Options: UPS, U.S. Postal Service

Membership Dues: $12 for U.S. membership, $18 for an International membership.

Membership Information, Contact:
Jane Clark Staple
P.O. Box 4168
Pittsburgh, PA 15202

Membership Benefits: Members receive a membership list and newsletter.

Fiber Designs

2446 Northwest 35th Terrace, Gainesville, FL 32605
Phone: (352) 373-0681
Services/Merchandise: They have 100% wool rug yarn. The yarn is 3-ply and has 300 yards per pound. The yarn is moth proofed, and it can be custom-dyed to match any samples or grading colors. Samples are available. The wool is $18 per pound plus shipping.
Payment Options: Check
Shipping Options: UPS
Minimum Order: No minimum order for retail sales.
Other Information: Workshops are available on rug weaving and dyeing.
Special Discounts/Offers: Wholesale to qualified businesses and professional weavers.
Catalog: Free upon request.

Fiber Fantasy Knitting Products

6 Hunters Horn Court, Owings Mills, MD 21117
Phone: (410) 363-1160, (800) 242-KNIT
Fax: (410) 581-9525
Services/Merchandise: They have videos and accessories for hand and machine knitting.
Payment Options: Check, Money Order, MC, Visa, Amex, Discover
Minimum Order: One item for retail. Wholesalers please inquire for rates.

Fiber Statements

46 Clinton Street, Sea Cliff, NY 11579
Phone: (516) 676-3342
E-mail: parodgers@aol.com
Services/Merchandise: Pat Rodgers offers videos, and she travels to lecture and teach classes and workshops.
Payment Options: Check, Money Order
Author's Note: I met Pat online on AOL, and she has been nothing but polite and helpful from the start. Her brochure is one of the best I have seen in quite some time, and her class topics and workshops are extensive. I look forward to meeting her someday and seeing her work first-hand.

The Fiber Studio

9 Foster Hill Road, P.O. Box 637, Henniker, NH 03242
Phone: (603) 428-7830
Services/Merchandise: They have unusual yarns for knitters and weavers, spinning wheels, and natural fibers such as silk, alpaca, camel hair, flax, cotton, and a large assortment of wools, both dyed and undyed, for the handspinner. They have natural fiber coned yarns for machine knitters and weavers. Their knitting yarns include brand names, closeouts, and an assortment of handpainted rayons, wools, cottons, mohairs, and chenilles. They also have books, natural and chemical dyes, and buttons for the fiber artist.
Payment Options: MC, Visa
Shipping Options: UPS, U.S. Postal Service
Minimum Order: $15
Other Information: The Fiber Studio, a family business for 20 years, is housed in a 200 year-old barn, located in rural New Hampshire. In addition to the yarns and equipment they sell, they also manufacture wood buttons.

The Fiber Studio specializes in handpainted variegated yarns in many natural fibers. They have a number of artists dyeing the yarns for them, which makes them unique. Unfortunately, these are difficult to accurately portray in a catalog, and they are only sold in the shop.

Their shop also features a line of rayon chenille yarns, which are very popular with weavers, machine knitters, and handknitters. These are included in their sample set.

The books sold by The Fiber Studio include topics in traditional, ethnic, and contemporary knitting, all types of weaving techniques, basketry, fimo, beading, spinning, and dyeing.

They carry beads from around the world, that are available for purchase in their shop.

The fibers available through mail order include Brown Sheep Wools, Classic Elite, Montera, mohairs, cottons, Shetlands, Crystal Palace Monterey, Henry's Attic cottons and wools, chenilles, cotton flakes, 8/2 cottons, silks, pearl cottons and more.
Special Discounts/Offers: Quantity discounts on yarn.
Catalog: Send $1 for a books and equipment catalog, $4 for doll hair fiber samples, $4 for spinning fiber samples, and $5 for yarn samples.

The Fiberfest Magazine/Stony Lonesome Press

P.O. Box 112, Hastings, MI 49058
Phone: (616) 765-3047
Fax: (616) 765-3538
Services/Merchandise: *The Fiberfest Magazine* contains a mixture of articles on fiber crafts, including handspinning, weaving, felting, dyeing of natural fibers such as wool, cotton, linen, angora, mohair, and cashmere, and information about raising fiber-producing animals, processing fibers, making finished products, and marketing.
Payment Options: Check, Money Order, MC, Visa
Shipping Options: U.S. Postal Service
Other Information: The magazine grew out of the Fiberfest Festival, which will celebrate its 13th year in 1996. The magazine is staffed by many of the same experienced people who have, for many years, contributed their time to making the Festival the largest and most well-known fiber gathering of its kind.

The magazine comes four times a year. Subscription prices are: $20 in the U.S., $30 in Canada, $42 to other countries.
Special Discounts/Offers: Wholesale to qualified businesses.
Author's Note: One of the issues I received has a great article about handfelting a pair of slippers with no seams. The article is very clear and shows each step by illustration. This magazine is a great resource for anyone interested in fibers, including spinners, weavers, knitters, and anyone with an inquisitive mind.

Fiesta Yarns

P.O. Box 2548, Corrales, NM 87048
Phone: (505) 897-4485
Fax: (505) 897-4485
E-mail: laboheme@rt66.com
Services/Merchandise: They have hand-dyed natural fibers in exquisite colors. The yarns come in many fibers, including mohair, cotton, wool, rayon, linen, silk, and combinations.
Payment Options: MC, Visa
Minimum Order: $100
Other Information: Color cards are available for $10 each. The company has been in business for 15 years, and emphasizes quality of merchandise and service.

Fire Mountain Gems
Wholesale to the Public

28195 Redwood Highway, Cave Junction, OR 97523
Phone: (800) 423-2319
Fax: (800) 292-3473
Services/Merchandise: They have beads of all makes and sizes, including seed and bugle beads, and Delica beads. They also have jewelry findings, jewelry-making books, fetishes, cabochons, tools, settings, diamonds, beading hoops, threads, and looms.
Payment Options: Check, Money Order, MC, Visa, Amex, Discover, COD
Shipping Options: UPS, U.S. Postal Service
Minimum Order: $50
Other Information: Fire Mountain Gems is a wholesale company that carries thousands of jewelry making supplies and findings. They have the best service around because they go the extra mile for their customers.
Catalog: $5

Fireside Fiberarts

P.O. Box 1195, Port Townsend, WA 98368
Phone: (360) 385-7505

Fax: (360) 437-0733
Services/Merchandise: They make Jack Looms, tapestry looms, and weaving accessories. They are innovators in custom-made equipment that makes weaving more comfortable and efficient. They also offer furniture that reflects quality craftsmanship using cherry, and/or walnut. They will work with a weaver to repair or upgrade a loom.
Payment Options: Call for information.
Shipping Options: UPS, U.S. Postal Service, Freight.
Minimum Order: No minimum order.
Other Information: Fireside Fiberarts has intentionally kept their business small to continue creating the quality looms that are their specialty. They've been making looms for 23 years, and all of their products are warranted for two years.
Catalog: $3

Fishmans Fabrics

1101 South Des Plaines Street, Chicago, IL 60607
Phone: (312) 922-7250
Fax: (312) 922-7402
Services/Merchandise: They offer a custom swatch service that features an extensive selection of silks, linens, cottons, and velvet. Everything for the bride, the mother of the bride, and bridesmaids. All they ask is that your requests be as specific as possible. There is no charge for samples.
Payment Options: Check, MC, Visa, American Express, Discover
Shipping Options: UPS
Minimum Order: No minimum order.
Other Information: They've been in business for over 80 years.
Special Discounts/Offers: 10% off first order with the mention of *Sew Far Sew Good*.

Fiskars, Inc.
Wholesale Only

7811 West Stewart Avenue, P.O. Box 8027, Wausau, WI 54402-8027
Phone: (715) 842-2091
Fax: (715) 848-5528
WWW: http://www.fiskars.com
Services/Merchandise: They have an extensive inventory of scissors, rotary cutters, mats, rulers, rotary paper trimmers, rotary blades, craft tools, snips, paper edgers, razor knives, compasses, protractors, student rulers, dictionaries, how-to books, children's creativity paints, sponges, stencils, and paint brushes.
Payment Options: Approved credit
Minimum Order: $1,000 to open an account. $750 for each re-order.
Other Information: Fiskars has been in business since 1649. They are a major supplier of quality products for the office, student, educational, crafts, sewing, quilting, and home/housewares markets.

Fittingly Sew® (Bartley Software, Inc.)

72 Robertson Road, Box 26122, Nepean, ON K2H 9R6, Canada
Phone: (613) 829-6488, (800) 661-5209
Fax: (613) 829-6488
E-mail: 72133.3102@compuserve.com
Services/Merchandise: *Fittingly Sew®* is an innovative software program for Macintosh and Microsoft Windows. It's used for fitting and designing clothing patterns. You can start with either a standard-sized or a custom-fitted pattern, then use on-line tools rather than erasers and pencils, save a copy at any stage, make more changes on-line, then print the copy you like most.

When you are designing, you can do the following, add fullness and pleats, change the shape of curves, transfer darts, lengthen or shorten pieces, make facings, and create yokes. You can set seam allowances from 0-2 inches (0-5 cm), and they are automatically adjusted whenever a piece changes shape. You can also plan layouts and determine fabric requirements right on the screen.

Fittingly Sew® prints to desktop printers using standard paper sizes. Any   portion or all of a pattern can be printed. The pages are taped or pinned together to get a full-sized pattern, which includes seam allowances, straights of grain, and piece information.
Payment Options: Check, Money Order, MC, Visa, Amex, School Postal Orders
Shipping Options: Courier
Minimum Order: One unit.
Other Information: Demonstration programs are available for both the Macintosh and Windows versions. These demos provide most of the functionality of full programs. You can create patterns consisting of up to five pieces based on the pants or skirts slopers. With the demo versions, you can print the patterns but you can't save them.
Special Discounts/Offers: Wholesale to qualified businesses. Educational discounts available with a minimum purchase of two programs. Call for a complimentary copy of the demo version.
Author's Note: I agree with Susan Bennet's summation of Fittingly Sew®, as it appeared in *Threads Magazine*, September '95.

"If you enjoy both designing your own patterns and working on your computer, then *Fittingly Sew®* is a powerful choice."

Fouché Patterns

2121 Bryant Street, San Francisco, CA 94107

Four Seasons Knitting Products

143 Ashdale Avenue, Winnipeg, MB R2H 1R1, Canada
Phone: (204) 233-4446
Fax: (204) 231-3389
Services/Merchandise: They are a mail order source of books and videos for handknitters, and they have a growing selection of items for spinners. They carry Addi Turbo needles and yarn from the Shetland Islands. Kits and patterns are available, as are design tools for knitters.
Payment Options: MC, Visa
Shipping Options: U.S. Postal Service
Other Information: They are a mail order business that began in 1993. They supply an excellent range of items for knitters and are always adding to their selection.
Special Discounts/Offers: 10% discount on first order with the mention of *Sew Far Sew Good*.
Catalog: Free upon request.

Frank Williams' Hemp Co.

5806 North Vancouver, Portland, OR 97217
Phone: (503) 286-4149
Services/Merchandise: They have hemp spinning fiber, threads, soft twine, yarns, and fabrics in natural and 24 organically dyed colors. They also carry the book *Hemp! For Textile Artists*.
Payment Options: Check, Money Order, MC, Visa
Shipping Options: UPS, U.S. Postal Service
Minimum Order: No minimum order.
Catalog: A selection of samples is $2, and a color chart is $10.

Fresh Water Pearl Button Company

622 Locust Place, Sewickley, PA 15143
Phone: (412) 741-4201
Fax: (412) 741-4202
E-mail: 73562.1377@compuserve.com
Services/Merchandise: They have the widest assortment of genuine freshwater pearl buttons in the U.S. This selection includes shirt buttons, fish eyes, self-shanks, carved buttons, and sequins. Buttons are available in ivory and nine hand-dyed colors.
Payment Options: Check, Money order
Minimum Order: No minimum order.
Other Information: Carved earlier this century from Midwestern river shells, these uniquely lustrous buttons feature individual variations in texture and grain. Today, when buttons are machine-stamped by the thousands from plastic sheets, freshwater pearls provide an exquisite alternative. These buttons are the perfect choice for fine silk, wool, cotton, and linen. There is a $4 shipping charge.
Special Discounts/Offers: Buttons are sold in bulk to retail and mail order customers and on printed cards for sale in stores. Vendors with a resale number qualify for wholesale prices. Individuals who help them land a retail account in their favorite fine fabric store or yarn shop will receive a $30 credit on their next mail order purchase.
Author's Note: These people are very friendly and enthusiastic about

---

Acid-washing silk...

Finish the raw edges of your silk charmeuse, broadcloth, or china silk by serging or using fray check.

Fill your washing machine with hot water and add 3 cups of vinegar. Allow the vinegar to mix with the water, then put the fabric in the water. Allow it to be agitated for 15 minutes, then run it through the rinse and spin cycles.

Dry the silk completely. If the sueded effect is not noticeable enough for you, you may repeat the entire process up to three times.

Remember, silk may shrink, so allow extra yardage when acid-washing.

Beaded twisted fringe...

String all the beads for both sides of the twisted fringe onto your thread. Lay your project down on the table. Drop your needle and grab your thread just below the strung beads. Now, just roll the thread between your thumb and fingers several times until the thread starts to "kink" up.

To see if you have enough twists in the fringe, pick up your project and bring the fringe thread up to the bottom of the bag and hold it there (don't let go of the string—or it will untwist). The beaded string of beads should twist all by itself.

If there isn't enough twist in the fringe, twist the thread some more.

If you want a larger bead at the bottom of the fringe, string half of the beads, a large bead, a small bead, then bring the needle back through the large bead and thread the other half of the beads. Now you just twist, and you will get the same result, only with a large bead decorating the end of your fringe.

Tip provided by: Barbara L. Grainger Enterprises Page 246

their work, and their T-shirt has a great Fifties design on it. Their buttons are beautiful, with a luster that cannot be duplicated in stamped plastic. Just the perfect touch of class.
Catalog: A sample card is $15 and includes 15 individual buttons in a variety of styles, sizes, and colors.

Friends Patterns
310 Snyder Branch Road, Scottsville, KY 42164-8720
Services/Merchandise: They offer patterns of a simple and plain nature, complete with illustrated instructions. They have modest clothing patterns for women's dresses, aprons, slips, bloomers, tights, cloaks, coats, head coverings, and bonnets. For men, there are shirts, trousers, broad fall pants, overalls, coveralls, coats, coat-type shirts, and vests. The same variety is available for children, as are patterns for Amish quilts and dolls.
Payment Options: Check, Money Order
Shipping Options: U.S. Postal Service
Other Information: This company states that its purpose is to offer modest and plain patterns in keeping with Amish and Mennonite traditions. The patterns are for functional clothing and are printed on sturdy paper—not tissue paper—so they can be used many times.
Special Discounts/Offers: Wholesale to qualified businesses.
Catalog: $1

Frostline Kits
The Original Sewing Kit Company
2525 River Road, Grand Junction, CO 81505
Phone: (303) 241-0155, (800) KITS USA
Fax: (303) 242-9312
E-mail: frostline@qli.backboard.com
WWW: http://www.backboard.com/~frostline
Services/Merchandise: They have kits for making your family's outdoor work, play, or travel clothes. The kits are designed by people who spend time out of doors.
Payment Options: Check, Money Order, MC, Visa, Amex, Discover, COD
Other Information: All of Frostline's kits are pre-cut, and include everything you need (even thread) to make a professional, high quality product at a fraction of the cost of store purchased items.
Catalog: $2

G Street Fabrics
11854 Rockville Pike, Rockville, MD 20852
Phone: (301) 231-8998
Services/Merchandise: They have fabrics, buttons, an education/con-

sulting service, quilting supplies and newsletter, tours, classes, notions, patterns, books (over 4,000 titles), fabric covered belts and buttons, and custom labels.
Payment Options: Check, Money Order, MC, Visa, Amex, Discover
Shipping Options: UPS, U.S. Postal Service
Minimum Order: $5
Membership Dues: You can join G Street's club for $40 per year.
Membership Benefits: You get the Notion of the Month at a 25% discount. You also get 720 swatches per year and special notice of sales.
Catalog: Free brochures upon request.

Gaelic College Craft Shop
Box 9, Baddeck-Victoria Co., NS B0E 1B0, Canada
Phone: (902) 295-3441
Fax: (902) 295-2912
Services/Merchandise: They have about 200 bolts of various tartans imported from Scotland, as well as other yard goods. They also have many Gaelic items, including jewelry, kilt pins, and more.
Payment Options: Check, Money Order, COD, MC, Visa, Amex
Minimum Order: No minimum order.

Garden of Beadin'
752 Redwood Drive, Garberville, CA 95542
Phone: (707) 923-9120

Gettinger Feather Corp.
16 West 36th Street, New York, NY 10018
Phone: (212) 695-9470
Fax: (212) 695-9471
Services/Merchandise: They have feathers and feather products, including feather boas, feather fans, ostrich plumes, peacock feathers, and more. Their feathers are perfect for crafts, dress trade, millinery, fishing, etc.
Payment Options: Check, Money Order
Shipping Options: UPS
Minimum Order: $25
Special Discounts/Offers: Wholesale to retailers.

Ghee's
2620 Centenary, #2-250, Shreveport, LA 71104
Phone: (318) 226-1701
Fax: (318) 226-1781
Services/Merchandise: They have handbag patterns and hardware,

such as frames and locksets. They also have vest patterns and books on fabric embellishment and manipulation.
Payment Options: Check, Money Order, MC, Visa
Shipping Options: UPS, U.S. Postal Service
Author's Note: *Texture With Textiles* and *More... Texture With Textiles* by Linda McGehee are both great books full of innovative techniques, inspirational photographs, and fun project ideas. If you have the embellishment bug, these books are a great way to learn a variety of techniques.
Catalog: Free upon request.

Ginger's Needleworks
905 East Gloria Switch Road, Lafayette, LA 70507
Phone: (318) 232-7847
Services/Merchandise: They have quilting supplies and fabrics, books, patterns, and yarns.
Payment Options: Check, Money Order, MC, Visa, Amex, Discover
Shipping Options: UPS, U.S. Postal Service
Catalog: $2

Ginsco Trims
242 West 38th Street, New York, NY 10018
Phone: (212) 719-4871

The Glass Giraffe
110 Depot Street, Waynesville, NC 28786
Phone: (704) 456-6665
Fax: (704) 456-6665
E-mail: GlassGiraf@aol.com, or NXUB32A@prodigy.com
WWW: http://www.crescendoweb.com/GlassGiraf/index.html
Services/Merchandise: They make torchworked hot glass beads, marbles, and buttons, and they specialize in large and dichroic beads. They have hot glass supplies, retail and wholesale. They also teach hot glass beadmaking across the country. They would be willing to teach for any organization, so please call for more information.
Payment Options: Check, MC, Visa
Shipping Options: UPS, U.S. Postal Service
Minimum Order: No minimum order, but there is a $5 surcharge for orders under $20.
Other Information: The Glass Giraffe also teaches stained glass making, and they sell stained glass supplies wholesale and retail.
Special Discounts/Offers: Specials are posted on their home page and mailed quarterly to their mailing list. Wholesale to qualified businesses.
Author's Note: Someone gave rave reviews of the Glass Giraffe and their products on the Prodigy Beading Board.

The Gleaners Yarn Barn
P.O. Box 1191, Canton, GA 30114
Phone: (770) 479-5083
Services/Merchandise: They have first quality mill-end yarns at low mill-end prices. Yarns are 2- and 3-ply, and come in natural, synthetic, and blended fibers, and in various sizes and types. New items are added constantly.
Payment Options: Check or Money Order
Shipping Options: UPS, U.S. Postal Service, Freight
Minimum Order: $15
Membership Dues: $3 for current set of samples and mailings for one year.
Other Information: They have 21 years of satisfied customers behind them.

GLP International
153 South Dean Street, Englewood, NJ 07631-3183
Phone: (201) 871-1010
Fax: (201) 871-0870
Services/Merchandise: They have magazines published by Burda and Gruner & Jahr on many subjects, including sewing, knitting, and needlecrafts. The magazines contain patterns, charts, iron-on transfers, and detailed instructions.
Payment Options: Check, Money Order, MC, Visa, Amex
Shipping Options: UPS, U.S. Postal Service
Minimum Order: No minimum order.
Other Information: The magazines are published in English, Spanish, and other languages. Call for publishing dates of annual issues.
Special Discounts/Offers: Wholesale to qualified businesses; call for details.
Author's Note: Although I have been familiar with GLP for quite some time, the range of their patterns and publications still astounds me.

Goldblatt Industrial Sewing Machine Company
1511 Milwaukee Avenue, Chicago, IL 60622
Phone: (312) 486-1784, (800) 356-1784
Fax: (312) 486-2665
Services/Merchandise: They have new and used industrial and household sewing machines, sergers, blind stitchers, and other specialized sewing equipment, including industrial steam irons, cutters, and household presses.
Payment Options: Money Order, MC, Visa, Amex, Discover
Shipping Options: UPS, COD
Minimum Order: No minimum order.
Other Information: They have been serving Chicagoland for over 65 years.
Special Discounts/Offers: 50% off CM-500 Portable Blindstitch.

A few additions to the previous note...

If you bring your needle back into the same bead your fringe started from, your fringe will become too crowded. Try bringing the thread back through the next bead.

Also, try using thin thread and doubling it when making fringe. The two threads will twist around each other much easier than one thread, and when you drop the needle to twist the thread, it can't fall off.

A little beeswax on your fingers will make twisting the thread easier.

Tip provided by: Roni Hennen Prodigy member, beading teacher and enthusiast.

Another road to twisted fringe...

Thread needles on both ends of a string at least three times longer than you want your final product.

1. String a bead on each needle, slide them to the bottom, and tie a right-over-left knot.

2. String a bead on each needle, slide them to the bottom, and tie a right-over-left knot.

And so on.

It is very time consuming, but for the perfect finish to a project that has already taken time, it is beautiful.

Tip provided by: Chris Phillips Prodigy member, beading enthusiast.

Good Wood

Route 2, Box 447A, Bethel, VT 05032
Phone: (802) 234-5534
Services/Merchandise: They have a variety of high quality, small weaving looms, warping boards, and other accessories. All looms are particularly suited to new weavers, young weavers, and as travel looms for anyone and everyone. They have Good Wood InchWorms for making knitted cord and weaving project kits for use with Good Wood looms.
Payment Options: Check, MC, Visa
Shipping Options: UPS, U.S. Postal Service
Minimum Order: No minimum order.
Other Information: All Good Wood products are carefully designed to work well and be pleasing to look at. Looms are sanded smooth and finished with non-toxic oil (except for the loom kit, which the customer finishes). Good Wood's magic heddle is designed to make weaving easy and fast. The magic heddle enables the weaver to warp the loom without threading the warp through holes or slots. This way there is very little or no warp waste.

They use only native hardwood (except for the loom kit, which may include pine). There are no plastic parts. The weaving projects contain only natural fibers, and they are excellent for new weavers. Good Wood InchWorms are available to make knitted cord with a circumference of 3, 4 or 5 stitches. All instructions are clear and easy to follow.

Loom prices range from $23 for a small frame loom kit to $290 for their cherry Slant Loom.
Special Discounts/Offers: Quantity discounts to retail customers. Wholesale to qualified businesses.
Author's Note: I had fun with the four-pin InchWorm they sent me. After I got the hang of it, my cord even began to look like the cord sample they sent me.

Gossamer Threads & More

575 Fourth Avenue, Durango, CO 81301
Phone: (970) 247-2822
Services/Merchandise: Lace knitting is their specialty. They have needles from size 7-0 to size 35, lace books, yarn, cob web, and lace lots. They also have the Lucky 15 Club, which you can call to about.
Payment Options: Check, Money Order, MC, Visa, COD
Shipping Options: FedEx
Special Discounts/Offers: 10% discount on first order with the mention of *Sew Far Sew Good*.
Catalog: Free upon request.

Gramma's Graphics

Department SFSG-P6, 20 Birling Gap, Fairport, NY 14450-3916
Phone: (716) 223-4309
Fax: (716) 223-4789
E-mail: 70671.321@compuserve.com
Services/Merchandise: Discover the secret of Sun Printing right in your own back yard. They offer kits to blueprint on material. Anything opaque can be printed: a treasured family photo, a pressed fern or flower, lace, a wedding invitation, a favorite verse, a college seal, a feather, a child's drawing—you name it, you can print it. Along with the original, complete Sun Print kits, they offer refill kits.
Payment Options: Check, Money Order
Shipping Options: UPS, U.S. Postal Service
Minimum Order: No minimum order for retail. 24 kits for wholesale.
Other Information: Personalizing the fabric you work with results in unique quilts, pillows, T-shirts, wallhangings, placemats, handbags, doll faces, etc. The applications are as broad as your imagination.

Gramma's Graphics has been in business since 1980, when the owner made an Heirloom Portrait Quilt to celebrate her grandmother's 100th birthday. The process dates back to 1842, and she has had great fun re-introducing it to today's quilters, sewing enthusiasts, schools, scouts, and senior groups.

The Sun Prints are unconditionally guaranteed.
Special Discounts/Offers: Wholesale to qualified businesses.
Catalog: $1 and a SASE.

Grand View Country Store

U.S. Route 2, Randolph, NH 03570
Phone: (603) 466-5715, (800) 898-5715
Services/Merchandise: They have 100% wool yarn from their own sheep, plus hundreds of other beautiful yarns, knitting classes, weekend Knit-Ins, and a newsletter/mini-catalog sent out twice per year.
Payment Options: Check, Money Order, MC, Visa
Minimum Order: No minimum order.
Other Information: tHey offer Two Days in a Yarn Shop - Mountains, Muffins, and Mohair! Knitters arrive Friday evening in time for a get-acquainted reception. After spending the night in their cozy guest rooms, knitters are served a New England breakfast, and then spend the entire day shopping for yarn and projects, and participating in mini-workshops of their choice: Fair Isle Knitting, Circular Knitting, The Anatomy of a Sock, Intarsia, Fleece-Stuffed Mittens, Cable Knitting, Lace, and more.

The neighboring town of Gorham has many restaurants where knitters can dine on Saturday evening. Night-owls are invited to knit and socialized as late as they wish before turning in. Sunday morning, after another home-cooked breakfast, knitters may finish or get help with individual projects before heading for home.
Special Discounts/Offers: 10% discount on first order with the mention of *Sew Far Sew Good*. Wholesale to qualified businesses.
Author's Note: See the Company Appendix for a knitted vest pattern

from Grand View Country Store.
Catalog: $3 for the first year, and you will continue to receive them with further purchases.

Granny's Quilts
4509 West Elm Street, McHenry, IL 60050
Phone: (815) 385-5107
Services/Merchandise: They have 2,500 bolts of cotton fabrics. All new quilting books are carried in stock, as well as many sewing books. They have hundreds of patterns for quilts, dolls, and projects, as well as silk ribbons, books, supplies, Viking and Pfaff sewing machines and sergers and all accessories, and machine embroidery supplies. They also have the following threads: silky YLI, Swiss Metrosene, and Madeira. They have an extensive variety of quilting and sewing notions.
Payment Options: Check, Money Order, MC, Visa, Discover
Shipping Options: UPS, U.S. Postal Service
Minimum Order: $15
Other Information: They have 20 years in the quilting and sewing retail business.
Special Discounts/Offers: 10% discount on first order with the mention of *Sew Far Sew Good*.

Grant Moser
(Moser Documentation Services)
316A Pinos Altos St., Silver City, NM 88061.
Phone: (505) 388-2486
E-mail: GrantMoser@aol.com
Services/Merchandise: Grant is a writer, editor, and designer who has been freelancing in desktop publishing for five years. During that time, he has designed, written, and/or edited eighteen books, ranging in length from 20 to 2200 pages. Most of this work has involved user/reference manuals for interactive CD authoring tools and systems, but he has also created style manuals, a user/reference manual for an on-line service for audio/video repair technicians, and edited *Sew Far Sew Good*.

In addition to his freelance work, Grant has experience in laying out, writing, and editing a consumer health publication, and writing a full array of legal documents (he used to be a lawyer). In the past two years, he has won two Awards of Excellence in juried competitions sponsored by the Society for Technical Communication.

If you have any kind of document or publication that needs designing, writing, or editing, Grant can help you.
Other Information: Work rates and payment methods are negotiable.
Author's Note: I have known Grant for years, and I wholeheartedly recommend him. His editing feats in Sew Far Sew Good were nothing short of miraculous. He took a half-formed idea from gibberish to a well thought-out publication in less than a quarter of the time he should

have had.

Great Divide Weaving School
Box 9018, Divide, CO 80814
Phone: (719) 687-3249
Services/Merchandise: They offer tapestry weaving classes in one-and two-week sessions.
Payment Options: Check, Money Order
Tuition Cost: $525 for a one-week course, $1,000 for a two-week course.
Other Information: Tuition includes all the materials you will need for your course, lodging, and one meal per day.
Special Discounts/Offers: $50 off for those who attend school with a friend or spouse.
Catalog: Free brochure upon request.

Great Northern Weaving
P.O. Box 462, Kalamazoo, MI 49004
Phone: (616) 341-9752, (800) 370-7235
Fax: (616) 341-9525
Services/Merchandise: They have supplies for rug weaving, including fabric by the pound, warps, rag roping, fillers, and fuzzy looper natural and colored. They have braiding supplies, including Braidaid tools, reel ad, and wool and cotton fabric by the pound. They have crochet supplies, including fabric by the pound, cotton yarn, and discount bulk yarns. They also offer bulk yarns in mixed fibers, wools, and books on weaving, braiding, and rug crocheting.
Payment Options: Check, MC, Visa
Shipping Options: UPS, COD
Minimum Order: No minimum order, but a $3.50 handling charge for orders under $40.
Other Information: Great Northern Weaving has been providing fast service to weavers, crocheters, and sewers for 10 years. Their prices are discounted, and all prices include shipping.

Mail order is their specialty, but they now have a store at 1414 West F Street open Mon. - Fri., 9 - 4.
Catalog: $2 for a price list and sample card, which is refundable with purchase. A price list only is free.

The Green Pepper
1285 River Road, Eugene, OR 97404
Phone: (541) 689-3292
Fax: (541) 689-3591
Services/Merchandise: They have patterns, fabrics, and hardware and zippers for outerwear, sportswear, and bags. Their fabrics include, ultrex, water-repellent nylons, and polartec fleeces. The patterns are

---

Cutting decorative cording without fraying...

To prevent decorative cording from fraying, wrap transparent tape firmly around the area to be cut. Use a piece of tape wide enough so that you can cut through the middle of it, leaving half on the other piece of cording. Leave the tape in place until you have sewn the cording onto your project.

Tip provided by: Prym-Dritz Corporation Page 325

Organize your space...

Closet organizers with clear plastic fronts are great for keeping your sewing room organized. They come in various sizes and shapes. A shoe organizer will hold smaller fabric pieces and notions, while a sweater organizer holds larger yardages of fabrics.

easy to make and they're designed for the home sewer.
Payment Options: Check, Money Order, MC, Visa
Shipping Options: UPS, U.S. Postal Service
Minimum Order: No minimum order.

Greenberg & Hammer, Inc.

24 West 57th Street, New York, NY 10019
Phone: (212) 246-2835
Fax: (212) 765-8475
Services/Merchandise: They have notions and dressmakers supplies, and a large selection of the basic tools and supplies needed to create a professional looking garment.
Payment Options: MC, Visa, Amex
Shipping Options: UPS, U.S. Postal Service, FedEx, Airborne Express
Minimum Order: $10
Other Information: Greenberg & Hammer contributes samples and information to authors doing research for articles related to sewing. Please contact Frank Piazza for more information.
Special Discounts/Offers: 10% discount on first order with the mention of *Sew Far Sew Good*.

Grey Owl Indian Craft

132-05 Merrick Boulevard, Jamaica, NY 11434-0468
Phone: (718) 341-4000
Fax: (718) 527-6000
E-mail: tke315@aol.com
Services/Merchandise: They offer American Indian crafts and supplies.
Payment Options: MC, Visa, Amex, Discover
Minimum Order: $20
Catalog: $3 for a 200-page color catalog.

Gutcheon Patchworks

917 Pacific Avenue #305, Tacoma, WA 98402
Phone: (206) 383-3047

The Gypsy's Bead Shoppe

117 West State Street (Route 38), Geneva, IL 60134
Phone: (708) 208-1663
Fax: (708) 208-1670
E-mail: Coming soon!
Services/Merchandise: They have 200 colors of beads in many styles

and materials, including seed beads (Czech and Japanese), bugle beads, filled beads, Austrian crystals, semi-precious stones, and Fimo. They also carry tools, books, findings (both sterling and gold-filled), a large selection of charms, sterling chain, cording, and collectible and antique jewelry.
Payment Options: Money Order, MC, Visa, Discover
Membership Dues: Free Bead Club
Membership Benefits: Members receive a newsletter, free patterns, discounts, and a punch card ($5 off merchandise with a full card).
Other Information: In addition to beads, Gypsy's has gift certificates, hairwraps, candles, essence oils, incense, handmade clothing, wall hangings, patches and stickers, rings, beaded artwork, and they host birthday parties.
Special Discounts/Offers: 10% discount on first order with the mention of *Sew Far Sew Good*.
Catalog: $2 for a price list.

H.E. Goldberg & Co.

9050 Martin Luther King Way South, Seattle, WA 98118
Phone: (206) 722-8200, (800) 722-8201
Fax: (206) 722-0435
Services/Merchandise: They have furs for sewing, beads, and beading supplies.
Payment Options: Money Order, MC, Visa
Shipping Options: UPS, U.S. Postal Service, FedEx, COD.
Minimum Order: No minimum order.
Other Information: They have been in business since 1912. They are also buyers and collectors of raw fur skins from original sources in the Northwest, Canada, and Alaska.
Special Discounts/Offers: Volume discounts on the following schedule:

$1,000–$1499	7 1/2 % Discount
$1500–$1999	10% Discount
$2000 +	12 1/2 % Discount

A 12 1/2 % discount is offered to accredited educational institutions.
Catalog: $1

Halcyon Yarn

12 School Street, Bath, ME 04530
Phone: (207) 442-7909, (800) 341-0282
E-mail: squombus@eworld.com
Services/Merchandise: They are a mail order yarn store, specializing in natural fiber yarns for weavers, knitters, and rug hookers/punchers. They have a full line of natural spinning fibers. They offer over 900 titles of books, magazines, and videos. They sell looms, spinning

wheels, knitting notions, dyes, cloth strippers, rug hooking frames, tatting supplies, kumi himo stands and bobbins, bobbin lace supplies, and children's looms.

They also have yarns, both brand names and a full line of yarns spun and dyed exclusively for Halcyon Yarn, in everything from heavy rug wools to the finest silks.

Payment Options: Check, MC, Visa
Shipping Options: UPS
Minimum Order: Orders under $15 are charged $3 for handling.
Other Information: Halcyon Yarn offers classes, too. Learn to spin, weave, knit, dye, crochet, hook, and more.
Special Discounts/Offers: Bulk pricing on yarn, spinning fibers, and books.
Author's Note: Although the title says "yarn", Halcyon Yarn has many things the home sewing enthusiast should not be without. I recommend the kits and books for children to keep them busy and entertained while they learn. What a great way to get them interested in fibers.
Catalog: Free information packet upon request.

You can also get:

- Yarn Store In A Box® - A complete set of yarn sample cards, an equipment catalog, a book list, and a price list. This is most suitable for weavers.
- Maine Collection - An abridged edition of the Yarn Store In A Box® containing only those yarns suitable for hand and machine knitting or crocheting. It also contains an equipment catalog, book list, and price list.
- Kingfisher Collection - Their sample box for rug hookers and rug punchers. It contains sample cards of their rug wools and their monk's cloth, as well as the equipment catalog, book list, and price list.
- Merrymeeting Collection - Their sample box for spinners. It includes a sample card for all the spinning fibers they sell and the equipment catalog, book list, and price list.

The benefits of owning a sample collection are that you receive updated sample cards of new yarns/fibers at no cost as they become available.

Hamilton Eye Warehouse

Box 450, Moorpark, CA 93021
Phone: (805) 529-5900
Services/Merchandise: They have glass and acrylic eyes in 13 colors and different styles. Eye sizes range from 8mm to 30mm.
Payment Options: Check, Money Order, MC, Visa
Minimum Order: No minimum order.
Special Discounts/Offers: Wholesale and quantity discounts. Free

paperweight eyes with a $75 net paperweight order.

Hancock's

3841 Hinkleville Road, Paducah, KY 42001
Phone: (502) 443-4410, (800) 845-8723
Fax: (502) 442-2164
E-mail: dsingbear@aol.com
Services/Merchandise: Hancock's offers a full catalog of quilting and sewing supplies, as well as a full-color catalog for drapery and upholstery fabrics. The quilting catalog offers all the basics for the patchwork enthusiast, including a wide assortment of battings, a variety of widths in muslin, 50 colors in Spring's Cotton Belle broadcloth, 50 colors in Kona Cotton broadcloth, notions, patchwork patterns and books, and a large selection of prints from well-known manufacturers such as Hoffman, Debbie Mumm for South Seas, Timeless Treasures, and more.
Payment Options: Check, Money Order, MC, Visa, Discover
Shipping Options: UPS, U.S. Postal Service,
Minimum Order: No minimum order.
Other Information: *Hancock's Home Decorating Catalog* is a full-color publication featuring the latest drapery and upholstery fabrics from the U.S. and abroad. Decorative trims, tassels and cords, pre-made bedding products, and window treatments are also featured.
Catalog: $2, which is refundable with purchase.

Handweaver's Guild of America, Inc.

2402 University Avenue, Suite 702, St. Paul, MN 55114-1701
Phone: (612) 646-0802
Fax: (612) 646-0806
E-mail: 73744.202@compuserve.com
Services/Merchandise: The Handweaver's Guild of America is a non-profit organization dedicated to bringing together weavers, spinners, dyers, basketweavers, patrons, and educators who are interested in the fiber arts. HGA was formed in 1969 to encourage excellence in contemporary fiber arts and to support the preservation of techniques and traditions in textiles.
Payment Options: Check, MC, Visa
Shipping Options: UPS, U.S. Postal Service, FedEx
Minimum Order: No minimum order.
Membership Dues: Individual Membership $30 per year or $58 for two years. Family Memberships are $40 a year. International Memberships add $5 for surface delivery, or $20 for airmail.
Membership Benefits: Members receive the quarterly magazine *Shuttle, Spindle, & Dyepot*, access to a beginner's hotline and an e-mail network. Members are also invited to Convergence, HGA's biennial meeting of fiber artists from around the world. Members can obtain

Fashion...

A king there was who lost
an eye
In some excess of passion;
And straight his courtiers
did try
To follow the new fashion.

Each dropped one eyelid
when before
The throne he ventured,
thinking
'Twould please the King.
That monarch swore
He'd slay them all for
winking.

What should they do, they
were not hot
To hazard such disaster;
They dared not close an
eye–dared not
See better then their master.

Seeing them lacrymose and
glum,
A leech consoled the weepers:
He spread small rags with
liquid gum
And covered half their
peepers.

The court all wore the
stuff, the flame
Of royal anger dying.
That's how court plaster
got its name,
Unless I'm greatly lying.

Poem by:
Ambrose Bierce

slide kits and textile sample kits, and take part in juried shows and exhibitions. HGA's Learning Exchange is also available to members.

Handweaver's Guild of America, Inc./Small Expressions
1129 Sunnymeade Drive, Jacksonville, FL 32211
Phone: (904) 720-0496
Fax: (904) 724-4646
Event Information: This year, Small Expressions will be held in conjunction with Convergence '96.
Payment Options: Check
How Many Years: 12 years.
Time of Year/Month: Summer, usually July.
Approximate Costs: $16 for members, $30 for non-members.

Handy Hands, Inc.
Route 1, Box 4, Paxton, IL 60957
Phone: (217) 379-3976
Fax: (800) 617-8626
Services/Merchandise: They have books, a catalog of tatting books and supplies, and the *Helping Hands Newsletter* for tatters. The newsletter keeps you up-to-date on what's going on in the realm of tatting and includes several patterns.
Payment Options: Check, Money Order, MC, Visa
Shipping Options: UPS, U.S. Postal Service
Minimum Order: No minimum order.
Catalog: Free with a SASE, or call for free issue.

Hansa Corp.
3039 Lyndale Avenue South, Minneapolis, MN 55408
Phone: (612) 821-1072
Fax: (612) 821-1074
Services/Merchandise: They have handmade Venetian glass beads from Venice, Italy, and antique German cases and boxes for sewing goods.
Payment Options: Check, Visa
Shipping Options: UPS, FedEx
Minimum Order: $100
Catalog: $3

Hard-to-Find Needlework Books
96 Roundwood Road, Newton, MA 02164
Phone: (617) 969-0942
Fax: (617) 969-0942

E-mail: needlewk@tiac.net
WWW: http://www.ambook.org/bookstore/needlework
http://www.tiac.net/users/needlewk
Services/Merchandise: They have over 10,000 in-print and out-of-print books on all forms of the needlearts, including beadwork, color and design, bargello, stitchery, crewel embroidery, cross-stitch, quilting, knitting, crochet, canvaswork, needlepoint, dolls and doll making, lacemaking, textiles, and weaving, fashion and sewing, buttons, tatting, samplers, rug hooking, and rare books. Specify your special interest.
Payment Options: Check, Money Order, MC, Visa, Discover
Shipping Options: UPS, U.S. Postal Service
Minimum Order: No minimum order.
Catalog: $1 by mail. Catalogs can be downloaded from the above WWW sites.

Harpagon/Sideline Design
19620 Shoreland Avenue, Rocky River, OH 44111
Phone: (216) 356-2535
Services/Merchandise: They have the book *"I Do" Veils - So Can You* by Claudia Lynch. This is the first comprehensive guide to making bridal headpieces and veils. It includes directions for making bows, handmade flowers, tiaras, and all types of hats and headpieces. The information is easy to understand, with plenty of good illustrations.

Harper House
P.O. Box 39-OP, Williamstown, PA 17098
Phone: (717) 647-7807
Fax: (717) 647-2480
Services/Merchandise: They have historically correct sewing patterns for men, women, and children, and patterns and dress cloth for porcelain fashion dolls. They have books on costume, textiles and needlearts history. They offer reproduction needlework tools, notions, findings, and historical gift items.
Payment Options: Check, Money Order, MC, Visa, Amex
Shipping Options: UPS, U.S. Postal Service
Minimum Order: No minimum order.
Catalog: $6

Harriet's TCS/Harriet's Patterns
6 Parkview Avenue, Winchester, VA 22601
- or -
P.O. Box 1363, Winchester, VA 22604
Phone: (540) 667-2541
Fax: (540) 722-4618

Isn't growing hemp in America illegal for a reason?

The fact is that hemp grown for fiber–whether by George Washington in 1790, by Kentucky growers in 1935, or by English farmers in 1994–has never contained psychoactive qualities. If one were to roll leaves from an industrial hemp plant into a cigarette and smoke them, no euphoric effects would be noticed, even if a thousand hemp cigarettes were smoked. The potentially psychoactive chemical in hemp is delta-9 tetrahydrocannabinol (THC). A plant cultivated for marijuana has 3 to 15 percent THC content or more, while industrial hemp generally contains one percent or less.

Tip quoted from:
Industrial Hemp Hemptech

Services/Merchandise: They have men's, women's, and children's period patterns, reproductions, and rentals circa 1600-1945. They also have fabrics and supplies for making reproductions, and custom and ready-made corsets and crinolines.
Payment Options: Check, Money Order, MC, Visa, Amex, Discover
Shipping Options: UPS, U.S. Postal Service, FedEx
Minimum Order: $15
Other Information: They have 30 years experience in researching, museum study, graduate school, and designing for clients worldwide. Authentic sewing techniques are used on all reproductions; they create modern heirlooms.
Special Discounts/Offers: Wholesale to qualified businesses.
Catalog: $10 for a patterns and clothing catalog, $10 for a catalog of rentals with color photos.

Harriet's Treadle Arts
6390 West 44th Avenue, Wheat Ridge, CO 80033
Phone: (303) 424-2742, (800) 592-2742
Fax: (303) 424-1290
Services/Merchandise: Specializing in supplies for the machine quilter, they carry a wide range of cotton batting, threads by Mettler and Sulky, DMC machine embroidery thread, 100% cotton fabrics, books, notions, and a lovely selection of silk ribbon and floss, as well as French wired ribbon and organdy ribbons. They expect to have all the necessary supplies for Australian wool embroidery in the near future.
Payment Options: Check, Money Order, MC, Visa, Discover
Shipping Options: UPS, U.S. Postal Service if requested.
Minimum Order: No minimum order.
Other Information: They offer the following books: *Home of Heirloom Machine Quilting* and *Mastering Machine Appliqué* by Harriet Hargrave. They are the complete source for Hobbs Heirloom Battings, and The Harriet Hargrave Collection of Reproduction Washgood and Shirting Fabrics by P&B Textiles.

Harris Publications
1115 Broadway, New York, NY 10010
Phone: (212) 807-7100
Services/Merchandise: They are the publishers of the following needlework, craft, and quilting magazines: *White Crochet, Country Afghans, Country Crochet, Christmas Crochet, Country Quilts, Quilts, Quilt Almanac, Miniature Quilts,* and *Big Block Quilts.*

Haywood Community College
Production Fiber Department, Freedlander Drive, Clyde, NC 28721-9454
Phone: (704) 627-4672
Fax: (704) 627-3606
Services/Merchandise: Haywood offers a comprehensive weaving program. Subjects include: weaving, dyeing, woven clothing construction, marketing, and business. For more information, contact Catherine Muerdter, Fiber Instructor at Haywood Community College.

Hedgehog Handworks
(Purveyors of Fine Needlework Supplies)
P.O. Box 45384, Westchester, CA 90045
Phone: (310) 670-6040
Services/Merchandise: They offer millinery supplies, including buckram, wire, thread, tape, and books. They also have real metal threads (bullion) in gold, silver, and copper, spangles in gold and silver, and Japanese threads. They carry silk ribbon in 2mm, 4mm, 7mm widths, Trebizond twisted silk thread, Au ver a Soie silk thread, Caron Collection silk and cotton threads, and vegetable-dyed lambswool for stitching (Broider Wul).

They have many unusual needlework tools, such as tambour hooks, lucets, tatting needles and shuttles; fancy scissors, tools, needle cases and thimble cases. They sell charts for needlework (cross-stitch) and fabrics (evenweave). They also have costuming supplies, including corset stays (bones), hoop wire, pewter clasps and buttons. They have hundreds of books on needlework, lace making, costuming (many periods), hatmaking, calligraphy and illumination, papermaking and book arts.
Payment Options: Check, Money Order, MC, Visa
Shipping Options: UPS, U.S. Postal Service, FedEx
Minimum Order: No minimum order.
Other Information: Special orders are never a problem and there is no extra charge.
Author's Note: Not only is the owner of Hedgehog Handworks friendly and quick (she returned my questionnaire within 10 days), but the 92-page catalog is full of beautiful needlework collectibles and supplies.
Catalog: $5, which is refundable with a $30 purchase.

Heirloom Knitted Lace
109 West 4th Street, Hermann, MO 65041
Phone: (753) 486-2162
Services/Merchandise: They do pattern research and troubleshooting for lace knitters, and make references for supplies for lace knitters. Gloria offers six books of patterns for lace knitting.
Payment Options: Check, Money Order
Shipping Options: UPS, U.S. Postal Service
Minimum Order: No minimum order.
Other Information: Gloria offers a money back guarantee. She has been lace knitting and collecting old patterns for 45 years, and in busi-

---

Hemp growing required...

Hemp production was so important for commerce that in 1640 the Governor of Connecticut declared that every citizen must grow the plant.

Tip quoted from: Industrial Hemp Hemptech

Argyll socks...

Although the first pair of argyll socks bearing this familiar pattern was most likely knitted with love in the traditional plaid pattern of the clan of Campbell of Argyll, there ends the resemblance. From light green crossed with dark green, and narrow independent crosslines of white, we now see the pattern in department stores, resplendent in a myriad of bright colors.

ness for 10 years. All orders are shipped within 24 hours.

Lace knitting, once almost forgotten, is now enjoying a renaissance, and each book of patterns is unique.

It is impossible to describe the wonder of knitted lace; you would really have to see the patterns Heirloom offers. They are beautiful when framed, and if they are knitted with heavier yarn and larger needles, they make breathtaking shawls.

The pattern sizes available range from 2″ to a full-sized tablecloth.

Special Discounts/Offers: 10% discount on first order with the mention of *Sew Far Sew Good*. Wholesale to qualified businesses.

Author's Note: Gloria enclosed a beautiful knitted lace doily from her book *Knitted Lace In Miniature*. You can see the doily on the bottom left of the front cover of this book.

Heirloom Woven Labels

Box 428, Morristown, NJ 08057
Phone: (609) 722-1618
Fax: (609) 722-8905
Services/Merchandise: They offer woven fabric labels.
Payment Options: Check, Money Order, MC, Visa
Shipping Options: U.S. Postal Service
Other Information: Because these labels are woven, the colors remain fast and the quality is superior. Their labels are offered in small quantities and at reasonable prices. They are great for individuals who take pride in producing unique articles, as well as for those who wish to identify articles to prevent loss.
Special Discounts/Offers: 10% discount on first order with the mention of *Sew Far Sew Good*.

Heirlooms Forever

3112 Cliff Gookin Boulevard, Tupelo, MS 38801
Phone: (601) 842-4275
Fax: (601) 842-2284
Services/Merchandise: Heirlooms Forever specializes in heirloom sewing, smocking, children's fabrics, patterns, and quilting. They manufacture, distribute, and own the patent on The Smocking Board. This is a device used to hand-smock material.
Payment Options: Check, Money Order, MC, Visa, Amex, Discover, Home Source, Bernina and Pfaff credit cards
Other Information: Heirlooms Forever started in 1984 with about 100 smocking design plates and 100 yards of fabric. They now own a 4,000 square foot building with over 1,000 bolts of fabric, thousands of yards of lace, and Bernina, Pfaff, Viking, and White sewing machines and sergers. They also carry hundreds of specialty patterns, along with the Burda and Kwik-Sew pattern lines.

Special Discounts/Offers: 10% discount on first retail order with the mention of *Sew Far Sew Good*.

Helyn's Hoops

911 City Park, Columbus, OH 43206
Phone: (614) 443-9988
Services/Merchandise: They have the Hoop-de-Deux, the original border hoop designed by Gay Dell, and her Cinch Hoop–a round, single-ring, wooden quilting hoop with a groove to accommodate a bungee cord and a cinch heart fastener as the outer ring. They also have *Emma Sings: The First Quilters Song Book* by Gay Dell, complete with quilting designs.
Payment Options: Check, Money Order, COD
Minimum Order: One item retail. Low wholesale.
Other Information: Helyn's Hoops shares space with Picking Up The Pieces Quilt Shop (their retail shop).
Special Discounts/Offers: Wholesale to qualified businesses.
Catalog: Free flyer upon request.

Hemp BC

21 Water Street, Suite 405, Vancouver, BC V6B 1A1, Canada
Phone: (604) 669-9052, (800) 330-HEMP
Fax: (604) 669-9038
E-mail: memery@hempbc.com
WWW: http://www.hempbc.com
Services/Merchandise: They have many interesting items–but I have included them primarily for their hemp fabrics.
Payment Options: Check, Money Order, MC, Visa
Author's Note: Hemp BC is very active on the cannabis scene, so requesting a catalog or viewing their web page is not for the timid.

Hemp Textiles International Corp.

3200 30th Street, Bellingham, WA 98225-8360
Phone: (360) 650-1684
Fax: (360) 650-0523
E-mail: hti@hemptex.com~hti
WWW: http://www.hemptex.com
Services/Merchandise: Hemp Textiles International Corp. offers wholesale Chinese hemp fabrics, as well as yarns for weaving and knitting. They also stock hemp fibers for spinning, papermaking, and decoration.
Payment Options: Check, Money Order
Shipping Options: UPS
Minimum Order: $25

Other Information: Hemp Textiles International Corp. is the U.S. leader in research and development of American-made hemp textile products. They will be introducing the first hemp/cotton knit fabric, HempCot, in 1996, as well as HempCot T-Shirts and their trademarked hemp/wool blended yarn, HempWol.

Heritage Looms

Route 6, Box 731E, Alvin, TX 77511-9411
Phone: (409) 925-4161
Fax: (409) 925-4506
E-mail: 76151.3705@compuserve.com
Services/Merchandise: They manufacture looms and handweaving equipment. They have stock items and manufacture custom-ordered weaving supplies.
Payment Options: Check, Money Order, MC, Visa
Shipping Options: UPS, U.S. Postal Service
Catalog: $1.50

Herrschners, Inc.

2800 Hoover Road, Stevens Point, WI 54481
Phone: (715) 341-4554, (800) 441-0838
Services/Merchandise: They have yarns, quilt blocks and kits, DMC floss and threads, fabrics, needlework kits and accessories, and sewing notions.
Payment Options: Check, Money Order, MC, Visa, Amex, Discover
Shipping Options: UPS, U.S. Postal Service
Other Information: Established in 1899, they are the largest mail order craft company in the world.
Catalog: Free upon request.

HH Designs

P.O. Box 183, Eastchester, NY 10709
Services/Merchandise: They have candlewicking and needlework kits.
Payment Options: Money Order
Shipping Options: U.S. Postal Service
Minimum Order: No minimum order.
Author's Note: The catalog shows beautiful, unique pieces that stand alone as works of art.
Catalog: $2

High Country West Needleworks

Suite 201, 114 North San Francisco Street, Flagstaff, AZ 86001
Phone: (520) 779-2900
Services/Merchandise: They have handpainted needlepoint canvasses, needlepoint kits, needlepoint learning kits, European threads (available only at their store), evenweave fabrics, leather, and hides.
Payment Options: Check, Money Order, MC, Visa
Shipping Options: UPS, U.S. Postal Service, FedEx
Other Information: High Country Needleworks provides one-on-one consulting and custom work for needlework canvasses, and they offer their own line of handpainted canvasses.

They also offer custom needlepoint finishing. Customers should call to make an appointment to send in their work. Turn-around time is three to four weeks.
Special Discounts/Offers: 10% discount with the mention of _Sew Far Sew Good_. Wholesale to qualified businesses.
Catalog: $3.50

The Hillsinger Company

1125 Northeast Failing Street, Portland, OR 97212
Phone: (503) 280-8789
E-mail: hillsinger@northwest.com
Services/Merchandise: The Hillsinger Company offers The Perfect Bead Box™. It's the perfect solution to the beadworker's problem of how to carry your work with you. Across the room, or around the world, this little case goes with you. Designed by a professional beadworker, The Perfect Bead Box™ lets you carry your beads, tools, supplies, and projects in one compact, attractive case. Even very small beads will not spill or get mixed up. There's a place for everything, including larger beads up to $\frac{1}{2}$" in diameter. Your bead collection deserves to travel in this handsome case.
Payment Options: Check, Money Order, Visa
Shipping Options: UPS, U.S. Postal Service, FedEx
Minimum Order: No minimum order for retail. For the wholesale minimum, please inquire.
Other Information: Hillsinger Fine Hand Beadwork offers custom beadwork pattern design. If you have a photo, or favorite image, they can turn it into an easy-to-read pattern in the size, scale, and colors you specify.

Coming soon from Hillsinger: The Perfect Bead Loom™ and a range of bead storage and display items for home, retail, and trade show use.
Special Discounts/Offers: Wholesale to qualified businesses.
Author's Note: I "speak" (via modem) quite frequently to the owner/operator of Hillsinger, and she is a wonderful person who is always ready to help. You will find her on the Prodigy Beading Board. I have great feelings about her and this company.
Catalog: Free brochure upon request.

Tying an ascot...

Leaving one side of your scarf much shorter, tie a knot in front of your neck. Take the longer end of the scarf and weave it up and under the knot from behind. Adjust the end so that it covers the knot.

Sewing Circles

If your machine does not have a circle sewing accessory, or you have not purchased the one that goes with your machine, here is how to have one for the price of a thumb tack and a couple inches of masking tape:

Decide the size of the circle you want to stitch. Measure half that distance horizontally from the needle of your machine. (To the right and/or left will be explained later.) Stick your thumb tack (flat head) into the center of a two-inch piece of masking tape and place on your sewing machine, with the point of the tack sticking up, over the point you just measured. Make sure the masking tape is firmly adhered to the sewing machine. Mark the center of the circle to be stitched onto your fabric and place this mark over the point of the thumb tack.

If you are making a very small circle, you may need to cut away some of the masking tape to avoid covering your feed dogs. Also make sure the presser foot clears the tack.

Cont.

Hinterberg Design, Inc.
2805 East Progress Drive, West Bend, WI 53095
Phone: (800) 443-5800
Fax: (414) 338-3852
E-mail: hinterbera@hnet.west-bend.wi.us
Services/Merchandise: They have quilting frames, floor standing quilting hoops, and the Easy Build quilting frame kit.
Payment Options: Check, Money Order, MC, Visa, Amex, Discover
Shipping Options: UPS, U.S. Postal Service
Catalog: Write or call for free information.

Historic Needlework Guild
P.O. Box 718, Insomac, PA 15127
Phone: (412) 635-8187
Fax: (412) 635-8474
Services/Merchandise: This is a guild devoted to promoting historic needlework, from 1650-1850. They focus on techniques of the day, including cross-stitch, drawn thread, pulled thread, stumpwork, and more. Readers learn through design, articles, and educational information about this interesting era in needlepoint history.
Payment Options: Check, Money Order, MC, Visa
Shipping Options: UPS, U.S. Postal Service
Membership Dues: $25
Membership Benefits: Members receive the quarterly newsletter *Fine Lines*, and discounts on materials as presented.
Other Information: They offer mail order for materials relating to historical needlework, as well as seminars, trips, and classes in various areas of the country. Send a SASE for more information.
Special Discounts/Offers: Wholesale newsletter to retailers.

History International, Inc.
424 South Craig Street, Pittsburgh, PA 15213
Phone: (412) 681-8815
Fax: (412) 422-8177
E-mail: history@citynet.com
Services/Merchandise: They guarantee the lowest prices in the U.S. for bone beads. Orders are shipped within 48 hours of receipt.
Payment Options: MC, Visa
Shipping Options: UPS, U.S. Postal Service
Minimum Order: $35
Other Information: Check out their site @craftvillage.com
Special Discounts/Offers: $5 discount on faxed orders over $100. Wholesale to qualified businesses.
Catalog: Free if you send a 9" x 12" double stamped envelope.

Hobbs Bonded Fibers
Wholesale Only
P.O. Box 2521, Waco, TX 76702-2521
Phone: (817) 741-0040
Fax: (817) 772-7238
Services/Merchandise: They have batting in polyester, cotton and poly, and 100% cotton (organic). They have all wool batting and fiberfill, both packaged and in bulk. They also have pillow forms that are 12" x 12" through 27" x 27".
Payment Options: Check
Shipping Options: UPS, RPS
Minimum Order: 4 cartons of assorted rolls.
Catalog: Free, but you must send your resale number.

Home-Sew
P.O. Box 4099, Bethlehem, PA 18018-0099
Phone: (610) 867-3833
Fax: (610) 867-9717
Services/Merchandise: They have many laces (Cluny, Venice, nylon, poly, eyelet, and more), elastic, satin and velvet ribbon, ricrac, tape, appliqués, specialty threads on cones or spools, zippers, snaps, hooks and eyes, buttons, Velcro dots, belts and buckles, pins, needles, scissors, doll parts, interfacings, shirring, pleater tape, tasseled and moss fringe, and cording.
Payment Options: Check, Money Order, MC, Visa
Shipping Options: UPS, U.S. Postal Service (Postage free on orders over $45)
Minimum Order: $5
Other Information: Home-Sew makes it easy for you to see trims before you buy–just join the Sample Club. For 50¢ you'll receive three samples of lace, trim, ribbon, and elastic each year. These are not pictured in the catalog.
Author's Note: It was very nice to receive the sample mailing of trims. Seeing and touching what you're about to buy is always best. Their 32-page catalog is well-organized and easy to use, with clear photographs of the trims and notions.
Catalog: Free within the United States.
Canadian Readers: Home-Sew also offers a bilingual catalog for $1 Canadian (*Parlez-vous français?*), available from Home-Sew Canada Inc., B.P./87, 3285 1 ere Rue, Local 3, St. Hubert, Quebec J3Y 5S9.

Homestead Needle Arts
12235 South Saginaw Street, Grand Blanc, MI 48439
Phone: (810) 694-3040
Fax: (810) 694-0370
Services/Merchandise: They have handpainted needlepoint and canvasses, charted needlepoint designs, a wide variety of threads

(cotton, wool, rayon, silk, and metallics), and many novelty fibers. They also have books, canvas, stitching tools, and beads.

Payment Options: Check, Money Order, MC, Visa, Discover
Shipping Options: UPS, U.S. Postal Service

House of Fabrics/So Fro Fabrics/Fabricland

13400 Riverside Drive, Sherman Oaks, CA 91423
Phone: (818) 385-2128
Services/Merchandise: These stores have fabrics, crafts, notions, florals, bridal fabric, home decorating supplies, trims, ribbons, laces, yarn, and stitchery supplies. See your local white pages for a store near you.

House of Russia

3901 North Field Road, Box 4551, Austin, TX 78765-4551
Phone: (512) 795-3535

House of White Birches

306 East Parr Road, Berne, IN 46711
Phone: (219) 589-8741
Fax: (219) 589-8039
Services/Merchandise: They offer *Quick and Easy Quilting* and *Quilt World Magazine* for $14.94 for six issues per year. They also have the Quilt Pattern Club.
Payment Options: Check, Money Order, MC, Visa, Discover
Shipping Options: UPS, U.S. Postal Service
Minimum Order: No minimum order.
Other Information: They also have catalogs and magazines on crochet, knitting, plastic canvas, cooking, doll collecting, and nostalgia.
Catalog: A free quilt patterns and supplies catalog upon request.

Hunt Valley Cashmere

6747 White Stone Road, Baltimore, MD 21207
Phone: (410) 298-4343
Fax: (410) 298-3579
Services/Merchandise: They have 100% cashmere fibers and yarns.
Payment Options: Check, Money Order, MC, Visa
Shipping Options: UPS, FedEx
Minimum Order: No minimum order.

I Love Needlework Fair

836 B Southhampton Road #285, Benecia, CA 94510

I.T.C./Italian Trading Company

P.O. Box 20875, Louisville, KY 40250-0875
Phone: (502) 896-6780
Fax: (502) 896-4018
Services/Merchandise: They have the *Professional Alteration Secrets Video Series* that shows you how to do alterations at home like the professionals. Part I–Trouser Alterations. Part II–Hems on Slacks & Skirts.
Payment Options: Check, Money Order, MC, Visa, Discover
Minimum Order: No minimum order.

Ident-ify Label Corp.

P.O. Box 140204, Brooklyn, NY 11214-0204
Phone: (718) 436-3126
Fax: (718) 436-3126
Services/Merchandise: They are manufacturers of clothing labels. Name tapes, woven labels, and custom labels with your logo are also available.
Payment Options: Check, Money Order, MC, Visa
Shipping Options: U.S. Postal Service
Minimum Order: 40 labels
Special Discounts/Offers: 10% discount on first order with the mention of *Sew Far Sew Good*.

Imagination Station

7571 Crater Lake, Highway 101, White City, OR 97503
Phone: (541) 826-7954, (800) 338-3857
Fax: (541) 826-7955
Services/Merchandise: They are a photo-to-fabric transfer service for quilters, crafters, and sewers.
Payment Options: Check, MC, Visa, Carte Blanc, Diner's Club
Shipping Options: U.S. Postal Service, UPS, FedEx
Minimum Order: No minimum order.
Other Information: They also offer photo T-shirts, caps, sweatshirts, BBQ aprons, book totes, and calendars.
Catalog: Free brochures. Please specify: Quilt, Family Calendar, or Adult Calendar.

In Cahoots

P.O. Box 72336, Marietta, GA 30007-2336
Phone: (800) 95 CAHOOTS
Fax: (770) 992-9678
Services/Merchandise: They have wearable art patterns, including pin weaving, machine embroidery, and piecing techniques. They also have a needle and thread guide book, covering sewing and specialty needles and threads. They also teach wearable art and machine embroidery

The tack works as a steering point for a perfect circle.

This technique will work for satin stitching, decorative stitching, and even lettering. If you are going to use this technique for anything other than lettering, it will be your choice as to which side of the needle you feel comfortable placing the tack.

If you are giong to use it for lettering, you will have to decide how you want the lettering to look.

For the lettering to be upright on the top half and upside-down on the bottom half of the circle, you will have to place the tack on the left side of the needle and stitch the complete circle.

For the lettering to be upright on the top and bottom, you will have to place the tack on the left side of the needle to stitch the top half, and to the right of the needle to stitch the bottom half of the circle.

Tip provided by: Lana L. Jones AOL member, sewing enthusiast.

What is a devil's darning needle?

A dragonfly.

classes in shops, to guilds, and at shows.
Payment Options: Check, Money Order, MC, Visa
Shipping Options: UPS, U.S. Postal Service
Minimum Order: No minimum order for retail.
Other Information: All pattern instructions are classroom tested and very thorough. Pattern instructions include information on machine set-up for all techniques, plus specialty needles and thread advice.
Special Discounts/Offers: 10% discount on first order with the mention of *Sew Far Sew Good*. Wholesale to qualified businesses.
Author's Note: The ladies at In Cahoots sent several of their patterns for my perusal. I was pleasantly surprised at the detailed instructions for constructing the garments. They go through each project step-by-step for beginners and add a lot of embellishment suggestions for those more familiar with garment construction techniques.
Catalog: Free upon request.

Infiknit

407 Roe Hampton Avenue, Toronto, Ontario M4P 1S3 Canada
- or -
(In the U.S.) 2315 Whirlpool Street, Suite 274, Niagara Falls, NY 14305
Phone: (416) 487-9401, (800) 408-1522
Fax: (416) 487-9401
E-mail: ctomany@interlog.com
Services/Merchandise: They have Foxfibre handknitting yarn, and organic cotton textiles. They also have Ann Norling patterns, Thomas The Tank Engine patterns, kits for knitted teacups, videos, Debbie New Notecards (knitting motifs), kits for knitting, jewelry, buttons from natural and recycled sources, and small knitting needles.
Payment Options: MC, Visa
Minimum Order: No minimum retail. $50 wholesale.
Other Information: They manufacture goods in organic cotton.
Special Discounts/Offers: Wholesale to qualified businesses.

International Fabric Collection

3445 West Lake Road, Erie, PA 16506
Phone: (814) 838-0740, (800) 462-3891
Fax: (814) 838-9057
Services/Merchandise: They have imported cottons from Italy, Africa, Japan, Australia, India, Bali, and other countries. They carry Liberty of London™ Tana lawns and craft cottons. They also have Tire silk threads, silk embroidery thread, silk ribbons for embroidery, stencils and threads for sashiko, and radiance, bouclé, and chenille threads for embellishment. They also carry the entire line of Eastwind Art patterns and create kits for some of their patterns.
Payment Options: Check, Money Order, MC, Visa, Discover
Shipping Options: UPS, U.S. Postal Service

Minimum Order: $\frac{1}{4}$ yard of fabric.
Other Information: Most of their business is by mail order. International Fabric Collection can be found at several quilt shows each year. They try to carry books, fabrics, and supplies that are not available anywhere else.
International Fabric Collection has a shop open every Thursday. They request that customers call to schedule appointments for other times of the week.
Special Discounts/Offers: 10% discount on first order with the mention of *Sew Far Sew Good*.
Author's Note: The color catalog they sent is beautifully done and full of gorgeous fabrics. It's worth sending off for this one.
Catalog: $3, charged only once. You will receive yearly catalogs at no charge thereafter.

International Old Lacers, Inc.

9 Lakemont Highlands, P.O. Box 305, Lakemont, GA 30552-0305
Phone: (706) 782-7166
Payment Options: Check, Money Order (checks may be accepted in overseas currency. Apply to treasurer for rates)
Membership Benefits: IOLI offers seminars and classes to members in a variety of lacemaking technique, including bobbin and needle laces, tatting, knitting, and Battenburg. You also get a directory of local IOLI chapters and members throughout the United States, Canada, Puerto Rico, and 25 foreign countries, plus a quarterly bulletin of events, patterns, ideas and news of lace activities. They have a library of slides, books, and videos, and resource information on lace teachers. They also sponsor an annual convention offering lacemaking, related classes, and an idea exchange.
Membership Dues: $27.50 U.S. first class, $19 U.S. third class, Canada $27.50 (U.S.), Air Mail Europe $37.50 (U.S.), Air Mail Pacific $40 (U.S.), Surface $27.50 (U.S.)
Membership Information, Contact:
    IOLI Treasurer, Lee Daly
    10 Elm Street, Newton
    NJ 07860-2016
Other Information: IOLI is an association, roughly 1,600 strong, of people who share an interest in the beauty and intrigues of lace. They encourage others to:
    Make lace to study and recreate historic old laces, or design and make contemporary pieces.
    Study antique laces to identify and appreciate inherited pieces to enjoy the history and beauty of ancient museum pieces.
    Collect old lace to preserve examples of craftsmanship of ages gone by.
Catalog: $2, for a sample bulletin. Contact the Editor, IOLI Bulletin, 2737 Northeast 98th, Seattle, WA 98115.

Interweave Press

201 East 4th Street, Loveland, CO 80537
Phone: (970) 669-7672, (800) 645-3675
Fax: (970) 667-8317
Services/Merchandise: They offer the fiber and craft related magazines *Handwoven*, *Spin-Off*, and *Piecework*, and related book titles. They also have the special issue/interest magazines *Interweave Knits* and *Interweave Beadworks*.
Payment Options: Check, Money Order, MC, Visa, Amex, Discover
Shipping Options: UPS, U.S. Postal Service, RPS
Other Information: Interweave Press has been in the business for 20 years. They do business with individuals, specialty shops, and mail order companies interested in fiber crafts.
Minimum Order: No minimum order.
Catalog: Free upon request.

Isaacson & Kater (I&K) Button Co.

2530 Superior Avenue, Cleveland, OH 44114
Phone: (800) 426-3526
Fax: (800) 528-1634
Services/Merchandise: They have buttons by the pound at the following costs:

- Bright Assortment #8B–$8 per pound
- Pastel Assortment #8P–$8 per pound
- Fall Assortment #8F–$8 per pound
- Metal Assortment #10M–$10 per pound
- Specific Color #11–$11 per pound

Also available are mother of pearl buttons, abalone shell buttons, akoya shell buttons, and assorted metal buckles for 20¢-30¢ each. Send your payment with your order and it will be shipped within 24 hours.
Payment Options: Check, Money Order.
Shipping Options: UPS, $3.50 first pound, $1 for each additional pound.
Minimum Order: $25
Special Discounts/Offers: 10% discount on first order with the mention of *Sew Far Sew Good*. Wholesale to qualified businesses.

Islander Sewing Systems

P.O. Box 66, 407 Northeast E Street, Grants Pass, OR 97526
Phone: (541) 479-3906, (800) 944-0213
Fax: (541) 479-3906
Services/Merchandise: They have videos, books, and lectures, and demonstrations in the U.S. and Canada. They also offer consultation services.
Payment Options: Check, Money Order, MC, Visa, Discover, COD
Shipping Options: UPS, U.S. Postal Service, FedEx

Minimum Order: No minimum order for retail. 6 or more of any video, and 12 or more of any book for wholesale.
Other Information: Margaret Islander also administers the Islander School of Fashion Arts in Grants Pass, Oregon.
Special Discounts/Offers: 10% off a purchase of all seven of Margaret's videos. Buy all three volumes of *Galaxy Sewing Techniques* for $99.95. Buy *Industrial Shortcuts I & II* and *Shirts, Etc!* I & II for $95.
Catalog: Free brochure upon request.

Ivy Imports, Inc.

6806 Trexler Road, Lanham, MD 20706
Phone: (301) 474-7347, (800) 7 TEXCOL
Fax: (301) 441-2395
Services/Merchandise: They have quality products for silkpainting, including dyes, paints, silk, books, videos, and instruction.

They also offer *The Silkworm*, an international networking newsletter for silk painters, fabric painters, creative sewers and quilters, and textile/fiber artists. Silkpainting is a relatively new art form. The techniques can be used on all fabrics, and are therefore very valuable to all creative textile artists. This newsletter is for individuals on all levels of skill–from the beginner to the professional. Information about techniques is included, along with marketing tips and teaching opportunities. Books are periodically reviewed. The editor, Anne Sendgikoski, welcomes articles, letters, and comments from the readers.

Write to *The Silkworm* at:
P.O. Box 887
Riverdale, MD 20738
Payment Options: Check, Money Order, MC, Visa Discover, COD
Shipping Options: UPS, U.S. Postal Service
Minimum Order: No minimum order.
Special Discounts/Offers: Mention *Sew Far Sew Good* when subscribing to *The Silkworm* and receive an additional two issues.

Jackie Fears

2931 St. Johns Avenue, Billings, MT 59102
Phone: (406) 656-9829
Services/Merchandise: They have patterns for crafts and costumes, and for men's, women's, and children's clothes.
Payment Options: Check, Money Order
Minimum Order: No minimum order.
Other Information: They offer discounted patterns, including Jackie Fears and popular brands. The cost is 50¢ for each pattern plus postage.
Catalog: $5 for a list of patterns, which is refundable with a purchase of 10 or more patterns.

Skirt styles...

Mini

Chinese symbols...

Hemp

Silk

Jacquart Fabric Products, Inc.

1238 Wall Street, Ironwood, MT 49938
Phone: (906) 932-1339
Fax: (906) 932-1579
Services/Merchandise: They have zippers, Velcro, Val-A-Cement, Zipper Ease, knit bottoms, collars, cuffs, thread, webbing, blue jean buttons, dot snaps, buckles and fasteners to be used with webbing, and more.
Payment Options: Check, Money Order, MC, Visa
Shipping Options: UPS.
Minimum Order: No minimum order.
Other Information: Jacquart Fabric Products, Inc., is a family-owned business that sold its first product in 1958. Since then, they have grown with their employees to sell a wide range of services and products, which include a retail bag and repair shop, an upholstery shop that reupholsters and builds finished products for home and industry, a mail order zipper business, a canvas shop that makes retail and wholesale boat covers and tarps of any shape or size, a custom sewing shop that makes a wide variety of specialty items, and a production line. Some of the products from this line are orthopedic pillows, duffel bags, dryer bags, air filters, aprons, covers, gym floor covers, dog and cat beds, air conditioner covers, sample cases, tool pouches, safety curtains, taps, and custom bags. The products and possibilities are endless. They are very energetic, creative, and are willing to tackle any project.
Catalog: $2, which is refundable with first order and the mention of <u>Sew Far Sew Good.</u>

Jaggerspun

P.O. Box 188, Water Street, Springvale, ME 04083
Phone: (207) 324-4455
Fax: (207) 490-2661
Services/Merchandise: They offer yarns wholesale, retail, and through the mail. Their yarns include 100% wool, 50% wool/50% silk, heather, and superfine Merino on cones for machine knitting, weaving, and handknitting.
Payment Options: Check, Money Order, MC, Visa
Shipping Options: UPS, U.S. Postal Service, FedEx
Minimum Order: ½ pound.
Other Information: Jaggerspun is a division of Jagger Brothers, Inc. Jagger Brothers has been spinning fine quality worsted yarn since the turn of the century.
Special Discounts/Offers: Wholesale to qualified businesses.
Catalog: $6

James W.M. Carroll Antiques

P.O. Box 239, Franconia, NH 03580

Phone: (603) 823-8446
Services/Merchandise: They have vintage and antique yard goods, scrap, quilts, tops, buttons, beads, trim, lace, linens, and other sewing items.
Payment Options: Check, Money Order
Shipping Options: UPS, U.S. Postal Service.
Minimum Order: No minimum order.
Catalog: $3

Jean Hardy Pattern Company

2151 La Cuesta Drive, Santa Ana, CA 92705
Phone: (714) 544-1608
Fax: (714) 544-1608
Services/Merchandise: They have patterns for riding apparel in English, western and saddleseat styles. They also have western dusters, western wedding clothes, and general western wear.
Payment Options: Check, Money Order, MC, Visa
Catalog: $1

Jehlor Fantasy Fabrics

730 Andover Park West, Seattle, WA 98188
Phone: (206) 575-8250
Fax: (206) 575-8281
Services/Merchandise: They have a variety of specialty fabrics and trims for special occasions, including cracked ice fabrics, handbeaded laces, sequined fabrics, metallic sheers, brocades, lamés, satins, chiffons, organzas, velvets, bridal fabrics, spandex, stretch satin, stretch velvet, super stretch spandex, stretch nude sheer, rhinestones, glass beads, glass sew-on jewels, beaded and sequined appliqués, trims, pearls, fringe, and feathers.
Payment Options: Check, MC, Visa, Discover
Shipping Options: UPS, U.S. Postal Service
Minimum Order: No minimum order.
Other Information: Jehlor Fantasy Fabrics can help you with your own one-of-a-kind creations. They also provide a swatching service.
Special Discounts/Offers: 15% discount on full bolt purchases. 15-20% discount for volume purchases to qualified businesses.

JHB International

Wholesale Only
1955 South Quince Street, Denver, CO 80231
Phone: (303) 751-8100
Fax: (303) 752-0608
Services/Merchandise: They have hundreds of types of buttons.
Payment Options: Check, Money Order, COD, Terms

Minimum Order: $50 for the first order, $30 for re-orders. There is also a minimum of either six cards, or one dozen buttons per style ordered.

Other Information: Thirty-seven years and counting!

Author's Note: Their catalog has a large selection of beautiful buttons. It would take any designer just a few minutes to meet their minimums.

Jiffy® Steamer Company

P.O. Box 869, Union City, TN 38281

Phone: (901) 885-6690

Fax: (901) 885-6692

Services/Merchandise: Professional steamers for home and commercial use.

Other Information: Serving enthusiasts and professionals since 1940.

Jill McIntire Designs

By Appointment Only

3032 North Lincoln Street, Spokane, WA 99205

Phone: (509) 325-8353

E-mail: 75610.274@compuserve.com

Services/Merchandise: JMD offers a scanning service for people with Baby Lock Esante and Espree embroidery machines, as well as the Brother and Bernina compatibles. They will scan your design (no copyrighted designs, please send for guidelines), or you can choose designs from their collection. The scan will be placed on an embroidery card compatible with the machine you indicate. You may supply your own card or buy it from them. Personalized instruction is available. They also have a line of patterns for baby activity toys.

Payment Options: Check, Money Order

Shipping Options: UPS, U.S. Postal Service

Other Information: Since her son was born, Jill discovered that the pattern companies make the cutest patterns only for little girls. In ready-to-wear, the great looking boys' clothes are embroidered, so she has created her own line of adorable embroidery cards for boys. Future plans include marketing designs in ready-to-scan form to current scanner owners.

Special Discounts/Offers: 10% discount on first order with the mention of *Sew Far Sew Good*. For every 10 designs scanned onto an embroidery card, the 11th one is free.

Catalog: $1, which is refundable with order or free with a 6" x 9" SASE with 2 stamps.

Joyce's Fabrics

66 Cedar Street, P.O. Box 381-SFSG, Morrisville, NY 13408

Phone: (325) 684-3365

Services/Merchandise: They have unusual fabrics, including camouflage, Thinsulate, and Polartec. They also have chamois cloth, nylon outerwear (Ultrex, Supplex, nylon taffeta, quilted outerwear), waffle-weave thermal knits, sweatshirt fleece with dyed-to-match ribbing, 100% cotton knits (solids, prints), rib knits (over 25 colors), mesh knits, 2-way stretch activewear (swimwear lycra, cotton/lycra), children's prints (knits, cottons, denims, corduroy—many OshKosh), denims, woven plaid shirting flannels, and 100% cotton sleepwear flannels. They also have patterns, including Kwik-Sew, Stretch & Sew, Great Fit Patterns for larger sizes, and Sunrise Designs for children.

Payment Options: Check, Money Order, MC, Visa, Discover

Shipping Options: UPS, U.S. Postal Service

Minimum Order: $10

Other Information: They were established in 1974, and specialize in hard-to-find fabrics and patterns in addition to basic sewing supplies.

Catalog: $2 and a 9" x 12" SASE.

Judy's Heirloom Sewing

13560 East Zayante Road, Felton, CA 95018

Phone: (408) 335-1050

Services/Merchandise: They have imported fabrics, laces, books, notions, silk ribbons, mokuba ribbons, smocking supplies, embroidery supplies, Brazilian embroidery supplies, DMC threads, a complete line of Dell patterns, and a complete line of heirloom sewing supplies.

Payment Options: Check, Money Order, MC, Visa, Discover

Shipping Options: UPS, U.S. Postal Service

Minimum Order: No minimum order.

Special Discounts/Offers: 10% off orders over $100.

Catalog: $6 for an 80-page catalog, which is refundable on orders over $50.

K & K Quilteds

Route 23 Main Street, P.O. Box 23, Hillsdale, NY 12529

Phone: (518) 325-4502

Fax: (518) 325-6625

E-mail: e.qrs@taconic.net

Services/Merchandise: They have an eight-room quilt restoration studio with a large inventory of vintage fabrics for restoration work. They also have a fabric library with 18th-20th century vintage fabrics. They do custom restoration and reformatting of quilts, and they carry the book *Quilt Restoration: A Practical Guide* by Camille Cognac. In October 1996, they will have a new book by the same author, *Fragile Beauties: Victorian Quilt Restoration*.

Payment Options: Check, Money Order, MC, Visa, Amex, Discover

Shipping Options: UPS, U.S. Postal Service

Minimum Order: No minimum order.

Too tense?

Needle thread too loose

Needle thread too tight

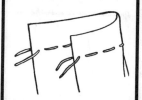

Correct tension

Beading by machine...

Thread your machine with wondersoft invisible thread and a cotton thread that matches your fabric.

You must use a very small needle, such as a 6/0 or 7/0.

Take one stitch, pull up the bobbin thread, and position your bead on your needle. Take a stitch inside your bead, then go back to your starting place. Take a stitch or two very near the edge of the bead, stitching around it.

Move to the next spot you need a bead to be placed, and repeat the steps.

Other Information: They have fifteen years in business, and are the home of the Quilt Restoration Society. In the summer, they are open Thurs. - Mon. During other seasons, call for weekend hours.

Kasuri Dyeworks

1959 Shattuck Avenue, Berkeley, CA 94704
Phone: (510) 841-4509
Fax: (510) 841-4511
Services/Merchandise: They have traditional Japanese fabrics, sashiko supplies, dyes, and books.
Payment Options: Check, Money Order, MC, Visa, Amex, Discover
Shipping Options: UPS, U.S. Postal Service
Minimum Order: $20 for credit card orders.
Catalog: $7.50, plus $5 shipping for a mail order video catalog that is two hours long. Updates are available, and you can send in your old catalog to receive an update for $5.

Kay Guiles Designs

P.O. Box 855, Petal, MS 39465
Phone: (601) 582-8312
Services/Merchandise: They carry products published by Kay Guiles Designs, including girls' patterns, smocking plates, collar booklet, books, and patterns for 18" vinyl dolls to match their girls patterns. They also custom design christening gowns.
Payment Options: Check, Money Order, MC, Visa, COD
Shipping Options: UPS, U.S. Postal Service
Minimum Order: No minimum order.
Other Information: They produce a line of unique heirloom patterns and designs. The designs are traditional, but they've added a touch of freshness.
Catalog: Free if you send a SASE.

Kaye Wood Publishing Company, Inc.

P.O. Box 456, West Branch, MI 48661
Phone: (517) 345-3028
Fax: (517) 345-3049
Services/Merchandise: They have the public television video series from *Quilting For The '90s* and *Strip Quilting With Kaye Wood*. They also have books and Starmaker Tools designed by Kaye Wood, along with products, patterns, and notions used in both programs.
Payment Options: Check, Money Order, MC, Visa, Discover
Shipping Options: UPS, U.S. Postal Service
Catalog: Free upon request.

KC Publishing

700 West 47th Street, Suite 310, Kansas City, MO 64112
Phone: (816) 531-5730
Fax: (816) 531-3873
Services/Merchandise: They have *Workbasket*, the world's largest needlework and crafts magazine, and books, patterns, and kits. They also sponsor the Classic Pattern and Craft Club. The club is designed especially to help creative people get the most enjoyment out of needlework and crafts.
Payment Options: Check, Money Order, MC, Visa, Amex, Discover
Shipping Options: UPS, U.S. Postal Service, FedEx
Minimum Order: No minimum order.
Membership Dues: $19.95 for one year.
Membership Benefits: Members get 50 Classic Patterns free, a retail value of over $45, and regular shipments of Classic Patterns. Members can also get discounted books, patterns, and kits, 50% discounts on Classic Patterns, accident insurance, car rental discounts, and more.
Catalog: Call for a copy of their catalog.

Keepsake Quilting

Box 1618, Centre Harbor, NH 03226
Phone: (800) 865-9458
Fax: (603) 253-8346
Services/Merchandise: They have a huge inventory of fabrics and supplies for quilting, including matched fabric bundles, notions, kits, and patterns. They also have a swatch club to help you make the most of the hundreds of fabrics they have to offer.
Payment Options: Check, Money Order, MC, Visa
Shipping Options: UPS, U.S. Postal Service
Minimum Order: No minimum order.
Membership Dues: $14.99 per year
Membership Benefits: Members receive catalog updates, *The Keepsake Quilter* newsletter, 600 cotton fabric ordering swatches, and $40 worth of money saving coupons. Members are also invited to take part in the Quilt Consignment Program.
Other Information: Keepsake Quilting is the largest quilt shop in America, with over 6,000 bolts of cotton-quilting fabric. They welcome bus tours, and you can call for information and accommodation suggestions.
Catalog: Free 128-page color catalog of quilting supplies.

Ken Quilt

111 Pattie, Wichita, KS 67211
Services/Merchandise: They have quilting machines.

Key West Hand Print Fashions

201 Simonton Street, Key West, FL 33040
Phone: (800) 866-0333

The Kirk Collection

1513 Military Avenue, Omaha, NE 68111-3924
Phone: (800) 398-2542, (402) 551-0386 (International inquiries)
Fax: (402) 551-0971
E-mail: kirkcoll@aol.com
Services/Merchandise: They have authentic antique fabrics, quilts, taps, blocks, lace, buttons, and trims. They have crazy-quilt fabrics and embellishments, needles, note/postcards, cotton batting, hard-to-find notions, silk ribbon, and preservation supplies and materials. They have books on a variety of topics, including silk ribbon embroidery, quilting, dyes, and textiles. They also offer the Gold Club.
Payment Options: Check, Money Order, MC, Visa, Amex, Discover
Shipping Options: UPS, U.S. Postal Service, Fed Ex (additional charge)
Minimum Order: No minimum order.
Membership Benefits: Members receive special bulletins and private sales.
Other Information: Kirk Collection has a cyberspace shop on the Microsoft Network in the Crafters Marketplace; the shortcut is Go Kirk. Real live shop hours are Tues. - Sat., 10 - 5. Call for map and driving directions.
Special Discounts/Offers: $5 off one order with the mention of *Sew Far Sew Good*.

Kite Studio

5555 Hamilton Boulevard, Wescosville, PA 18106
Phone: (610) 395-3560
Fax: (610) 395-3560
E-mail: kbi.ferrel@microserve.com
Services/Merchandise: They are a retail supplier of all supplies for making kites and banners. They also offer the Kite Builders International club.
Payment Options: Check, Money Order, MC, Visa
Minimum Order: No minimum order.
Membership Dues: $20 per year
Membership Benefits: Members get 10% off regular prices, special sales, and a newsletter.
Other Information: All their fabrics come from high quality manufacturers, so they guarantee your satisfaction. They boast one stop shopping and feel it is evident by their catalog. They have monthly sales on different colors and types of fabric.
Special Discounts/Offers: 10% discount on first order with the mention of *Sew Far Sew Good*.

Author's Note: *The KBI Newsletter* is full of great kite ideas for the experienced kite builder and the novice. Hmmm, I wonder if I can fit in another hobby?

The Knitting Guild of America

P.O. Box 1606, Knoxville, TN 37901
Phone: (615) 524-2401
Fax: (615) 521-6034
Services/Merchandise: They have *Cast-On* magazine, educational programs, educational videos, a national convention, regional conferences, and correspondence courses.
Payment Options: MC, Visa
Shipping Options: UPS, U.S. Postal Service
Membership Dues: $23 per year in the U.S., $30 per year in Canada, and $38 per year in other countries.
Membership Benefits: Members receive five issues of *Cast-On*, can enter a design competition, and have access to local chapters.

Koigu Wool Designs

Rural Route #1, Williamsford, Ontario N0H 2V0, Canada
Phone: (519) 794-3066
Fax: (519) 794-3066
Services/Merchandise: They have 100 sweater kit designs, 100% wool yarn for knitting in 150 hand-dyed colors, other natural fibre yarns (Mohair, wool and silk blends, etc.), and handmade sweaters.
Payment Options: Check, Money Order, MC, Visa
Shipping Options: U.S. Postal Service, Canadian Postal Service
Minimum Order: No minimum order.
Special Discounts/Offers: Wholesale to qualified businesses.
Catalog: They have a color catalog for $5, which is refundable with your first purchase. They also have a shade card for $10.

Kreinik Mfg. Co., Inc.

Wholesale Only
3106 Timanus Lane, Suite 101, Baltimore, MD 21244
Phone: (800) 537-2166
Fax: (410) 281-0987
Services/Merchandise: They have silk threads, including Silk Mori, Silk Sereica, Soie D'Alger, Soie Gobelin, Soie Perlee, Soie Noppee, Soie Platte, and Ping Ling.
They also have metallic threads, including blending filament, cord, cable, metallic braid, metallic ribbons, Ombre, and Japan threads.
Payment Options: Check, Money Order, MC, Visa, Amex, Discover
Other Information: Call Kreinik Customer Service for a retailer near you.

Get fired up...

Tests have shown that hemp fibers remain unchanged at heats of nearly 700 degrees. And, according to the Chinese Academy of Sciences, fabrics with at least a 50-percent hemp content block the sun's UV rays more effectively than do other fabrics.

Compared to cotton fibers, hemp fibers are longer, stronger, more lustrous and absorbent, and more mildew resistant. Hemp fabrics also keep the wearer cooler in the summer and warmer in the winter than do cottons or synthetics.

Tip quoted from:
Industrial Hemp
Hemptech

Special Discounts/Offers: Send a SASE for a free gift.
Author's Note: Kreinik sent a wonderful array of samples from their selection of metallics, bullions, and silk threads. The selection is amazing and the colors are gorgeous. They have also provided information (see the Company Appendix of this book) about silk threads, metallic threads, and their use.

L J Originals

516 Sumac Place, DeSoto, TX 75115
Phone: (214) 223-6644
Fax: (214) 223-1431
Services/Merchandise: They have the TransGraph-X®, which enables you to create your own counted needleart kit.

TransGraph-X® clear plastic grid overlays instantly convert photos and drawings into counted needleart charts without hand-charting. Simply overlay any color photo, picture, or drawing with the selected TransGraph-X® clear plastic grid to create an instant chart. Stitchers can then follow the colors that show through each square of the grid instead of the symbols as used on pre-charted designs.
TransGraph-X® eliminates hand-charting, additional costs for expensive colored pens and pencils, and hidden costs for replacement graphs. The top quality, clear plastic grids can be used countless times to produce an unlimited variety of personalized needleart. Reproduce photos, children's drawings, family crests, portraits, fabric designs, greeting cards—the list is endless.

You can enlarge and reduce effortlessly. Original art is often unavailable in the desired size for final reproduction. Therefore, it is important that designers can easily make size adjustments. The variety pack provides the flexibility to enlarge and reduce effortlessly. To duplicate, use a graph with the same count as the cloth. To enlarge, choose a graph with more squares per inch than the cloth. To reduce, choose a graph with fewer squares per inch than the cloth.
Payment Options: Check, Money Order, MC, Visa, Amex
Minimum Order: One kit retail. $35 minimum for wholesale.
Other Information: TransGraph has been featured on TV on *Aleene's Creative Living with Crafts*. This product has been marketed since 1980, and is also available with instructions in English, German or French.
Special Discounts/Offers: Wholesale to qualified businesses.

L. C. Smith's

P.O. Box 176, Medford, OR 97507
Phone: (541) 772-0432
Fax: (541) 772-7671
Services/Merchandise: They have beads, books, glass blowing supplies, displays and trays, best-buy tools, marbles, silver, gold, and other craft metals.

Payment Options: MC, Visa
Shipping Options: UPS, U.S. Postal Service, COD
Minimum Order: No minimum order.
Special Discounts/Offers: They offer volume price discounts and a special discount on your first order.
Catalog: $2

Labours of Love Heirloom Sewing Supplies, Inc.

3760 Old Clayborn Road, Rural Route #9, Abbotsford, BC V3G 1H8, Canada
Phone: (604) 853-9132
Fax: (604) 853-9142
E-mail: heirloom@direct.ca
Services/Merchandise: They have heirloom sewing supplies, fine cottons and heirloom silks, French lace and embroideries, silk ribbons, French wire edge ribbons, vintage bear-making supplies, books, videos, patterns, and all related notions. Getaway sewing weekends are in the fall and spring.
Payment Options: Check, Money Order, MC, Visa
Shipping Options: Canada post expedited.
Minimum Order: No minimum order.
Other Information: They were established in 1990 and are recognized as Canada's premier mail order service for fine sewing. The owner is Debra Justice, a well known international keynote speaker.
Special Discounts/Offers: Free shipping on first order with the mention of *Sew Far Sew Good*. Wholesale to qualified businesses.
Catalog: Free upon request.

Labours of Love Heirloom Sewing Retreat

3760 Old Clayburn Road, Abbotsford, BC V3G 1H8, Canada
Phone: (604) 853-9132
Fax: (604) 853-9142
E-mail: heirloom@direct.ca
Event Information: All classes are taught by Debra Justice, so you can learn in small, uninterrupted 3-day seminars. You can learn heirloom sewing on a Victorian nightgown, lace shaping, sharks tooth, shadow embroidery, fancy pintucks, and vintage ribbon-work. Each class has a Saturday evening seminar and reception.
Payment Options: Check, Money Order, MC, Visa
How Many Years: 2 years
Time of Year/Month: October and May
Approximate Costs: $245 Canadian per class, plus kits that cost approximately $150. Lunch is included in the class cost.
Other Information: Kit fees are due the last day of retreat. Call them to register. Enrollment is limited, so you should call early.
Special Discounts/Offers: 10% off for registrations and tuitions

received eight weeks prior to the class.

Lace Heaven, Inc.
2524 Dauphin Island Parkway, Mobile, AL 36605
Phone: (334) 478-5644
Fax: (334) 450-0589
Services/Merchandise: They have books, buttons, fabrics, lace, children's and women's patterns, zippers, thread, and trims.
Payment Options: Check, Money Order, MC, Visa, Discover
Shipping Options: UPS inside continental U.S., U.S. Postal Service outside U.S.
Minimum Order: $10 retail. $100 wholesale.
Other Information: The store is open Tues. - Fri., 10 - 4. However, they are often in the store on Monday and Saturday. They will take orders at any time they are there. Orders can be faxed 24 hours per day.

Everyone who works at Lace Heaven sews, and will be happy to answer any of your questions. The store is run completely by women with families, so they understand many of your sewing problems. They will always try to answer questions and match colors.

Lace Heaven has been in business for over ten years. They carry over a million yards of lace in stock at all times, with over 2,400 patterns and colors to choose from.
Special Discounts/Offers: 10% off first order of $25 or more with the mention of _Sew Far Sew Good_.

The Lace Merchant
P.O. Box 222, Plainwell, MI 49080
Phone: (616) 685-9792
Fax: (616) 685-5043
Services/Merchandise: They have books, antique and vintage embroidery and needlework, antique and vintage laces, and _The Old Lace and Linen Merchant_ newsletter.

Bulletin boards, classified ads, and display ads in the newsletter will bring together buyers and sellers of antique lace, linens, pre-Edwardian clothing, and textiles. The newsletter serves as a price reference for dealers, collectors, and private sellers. It also provides information on where to have lace identified and evaluated, and how to wash, use, display, and store old lace and textiles. Send a SASE for a sample copy.
Payment Options: Check, Money Order, MC, Visa

The Lacemaker
176 Sunset Avenue South, Edmonds, WA 98020-4134
Phone: (206) 670-1644
Fax: (206) 774-1219

E-mail: 102254.314@compuserve.com
Services/Merchandise: They have everything you need for lacemaking, embroidery, and many other lost arts. They have books, supplies, kits, fabrics, and dyes.
Payment Options: Check, Money Order, MC, Visa, Amex
Shipping Options: UPS, U.S. Postal Service
Special Discounts/Offers: Wholesale to qualified retailers.
Catalog: $5

Lacis
3163 Adeline Street, Berkeley, CA 94703
Phone: (510) 843-7178
Fax: (510) 843-5018
Services/Merchandise: Lacis offers an extensive selection of threads, ribbons, and supplies for lacemaking, embroidery, and costuming. They publish over 60 books relating to needlework and costuming, and maintain an inventory of over 3,000 titles relating to textiles and costuming in English and foreign languages. They manufacture specialized lace making tools, sew-on purse frames, exotic tatting shuttles, reproduction needlework tools, reproduction bridal "orange-blossom" flowers, tassel forms, hand-dyed bias cut silk embroidery ribbon, and tatting needles. They distribute DMC Floche and other cotton threads, Edmar Brazilian embroidery threads and Japanese Bunka threads. You can also find a wide selection of period images on silks and other fabrics for quilts and other projects. A photo transfer service is provided for transferring your own images or documents to fabric. The retail store offers an extensive selection of vintage garments, with an emphasis on bridal and whitework, while a gallery offers antique lace and textiles dating from the 14th century, as well as fine vintage linens.
Payment Options: Check, Money Order, MC, Visa
Shipping Options: UPS, U.S. Postal Service
Minimum Order: No minimum order.
Other Information: Established in 1965, Lacis also has a separate wholesale division offering books, tools, and notions to the needlework industry. They exhibit at TNNA, INRG, SE Fabric, and Quilt Market trade shows. The retail store is located at 2922 Adeline Street in Berkeley, CA.
Special Discounts/Offers: Wholesale to qualified businesses.
Catalog: $5

Lark Books
50 College Street, Asheville, NC 28801-2896
Phone: (704) 253-0467, (800) 284-3388
Fax: (704) 253-7952
Services/Merchandise: They have books, magazines, kits, and furniture based on a wide variety of crafts.

Hair scrunchees...

Cut any piece of 45" fabric cross-wise, at least 6" wide.

Fold this in half lengthwise, and sew a 1/4" seam the full length of the tube.

Sew a 7" piece of elastic on one end of your tube to the wrong side of the fabric.

Turn the fabric right side out, and pull the elastic through.

The fabric will "scrunch" as you pull the elastic. When it is through, secure the free end of the elastic and sew the ends of your scrunchee together.

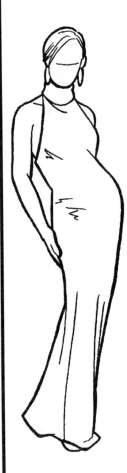

Dress styles...

Evening Gown

Payment Options: Check, Money Order, MC, Visa, Amex, Discover
Shipping Options: UPS
Minimum Order: No minimum order.
Special Discounts/Offers: Special discounts on many items.

The Leather Factory

Department SEWCAT, P.O. Box 50429, Fort Worth, TX 76105
Phone: (817) 496-4414
Fax: (817) 496-9806
Services/Merchandise: They have leathers of all types for garments. They also have moccasins. They carry jewelry, accessories, metal buttons, conchos, spots, and nailheads. They have leather and vinyl lace, dyes, paints and finishes for leather, and thread for sewing leather by hand or by machine. They will fit garment patterns to leather at no cost when you order from them. They also have a wholesale club.
Payment Options: Check, Money Order, MC, Visa, Amex, Discover
Membership Dues: $25 per year.
Membership Benefits: Members receive wholesale prices and a bi-monthly newsletter.
Other Information: They offer fast service from over 20 warehouse locations.
Special Discounts/Offers: Free catalog with the mention of *Sew Far Sew Good*.
Catalog: $3

Leather Unlimited

7155 Highway B, Department SFSG96, Belgium, WI 53004-0905
Phone: (414) 994-9464
Fax: (414) 994-4099
Services/Merchandise: They have leather, sheepskin, tools, findings, kits, patterns, and books. They also have leather accessories, including handbags, vests, chaps, and belts to decorate in any way you wish.
Payment Options: Check, Money Order, MC, Visa, Discover
Shipping Options: UPS, U.S. Postal Service, RPS, Freight
Minimum Order: $40
Special Discounts/Offers: 5% discount on first order with the mention of *Sew Far Sew Good*. Wholesale to qualified businesses.
Catalog: $2, which is refundable with purchase.

Ledgewood Studio

6000 Ledgewood Drive, Forest Park, GA 30050-3228
Phone: (404) 361-6098
Fax: (404) 361-5030
Services/Merchandise: They have beads, buttons, costuming supplies, fabrics, feathers, hatmaking supplies, laces, fur, rhinestones, dress pat-

terns for dolls, silk ribbons for embroidery, thread, and yarn.
Payment Options: Check, Money Order, MC, Visa
Shipping Options: U.S. Postal Service
Minimum Order: No minimum order for check or money order, but a $50 minimum on MC and Visa.
Other Information: Most of the merchandise is small and specialized for doll costuming. Many items, such as laces and trims, are suitable for full-sized clothing. The dress patterns for dolls are published by the owner.
Catalog: $2, and a business sized, SASE, triple stamped.

Leesburg Looms, Inc.

201 North Cherry Street, Van Wert, OH 45891
Phone: (419) 238-2738, (800) 329-9254
Services/Merchandise: They have floor and table looms, and weaving supplies.
Payment Options: Check, MC, Visa
Shipping Options: UPS, Looms shipped by freight.
Minimum Order: No minimum order.
Catalog: Free catalog upon request.

Left Bank Fabric

8354 West 3rd Street, Los Angeles, CA 9000
Phone: (213) 655-7289

Lefthanders International

P.O. Box 8249, Topeka, KS 6608
Phone: (913) 234-2177

Leisure Arts

P.O. Box 5595, Little Rock, AZ 72215
Phone: (501) 868-8800

Lifetime Career Schools

101 Harrison Street, Archibald, PA 18403
Phone: (717) 876-6340
Fax: (717) 876-1682
Services/Merchandise: They offer in-home training programs, including Sewing/Dressmaking, Doll Repair, and Small Business Management.
Other Information: Lifetime Career Schools is an accredited member of the Distance Education and Training Council. They are very proud that LCS has had this status since the inception of the accrediting pro-

gram in 1956. They are also licensed by the Pennsylvania State Board of Private Licensed Schools.

Each one of these hobby/career training programs is hands-on, so that you learn by doing and enjoy the money-making potential long before you finish the program.
Catalog: Free upon request.

The Linen Fabric World
1246 Bird Road, Miami, FL 33146
Phone: (305) 663-1577
Fax: (305) 661-7385
Services/Merchandise: Their fabrics are 100% linen, mostly imported from England, Belgium, and Ireland. The fabrics range from 54" - 60" width, and are carried in three weights:

Sandy is the heaviest of the three and is suitable for jackets, pants, tablecloths, and upholstery.

Karmen is a medium weight linen for dresses, blouses, and skirts.

Caracas is the lightest of the three, and is used for children's clothing (this is known as the handkerchief weight).

Each weight has a color card with 20 or more colors.

They also offer more seasonal fabrics, like spring wool, at very competitive prices and 100% raw silk in fashionable colors. In addition, they will be adding notions, buttons, and trims in the near future.
Payment Options: Check, Money Order, MC, Visa
Shipping Options: UPS, U.S. Postal Service (2 day priority)
Minimum Order: No minimum order.
Membership Dues: $5 annually, which is refundable with your first order of $20 or more.
Membership Benefits: Customer receives a package containing: color cards, updates on new colors, sales, fashion tips, 20% discount on all fabrics and further discounts on volume purchasing.
Other Information: Even though their main product is 100% linen fabric, they encourage their customers to let them know of special needs in other areas of sewing products, such as buttons, trims, and notions.
Special Discounts/Offers: Special prices on volume purchasing. A 20% discount on the regular price is included on the retail list of prices.

Live Guides, Inc.
10306, 64th Place West, Mukilteo, WA 98275
Phone: (206) 353-0240
Fax: (206) 361-6188
Services/Merchandise: They have accessory findings, classes and instruction, custom patterns, videos, serging equipment, and serging and sewing notions.

Payment Options: Check, Money Order, MC, Visa
Shipping Options: UPS, U.S. Postal Service

Logan Kits
Route 3, Box 380, Double Springs, AL 35553
Phone: (205) 486-7732
Fax: (205) 486-0070
Services/Merchandise: They have bra underwires, lingerie kits, pound and yard goods, tricot, cotton, lycra, cotton/lycra blends, power net, lace, elastic, interlock, plaids, jersey, sweatshirt fleece, collars, thread, towels, Sew Lovely patterns, Kwik-Sew patterns, Stretch & Sew patterns, ribbing, robe velour, quilt battings, spandex, and sewing books.
Payment Options: Check, Money Order
Shipping Options: UPS
Minimum Order: $5 retail. $50 wholesale.
Other Information: They ship within 3-7 working days.
Special Discounts/Offers: Free patterns with selected bundles of jersey, interlock, and sweatshirt fabrics.
Catalog: $1.50 each for retail and wholesale brochures. Brochures are printed twice a year in the spring and fall.

Londa's Sewing, Etc.
404 South Duncan Road, Champaign, IL 61821
Phone: (217) 352-2378
Fax: (217) 352-3389
Services/Merchandise: They have classes, fabrics, and 10 patterns that feature heirloom sewing, but could be made without it. Explicit directions for general sewing and heirloom sewing are included.
Payment Options: Check, Money Order, MC, Visa, Discover
Shipping Options: U.S. Postal Service
Minimum Order: $5 or one pattern.
Other Information: The retail store grew out of the pattern line Londa's Elegant Creations. Their teaching philosophy is, "Students should learn all they can from all sources, and come up with their favorite techniques. No way is always right."
Special Discounts/Offers: All patterns are discounted to $2.50.
Catalog: $1.75

Loompal
4223 Lost Lane, Las Cruces, NM 88005
Phone: (505) 523-9039
Services/Merchandise: They offer covers to protect your loom. The Loompal cover is heavy enough to resist accidental spills, protect your valued loom during travel, and keep the sun from drying out that

Dress styles...

A-Line

Dress styles...

Princess Seamed

special wood or fading your project. The Loompal cover keeps house pets from catching your sewing in their claws, protects needles and pedals from small hands, and eliminates periodically dusting your loom.

Payment Options: Check, Money Order
Shipping Options: UPS, U.S. Postal Service
Other Information: Your satisfaction is guaranteed.
Special Discounts/Offers: Wholesale to qualified businesses.
Catalog: Send a SASE for a free brochure.

Louët
P.O. Box 267, Ogdensburg, NY 13669

M & J Trimming Co.
1008 6th Avenue, New York, NY 10018
Phone: (212) 391-6200
Fax: (212) 764-5854
Services/Merchandise: They have trims, trims, and more trims!
Payment Options: Check, Money Order, MC, Visa, Amex
Shipping Options: UPS, U.S. Postal Service, FedEx
Minimum Order: $50
Other Information: They have over 8,000 trims in inventory.
Author's Note: I have been inside the store on Sixth Avenue, and it's a wonderland of trims and tassels. They have trims arranged in every square inch, and it took me several minutes of stunned silence to grasp the enormity of it all. Their catalog gives you a good idea of the trims they carry, but they have so much more. Call if you are looking for something specific.
Catalog: Free upon request.

M & M Trims
91 South Main Street, Wilkes Barre, PA 18701
Phone: (717) 825-7305
Fax: (717) 825-7463
Services/Merchandise: They have Swarovski rhinestones, beads, sequins, pearls, mirrors, feathers, appliqués, nailheads, and more. You can buy wholesale and save.
Payment Options: MC, Visa, Discover
Shipping Options: UPS
Catalog: $1, plus a SASE for catalog.

M's Fabric Gallery
200 South 21st Street, Birmingham, AL 35233
Phone: (205) 323-7755

Fax: (205) 323-1522
Services/Merchandise: They have drapery and upholstery fabrics, decorative trims, wood poles, wrought iron wimpoles, and finials for decorating.
Payment Options: Check, Money Order, MC, Visa
Shipping Options: UPS
Minimum Order: No minimum order for supplies in stock.

MagEye's-MFD Enterprises
222 Sidney Baker South, Suite 204, Kerrville, TX 78028
Phone: (210) 896-6060
Fax: (210) 896-6064
E-mail: amigo@hi/conet.com
Services/Merchandise: They have a hands-free, head-mounted magnifier for quilting, sewing, and other close work. The magnifier has an optical quality acrylic lens, and greater power is available by switching lenses. A slip-on, cushioned headband fits all head sizes. You adjust focus and enlargement by moving the object closer to or farther away from the lens. The visor swings out of the way when not in use. It works well with or without prescription glasses, travels well, and makes a great gift.
Payment Options: Check, MC, Visa
Shipping Options: UPS
Author's Note: MagEye's sent a sample magnifier for me to try, and I really have to admit, it made things much clearer and reduced my eye strain. My eyes were less tired after an hour of close work than ever before. I would definitely recommend this for anyone working with delicate stitches, beads, embroidery, or other close work.

Magic Cabin Dolls
Route 2, Box 39, Westby, WI 54667
Phone: (608) 634-2848
Fax: (608) 634-2877
Services/Merchandise: They have natural fiber dolls and doll making supplies. They also offer ethnically diverse skin fabrics, yarns, wool stuffing, patterns, kits, tools, books, clothing, and accessories.
Payment Options: MC, Visa
Other Information: This is their eighth year in business.
Special Discounts/Offers: Quantity discounts are available.
Catalog: Free catalog upon request. $5 for swatches of skin fabrics and hair yarns.

Magic Fit Patterns
P.O. Box 606, Anacortes, WA 98221
Phone: (360) 293-2688, (800) 477-6355

Fax: (360) 299-0383

Services/Merchandise: They have Custom Fit Dress and Pants patterns, French curves, vellum paper, and a how-to video.

Payment Options: Check, Money Order, MC, Visa

Shipping Options: UPS, U.S. Postal Service

Minimum Order: No minimum order.

Other Information: Magic Fit Patterns are custom-fitted to a specific figure using 14 basic measurements. After you purchase the pattern, measure and draw it yourself, or have a Magic Fit consultant draw it for you. There are over 820 design possibilities for the dress pattern, seven with the pants pattern. The Dress Pattern and Pants Pattern kits come with the following:

    Dress Kit: Pattern Front - Master
                      Pattern Back - Master
                      Pattern Sleeve - Master
                      Bust Dart Marker
                      Curve Tools
                      Dart Tool
                      Instruction Manual

    Pants Kit: Pattern Front - Master
                      Pattern Back - Master
                      Waistband and Pockets - Master
                      Curve Tools
                      Instruction Manual

There is a how-to video available for customers who would prefer to see the techniques demonstrated. This system is sold retail and wholesale from the home office.

They are setting up a network of consultants around the country who will retail Magic Fit Products. This is a wonderful home business opportunity. Call (800) 477-6355 for more information.

Author's Note: Magic Fit sent me a copy of their how-to video, and it is excellent. The pattern kits have everything you need to get started on the way to custom-fit tailoring or sewing, but I really suggest you see the video as well. It's inspiring!

Mallery Press

4206 Sheraton Drive, Flint, MI 48532

Phone: (800) A STITCH in North America only, (810) 733-8743

Fax: (810) 733-7357

E-mail: amisimms@aol.com

WWW: http://quilt.com/amisimms

Services/Merchandise: Mallery Press carries books by Ami Simms, including *Every Trick in the Book*, *Invisible Appliqué*, *How to Improve Your Quilting Stitch*, and others.

Payment Options: Visa, MC

Shipping Options: UPS, U.S. Postal Service

Special Discounts/Offers: $1 off any two or more books with the mention of *Sew Far Sew Good*.

Other Information: Autographed copies upon request.

Author's Note: Ami's books are fun, and filled with her unique sense of humor. They are easy to follow, and full of interesting information, told as only Ami can. She sent postcards of some of her quilts, including her whimsical bikini quilt, which more than any, shows her sense of fun and frolic.

Catalog: Free upon request.

The Mannings Handweaving School & Supply Center

1132 Green Ridge Road, P.O. Box 687, East Berlin, PA 17316

Phone: (717) 624-2223

Services/Merchandise: They have books and magazines for knitting, weaving, spinning, and dyeing. They also have knitting patterns, looms, spinning wheels, yarns, fibers, natural dyes, knitting needles and supplies, weaving shuttles, bobbins and tools, spindles, hand carders, and drum carders.

Payment Options: Check, Money Order, MC, Visa, Discover

Shipping Options: UPS, U.S. Postal Service

Minimum Order: No minimum order.

Other Information: Service, service, service. They make every effort to get whatever a customer is looking for; if they have it in stock, they ship it the same day they get the order.

Manny's Millinery Supply Center

26 West 38th Street, New York, NY 10018

Phone: (212) 840-2235

Fax: (212) 840-2236

Services/Merchandise: They have everything for ladies' hatmaking, including trims, equipment, blocks, hat boxes, displays, hat bodies, and trimmed and untrimmed hats. They also provide custom-blocking of felt and straw hats.

Payment Options: Check, Money Order, MC, Visa, Amex

Minimum Order: Three hats, or $25 of assorted trims, or one hat and $15 of assorted trims.

Maple Hill Software

Maple Hill, Plainfield, VT 05667

Phone: (802) 454-7310

Fax: (802) 454-7310

Services/Merchandise: They have *Patternland Weave Simulator* design software for weaving and publication, for IBM compatibles. It features numeric or graphic drafts, on graph paper. Direct Loom Control is optional. A Windows version of *Patternland Weave Simulator*, *Weave Publisher* and *Pattern Grapher* is under development. PWS 5.1 demo

Dress styles...

Jumper

Large buttons won't fit?

Has this ever happened to you?

You find some really beautiful buttons at the store (or in a catalog) that would look great with a silk shirt you have. The problem is that not only are the buttonholes too small, but the placket is not wide enough to enlarge them.

Well, here is an easy solution to that problem:

Take the existing buttons off that shirt and save them. Where the buttons were, put in a second set of buttonholes, perfectly aligned with the originals.

Now, sew each new button to one of the shirt's original buttons, leaving a thread shank. Button the smaller buttons through each pair of holes, and your larger buttons will adorn the front of your blouse as if they had been meant to.

disk $10 charge is good toward program purchase of the full version of PWS.
Payment Options: Check, Money Order, MC, Visa
Shipping Options: U.S. Postal Service

Margola Corporation
Wholesale Only
48 West 37th Street, New York, NY 10018
Phone: (212) 695-1115
Fax: (212) 594-0071
Services/Merchandise: They sell Czech glass rhinestones, beads, acrylic rhinestones, settings, nailheads, pearls, embroidered trim, Czech seed beads, fire-polish beads, fashion beads, and jewelry findings.
Payment Options: MC, Visa
Shipping Options: UPS
Minimum Order: $50
Other Information: Margola imports many items from all over the world. They service the jewelry, apparel, craft, and bridal industries.

Marilyn's Button Sales
Wholesale Only
10121 Evergreen Way, #628, Everett, WA 98205
Phone: (800) 422-1434
Services/Merchandise: They specialize in unique, artisan-made buttons in various materials, including fused glass, pewter, fine porcelain, silver, nickel-silver, bone, shed antler, acrylics, novelties, antiques, and collectibles; there are hundreds to choose from.
Payment Options: Open Accounts/Checks, MC, Visa
Minimum Order: No minimum order.
Other Information: They offer fast and personal service, and have a national reputation. They have been in business since 1989 as Marilyn's Sales & Associates.
  Terms on open accounts are 5% 15 day/net 30 days.
Catalog: $15 full color catalog.

Marinda Stewart
P.O. Box 402, Walnut Creek, CA 94597
Phone: (510) 938-4391
Services/Merchandise: Marinda Stewart specializes in women's clothing patterns with interesting details and embellishment techniques. The focus is on a flattering fit as well as fashion appeal. Along with fashion patterns, there are several dolls, some clothing accessories, and a few home decorating items.
Payment Options: Money Order, Personal Checks
Shipping Options: UPS, U.S. Postal Service

Minimum Order: One item for retail sales.
Other Information: Marinda has been teaching and designing for twenty years, and her work has been featured in countless books, magazines, and invitational shows.
Catalog: Send a SASE for a free catalog. A wholesale catalog is available for stores. Please mention Oracle Publications when requesting a catalog.

Marine Sewing
6801 Gulfport Boulevard South, South Pasadena, FL 33707
Phone: (813) 345-6994, (800) 713-8157
Fax: (813) 347-1424
Services/Merchandise: They have canvas and other outdoor fabrics and notions, upholstery supplies, flag cloth and other nylon fabric, cotton duck, hook and loop, webbing, sunbrella, vinyl coated mesh, rot-resistant thread, and zippers.
Payment Options: MC, Visa, Amex, Discover
Shipping Options: UPS, U.S. Postal Service
Minimum Order: No minimum order.
Other Information: Marine Sewing has everything a home sewer needs to make their yacht canvas, and do upholstery. Advice is free with any purchase.
Special Discounts/Offers: Discounts to qualified businesses.

Marlene's Decorator Fabrics
301 Beech Street, Department 2J, Hackensack, NJ 07601
Phone: (800) 992-7325
Fax: (201) 843-5688
Services/Merchandise: Decorator Fabrics offers 34-60% off on all national fabric brands. They buy first quality direct from the country's leading sources. Orders are processed the day they are received. Some brands they offer are Angie, Ametex, Kaufman, Covington, J.A. Barrow, Kranst, Kasmer, and Durales.
Payment Options: Money Order, MC, Visa
Shipping Options: UPS
Minimum Order: 4 yards retail (with discount). 15 yards wholesale.
Other Information: They have 25 years of experience in decorator fabrics. It is important to them that their customers are satisfied.
Catalog: You can get a brochure by sending them a SASE.

Mary Ellen & Co.
29400 Rankert Road, Department SF, North Liberty, IN 46554
Phone: (219) 656-3000, (800) 669-1860
Fax: (219) 656-3000
E-mail: 71562.2136@compuserve.com

Services/Merchandise: They have historical sewing patterns from the 1830s to the 1890s for beautiful wedding gowns, capes, corsets, and undergarments. They also have corset kits, books on clothing, costuming, hatmaking, needlecraft, sewing, quilting, dolls, and hoop boning, doll making supplies, sewing notions and accessories. They also have many Victorian accessories and gifts.

Payment Options: Check, Money Order, MC, Visa

Shipping Options: U.S. Postal Service, UPS

Minimum Order: No minimum order.

Other Information: Mary Ellen Smith has over 17 years of experience with Victorian 1800s items, and she is an assistant staff member for CompuServe's Living History Forum. She offers assistance with historical sewing patterns, Victorian wedding gown patterns, and corset and camisole patterns to their sewing customers.

Mary Ellen & Co. assists museums, The National Park Service, theatre groups, gift shops, bridal shops, old time photo studios, and historical home tours with costuming guides, clerks, and staff. Most items are kept in stock, ready for immediate shipping.

Special Discounts/Offers: Wholesale to qualified businesses.

Author's Note: Mary Ellen & Co. also carries a wide variety of gifts and bridal accessories. I'd suggest her catalog to anyone with even a passing interest in vintage fashion; it is sure to make you an enthusiast in no time.

Catalog: $3, which is refundable with purchase, or free by request with any order.

Mary Jane's Cross 'N Stitch

Mail Order Only

1948 Keim Court, Naperville, IL 60565

Phone: (708) 355-0071, (800) 334-6819

Fax: (708) 355-0396

Services/Merchandise: They have books, kits, accessories, fabrics, and fibers for counted cross-stitch.

Payment Options: Check, Money Order, MC, Visa, Discover

Minimum Order: No minimum order.

Other Information: They have a newsletter that is mailed six times a year. They have been specializing in counted cross-stitch supplies since 1977. Special orders are welcome.

Catalog: $7.50. $5 is refundable with your first $30 order.

Mary Roehr Books & Video

500 Saddlerock Circle, Sedona, AZ 86336

Phone: (520) 282-4971

Services/Merchandise: They have books and videos on sewing,

fitting, and sewing as a business, as well as a sewing cartoon book.

Payment Options: Check, Money Order

Shipping Options: U.S. Postal Service

Other Information: Mary Roehr has a B.S. in Clothing and Textiles, and has operated her own custom tailoring business for more than 20 years. She has taught thousands of students how to tailor, alter clothing, and start sewing businesses of their own.

Mary Wales Loomis

1487 Parrott Drive, San Mateo, CA 94402-3632

Phone: (415) 345-8012

Fax: (415) 345-3206

Services/Merchandise: They have the book *Make Your Own Shoes*.

Payment Options: Check, MC, Visa

Shipping Options: UPS (for large wholesale orders), U.S. Postal Service

Minimum Order: One book.

Special Discounts/Offers: Wholesale to qualified businesses.

Author's Note: Mary sent me a copy of her book, and I got extremely excited reading her simple instructions. These are shoes that you make yourself, not old shoes re-covered. My head is filled with ideas for custom shoes.

Mary's Productions

Box 87 SFSG, Aurora, MN 55705

Phone: (218) 229-2804

Fax: (218) 229-2533

Services/Merchandise: They carry creative sewing and appliqué books by Mary Mulari. They also have sewing-themed notecards.

Payment Options: Check, Money Order, MC, Visa, Discover

Shipping Options: UPS, U.S. Postal Service

Minimum Order: One book.

Other Information: Mary's Productions has been in operation since 1983, the year Mary Mulari published her first book, *Designer Sweatshirts*. She continues to write about and teach creative sewing with appliqué and embellishing sweatshirts and other clothing. She has also written a book about making your own travel accessories, has designed patterns for *McCalls'*, and has appeared as a frequent guest on *Sewing With Nancy*.

Special Discounts/Offers: Discount coupons will be sent to those who mention *Sew Far Sew Good* when requesting a catalog.

Author's Note: Mary sent me a copy of her book of travel accessories, and I can't wait until I have the time to spend making some of her items for our upcoming trips to consumer shows across the country.

Catalog: Catalogs and brochures can be requested with a SASE.

Hat styles...

Cap

Top

Bowler

Ten Gallon

Fusible banner making...

Rather than stitching around the edges of a banner piece with a fusible thread, then bonding the pieces in place, try using a liquid fusible to save time and one step at the sewing machine.

Master Designer

P.O. Box 1667, North Riverside, IL 60546
Phone: (708) 780-1769
Fax: (708) 780-0076
Services/Merchandise: The Master Designer book series offers comprehensive, self-instructed methods of pattern drafting, garment designing, and tailoring.
Payment Options: Check, Money Order, MC, Visa
Minimum Order: No minimum order.
Other Information: Master Designer has been providing schools with books on pattern drafting, designing, and tailoring for more than 55 years. Many of the finest fashion schools in the country use Master Designer books in their curricula. Among these schools are:
- Fashion Institute of Technology, New York, NY
- Philadelphia College of Textiles and Science, Philadelphia, PA
- Los Angeles Trade and Technical College, Los Angeles, CA

These books contain the findings of years of research. The material is of interest to the home sewer, student, or specialist in the field.

Material Memories

P.O. Box 39, Springville, NY 14141
Services/Merchandise: This company offers full-size and easy to sew patterns. Patterns include Raggedy Ann, Topsy Turvey, Amish, Folk, and Angels. Also available are patterns for delightful Rabbits, Merlina, and old-fashioned African American and Santa dolls.
Payment Options: Call to ask.
Shipping Options: Free postage.
Other Information: They've been in business for over twelve years. The price for patterns has not gone up, and the postage is free—a great bonus.
Special Discounts/Offers: Free catalog with the mention of *Sew Far Sew Good*.
Catalog: $1

Mediaeval Miscellanea

6530 Spring Valley Drive, Alexandria, VA 22312
Phone: (703) 642-1740
Fax: (703) 642-1740
Services/Merchandise: They have Mediaeval and Renaissance costume patterns, available either by mail order or at events. Their office is open by appointment.
Payment Options: Check, Money Order, MC, Visa
Shipping Options: UPS, U.S. Postal Service, FedEx
Other Information: In business since 1982, the owner is a professional costumer specializing in these eras since 1970. All of the designers are also professionals. They are very helpful and will refer customers to various sources as necessary.
Special Discounts/Offers: Wholesale to qualified businesses.
Catalog: Free upon request.

Meredith Stained Glass Center, Inc.

1701-G Rockville Pike, Rockville, MD 20852
- or -
1840-17 Cherry Lane, Laurel, MD 20707
Phone: (301) 770-6930, (301) 953-1740, or (800) 966-6667
Fax: (301) 770-6931, (301) 490-3613
Services/Merchandise: They have supplies for making glass beads, buttons, marbles, and other glass goods. They have glass rods, equipment, and classes in glass crafts. They also have a complete line of supplies for stained glass and fusing crafters.
Payment Options: MC, Visa, American Express, Discover, (the Laurel location also accepts bank debit cards)
Shipping Options: UPS
Special Discounts/Offers: One-time 10% discount on first order with the mention of *Sew Far Sew Good*.

MHC

2852 Jeff Davis Highway, Suite 109, Box 11, Stafford, VA 22554
Phone: (540) 720-6758
Fax: (540) 720- 1734
Services/Merchandise: They have the Lazy Sharyn rotary tables with cutting mat, quilt patterns, and quilt hangers.
Payment Options: Check, Money Order, MC, Visa, Discover
Shipping Options: UPS
Minimum Order: No minimum order.
Other Information: These rotary tables are made of sturdy wood and heavy bearings, enabling the cutting of any fabric without the table bowing or breaking. Custom-made tables are available.
Special Discounts/Offers: Free shipping of first order with the mention of *Sew Far, Sew Good*.
Catalog: $2, which is refundable with your first order.

Michael James/Studio Quilts

258 Old Colony Avenue, Somerset Village, MA 02726-8601
Phone: (508) 672-1370
Fax: (508) 676-8601
Services/Merchandise: Michael James teaches beginner to advanced level workshops in color and design. The workshops are not restricted to quiltmakers. The workshops are comparable to foundation level art school courses, and are useful for aspiring colorists/designers in widely varying media.

Michael James also lectures on his own work and other contemporary art quilts.

Other Information: Prices are $600 for a lecture (negotiable, depending on anticipated size of audience), and $1,800 for a 3-day intensive workshop, plus expenses. Call or write for more information.

Mimi's Books & Patterns for the Serious Dollmaker

300 Nancy Drive, P.O. Box 662, Point Pleasant, NJ 08742
Phone: (908) 899-0804
Fax: (908) 714-9306
Services/Merchandise: They have books and detailed teaching patterns for realistic dolls.
Payment Options: Check, MC, Visa
Shipping Options: UPS
Special Discounts/Offers: Wholesale to qualified businesses.
Author's Note: Mimi sent almost too much information for me (or this book) to absorb. Her generous nature also shines through in her magazine, *Let's Talk Dollmaking.* This is one of the most comprehensive works I have seen on this subject, and Mimi's whimsy and enthusiasm really make it a joy to read.

In their book, *New Clays for Dollmaking*, Mimi and Jim give comprehensive insights into working with cellular and polymer clays, how they are formed, and why they react the way they do to different heats and pressures. I would suggest this as necessary reading for anyone interested in learning more about working in these media, whether for dolls, beads, buttons, or sculpture.

To delve deeper into Mimi's wonderful sense of humor, I must give you a sample of the inspirational wording that accompanies her *Happy Birthday Honey Doll Pattern and Instruction Book*:

"Mary was feeling tired and fat and fifty when she discovered that Victoria's Secret sold intimate apparel in size 2X.

Smiling to herself, she planned a birthday party for her honey. She baked a chocolate cake and served it with champagne, added some naughty videos, and her own special gift wrap..."

To say the least, the doll that results takes itself none too seriously, and allows room for personalization. Her other patterns offer the same enjoyment in creation and flexibility in construction techniques.

They also offer the *Dollmaker's Sourcebook*, full of sources, clubs, and useful information. Well worth it for anyone interested in doll making.
Catalog: Free if you send a SASE.

Mimi's Fabrications

4836 South Main Street, Waynesville, NC 28786
Phone: (704) 452-3455, (800) 948-3455

Services/Merchandise: They are Elna sewing machine dealers. They also have books, blank fabrics, buttons, custom services, doll and soft toy making supplies, embroidery supplies, fabrics, classes, lace, videos, patterns, kits, quilting and patchwork supplies, sewing notions, silk ribbon embroidery, and smocking supplies. Retail sales only.
Payment Options: Check, Money Order, MC, Visa.
Minimum Order: $15
Special Discounts/Offers: 10% discount on first order with the mention of *Sew Far Sew Good*.
Catalog: $5

Mindsun

1007 Mohawk Trail, Andover, NJ 07821
Phone: (201) 398-9557
Fax: (201) 398-8082
Services/Merchandise: They have *Mindweave* weaving software.
Payment Options: Check, Money Order, MC, Visa
Shipping Options: U.S. Postal Service
Minimum Order: One unit.
Special Discounts/Offers: $95 is the current discount price.
Catalog: Free upon request.

Minifest

P.O. Box 369, Cedar Mountain, NC 28718
Phone: (704) 884-7667
Event Information: The only show and seminar devoted exclusively to miniature quilts. Classes are offered during the run of the show.
Payment Options: Check, Money Order
Shipping Options: UPS, U.S. Postal Service
Time of Year/Month: Early Summer.
Approximate Costs: $50 for each full-day class.
Other Information: Classes are taught by nationally known teachers who specialize in miniature quilts. There are cash awards and an annual Singer Featherweight drawing.
Catalog: Free upon request.

Miss Maureen's Fabrics and Fancies

1151 Hillcrest Road, Suite East, Mobile, AL 36695
Phone: (334) 639-8270, (334) 639-8271, (800) 633-0991
Services/Merchandise: They have heirloom and fine fabrics, including silks, linens, cottons, wools, and blends. They have several brand name lines of threads, such as Kreinik, Petals, YLI, Minnamurn, Waterlillies, and Watercolors. They also have Anchor threads and flossses, overdyed threads, and ribbons. They carry the line of Hendler satin ribbons, silk

Coat styles...

Clutch

Qiviut, golden fleece of the Arctic...

Quiviut is the under-fleece of the musk ox. It is extremely soft, and much stronger than cashmere .

threads, flosses, and ribbons. In addition to these products, they also carry patterns, smocking plates, cross-stitch designs, mother of pearl buttons, Swiss embroideries, and designer buttons. They also have a wide selection of laces, including French, English, German, domestic, antique, Cluny, and Battenburg.

Payment Options: Check, MC, Visa, Amex
Shipping Options: UPS, U.S. Postal Service
Minimum Order: No minimum order.
Other Information: They have classes taught by nationally known sewing and needlearts teachers, including classes on smocking, tatting, basic sewing, hand and machine heirloom sewing, all types of embroidery, custom sewing, and designing. The owner writes for *Creative Needle* magazine.
Special Discounts/Offers: Purchase $200 in merchandise and receive free shipping and handling.
Catalog: $2.50 and fabric swatches for $5.

Morning Light Emporium

P.O. Box 1155, Paonia, CO 81428
Phone: (970) 527-4493
Fax: (970) 527-4493
E-mail: mle@wic.net
Services/Merchandise: They have glass beads in many styles, including crow, pony, seed in sizes 11 and 14, bugles, Czech fire-polish, rounds, chevrons, bone, metal, and more. They also have beading thread, needles, and instruction books.
Payment Options: Check, Money Order, MC, Visa
Shipping Options: UPS, U.S. Postal Service
Minimum Order: No minimum order.
Other Information: They also sell through A Haggle of Vendors Emporium, which is located at 510 Main Street in Grand Junction, Colorado.
Catalog: Free upon request.

Morning Star Indian Gallery

1236 Sheridan Avenue, P.O. Box 2343, Cody, WY 82414
Phone: (307) 587-6577
Fax: (307) 587-4383
Services/Merchandise: They specialize in Native American and mountain man craft and bead supplies. They have instruction, history, and general information books. Patterns are also available.
Payment Options: Money Order, MC, Visa
Shipping Options: UPS
Minimum Order: No minimum order.
Other Information: Owner Debbie Harrington is an enrolled member of the Sault Ste. Marie Tribe of Chippewa Indians. As a child, she was

given the name of Morning Star. She traveled to Pow Wows, danced, made crafts, and developed her own beading skills. Her work has won awards and has been shown in galleries across the U.S.
Catalog: $3, which is refundable with purchase.

Mother Nurture

916 Royal Blackheath Court, Naperville, IL 60563-2304
Phone: (708) 420-4233 (area code changes to 630 after Aug '96)
E-mail: sgustafs@maui.netwave.net
Services/Merchandise: Mother Nurture specializes in everything for breastfeeding, pregnancy, and beyond. They offer patterns for discreet nursing at discounted prices. Some of these patterns are available exclusively through Mother Nurture, and many others are hard to find.

They also offer *Sewer Guide*, a book to help you modify clothes you already own and adapt conventional patterns to breastfeeding. It applies to over 100 styles of clothing and costs $10.
Payment Options: Check, Money Order, MC, Visa
Special Discounts/Offers: 10% discount on first order with the mention of *Sew Far Sew Good*. Wholesale to qualified businesses.
Catalog: $3

Mountain Colors

P.O. Box 156, Corvallis, MT 59828
or
4072 Eastside Highway, Stevensville, MT 59870
Phone: (406) 777-3377
Services/Merchandise: They have multi-colored handpainted yarns in colors inspired by the Rocky Mountain West. The yarns are available in wool, mohair, alpaca, and novelty yarns for knitting, crocheting, and weaving. They have kits with patterns and yarn for various sweaters, vests, hats, scarves, mittens, shawls, and throws.
Payment Options: Check, Money Order, MC, Visa
Shipping Options: UPS, U.S. Postal Service
Minimum Order: No minimum order.
Other Information: Mountain Colors is a cottage business located in the beautiful Bitterroot Mountain Valley and established to sell multi-colored hand-dyed yarns and fibers. Their 17 luscious colors have been inspired by the mountains, meadows, and woodlands that surround them.

They use a variety of techniques and colors to give their yarn a one-of-a-kind look. They have studied and tested to come up with color combinations that will be fun and interesting to use in knitting and weaving. They handpaint every skein of yarn with up to eight colors. That means that though two skeins may have the same color name, no two skeins are exactly alike.

Their business began in 1992, when they had young children at home. Due to limited opportunities in their area, they decided they needed to create jobs for themselves. They saw a need for high-quality wools in handpainted colors for those wanting one-of-a-kind finished goods. As Mountain Colors has grown, they have been able to hire other women with young children. Their employees work from their homes, which allows them to schedule their own time.

All of their yarns are also available undyed for purists and home-dyers.

Special Discounts/Offers: Quantity discounts. Wholesale to qualified businesses.

Author's Note: Their yarns are featured on the back cover, but the picture simply cannot do justice to the brilliant array of gorgeous colors they have available. I think that $5 is a small price to pay to have a look (and feel) at these unique, beautiful yarns.

Catalog: $5 for a catalog and sample cards.

Mountain Mist/The Stearns Technical Textiles Company

100 Williams Street, Cincinnati, OH 45215-4683
Phone: (513) 948-5276 or (800)-345-7150
Fax: (513) 948-5281
Services/Merchandise: Mountain Mist manufactures a complete line of 100% bleached cotton batting, blue ribbon cotton batting, quality polyester batting, quilt light polyester batting, fatt batt polyester batting, pillowloft, pillow forms, fiberloft stuffing, wonderloft stuffing, and their Mountain Mist historic quilting stencils.
Payment Options: MC, Visa, Check, Money Order
Shipping Options: UPS, U.S. Postal Service, RPS
Other Information: In 1996, the Mountain Mist division of the Stearns Technical Textiles Company celebrated 150 years of experience and service in quiltmaking. A century and a half of quilt batting and quilt pattern tradition are accomplishments of which they are very proud. Throughout the 150 years, Mountain Mist has felt the obligation to be a resource for both beginners and experienced quilters. If you have any questions concerning quilting, or about any of the Mountain Mist products, please call Miss Phoebe Edwards. She is their resident expert on quiltmaking and will be happy to assist you.

Phoebe may be reached 8:30 - 4:30 EST at (800) 345-7150, or write to:

Miss Phoebe Edwards, c/o Mountain Mist
100 Williams Street, Cincinnati, OH 45215-4683.

---

mRAYO'S Fiberworks

506 Baylor Court, Benicia, CA 94510-1329
Services/Merchandise: They carry the book *Machine Embroidery:*

Stitches and Techniques Workbook.

Murielle Roy & Co.

67 Platts Mill Road, Naugatuck, CT 06770

The Musk Ox Company

633 Fish Hatchery Road, Hamilton, MT 59840
Phone: (406) 363-6818
Services/Merchandise: They have the only private wool production herd of musk oxen in the world. They are proud to offer clean, handcombed fiber and pure musk ox yarn in natural and colored shades.
Payment Options: Check, Money Order, MC, Visa
Author's Note: The musk ox fiber they sent as a sample is one of the softest fibers I have ever felt. It may be my imagination, but it felt very warm, almost like it generated it's own warmth. Absolutely beautiful!
Catalog: $4 and a SASE for samples and brochure.

Nancy's Notions

P.O. Box 683, Beaver Dam, WI 53916-0683
Phone: (414) 887-0391, (800) 833-0690
Fax: (800) 255-8119
Services/Merchandise: They have notions, books, fabrics, patterns, videos, threads, ribbons, snaps, and zippers.
Payment Options: Check, Money Order, MC, Visa, Discover
Shipping Options: Airborne Express
Minimum Order: No minimum order.
Other Information: 100% satisfaction is guaranteed. They have qualified customer service representatives you can call at (800) 245-5116. They also have the Video Rental Club. The knowledgeable staff at Nancy's Notions will take your order quickly and accurately, package your order carefully, and send it out to you. Each product is tested, and they are always looking for new sewing, quilting, and serging items that will make your sewing time more efficient and pleasurable.
Author's Note: They carry just about every notion imaginable, and some I haven't imagined. A must for any sewing gadget enthusiast.
Catalog: Free *Best of Nancy's Notions* catalog upon request, and a full-sized catalog of over 160 pages with first order.

National Academy of Needlearts

10300 Cherokee Road, Richmond, VA 23235
Phone: (804) 320-1437

Skirt styles...

Pegged

Fax: (804) 320-9654
Services/Merchandise: The Academy's goal is to provide the highest standards of needlework education to all needle artists who are interested in furthering their embroidery skills as technicians, artists, or teachers.
Membership Dues: Graduates $25, Associates $15, Friends - any amount.
Membership Benefits: Members receive the quarterly newsletter and can attend the annual assembly for classes and lectures. The academy also offers teacher certification, judging certification, and an honors program.

National Quilting Association
P.O. Box 393, Ellicot City, MD 21041-0393
Phone: (410) 461-5733

National Thread & Supply
695 Red Oak Road, Stockbridge, GA 30281
Services/Merchandise: They have a wide assortment of threads, notions, buttons, scissors, drapery, hardware, press boards, irons, and related supplies, equipment, and books.
Payment Options: Check, Money Order, MC, Visa, Amex, Discover
Shipping Options: UPS, U.S. Postal Service, FedEx, COD
Minimum Order: $20
Other Information: Their slogan is, "The professional's choice since 1948."
Catalog: Free upon request.

The Natural Fibre Club of Canada
143 Ashdale Avenue, Winnipeg, MB R2H 1R1, Canada
Phone: (204) 233-4446
Fax: (204) 231-3389
Services/Merchandise: This is a club dedicated to natural fibers.
Payment Options: MC, Visa
Membership Dues: $15 U.S. per year.
Membership Benefits: Members receive the quarterly newsletter, fibre and yarn samples, and discount coupons.

Needleart Guild
2729 Oakwood NE, Grand Rapids, MI 49505
Phone: (616) 361-1531
Fax: (616) 361-2616
Services/Merchandise: They have quilting patterns and quilting stencils for both full-size and miniature quilts, and a complete line of

quilting notions, including raised edge quilters' thimbles. They have an extensive line of needles for appliqué, basting, and quilting, and handcrafted jewelry for stitchers.
Payment Options: Check, Money Order, MC Visa
Shipping Options: UPS, U.S. Postal Service
Other Information: They have offered mail order quilting supplies since 1932.
Special Discounts/Offers: Wholesale to qualified businesses.
Catalog: Retail catalog $2, or free with order. Free wholesale catalog.

The Needlecraft Shop
103 North Pearl Street, Big Sandy, TX 75755
Phone: (903) 636-4011
Fax: (903) 636-4088
Services/Merchandise: They have a club offering frequent stitcher points that can be used for The Needlecraft Shop patterns, supplies, and other goods. They have crochet kits, books, dolls and doll kits, and ideas and stories from needlecrafters all over the country.
Payment Options: Check, Money Order, MC, Visa, Discover
Shipping Options: UPS, U.S. Postal Service
Membership Dues: $15 per year.
Membership Benefits: Members get up to 70% off Needlecraft Shop and other patterns, and publications. Members also receive their newspaper.
Other Information: The club was founded to preserve and promote the skill of needlecraft as a vital part of our cultural tradition.
Special Discounts/Offers: Earn free points that can be redeemed for patterns and supplies.

Neighbors and Friends
P.O. Box 294402, Lewisville, TX 75028-4402
Phone: (214) 539-1073
WWW: http://www.craft.com./nbr_frnd
Services/Merchandise: *Neighbors & Friends Arts & Crafts Market Guide* is a monthly magazine of business articles for professional crafters. It includes show opportunities, lists of wholesale suppliers and craft malls, and more. Exposure is national. Regular subscription price is $21. For a single issue send $2.
Special Discounts/Offers: Special subscription rate of $18 with the mention of *Sew Far Sew Good*.

New England Quilt Museum
18 Shattuck Street, Lowell, MA 01852
Phone: (508) 452-4207
Fax: (508) 452-5405

Services/Merchandise: They offer classes and lectures, and have changing exhibitions of antique, traditional, and contemporary quilts. They also offer various quilting-related products.

Payment Options: Check, Money Order, MC, Visa

Membership Dues: $30, $15 for Seniors

Membership Benefits: Members receive free admission to the museum, discounts, and a newsletter.

Special Discounts/Offers: 10% discount on first order with the mention of _Sew Far Sew Good_.

Nimble Thimbles

704 Fairview Avenue, South Pasadena, CA 91030

Phone: (818) 403-5792

Fax: (818) 403-5792

Services/Merchandise: They offer custom-made patterns. They also offer the pattern books _How to Make Lazy Lucy, a Cute Doll You Can Make from Any Scraps You May Have, Pants, Pants, Pants–and How to Make Them Fit_, and _T-Shirt Masterpiece_, which has 10 cute, comfortable and flattering outfits from T-shirts.

Payment Options: Check, Money Order

Minimum Order: No minimum order.

Special Discounts/Offers: 10% discount on first order with the mention of _Sew Far Sew Good_. Wholesale to qualified businesses.

Author's Note: The owner sent me pictures of her patterns, a copy of her book _Pants, Pants, Pants–and How to Make Them Fit_, and a copy of her Lazy Lucy pattern, which appears in the Company Appendix. Her instructions are very easy to follow, and her ideas for T-shirt clothing are ingenious.

Catalog: $2, which is refundable with an order. You can also get the catalog free of charge via fax-on-demand systems. Please call from a fax machine.

Nina Designs

P.O. Box 5766, Santa Fe, NM 87502

Phone: (505) 982-1214, (800) 336-6462

Fax: (505) 982-1321

E-mail: nina@nets.com

Services/Merchandise: They have sterling silver beads, clasps, earring tops, pendants, charms, chains, buttons, and headpins, handmade in Bali. They also have handcarved beads of cow bone made in Bali.

Payment Options: MC, Visa, COD

Shipping Options: UPS

Minimum Order: $50 retail. $100 wholesale.

Nolting Mfg., Inc.

Route 3, Box 147, Highway 32 East, Stover, MO 65078

Phone: (573) 377-2713

Fax: (573) 377-4451

Services/Merchandise: Nolting offers four sizes of hand-guided, long-arm quilting machines with tables and accessories, a sit down long arm model quilting machine with table, and a computerized quilting machine with table that runs in computer mode or out of computer mode.

Payment Options: Check, Money Order, MC, Visa, Discover, COD

Shipping Options: UPS

Minimum Order: $25

Other Information: Nolting is the original manufacturer of these quilting machines and still manufactures them at their shop in the U.S.A.

Special Discounts/Offers: Information available for distributors and dealers.

Catalog: Free upon request. The video catalog is $14.95.

Nordic Fiber Arts

   Mail Order Only

4 Cutts Road, Durham, NH 03824-3601

Phone: (603) 868-1196

Services/Merchandise: This is your only complete source for Rauma Yarns—the yarns preferred by Norwegian craftspeople and featured in the books _Sweaters: Twenty-eight Contemporary Designs in the Nordic Tradition_ and _More Sweaters: A Riot of Color, Pattern and Form_, both by Tone Taklle and Lise Kolstad. They will have another book translated by Interweave Press, again featuring Rauma yarns. This yarn is also featured in _Folk Socks_ by Nancy Bush. They also offer customized kits, books, specialty items, knitting needles, buttons, and clasps. They will ship orders within 48 hours of receipt.

Payment Options: Check, Money Order, MC, Visa

Shipping Options: UPS, U.S. Postal Service

Minimum Order: No minimum order.

Other Information: Nordic Fiber Arts travels to major knitting shows and conventions for consumers, and they offer assistance with any of their designs.

Special Discounts/Offers: 10% discount on first order with the mention of _Sew Far Sew Good_.

Catalog: Free upon request.

Northeast Quilters Association

2717 Main Street, Glastonbury, CT 06033

Phone: (860) 633-0721

Services/Merchandise: Quilt festival each July.

Coat styles...

Princess-Seamed

Jacket styles...

Safari

Bolero

Northwest Tag & Label, Inc.

2435 SE Eleventh Avenue, Portland, OR 97214
Phone: (503) 234-1054
Fax: (503) 234-1294
Services/Merchandise: They have custom-printed fabric labels, logo labels, care/content labels, and in-stock labels.
Payment Options: Check, Money Order, MC, Visa, COD
Shipping Options: UPS
Minimum Order: 250 labels.
Catalog: $1, which is refundable with order.

Norton House

P.O. Box 579, 1836 Country Store Village, Wilmington, VT 05363
Phone: (802) 464-7213
Fax: (802) 464-8826
Services/Merchandise: They have an incredible selection of cottons for quilters, along with all of the books, patterns, and notions to make quilts or related projects. They also have gifts, including quilts and completed items.
Payment Options: Check, MC, Visa
Shipping Options: UPS, U.S. Postal Service
Minimum Order: No minimum order.
Other Information: They have been in business for 29 years and provide excellent customer service and quilting classes. Their charming New England house, circa 1760, is listed on the National Register of Historic Sites, and the retail shop and restaurant are open daily all year. Fabric coordination and selection is provided at no charge.
Special Discounts/Offers: Bonus Card Club: $20 in Free merchandise for every $190 spent.

Norwood Looms, Inc.

P.O. Box 167, Fremont, MI 49412
Phone: (616) 924-3901
Fax: (616) 924-2895
Services/Merchandise: They make handcrafted, furniture-quality handweaving looms, quilting hoops, and frames. All are made of solid northern cherry or hard rock maple, and smooth sanded with a clear finish.
Payment Options: MC, Visa
Minimum Order: No minimum order.
Other Information: Norwood Looms was incorporated in 1939, and they have been at the same location since 1964. They are a small company with a reputation for quality craftsmanship and customer service.
Catalog: $2 for a color brochure of looms and accessories. Send a SASE for a color brochure of quilting hoops and frames.

O.F.A.

P.O. Box 668496, Charlotte, NC 28266-8496
Services/Merchandise: They have traditional African patterns and doll patterns. Patterns can be cut in your size from African fabrics in stock.
Payment Options: Money Order
Shipping Options: UPS, U.S. Postal Service
Other Information: O.F.A. considers itself to be the first traditional African pattern supplier for the home sewer. They have patterns for women, men, children, and dolls.
Catalog: Send $2 money order for brochure.

Oiye Buttons

8640 Northwest Bailey, Portland, OR 97231
Phone: (503) 286-5511
Services/Merchandise: They have handmade porcelain buttons and pins, in a large assortment of sizes, colors, and styles (especially animals and flowers).
Payment Options: Check, Money Order
Shipping Options: UPS, U.S. Postal Service
Minimum Order: No minimum order.
Other Information: These buttons are made of porcelain clay and fired to temperatures of up to 2,400°F. Heavy duty thread is best for sewing these buttons onto your garment. Turn your garment inside out, or place it in a pillowcase, for added protection before machine washing and drying.
Special Discounts/Offers: Wholesale to qualified businesses.
Author's Note: Very tasteful, unique buttons; I love them.

Old Style Trading Company

230 East Rangely Avenue, Rangely, CO 81648
Phone: (970) 675-2017
Services/Merchandise: They have one-of-a-kind items, beads, beading classes by appointment, books, leather, furs, videos, and feathers.
Payment Options: Check, Money Order
Shipping Options: UPS, U.S. Postal Service
Minimum Order: No minimum order.
Other Information: They have several sources for beads. If you are having trouble finding a color, or if you need to match a color, they will attempt to help you.
Catalog: $2, which is refundable with purchase.

Open Chain Publishing, Inc.

P.O. Box 2634, Menlo Park, CA 94026-2634
Phone: (415) 366-4440

Fax: (415) 366-4455
Services/Merchandise: They have *Creative Machine Newsletter*, a 48-page forum for people who love sewing machines and sergers the way others love cars or computers. It contains extensive book, video, and pattern reviews, articles, resource listings, an information exchange, and lots of laughs.
Shipping Options: UPS, U.S. Postal Service
Other Information: They have some selected books by Robbie Fanning, like *The Complete Book of Machine Quilting*, second edition, as well as a yearly *Sewing Machine/Serger Survey* ($25), and the *Sewing Machine Blue Book* ($20).
Author's Note: Robbie is a very nice lady, and she is very well informed about her subjects. She has graciously contributed an article about copyright to the Company Appendix

Optional Extras, Inc.

55 San Remo Drive, South Burlington, VT 05403
Phone: (800) 736-0781
Fax: (802) 864-5030
Services/Merchandise: They have a complete range of beads and jewelry components for the serious beader and hobbyist, an incredible book selection, and basic tools.
Payment Options: Check, Money Order, MC, Visa, Discover, COD
Shipping Options: UPS
Minimum Order: No minimum order.
Catalog: $1

Oracle Publications

1226 Carroll Avenue, Ames, IA 50010
Phone: (515) 233-6226
Fax: (515) 233-6744
E-mail: oraclepubl@aol.com or ljbc20b@prodigy.com
Services/Merchandise: They have small business image and marketing services.

They also have a finder system. For a $5 fee, they will find at least one source for rare or unique items you want that are sewing or fiber-related.

They also have *Sew Far Sew Good*, and coming soon, a cooking sourcebook, and a professional education opportunities sourcebook.
Payment Options: Check, Money Order, MC, Visa, COD. Terms available.
Shipping Options: UPS, U.S. Postal Service
Other Information: They are a small business whose owners have backgrounds in crafts, cooking, journalism, graphic design, and promotions. Their services are guaranteed and personalized to suit businesses or individuals.

They are setting aside a percentage of profits from *Sew Far Sew*

Good to benefit needy children. They are looking for volunteers to decorate muslin dolls for children in homeless shelters across the country.

Oracle Publications will also be offering contemporary needlework and embroidery patterns from a collection of work left by Heather's mother, Jacqueline Ahrens, who passed away as a result of breast cancer. They're looking for volunteers to test some of the patterns and give feedback on the designs. Twenty-five percent of profits from each of these designs will be donated to benefit breast cancer research.

Please call or write for more information.
Special Discounts/Offers: Wholesale to qualified retailers and distributors. Call or write for rates.
Author's Note: Thank you for purchasing this book. We've made every effort to make *Sew Far Sew Good* a book that you will find informative, entertaining, and pleasing to use. We'd love to hear your comments on what we can do better, or what we've done right. We are dedicated to improving each updated edition.

Oregon Buttonworks

174 Cross Place, Eugene, OR 97402
Phone: (541) 484-0434
E-mail: buttonups@aol.com
Services/Merchandise: They have gemstone buttons—hand-cut, drilled, and polished—from a variety of stone material.
Payment Options: Check, Money Order
Shipping Options: U.S. Postal Service
Other Information: Each button is unique, but care is taken when creating a matched set. The buttons can be machine washed and dried without scratching or breaking. Any broken button will be replaced.

Some of their most popular buttons are fashioned from picture, poppy, and rain forest jaspers, and from crazy lace agate.

Special orders are welcome. Just let them know which stone interests you, and they'll try to find it. Oregon Buttonworks will also try to match fabric and yarn swatches.
Author's Note: The flier that they send out shows some of the buttons from their standard and premier collections. I have always had a love affair with different rocks, stones, and minerals, and these buttons touch that part of me. The colors cover the spectrum and capture the imagination. Worth the envelope and stamp.
Catalog: Send a SASE for a color flier.

Oregon Rule Company

P.O. Box 5072, Oregon City, OR 97045
Phone: (503) 657-8330
Fax: (503) 655-8040
Services/Merchandise: Oregon Rule Company provides self-adhesive rulers constructed from Mylar plastic in various widths and lengths. The rulers can be placed on sewing machines or sewing tables at a

Jacket styles...

Blazer

Chanel/Box

Bodywear styles...

Catsuit

fraction of the cost of metal yardsticks. You can get rulers that read left-to-right, right-to-left, up, down, or rulers that read left and right from a zero centerpoint. Special orders are no problem. The Easy Reader 36" is $4.95, the 72" is $8.95.
Payment Options: Check, Money Order, COD
Shipping Options: UPS, U.S. Postal Service, FedEx
Minimum Order: $15
Other Information: ORC originated in 1983 to provide unique and specific measuring devices for all types of applications.
Special Discounts/Offers: Quantity discounts. Wholesale to qualified businesses.

Oregon Street Press

2145 Oregon Street, Berkeley, CA 94705
Services/Merchandise: They have the book *Polychromatic Screen Printing* by Joy Stocksdale.
Author's Note: This is a very interesting method of silkscreening; all of the colors are painted on a single screen, then transferred to the cloth with one pull of the squeegee.

The technique is clearly explained, and photos and illustrations enhance the text of the book.

Oregon Tailor Supply Co.

P.O. Box 42284
Phone: (800) 678-2457
Fax: (503) 232-9470
Services/Merchandise: They offer dressmakers' and tailors' supplies.
Payment Options: MC, Visa
Shipping Options: UPS
Minimum Order: $5

Oregon Worsted Company/Mill End Store

9701 Southeast McLoughlin Boulevard, Portland, OR 97222
Phone: (503) 786-1234
Fax: (503) 786-2022
Services/Merchandise: They have a large selection of fabrics in many styles, including bridal, fashion, juvenile, outerwear, quilting, costume, couture, and home decorating. They have an excellent selection of materials, including cotton, rayon, polyester, silk, wool, nylon, acetate, and fur. They also have batting, laces, sequins, linings, notions, and yarns.
Payment Options: Check, Money Order, MC, Visa, Discover
Shipping Options: UPS.
Minimum Order: $15
Membership Benefits: Guild discounts, 10% off with proof of mem-

bership.
Other Information: A swatching service is available, as well as special orders.

Oriental Silk Company

8377 Beverly Boulevard, Los Angeles, CA 90048
Phone: (213) 651-2323
Fax: (213) 651-2323
Services/Merchandise: Oriental Silk Company offers only the finest imported silks, woolens, porcelains, hand embroideries, and linens from China and the Orient. They have an incredible color selection and great prices.
Payment Options: Check, Money Order, MC, Visa
Shipping Options: UPS
Minimum Order: One yard per cut.
Other Information: Oriental Silk Company has been family-owned and operated for over 20 years. They serve a diverse customer base, including home sewing enthusiasts, couture designers, clothing manufacturers, and Hollywood costumers. Their store hours are Mon. - Sat., 9 - 6.
Special Discounts/Offers: 10% discount to schools. Wholesale to qualified businesses.
Author's Note: The price list really shows some excellent buys. I can't wait for *Sew Far Sew Good* to be done, so that I can get some silk and sew again.

Original Sewing & Craft Expo

26612 Center Ridge Road, Westlake, OH 44145
Phone: (216) 899-6300, (800) 699-6309
Fax: (216) 899-6302
E-mail: sewncraft@aol.com
Services/Merchandise: This is a traveling, three-day, sewing and craft consumer exposition with exciting sewing, quilting, tailoring, home decorating, needlework, and craft classes featuring nationally acclaimed instructors. Each show has fabulous fashion events, a large retail exhibit hall with all the newest and best in sewing and crafting, make-it-take-it-crafts, home decorating presentations, hands-on workshops, seminars, displays, and much more. In addition, a sourcebook containing tips, techniques, projects, and instructions from instructors and exhibitors is available.
Payment Options: Check, MC, Visa
Other Information: Register for classes by mail, phone, fax, or at the Expo. Consumers learn about all the most up-to-date techniques and products in the sewing and craft industry. The ever-changing Seasonal Decorating Craft Studio lets everyone try the latest products while creating delightful projects in less than an hour. The numerous Exhibit Hall booths support and extend the classroom experience. Everyone is

welcome to attend for one, two, or three days.
Special Discounts/Offers: Free brochure, free General Admission. Class discounts available when registering in advance.

Ornament

P.O. Box 2349, San Marcos, CA 92079
Phone: (800) 888-8950
Fax: (619) 599-0222
Services/Merchandise: They have the book *Collectible Beads* by Robert K. Lui and *Ornament Magazine*.

Ornamental Resources

P.O. Box 3010-SS, 1427 Miner Street, Idaho Springs, CO 80452
Phone: (303) 279-2102, (800) 876-6762
Fax: (303) 567-4245
Services/Merchandise: They have rare and old glass beads and buttons, stones, pendants and tassels, and beads of metal, bone, horn, shell, ceramic, stone, wood, and plastic. They also have feathers, findings, chain, handbag frames, rhinestones, books, tools, seed beads, pony and bugle beads, beading thread, needles, and glass sew-ons.
Payment Options: Check, Money Order, MC, Visa, Amex, Discover
Shipping Options: U.S. Postal Service, UPS, Fed Ex
Minimum Order: $25
Other Information: For over 25 years, Ornamental Resources has provided bead workers, jewelry designers, production craft workers, and costume designers with one-stop shopping. They specialize in unique, rare, and vintage pieces, but make sure that basic beads, charms, tools, and supplies are also available for prompt shipping. If you would rather design and create than expend energy tracking down supplies, they can help you put it all together.
Special Discounts/Offers: Quantity discounts on many items.
Author's Note: The catalog is overwhelming. The choices are practically endless. I've tried very hard to do justice to their huge inventory, but you really have to sit down with the catalog for an hour or more to grasp the full extent of their selection. This one is a must for anyone interested in making their own jewelry.
Catalog: $15 for 300 pages (B&W) in a 3-ring binder, including supplemental updates.

Outdoor Wilderness Fabrics

16195 Latah Drive, Nampa, ID 83651
Phone: (208) 466-1602, (800) OWF-SHOP
Fax: (208) 463-4622
Services/Merchandise: They have Polartec by Malden, waterproof breathables, coat fabrics, coated nylons, insulations, hardware, and patterns.
Payment Options: Check, Money Order, MC, Visa, Discover, COD
Shipping Options: UPS, U.S. Postal Service
Minimum Order: No minimum order.
Other Information: The owners take pride in the personal service and commitment they offer to each of their customers. They try to meet the needs of ALL. Any customer can purchase small yardage with no minimum order requirements or cut fees. The wholesaler can purchase any size yardage or amount of hardware with only a $30 minimum order; no cut fees are applied. They also offer additional price cuts for overrun fabrics, full rolls, 15 yard cut pieces of Polartec for the full roll discounted price, plus 5% for handling bulk prices on hardware.
Author's Note: Outdoor Wilderness Fabrics sent me the sample fabrics set that can be ordered for $5. The range of color available in Polartec is huge, as are their other fabric selections. If you love the great outdoors, and love to sew, you can't afford to miss their products.
Catalog: $5 for a full set of fabric samples.

Oxford Craft Software

P.O. Box 208, Bonsall, CA 92003
Phone: (619) 723-0141, (800) 995-0420
Fax: (619) 723-6196
Services/Merchandise: They have the *X-Stitch Designer: Premium Plus*, computer cross-stitch charting program for Windows (IBM), for $499.95. A retail version is also available by mail order for $129.95. *X-Stitch Designer for Lace* will be launched this year (1996).
Payment Options: Check, Money Order, MC, Visa, Discover
Shipping Options: U.S. Postal Service, FedEx
Membership Benefits: They have a user group in the U.K., and hope to start one in the U.S.
Other Information: Their programs are endorsed by Anchor, DMC, Madeira, Patternayan, and Paterna. Most top designers use their *Premium Plus* program.
Special Discounts/Offers: Their retail program is sold with a 40%-50% discount on purchases of five or more.
Catalog: Free upon request.

P.L. Greene's Country Jumpers & Hand Painted Ceramic Buttons

1100 Olive, New Haven, MO 63068
Phone: (314) 237-2992
Services/Merchandise: What Wonderful Buttons are all made of durable ceramic and come in a wide range of shapes and designs. They use seven different colors: black, red, green, gold, mauve, purple, and blue. They have adorable cats, dogs, elephants, geese, swans, horses, pigs, chickens, rocking horses, and cows. They have a Christmas series,

Your own iron-ons...

How would you like an easy way to transfer a pattern with an iron, rather than tracing it?

Take your design to the local copy center and ask to have it copied onto vellum. That's all you need to do. Your personal transfer is ready.

Tip provided by: Atlanta Puffections Page 243

and also offer houses, sailboats, lady bugs, and bumble bees. They have a large, colorful variety of florals, irises, roses, shasta daisies, and ovals, circles, and hearts. They have needleart buttons for quilters and knitters, featuring the tools of the craft in all colors. The buttons are all created by local artisans in New Haven and Hermann, Missouri. They are painted with a white background, and they are beautiful and truly unique, and as the name implies, just Wonderful.

Payment Options: Check, Money Order, MC, Visa
Shipping Options: U.S. Postal Service
Minimum Order: 10 buttons retail. 100 buttons wholesale.
Special Discounts/Offers: Wholesale to qualified businesses.
Catalog: $2 for a brochure.

Palmer/Pletsch Publishing

P.O. Box 12046, Portland, OR 97212-0046
Phone: (503) 274-0687
Fax: (503) 274-1377
Services/Merchandise: They have books, videos, kits, and some unusual notions. They also have a full range of classes for the sewing enthusiast.
Payment Options: Check, Money Order, MC, Visa
Shipping Options: UPS, U.S. Postal Service, FedEx
Minimum Order: $10
Special Discounts/Offers: Wholesale to qualified businesses.
Catalog: Free upon request.

Paperdolls' Design

P.O. Box 182067, Shelby Township, MI 48318-2067
Phone: (810) 739-2679
Services/Merchandise: They have stretch fabrics, including lycra solids and prints, illusion, lace, knits, and velvets. They also have non-stretch fancies: velvets, pre-beaded chiffons, lycra, and knits. They cater mainly to roller and ice skaters, but also serve persons requiring activewear fabrics for various sports.
Payment Options: Check, Money Order, MC, Visa, Discover
Shipping Options: UPS, U.S. Postal Service, COD
Minimum Order: No minimum order.
Other Information: Their business is primarily mail order. They carry over 150 types of fabrics and colors. Their stock is not rotated like many fabric retail stores. They offer these fabrics year-round. Every month a specific fabric is discounted up to 25%.

Designing services are offered for skaters, and they have 20 years of experience in sewing and designing skate costumes.

Paperdolls' Design offers a monthly newsletter for $5 for 6 months. The newsletter offers sewing tips, skate humor, and a sewing topic of the month in lengthy discussion.

Special Discounts/Offers: 10% discount on first order with the mention of *Sew Far Sew Good*.
Author's Note: The sample newsletters she sent are fun, lighthearted reading, with good information, tips, and humorous insights into the world of skating competitions.
Catalog: They have swatch sample packets, including stretch fabrics (basic), non-stretch fabrics (basic), and fancies (including pre-beaded), for $6 each. The cost of each is applied to your first order.

Park Bench Pattern Company

5423 Mary Lane Drive, San Diego, CA 92115-1328
Phone: (619) 286-6859
Fax: (619) 287-0841
Services/Merchandise: They design and carry 16 patterns, including dresses, jackets, pants, a 3-piece outfit, and a 6-piece outfit. They have pattern design kits for each pattern. They offer design ideas, finishing options, additional sizing instructions, embellishing ideas, and more. They have a semi-annual newsletter, and offer trunk shows, lectures, and classes for retail sewing stores, sewing clubs, etc.
Payment Options: Check, MC, Visa
Shipping Options: UPS, U.S. Postal Service
Minimum Order: No minimum order.
Other Information: Park Bench Pattern Company has been operating since 1993. They are an independent pattern company specializing in easy-to-make, easy-to-wear garment patterns for the home sewer. These are modern patterns that are an exciting alternative to the mainstream home sewing patterns, designed for the real woman who wants stylish, comfortable garments that are fashionable year after year. The garments made from their patterns are simple, practical, and timeless. Park Bench Patterns:

- Have strong simple shapes that make them easy to sew.
- Inspire imagination and creativity.
- Lend themselves to the sewer's individual design.
- Are not tailored or structured (precise sewing not required).
- There are no rules with Park Bench patterns. If it works for you, it's right.

The pattern instructions are clear and easy to follow. Designed for lots of ease (6"-10"), Park Bench Patterns come in one size and adjust up and down with little effort. They are a favorite with dressmakers, quilters, handweavers, wearable art enthusiasts, and fabric painters, and they have lots of open areas for embellishing.

Design kits are available for each pattern. Each kit contains templates of the garment, sewing hints, and numerous design ideas. Using colored pencils or fabric swatches, you can create your own design.

Park Bench Patterns are exhibited at sewing shows and conventions throughout the country. Mary Lou is also available to present trunk shows, lectures, and classes featuring her Park Bench Collection.

Special Discounts/Offers: Wholesale to qualified businesses. Discounts to sewing teachers.
Author's Note: Mary Lou sent me her Elm Street Park pattern and the design kit to go with it. She has a lot of fun with her suggestions on embellishing and personalizing the pattern. I am looking forward to stealing time away to play with this new toy. She even gives you coloring pages to design your new garment. Check these patterns out; they are sure to appeal to everyone.
Catalog: $3

Past Patterns

P.O. Box 2446, Richmond, IN 47374
Phone: (317) 962-3333
Fax: (317) 962-3773
Services/Merchandise: Their historical patterns catalog features 108 patterns from 1829-1950 for women, men, children, brides, and full figures. They have workshops for constructing historical clothing.
Payment Options: Check, Money Order, MC, Visa, Discover
Shipping Options: UPS, U.S. Postal Service
Minimum Order: No minimum order.
Other Information: Past Patterns has been in business since 1979.
Special Discounts/Offers: 50% discount to qualified businesses.
Catalog: $4

Patchogue Sewing Machine Center, Inc.

75 East Main Street, Patchogue, NY 11772
Phone: (516) 475-8282
Services/Merchandise: Sewing machine accessories.

Patchworks

6676 Amsterdam Road, Amsterdam, MT 59741
Phone: (406) 282-7218
Fax: (406) 282-7322
E-mail: ptchwrks@alpinet.net
WWW: http://www.alpinet.net/~ptchwrks/
Services/Merchandise: They specialize in providing reproduction cotton fabrics to quilters for specific time periods between 1775 and 1940. They have a catalog and provide a sampling service. They also have visuals of the latest arrivals in the What's New section of their home page on the World Wide Web. Mainly a mail order company, but they sell to walk-in customers. They have supplied custom-made quilts and yardage to customers in the television and movie industries, to living history museums, re-enacting groups, and opera and theater companies.
Payment Options: Check, Money Order, MC, Visa, Amex
Shipping Options: UPS, U.S. Postal Service, FedEx, Airborne Express

Minimum Order: ½ yard.
Other Information: Patchworks offers programs and workshops on fabric dating and reproduction cottons. These programs include the story of *The Indigo Quest*, the 16-month search for the mill that still prints English-style Indigo prints of the 1860s, and stories about other fabrics still being produced around the world by craftsmen using traditional methods.

Samples from Patchwork are available.
Catalog: $1

Patria Gardens Video

Box 120, West Fulton, NY 12194
Phone: (518) 827-5937, (800) 383-3824
Fax: (518) 827-5937
Services/Merchandise: They have the video *Learn to Make Slipcovers, The Removable Upholstery* by Clare Driscoll. This straightforward instructional video was produced by a custom slipcoverer for the sewers on her 3-6 month waiting list who were hesitant to tackle their own furniture. Driscoll goes over tools, fabric selection, terminology, measuring for yardage, blocking out, making cording, and sewing each section. The slipcover is made directly on the furniture without making a muslin pattern—no confusing diagrams or drawings to decipher. Reviewed and recommended by *Video Librarian*, *ALA Booklist*, and *Video Rating Guide For Libraries*. $29.95, plus $4 for shipping (NY add sales tax).

They also have *Learn to Make Throw Pillows and Cushions* by Clare Driscoll. This hands-on video leads sewers through the steps necessary to produce the most simple throw pillows and the more complex self-welted, boxed cushions found on numerous furniture pieces. Beginners and the more advanced sewer will find helpful tips and straightforward instructions. Running time and price to be announced.
Payment Options: Check, Money Order, MC, Visa
Shipping Options: U.S. Postal Service
Special Discounts/Offers: Free shipping with the mention of *Sew Far Sew Good*.

Patterns of History

816 State Street, Suite SF, Madison, WI 53706-1488
Phone: (608) 264-6428
Fax: (608) 264-6533
Services/Merchandise: They have patterns based on the 19th-century garments in the collections of the State Historical Society of Wisconsin, including gowns from 1835, 1840, 1857, 1865, 1876, 1881, 1888, 1893, and 1896, a man's suit from 1878, and a bustle from 1873.
Payment Options: Check, Money Order, MC, Visa
Shipping Options: UPS, U.S. Postal Service

Specialty yarns...

Snarl

Garment ease for children

For the arm...	
Upper arm:	2–2 1/2"
Elbow:	2"
Forearm:	3/4"–1"
Wrist:	3/4"
Inside Seam:	1/4"
Outside Length:	1/4"
For the upper body...	
Neck:	1/4"
Chest:	1"
Waist:	1"–1/2"
Shoulder to Waist:	1/4"
Shoulder to Crotch:	1 1/2"
For the lower body...	
Waist:	3/4"–1"
Hips:	1 1/2"–1 3/4"
Crotch Depth:	3/4"–1"

Other Information: Every year, a new pattern is added to the series.
Special Discounts/Offers: Wholesale to qualified businesses.
Catalog: Free brochure upon request.

Patternworks

P.O. Box 1690, Poughkeepsie, NY 12601
Phone: (914) 462-8000
Fax: (914) 462-8074
E-mail: knit@patternworks
WWW: http://www.patternworks.com
Services/Merchandise: They have knitting patterns, yarn, supplies, kits, and books. They also have spinning wheels, books, and fibers, and felting kits.
Payment Options: Check, Money Order, MC, Visa, Amex, Discover
Other Information: Patternworks has been selling knitting supplies to knitting enthusiasts since 1979. Their 56-page catalog is packed with yarns, needles and other tools, books, videos, software–everything to inspire and aid the knitter.
Author's Note: I don't think I've ever seen such an astonishing array of patterns for knitting. There are patterns for sweaters, socks, hats, bags, suits, dog sweaters, slippers, a full length "fur" coat, and much more, in a beautiful catalog that's a source of inspiration. They also carry a unique collection of buttons to complement their yarns. Although I cannot knit yet, I'm going to learn so I can make some use of this wonderful resource.
Catalog: $3

Peas & Carrots

(A Division of Weidman Design)
9217 Brechin Drive, Charlotte, NC 28277
Phone: (704) 544-0006
Fax: (704) 544-0006
Services/Merchandise: Peas & Carrots, a division of Weidman Design, specializes in easy to sew patterns in sizes 0-4T for children. They strive for style and comfort for the child and washability for the busy parent. Their one-of-a-kind designs for preschoolers have been created to give your child that unique look for all occasions–little ones need Peas and Carrots every day.
Payment Options: Check, Money Order
Shipping Options: UPS, U.S. Postal Service
Minimum Order: No minimum order for retail. 12-pattern minimum for wholesale.
Other Information: Included with each pattern is an identical pattern for an 8" stuffed animal to wear. Now, little friends can wear the same outfit you make for your child.
Special Discounts/Offers: 10% discount on first order (wholesale or retail) with the mention of *Sew Far Sew Good*.
Catalog: 50¢, which is refundable with an order.

Peddler's Wagon

Mail Order Only
P. O. Box 109-50, Lamar, MO 64759-0109
Phone: (417) 682-3734
Services/Merchandise: They sell older and out-of-print needlework and quilting books by mail. Their book subjects include needlepoint, embroidery, cross-stitch, samples, rug hooking, and quilting. They are closing out most magazines at $2 each.
Payment Options: Check, Money Order, MC, Visa
Shipping Options: U.S. Postal Service
Minimum Order: $10
Other Information: This husband and wife business was established in 1985.
Catalog: $3 for 3 mailings, which is refundable with a $25 order.

Pegee of Williamsburg Patterns From Historie

P.O. Box 127, Williamsburg, Virginia 23187-0127
Phone: (804) 220-2722
Services/Merchandise: They have the Patterns From Historie Pattern Series circa 1776. The patterns are for a lady's dress and cloak, a girl's dress, a man's and a boy's waistcoat, a man's military/civilian coat, Scarlett O'Hara's barbeque party dress, Scarlett O'Hara's hoop skirt, a green Velveteen Portieres dress, Bonnie's blue riding habit, and more.
Payment Options: Money Order, Cashier's Check
Shipping Options: UPS, U.S. Postal Service
Minimum Order: No minimum order.
Other Information: Pegee Miller is a fashion designer who specializes in the preservation of historic clothing designs; her first historic patterns were copyrighted in 1972. The original historic garment is carefully researched, a pattern is developed, and a replica of the original garment is made. The resulting pattern, with detailed sewing instructions and illustrations, is then printed and made available to the public.
Special Discounts/Offers: 10% discount on first order with the mention of *Sew Far Sew Good*. Wholesale to qualified businesses.
Catalog: $2

Pennywise Fabrics

1650 Highway 124, Box 305, Harrisburg, MO 65256
Phone: (573) 874-1096
Services/Merchandise: They carry fabric from natural fibers only, such as 100% cotton, linen, wool, and silk. They do not carry synthetic fabrics or blends.

Payment Options: Check, Money Order
Shipping Options: UPS, U.S. Postal Service
Minimum Order: No minimum order.
Membership Benefits: After your first fabric order, mailings are sent twice per year at no charge.
Other Information: Current prices range from $1.55 per yard to $10.50 per yard. While the inventory varies, they try to stock a wide range of fabric types, including denims, twills, calicoes, terrys, batiste, suitings, jacquards, corduroys, velveteens, and more.

Pennywise Fabrics frequently sells fabric by the bolt to small businesses and dressmakers. On request, they will try to locate any fabric not currently in stock.
Special Discounts/Offers: Fabrics by the bolt at reduced prices.
Author's Note: The fabric samples they sent me were varied and definitely pennywise. There is a beautiful angora/silk/lambswool blend knit for $10 per yard, silks for $6 per yard, and wools for $4.75 per yard.
Catalog: $3 for a set of 100+ swatches of current stock.

Pepper Cory

1527 Ann Street, Beaufort, NC 28516
Phone: (919) 728-5110
Fax: (919) 728-5110
Services/Merchandise: They offer classes and instruction, and quilting and patchwork supplies.

A professional teacher of quilting since 1975, Pepper Cory imparts her knowledge to students at quilt guilds, special events such as conferences and trade shows, and through retail quilting and craft shops. She has taught in 42 states and overseas in England, France, Belgium, the Netherlands, Germany, and Australia. She is also an experienced quilt judge. She gives lectures, and her classes are half-day or full-day. Her books are, *Quilting Designs from the Amish, Quilting Designs from Antique Quilts, Crosspatch-Inspirations in Multi-Block Quilts,* and *Happy Trails-Variations on the Classic Drunkard's Path Patterns.* Her fifth book is *The Signature Quilt,* co-authored with Susan McKelvey.

Her 200+ stencil collection for quilting and painting is available from Quilting Collections by D. J., Inc., and her Drunkard's Path templates are available from Quilter's Rule International.
Other Information: Pepper's latest project was a commission quilt for Oxmoor House Press. Her dramatic star sampler quilt, Starry Night Sampler with Northern Lights sashing, is their calendar quilt for 1997.

Personal FX

P.O. Box 664, 1085 Pine Street, Moss Beach, CA 94038
Phone: (415) 728-8611, (800) 482-6066
Fax: (415) 728-1910
Services/Merchandise: They have beads in jade, turquoise, rose

quartz, baltic amber, glass, pearls, bone, horn, metal, serpentine, and sterling silver, They also have buttons, hunan tree resin carvings and stringing material. They offer a restringing service, custom design work, and designer bead search. They are adding a line of hand-dyed silk ribbon.
Payment Options: Check, Money Order
Shipping Options: UPS, U.S. Postal Service
Minimum Order: $25
Special Discounts/Offers: They offer quantity discounts and a 20% discount to designers with a current resale license.
Author's Note: The Personal FX catalog has the most beautiful design I have seen so far. The colors are vibrant and make you want to pick the beads up off the pages. The jewelry that is shown is worthy of the highest honors—you'll really have to see their presentation to believe it.
Catalog: $6.70 ($5, plus $1.70 postage), which is refundable with first order.

Personal Threads Boutique

8025 West Dodge Road, Omaha NE 68114-9793
Phone: (402) 391-7733
Services/Merchandise: They have books, magazines, a huge selection of yarns, kits (theirs and Vogue's), needlework findings, and weaving, tatting, and needlepoint supplies.
Payment Options: Check, Money Order, MC, Visa
Shipping Options: UPS
Minimum Order: $25
Special Discounts/Offers: 25% discount on first order.
Catalog: Free catalog and newsletter upon request.

Photo Textiles

P.O. Box 3036, Bloomington, IN 47402-3063
Phone: (800) 388-3961
Fax: (812) 334-3656
E-mail: phototex@aol.com
Services/Merchandise: They specialize in the transfer of photos and artwork to fabric, exclusively printed labels, and the duplication of antique fabrics. The photo transfer images are permanent, washable, iron-able, and won't crack or peel. They transfer the laser copies onto pre-washed, white 100% cotton, with a minimum one-half inch border on all sides. The process uses extreme heat, pressure, and chemicals.
Payment Options: Check, Money Order, MC, Visa
Shipping Options: UPS, U.S. Postal Service, FedEx, COD
Minimum Order: $19.45
Special Discounts/Offers: 10% discount on $100 order.
Catalog: Free upon request.

Pants styles...

Jodphurs

Patterns without the counting...

Multi-colored hand-painted yarns work well as the pattern yarn in a Fair Isle design, providing color changes without having to change strands of yarn.

Fast, fun & easy.

Tip provided by:
Mountain Colors
Page 310

Picking Up The Pieces Quilt Shop

911 City Park, Columbus, OH 43206
Phone: (614) 443-9988
Services/Merchandise: They have an Enchanted Attic, designed to house fabrics no longer available. They offer a special service for quilters who find they just need enough to finish the quilt started 10 years ago. They have all of the Helyn's Hoops lines. They offer classes, and they try to stay current and invent new techniques. They have the basics in fabrics, books, and quilting supplies.
Payment Options: Check, Money Order
Other Information: They are located in the historic German Village area of Columbus, Ohio. Customers can park in the driveway when space is available, and will be greeted by the shop mascot, Emmy (a cocker spaniel).
Special Discounts/Offers: 10% discount on fabrics bought for a class project with payment of class fee.

Pieces

P.O. Box 1135, 1051 Braddock Drive, Breckenridge, CO 80424
Phone: (970) 547-0917, (800) 875-3723
Services/Merchandise: Pieces carries fabric, buttons, yarns, patterns, and some notions. Ethnic, ethnic inspired, and whimsical describe the available styles. They have a small but carefully chosen selection. Fabrics are mostly cottons with a few rayons, polyesters, poly/cotton tapestries, and washable felts. There is a nice assortment of cottons from Africa, including batiks, mudcloth, ramie, Guatemalan Ikats, Indonesian rayon batik sarongs, cotton batik sarongs, and batik paintings, and handloomed cottons from Nepal. American companies represented include Alexander Henry, Hoffman, Moda, South Sea Islands, P & B, Mission Valley Textiles, and Peter Pan. Cottons are mostly in the $7-$10 per yard range.

The button selection is wonderful. Buttons are from three major button companies and a few independent companies specializing in handcrafted buttons. There are shell, metal, horn, bone, plastic, Fimo, and glass buttons in a variety of styles. They will also try to track down a specific button for you to match your fabric. Once again, the styles lean toward ethnic and whimsical.

Yarns are from Reynolds, Brown Sheep, Plymouth, Rowan, Patons, Berroco, Unger, and Classic Elite. They have bamboo knitting needles from Plymouth. They will do special orders for items not in stock.

Patterns include Burda, Pavelka, K.P. Kids & Co., Kindred Spirits, Indygo Junction, Pieces From My Heart, From the Powder Mill, Wild Goose Chase, Out on a Whim, Star Quilt Co., and Folkwear. They also have patterns from Wildwood Collection, One Crazy Quilter, and Tynnebelles Quilts (miniature foundation pieces), which are all Colorado based designers. They have some select knitting patterns.
Payment Options: Check, Money Order, MC, Visa

Shipping Options: UPS, U.S. Postal Service
Minimum Order: No minimum order.
Other Information: They try to find fabrics, buttons, and yarns that are less common than one generally finds in big fabric stores. The products are good quality at suggested retail prices. Their customers say they have an eye for color and style, and a selection that they usually can't find elsewhere. They offer personalized service, because their business is part of their life. Their shop is by their home and open by appointment.
Special Discounts/Offers: 10% discount on first order with the mention of *Sew Far Sew Good*. The cost of the swatch pack is refundable.
Catalog: $5, which is refundable with order.

The Pin Cushion

2307 North Alexander, Baytown, TX 77520
Phone: (713) 427-6414
Fax: (713) 428-1030
Services/Merchandise: They carry fashion fabrics, denim, silk, heirloom fabrics, laces, lingerie fabrics, swimwear fabrics, beaded laces, and towelling. They have over 2,400 bolts of quilting fabrics, and carry silk ribbon and embroidery supplies. They offer classes in basic sewing, quilting, embroidery (hand and machine) crafts, and more. They are the largest Viking Sewing Machine Dealer in their area.

The Pin Cushion hosts The Art of Sewing Extravaganza in February, which offers sewing product displays, contests (patterns, children's sewing, quilting, and wearable art), and sewing celebrities, who give lectures and demonstrations. Registration is $5.
Payment Options: Check, Money Order, MC, Visa, Amex
Shipping Options: UPS
Membership Benefits: Quilt Guild and ASG members receive a special discount.
Other Information: Their motto is: "Quality, Service & Education." They don't just help people learn to sew, they teach them to love sewing.
Special Discounts/Offers: 10% discount on your first order with the mention of *Sew Far Sew Good*.

Pioneer Quilts/Spearfish Canyon Quilter's Spree

801 Columbus, Rapid City, SD 57701
Event Information: The Spearfish Canyon Quilter's Spree is a 3-day quilting seminar held in the heart of the beautiful Black Hills of South Dakota. It features two nationally known quilting teachers in a rustic, relaxing atmosphere. A perfect quilting vacation to de-stress yourself from this fast-paced society.
Payment Options: Check, Money Order

How Many Years: 2 years
Time of Year/Month: July
Approximate Costs: $200-$300 would include classes, meals, and lodging.
Other Information: Spearfish Canyon is located 60 miles from Rapid City, SD, on National Scenic Highway 14A. It has fabulous natural panoramas as seen in the movie *Dances With Wolves*. Guaranteed to be conducive to learning and relaxation. Camping, fishing, and hiking are also available.

PJS Publications

Box 1790, Peoria, IL 61656
Phone: (800) 289-6397 to contact *Sew News*
(800) 444-0454 to contact *Serger* & *Sewing Updates*
Services/Merchandise: *Sew News* magazine is a fashion sewing publication covering current fashion and fabric trends, sewing projects and techniques, new products, sewing machines, and special offers.

Serger Update is a newsletter featuring a wide variety of innovative serger how-to's—from fashion to home decoration—by top serger experts, plus the newest techniques, products, and tips.

Sewing Update is a newsletter featuring fashion sewing how-to's by industry professionals, plus innovative ideas, technical data, questions and answers, and product, equipment, and pattern news.

Sew 'N' Go Tours are tours designed to showcase fabric and industry resources in a particular geographic area. Visits are made to sewing manufacturing facilities, fabric stores, and to sewing celebrities. Shopping discounts are offered by most merchants for group participants.
Payment Options: Check, Money Order, MC, Visa, Direct Billing
Minimum Order: No minimum order.
Special Discounts/Offers: *Sew News* is available for wholesale to qualified businesses, with a 10 copy minimum (contact Diane Ashens, 800-521-2885).
Author's Note: I love *Sew News*, and I've just subscribed to *Sewing Update* and *Serger Update*. PJS sent me a sample of each, and they are jam-packed with great ideas and solutions to make your work easier.

Planet Bead

714 North Broadway, Milwaukee, WI 53202
Phone: (414) 223-1616
Services/Merchandise: They have a diverse selection of beads of every origin, including new and antique beads.
Payment Options: MC, Visa, AmEx
Special Discounts/Offers: 10% discount to qualified businesses.

Portland Bead Society

P.O. Box 10611, Portland, OR 97210
E-mail: beadport@hevanet.com
Services/Merchandise: Society meetings are held on the third Wednesday of every month at 7 p.m., except July, August, and December. The Annual Winter Bead Bazaar takes place on the first weekend in November. Meetings and the Bead Bazaar are held at Montgomery Park in Portland.
Payment Options: Check
Membership Dues: $10 for an individual, $15 for a family, $20 for a business.
Membership Benefits: Members can attend monthly meetings and get free admission to the annual Winter Bead Bazaar.

Power Sewing

185 Fifth Avenue, San Francisco, CA 94118
Phone: (415) 386-0440
Fax: (415) 386-0441
Services/Merchandise: They have books and videos on sewing techniques.
Payment Options: Check, Money Order, MC, Visa
Shipping Options: UPS, U.S. Postal Service, FedEx
Other Information: Sandra Betzina is a syndicated columnist and contributor to several national magazines.
Author's Note: I have owned *Power Sewing* for about a year, and they sent a copy of *More Power Sewing* for my perusal. Both are chock-full of time-saving techniques, tips, and a no-nonsense approach to fitting. Although the first book is very thorough, the information in *More Power Sewing* is entirely new and just as useful. I look forward to acquainting myself with more of Sandra Betzina's books and videos.
Catalog: Free upon request.

Practical Applied Logic, Inc.

228 Dry Brook Road, Owego, NY 13827
Phone: (607) 687-2793
Fax: (607) 687-3201
Services/Merchandise: They have bead pattern design software.
Payment Options: Check, Money Order
Shipping Options: U.S. Postal Service
Other Information: Send for a brochure and order blank.
Special Discounts/Offers: 10% discount on first order with the mention of <u>Sew Far Sew Good</u>. Wholesale to qualified businesses.

Prairie Edge/Sioux Trading Post

606 Main, Rapid City, SD 57701
Phone: (605) 348-4822

Did you know...

Cotton batting has withstood the tests of time. If quilts with cotton batting is washed properly and cared for, they can last for hundreds of years. On the other hand, we are seeing quilts with polyester batts breaking down after as little as 20 years. If you invest 200 to 400 hours hand-quilting a quilt, don't you want your investment to last? As a friend of mine said, "Quilters today take so much trouble to use 100% cotton for their tops and backs. Why would they put garbage bags in the middle?"

There is another compelling reason to use cotton batting—the way light reflects from your quilts. Look at an old quilt made with cotton batting. It has thousands of facets, much like a well-cut diamond, each creating a surface to bounce light back to the eye. A polyester batt creates a series of rounded humps, all the same height, bringing much less light back to the viewer. Give your new quilts the vibrancy of fine antique quilts by giving them the gift of light—a good cotton batting.

Tip provided by:
The Kirk Collection
Page 299

Long sleeve styles...

Bishop

3/4

Fax: (605) 348-9624
Services/Merchandise: They have craft supplies, beads, and books. Most of what they offer is for ceremonial use.
Payment Options: MC, Visa, Amex
Shipping Options: UPS, U.S. Postal Service
Minimum Order: No minimum order.
Special Discounts/Offers: Discounts to schools.

Prairieland Quilts

107 North Second, P.O. Box 458, Cissna Park, IL 60924
Phone: (815) 457-2867, (800) 391-2867
Fax: (815) 457-2577
Services/Merchandise: Prairieland Quilts is a full-service quilting store offering the very latest in books, patterns, supplies, notions, and, of course, 100% cotton fabric. From the Homespuns to Christmas prints, flannels to calicos, they have it all. Prairieland Quilts also offers classes on quilting, and machine or handquilting services. They also have finished quilts and a complete line of embroidery supplies. Gift items are available and include collectable Amish quilt figurines, decorative tins, wooden pictures and puzzles, paintings, quilt hangers, lapel pins, and more. Prairieland Quilts is an authorized dealer for New Home/Janome sewing machines. They also service all makes of sewing machines and have used machines for sale.

Visiting the store is a fun experience. Project samples are everywhere, the staff is most helpful, and they're open Mon. - Fri. 9 - 5 and Sat. 9 - 3. Mail order is available through their 800 number, with free shipping on orders over $25. Their newsletter, *Notes from the Prairie*, is published quarterly and is full of humor, quilting tips, seasonal recipes, quilting industry news, and all the new products available to quilters. These are just some of the reasons to make Prairieland Quilts one of your favorite places.
Payment Options: Check, Money Order, MC, Visa, Discover
Shipping Options: UPS
Minimum Order: No minimum order.
Special Discounts/Offers: 10% discount on first order with the mention of *Sew Far Sew Good*.
Author's Note: Prairieland Quilts was very helpful and friendly when I called. They sent a sample of their newsletter, and it's a hoot.

Preemie-Yums

2260 Gibson Woods Court Northwest, Salem, OR 97304-1700
Phone: (503) 370-9279
Fax: (503) 370-9279
Services/Merchandise: Preemie-Yums offers patterns, pre-cut kits, and ready-to-wear items sized exclusively for low birth-weight infants of 4

to 6 pounds.
Payment Options: Check, Money Order, MC, Visa
Shipping Options: UPS, U.S. Postal Service
Minimum Order: No minimum for retail orders. 12 patterns (4 of each style) for wholesale orders.
Other Information: Patterns include easy to follow instructions, a fabric and notions guide, and suggestions for the use of monitors and IV tubing. The pre-cut kits are complete with fabric, notions, and instructions for constructing each garment.
Special Discounts/Offers: 10% discount on first order with the mention of *Sew Far Sew Good*. Wholesale to qualified businesses.
Catalog: $1.50 with a SASE.

Primrose Lane

1120 Royal Palm Beach Boulevard, #119, Royal Palm Beach, FL 33411
Phone: (407) 795-4250, (800) 218-7611
Fax: (407) 791-9116
E-mail: primlane@aol.com
Services/Merchandise: They have doll clothing patterns, with fully illustrated, easy-to-follow instructions, and designs for both porcelain and popular vinyl dolls. Childrens patterns, marketed under the name Baby Rose will be available beginning the Summer of '96. These patterns will have the same easy-to-follow, fully illustrated instructions as their popular doll clothing patterns.
Payment Options: Check, Money Order, MC, Visa, Amex, Discover
Minimum Order: No minimum for retail orders, $80 minimum for wholesale (established accounts have no minimum on re-orders).
Other Information: Their slogan, "The doll clothes you wish you could wear", accurately describes their unique patterns. They believe sewing should be fun, and sewing for dolls should be as much fun as playing with them! Their patterns explore many different facets of needlework, including smocking, heirloom sewing, traditional embroidery, silk ribbon embroidery, stenciling, leatherworking, beading, appliqué, and quilting. Each pattern has been graded for difficulty (beginner, intermediate, advanced), so customers can choose patterns geared for their own level of expertise. Full-size pattern pieces and fully illustrated instructions make these patterns a joy to use. Three different catalogs are currently available:

- Porcelain Collection: Patterns for various sizes of porcelain dolls.
- Primrose Lane Collection: Patterns for popular 18" vinyl dolls and 15" baby dolls.
- The Baby Rose Collection: Patterns for infants and girls.

Special Discounts/Offers: Wholesale to qualified businesses.
Catalog: $2 each.

Pro Show, Inc.

P.O. Box 369, Monroeville, PA 15146
Phone: (412) 325-5689
Fax: (412) 325-5699
E-mail: creatvinsp@aol.com
Event Information: They put on Creative Inspiration™, a three-day consumer event that showcases the latest in sewing, quilting, wearable art, needlearts, crafts, and more. Activities include hour-long seminars from nationally recognized educators, demonstrations, make-it-take-it projects, and fashion presentations. There are over 100 exhibition booths where consumers can examine and purchase the newest supplies, machinery, tools, and services from local and national retailers and manufacturers.
Payment Options: Check, Money Order, MC, Visa
Time of Year/Month: Spring and fall.
Approximate Costs: Admission $5, Seminars $7
Catalog: Free class and event schedule upon request; call (800) 249-3154 to be placed on the mailing list.

Professional Association of Custom Clothiers

P.O. Box 8071, Medford, OR 97504-0071
Phone: (541) 772-4119
Fax: (541) 770-7041
Services/Merchandise: The Professional Association of Custom Clothiers is a nationwide, professional organization. Founded in 1991, PACC targets the needs of custom clothiers working in the home, or in commercial settings. PACC is a non-profit national resource run by a national board. The primary purpose of PACC is to provide networking, education, and support for sewing professionals.
Payment Options: Check, Money Order
Membership Dues: $50 per year. Local dues vary by chapter.
Membership Information, Contact:
  Jean Fristensky, PACC
  P.O. Box 8071
  Medford, OR 97504-0071
Or, contact your local chapter.
Membership Benefits: Members get networking and support from fellow clothing professionals, a subscription to the quarterly national newsletter, and information on supplies, products, and business services. Professional discounts are available through chapter-run group-buy programs. Jurying services and dressmaker referral services are provided. There is a membership directory, and members have educational opportunities via seminars and classes on the local and national level, often with member discounts.

Promenade's Le Bead Shop

1970 13th Street, Boulder, CO 80302
Phone: (303) 440-4807
Fax: (303) 440-8714
Services/Merchandise: They specialize in seed beads from the Czech Republic and Japan. They also have a full line of Czech and Austrian crystal beads, kits, charms, jewelry notions, sequins, rhinestones, costuming supplies, instruction books on beadwork design, beadwork supplies, and semi-precious beads.
Payment Options: Check, Money Order, MC, Visa, Amex
Shipping Options: UPS, U.S. Postal Service
Minimum Order: $20
Special Discounts/Offers: 20% off $100 for wholesalers only.
Catalog: $2.50, which is refundable with purchase.

Prym-Dritz Corporation
  Wholesale Only

P.O. Box 5028, Spartanburg, SC 29304
Phone: (864) 576-5050
Fax: (864) 574-3847
Services/Merchandise: In addition to straight pins and safety pins, Prym-Dritz manufactures and distributes a wide range of notions for sewing, quilting, crafts, and home decorating.

Prym-Dritz notions include marking tools, rulers, pressing equipment, needles, snaps, hooks and eyes, 4-part snap fasteners, eyelets, grommets, cover buttons and buckles, shoulder pads, and more. In recent years, Prym-Dritz has expanded its products to include Dylon Cold Water Dyes, Fuzzy Touch by Hix iron-on velour letters, numbers and sports motifs, Interior Expressions decorator rods and finials, sew-in and iron-on drapery tapes and accessories, upholstery supplies, and Hollywood Trims, a beautiful line of decorator trims (cording, fringe, braid, welting, tassels, tiebacks, and chair ties) for pillows, upholstery, valances, draperies, and more.
Other Information: Prym-Dritz products are widely available in fabric and craft stores.

The Prym-Dritz Corporation is family-owned and operated by the Prym Consumer Company of Stolberg, Germany. The company was founded by William Prym over 400 years ago and is the largest manufacturer of straight pins and safety pins in the world. In 1924, Hans August Prym established William Prym of America in New York City as an importer and exclusive sales agent for William Prym of Stolberg, Germany. During the 1940s, Hans Prym moved the company to Dayville, Connecticut, and started a manufacturing facility. Dritz was founded in the 1940s by John Dritz, who was a distributor of sewing notions. Prym acquired the Dritz Company in 1988. All U.S. Prym-Dritz operations were centralized in Spartanberg, South Carolina, in 1990.
Special Discounts/Offers: To receive a free *Know Your Notions*

Long sleeve styles...

Shirt

Bell

brochure from Prym-Dritz, send a SASE to:

> Customer Service, Prym-Dritz Corp.
> Department SFSG
> P.O. Box 692
> Spartanburg, SC 29304-0692

Author's Note: Although anyone who has walked around a fabric store knows the Dritz product line, not everyone knows the extent of their line of products. If you are interested in home decoration, inquire about Prym-Dritz's Hollywood Trims line at your local fabric store; you will be amazed at the extent of their collection.

Prym-Dritz has also very graciously contributed several tips and tricks for *Sew Far Sew Good*.

Qualin International

P.O. Box 31145, San Francisco, CA 94131-0145
Phone: (415) 333-8500
Services/Merchandise: They have ready-to-dye silk scarves, clothing, fabric, threads, neckties, pillowcases, ribbons, accessories, fabric dyes, brushes, fabric stretchers, and steamers.
Payment Options: Check, Money Order, COD
Minimum Order: No minimum order.
Special Discounts/Offers: Wholesale to qualified businesses.

Queen Ann's Lace

715 East Vine Street, Kissimmee, FL 34744
Phone: (407) 846-7998
Fax: (407) 846-7773
Services/Merchandise: They have quiltmaking supplies, including 100% cotton fabrics, thread, patterns, books, and tools. Their painting supplies include acrylic paints, brushes, and books. Their silk ribbon embroidery supplies include ribbon, needles, and books.
Payment Options: Check, Money Order, MC, Visa
Shipping Options: UPS, U.S. Postal Service
Minimum Order: No minimum order.
Membership Benefits: 10% discount to Quilt Guild Members who show a membership card.
Other Information: They have a punch card good for $20 in free merchandise when it is filled.

Quest Beads & Cast, Inc.

49 West 37th Street, 16th Floor, New York, NY 10018
Phone: (212) 354-0979
Fax: (212) 354-0978
Services/Merchandise: They have castings, beads, charms, custom castings, and jewelry components.

Payment Options: Check, Money Order, MC, Visa, COD
Shipping Options: UPS, U.S. Postal Service
Minimum Order: $100
Catalog: $5

Quest Outfitters

2590 17th Street, Box B, Sarasota, FL 34232
Phone: (941) 378-1620
Fax: (941) 377-5105
Services/Merchandise: They have fabrics for outdoor wear and gear, including cordura, packcloth, polartec fleece, insulations, etc. They have a wide variety of zippers, and continuous zippers from the roll. For fasteners, they have D-rings, side release buckles, snaps, and eyelets and grommets. They have webbing, drawcord, stretch seam binding, and seam sealing tape. They have men's, women's, and children's jackets, pants, ski suits, ponchos, vests, scuba suits, long underwear, and bike wear.
Payment Options: Check, Money Order, MC, Visa
Shipping Options: UPS, U.S. Postal Service
Minimum Order: No minimum order.
Other Information: All orders are shipped the day they are received, if received by noon. The free catalog includes a listing of supplies offered, as well as general information and tips regarding sewing with outdoor fabrics and supplies. Swatches of each fabric are available.
Special Discounts/Offers: Volume discounts are available for everyone.
Catalog: Free upon request.

Quilici Fay Productions

85 Liberty Ship Way, Suite 104, Sausalito, CA 94965
Phone: (415) 331-5324
Fax: (415) 383-9629
Event: Fall Colors... Fashion, Fabric, Fiber & Fun
Payment Options: Check
How Many Years: 3 years
Time of Year/Month: October (19th and 20th in '96)
Other Information: Fall Colors features supplies, equipment, and services for the fiber enthusiast—beginner or expert, hobbyist or professional. Set in a showcase of Bay Area Fiberart, the public will enjoy fashion shows, demonstrations, and a wide variety of quality vendors. There is also a gallery for attendees to wander through.
Special Discounts/Offers: Free admission when you bring your copy of *Sew Far Sew Good* to be signed by Heather.

Quilt in a Day

1955 Diamond Street, San Marcos, CA 92069

Phone: (619) 591-0081, (800) 777-4852
Fax: (619) 591-4424
Services/Merchandise: Quilt in a Day is a publisher and retail store. They've published over 50 quality quilting instruction books in over 16 years. The author, Eleanor Burns, can be seen on over 125 PBS stations nationwide. Quilt in a Day offers quilting classes in their on-site teaching facility, opportunities to purchase quality fabrics and notions from their retail store, and a chance to tour their video production studio.
Payment Options: MC, Visa, Discover, Terms Available
Shipping Options: UPS, U.S. Postal Service
Minimum Order: Varies by classification: distributor, wholesaler, retailer.
Other Information: Quilt in a Day offers educational programs via PBS, on-site classes, and educational videos.
Special Discounts/Offers: 10% discount on first order with the mention of *Sew Far Sew Good* for all retail sales from retail store.
Author's Note: The two books I was sent are profiled in the Books Section. The *Christmas Quilts and Crafts* book is especially pleasing and full of life. *Star Log Cabin Quilts* has very simple instructions and plenty of how-to illustrations.

The Quilt Rack

605 Kansas Plaza, Garden City, KS 67846
Phone: (316) 275-8786
Services/Merchandise: They have a large selection of quilting fabrics, embroidery thread, patterns, and notions.
Payment Options: Check, Money Order
Shipping Options: UPS, U.S. Postal Service
Minimum Order: No minimum order.
Other Information: The Quilt Rack offers classes in quilting, silk ribbon embroidery, smocking, hardanger, and needlepoint. A local club meets once a month with a different project each month. New techniques, new tools, and color variety are accented. In-store demos are available on new items.
Author's Note: I first came across the name "The Quilt Rack" in one of the bulletin boards I frequent on-line. After that, the name kept popping up as a haven for quilting enthusiasts in the Midwest. Although I have not been there, it is held in very high regard by many, and their selection of supplies and equipment is considerable.

Quilt Restoration Society

P.O. Box 337, Hillsdale, NY 12529
Phone: (518) 325-4502
Fax: (518) 325-6625
E-mail: e-qrs@taconic.net
Services/Merchandise: The Quilt Restoration Society serves as a center for sharing information about quilt restoration techniques, products, and tools used by quilt restorers throughout the world. Centuries-old, the art of quilt restoration remained a hidden household occupation from the mid-twentieth century to the present time. Preserved and maintained within the home, all family linens were regularly restored in order to guarantee their continued usefulness within their appropriate context. Many precious textiles have survived into the twentieth century because they were painstakingly cared for by the owner within the domestic setting. Fine sewing, mending, and darning skills were used on a weekly basis, and these skills, so universally applied to all household linens, have been neglected and are now being re-examined and re-learned by quilt restorers

The *Quilt Restoration Society Newsletter* serves as a vehicle for discussion, sharing, and teaching the time-honored methods used to extend the practical use of textiles. Many quilt restoration methods used by restorers today were part of the daily life for women across the centuries, who sought methods to preserve their household linens. Antique textiles—quilts, linens, and clothing that have survived—exemplify the methods used by seamstresses, dressmakers, and quilters in previous centuries. Today, new products and methods add to the compendium of knowledge and allow the present day quilt restorer to utilize methods earlier quilt restorers would have embraced. After a half-century of neglect, these methods and skills are shared. Major quilt restoration projects are featured, and new methods and techniques are explored.

All quilt restorers are encouraged to network with fellow members via *The Quilt Restoration Society Newsletter*, so that an on-going hotline of new products and techniques can be examined by fellow quilt restorers around the world. The newsletter alleviates the domestic isolation of this labor-intensive profession and creates a public forum for international sharing.
Payment Options: Check, Money Order, MC, Visa, Amex, Discover
Shipping Options: UPS, U.S. Postal Service
Minimum Order: No minimum order.
Membership Dues: $25 in the U.S. and Canada, $35 in other countries.
Membership Benefits: 20% discount on all publications, conferences, and directories.

The Quilting B

232 Second Street Southeast, Cedar Rapids, IA 52401
Phone: (319) 363-1643
Services/Merchandise: They have a wholesale and retail line of over 35 yarns and fibers for doll hair and Santa beards. They also own and operate a retail quilting shop.
Payment Options: Check, Money Order
Shipping Options: UPS
Minimum Order: Retail, none. Wholesale please inquire.
Catalog: Sample ring of fibers $5, plus $1.75 for shipping.

it, criticized the color, and then went home empty-handed. I couldn't deal with it.

Eventually it became obvious that it was the perfect solution, and it kept dancing in my dreams. So, after about a week, I went back, stared at it some more, and bought it. It wasn't even expensive.

So far, no one has seemed to notice it's a bullet case (my family was never big on hunting, and probably wouldn't know a bullet from a lipstick).

Although I am not big on supporting that type of manufacturer, I have considered sending them a photo of the beautiful rainbow of beads it carries!

Entertainment provided by:
Esther Liberman
Prodigy member, beading enthusiast.

*A great way to use
water soluble
stabilizer scraps...*

*Save them until you
have a handful; place
them into a spray bottle,
and fill it with water. It
is the perfect thing to
add just a little stability
here and there with a
squirt.*

The Quilting Bee

357 Castro Street, Mountain View, CA 94041
Phone: (415) 969-1714, (800) 492-6397
Fax: (415) 969-2419
E-mail: quiltbee@iwe.com
WWW: http://www.iwe.com/quiltbee
Services/Merchandise: They have fabric, books, notions, and Viking, White, Bernina and Euro-Pro sewing machines, sergers, and accessories. They have the largest selection of quilting and sewing classes on the West Coast. Their clubs include Viking Club, Bernina Club, and various Serger Clubs. Mail orders are welcome.
Payment Options: MC, Visa, Bernina Credit Card, Homesource
Shipping Options: UPS, U.S. Postal Service
Minimum Order: No minimum order.
Membership Benefits: 10% discount to quilt and sewing guild members.
Special Discounts/Offers: Call for their newsletter. It has coupons, sale dates, and more.
Other Information: They specialize in customer service and special orders. They'll try to find any quilting or sewing supply you might need. Tours are welcome.

Quilting Books Unlimited

1911 West Wilson, Batavia, IL 60510
Phone: (708) 406-0237
Fax: (708) 406-0238
Services/Merchandise: They have over 1,200 books on quilting, notions, and cotton fabrics.
Payment Options: Check, Money Order, MC, Visa, Amex, Discover
Shipping Options: UPS, U.S. Postal Service
Minimum Order: No minimum order.
Other Information: They carry the unusual as well as the usual in quilting books, with an emphasis on quality service. They sell at shows in Houston, Texas, Paducah, Kentucky, Lancaster, Pennsylvania, Indianapolis, Indiana, the National Quilting Association Show (which moves), and others.
Special Discounts/Offers: 10% discount for orders of $100 or more. 20% discount for orders of $200 or more.
Catalog: $1

Quilting From The Heartland

111 East Fifth, Starbuck, MN 56381
Phone: (612) 239-4044
Services/Merchandise: They carry the quilting books, videos, templates, and notions from the show *Quilting From The Heartland* with Sharlene Jorgensen. Their catalog matches each product with a section of the series, so you are able to get exactly what you need for your projects.
Payment Options: Check, Money Order, MC, Visa, Discover, COD
Shipping Options: UPS, FedEx
Minimum Order: No minimum for retail. $60 Wholesale. $400 Distributor.
Other Information: Their company is family-owned and operated. They call themselves "The little company with the big heart."
Author's Note: They sent me copies of the books *Fan-Tastic*, and *Quilting From The Heartland-400 Series*. Both are very good, and include full-color photographs, colored instruction illustrations, and a quick-reference guide to the materials you will need for the featured projects. I was particularly drawn to *Fan-Tastic*, however, because the quilts pictured are so very beautiful, and the colors appeal to my aesthetics. Two thumbs up for both.

Quilts & Other Comforts

(The Retail Mail Order Division of Leman Publications, Inc.)
1 Quilters Lane, P.O. Box 4100, Golden, CO 80402-4100
Phone: (303) 278-1010, (800) 881-6624
Fax: (303) 277-0370
Services/Merchandise: If you like quilts or patchwork, sewing or crafts, or gift items with a country flair, Quilts & Other Comforts will delight you. Since 1969, Quilts & Other Comforts has been dedicated to quality merchandise and service especially for quiltmakers. Among the many outstanding products their company produces are two of the most popular and important quilt magazines on the market today–*Quilters Newsletter Magazine* and *Quiltmaker*.
Here are the basic categories of products in their catalog you'll find interesting:

- Easy projects made with beginners in mind.
- Unique items to decorate your home or to give as gifts.
- Quilt projects designed to save you time.
- Color choice and fabric selection made easy.
- Quilt patterns and fabric-craft projects from traditional to contemporary, from mini to king, and every shape and size in between.
- Several exclusive products you can't buy in any store or from any other mail order catalog.
- Over 600 patterns, books, fabrics, and products especially for quilters, of which more than one-third are always brand new.
- Exclusive Quilts & Other Comforts Fabric Club, featuring a bi-monthly newsletter with a pattern and a packet of 5 die-cut cotton fabric squares. Special product discount to members.

They know that quilts are important to millions of people around the world–they are lovely to look at, collect, sleep under, give away as special gifts, and to decorate with and pass down to children and friends. If you have ever felt that quilts are special, Quilts & Other Comforts will delight you.

Payment Options: Money Order, MC, Visa, Amex, Discover
Shipping Options: UPS, U.S. Postal Service
Catalog: Free catalog, upon request, of over 600 products for quilters. Mailed several times per year.

Quilts By the Oz

3201 23rd Avenue, Moline IL 61265
Phone: (309) 762-9673
Fax: (309) 762-1869
Services/Merchandise: Quilts By the Oz does custom quilting, and stocks over 2,500 bolts of 100% cotton quilting fabric. Their button bins are full of over 250 styles of buttons. Customers can pick out the buttons of their choice for 10¢ each or 25¢ each for metal or wood buttons. Buttons can also be purchased at bulk prices per pound.
Payment Options: Check, Money Order, MC, Visa, Amex, Discover
Shipping Options: UPS, U.S. Postal Service
Minimum Order: No minimum order.
Membership Dues: Their Sewer's Super Saver Society is $12 per year.
Membership Benefits: Members receive 12% off all non-sale merchandise. If they buy 12 books, they get one free.
Other Information: Quilts By the Oz stocks a large and current assortment of quilting books, patterns, threads, and notions, and sells 5" charm squares of 100% pre-washed cotton fabric.
Special Discounts/Offers: 10% discount on first order with the mention of _Sew Far Sew Good_.

QuiltSoft

P.O. Box 19946, San Diego, CA 92159
Phone: (619) 583-2970
Fax: (619) 583-2682
E-mail: quiltsoft@aol.com
Services/Merchandise: They have quilting software for Windows and Mac, and CDs of fabrics. More CDs are added as they become available. They also have add-on block libraries.
Payment Options: Check, Money Order, MC, Visa, Amex
Shipping Options: U.S. Postal Service, UPS, FedEx
Minimum Order: One unit retail. Four units wholesale.
Other Information: Quiltsoft has the original software for both Windows and Mac.
Special Discounts/Offers: 10% discount on first order with the mention of _Sew Far Sew Good_. Wholesale to qualified businesses.

Catalog: Free upon request.

The Rain Shed, Inc.

707 Northwest 11th Street, Corvallis, OR 97330
Phone: (541) 753-8900
Services/Merchandise: They have retail fabrics for outdoor and active wear.
Payment Options: Check, Money Order, MC, Visa, Discover
Shipping Options: UPS, U.S. Postal Service
Minimum Order: No minimum order.
Other Information: They are mainly a mail order business, but they have a store open Tues. - Sat. They print one catalog every year.

The Rain Shed has been in business since 1977. They make every effort to assemble products for the home sewer to make professional garments and gear.
Author's Note: Their catalog has sewing tips, as well as their products.
Catalog: $1

Ranita Corporation

P.O. Box 5698, Eugene, OR 97405-0698
Phone: (541) 344-0422
Fax: (541) 344-3944
Services/Merchandise: They have the embellishment book _Wrapped in Fabrique_™ and the Sure-Fit Designs™ fitting system, with kits for dresses, pants, shirts, and children. They also have threads, "fringy and fuzzy" yarn for couching, netting, machine embroidery needles, plastic embroidery hoops, and videos.
Payment Options: Check, Money Order, MC, Visa
Shipping Options: UPS, U.S. Postal Service
Special Discounts/Offers: 10% discount on first order with the mention of _Sew Far Sew Good_.

Ree's Creative Ideas

P.O. Box 70805, Tuscaloosa, AL 35407
Phone: (205) 556-3838
Fax: (205) 553-3277
Services/Merchandise: They have appliqué kits. Each kit is fused to a perma-press fabric, handcut, and mounted on card stock. You simply take the kit out of the ziploc bag, iron it down, and stitch around. Directions for the appliqué and the notions you will need are included in each kit. Over 100 designs are available.
Payment Options: Check, Money Order, MC, Visa
Shipping Options: UPS, U.S. Postal Service, FedEx, COD
Minimum Order: No minimum order for retail. $25 minimum for wholesale.

Skirt styles...

Broomstick

Skirt styles...

A-Line

Other Information: The appliqué kits are a great way to liven up store-bought or homemade clothing for yourself or for gifts to others.
Special Discounts/Offers: 10% discount on first order with the mention of *Sew Far Sew Good*, for both wholesale and retail accounts. Wholesale to qualified businesses.
Catalog: Free black and white catalog with line drawings available upon request. For a color catalog, send $5, which will be refunded with your first order.

Renaissance Buttons

826 West Armitage, Chicago, IL 60614
Phone: (312) 883-9508
Fax: (312) 883-9516
Services/Merchandise: They have beautiful and unusual buttons from around the world in a kaleidoscope of colors, textures, and sizes. Customers choose from handcarved horn, etched mother of pearl, natural tagua nut, plastics from the 1940s, vintage and modern glass, and antique collectibles.
Payment Options: Check, Money Order, MC, Visa
Shipping Options: UPS, COD
Minimum Order: $10
Other Information: For your unique creations. Renaissance Buttons specializes in individual mail order requests. Send them your swatches and specifications, and they will send you photocopies or sketches from their assortment of fine contemporary and antique buttons. Include a SASE for response and seasonal brochure.
Author's Note: Renaissance Buttons sent a beautiful sampling of buttons, and I was hard-pressed to decide which of them was more intriguing. You can see two of their buttons on the back cover of this book.

Revelli

1850 Union Street #1645, San Francisco, CA 94123
Phone: (415) 673-6313
Fax: (415) 673-3525
Services/Merchandise: They have books, kits, and videos designed to help you discover your own colors, styles, and decorating personality.
Payment Options: Check, Money Order, MC, Visa
Shipping Options: UPS, U.S. Postal Service, FedEx
Minimum Order: $10
Other Information: Clare Revelli has spent her entire career in fashion and design. She has designed for several of New York's top fashion houses and has spoken internationally on personal color.
Special Discounts/Offers: 40% discount on wholesale orders of 12 or more items to qualified businesses.
Catalog: Free brochure upon request.

Ribbons & Roses

(A Division of O'Tauma Systems, Inc.)
13626 Dornock Court , Herndon, VA 22071
Phone: (703) 435-0150
Fax: (703) 787-7558
Services/Merchandise: They have 2mm, 4mm, 7mm, 13mm, and 32mm silk ribbon, Mokuba ribbon, books, *Inspirations* (an Australian embroidery magazine), YLI threads, DMC machine embroidery thread, patterns, and notions.
Payment Options: Check, Money Order
Shipping Options: UPS
Minimum Order: No minimum order.
Other Information: Ribbons & Roses also offers silk ribbon embroidery classes. Although they're a mail order business, they do see customers and friends by appointment, so give them a call if you are in the area. They will accept pictures of your work for their newsletter, and would like any information about guilds or clubs, as a service to their readers.
Special Discounts/Offers: 10% discount to guilds.
Author's Note: In my search for more options in silk ribbon colors and sizes than what was offered in my only local store, I found Ribbons & Roses. It took less than a week to receive my catalog, and I was delighted by the variety of ribbons (185 in various sizes). They also carry wool embroidery thread, an extensive line of books on embroidery, quilting, and sewing, and some unique fabrics. With their service and selection, I recommend them highly.
Catalog: $2, which is refundable with purchase.

Richard The Thread

8320 Melrose Avenue, #201, Los Angeles, CA 90069
Phone: (213) 852-4997
Fax: (213) 852-1604
Services/Merchandise: This is a costume and notions house with a wide range of products for tailoring, dressmaking, corsetry, and millinery. Their customers include studios, professional theaters, and colleges and universities. They also carry dressforms and their own line of historical patterns.
Payment Options: Check, Money Order, MC, Visa
Shipping Options: UPS, FedEx, COD
Minimum Order: $25
Other Information: Send them a sample of what you're looking for in quantity, and they'll do their best to locate the hard-to-find.
Catalog: $3, which is refundable with order.

Rings & Things

Wholesale Only

P.O. Box 450, Spokane WA, 99210-0450

Phone: (800) 366-2156

Fax: (509) 838-2602

E-mail: pollarue@aol.com

Services/Merchandise: They have earwires, posts, bar pins, hat pins, hair sticks, button covers, suspender clips, barrett backs, Fimo, Sculpey, Friendly Plastic, and earring display cards. They also have beads in glass, bone, metal, ceramic, horn, crystal, gemstone, and a little bit of plastic. They have Swarovski lead crystal, a wide variety of stringing cord and other stringing supplies, and new kits and supplies for "Y" and other beaded chain necklaces.

Payment Options: Check, Money Order, MC, Visa

Shipping Options: UPS, U.S. Postal Service, FedEx

Minimum Order: No minimum order, but there is $4 service charge on orders under $50.

Special Discounts/Offers: 10% discount on first order with the mention of *Sew Far Sew Good*. Wholesale to qualified businesses.

Catalog: $2, which is refundable with purchase.

River Gems & Findings

6901 Washington Northeast, Alberquerque, NM 87109

Robin's Bobbins & Other Things

1674 Murphy Highway, Mineral Bluff, GA 30559-9736

Phone: (706) 374-6916

Services/Merchandise: They have hard-to-find bobbin and needle lace supplies, and a wide assortment of pillows, bobbins, threads, pins, shuttles, carrying cases, and books.

Payment Options: Check, MC, Visa

Shipping Options: UPS, U.S. Postal Service

Other Information: They put on workshops in many areas of bobbin lace, for beginner to advanced lacemakers.

Special Discounts/Offers: 10% discount for teachers and resalers on most products with an order of $100 or more.

Catalog: $1

RolyKit

Distributed Exclusively by QVC

Phone: (800) 345-1515

Services/Merchandise: They have RolyKit–The Roll-Up Case That Keeps Things In Place®. It is uniquely designed to simply roll out on any flat surface, then roll back up into a compact carrying case that fits just about anywhere. Each kit snaps shut with a patented interlocking device that keeps contents intact, even when the kit is upside down. Each model also has adjustable compartments for a variety of uses.

Other Information: Three sizes are available:

- S11: 11-27 adjustable compartments, 7H x 11 x 8G rolled. More than 240 cubic inches of storage capacity.
- S14: 14-38 adjustable compartments, 8G x 11 x 9H rolled. More than 310 cubic inches of storage capacity.
- S18: 14-36 adjustable compartments 11H x 11 x 9H rolled. More than 680 cubic inches of storage capacity.

Author's Note: These are great for any sort of small notions–even beads. Products don't get mixed up in this handy holder.

Running Stitch Studio

1029 Northeast 90th, Seattle, WA 98115

Phone: (206) 523-4367

Services/Merchandise: The Running Stitch Studio is a custom interior workroom that offers sewing and quilting services to interior designers and retail customers. They sew custom bedding, window treatments, pillows, and more. They also quilt patchwork quilt tops and do antique quilt repair.

Payment Options: Check, Money Order

Shipping Options: UPS, FedEx

Minimum Order: No minimum order.

Other Information: Running Stitch Studio has operated for over 15 years, offering quality artistic machine-quilting for patchwork enthusiasts who love to piece tops, but don't have the time or the inclination to quilt them. They also work on antique quilt tops that have never been finished. The quilting design is specifically chosen for the individual quilt. It is hand-guided machine quilting (not programmed), which offers a wealth of design possibilities. Custom patchwork quilts can also be ordered.

Special Discounts/Offers: 10% discount on first order with the mention of *Sew Far Sew Good*, for retail orders. 15% discount for wholesale orders.

Author's Note: Running Stitch Studio sent a picture of one of their pieces–an antique quilt top quilted in their store. It was a beautiful, intricate masterpiece, and more work than I would like to do, even with a machine.

Rupert, Gibbon & Spider

P.O. Box 425, Healdsburg, CA 95448

Phone: (707) 433-9577, (800) 442-0455

Fax: (707) 433-4906

Pants styles...

Stirrup

Specialty yarns...

Chenille

Services/Merchandise: They have silk, cotton, rayon, and hemp fabrics. They also have paints and dyes, accessories for batik and tie-dye, easels, frames, and stitchery and embroidery frames.
Payment Options: Check, MC, Visa
Shipping Options: UPS, FedEx, RPS
Minimum Order: $50
Other Information: Rupert, Gibbon & Spider manufactures the Jacquard line of paints and dyes for textiles. They also import silk from China at very good prices.

Saf-T-Pockets

822 Northwest Murray Boulevard, Portland, OR 97229-8568
Phone: (503) 643-1968
Fax: (503) 643-0764
Services/Merchandise: Creative Clothing for Carefree Travel is their line of travel clothing patterns.
Payment Options: Check, Money Order
Shipping Options: UPS, U.S. Postal Service
Minimum Order: No minimum order.
Other Information: Saf-T-Pockets Patterns feature lots of pockets, mostly concealed, to allow purse-free, hands-free travel. These clothes aren't just for foreign trips to exotic places, they are just as useful for grocery shopping or hiking. They're great for young mothers, photographers, and artists, too. Each pattern contains great ideas for embellishment and fabric choices, as well as a section featuring coordinating but compact travel wardrobes. Patterns are multi-sized for sizes 6-20 and are printed on tissue.
Special Discounts/Offers: $1 off first pattern purchase with the mention of *Sew Far Sew Good*. Wholesale to qualified fabric stores and instructors, with a minimum order of six patterns.
Catalog: Send a SASE for brochure.

Salt Spring Island Fibre Studios

121 Mountain Road, Salt Spring Island, BC V8K 1T8, Canada
Phone: (604) 653-4033
Fax: (604) 537-9930
E-mail: susanb@islandnet.com
Services/Merchandise: They have handspun, hand-dyed yarns in medium, fine, and extra fine weights. They have millspun, hand-dyed yarns in medium and fine weights. They have wool, alpaca, mohair, and llama yarns, complex and straightforward patterns, and kits with their yarns. They have handwoven skirt lengths to match yarns, and they will knit dog hair for you.
Payment Options: Check, Money Order, MC
Special Discounts/Offers: 10% discount on first order with the mention of *Sew Far Sew Good* (except for catalog).

Catalog: $10 for a catalog and complete sample card. $5 is rebated with first order.

Sandeen's Scandinavian Art, Gifts & Needlecraft

1315 White Bear Avenue, St. Paul, MN 55106
Phone: (612) 776-7012, (800) 235-1315
Services/Merchandise: They have brackets for bellpulls and wallhangings, imported Scandinavian kits for pillows, bellpulls, table runners, and wallhangings, fabric, threads, instruction books, and patterns. They have a complete selection of art supplies for painters specializing in Rosemaling (Norwegian folk art), Dalamalning (Swedish folk art), Bauernmalerei (Austrian folk art), and decorative painting of all kinds. This includes blank woodenware, patterns, instruction and pattern books, brushes, paints, and backgrounding and transferring materials, for both oil painting and acrylic painting.
Payment Options: Check, Money Order, MC, Visa, Amex
Shipping Options: UPS, U.S. Postal Service
Minimum Order: One item.
Other Information: They have been in business for 40 years in their present location, and have taught Rosemaling for 40 years after extensive study and travel in Europe. Try to visit their picturesque gift shop, reminiscent of the shops you have visited in Europe, and choose first-hand, the materials for your favorite folk art. Need help? Ask them. Need advice? They will do their best to help you choose. Mail orders are also welcome.
Catalog: Needlecraft catalog $3, which is refundable on first order. The art supply catalog is $2, which is refundable on first order.

San Diego Quilt Show

P.O. Box 12600, El Cajon, CA 92022-2600
Phone: (619) 461-7321

Sawyer Brook Distinctive Fabrics
Mail Order Only
P.O. Box 1800, Clinton, MA 01510-0813
Phone: (508) 368-3133
Fax: (508) 365-1775
Services/Merchandise: Sawyer Brook is a mailorder fashion fabric service, featuring high quality, unique fabrics for the home and professional sewer. Each fashion season—Fall/Winter and Spring/Summer—they publish three brochures filled with tempting swatches of fine wools, luxurious silks, silky cottons, imported rayons, and much more. In addition, they offer a line of specialty buttons to enhance the fabrics in their seasonal collections.
Payment Options: Check, Money Order, MC, Visa

Shipping Options: UPS, U.S. Postal Service
Minimum Order: One yard.
Membership Dues: $10 per season (Fall/Winter, Spring/Summer)
Other Information: Sawyer Brook is staffed by fabric specialists who not only know their fabrics well, but are expert seamstresses and can respond knowledgeably to customers' questions on garment construction, appropriate fabric choices, and best match lining, notions, and buttons.
Special Discounts/Offers: New Subscriber Bonus! Free shipping on your first order with the mention of *Sew Far Sew Good*.
Author's Note: Sawyer Brook sent me a sample of their mailings for Fall/Winter 1995, and all the others since then. They are very generous with the amount they send, and all the high quality fabrics are beautiful. I am consistently amazed at the prices. I have been sent a few of the same fabrics (or very similar ones) for three times the amount Sawyer Brook was charging. Since their fabrics are top quality, they are not a discount store. The care they put into coordinating their swatch sets and informing their customers shows through.
Catalog: $10 for an entire season's brochures. If you place an order of $25 from the current season, you will receive the next season's catalogs free. Reminders are placed in the last catalog of each season.

SAX Arts & Crafts

2405 South Calhoun Road, P.O. Box 51710, New Berlin, WI 53151-0710
Phone: (800) 558-6696 (answered 24 hours a day)
Fax: (414) 784-1176
Services/Merchandise: Fabric paints and dyes, and brushes.
Payment Options: Check, Money Order, Telecheck, MC, Visa, Amex, Discover
Shipping Options: UPS
Minimum Order: $10
Other Information: 100% satisfaction is guaranteed on the quality of products listed in their catalog. Their Customer Service Hotline is (800) 522-4278.
Author's Note: I love their catalog. It has everything your art desires.
Catalog: $5, which is refundable with purchase. No charge for schools and institutions when ordered on official letterhead.

The Scarlet Letter

Mail Order Only
P.O. Box 397, Sullivan, WI 53178
Phone: (414) 593-8470
Fax: (414) 593-2417
Services/Merchandise: They have over 150 museum reproduction counted thread and silk-screened sampler kits, with designs that date from 1625 to 1840. They also have materials for sewing historic samplers, including exclusive flax linens in many different thread counts, silk threads, needles, and antique reproduction sewing tools. They make custom-made period style frames from tiger and birdseye maple, flame birch, Carpathian elm and walnut burls, and hand-grain painted woods. Archival mounting of needlework is provided with the framing service. The mail order catalog includes a large selection of books on antique samplers and early textiles. Genuine antique samplers are also available for sale.
Payment Options: Check, Money Order, MC, Visa, Amex
Shipping Options: UPS, U.S. Postal Service, FedEx
Catalog: $4

Schoolhouse Press

6899 Cary Bluff, Pittsville, WI 54466
Phone: (715) 884-2799, (800) YOU-KNIT
Fax: (715) 884-2829
Services/Merchandise: They have complete supplies for handknitting, including wool, needles, books, videos, buttons, kits, wool winders, swifts, and more. They also offer *Wool Gathering*, a newsletter, for $15 for three years.
Payment Options: Check, Money Order, MC, Visa, Discover
Shipping Options: UPS, FedEx, Parcel Post
Other Information: Schoolhouse Press has been supplying handknitters exclusively since 1959.
Special Discounts/Offers: Full wholesale discounts on all books and videos to qualified businesses.
Catalog: $3 for a catalog and a wool sample card.

Sealed With A Kiss, Inc.

1024 East Noble, Guthrie, OK 73044
Phone: (405) 282-8649
Services/Merchandise: They have unique picture-knit sweater patterns for women and children. Kits and coordinating buttons and earrings are available as well. The current series of patterns includes State Pride, Holidays & Other Happenings, Professions & Pastimes, SWAK International, and SWAK Kids.
Payment Options: Check, Money Order, MC, Visa
Shipping Options: UPS, U.S. Postal Service, FedEx
Minimum Order: No minimum order for retail sales.
Other Information: Sealed With A Kiss is a home-base, mother/daughter owned business that offers personal service to all their customers. They are in their third year of offering whimsical designs to knitters.
Special Discounts/Offers: 10% discount on first order with the mention of *Sew Far Sew Good*. Wholesale to qualified businesses.

Skirt top styles...

Paper Bag Waist

Elastic

Short sleeve styles...

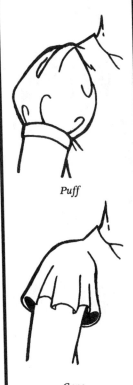

Puff

Cape

Roll

Author's Note: The catalog has line art of the patterns available, as well as a photograph of five sweaters on the cover. They use fun colors and a great sense of style to create each of these wearable works of art.
Catalog: $1

Seattle Fabrics, Inc.
3876 Bridge Way North, Seattle, WA 98103
Phone: (206) 632-6022
Fax: (206) 632-0881
Services/Merchandise: They have outdoor gear supplies and patterns.
Payment Options: Check, MC, Visa
Shipping Options: UPS, U.S. Postal Service, COD
Minimum Order: $10
Special Discounts/Offers: Wholesale to qualified businesses.

The Seraph Textile Collection
420 Main Street, P.O. Box 500, Sturbridge, MA 01566
Phone: (508) 347-2241, (800) X-SERAPH
Fax: (508) 347-9162
Services/Merchandise: They have authentic handloomed, homespun wool in light and medium weights. They also have over 80 authentic patterns. They are one of the first companies to reproduce handloomed fabric, and they have a large selection.
Payment Options: Check, Money Order, MC, Visa
Minimum Order: No minimum retail. 25 yards wholesale.
Author's Note: You can see a sample of their fabric in the fabric square on the back cover.
Catalog: $5 for a retail catalog. $3 for a wholesale catalog.

Seventh Annual Quilt/Surface Design Symposium
464 Vermont Place, Columbus, OH 43201

Sew Natural-Fabrics By Mail
Mail Order Only
521 N. Essex Drive, Lexington Park, MD 20653-1658
Phone: (301) 863-5952
Services/Merchandise: They have 100% cotton, wool, and linen fabrics. Their woven fabrics include denims (in several weights), twill, sheeting, flannel, chamois, feather corduroy, and diaper fabrics. Their knit fabrics include interlock, sweatshirt fleece, French terry, T-shirt jersey, rugby, and all weights and widths of ribs. They also carry Ultrex, wool and cotton quilt batting, Kwik-Sew patterns, Stretch & Sew patterns, and other patterns.

Payment Options: Check, Money Order, MC, Visa
Shipping Options: UPS, U.S. Postal Service
Other Information: Their catalog comes four times a year and has swatches of fabrics. They are a home business and willing to work with you to find anything you may want.
Special Discounts/Offers: Free shipping on first order with the mention of *Sew Far Sew Good*.
Catalog: $2. They send a $5 coupon with their catalog.

Sew Sassy Lingerie
9009-C South Memorial Parkway, Huntsville, AL 35802
Phone: (205) 883-1209, (800) 67-SASSY
Services/Merchandise: They have a complete line of lingerie fabrics, tricot with matching lace elastics, sheer slip straps, all-over stretch lace, charmeuse, re-embroidered lace, light-weight knits, and specialty elastics. They also have many different bra patterns and accessories, including underwires, bra rings and slides, front and back closures, and other notions. They carry lycra for swimsuits and costumes, specialty fabrics, and sewing instruction books on how to sew with lycra. They stock the complete line of Stretch & Sew, and Kwik-Sew patterns.
Payment Options: Check, Money Order, MC, Visa
Minimum Order: $20.
Catalog: $2, which is refundable with first order.

Sew-Pro Workshop
2315 B Forest Drive, Suite 50, Annapolis, MD 21401
Phone: (800) 355-1137
Fax: (410) 798-1951   .
Services/Merchandise: They have books and videos and the tailoring supplies used in the books and videos. These supplies include 100% cotton twill tape, Silesia pocketing fabric, waistband curtain, pants pocketing, trouser zippers, full canvas coat fronts with padding, canvas chest pieces with padding, Armo Weft, Whisper Weft, SofBrush fusible interfacings, and more.
Payment Options: Check, Money Order, MC, Visa
Shipping Options: UPS, U.S. Postal Service
Minimum Order: No minimum order.
Catalog: Free price list upon request.

SewBaby!
P.O. Box 11683, Champaign, IL 61826
Phone: (800) 249-1907
E-mail: sewbaby@prairienet.org
WWW: http://www.prairienet.org/sewbaby/homepage

Services/Merchandise: SewBaby tries to provide everything you need–patterns, fabrics, and notions–to make department store quality children's garments. They carry patterns from over 20 small, independent companies for children's clothing, soft toys, and baby necessities. A few of the companies they carry are: K.P. Kid's and Co., BearWear, Peas & Carrots, Sew Little, and Sunrise Designs. They are also a source for Kwik-Sew and Stretch & Sew patterns, as well as their home catalogs. They have a bonus pattern program; if you order four patterns or books (adult patterns, too), they'll give you the fifth one free (lowest value is free).

They stock juvenile knits, printed corduroys, denim dobbie plaids, waterproof Ultrex, taffeta vinyl, and a wide assortment of stretch terry in both solids and prints. They carry the K.P. Kid's line of woven cotton prints.

They are a source for Snap Source snaps and snap tools. They carry 15 colors, in both the open ring and capped styles, in size 16. They also carry 12 colors of size 20–the preferred size for outerwear.

Additional products include squeakers, Jiffy Grip (for the bottoms of booties), and size labels. They also have an extensive selection of Healthtex knit trim that they sell in grab bag fashion.
Payment Options: Check, Money Order, MC, Visa
Shipping Options: UPS, U.S. Postal Service
Minimum Order: No minimum order.
Other Information: They publish a quarterly newsletter that features new fabric swatches, reader tips, designer profiles, and book excerpts. To subscribe, submit your favorite sewing tip or send $2.
Special Discounts/Offers: $5 discount on a fabric purchase of five yards or more with the mention of *Sew far Sew Good*.
Catalog: Free catalog upon request. Swatches of all of their fabrics, $2.

Sewing Emporium/Sew-Easy Products

1079B 3rd Avenue, Chula Vista, CA 91910
Phone: (619) 420-3490
Fax: (619) 420-4002
Services/Merchandise: They re-manufacture many sewing machine parts and accessories. They also provide machine overhaul, repair, and rebuild services to dealers and the general public. They stock nearly 10,000 parts and have access to over one million parts for domestic and commercial machines.
Payment Options: Check, Money Order, MC, Visa, Amex, Discover, COD
Shipping Options: UPS, U.S. Postal Service, FedEx
Other Information: They promote the art and science of home sewing, provide machine availability at a reasonable price, and assist customers in the pursuit of their objectives. They are a member of AHSCA and of TNNA.
Special Discounts/Offers: Special prices to groups, guilds, and teachers. Wholesale to qualified businesses.
Catalog: $4.95, which is refundable with order.

Sewing Machine Exchange

1131 Mission Street, San Francisco, CA 94103
Phone: (415) 982-3003

Sewing Sampler Productions, Inc.

P.O. Box 39, Springfield, MN 56087
Phone: (507) 723-5011
Fax: (507) 723-6231
Services/Merchandise: They have newsletters devoted to fashion sewing for adult women and to fashion sewing for children. They have fashion fabric from famous ready-to-wear manufacturers, including OshKosh, Absorba, and Lee, and 100% cotton interlock, cotton/lycra, ribbing, and French terry. They also have colored enamel snaps, and books related to fashion sewing.
Payment Options: Visa, MC, Discover
Shipping Options: UPS, U.S. Postal Service
Other Information: A sample newsletter is $3, and a sample swatch mailing is $3. A one year swatch subscription is $10.
Special Discounts/Offers: 25% discount on books with the mention of Sew Far Sew Good. 10% discount on fabric to newsletter subscribers.
Catalog: Free upon request.

Sewing Supplies, Inc.

142 Medford Avenue, Patchogue, NY 11772
Phone: (516) 475-8282
Services/Merchandise: They specialize in hard to find parts and accessories for sewing machines. They also have over 35 titles of books.
Payment Options: Check, Money Order, MC, Visa, Amex
Other Information: They are listed in *Gail Brown's Ultimate Serger Answer (Source) Book*. Customer service at Nancy's Notions may refer you to Sewing Supplies, Inc. if you have questions about machine parts and compatabilities.
Special Discounts/Offers: 10% discount on first order with the mention of *Sew far Sew Good*.
Catalog: $3, which is refundable with purchase.

SewStorm Publishing

944 Sutton Road, Cincinnati, OH 45230-3581
Phone: (513) 232-5403
E-mail: sewstorm@aol.com
Services/Merchandise: They have books, booklets, and newsletters for sewing professionals, and they teach to groups.
Payment Options: Check, Money Order, MC, Visa
Shipping Options: UPS, U.S. Postal Service
Minimum Order: No minimum order.

Short sleeve styles...

Cap

Melon

Plain

Other Information: They specialize in helping sewing-related businesses find success.
Special Discounts/Offers: Wholesale to qualified businesses. 25% discount on purchases of five or fewer books.

SewSweet Dolls from Carolee Creations

787 Industrial Drive, Elmhurst, IL 60126
Phone: (708) 530-7175
Fax: (708)530-8489
Services/Merchandise: *SewSweet Dolls* is a full-color, 32-page catalog featuring over 200 unique doll and animal patterns. Patterns are full-sized and easy to sew, with clear instructions and easy sewing methods. Hard-to-find doll making supplies are also offered in the catalog.
Payment Options: Check, Money Order, MC, Visa, Discover
Shipping Options: UPS, U.S. Postal Service
Minimum Order: No minimum order.
Other Information: The staff at Carolee Creations prides itself on prompt and courteous service. They've been in business for over 25 years and are now reaching a second generation of doll makers. Many customers say that a mother or grandmother made a SewSweet Doll for them, and now they want to do the same for their children.

Shipwreck Beads

2727 Westmoor Court Southwest, Dept. OP, Olympia, WA 98502
Phone: (360) 754-BEAD
Fax: (360) 754-2510
Services/Merchandise: They have a wide variety of beads, including Czech lamp and glass, gemstone, cut lead crystal, seed, bugle, metal, wood, bone, hare pipe, and buffalo horn beads. They also have an assortment of metal charms, findings and accessories, and a large selection of books.
Payment Options: Check, Money Order, MC, Visa, Discover, Terms Available
Shipping Options: UPS, U.S. Postal Service
Minimum Order: $25 mail order. 1¢ in their store (!)
Other Information: Shipwreck Beads was established in 1969, and began the bead industry's first catalog. The catalog has photos of beads at exact sizes and a 90-page price list. Sales flyers and information on upcoming shipments are included.
Special Discounts/Offers: Wholesale and distributor prices are available.
Catalog: $4

Shuttle-Craft Books

P.O. Box 550, Coupeville, WA 98239

E-mail: scb@whidbey.net
Services/Merchandise: They have 40 books and monographs relating to weaving and feltmaking by Madelyn van der Hoogt, Anita Mayer, Pat Mayer, Pat Spark, Margaret Windeknecht, Virginia Harvey, Mary Atwater, and Harriet Tidball.
Payment Options: Check, Prepaid
Shipping Options: UPS, U.S. Postal Service
Minimum Order: No minimum order.
Other Information: The titles available include *Complete Book of Drafting* by Madelyn van der Hoogt, *Fundamentals of Feltmaking* and *Scandinavian-Style Feltmaking* by Pat Spark, *Handwoven Clothing, Felted to Wear* by Anita Mayer, and *Byways in Handweaving* by Mary Atwater. Write for a free catalog or visit them on the internet at the above e-mail address.

Sievers School of Fiber Arts

Jackson Harbor Road, Washington Island, WI 54246
Phone: (414) 847-2264
Services/Merchandise: They offer classes in all fiber arts from May to October and have dormitory facilities. They have Sievers weaving looms, yarns, books, fabrics, basketry supplies, fiber art supplies, fine handmade crafts, and fiber art from the students and teachers at Sievers School of Fiber Arts.
Payment Options: Check, Money Order, MC, Visa
Shipping Options: UPS, U.S. Postal Service
Tuition Cost: Varies according to class.
Minimum Order: No minimum order.
Other Information: The school has offered classes in weaving, quilting, basketry, spinning, papermaking, surface design, and more since 1979. 35 instructors teach over 60 week-long and weekend classes between May and October. A dormitory is located on school grounds.

For over 25 years, Sievers Looms has been selling plan sheets to build your own loom. Today, both plan sheets and loom kits are available in two sizes: 15" Four-Harness Table Loom and 36" Four-Harness Floor Loom. Loom kits are available in birch or cherry lumber and are sold by mail order. Weaving equipment and accessories are also offered through the catalog.

Yarns, books, fabric, basketry, and fiber art supplies are sold, along with original fiber art and fine crafts handmade by Sievers students and teachers. The retail shop is located in a turn-of-the-century schoolhouse at Sievers School of Fiber Arts.
Special Discounts/Offers: 10% discount on loom purchase when you are attending a class at Sievers School.
Catalog: Free class list. $2 for a loom and weaving accessories catalog.

Silk Gardens

P.O. Box 369, Cedar Mountain, NC 28718
Phone: (704) 884-7667
Services/Merchandise: They have hand-marbled and handpainted silk ribbon.
Payment Options: Check, Money Order
Shipping Options: UPS, U.S. Postal Service
Minimum Order: $8
Other Information: They believe that they are the only source for hand-marbled ribbon.
Catalog: Free upon request.

The Silk Tree

#15, 1551 Johnston Street, Vancouver, BC V6H 3R9, Canada
Phone: (604) 687-7455
Fax:(604) 465-0976
Services/Merchandise: They have a wide range of silk yarns and fibers, including singles, cords, bouclés, ribbon, and chenille in natural and 52 colors. Small skeins are available for embroidery. They also have silk batting for quilting.
Payment Options: Check, Money Order, MC, Visa, American Express
Shipping Options: U.S. Postal Service
Other Information: They are celebrating 16 years of mail order silks to customers in Canada, the U.S.A., and around the world.
Special Discounts/Offers: 10% discount on first purchase with the mention of _Sew Far Sew Good_. Also, 10% off orders over $200 and 20% off orders over $400, all of the time.
Catalog: $5

Silkpaint Corporation

P.O. Box 18 SFSG, 18220 Waldron Drive, Waldron, MS 64092
Phone: (816) 891-7774
Fax: (816) 891-7775
Services/Merchandise: They have the Airpen® to draw lines without squeezing a bottle. Just fill the cartridge with paint, glue, or silkpainting resist, plug in the electric air pump, and draw smooth and flowing lines.

They also have Fiber-Etch® Fabric Remover. It removes fabric from cutwork without cutting. Apply gel, iron, and rinse fabric. Fiber-Etch® is the winner of the 1995 Innovation Award and the 1996 Home Economics Healthy Living Award. They also carry a complete line of French dyes and silk painting supplies.
Payment Options: Check, Money Order, MC, Visa
Shipping Options: UPS, U.S. Postal Service
Minimum Order: No minimum order.
Other Information: SilkPaint is the manufacturer of Fiber-Etch®, The Airpen®, and other quality products. Orders are filled within 24 hours.

Special Discounts/Offers: Free booklet–_Teaching Classes and Making Display Samples with Fiber-Etch®_–with the mention of _Sew Far Sew Good_.
Catalog: Free upon request.

Sloppy Joes Casualwear

One 20th Street, Paris, KY 40361
Phone: (606) 987-5228

Smocking Arts Guild of America

4350 DiPaolo Center, Glenview, IL 60025
Phone: (847) 390-SAGA
Fax: (847) 699-6369
Services/Merchandise: They offer classes in smocking, heirloom sewing, and other needlearts through regional weekend seminars and the annual national convention. They have correspondence courses in sewing, chapter programs, and artisan programs featuring 3 levels of achievement in each of the three years for smocking, fine handsewing, and fine machine sewing. Members receive 5-6 issues of _SAGANEWS_, a newsletter with patterns, tips, and club news. SAGA has traveling trunk shows of garments, and a design show of original sewn garments and items at the annual convention. There are 170 chapters of SAGA in the U.S. and Canada and many foreign members.
Payment Options: Check, Money Order, MC, Visa
Membership Dues: Memberships for the calendar year are $28 January-March, $21 April-June, $14 July-September, and $7 October-December.
Membership Benefits: SAGA members enjoy education and the camaraderie of needlearts enthusiasts.

The Smocking Horse Collection

5 Parkway Drive, Olmsted Falls, OH 44138
Phone: (216) 235-2035, (800) 910-2035
Fax: (216) 235-0578
Services/Merchandise: They have fabric cards of all their fabrics. The customer purchases the type of card wanted, and the cost is deducted from the first order. Their mail order business represents a portion of what is sold and done in their charming, Victorian cottage store. Store hours are Mon. - Sat., 11 - 5, and Thurs. 11 - 9. They have hundreds of quality fabrics, laces, and notions, and every day, they have classes going.
Payment Options: Check, Money Order, MC, Visa, Discover
Minimum Order: No minimum retail. $35 wholesale for a first time order.
Other Information: They only sell quality fabrics, notions, books, etc. Their goal is to put quality back into sewing.

Neckline styles...

Deep Square

Wide V

Bateau

Vest syles...

Weskit

Fingertip

Special Discounts/Offer: Three newsletter and catalog mailings for $3 a year. Two coupons for $5 off with a $20 purchase.

Catalog: If you're just buying a catalog and no subscription, the cost is $2, which is refundable with your first order.

The Snap Source, Inc.

P.O. Box 99733, Troy, MI 48099

Phone: (810) 585-2234, (800) 725-4600

Services/Merchandise: The Snap Source, Inc., carries one of the nation's largest selections of colorful, long-prong snap fasteners, and an award winning snap-attachment tool.

Payment Options: Check, Money Order, MC, Visa, COD

Shipping Options: UPS, U.S. Postal Service, FedEx

Minimum Order: No minimum order.

Other Information: The Snap Source is dedicated to providing the home sewing and crafting industries with quality snap-attaching products. They're redefining the art of attaching snaps. All of their products are American made, and feature easy-to-use instructions and a 100% satisfaction guarantee.

Special Discounts/Offers: 20% discount on first order with the mention of *Sew Far Sew Good*. Wholesale to qualified businesses.

Author's Note: The selection of colors and sizes I received from The Snap Source is amazing. They truly have anything you will ever need in snaps.

Catalog: Free upon request.

Snowgoose

P.O. Box 27805, Denver, CO 80227

Phone: (303) 934-5168

Services/Merchandise: They have lacemaking supplies, beginner kits, and hard-to-find tools.

Payment Options: Check, Money Order, MC, Visa

Shipping Options: UPS, U.S. Postal Service

Minimum Order: No minimum order.

Other Information: If Snowgoose does not have what you're looking for, they will try to direct you to another source.

Special Discounts/Offers: Wholesale to qualified businesses on some items.

Catalog: Free upon request.

Software Directory for Fibre Artists

5010 50th Avenue, Camrose, AB T4V 0S5, Canada

Phone: (403) 672-5887

Fax: (403) 672-9570

E-mail: swp@ecinet.ab.ca

WWW: http://www.islandnet.com/rarodgers/directory.html

Services/Merchandise: *Software Directory for Fiber Artists* lists comprehensive information on 262 software programs, and profiles seven professionals who discuss how using a computer has changed their work.

Payment Options: Check, Money Order, MC, Visa

Minimum Order: One unit.

Other Information: The author began collecting information on weaving software in the mid-Eighties out of a personal interest. She was encouraged to make the information available to others and published the first edition of her book in 1986. This third edition is expanded to include all fiber-related software.

Special Discounts/Offers: Free demonstration disks with purchase of Directory, while supplies last.

Soho South

P.O. Box 1324, Cullman, AL 35056-1324

Phone: (205) 739-6114

Fax: (205) 734-6759

E-mail: sohosout@village.ios.com

Services/Merchandise: They specialize in Czech Republic glass beads, including seed beads in sizes 11/0, 8/0, 12/0 and 6/0 "E". They also have bugles, twisted bugles, 2-cut hexagon beads, heart, star, leaf, and teardrop shape beads, faceted fire-polish beads, Czech crystals, molded round glass beads, and many others. They also have gemstone beads, freshwater pearls, 14k gold-filled and sterling silver beads and findings, a large range of bead thread, bead cord, tools, and books. Customers receive listings of new bead arrivals and special purchases every 2-3 months. Their selection of silkpainting and batik includes Fabricarts liquid silk dyes, Procion H and Procion MX dyes, auxiliary chemicals, gutta and wax resists, silkpainting tools, and marbling supplies.

Payment Options: Visa, MC, Check, Money Order

Shipping Options: UPS, U.S. Postal Service Priority

Minimum Order: No minimum order, but a $1 shipping charge on orders under $50.

Other Information: You may wish to order their bead sampler #5 at a cost of $10 (some of the beads shown on the back cover of this book are from the sampler). A free catalog is included with your purchase of a bead sampler.

Special Discounts/Offers: Free shipping to readers of *Sew Far Sew Good*. Free bobbin of nymo beading thread with a $20 purchase and the mention of *Sew Far Sew Good*. 10% discount to qualified designers with $100 purchase. Prices on beads are less than retail, with quantity discounts on many items.

Author's Note: The bead sampler was sent to me, and I was so impressed that I used many of the beads on the back cover as examples.

Catalog: $2.50, which is refundable with your first purchase of $20 or more.

Sojourner

26 Bridge Street, Lamebertville, NJ 08530
Phone: (609) 397-8849
Fax: (609) 397-9240
Services/Merchandise: Sojourner stocks over 1,000 varieties of Czech Republic glass beads in hundreds of colors. They also carry about 50 varieties of seed beads in sizes 6, 10, and 11. The finishes available on the seed beads are opaque, transparent, foil lined, acid washed, and petrolated. Although Czech beads are the mainstay of their business, they also stock a wide selection of beads from Africa, and China, as well as an extensive line of sterling silver beads from Indonesia and India. Sometimes they are lucky enough to discover caches of vintage beads, which are then made available to customers. The Sojourner stocks all the findings necessary to make your own jewelry in both gold-tone and silver-tone, as well as some sterling silver. They carry approximately 10 different kinds of string, ranging from beading silk to two millimeter thick leather. Bead kits are available, ranging in price from $3 for a kit that will make one project, to $12 for a kit that will make four necklaces. Some special project kits are more expensive, but the average kit price is about $10. Due to their propensity for collecting, they also have a large inventory of vintage braids. Since these braids are not a big part of their business, it is best to call ahead if you would like to see them, so they can be hauled out of the attic.
Payment Options: Check, Money Order, MC, Visa, Discover
Minimum Order: No minimum order.
Other Information: Sojourner has a second summer-time only store in New Jersey. It is open from mid-May through mid-October. Although they only wholesale from the Lambertville location, the summer store is fully stocked with everything available from their wholesale location.

The Sojourner has been in business for 10 years. It is a mother/daughter partnership. A bead table is set up in the store, where you can design and make your projects. Tools are available, and the helpful and knowledgeable staff is always there to help you in any way they can.

Another part of Sojourner's business is importing art from all over the world. They often have pieces of antique textiles that would be of interest to fiber artists, including yard goods from Guatemala, handmade silks from Thailand, and chakla cloth from India, among other offerings.
Special Discounts/Offers: Wholesale to the public, with a $50 minimum.

Solo Slide Fasteners, Inc.

8 Spring Brook Road, P.O. Box 378M, Foxboro, MA 02035
Phone: (800) 343-9760
Fax: (800) 547-4775
Services/Merchandise: They have many sewing notions and supplies in packaged quantities.
Payment Options: Check, MC, Visa, Amex
Shipping Options: COD, Prepaid
Minimum Order: $30

Something Pretty

Route #1, Box 93C, Big Sandy, TN 38221
Phone: (901) 593-3807
Fax: (901) 593-3807
Services/Merchandise: They have custom buttons on request, with a minimum purchase of 12 for wholesale, and 6 for retail. They also have over 500 buttons in stock at this time, all 100% handpainted.
Payment Options: MC, Visa
Shipping Options: UPS, U.S. Postal Service
Minimum Order: $75 on the first order only
Other Information: They have been creating custom handpainted buttons since 1989.
Special Discounts/Offers: 10% discount on first order with the mention of _Sew Far Sew Good_. Wholesale to qualified businesses.
Author's Note: Something Pretty creates whimsical, fun ceramic buttons–great for kids or kids-at-heart.
Catalog: $2.50 for a color brochure.

Sonya Lee Barrington

837 47th Avenue, San Francisco, CA 94121
Phone: (415) 221-6510
Services/Merchandise: They have hand-dyed and marbled 100% cotton fabric in 300 colors.
Payment Options: Check, Money Order, MC, Visa
Shipping Options: UPS, U.S. Postal Service
Minimum Order: $10 for fabric, $5 for swatches.
Other Information: Sonya also teaches and lectures, and has over 27 years of experience as a quiltmaker.

SouthStar Supply Company

P.O. Box 90147, Nashville, TN 37209
Phone: (615) 353-7000
Fax: (615) 353-7155
E-mail: jfreb@aol.com
Services/Merchandise: SouthStar Supply Company is a distributor of spare parts, machinery, equipment, tools, and supplies used in the manufacture of sewn products, from patternmaking to cutting, sewing, and finishing.
Payment Options: MC, Visa, American Express
Shipping Options: UPS

Skirt styles...

Accordian Pleated

How did a wild carrot get the name Queen Anne's Lace?

Possibly after Anne of Bohemia. This is the story I have been told:

A small girl was brought to the attention of the queen. She showed the queen a pattern based on the flower of a wild carrot that she had been tatting. The queen graciously gave her leave to name the pattern for Her Majesty.

Other Information: SouthStar was founded in 1989 and has grown to become one of the largest suppliers to the U.S. sewn products manufacturing industry. SouthStar publishes a monthly catalog it will mail free to prospective customers, whether commercial enterprises or consumers.

Southwest Craft Center

300 Augusta Street, San Antonio, TX
Phone: (210) 224-1848
Fax: (210) 224-9337
E-mail: swcc@dcci.com
Services/Merchandise: The Southwest Craft Center offers courses and workshops taught by visiting artists in the disciplines of ceramics, fibers, metal, papermaking, photography, and surface design. Their approach to instruction allows students to work alongside professional artists, gaining both the technical expertise involved in the craft, and the business know-how necessary to make a living as a working artist.

The Fiber Studio focuses on the areas of on- and off-loom weaving, basketry, spinning, botanicals, and other techniques.

The Surface Design Studio offers courses in Complex Cloth Projects, Creative Expressions, Color Basics, and Beaded Tassels.
Tuition Cost: Call for more information.

Speed Stitch

3113 Broadpoint Drive, Port Charlotte, FL 33983
Phone: (800) 874-4115

Speigelhoff Stretch & Sew/Great Copy Patterns

4901 Washington Avenue, P.O. Box 085329, Racine, WI 53408-5329
Phone: (414) 632-2660
Fax: (414) 632-0152
Services/Merchandise: Their monthly newsletter offers swatches of current fashion knits, as well as up-to-date information on the latest Stretch & Sew and Great Copy Patterns. Twice per year, they send basic charts featuring dyed-to-match doubleknit, interlock, and rib in the latest fashion colors.

Great Copy features garment variations using Great Copy Patterns. Ruthann shops better ready-to-wear and designer stores to bring you the latest in fashion, and then makes it easy by adapting her Great Copy Patterns.
Payment Options: Check, Money Order, MC, Visa, Discover
Shipping Options: UPS, U.S. Postal Service
Minimum Order: No minimum order.
Membership Dues: $20 for 12 issues of *Great Copy Club*. $25 for 23 issues of *Fabrics by Mail*.

Membership Benefits: Subscribers receive a 10% discount on Great Copy Patterns, as well as other specials from their newsletter.
Other Information: Fabrics by Mail monthly swatches are exclusively knits and coordinates.
Special Discounts/Offers: Special discount on first order with the mention of *Sew Far Sew Good*.
Author's Note: They sent me a copy of *Polarfleece Pizzazz* by Ruthann Speigeloff and Judy Laube. It is packed full of great patterns and great ideas. The patterns are easy for the beginner, and the projects so useful that everyone will want to make them.
Catalog: Send a SASE with two stamps for a Great Copy brochure and mail order information.

Spinning Wheel

217 Main Street, Fordyce, AR 71742
Phone: (501) 352-7694
Fax: (501) 352-7694
Services/Merchandise: They have cross-stitch books from Leisure Arts, Gloria & Pat, Lavendar and Lace, and more. They also have DMC embroidery floss, Anchor embroidery floss, Kreinik threads, overdyed floss, Medici yarn, and Marlitt threads. Leisure Arts hard cover books include *Spirit of Christmas*, *Holiday Cooking and Decorating*, and *Southern Living Christmas*.
Payment Options: Check, Money Order, MC, Visa
Shipping Options: UPS, U.S. Postal Service
Minimum Order: No minimum order.
Other Information: Spinning Wheel is a family-owned business run by Beth Greene and her daughter, Gwynne Workman. They have been in business since 1987. They opened their shop because they love needlearts and thought others would get the pleasure they do from creating beautiful things. They take pride in trying to help each customer match his/her individual needs and tastes with the appropriate merchandise. If they don't have what you need in stock, they will special order it if at all possible.

They look forward to seeing you (or hearing from you, if you can't make it to the store).
Special Discounts/Offers: 15% discount on first order with the mention of *Sew Far Sew Good*.
Catalog: $4, which is refundable with purchase.

Stevie Didn't Do It.

3466 Route 973 East, Cogan Station, PA 17728
Phone: (717) 321-9156
Services/Merchandise: Stevie is a craftsman working in polymer and specializing in high quality beads, but he also makes some wearable items—buttons, bubble blowers, pins, and more.

Payment Options: Check, Money Order, Pre-Paid, COD
Shipping Options: UPS, U.S. Postal Service
Minimum Order: $20
Author's Note: Stevie did it! A couple of times! He sent us exceptionally well-crafted beads that are too good to string and wear. The color schemes and designs are impressive and too pretty to risk losing, so I intend to keep them in a fire-proof safe.

Stitches Great Fiber Getaways

420 North Fifth Street, Suite 310, Minneapolis, MN 55401
Phone: (612) 288-0068
Fax: (612) 288-0069
E-mail: stitchsinc@aol.com
Services/Merchandise: Stitches was the originator of the sewing vacation and has been frequently copied since being formed nine years ago. They invite the fiber lover (along with her friends, relatives, even husbands) to join with a group of fun-loving women who share the same interests and sense of adventure. Stitches offers customized, guided tours throughout the world. Each tour includes fiber points of interest, including classes, behind-the-scenes museum exhibitions, and visits with local designers. Time is always made for fabric and fiber shopping, unique and unusual tours of the area, and there's plenty of free time for individual exploration. They specialize in the single woman traveler and will arrange suitable roommates or provide single accommodations upon request. They work with each individual to ensure that her specific travel agenda is met. They hire the best, most knowledgeable, fun-filled group of women possible. They admit that their prices are higher than some other tour companies, but they fly to all their destinations, stay at deluxe hotels, and include all ground transportation, museum and some class fees, and meals when indicated. They say they out-service all of their competitors.
Payment Options: Check, Money Order, and individualized payment plans
Other Information: Their hands-on workshops and seminars have featured Claire Shaeffer, Shermane Fouche, and Roberta Carr. In 1996, they are welcoming Linda McPhee. Stitches will gladly bring a workshop or seminar to any area of the country upon request, as they did for Roberta Carr in Dallas. For $3, Stitches will send you their current calendar.

Stone Age

4114-17 Crooked Tree, Wyoming, MI 49509
Phone: (616) 532-6324
Services/Merchandise: They have heirloom quality gemstone buttons, button covers, earrings, cufflinks, and tuxedo sets.
Payment Options: Check, Money Order

Shipping Options: UPS, U.S. Postal Service
Minimum Order: $50
Other Information: Stone Age offers you an impressive choice of custom-crafted, heirloom-quality accessories.

They have magnificent gemstone buttons, featured in *Women's Wear Daily* as a top trend. They have faceted gemstones, cabochons, and gemballs—from opals to peridot to aquamarine to amber. Alive to every movement, moonstones and starstones are just the thing for that unforgettable wedding gown or cocktail dress. Electric blue lapis lazuli, green jade, and black onyx provide the perfect accent for a very special shirt. Stones come in sizes from $\frac{1}{4}$ inch—for a stunning blouse, a youngster's outfit, or a christening robe—up to 1' inch+ for dramatic overcoats. They also have sterling silver, gold-filled, and gold-plated settings. Customers who know the color button they want, but are not sure of the color of a particular stone, may send a color sample to match.

They have exceptional gemstone button covers to wear as a neckline centerpiece for that special banded-collar shirt or blouse. Over the Top gemstone button covers are offered in 24 superior gemstones—from star sapphire to gem opal to emerald—in sterling silver and 24k gold over sterling settings. You can also purchase matching cufflinks and tuxedo sets, so you can make a matching pair. All covers and sets are packaged with deluxe velour-covered, metal frame presentation boxes, and are perfect for weddings and all formal occasions. Stone Age button covers are also supplied with a pin and a clutch, allowing them to be worn on the lapel of a jacket—or most anywhere else, as well as over a button.
Special Discounts/Offers: Wholesale to qualified businesses.
Catalog: $2.50 for a price list, which is refundable with purchase.

Stone Mountain & Daughter Fabrics

2518 Shattuck Avenue, Berkeley, CA 94704
Phone: (510) 845-6106
Fax: (510) 845-6114
E-Mail: zan3@aol.com
Services/Merchandise: They have a large selection of cottons in prints and solids, silk in designer prints and solids, and N.Y. Designer wools. They also have a fantastic selection of linen, rayon, bridal fabrics, polysilkies, half-priced fabrics, a wall of special buttons, a full selection of notions, and many patterns. Mail order is available by request.
Payment Options: Check, Money Order, MC, Visa, Amex, Discover
Shipping Options: UPS
Minimum Order: $\frac{1}{8}$ yard.
Other Information: This father/daughter business started 15 years ago and continues to grow and serve the community in many wonderful ways. The fabrics are discounted to ensure a fast turnover, and there are always plenty of fabrics to go crazy over. It's well worth the trip to visit their store—the last of the great, independent full fashion stores.

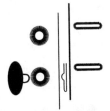
Special Discounts/Offers: 10% discount on first order of non-sale items with the mention of *Sew Far Sew Good*.

Straw Into Gold

3006 San Pablo Avenue, Berkeley, CA 94702
Phone: (510) 548-5241
Fax: (510) 548-3453
E-mail: straw@straw.com
WWW: http://www.straw.com
Services/Merchandise: The store has a large book area, with books on all fiber, textile, and yarn topics, and 6,000 square feet of yarn on balls, cones, and skeins. They also have spinning wheels and supplies, classes, equipment, and tools. They specialize in natural fibers.
Payment Options: Check, Money Order, MC, Visa, Discover
Shipping Options: UPS, U.S. Postal Service
Minimum Order: No minimum order, but there may be a handling fee on small orders.
Other Information: Straw Into Gold started in 1971 as a spinning shop and has added yarns and books over the years. This is their 25th year in business.
Special Discounts/Offers: 5% discount card for customers who visit the store.
Catalog: Free if you send a SASE with two stamps.

Styles Check Company

22600-F Lambert Street, Suite 1203, Lake Forest, CA 92630
Phone: (714) 597-4944, (800) 356-0353
Fax: (714) 597-4949
Services/Merchandise: They have Sewing Checks—perfect for the enthusiast, or for touting your favorite hobby. These checks are not only fun, they meet all bank regulations. The Sewing Checks and many other fun and exciting designs are offered exclusively by the Styles Check Company.
Payment Options: Check, Money Order, MC, Visa
Other Information: Call for a free brochure.

Success Publishing

(S.O.S for Windows™)
5706 Edgepark Drive, Cleveland, OH 44142-1026
Phone: (216) 779-4844
Fax: (216) 779-4844
E-mail: success@acclink.com
Services/Merchandise: They have the Sewers Organization Software, *S.O.S. for Windows*, which includes a spiral-bound user manual.

Payment Options: Check, Money Order, MC, Visa
Shipping Options: U.S. Postal Service
Other Information: *S.O.S. for Windows* was developed by a sewer, just for sewers. It's software for the sewer who has everything, but can't find any of it. *S.O.S.* provides a quick and easy place to record all of your sewing items and to print listings of what you have for easy reference. No more digging through boxes or closets to find that elusive piece of black silk you want to use. You get 10 different menu options for entering or viewing all of your sewing related items, from fabric to books to patterns to machines. There are over 30 report options and 10 inventory forms that print on standard 8½ x 11 paper. You can print the inventory forms as you need them. There are no special forms to buy. *S.O.S. Pro* is scheduled to be released Fall 1996, for sewing professionals. It will include the standard *S.O.S.* software, plus invoicing, expense tracking, sales analysis, and more. To use *S.O.S.* for Windows, you need a 386 or better computer (IBM or compatible), Microsoft Windows and a mouse, a 3.5" floppy drive for installation diskettes, and 7 MB of hard disk space to load and begin using *S.O.S.*
Catalog: Free brochure upon request.

Sulky of America

3113 Broadpoint Drive, Port Charlotte, FL 33983
Phone: (813) 629-3199

Sunshine Artist Magazine

2600 Temple Drive, Winter Park, FL 32789
Phone: (800) 597-2573
Services/Merchandise: *Sunshine Artist* is America's oldest and largest arts and crafts show listing guide. Every September, they list and review the 200 best shows in the country. The magazine has many articles on running your own successful crafts business.
Payment Options: Check, Money Order, MC, Visa

Super Silk, Inc.

265 West 40th Street, New York, NY 10018
Phone: (212) 921-8211
Fax: (212) 921-0234
Services/Merchandise: They have silk fabrics, including charmeuse, chiffon, crepe de chine, dupioni, habotai, matka, noil, silk metallic, organza, taffeta, and tussah. Sample sets are $1 each, which is refundable with your first order.
Payment Options: Money Order, MC, Visa, Amex
Shipping Options: UPS, U.S. Postal Service
Minimum Order: One yard.

Special Discounts/Offers: 5% discount on first order with the mention of *Sew Far Sew Good*.

Author's Note: The samples sent with the company information are eye-popping (a few show up on the back cover of this book). They made me want to give up on this book, order hundreds of yards of silk, and re-create my wardrobe. Of course if I did that, I would not have the money to go anywhere and show off my new wardrobe, so I stuck with the book.

Surface Design Association

P.O. Box 20799, Oakland, CA 94620-0799

Phone: (510) 841-2008

Fax: (707) 829-3285

Services/Merchandise: The *Surface Design Journal* and the *SDA Newsletter* are published by the Surface Design Association. For sample copies of the journal and newsletter, send $7; back issues are $8.50 each.

Payment Options: Check

Shipping Options: U.S. Postal Service

Membership Dues: $45 per year. $25 for students with current ID.

Membership Benefits: Members receive four issues of the full-color *Surface Design Journal* and four issues of the *SDA Newsletter*.

Other Information: The purposes of the Surface Design Association are to provide leadership through education in the field of surface design, and to provide a forum for the exchange and evolution of ideas through conferences, study tours, and the *SDA Journal* and *Newsletter*. They've had conferences and tours for the last 20 years. Conferences are in odd years, and tour dates vary.

Special Discounts/Offers: Student discounts for conferences and memberships.

Suzanne Cooper, Inc.

5005 Kenilworth, Spring Branch, TX 78070

Phone: (210) 885-4533

Fax: (210) 885-7705

E-mail: suzycoop@aol.com

Services/Merchandise: They have the book *Dancing Light: Full-Color Charts for Beading,* which has 29 designs for amulet-purse necklaces. The book is $19.95, plus $2.50 shipping and handling. They also have an extensive line of stained glass design books, used by many for quilt, appliqué, and wearable art designs.

Payment Options: Check, Money Order, COD

Shipping Options: UPS, U.S. Postal Service

Minimum Order: One book.

Other Information: Suzanne's love of stained glass—and a 10 year

---

history of publishing books on the medium—was an inspiration for bead designs. Holding a tiny amulet purse is like holding a tiny stained glass window. Once you see the light dancing on the surface of the beads, you are hooked for life!

Special Discounts/Offers: Free shipping with the mention of *Sew Far Sew Good*. Wholesale to qualified businesses.

Author's Note: Suzanne is a Beading Bulletin Board buddy, and she's fun and quirky. She has a great wit, and (unfortunately) applies it to everything around her–including her beading charts. I even received her "Limited Edition Beaded Yard Butt" patterns in the mail one day. For those of you who do not know, a yard butt is a wooden yard ornament that looks like a lady bending over gardening–and you can see her bloomers!

Suzanne's *Simply Flowers* was given the Best Book 1995 award by the Glass Suppliers Association.

Catalog: Free upon request.

Suzanne Roddy, Handweaver

1519 Memorial, Conroe, TX 77304

Phone: (409) 441-1718

Fax: (409) 441-1718

Services/Merchandise: They have supplies and equipment for weaving, spinning, dyeing, lacemaking, knitting, and needlepoint.

Payment Options: Check, Money Order

Shipping Options: UPS, U.S. Postal Service

Special Discounts/Offers: 10% to professional weavers on yarns and fibers with a $100 purchase. A discount is available to retailers by arrangement.

Catalog: A price list on paper or disk (Windows 95) is $2, prepaid. A sample catalog for yarn is $20, for fiber is $15, and a combination is $25. Catalog costs are refundable with first $50 order.

Sweet Child of Mine

139 East Fremont Avenue, Sunnyvale, CA 94087

Phone: (408) 720-8426

Fax: (408) 720-8425

Services/Merchandise: They have heirloom sewing supplies, silk ribbon, books, and magazines.

Payment Options: Check, Money Order, MC, Visa

Minimum Order: No minimum order.

Special Discounts/Offers: Coupon specials for preferred customers.

Author's Note: I simply love the Petals line of silk ribbon that they carry.

Catalog: $5

Stabilizing seams...

To stabilize bias seams, such as shoulder seams, skirts, pants without waistbands, and pants pockets, try stitching the seam over twill tape.

Tip provided by:
In Cahoots
Page 293

Taos Mountain Wool Works

P.O. Box 327, Arroyo Hondo, NM 87513
Phone: (505) 776-2925
Fax: (505) 776-1374
Services/Merchandise: They have natural wool batting and felt. The felt is available in natural, black, red, and green.
Payment Options: Check, Money Order, MC, Visa
Shipping Options: UPS, U.S. Postal Service
Minimum Order: No minimum order retail. $100 minimum wholesale.
Other Information: Their wool batting is needle punched, and it has no chemicals. You can feel the difference.
Special Discounts/Offers: Wholesale to qualified businesses.
Catalog: Send a SASE for samples.

Taunton Press

63 South Main Street, Newton, CT 06470
Phone: (800) 888-8286
Services/Merchandise: They have *Threads Magazine,* books, and videos. All contain solid sewing, quilting, and embellishment information that is understandable and easy to use.
Payment Options: Check, MC, Visa, Amex, Discover

Taylor's Cutaways & Stuff

2802 East Washington Street, Urbana, IL 61801-4699
Services/Merchandise: They have fabric remnants and cutaway pieces sold by the pound, including satin, velvet, polyester, silk, cotton, fur, and more. They have pre-cut shapes for toys, crafts, and quilting, inexpensive project patterns, and empty tea baglets.
Payment Options: Check, Money Order, MC, Visa
Minimum Order: No minimum order.
Membership Dues: Their Needle & Thread Club is $5.
Membership Benefits: Members save 5% on every order, and get free patterns, additional discounts, credits, and surprise gifts.
Other Information: They have been serving crafters by mail since 1977.
Special Discounts/Offers: 10% discount on first order with the mention of *Sew Far Sew Good.*
Catalog: $1

Tea Cakes and Mud Pies

9869 Belmont Lane, Tuscaloosa, AL 35405
Phone: (205) 758-2532
Fax: (205) 758-2532
Services/Merchandise: They have sculpted dough doll heads, which may be used to make pins or magnets. The heads come unfinished, with directions and materials. Doll hair is in different styles, and they are cute.

Try their Dust Bunnies kit. This is a necessary tool for housecleaning, yet is also decorative. Kids will love to help out with the task of dusting when they can use this little fellow. A hand fits into a mitt in the dusting cloth which looks like a bunny with wiggly eyes and whiskers. The kit includes the materials and instructions for four dust bunnies. These may be sold in local stores or craft fairs. Patent Pending.

They also have Hand-Me-Down Hankies kits. This is a piece of sentiment that will be passed down from generation to generation. It is first a baby's bonnet, then a bride's hanky.
Payment Options: Check, Money Order
Shipping Options: UPS, FedEx
Minimum Order: $25
Special Discounts/Offers: 10% discount on first order with the mention of *Sew Far Sew Good.*
Catalog: $5, which is refundable with first order.

Tender Buttons

143 East 62nd Street, New York, NY 10021
Phone: (212) 758-7004
Fax: (212) 319-8474
Services/Merchandise: The shelves at Tender Buttons are bursting with imported French and Italian couturier buttons, along with a grand selection of pearl, wood, horn, Navajo silver, leather, ceramic, bone, ivory, and pewter buttons. Displayed on their walls is a large collection of antique and period buttons.
Payment Options: Check, Money Order
Shipping Options: UPS, U.S. Postal Service
Minimum Order: No minimum order.
Special Discounts/Offers: Wholesale to qualified businesses.
Author's Note: One button from a set of paperweight buttons that I purchased from their store is featured on the back cover. They have some of the most beautiful old and unique button sets I have ever seen. If you are ever in NYC, this is a must-see.

Tess' Designer Yarns

33 Strawberry Point, Steuben, ME 04680
Phone: (800) 321-TESS, (207) 546-2483
E-mail: tessyarns@mcimail.com
Services/Merchandise: They have hand-dyed yarns and fabrics in exceptional colors. The high quality fiber and fabric is hand-dyed with care for incredible softness. They have quality products at reasonable prices. Custom orders are welcome.
Payment Options: MC, Visa, Check, Money Order
Shipping Options: UPS, U.S. Postal Service

Membership Dues: The Frequent Buyer Club has a $50 annual fee.

Membership Benefits: Members receive a 20% discount on regular prices of yarns and silk, and a 10% discount on sale prices and special promotions.

Other Information: Tess Designer Yarns began on the coast of Maine as Pigeon Hill Farm. They use their experience with fiber animals to discern the highest quality fabric and yarns. They then process these as gently as possible, by hand, for premium quality products.

Special Discounts/Offers: 20% discount on first purchase with the mention of *Sew Far Sew Good*.

TestFabrics, Inc.

P.O. Box 420, Middlesex, NJ 08846

Phone: (908) 469-6446

Fax: (908) 469-1147

Services/Merchandise: They have fabric that is ready to accept color from dyes, fabric paints, etc. They also have ready-made silk and cotton scarves, cotton placements and napkins, aprons, and more.

Minimum Order: $25

Catalog: Free upon request.

Textile Arts Forum

DRUDING—3006 San Pablo Avenue, Berkeley, CA 94702

Phone: (510) 548-5243

E-mail: drudings@delphi.com

Services/Merchandise: If you have a computer and a modem, you can join the Textile Arts Forum at Delphi Custom Forum 135. The topics cover spinning, weaving, knitting, quilting, crochet, needlearts, non-loom, lace, tatting, quilting, and cross-stitch.

Membership Dues: $20 for 20 hours, or $10 for 4 hours.

Membership Information, Contact:
Susan Druding
3006 San Pablo Avenue
Berkeley, CA 94702

Membership Benefits: Members receive technical and historical facts, inspirational and helpful ideas, and exchanges.

Other Information: The Textile Arts Forum is a place for textile artists and crafters to exchange ideas and facts, and to help each other explore their fascination and addiction to fibers, yarns, and fabrics.

Special Discounts/Offers: Free 5 hour trial:
Dial by modem 1-800-695-4002
Press return once or twice
At Username, enter JOINDELPHI
At Password, enter CUSTOM135

Textile Reproductions

P.O. Box 48, 666 Worthington Road, West Chesterfield, MA 01084

Phone: (413) 296-4437

Fax: (413) 296-0036

Services/Merchandise: They have materials for needlework, costume and furnishing reproductions, and vegetable-dyed and natural color fibers for traditional handwork. They also have fabrics, trimmings, threads, yarns, felt, kits, patterns, books, and tools.

Payment Options: Check, Money Order, MC, Visa, Amex, Discover, COD

Shipping Options: UPS, U.S. Postal Service, FedEx

Minimum Order: No minimum order.

Other Information: Vegetable dyeing, the process that preceded mid-19th century chemical dyeing, is their cornerstone. Their careful selection of threads and fabrics results in historically accurate textiles.

Special Discounts/Offers: Wholesale to qualified businesses. Bolt prices on fabrics and trimmings. Educational discounts to established school programs.

Catalog: $4. $14 with swatches, which can be returned for credit.

Texuba

13428 Maxella Avenue #342, Marina Del Ray, CA 90292

Services/Merchandise: They have kimonos available through the trunk shows they produce.

That Patchwork Place

P.O. Box 118, Bothell, WA 98041-0118

Phone: (800) 426-3126

Thimbles by T.J. Lane/Integrity Patterns by T.J. Lane

9666 E. Riggs Road, Suite 401-247, Sun Lakes, AZ 85248-7410

Phone: (602) 895-2771, (602) 895-8074

Services/Merchandise: They have custom thimble designs in all sizes, made from sterling silver or gold. They also have Integrity Patterns.

Payment Options: Check, Money Order

Shipping Options: Postage paid by T.J. Lane to anywhere in the world.

Minimum Order: One item.

Other Information: They have been in business since 1972. Integrity Patterns are published full-size with directions. They trust the integrity of the consumer to pay $5 for a pattern after the garment is made and the consumer is satisfied.

Special Discounts/Offers: $10 discount on first purchase of thimbles or related items with the mention of *Sew Far Sew Good*. Quantity discounts for prepaid orders of 10 or more items.

Coat styles...

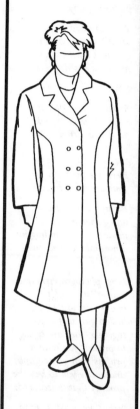

A-Line

Illusions...

Although Maggie Righetti explains this theory in her book, which focuses on knitting patterns, these truisms apply to any picture of any garment.

You can always tell what's wrong with the garment by the way the model is posed.

-OR-

Slender five-foot-ten-inch-tall models look good in anything.

Here are the tests for your dream garment:

Be aware—beware—of any garment whose model is not standing in a normal, relaxed position.

Most photographers and journalists do not know—nor do they care—how a garment is put together, they are trying to present you with a professional photograph, and entice you to buy the product that is featured.

What you need to do to protect yourself is to learn how to look at a picture of a garment that you are considering as a project. We don't just want you to look at the picture, though, we need you to see it.

For instance, look at the seams. Can you see them? Are they styled in

Cont.

Author's Note: T.J. Lane is a very creative woman, and her Integrity Patterns are beautiful and have easy-to-follow instructions. She sent me a beautiful sash belt with a silver thimble clasp, and a gorgeous silver thimble. She does absolutely lovely work.

Her pieced strip skirt with swirl hemline pattern is featured in the Company Appendix, so try it out. If you like it, please remember to send her $5—a small price to pay for a great pattern.

Catalog: Send four 32¢ stamps to receive a Thimble Brochure and an assortment of Integrity Patterns for garments with swirl hemlines.

Thimbles-n-Things

P.O. Box 301, 9288 West River Road, Phoenix, N.Y. 13135
Phone: (315) 695-2315
Services/Merchandise: They have craft, gift, and novelty items with a thimble theme, and sewing tools. They also have key chains, tote bags, refrigerator magnets, rubber stamps, stationery with a sewing theme, thimble and sewing lover's jewelry, bookmarks, telephone/address books, sewing kits, fabric covered thimble display boxes, charms, and charm holders.
Payment Options: Check, Money Order
Shipping Options: UPS, U.S. Postal Service
Minimum Order: No minimum order.
Other Information: The owner of Thimbles-n-Things is a member of the Empire State Thimble Collector's Club (president at this time), Thimble Collectors International, and the Thimble Guild.
Catalog: A catalog is available—a written list of merchandise and a small set of four photo albums to go along with the descriptions. The photo albums must be returned, but the merchandise list is for keeps.

Thimblers Are Us

P.O. Box 381807, Duncanville, TX 75138-1807
Phone: (214) 780-8278
Services/Merchandise: This club is dedicated to the study of thimbles and antique sewing accessories. They meet the third Saturday of January, April, July, and October. Meetings are held at various members' homes.
Payment Options: Check, Money Order
Shipping Options: U.S. Postal Service
Minimum Order: No minimum order.
Membership Benefits: They offer a Club Thimble in sterling silver when you join the club.

Thimble Collector's International

1952 White Feather Lane, Nokomis, FL 34275-5315
Services/Merchandise: Thimble Collectors International is an associa-

tion dedicated to thimbles.
Payment Options: Check, Money Order
Membership Dues: $15 per year (add $5 International), due on January 1st.
Membership Information, Contact:
Barbara Acchino
8289 Northgate Drive
Rome, NY 13440-1943
Send a SASE.
Membership Benefits: Members receive the TCI Bulletin and a membership directory. Members also have access to audiovisual rentals, library and research materials, and the members-only biennial convention.
Other Information: TCI is both an organization, formed by collectors, to introduce its international membership to the various aspects of thimble collecting. The purpose of TCI is to promote research and scholarship, and to disseminate information through its bulletin. They publish booklets on thimbles and related needlework tools for members. TCI also encourages friendship and service through the establishment of regional chapters.

Bulletins are published in January, April, July, and October. The publication provides information about thimbles and sewing tools, convention plans, regional group news, questions, answers, and a President's Message.

Slides of both private and museum thimble and sewing tool collections are available to groups or individual members for a nominal rental fee.

A collection of magazine and newspaper articles, bulletins, and research papers are available for private study and research. Photocopies are provided for a small fee.

A biennial convention is held in August of even numbered years. Speakers, workshops, and a sales mall are featured. Convention sites are rotated around the country.
Catalog: A sample copy of the bulletin is available for $3.

Things Japanese

9805 NE 116th Street, Suite 7160, Kirkland, WA 98034-4248
Phone: (206) 821-2287
Fax: (206) 821-2287
Services/Merchandise: They have a wide variety of silk products, including threads, Japanese Riba silk ribbon, Biasilk pre-cut silk bias, and silk tapes. The Tire line of silk threads, including embroidery, machine twist, line stitch, and buttonhole silk, is available in 171 colors. Things Japanese also offers instructional guides and kits to educate the consumer about uses and processes for silk notions.
Payment Options: Check, Money Order, MC, Visa
Minimum Order: $10

Other Information: Things Japanese has color cards for silk threads, and also offers samplers for previewing thread, ribbon, bias, silk dyes, and paints. They recommend that their customers keep in touch with them, as they are constantly discovering exciting new processes to extend the uses of their silk products.

Special Discounts/Offers: Wholesale to qualified businesses. Quantity discounts for retail sales.

Catalog: $1

The Thrifty Needle

3233 Amber Street, Philadelphia, PA 19134

Phone: (215) 423-3094, (800) 324-9927

Services/Merchandise: They have sweater blanks for the home sewing trade in cotton, acrylic, and wool. They also have books about sewing knits.

Payment Options: Check, Money Order

Shipping Options: UPS, U.S. Postal Service

Minimum Order: No minimum order.

Other Information: The Thrifty Needle is a 15-year old division of the 45-year old Oliver Knitting Company. They specialize in supplying the home sewer with the same fabric available to ready-to-wear manufacturers. The rib for the waist and sleeve cuff are already knitted onto the fabric of each sweater blank. They usually stock over 50 styles for you to choose from.

Special Discounts/Offers: Introductory discount coupon. Buy three blanks and get one free.

Catalog: $2

Timeless Impressions

P.O. 9205, Ogden, UT 84409

Phone: (801) 728-5778, (800) 984-5778

Fax: (801) 782-9146

Services/Merchandise: They have the Cool Band Kit—a fun and unique way to stay cool in the heat of summer. The kit includes a pattern with detailed instructions, and two packs Cool Crystals, the secret to making the Cool Band work. You supply the fabric and the labor, then simply soak the Cool Band in water for two minutes and stay cool all day. Wear it during all types of daily activities; it's for the serious and the armchair athlete.

Payment Options: Check, Money Order, MC, Visa

Shipping Options: UPS, U.S. Postal Service, COD

Minimum Order: No minimum order retail. $50 wholesale.

Special Discounts/Offers: Timeless Impressions is offering these discounts with the mention of *Sew Far Sew Good*:

Pattern kits that regularly cost $4.99 cost you only $3.50.

If you would like to make more Cool Bands, they are offering a buy three, get one free special for their Cool Crystals six-packs.

If it has just gotten too hot to sew, and you still want a Cool Band, you can purchase them pre-made for a 30% savings at $6.99.

Please note that shipping costs are not included.

Author's Note: The secret to cool crystals is that they absorb water until they are four times their original size. I just received my kits and crystals in the mail—too late to review them for this edition, but look for the conclusion in your update, after the hot summer is through, and I have put my cool bands to some good use.

Timeless Treasures

438 Bloomfield Avenue, Montclair, NJ 07042

Phone: (201) 783-7878

Fax: (201) 736-8736

Services/Merchandise: They have thousands of loose beads to satisfy any creative appetite. They have a tremendous selection, including glass, crystal, porcelain, enamel, vintage, trades, semi-precious, horn, bone, and metal beads. They have all sizes and unusual shapes from ancient times to recent manufacturers. They have beads from Venice, the Czech Republic, Germany, India, China, Indonesia, Japan, Turkey, and Africa. They carry instructional jewelry making books for beginners through advanced beaders. Their findings section is large, and all findings are available in base metals, sterling silver, gold-washed, gold-plate, and others. They have high quality Greek leather, satin cord, nylons, silk, tigertail, soft flex wire, and translucent cord. They have hundreds of charms and components, old glass buttons, some recent fun buttons, vintage tassels, bead components, and bead findings.

Payment Options: Check, MC, Visa, Discover

Membership Benefits: Their Bead Club is free. Members receive discounts on loose beads and findings.

Other Information: Timeless Treasures offers discounts to clubs and organizations. They try to keep their prices competitive, and the service and quality are superb. If they do not have what you need, they will make every effort to find it.

Special Discounts/Offers: 10% discount on first purchase with the mention of *Sew Far Sew Good*.

Tinsel Trading Co.

47 West 38th Street, New York, NY 10018

Phone: (212) 730-1030

Services/Merchandise: Tinsel Trading Co. specializes in antique trims, tassels, cords, fringes, etc., made from metallic threads. They also offer currently manufactured trims, tassels, and cords in all fibers. In addition, they carry antique flowers, antique glass and lace buttons, and antique metallic threads.

Payment Options: Check, Money Order, MC, Visa, Amex, Discover

---

a way that would flatter a body shape that in not "the ideal?" Have you made clothes with similar seam treatments and been happy with the results?

What about the collar, cuffs, and hem? How are they set on the body? Where does the hemline fall? Is it pushed up or tucked in, so that it doesn't cross exactly at the hip line? What about the sleeves on that sweater... why are they pushed up like that? Don't they end in the right place? Where does the neckline fall on the body? Is it a neckline that would be flattering to your face and figure?

What are the available sizes? If it says S,M,L, what measurements fit a size small?

With these thoughts in mind, continue looking at each portion of the outfit, judging it on the basis of wearability and "make-ability".

If you find that although your garment comes up short here and there, but you are willing to make adjustments, that is your choice. Just make sure to look first, so you don't find out after you have bought it.

Tip inspired by:
Chapter 1
Knitting in Plain English
by Maggie Righetti
©1986

Cont.

Which loom should you choose?

Your first loom could be an inkle loom or a rigid heddle loom. These looms are fairly easy to master. Regardless of the loom you choose, the width indicates how wide a fabric you will be able to weave. The length can be many yards on floor looms—it is more limited on rigid heddle or table looms.

Perhaps you would like a 4-harness loom as your first loom. The more harnesses a loom has, the more design possibilities it offers. Among 4-harness looms, a table loom is cheaper and can be moved easily, but is hand-operated and therefore much slower than a floor loom; because of its low weight and width, the weaving possibilities are limited. It is good for beginners, demonstration purposes, samples, and workshops. If it's your first loom, it can be used later for samples, research, and small projects.

A floor loom should be your choice if you have enough space. It is built strongly, works much faster than a table loom, offers more possibilities, and gives a better shed

---

Minimum Order: $25
Other Information: Tinsel Trading Co. is listed in Gerry Frank's *Where to Find It, Buy It, Eat It in New York*, with these comments:

"The personnel at Tinsel Trading claim it is the only firm in the United States specializing in antique gold and silver metallics, and they have everything from gold thread to lamé fabric. Tinsel Trading offers an amazing array of tinsel threads, braids, fringes, cords, tassles, gimps, medallions, edging, banding, gauze lamés, bullions, tinsel, fabrics, ribbons, soutache, trims, and galloons. All are genuine antiques, but many customers buy them for the accents they lend to modern clothing. The collection of military gold braids, sword knots, and epaulets is unexcelled anywhere in the city."
Catalog: A sample card of 21 threads is available for $3, plus 32¢ postage.

TLC Yarns

32022 8th Avenue South, Roy, WA 98580
Phone: (206) 843-2294, (800) 382-1820
Fax: (800) 701-2081
Services/Merchandise: TLC Yarns is a small, independent worsted spinning mill, specializing in 100% wool yarns, which they sell direct to craft yarn users.
Payment Options: Money Order, MC, Visa
Shipping Options: UPS, COD
Minimum Order: No minimum order.
Other Information: TLC is a family operation, running from great grandmother Mimi, who designed the distinctive logo, to great-grandson Harold, who waits patiently while Mother uses her state-of-the-art desktop publishing equipment to develop all of their promotional literature. Each step of the manufacturing of this fine yarn is watched over by family members, who are dedicated to producing the finest, most useful yarn for your very special projects. Their goal is to provide you with the material you need to experience the joy of creating something that will last more than one lifetime.

TLC Yarns would like to become the source for your special wool yarn needs. Their commitment to excellence keeps the yarns top quality, and "Made in the USA" pricing keeps them affordable.

TLC Yarns are natural, heirloom quality yarns that will last more than a lifetime. Their 100% wool yarns are dyed with environmentally friendly, bright, biodegradable, color-fast dyes, imported from Europe.

TLC Yarns also publishes *Wool Tips*, a quarterly newsletter that provides a forum for networking between natural fiber artists, and to promote crafts skills that are a part of our cultural heritage.
Special Discounts/Offers: 10% discount on first order with the mention of *Sew Far Sew Good*.
Catalog: Free color card upon request.

Treadle Yard Goods

1338 Grand Avenue, St. Paul, MN 55105
Phone: (612) 698-9690
Services/Merchandise: They have fabrics and patterns.
Payment Options: Check, MC, Visa, Discover
Shipping Options: UPS, U.S. Postal Service
Minimum Order: No minimum order.
Other Information: Treadle Yard Goods often tries to buy from small vendors who specialize in unusual fabrics and do not sell to chain stores. They also have several sources for designer overruns.
Special Discounts/Offers: 10% discount on first order with the mention of *Sew Far Sew Good*.

Treasures of the Past by Annie B. Wells

530 Bellevue Road, Nashville, TN 37221-3429
Phone: (615) 646-4123
Services/Merchandise: Patterns for children, and classes in heirloom sewing, silk ribbon embroidery, and pattern drafting.
Payment Options: Check, Money Order
Shipping Options: UPS, U.S. Postal Service
Minimum Order: $25
Other Information: This business is only three years old, and patterns are being added as money allows. They will travel to your heirloom quilt shop to teach.
Author's Note: The flyer shows several timeless patterns for boys and girls, including rompers, jumpers, and frocks.
Catalog: Free flyer upon request.

Trendsetter Yarns/Ornashi Filati
Wholesale Only

16742 Stagg Street, #104, Van Nuys, CA 91406
Phone: (818) 780-5497
Fax: (818) 780-5498
E-mail: trndstr@aol.com
Services/Merchandise: Handknitting yarns in cotton, linen, wool, and rayon classic fibers, and novelties with textures. They specialize in fiber fantasy for knitters, weavers, manufacturers, quilters, and the creative person in each of us.
Payment Options: Check, Money Order, MC, Visa, COD
Shipping Options: UPS
Minimum Order: $250 minimum, re-orders minimum of $50.

Tucson Bead Society

P.O. Box 14271, Tucson, AZ 85732-4271

Services/Merchandise: The society has monthly meetings, except in summer, a newsletter, and various group activities.
Payment Options: Check
Membership Dues: $20 per year (September renewal).
Membership Benefits: The society offers networking and guest speakers.

UltraScraps by D.M. Design

6626 W. 79th Avenue, Arvada, CO 80003
Phone: (800) 431-1032
Fax: (303) 456-1582
Services/Merchandise: They have Ultrasuede, Utrasuede light, and Ultraleather, sold by the yard or in cut squares in 70 different colors. Ultrasuede scraps are sold by the pound. They also carry books, notions, and patterns in cutwork by Ann Wall. A full swatch set on a keyring $5.
Payment Options: Check, Money Order, MC, Visa, Discover
Shipping Options: UPS, U.S. Postal Service
Minimum Order: No minimum order for retail. $150 for wholesale.
Special Discounts/Offers: Free catalog with the mention of _Sew Far Sew Good_. Wholesale to qualified businesses.

Unicorn Books and Crafts, Inc./Glimåkra Looms 'n Yarns/Frederick J. Fawcett, Inc.

1338 Ross Street, Petaluma, CA 94954-6502
Phone: (707) 762-3362
Fax: (707) 762-0335
Services/Merchandise: Unicorn Books and Crafts offers 2,000 titles of textile craft books. They offer handweaving looms and equipment.

Lacemaking and spinning equipment is offered under both the Unicorn and Glimåkra names. Imported weaving yarns in wool, linen, and cotton are offered under the Glimåkra and Fawcett names.
Payment Options: Check, Money Order, MC, Visa
Shipping Options: UPS, U.S. Postal Service
Minimum Order: No minimum order.
Catalog: $3

Unique Patterns Design

5670 Spring Garden Road, Suite 300, Dartmouth, NS B3B 1J4 Canada
Phone: (800) 543-4739
Fax: (800) 292-4331
E-mail: tstrans@fox.nstn.ca
Services/Merchandise: They have over 100 patterns in many styles of pants, dresses, skirts, blouses, jackets, and two-piece suits. The patterns are updated regularly. Their home measuring kit includes a measurement instructional video, a manual tape measure, a full-color catalog, and membership in the Unique Patterns Club for one year.
Payment Options: Check, Money Order, MC, Visa, Amex
Minimum Order: No minimum order.
Membership Dues: $34.95 U.S. for the first year and measuring kit, $15 U.S. for renewal.
Membership Benefits: Members receive newsletters, pattern updates, and discounts.
Other Information: Unique Patterns has developed a special program to alter patterns to a person's exact body measurements. The result is custom-fit patterns. There is no more need for alterations, just cut and sew.
Special Discounts/Offers: 10% discount on home measuring kit with the mention of _Sew Far Sew Good_.

The Unique Spool

407 Corte Majorca, Vacaville, CA 95688
Phone: (707) 448-1538
Fax: (707) 447-5161
Services/Merchandise: They have authentic African fabrics, as well as Australian prints, patterns for wearable art, quilts, and dolls. They have notions, books, wood spool holders, and a Unique Spool insert for tube-type threads. They also have beads, buttons, and necklaces from Africa.
Payment Options: Check, Money Order, MC, Visa, Amex, Discover
Shipping Options: UPS, U.S. Postal Service
Minimum Order: No minimum for retail. $25 for wholesale.
Membership Dues: The African Fabric Club has monthly mailings of seven fat quarters of fabric for $15 plus shipping and handling plus tax. New fabrics are added monthly.
Catalog: Send a large SASE with two 32¢ stamps.

Unique Techniques

3840 136th Avenue Northeast, Bellevue, WA 98005
Phone: (206) 885-5296
Fax: (206) 885-5296
Services/Merchandise: They offer seminars, workshops, educational videos and brochures, and fusible stabilizing tape from Japan.
Payment Options: Check, Money Order, MC, Visa
Shipping Options: U.S. Postal Service
Minimum Order: No minimum order.
Other Information: Judy's goal is to develop fool-proof construction techniques that save time without sacrificing quality, and to share this knowledge with others. She accomplishes this through her teaching, her video _Japanese Tailoring_, which includes many unique techniques, and her other instructional materials. She helps her students enjoy the

because of its greater depth.

Among floor looms, some are light and can be folded, others are heavier and take more space. If you plan on weaving mostly rugs, a heavy, sturdy loom such as the Glimåkra Standard, Glimåkra Regina, Leclerc Nilus 11, Harrisville Rug Loom, or the Clearbrook should be your choice.

Mechanically speaking, there are three types of looms:

Jack-type looms work as well for balanced weaving as for unbalanced weaving (one harness against three) because each harness frame is operated independently; however, the treadling is slightly noisier and harder than on counterbalance looms. Since the tension on the warp cannot be very high, non-elastic warps (linen, nylon) are not recommended on these looms.

Counterbalance looms are noiseless and have a faster and softer treadling than jack-type looms. They allow a high warp tension (important in rugweaving) and elastic warps (wool, cotton), as well as non-elastic warps. The shed is not perfect

Cont.

when weaving is unbalanced but with some looms the problem can be solved by adding a shed regulator.

Countermarch looms (such as Glimåkra's Ideal and Standard, the Cranbrook, and the Harrisville Rug Loom) combine the rising/sinking action of the counterbalance loom with the ability of the jack loom to open any shed, whether balanced or unbalanced. They are quiet, sturdy, and the favorite of many highly skilled weavers.

Tip provided by:
The Woolery
Page 354

tailoring process and gain skill and confidence as they produce professional looking garments.

Special Discounts/Offers: 10% discount on first order with the mention of *Sew Far Sew Good*. Videos wholesale to qualified businesses.
Catalog: Free upon request.

Universal Synergetics (UniSyn Beads)
P.O. Box 2840, Wilsonville, OR 97070-2840
Phone: (503) OAK-BEAD
Fax: (503) OAK-4FAX
E-mail: virginia@beadcats.com or carol@beadcats.com
Services/Merchandise: They have books, videos, glass seed beads in sizes 11 to 24, bugles, ponies, Japanese Delica beads, molded beads especially made for UniSyn, lampworked beads, cut beads in sizes 10 to 18, antique seed beads, innovative beading supplies (including lots of colored threads, needles, bead trays, and cases), kits, transparent graphs, findings, bead looms, bead knitting needles, and fast mail order service.
Payment Options: Check, MC, Visa
Shipping Options: UPS, U.S. Postal Service
Minimum Order: No minimum order for retail. $100 minimum for wholesale.
Other Information: Sample bead cards are available for purchase. These are an invaluable tool when designing beadwork. Actual beads are sewn to cards with stock numbers. They also offer expert advice by beadworkers Carol Perrenoud and Virginia Blakelock.
Special Discounts/Offers: Wholesale to qualified businesses.
Author's Note: They've got a fun catalog with many unique beads.
Catalog: $2, please specify retail or wholesale.

V. R. Alex, Ltd.
5815 Woodward, Downers Grove, IL 60516
Phone: (708) 963-4146
Fax: (708) 963-4330
Services/Merchandise: They have hundreds of handmade glass buttons, European molded buttons, and gold and platinum trimmed buttons.
Payment Options: Check, Money Order
Catalog: Send $3 and a SASE with two stamps. The $3 is refundable with purchase.

Vale Cottage Studio
4250 Alderbrook Avenue, SE, Salem, OR 97302-3912
Phone: (503) 364-6355
Services/Merchandise: They have old quilts, tops, cutter quilts, *New*

Stitches–Books III, IV, V, and VI, quilting stencils, crafts from old quilts, and old sewing tools. Vale Cottage Studio also offers quilt restoration, quilt appraisals, and they buy and sell vintage quilts (pre-1940).
Payment Options: Check, Money Order (Make checks payable to Dianna Vale)
Shipping Options: UPS, U.S. Postal Service
Minimum Order: No minimum order for retail. $30 for wholesale.
Other Information: Formerly Dianna's Quilting Supplies, Dianna Vale has been in business since 1978. She sells retail or wholesale, in studio, or by mail order.

The series of *New Stitches Original Quilting Designs* is self-published by Dianna Vale. Each book is spiral bound with a soft cover. All original designs are printed full-size and cannot be found in other publications. The designs are for use in borders, narrow and wide corners, and blocks large, small, square, or rectangular. The designs range from geometric to flowing, and can be used for trapunto, appliqué, candlewicking, stenciling, and shadow appliqué.
Special Discounts/Offers: 10% discount on first order with the mention of *Sew Far Sew Good*. Wholesale to qualified businesses.
Author's Note: Dianna sent two of her books and a few of her stencils. Her designs range from simple to intricately detailed, and from whimsical to elegant. There are not many books devoted exclusively to quilt stitching. Although your design and use of color are important, the stitching itself is what creates the functional beauty of a quilt. I would recommend these books for any quilter who wants to add the perfect finishing touch to a treasured item.
Catalog: $1 for a catalog that lists stencils and books.

Victorian Bridal and Gifts
Postal Station D, Box 543, Etobicoke, ON M9A 4X4, Canada
Phone: (416) 236-7255
Services/Merchandise: They have fabulous Victorian-style wares. They offer custom bridal gowns from the finest fabrics, dresses for bridesmaids, flowergirls, and mothers, headpieces, veils, handbags, potpourri pillows, hangers, garters, jewelry, fabric flowers, silk, ribbon embroidery, and more. The pieces are custom-made from beautiful fabrics and lace to complement your gown.
Payment Options: Check, Money Order
Special Discounts/Offers: 10% off bridesmaids' dresses when the bride orders her gown as well.
Catalog: $2

Victorian Video Production
P.O. Box 1540, Colfax, CA 95713
Phone: (916) 346-6184, (800) 848-0284
Fax: (916) 346-8887

Services/Merchandise: They have instructional videos on traditional and contemporary handcraft techniques. Their catalog includes over 150 in-depth instructional videos on appliqué, quilting, basketry, bead-work, crochet, knitting, tatting, bobbin lace and other lacemaking techniques, and all types of needlework–cross-stitch, embroidery, and needlepoint–plus rug making, spinning, dyeing, feltmaking, and a comprehensive series on handweaving.

Payment Options: Check, Money Order, MC, Visa, Discover
Shipping Options: UPS, U.S. Postal Service, FedEx, COD
Minimum Order: No minimum order.
Other Information: The major objectives of the company are to preserve the process of traditional handcraft techniques, to provide quality instructional material in the form of self-instructional video, and to preserve, on video, many talented craftspeople throughout the U.S. and other countries, who have made a major contribution to their craft through their own work, and their teaching and writing.
Special Discounts/Offers: 10% discount coupon order with the mention of *Sew Far Sew Good*. Wholesale to qualified businesses.
Catalog: Free upon request.

Virginia West

2809 Grasty Woods Lane, Baltimore, MD 21208
Phone: (410) 486-1519
Services/Merchandise: They have *A Cut Above* by Virginia West, a book on couture clothing for fiber artists, with 26 innovative designs for women's clothing, generously diagrammed and illustrated. They also have *Designer Diagonals* by Virginia West, a portfolio of 22 patterns for women's clothing designed on the bias, generously diagrammed and illustrated.

Together, these books offer almost 50 patterns for ingeniously designed women's clothing–startlingly simple to make, yet stylishly sophisticated.
Other Information: Virginia's experience comes from a background in designing and weaving fabrics; therefore, her layouts are economic of fabric and carefully planned. Sewers and fiber artists alike will find the books invaluable.
Author's Note: Each of Virginia's patterns shows a creativity and ingenuity of style that I have not seen in quite some time. Although it is mentioned above that she is very economical with fabric, it is difficult to understand just how economical her patterns are until you see them for yourself. Since her background is based in weaving, I can understand why she would find ways to get the most clothing out of each woven piece. I recommend these books to all sewers at all levels of skill.

Vogue Fabrics/Vogue Fabrics by Mail

718 Main Street, Evanston, IL 60202

Mail Order: 618 Hartrey Avenue , Evanston, IL 60202
Store Phone: (847) 864-9600
Store Fax: (847) 475-8958
Mail Order Phone: (847) 864-1270, (800) 433-4313 (for swatch-related calls only)
Mail Order Fax: (847) 864-0113
Services/Merchandise: They have designer collection fabrics from Liz Claiborne, Donna Karan, DKNY, Anne Klein, Calvin Klein, Ralph Lauren, Dana Buchman, Ungaro, Mizrahi, and many others. They also have a wide variety of silks, woolens, cottons, polyesters, bridals, rayons, and others.
Payment Options: Check, Money Order, MC, Visa, Amex, Discover
Shipping Options: UPS, U.S. Postal Service, FedEx
Minimum Order: No minimum order.
Membership Dues: $5 for one swatch set. $20 for a full year of six swatch sets.
Other Information: Due to their vast inventory, it is difficult for Vogue Fabrics to send out samples for general requests like "swatches of silk prints." However, if you have a specific item you need, like "a blue wool crepe", or "a peach sueded silk", they will send you the appropriate samples. If you have a print that you would love a bottom weight wool to coordinate with, or if you have a bottom weight and would like a silk print to coordinate, send them a swatch of your fabric and they will send you some swatches that go with it.

Since Vogue tries to keep their prices competitive, they go through millions of yards of fabric per year–many directly from designers. If you receive a swatch that you like, you should act quickly, because when they sell out of a particular fabric, they generally cannot order more.

The bi-monthly swatch sets focus on coordinated fabrics for the creation of your own unique ensembles, rather than just one or two garments. Their color stories usually have six fabrics, with top and bottom weights, solids and prints, and different fibers (silk, wool, rayon, polyester, etc.). Mail order and store prices are the same.

Waechter's Silk Shop

94 Charlotte Street, Asheville, NC 28801
Phone: (704) 252-2131
Services/Merchandise: They have 100% natural fiber fabrics, including silks, wools, cottons, linens, and "natural rayons", as well as 45,000 different buttons. They have Burda, Neue Mode, Style and New Look patterns, Bernina sewing machines, sergers and accessories, and designer end cuts from Armani, Ralph Lauren, Chanel, and others. They have a huge selection of Metrosene and Gutermann threads and Madiera threads, Handler interfacings and tailoring supplies, and Gingher and Mundial scissors. They also offer a swatch club.
Payment Options: Check, Money Order, MC, Visa
Shipping Options: UPS

Save those swatches...

Do you have an investment in swatches? Are you unable to think of anything to use them for? Try these ideas:

Using a good craft glue, like Sobo, use your fabric scraps to decoupage some wooden boxes for your sewing room. (I just recently used some of mine to create fashion rollerblades!)

Along the same lines, using a washable glue, cover your own funky buttons.

Use your swatches to make fabric beads (see page 7).

Sew enough squares together to make a hair scrunchee (see page 301).

Use them for a miniature quilt, for a child's beloved doll.

Piece enough swatches together in 1 1/12' squares to make a vest (piece just enough for the front, or for the front and back).

Hat styles...

Cloche

Breton

Hood

Watteau

Minimum Order: $15

Membership Dues: $20 per year for swatch mailings, $10 refunded on your first order.

Membership Benefits: Member receive notice of mail order only sales, newsletters, and pattern and button suggestions.

Other Information: Waechters has been in business since 1929 and has recently doubled the size of their store. They also carry 72" wide Irish linen for altarcloths and tablecloths.

Special Discounts/Offers: Wholesale to qualified businesses. 10% discount to churches.

Author's Note: Waechter's sent me several swatches, including silk noil for $10.98 per yard and some more expensive mohair blends for $65-$75 per yard. They also attached fiber content notices with the width, price, and cleaning instructions for the fabrics.

Wakeda Trading Post

P.O. Box 19146, Sacramento, CA 95819

Phone: (916) 485-9838

Services/Merchandise: They have beads, feathers, furs, bone items, and books.

Payment Options: Check, MC, Visa, Amex

Shipping Options: UPS, U.S. Postal Service

Minimum Order: No minimum order, but there is a shipping charge if an order is under $50.

Catalog: $2

Water Fountain Software, Inc.

13 East 17th Street, Third Floor, New York, NY 10003

Phone: (212) 929-6204

Fax: (212) 929-1025

Services/Merchandise: They have several kinds of Personal Patterns software for DOS or Windows.

Payment Options: Check, Money Order, All Major Credit Cards

Other Information: Personal Patterns software lets you prints full-sized clothes patterns from your PC in minutes.

Special Discounts/Offers: Demonstration versions of *Women's and Children's Basic Patterns* and *Women's Designer Jackets and Suits* are $10 each.

The Weaver's School

P.O. Box 1228, Coupeville, WA

Phone: (360) 678-6225

Services/Merchandise: They have one-day and five-day classes in weaving. All weave structures are covered thoroughly: warping, drafting, pattern weaving, coverlets, drawlooms and dobby looms.

Payment Options: Check, Money Order

Other Information: Here's a place where one can devote all waking hours to weaving, while staying in the fabulous bed-and-breakfasts of Whidbey Island.

Catalog: Send a SASE for a brochure.

The Weaving Works

4717 Brooklyn Avenue Northeast, Seattle, WA 98105

Phone: (206) 524-1221

Fax: (206) 524-0250

Services/Merchandise: They have knitting and weaving yarns and supplies, handspinning fibers in wool, cotton, silk, flax, blends and exotic fibers, and hand papermaking supplies and equipment, dyeing supplies, textile printing inks, silkpainting supplies, natural dyes, basketry materials, and a large selection of books (over 1,800 titles).

Payment Options: Check, Money Order, MC, Visa, Discover

Shipping Options: UPS, U.S. Postal Service

Minimum Order: No minimum order.

Other Information: They offer many classes on beginning and advanced techniques in all of the above topics.

Special Discounts/Offers: 10% on single-purchase orders of yarn over $200.

Wendy Schoen Design

308 Crystal Street, New Orleans, LA 70124

Phone: (504) 288-9720

Fax: (504) 895-1479

Services/Merchandise: Wendy Schoen Design carries heirloom embroidery for boys, Petite Poche Patterns, Wendy Schoen Design Needles, mother of pearl buttons, specialty embroidery scissors, specialty threads, and hard-to-find sewing supplies.

Payment Options: MC, Visa, Amex, Discover

Other Information: Wendy Schoen is a self-published designer of embroidery designs for the heirloom sewing industry.

Special Discounts/Offers: Wholesale to qualified businesses.

Westbrook Bead Co.

16641 Spring Gulch Drive, Anderson, CA 96007

Phone: (916) 357-3143

Services/Merchandise: Westbrook Bead Company is a small specialty company handling antique beads and reproductions of old beads. They have beads that can't be found in other shops. They also have, old trade beads, seed beads, findings, and stringing supplies.

Payment Options: Check, Money Order, MC, Visa

Shipping Options: Next day shipping.

Minimum Order: No minimum order for check or money order. $25 minimum for MC or Visa.

Other Information: Their catalog is published annually, with updates through the year. Westbrook has been in business for eight years. The business is mail order; however, there is a showroom which is open by appointment.

Special Discounts/Offers: 10% discount on orders of $100 or more.

Catalog: $2

Wheeler Arts

66 Lake Park, Champaign, IL 61821-7132

Phone: (217) 359-6816

Fax: (217) 359-8716

E-mail: wheelers@aol.com

Services/Merchandise: They have electronic clip art on diskettes for Macintosh and PC (IBM or compatible). Their *Quick Art* images include clothing, sewing, crafts, textures, and patterns. The top-quality drawings and cartoons are on 3.5" high-density disks. The image formats are TIFF in self-extracting archives for the Mac, and PCX for DOS/Windows. The images are all in resizeable black and white. A paper pictorial index accompanies each subject.

Payment Options: Check, Money Order, MC, Visa, COD

Shipping Options: UPS for USA, U.S. Postal Service for other countries

Other Information: Wheeler Arts, a family-owned design studio since 1973, is run by the Wheeler husband-and-wife team. One of their creations is the *Quick Art* collection of over 100 subjects available for computer applications. These images enhance the look and increase the readability of business publications and personal communications—perfect in newsletters, catalogs, cards, and ads. Quick Art is also offered on CD-ROM, *Deluxe 1 and Deluxe 2*. Each CD has 3,200 images in over 50 subjects from animals to western, including sewing. Many of the new images are drawn from lists of requests on User Reports sent in by customers. (Thank you for all the positive comments and great ideas for future collections.)

Special Discounts/Offers: 20% discount on first order with the mention of *Sew Far Sew Good*.

Author's Note: The clip art CD-ROM was sent to me for review, and I think is a well-rounded collection. The sewing and craft clip art has quite a few realistic drawings, as well as some having a more whimsical nature. I used a few of the pin images from this collection on the cover of this book.

Catalog: Free brochures upon request.

Whetstone Hill Publications

P.O. Box 331, Swansea, MA 02777-0331

Phone: (508) 324- 4148

Fax: (508) 676-8601

Services/Merchandise: They retail and wholesale the book *Micheal James Studio Quilts*, and have retail-only sales of *The Quiltmaker's Handbook* and *The Second Quiltmaker's Handbook* by Micheal James.

Payment Options: Check, Money Order, MC, Visa, Discover

Shipping Options: UPS, U.S. Postal Service, FedEx

Minimum Order: One book.

The Whole Bead Show

3424 Silverado Trail, St. Helena, CA 94574

Phone: (707) 963-2554

Fax: (707) 963-1178

Services/Merchandise: This is a wholesale and retail show with all kinds of beads, findings, and jewelry making supplies.

Payment Options: Check, Money Order, MC, Visa, Amex, Discover

Other Information: Call (800) 292-2577 for buyer and exhibitor information, wholesale and retail pre-registration, discount hotel and travel information, class descriptions and schedules, and to get on their mailing list.

Willie's...By Mail

1837 Indiana Northeast, Albuquerque, NM 87110

Phone: (800) 453-9125

Wonderful World of Hats

897 Wade Road, Siletz, OR 97380-9724

Phone: (541) 444-2203

Services/Merchandise: They offer the Hatmaker/Designer Home Study Courses. There are 15 information-packed, illustrated study units, each with a step-by-step video for making the classic styles in the lesson. You learn to make hundreds of designer creations. Lessons include designing, refurbishing, pattern drafting, construction, blocking felt, straw, and buckram, making fur and faux fur hats, and wedding and evening millinery. Learn how to have a business out of your own home, truly on a shoestring. They also offer the Shoe Covering course (one book) for $20, and the *Hat Lover's Dictionary* (illustrated) for $15.

Payment Options: Check, Money Order

Shipping Options: UPS, U.S. Postal Service

Minimum Order: One lesson.

Special Discounts/Offers: Libraries and schools receive 10% off.

Author's Note: The introductory video shows some hats that you will learn to make in their courses. The hats shown are made by students and are beautiful. I am seriously considering this course as a great way to learn a new hobby. I could make my own hats—better than anyone else could, and to match the clothes I make.

Are your double-breasted jackets getting too tight?

Too-tight jackets are never flattering, especially double-breasted jackets. I have heard of two quick methods for alleviating this situation:

Move the outside row of buttons in, to add more ease and to give the look of a narrower silhouette.

Take out a set of buttons, and make it a single-breasted jacket.

Catalog: The catalog and information video are $9 (Canada add $5, other countries add $10).

Wood Forms

P.O. Box 637, Henniker, NH 03242
Phone: (603) 428-7830
Services/Merchandise: Wood Forms offers exotic wood buttons in three round sizes and three toggle sizes. The buttons are available in four wood types: bubinga (reddish brown), kingwood (purple-red), rosewood (dark brown), and zebrawood (tan with black stripes). The buttons have a lacquer coating to protect the wood. They are sold by mail order and can be found in yarn shops across the U.S. Button samples are $2.
Payment Options: MC, Visa
Shipping Options: UPS, U.S. Postal Service
Minimum Order: $10 retail. 100 buttons per style and size for wholesale.
Special Discounts/Offers: Wholesale to qualified businesses.
Author's Note: The samples are beautifully formed and satiny smooth—just the thing for that handknitted sweater.
Catalog: Send a SASE.

The Woolery

R.D. #1, Genoa, NY 13071
Phone: (315) 497-1542
Fax: (315) 497-3620
Services/Merchandise: They have spinning wheels, accessories, fibers, looms, weaving accessories, knitting yarns, knitting kits, knitting supplies, dyes, and other supplies. They have books available on spinning, weaving, knitting, felting, raising fiber animals, dyeing, and many more subjects. Yarn samples are $3.
Payment Options: Check, Money Order, MC, Visa
Shipping Options: UPS, U.S. Postal Service, COD
Minimum Order: $20 minimum for credit card sales.
Other Information: The Woolery's goal is to offer an ever-expanding line of quality spinning, weaving, knitting, and fiberarts supplies. You will find a knowledgeable staff there, ready to help you select just what you need. Whether you are a novice or someone with years of experience, they encourage you to consider them as your source for supplies and advice. They use everything they sell and have practical experience to share.
Special Discounts/Offers: 10% off on orders of 6 books or more. Free shipping and discounts on spinning wheels, looms, and drum carders.
Catalog: $2 by cash or check, $3 by credit card.

XRX, Inc.

P.O. Box 1525, Sioux Falls, SD 57101-1525
Phone: (605) 338-2450
Fax: (605) 338-2994
Services/Merchandise: They have *Knitters Magazine*, *Weavers Magazine*, and *Ethnic Socks & Stockings* by Priscilla Gibson-Roberts. They put on the yearly Stitches Knitters Fair, which offers classes and a market. They also offer Navigating Photoshop workshops.
Payment Options: MC, Visa, Discover, Amex
Shipping Options: UPS, U.S. Postal Service, FedEx
Other Information: Stitches has approximately 80 classes and 150 exhibitors and is usually held in the Fall. Navigating Photoshop has workshops around the country all year round.
Special Discounts/Offers: Wholesale to qualified businesses.

Yarn Barn

918 Massachusetts Street, Lawrence, KS 66044
Phone: (913) 842-4333, (800) 468-0035
Services/Merchandise: They are a complete service store for knitting, weaving, spinning, and dyeing. They carry over 700 fiber-related books, and a large and competitive selection of looms and spinning wheels. They've been in business for 25 years.
Payment Options: Check, MC, Visa, Discover
Shipping Options: UPS, U.S. Postal Service
Special Discounts/Offers: They have the following bulk prices on yarns: $100 - 10% off, $150 - 15% off, $200 - 20% off.
Catalog: Three catalogs are available—please request specific one(s) and send $1 for each: Knitting and Crochet Catalog, Weaving, Spinning, and Dyeing Catalog, Equipment Catalog.

Yarns International

5110 Ridgefield Road, Suite 200, Bethesda, MD 20816
Phone: (301) 913-2980
E-mail: yarns2u@aol.com
Services/Merchandise: They have knitting yarns, mostly in natural fibers, accessories, patterns, books, and classes. They carry the complete line of Alice Starmore and Dale of Norway yarns, plus a good selection of Rowan, Annabel Fox, Mamos Schaefer, Classic Elite, Missoni, and Muench.
Payment Options: Check, Money Order, MC, Visa
Shipping Options: UPS, U.S. Postal Service
Minimum Order: No minimum order.
Other Information: They have a "Yarn of the Month" which is on sale at 15% for a sweater quantity. They have a free quarterly newsletter, a book list, and they offer a yarn list which includes price, gauge, and yardage information.

Special Discounts/Offers: 10% discount on first order with the mention of *Sew Far Sew Good*.

Zoodads-Simply Kidz Fabrics

1086 Willett Avenue, East Providence, RI 02915
Phone: (401) 437-2470
Fax: (401) 437-0128
Services/Merchandise: They specialize in fabrics for boys. Their catalog and swatches are mailed out every three months. The fabrics carried are fun, and range from brightly colored to pastels. Fabrics change from catalog to catalog, so order early for best selections. Since they have four boys, they know how hard it is to find fabrics for them and are always looking for fabrics that they know boys will like. Stop in and visit their store if you are in the area. They try to please everyone, so if you have any suggestions, please send them in.

They have a wholesale catalog on ready-to-wear Polartec hats, mittens, and jackets. If you have not used Polartec to keep you and your kids warm, it's time you did.
Payment Options: Check, Money Order, MC, Visa, Amex, Discover
Minimum Order: Credit card minimum $20.
Membership Dues: $6 yearly
Other Information: This is a family-owned business, started four years ago. They carry fabrics from Osh Kosh, Carters, Health Tex, and many more. Fabrics include knits, interlocks, cottons, and cotton blends. Many are novelty prints of pastel or primary colors that kids love to wear.

They also take requests for any fabrics, notions, or patterns you may be looking for.
Special Discounts/Offers: $2 off first order with the mention of *Sew Far Sew Good*.

Zuni Mountain Lodge

HC-62, P. O. Box #5114, Thoreau, NM 87323-9515
Phone: (505) 862-7769
Services/Merchandise: They offer a Navajo rug weaving workshop (April, March, Oct. of 1996).

Bias placement made easy...

If you have trouble placing your bias strips for finishing, try using a glue stick.

The glue stick will hod ithe strip in place, and wash right out.

Tip provided by:
Kelly Karvonen
AOL member, sewing enthusiast

Company Appendix

Consumer information generously provided by various companies for your benefit.

The Beauty of Stitching with Silk

Silk is an animal fiber made from the cocoons of the silkworm. In tracing the history of silk use in the United States, it becomes apparent why people have little knowledge of it. At the beginning of the 1940s, when Japan went to war with the U S., the silk supply literally dried up overnight. In response to this void, chemical companies successfully developed many synthetic fibers for commercial use. Rayon and synthetics such as nylons, acrylics, and polyesters replaced silk almost instantly. As a result, for the past 45 years, people have looked upon silk as rare, expensive, and delicate.

With the recent rising interest in natural fibers, people have begun to acknowledge cotton and silk for the wonderful, practical fibers they are. Cotton, being the more familiar domestic yarn, has acquired an automatic acceptance among needleworkers. Silk, on the other hand, being more mysterious and imported, is only now gaining popularity among stitchers.

Silk differs from cotton in that it possesses greater strength—1.4 times as strong as steel of the same diameter—and a translucency that absorbs and reflects light, giving the finished product a beautiful, shimmering luster. Silk also has three times more yardage per pound than cotton of equal diameter. Because of its smooth surface, silk flows easily through Aida, canvas, or any other fabric you choose to work with. Completed projects gain an immediate heirloom quality and are saved by generations af loving families or friends.

Silk is easier to use than cotton because it is smooth where cotton is fuzzy. This difference is due to differing cellular structures, which allows silk to remain lustrous and strong, while cotton loses its luster and strength over time. In fact, archeologists found that silk in China, buried in tombs for 3,000 years, was the only fiber that remained intact and recognizable. Also, in Sweden, while dredging a channel in the harbor where an old warehouse had burned, black silk skeins buried under mud for 27 years were discovered. After washing, they found that the color, strength, and luster still remained.

More and more needleworkers realize that their time, energy, and resources are limited in today's busy world. In response to these factors, and to the fact that there are a growing number of beautiful designs out on the market to be stitched, customers are asking for finer materials, and silk is therefore becoming increasingly more popular.

To meet the demand, Kreinik Mfg. Co., Inc., offers stranded silks in over 300 vibrant colors. Kreinik recommends that you order enough of each color for your project to obtain the same dye lot. To ensure lasting beauty, if your piece becomes soiled, have it dry cleaned. Do not wet block any silk work. If you are using silk for highlights only, finish the work on all other areas first, block the work, and then complete the canvas with the silk. This process also applies when you use silk to highlight with any other yarns. As with all needlework projects, use a frame or hoop while stitching. This allows you to stitch more evenly and prevents mishaping of your piece.

The Magic of Metallic and Metal Thread Embroidery

Metallic and metal thread work are the most exciting techniques available to the embroiderer today. The skill needed to achieve beautiful and dramatic effects in a design is simple and can be learned with some easy to follow techniques.

Before it is explain why and how to easily incorporate metallic and metal threads into your stitching, it is fascinating to know a little history about their use. The whole history of metal thread embroidery goes back so far into the past that its origins are lost. Embroidery was in use in China at least three thousand years B.C., but we do not know precisely when gold thread was introduced. In the Bible, the use of gold and silver embroidery is mentioned on a number of occasions. Today metallic and metal thread is still used for ecclesiastical and ceremonial items.

Metal thread in textile decoration probably owes its importance to the symbolic significance attached to gold. The brilliance of gold threads represents the magical power of the sun. Gold is a word that has meaning for all people in all societies. Throughout history, we find that gold and precious metals have intrigued people and have been incorporated into all areas of artistic expression on society—e.g. jewelry, textiles, fashion, and even architecture.

In embroidery, while the words, "metal" and "metallic" are often used interchangeably, the two terms do not have the same meaning. To be a true "metal", the greatest percentage of the thread must be either a metal or a metal compound. The term "metallic" is correctly applied to all those threads which appear to be made of metal, but which are actually composed of a synthetic material or polyester. Gold, by definition, is a metallic element, highly malleable and free from liability to rust. Incorporating gold in fiber art has challenged the textile craftsman since ancient times and continues to challenge us today.

There are many different types of metal threads. The play of light and firm texture that metal brings to embroidery is exciting. Though called "threads", metal threads are NOT put in the eye of a needle and "sewn". These threads are attached to a fabric or canvas with small stitches of another thread. This technique is called "couching".

Modern technology and knowledge of fiber construction has enabled Kreinik to create metallic threads that are very soft, easy-to-use, and non-tarnishing. Today, colored threads with a metallic finish have gained widespread acceptance among needleworkers because the wide range of effects that they add to designs. Whether you want to add brilliance or realistic subtlety, metal and metallic thread embroidery can create the effects of light and multiple dimension. If you think of metal and metallic threads as a light source, you can enhance the appearence of water, snow, plants, flowers and birds. Consider also that the light source can be sunlight, artificial light, moonlight, or starlight. The possibilities are endless!

By learning the basic materials and techniques used with metal and metallic thread embroidery, you will be able to incorporate multiple fibers into your designs and achieve more realistic and dramatic effects than are possible when using a single thread type. Whether you currently use cotton or silk threads in cross stitch, wool or silk threads in needlepoint, or perle cotton in crochet, by simply adding the appropriate metal or metallic thread, you can transform a flat, one-dimensional, single thread type design into a more visually attractive and stimulating two -dimensional multiple thread type picture.

Types of Metal Threads:

Metals: Yarns made of metal wire—round or flat or thin films of metal (gold, silver or platinum) bonded to a paper back and then slit and wound on a core to give a threadlike appearance.

Passing Threads: Threads that are generally cored (metal or metallic thread wound on a fibrous core), which can be used in the same manner as a sewing thread.

Bullion (Bul-yen): Wire-like metal that is wound on a mandril to have a close, spring-like appearance. Small pieces are cut from the main body, and a thread is passed through the hollow core to fasten the bullion to the work. Bullion is available in gold or silver, and in bright (shiny), matte (dull) and frieze (faceted).

Frieze (Frez): A textured yarn that is crisp and angular, which gives it a faceted look..

Faconnee: A textured gold or silver bullion that has a spiral configuration.

Jaceron (Jas-er-on) or Pearl Purl: A heavy wire of gold or silver, coiled to have a beadlike appearance, and is generally used for outlining.

Cordonnet (Kor-doan-nay) or Crinkle: A metallic or metal trim that has a cotton core and a twisted, serpentine appearance. Cordonnet is similar to a miniature rick-rack.

This information was provided by:
Kreinik Mfg. Co., Inc.

Page 299

Tweed Mohair Vest

Finished Sizes:

36 (40, 42) (44, 48)"

Materials:

Tweed Mohair Yarn, or similar weight yarn; 43gr/93 yard balls—4 (4,5) (5,6)

Needles:

Size #8 and #10 or #10½

Gauge:

3½ sts=1" (very important!)

Back:

With smaller needles cast on 59 (67,71) (75,83)sts. RDW 1: (Broken Rib) *K2,P2, repeat from * across, ending K2, Pl. Repeat Row 1 for 1½" for rib. Change to larger needles and inc. 3sts evenly spaced across row. Work in stockinette stitch until piece measures 12–13" or desired length to underarm, ending on a P row. Next row bind off 5sts, Knit across (*). Next row bind off 5sts, K next 4sts, P across, K last 4sts. Continue working in st. stitch, knitting first and last 4sts of every row, until piece measures 20 (21,22) (22,23)" or desired length to shoulder. Bind off.

Front:

Work same as back to (*). Next row, bind off 5sts, Knit next 4sts, Purl to within 4sts of center, place a marker, K8, place a marker, P to last 4sts, K4. V-NECK SHAPING: Row 1: Knit. Row 2: K4, P to marker, slip marker, K8, slip marker, Purl to last 4 sts, K4. Row 3: Knit. Row 4: Repeat row 2. Row 5: (lst Dec row) K to 2sts before marker, Sl 1, Kl, Psso, slip marker, K4, attach another ball of yarn, K4, slip marker, K2 tog, K across. Continue working both sides, decreasing 1 stitch every knit row each side until 19 (19,19) (21,23)sts remain. Work even until piece measures same as back. Bind off. Sew side seams. Sew shoulder seams.

This Pattern was provided by:

Grand View Country Store

Page 284

Do You Understand Copyright?

The newsletter editor of the guild receives a promotional package from the *Creative Machine Newsletter* showing a clever way to sew on buttons. She cuts out the drawings and text and then pastes it up in her next newsletter. ***This is a violation of copyright.***

A teacher of a machine-quilting workshop at a store passes out handouts to his class. The handouts have photocopies from the books of Deb Wagner, Harriet Hargrave, Hari Walner, Maureen Noble, and the Fannings. ***This is a violation of copyright.***

Someone digitizes a *Calvin and Hobbes* drawing and uploads it to the internet BBs. Others download it and stitch it out. ***This is a violation of copyright.***

A once-in-a-while craftsperson makes vests from Linda McGehee's patterns and sells 25 of them at a holiday boutique. ***This is a violation of copyright.***

A person with a New Home 8000 sets up her machine at the guild quilt show and stitches KanScan quilt designs on people's totebags to raise money. ***This is a violation of copyright.***

The concept behind copyright protection is that the minute you create something–a pattern, design, poem, article, story, play, drawing, sculpture, photo, film, dance, song, symphony, or sound recording—it is yours, fully protected by copyright. No one can copy all or part without your permission. "But I was raising money for the church," explains someone who made 50 Judi Maddigan Fidget bear puppets for sale. A copyright holder has nothing against raising money for your church, but she is being denied income. You are making money from a pattern that took Judi or another designer a long time to perfect. You're not adequately sharing the income with the designer by buying one copy of her book. This is a violation of copyright.

And that's the crucial question to ask yourself any time you want to use copyrighted material. "Am I denying income to the creator of this original material?" If the answer is yes, you must have permission or pay a licensing fee before you can use all or part of the material.

The law allows certain use without permission or payment of a fee. One instance is in reviewing books or patterns. "Fair use" is allowed, although what that constitutes is constantly being challenged in the courts. You can usually quote up to 250 words of a book without permission, especially if the publisher is going to benefit from the publicity.

Another gray area of permission is the classroom. Teachers are allowed to reproduce part of a work, such as a single magazine article, if it is for educational purposes. Otherwise, each student would have to purchase an entire magazine in order to read one article. Note that this teaching exemption does not apply to teachers outside nonprofit institutions. Robbie Fanning (from *Creative Needle*) is constantly shocked at the handouts in store sewing classes—blatant copyright infringements and usually without attribution. Most authors know about these practices, are helpless to prevent it, and merely wish teachers would use their names and books on the material, but even with attribution, without permission, this is a violation of copyright.

The staff at *Creative Machine Newsletter* are often asked by guilds if they can reproduce one of their Know Your Tools articles. These articles take months to research, test, and write. In addition to the cost of phone calls and postage, there is Robbie's time, Gaye's time, the proofreader's time, the artist's fees, and the printer's fees. They hope to attract new subscribers with such in-depth articles, as well as to satisfy your curiosity about a subject. If a guild wants to pay a small reprint fee, we are certainly willing to license one-time use. But if the article is reprinted without permission, they are denied income. This is a violation of copyright. They always feel like a Scrooge when they explain their policy because they understand the kindness behind it ("Hey, good article— I'm going to share it with all my sewing buddies!"), but they'd also like to stay in business.

The two hot areas of copyright law of interest to writers are the embroidery designs on the new sewing machines and electronic rights. House and Senate bills known as The NII Copyright Protection Act of 1995 are especially investigating the meaning of "electronic transmission" as an act of publishing.

Again, ask yourself if you are denying the creator income. If you stitch a design from a sewing machine for your own pleasure or on gifts for your loved ones, no one objects. If you stitch designs for sale or for distribution to many other stitchers, this is a violation of copyright. Actually, the sewing machine companies usually do not own the copyright on their designs. They have been granted permission to include them on the machine by the creator, often an individual or small company. If you stitch out the design and sell it, you are violating the copyright of the creator, not the sewing machine company.

Copyright infringement on the on-line services is one giant horror. We all cherish the tone of sharing and enthusiasm. Nevertheless, when one person has a question about her Viking #1+ and someone else uploads the entire answer that appeared in a recent *Creative Machine Newsletter*, this is a violation of copyright. They would never pursue amateurs, of course. Consumers often don't realize what they've gone through (read, "dollars spent") to answer that question.

But commercial use of their research and writing is a different story. Writers are just beginning to understand the horrors of giving up electronic rights. It's similar to when a down-and-out songwriter sold a ditty for $100 that later brought in millions for the publisher. This is contrary to the spirit of our country, which is fairness. If someone grossly benefits from someone else's creation, it is only fair to share the wealth. That's why the creators of Superman, Jerry Siegel and Joe Shuster, who sold all rights to their creation for $130 in the Depression, later received $20,000/year plus medical benefits for life.

Many magazines are putting their contents onto the on-line services. When anyone can log in and read it or download it, how do the magazines make money? By receiving royalties from the on-line services and by delivering that many more bodies to their advertisers. But the writers of the articles don't benefit. We don't receive additional money every time someone reads their article for free. Writers make their money by creating something that can be sold over and over in various forms—articles, pamphlets, books, films, videos. Each time their material is used, they make a little more money. (That's why you won't see many of the big sewing names writing for magazines in their field. Some of the magazines insist on buying all rights, and authors are not willing to give them up for the small amount of money paid. It's not worth it.)

Think twice the next time you take someone else's design, pattern, writing, or drawing public, so you don't commit what Peggy Bendel of *Sew News* calls a "copywrong."

This material was paraphrased and used with permission from:
Creative Machine Newsletter, Published by:
Open Chain Publishing
Pag 314

This material is not intended to act as a replacement of qualified legal advice. If you have questions regarding copyright, please contact a lawyer licensed to advise on copyright law.

INTEGRITY PATTERNS

T.J Lane introduces a marketing concept that presents the product first, tells you how to use it, and trusts your integrity to pay after successfully completing the project.

Copy this page twice. Cut one pattern piece from each page.
There are three pieces to each swirl panel, but the long one needs no pattern.

1. Cut Strips 4" x 45"
Cut at least 12 strips for hips up to 30 inches, 14 strips for 40", 18 strips for 50", 20 strips for 60", 22 strips for 70".

2. Stack Strips Right Sides Up
With ends and edges carefully aligned, to use rotary cutter.

3. Place Pattern Pieces Right Side Up
Put the small one with the capital letter A at the tip end of the strip.
Make cuts in order, HA, HAC, HB, bD.

4. Piece Enough Swirl Panels For Your Size
Sew 1/4" seams: first sew small piece to medium one along the matching straight edges (Aa to Bb). Sew the long edge (CD) of the medium one to the straight edge of the long one. Finish seams and press towards small pattern piece.

5. Sew Swirl Panels Together, Waist To Hem
Dot H to dot h. Finish seams and press. Hem by folding 1/4" and stitching with 3-way zig-zag over the raw edge. Press.

Finish Waist
Make a buttonhole on a seam 1/4" from the top edge of skirt
Fold 1 1/4" toward inside, 3-way zig-zag over raw edge and along top edge. Insert elastic with strings on ends. Tie strings at waist.

Pieced Strip
Skirt With
Swirl Hemline

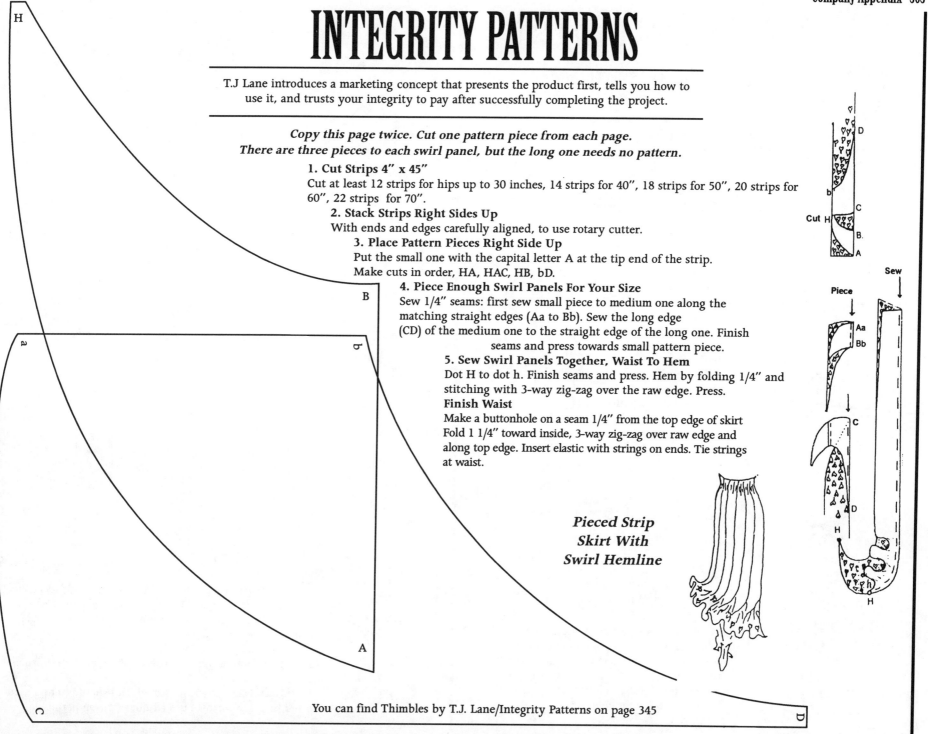

You can find Thimbles by T.J. Lane/Integrity Patterns on page 345

LAZY LUCY PATTERN

From Nimble Thimbles

page 313

You can make this cute doll from any fabric you have around your house. Try calico prints, gingham checks, or any color of the rainbow.

You can make this doll into a green elf or Santa's helper for Christmas... or a bunny for spring... or a cupid for Valentine's Day. Your limit is your imagination.

All of the seams have a 1/4" allowance, so all you have to do is match the edge of the fabric with the side of the presser foot on your sewing machine.

You will need two little 1/4" buttons for eyes. Be creative. What color eyes would you like her to have? Blue, brown, black? You will also need one small, half-ball, covered button for the nose. For hair, you will need some 1/4" ribbon or yarn. Again, remember to be creative. Last, but not least, you will need some fiberfill to stuff her with.

If you like this pattern, Please send $5 to Nimble Thimbles

—or—

Buy the complete pattern. It includes a full-sized pattern, easy step-by-step sewing instructions, along with a bunny outfit, a cupid outfit, a Halloween outfit, a summer bikini, a Christmas helper outfit, and a traditional baby bonnet and diaper outfit. All for only $15.

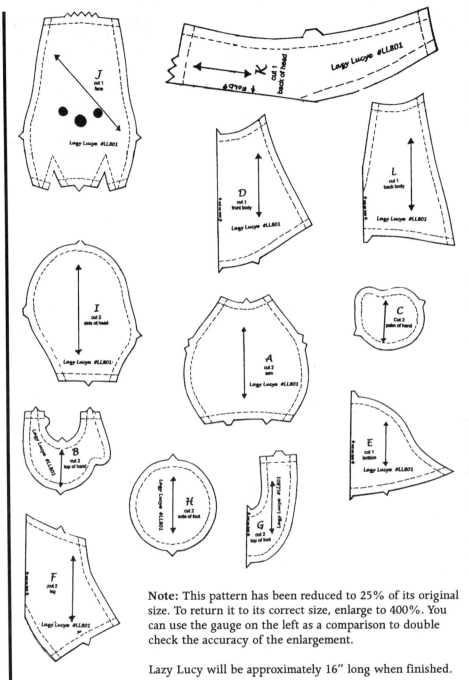

Note: This pattern has been reduced to 25% of its original size. To return it to its correct size, enlarge to 400%. You can use the gauge on the left as a comparison to double check the accuracy of the enlargement.

Lazy Lucy will be approximately 16" long when finished.

Lazy Lucy is copyright protected, and should not be used other than for personal use without written permission

Sew Saavy Or…
How To Not Spend All That Time And Effort Sewing Clothing That You Will End Up Throwing In The Garbage Or Storing In The Closet!

There is not a fast, easy garment that does not require at least a modest amount of time and effort. Even the construction of a simple T-shirt can prove aggravating when you find it has shrunk 6" after the first wash. It is even worse when you construct a more complex garment, requiring several precious nights, or a weekend of preparing, cutting and sewing, only to end up relegating it to the trash heap or stuffing it in a hidden corner of your clothes closet. But how are you to know what to choose for your projects without taking a two year textile course?

Well, there are basic principles you can employ to prevent premature garment death. The first is to be aware of the nature and characteritics of fabrics and interfacings. The second is to choose your fabric store carefully. Have you ever noticed that there are hundreds of people who work in fabric stores who do not seem to know more about fabric than you do? In fact, the last time you dealt with such an individual, you might have even remarked, "Why s/he doesn't even know as much about fabric and sewing as I do!". I am not saying this is true of all fabric sales clerks, just that there are an awful lot of them out there. This makes it important for you to be aware of the nature of the beast and the strange things some clerks will say when faced with a question they cannot answer. To illustrate, I will address some of the fabric lies I have been told.

"Oh, that is pre-shrunk".

This is one of my favorites. If it does not say pre-shrunk on the label, do not believe the clerk! Buy the fabric if you love it, but be aware that if it is 100% natural fiber, it will shrink even after it has been pre-shrunk. If you are using a commercial pattern, the extra yardage required by the pattern company will usually be sufficient to compensate for any loss through shrinkage. You should pre-shrink all natural fiber fabrics. Use the same method that you would to wash the garment; for example, if you intend to dry-clean the garment, you must dry-clean the fabric to pre-shrink it.

Having said this, I must contradict myself. There are some fabrics that are easier to handle for sewing purposes with the factory (kind of like starch) still in the fabric. If you wash out the sizing while pre-shrinking, the fabric will become soft and unmanageable. To prevent this, you must calculate the shrinkage of the fabric. Cut two 10"x10" squares of fabric. Clearly mark the grain with an indelible marker. Serge the edge without cutting. Wash in hot water in the washer, dry in the dryer. Measure the results and calculate your percentage of shrinkage (i.e. 1" is 10% of 10"). If you are making pants that have a 40" pattern piece, you would add about ½" to the height of the crotch and 3½" to the outseam and inseam. That would give you 4", or 10% of 40". Repeat this operation on the width of the pattern. We use this method for making jeans that are garment washed.

"It is 100% natural fiber. I don't know how it got that unknown fibers label on it."

Whenever a fabric is unidentified, don't assume what fibers it is made from by looks alone—not when there is such a simple method of determining whether it is a natural or synthetic fiber. The old burn test is the clearest indicator. Snip a small piece off the fabric and hold over a flame in a safe place, preferably over a sink. If you use a match, be sure to allow the sulfer to burn off before burning the fabric. If the fabric burns and melts, it is definitely a synthetic. This means it will be harder on your sewing machine, more difficult to sew, and less forgiving. If you still love it, take home a quarter-meter and test it on your sewing machine and iron. Many stores will put a piece of fabric away for you for a couple of days while you make your decision.

If your test sample burns and forms an ash, it is most likely natural fibers. It could also be rayon or acetate, which are man-made fabrics with cellulosic fibers. Rayon you should be able to spot by the soft, drapey feel of the fabric. Acetate will dissove in acetone (nail polish remover) and feels papery and stiff. Satin linings are generally acetate. All other natural fibers will burn and leave an ash. If the smell of the smoke is like burning paper, the fabric is a cotton or a linen. If the smoke has an odor of burning hair, it is either silk, wool, or a specialty hair fiber such as alpaca or cashmere. We often find treasures in the bargain shelves of chain stores, because no one knows what the fibers are. My last find was a 20 meter piece of charcoal grey linen that I picked up for peanuts.

"It's a very high thread count."

First of all, the only way to be sure of a thread count is to, you guessed it, count. The simplest way to count threads is to buy a linen tester. This is a magnifying glass in a little square metal frame suspended over another little square metal fram measuring either ½" or 1" square. These can ususally be found in specialty shops that carry telescopes and magnifying glasses. Occaisionally, the finer fabric stores will carry them. If you don't want to buy one of these little devils, you can cut a piece of cardboard with a window exactly ½" or 1" square and use an ordinary magnifying glass to count how how many threads per inch in both directions. I strongly suggest this if someone is selling you expensive fabric on the basis of thread count. I have seen percales sold as 280 x 280 with no more than 80 x 120 thread count. You still have to keep in mind, however, that thread count is not the sole indicator of quality.

When looking at a fabric to ascertain quality, you must also examine things such as the twist of the yarn, the length of the fibers, and the colorfastness and quality of the print or dye. Examine the twist of the yarn by unravelling the yarn from the fabric and untwisting it. If it is very curly, it is a high twist yarn. If it is more straight, it has a lower twist. Higher twist yarns are more desirable. Use the same procedure to examine the length of the staple fiber. Untwist the fibers; the longer the fiber, the better the quality of the fabric. Colorfastness is a trick unto itself. Rub a piece of white fabric against the color fabric. If some dye rubs off or migrates, the dye in the fabric will not remain colorfast and bright after several washes. Purchase several inches of the fabric and wash it as you would the finished garment to test for colorfastness. High thread count, high twist yarn, long staple fibers, and high quality prints and dyes are all indicators of high quality fabric. Once these elements have been examined, you can feel safe purchasing the fabric.

"That's a very good quality fabric and it's cheap."

Buyer Beware! Almost without exception, you get what you pay for. You have to examine reasons for the price. Vintage fabric from designer roll-ends, and the fashion houses of New York, Los Angeles, and even Europe, can find their way to your local fabric store. Designer discounts are good, designer duds are not! Scrutinize any designer or fashion house roll-ends as you would any other fabric. Examine the feel, hang, and look of the fabric. Take a look at the drape in a mirror. Don't buy just because of the designer name, and don't assume quality; use your judgement. Fold the fabric and hold it up to a light or window. A lot of fuzzy ends indicates that the staple yarn is very short. This is not desirable in natural fibers. The more fuzzies on the folded edge of the fabric, the poorer the fabric quality—even if it has a designer name on it.

"That will soften up once it's washed."

Maybe it won't! It depends on the weave of the fabric and the type of finish. If the fabric is finished with sizing, there is a good possibility the sizing will wash out. However, some finishes are not washable. These finishes will remain in the fabric, and the fabric will remain stiff. Again, purchase several inches of the fabric and wash it several times as you would the garment. You will immediately know if the finish comes out and if the fabric will soften up.

Somebody one recommended that I use pillowticking for pocketing. The problem? Pillow ticking is woven together so tightly that no matter how many times it was washed, it distorted the way the pockets hung. I almost always buy in quantity, so I had enough pillow ticking for several pairs off pants pockets. Fortunately the stiff quality of the fabric was sufficient for it to be used as interfacing in waistbands, and I did not lose anything. It did teach me to always test my fabric.

"A fusible interfacing would be fine for that."

Don't let anybody tell you that there is an interfacing that can be used for all garments. This is a fallacy. Interfacings are made in a zillion different possible combinations and possibilities because there are so many kinds of fashion fabric. Each kind requires its own interfacing, How do you determine the appropriate kind of interfacing? I'll repeat myself—you have to feel the interfacing and fabric together. You actually have to use the interfacing on the fashion fabric to feel the hand and to determine the kind of look you want in your garment. At the studio, we always test the interfacing with the fashion fabric before we assemble a piece of clothing. This prevents everyone from having to participate in the arduous task of ripping. Ripping is one of our least favorite activities. Please make it a point to test your interfacing with your fashion fabric so there is no need to rip.

"You can use a polyester gabardine. It will look just as nice, and it's a lot less expensive."

In the short term, it might look almost as nice. One of the things about the nature of polyester is the 100% guarantee that it will pill in the areas that you don't want it to. Imagine the delightfull appearance of little fuzzy balls on abraded areas of your clothes (wallet pocket, knees, and the area on which you sit the most). This gives an unkempt look to clothes. Generally, you spend a great deal of time putting the clothing together–cutting sewing, and finishing. Much love and work goes into the clothing, and it is aggravating to have signs of wear after only a few wearings. It is advisable to choose an alternate fabric. Use a wool gabardine. In the long run, it is less expensive than poly, as the garment life will exceed that of poly by at least 10 times. While ironing polyester, even with a press cloth, you will find interesting shiny streaks can be created by the iron's heat. Even if this occurs on wool, it will be easily removed from the wool with a solution of one part vinegar to one part water. The marks are more permanent with poly. If those marks appear on polyester, it is usually an indicator that you have melted it. Some polyesters are actually as costly as natural fibers, and natural fibers are longer lasting and more forgiving. If you are trying to save time on ironing, you are losing something else–like quality, durability and appearence.

"No, I wouldn't line that."

One of the reasons I think many people shy away from linings is to facilitate making the garment. Often, people think linings are complicated to make and add construction time. A lining will actually help the hang and appearannce, and may extend garment life. A lining is easy to make using guidelines from many of the more popular sewing books.

Try to make a lining out of rayon, acetate, silk, or a blend. Natural fibers do not create as much static electricity as synthetics, they breathe better, and they are more comfortable to the body. You might come across some higher-end, high-tech linings made out of microfiber, blends of acetate, rayon, triacetate, or cotton combined with a small percentage of nylon. If you see this kind of lining, it is generally European and quite expensive, but it gives more breathability and comfort. The small percentage of the nylon prevents creasing and wrinkling of the fibers and the fabric. Try to choose a weight of lining that is appropriate to your fashion fabric and to your garment. Again, with linings, just as with interfacings, there are different types and weights. You want to ensure you have the proper lining for your garment. Hold the lining together with the fashion fabric and feel the drape and hang. If the lining and fashion fabric feel good together, that is they are not too stiff, the lining does not change the character or the drape of the fabric, and it is the appropriate lining to use. If it sounds like I am repeating myself, that is because I am. The same old rule applies. Test everything together. Take that five or ten extra minutes to ensure that you are using the right materials. If you take these steps, you might end up saving yourself hours constructing the garment. Or, better yet, you might save that garment from the trash heap or the closet corner.

An element that is often overlooked is the fabric store itself and it's staff. This detail is very important because the store can be your lifeline to a well-made project. Let's examine some fabric sources: the independent store, Uncle Joe who is visiting Hong Kong, the large chain stores, and the discount fabric chains.

You may be wondering "what does it matter where I get my fabric, as long as I find the look at the price I want?"

Often, the price comes with service. Independent stores will generally be more expensive. The availability of high-end fabrics is generally greater. The clerks are also generally more knowledgable. Ususally you deal with the owner who has been working with fabric for many, many years, or because the store is independently owned, the owner will hire staff who are highly knowledgable and professional. This is definitely to the benefit of the customer. When you have difficult technical questions, the staff of the small independent stores generally have the answer to help you, or they know who to direct you to for help. You can also find workshops, seminars, or classes at these small independent stores. They are usually of interest to the customer, because the store owner takes care to cater to the primary interests of the customer and tailors the classes or courses around them. Again, service is markedly better in the smaller independents because there is less square footage to cover. Combined with the fact that an independently run store can consider special orders for customers, and again, usually the store owner and hand-picked personnel serve you.

When Uncle Joe goes to visit Hong Kong, I might give him a couple of bucks to buy me a couple of yards of silk. Be well aware of the fact that unless Uncle Joe knows a Chinese person, he will not be able to find silk for any less money than in North America. The selection is also limited, and you are not there to aid in the selection of your precious silk. You might ask for chartreuse (which is actually green), and he might think it is a wonderful shade of pomegranate pink.

You'll end up with useless fabric. I would not rely on this particular source as an outlet for discovering new, beautiful, and wonderful fabrics.

Chain stores are wonderful things. I just finished a treasure hunt in our local chain fabric store and came away with several pieces of lining, some nice bottomweights, and some nice fabric to make a jacket, all for $100. When I say lining, I mean that I bought 10 meters each of four. Every fabric store has its raison d'être. If I go to a chain store, I am looking for sales and bargains. I'm not looking for a fine worsted Italian gabardine or printed silk. I think I would drop dead if I ever saw such a fabric in a chain store.

I quite often send my students to the chain stores, tell them exactly what they need, and instruct them not to ask the sales clerks for help. This may be construed as snobby, but it's the safest way. I prefer to go into a chain store with one of my students rather than them asking anyone for help. Usually, the student knows more about fabric than the sales clerks. I am not trying to demean chain store sales clerks. However, they often know little about fabric, and they are often passing through the sewing world en route to a career or education in some other field. This does not bode well for the consumer who needs help in selecting fabric, and who may sometimes makes their choices based on inappropriate advice.

Another place to find outrageous bargains is the discount jobber. You can spot this one a mile away. There are no price tags on anything, and everything is piled in heaps. You don't know the fabric content because nothing is labeled. Sometimes tags and tickets have been yanked or ripped off the flats or rolls. Flats are the straight pieces of cardboard that are half the width of the actual goods. Fabric for retail stores is folded onto flats. Fabric for design house samples are generally put on rolls. If you see rolls of fabric in a store, it generally means the fabric was intended for a manufacturer. Therefore, when you see these fabrics in retail stores, they are from fashion seasons past. That is not important. What is important is that they are in your fabric store right now.

Use the tests and evaluations given to see if these fabrics are actually worth purchasing. Just because it was a roll-end or a mill-end, it doesn't mean it is good.

You spend so much time constructing a garment, you deserve to have it last. I can't say it often enough–examine, pre-shrink, and test. You will save yourself hours of work, maybe some money, and quite possibly your sanity and love of sewing!

The previous information graciously written exclusively for _Sew Far Sew Good_ by:
Lenora Elkin
Atelier Plateau Collection Menzwear
Page 243

Fashion & Fiber Glossary

I've compiled a list of some of the terms you will find in your travels through the world of fiber and textile arts.

BUTTON TERMS

Ball B
A globe-shaped, spherical button, usually with a shank.

Covered
A button made by covering a button mold with fabric, leather, or stitches.

Fish eye
A sew-through button whose holes are set in a recess shaped like a fish.

Passementarie
Fancy buttons trimmed with braid, beads, metallic threads, sequins, and so forth.

Self shank
A one-piece button with a hole through a protrusion in the back.

Sew-through
A button with holes pierced through it.

Shank
A button with a U-shaped loop attached to the back for the purposes of attaching the button.

Toggle
An oblong button attached to a loop on one side of the garment and fastened by pulling it through a similar loop on the other side of the garment.

BEAD TERMS & COLORS
Graciously provided by Ornamental Resources.

AB
Aurora Borealis. Rainbow effect coating on transparent glass.

Alabaster
Translucent white.

Alexandrite
Pale light sapphire to lilac.

Amethyst
Purple.

Aqua
Light to medium blue-green.

Baroque
Irregular or free-form in shape as in a nugget; or deviating somewhat from the regular form, as in baroque ball, and baroque oval.

Chalcedony
Translucent light blue.

Coral
Various tones of opaque pink, orange or red, sometimes striated.

Foiled
Transparent or translucent bead in which silver or gold foil has been trapped within the body or the surface of the bead.

Fuschia
Transparent to opaque vivid reddish-purple.

Garnet
Deep wine red.

Hematite
Metallic, dark grey.

Iris
Rainbow effect coatings on opaque glass.

Jade
Various tones of translucent to opaque green.

Jonquil
Yellow.

Linings
Metallic or other colored coatings on the interior (hole) surface of a transparent bead. (The effect of color lining is also sometimes achieved through a colored inclusion closely surrounding the hole.)

Matte
Designates very low-luster surface that may also be referred to as "frosted" or "Laliqued". Matted transparent beads become translucent..

Millefiori
Italian for "1,000 flowers"; decoration consisting of slices of multi-colored glass rods (canes), usually pressed smooth (marvered) while hot, into the surface of a core piece of glass.

Pearl, ceylon
Opaque to translucent, pearlescent coatings in various colors.

Periwinkle
Medium, soft, opaque blue.

Rondelle, belly
Flattened ball with center hole.

Smaragd
Bright green.

FABRICS & FIBER TERMS

Alpaca
Hair fiber from the semi-domestic alpaca or from the llama, both animals belonging to the camel family.

Angora
Hair of the angora rabbit.

Astrakhan yarn
Yarn with exaggerated loops and imitating Astrakhan lamb fur.

Balanced
A weave structure with the warp and weft similar in size and spacing.

Basket weave
A balanced weave structure with warp and weft threads paired or grouped.

Batik
The Javanese art and method (introduced to England by way of Holland) of executing designs on textiles by covering the materials with wax in a pattern, dyeing the parts left exposed, removing the wax, and repeating the process when more than one dye is used.

Batiste
The French word for cambric, applied to a fine light fabric of the same texture, but differently finished; usually of cotton or linen.

Bedford
A woven fabric with prominent cords running in the direction of the warp.

Bias
A line on a piece of fabric that is diagonal to the warp and weft; true bias is a 45º angle.

Binder yarn
A strong yarn used to keep weaker yarn components in place.

Black wool
Any wool that is not white, according to industry standards.

Bleach
To remove natural or applied color or impurities from yarn or fiber by chemical treatment .

Blends
The combination of two or more different fibers in a yarn or fabric.

Blocking
Placing fabrics or yarn into a stretched position during drying to achieve a formed shape.

Bobbin
A spool for winding the weft to be used in a shuttle for weaving.
A spool used for winding thread for the bottom thread for sewing .

Boucle
A French word used to describe a curly or looped yarn.

Broadcloth
A fine, plain weave fabric.

Brocade
A weave structure in which there are two wefts, a structural one and a decorative one that appears in the area of the pattern only.

Brushed yarn
A hairy-surfaced yarn produced by teasing some of the fibers out of the yarn structure.

Bulked yarn
Yarn that is loftier and fluffier than the original yarn as a result of different treatment tecniques.

Cable
To twist two or more folded yarns together.

Cambric
A kind of fine white linen, originally made at Cambray in Flanders; also applies to an imitation made of cotton yarns.

Camel hair
The underfleece of the Bactrian camel.

Canvas
A strong or coarse unbleached cloth originally made of hemp or flax; more often applied to similar cloth made of cotton.

Carding
Disentangling fibers and creating a web of evenly aligned fibers.

Cashmere
The hair of the cashmere goat, which lives in the Himalayan mountain regions.

Challis
A fine silk and worsted fabric, very pliable and without gloss.

Chambray
A kind of gingham with a linen finish; often applied to a light-weight, light-colored denim.

Chenille
A novelty yarn with tufts of fiber inserted between binder yarns to create a fuzzy, textured surface.

Chino
A cotton twill cloth, usually khaki in color.

Chintz
Originally, a name used for the painted or stained calicos imported from India; now, a name for cotton cloths printed with designs of flowers, etc, in a number of colors—generally not less than five—usually glaze-finished.

Cluny
The name of a town in the Saône-et-Loire department of France, used to designate a kind of net or bobbin lace; also lace made in this style.

Chantilly
Applied to a delicate lace made originally at Chantilly in France.

Combing
Aligning long fibers in preparation of worsted spinning.

Cone
Yarn wound on a conical support.

Corduroy
A course, thick-ribbed cotton fabric. The name is often assumed to have developed from cord-du-roi, or the kings' cord (Fr.), apparently a label of English invention (an 1807 French article speaks of "...this king's cord from England") for advertment purposes—who wouldn't want to wear the King's cords?

Count
The method of describing the thickness of yarn by stating the mass per unit length, or the length per unit mass.

Crepe (fr.) or Crape
A thin, transparent or translucent gauze-like fabric that is plain woven without twill of Crepe yarns, usually of silk or a similar staple, then mechanically embossed so as to have a minutely wrinkled surface.

Crepe yarn
A tightly twisted, cabled yarn.

Damask
A rich silk fabric woven with elaborate designs and figures, often in a variety of colors; also applied to fabrics of other fiber made in the methods of the original damasks, used most often for furniture coverings, curtains, etc.

Denim
A twilled cotton weave, in which the warp is usually colored, and the weft is white.

Double ply
Two single threads twisted together to form a single thicker thread.

Duck
A strong, untwilled linen or cotton fabric, lighter and finer than canvas.

Dupioni
A rough silk fabric or thread woven from threads from double cocoons; also applied to imitations made by other processes.

Dyeing
Changing the color of a fiber, yarn, or fabric.

Ecru
The unbleached color of raw fibers, usually a light brown or beige, also natural.

Fancy yarn
Yarn deliberately produced with irregularities, also fantasy yarns.

Felting
Interlocking of the scales on hair fibers, usually created by applying moisture and pressure to fibers to create a formed mass.

Fiber
The basic raw material of yarns, natural or man-made, whose length is much greater than its breadth.

Flax
The fiber used to make linen.

Fleece
The shorn covering of a sheep.

Gabardine
A variety of twill woven cloth, usually of fine worsted.

Gauze
A very thin, transparent fabric of silk, linen, or cotton.

Gingham
A kind of cotton or linen cloth, woven of dyed yarn, often in stripes, checks, and patterns.

Greige
Gray goods; also, the color between gray and beige.

Hair
Animal fibers other than sheep's fleece or silk.

Hand, Handle
The touch or feel of a yarn or fabric.

Hand spindle
Any spinning spindle that is rotated by hand, rather than by wheel or machine.

Hank
Yarn wound loosely into a package.

Harness
A single heddle shaft.

Heather
Combination of colors in one yarn giving a depth of color.

Heddle
String, wire, flat steel (or other material) that encircles a warp thread, for the purpose of pulling it up separately from other warp threads.

Homespun
A coarse and loosely-woven material made in imitation of homemade cloth.

Homespun yarn
Yarn resembling hand-spun yarn.

Hopsacking
Originally the material of which hop-sacks were made, a course fabric composed of hem and jute, now applied to dress fabrics with roughened surfaces.

Ikat
A weaving technique producing a blurred effect by using tie-dyed warp and/or weft yarns.

Inkle loom
A small portable loom consisting of a framework with numerous pegs around which the warp is wound.

Jersey
A sweater; also, a fine machine-knitted fabric worked in stockinette stitch.

Lamb's wool
Fleece from a sheep up to eight months old.

Lawn
A kind of fine linen resembling cambric.

Linen
Yarn spun from flax fiber, and the fabric woven from these yarns.

Luster
The light reflection of a fiber.

Madras
Cotton fabric produced in Madras, India, especially the brightly checked or striped cottons, the colors of which run together in laundering.

Mercerized Cotton
Cotton fiber that has been treated under tension with caustic alkali, to create a shiny surface and a stronger fabric or yarn.

Merino wool
Wool from Merino sheep.

Metallic yarn
Generic name for yarns which include metal in their structure.

Mohair
Hair of the angora goat.

Musk ox
Animal from arctic North America, which produces an extremely fine fiber, quivit.

Muslin
A general name for the most delicately woven fabrics, including many varieties, most often used to check the drape or fit of a pattern before final sewing.

Nap
The surface of a fabric formed by fibers standing at an angle to the plane of the fabric.

Natural fibers
Naturally occurring fibers from animal, vegetable, or mineral sources.

Novelty yarns
Yarns with special spinning, folding, or textural effects. See also Fancy yarns.

Oiled wool
Unscoured wool.

Organdie/Organdy
A very fine and translucent kind of muslin.

Oxford
Plain, basket or twill-woven cotton often used for suiting. It is generally a fairly heavy cloth in which two yarns travel as one in the warp, and on filling yarn is equal in size to the two warp yarns.

Percale
A closely woven cotton fabric originally of French manufacture, with a higher finishing than muslin, and without gloss.

Pile
A textured fabric surface formed by protruding threads at more or less perpendicular angles to the fabric.

Pilling
The accumulation of fuzzy, fiber balls on the surface of a fabric.

Piqué
A rather stiff cotton fabric woven in a strongly ribbed or raised pattern.

Plissé
A piece of fabric shirred or gathered into narrow pleats; a gathering of pleats.

Ply
The number of folds in a yarn.

Plying
Twisting several singles to form a folded yarn.

Pongee/Chefoo silk
A soft unbleached kind of Chinese silk made from the cocoons of wild silk worms, which feeds on oak leaves.

Poplin
A mixed woven fabric consisting of a silk warp and worsted weft, and having a good corded suface; also applied to imitations.

Pure new wool
Wool marked in this way has to be made of new wool fiber that has not been used in an industrial process before.

Raddle
A comblike tool that can be clamped to the treadle loom during the beaming process to keep the warp threads evenly spaced.

Ramie
A very white and silky vegetable fiber, generally heat-resistant.

Rigid heddle
A combination reed and heddle with eyes in every other tooth for the threading of alternate warp threads; by pushing the rigid heddle down or up, one forms alternate sheds.

S-twist
The counter-clockwise twist direction in which a yarn is spun.

Sateen
A cotton or woolen fabric with a glossy surface like that of satin.

Satin
A silk fabric with a glossy surface on one side, produced by a method of weaving in which the thread of the warp is caught and looped by the weft only at certain intervals.

Seersucker
A thin linen or sometimes cotton fabric, striped and with a crimped or puckered surface, originally made in India; also applied to imitations.

Shetland wool
Wool from the fleece of Shetland sheep; also, wool from the fleece of sheep crossbred with Shetland sheep.

Silk
The fibers spun by the caterpillar of the silk moth to protect itself in its cocoon.

Skein
A loosely wound package of yarn.

Slub
A lump or bulge in a yarn.

Spin
To turn prepared staple fibers into yarn by twisting them.

Spool
A small, cylindrical yarn or thread package.

Spun silk
Yarn that is staple-spun from silk waste.

Swatch
A small sample of fabric or yarn.

Swift
A skein holder.

Terry
The loop raised in pile weaving left uncut; an absorbent cotton or linen cloth used for making towels, beachwear, etc.

Top
A continuous roving made of combed fiber.

Tusseh
Wild silk; also spelled tusser, tussor, and tussore.

Twist
The action of spinning yarn; also, the direction of the spin.

Velour
A woolen dress fabric with a velvet pile.

Velvet
A textile fabric of silk, having a short, dense, and smooth piled surface; often applied to imitations.

Velveteen
A fabric having the appearance or surface of velvet, but made of cotton in place of silk.

Voile
A thin semi-transparent cotton or woolen material much used for blouses and dresses.

Warp
The longitudinal fixed yarns on a loom.

Web
A sheet of prepared fiber.

Weft
The crosswise yarns woven in and out of the warp.

Woof
Another name for weft.

Wool
The fiber from the fleece of sheep.

Woolen
Made of wool fiber; also, yarn spun on the woolen system; also fabric woven from this yarn.

Worsted
Yarn spun on the worsted system; also, fabric made from yarn spun on the worsted system.

Yarn
Any form of prepared fiber twisted into a continuous length.

Yarn size
The thickness or count of the yarn.

Z-twist
The clockwise twist direction in which a yarn is spun.

FASHION TERMS

These terms will describe a few basic styles you will want to become familiar with when purchasing patterns, designing garments, or describing a garment accurately. You will be able to find enlarged versions of some of these illustrations throughout the book. They are include here to offer an easy-reference for your design ideas.

BODICE STYLES

French dart

Princess

Strapless

Surplice

CUFF STYLES

Barrel/Band

Fitted

French

Gauntlet

Roll

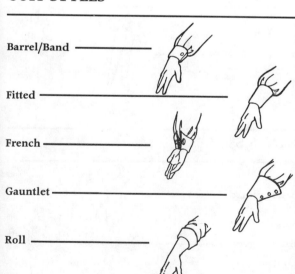

DRESS STYLES

A-line

Basic fitted

Cheongsam

Flapper

Jumper

Long dinner

Princess

Sheath

Slip

Tent

JACKET/OUTERWEAR STYLES

Blazer

Bolero

Box/Chanel

Capelet

Cardigan

Pea Jacket

Safari

Shawl

Ski

Stole

Sweater

Trench

LONG SET-IN SLEEVE STYLES

¾ length

Bell

Bishop

Juliet ————————

Leg-o-mutton ————————

Long fitted ————————

Long lantern ————————

Peasant ————————

Shirt ————————

NECKLINE STYLES

Bateau/boat ————————

Crew ————————

Decollette ————————

Deep cowl ————————

Deep square ————————

Drawstring ————————

Funnel ————————

Halter ————————

Keyhole ————————

Off-the-shoulder ————————

One shoulder ————————

Plain/jewel ————————

Scalloped ————————

Scoop ————————

Sweet heart ————————

U ————————

V ————————

Wide cowl ————————

Wide square ————————

PANTS LENGTHS

Listed by length, rather than alphabetically.

Hot pants ————————

Boy pants ————————

Jamaica ————————

Bermuda ————————

Deck pants ————————

Clam diggers ————————

Toreador ————————

Capri ————————

Slacks ————————

PANTS STYLES

Basic tailored ————————

Hip huggers ————————

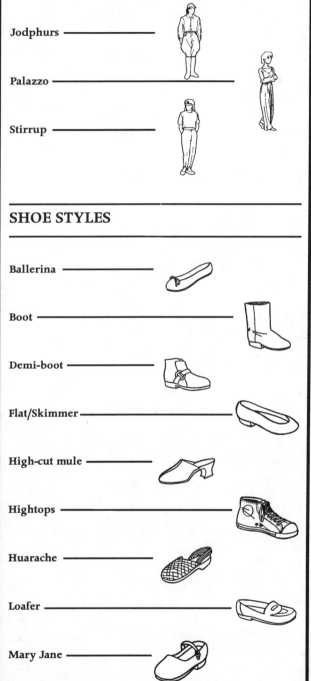

Jodphurs ————————

Palazzo ————————

Stirrup ————————

SHOE STYLES

Ballerina ————————

Boot ————————

Demi-boot ————————

Flat/Skimmer ————————

High-cut mule ————————

Hightops ————————

Huarache ————————

Loafer ————————

Mary Jane ————————

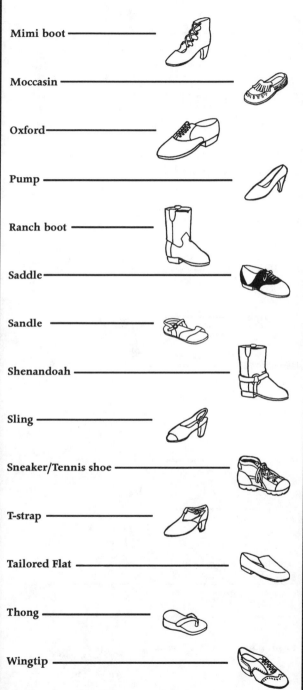

Mimi boot ————————

Moccasin ————————

Oxford ————————

Pump ————————

Ranch boot ————————

Saddle ————————

Sandle ————————

Shenandoah ————————

Sling ————————

Sneaker/Tennis shoe ————————

T-strap ————————

Tailored Flat ————————

Thong ————————

Wingtip ————————

SHORT SET-IN SLEEVE STYLES

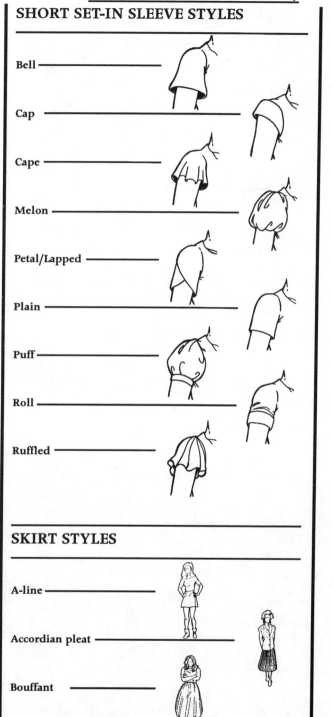

Bell ————————

Cap ————————

Cape ————————

Melon ————————

Petal/Lapped ————————

Plain ————————

Puff ————————

Roll ————————

Ruffled ————————

SKIRT STYLES

A-line ————————

Accordian pleat ————————

Bouffant ————————

Broomstick

Circular

Cluster-pleated

Dirndl

Flared

Full

Gored

Inverted pleat

Kilt

Long dinner

Mini

Pegged

Straight-fitted

Surplice

Tiered

Wrapped

SKIRT TOP STYLES

Banded

Bandless

Elasticised

Hip Hugger

Paper bag waist

Pointed

Yoke

VEST STYLES

Double-breasted

Fingertip

Long vest

Single-breasted

Weskit

WAISTLINE STYLES

Dropped

Empire

Midriff yoke

Normal-fitted

Pointed

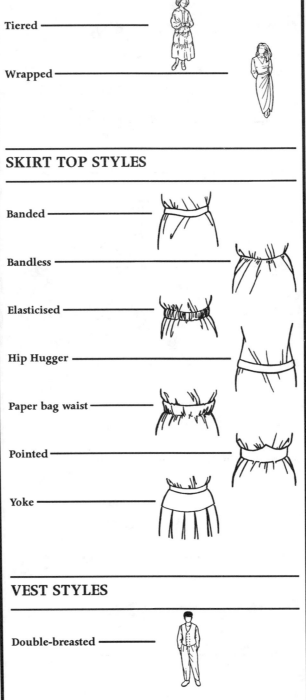
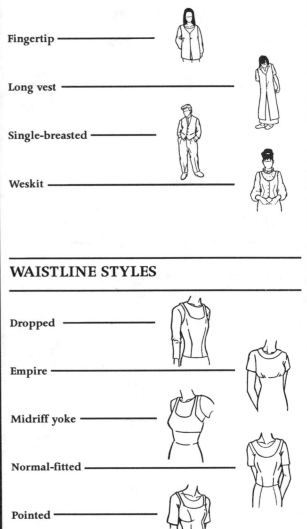

Special Thanks

―――――――――― +≡+≡+ ――――――――――

Although it would be impossible to thank everyone, I've included everyone I could.
Please know that you have my thanks, even if I've missed your name.

This book would not have been possible without the help and support of many people:

Gerard Smith has supported me through my days and nights, and loved and supported me in the darkest hours after my mother passed away.

Firstar Bank of Ames and its staff, particularly Verne Bates, Maggie Wilcox, and Sue Selby-Gore, have helped me work out the financial wrinkles.

Dave Hunziker was patient while we "set up shop" in various areas of the house, causing erratic mealtimes.

The women on the Prodigy Beading Board have supported me and kept me entertained.

AOL has helped keep me connected with the world.

My professors at ISU allowed me more flexibility than an average student and encouraged me in many ways.

Grant Moser flogged himself mercilessly to edit the scrambled mess I dared to call a book.

John and Marsha Ahrens gave me encouragement, despite their total lack of interest in "business".

Christopher Rich pulled through with the illustrations in record time.

Ken Patton has offered his advice and support, and most of all, his ideas on saving printing costs.

Michelle Rushing provided fast and accurate data-entry of hundreds of companies, for an unheard of price. You can reach her at The Office Assistant, (515) 276-5171 if you need similar services.

Bruce Meyerson edited our introductory letter so that companies would take us seriously.

Guilio Rammairone provided immoral support and free advertising in *Staten Island Parent* and *Brooklyn Parent* magazines.

Michael Golub helped us choose and purchase the Power Macintosh and other hardware when we needed it most.

Mary Dengler was there with soothing massages when the stress became too much.

Bibliography

Many different books, magazines, and other publications have provided me with information and inspiration for this book. They are listed here.

Bierce, Ambrose. The Devil's Dictionary. New York: Dover Publications, Inc.

Boyd, Margaret A. The Crafts Supply Sourcebook. Cincinnati: Betterway Books. ©1994

Brown, Rachael. The Weaving, Spinning, and Dyeing Book. New York: Alfred A. Knopf, Inc. ©1978

Burgess, Maryanne. Designer Sourcebook. Chicago: Carikean Publishing. ©1995

Creative Sewing Ideas. The Editors of Cy Decosse, Inc, in cooperation with the Sewing Education Department, Singer Sewing Company. Minnetonka, Minnesota: Cy Decosse Inc. ©1990

Crown, Fenya. The Fabric Guide for People Who Sew. New York: Grosset & Dunlap. ©1973

Dittman, Margaret. The Fabric Lover's Scrapbook. Radnor, Pennsylvania: Chilton Book Company. ©1988

Funk, Charles Earle Jr. & Sr. Horsefeathers & other Curious Words. New York: Harper & Row. © 1986

Gadney, Alan. Fabric & Fiber Contests. New York: Facts on File. ©1983

Gioello, Debbie Ann. Understanding Fabrics: From Fiber to Finished Cloth. New York: Fairchild Publications. ©1982

Green, Marilyn V. The Button Book. Radnor, Pennsylvania: Chilton Book Company. ©1991

Ingham, Rosemary & Covey, Liz. The Costume Technician's Handbook.

Portsmouth, New Hampshire: Heineman Educational Books, Inc. ©1992

Thompson, Bobbie Jean. Scarf Tying Magic. Washington, D.C.: Acropolis Books, Ltd. ©1988

Kenzle, Linda Fry. Embellishments: Adding Glamour to Garments. Radnor, Pennsylvania: Chilton Book Company ©1993

Le Mot Juste. New York: Vintage Books, A Division of Random House, Inc. Edited By: John Buchanan-Brown, Jennifer Cang, John Crawley, Barbara Galuska, Brendan McCabe, Gilman Parsons, Carol Steiger, and Kate Williams. © 1981

Lindahl, Judy. Decorating With Fabrics. New York: Butterick Publishing. ©1977

McCall's Sewing Book. Random House. ©1963

O'Neill, Jaime. What Do You Know: The Ultimate Test of Common (and Not So Common) Knowledge. New York: Bantam Books. © 1990

Pinkham, Mary Ellen. Mary Ellen's Giant Book of Helpful Hints. New York: Wings Press. © 1994

Professional Degree Programs in the Visual and Performing Arts. Princeton, New Jersey: Peterson's. © 1995

Quong, Rose. Chinese Written Characters, Their Wit and Wisdom. Boston: Beacon Press. © 1968

Randall, Bernice. When is a Pig a Hog, A Guide to Confoundingly Related English Words. New York: Prentice Hall. © 1991

Tuckman, Diane and Janas, Jan. The Complete book of Silk Painting. Cincinnati: F&W Publications, Inc. © 1992

Magazines, Journals, and Other Publications

Bead & Button. Seattle: Conterie Press

Butterick Home Catalog. New York: Butterick Co., Inc.

Chun, Rene. World's Oldest Fabric is Now It's Newest, New York Times: Styles, Sunday, June 25, 1995. New York Times. © 1995

Creative Needle. Lookout Mountain, Tennessee: Needle Publishing, Inc.

Handcraft Illustrated. Brookline, Massachusetts: Boston Common Press Limited Partners.

Industrial Hemp. Ojai, California: Hemptech. © 1995

Lapidary Journal. Devon, Pennsylvania: Lapidary Journal, Inc.

McCall's Patterns. New York: McCall Pattern Co.

Piecework, All This By Hand. Loveland, Colorado: Interweave Press.

Quilter's Newsletter Magazine. Golden, Colorado: Leman Publications.

Sewing Decor. Peoria, Illinois: PJS Publications.

Sew News. Peoria, Illinois: PJS Publications.

Vogue Patterns. New York: Butterick Co., Inc.

Index

Your page-by-page reference to <u>Sew Far Sew Good</u>.

Company Information Sheets

Your company listing is absoloutely free, just fill out the following forms, and return them to Oracle Publications. Photocopies are acceptable.

If you are interested in a free listing, I have included the forms for you to fill out that will provide us with the body of information to be included in the book. Include everything you consider to be important. Do not hesitate to write on separate sheets of paper, and include them with your completed form. Please note that I may need to edit information for clarity.

If you would like your company to have a more noticeable presence in Sew Far Sew Good, you are welcome to use any or all of the following suggestions.

Send samples: You are invited to send samples of any unique books, kits, novelties, etc. that you carry and think may be of interest to potential customers. I will choose some of the most interesting to be featured on the cover of the book. These items will be identified inside. I will also review any samples you send and include my review with your listing. Since these samples cannot be returned (except in special cases, please call), please send only a small quantity. All samples will be kept on file for further reference as the interactive CD-ROM and updated versions of Sew Far Sew Good go into production.

Offer ideas: Please include any tips or tricks that you think our readers may be interested in (a hint on how to use one of the products you offer?). I will try to make space enough for all. If we include your suggestion, you and your business will be credited on the same page.

Make a special offer: Offer a special discount for the readers of my book (ie. 10% off first purchase]. It will help you track inquiries and bring in new customers. If you decide to make a special offer, your organization will be listed on the cover with other companies offering discounts and specials to readers Sew Far Sew Good..

Note that throughout the book, there are obvious differences in the listings, depending on the amount of information we receive. I will be able to provide a more complete listing if you err on the side of wordiness, rather than brevity.

Include all unique or hard-to-find products or services you offer, they will help to set you apart from everyone else. If you have a catalog, please include a copy with your reply. It will greatly aid in making your listing as complete as possible.

Information Page for:
Mail Order/Clubs & Associations/Shops

COMPANY NAME:

CONTACT (not included in publication, for business use only):

ADDRESS:

PHONE/FAX/E-MAIL/WWW:

PAYMENT ACCEPTED (please circle):   Check   Money Order   MC   Visa   Amex   Disc   COD

MAIL ORDER: ☐ Yes ☐ No   SHIPPING OPTIONS (please circle):   UPS   USPS   FedEx

MINIMUM ORDER:

MEMBERSHIP DUES:

CLUB/ASSOCIATION BENEFITS:

SPECIAL DISCOUNTS/OFFERS (for example, 10% off first order with mention of book, wholesale to retailers, etc.):

SERVICES/MERCHANDISE   (please list all applicable, add another page if necessary):

OTHER INFORMATION, any information you would like prospective customers to know about, for example; company history or philosophy, etc. (add an extra page if necessary):

CATALOG PRICE (is it refundable with an order?)

Information Page for:
Contests/Travel Groups/Juried Shows/Retreats

COMPANY NAME:

CONTACT (not included in publication, for business use only):

ADDRESS:

PHONE/FAX/E-MAIL/WWW:

PAYMENT ACCEPTED (please circle):   Check   Money Order   MC   Visa   Amex   Disc

HOW MANY YEARS HAVE YOU BEEN HOLDING THIS EVENT?:

TIME OF YEAR/MONTH:

APPROXIMATE COSTS:

SPECIAL DISCOUNTS/OFFERS (for example, 10% off first reservation with mention of book, wholesale to retailers, etc.):

WHAT IS THE EVENT GEARED TOWARD, WHO WOULD BE INTERESTED?:

OTHER INFORMATION, any information you would like prospective customers to know about, for example; company history or philosophy, etc. (add an extra page if necessary):

List of Subject Headings

COMPANY NAME: _____

Here is the list of Subject Headings planned for my book. Please check all those that apply to your business, and I will do my best to make sure that your name is listed under each category.

Bear in mind that this page will also provide a helpful nudge, reminding you of services and merchandise that you offer, while you fill out your statement on the Information Page. Please return this page along with the others.

Also remember that under each subject heading will be a list of which products or services you offer. For instance, under silk, you could list crepe de chine, jacquard and noil. If you are as detailed as possible, your products will be listed in this way. If you do not provide this information, your company name will still appear.

- ☐ Accessory Findings
- ☐ Beads
- ☐ Blank Fabric/Clothing to Decorate
- ☐ Books/Magazines
- ☐ Business Resources Information for Small Businesses
- ☐ Business Suppliers/Wholesale
- ☐ Buttons
- ☐ Classes & Instruction Please list topics
- ☐ Clubs/Associations Local Guilds & National Associations
- ☐ Contests/Shows Regular Shows, Yearly Judgings, etc. Please list season/month held, general description, and deadlines for entries, reservations, retail enquires.
- ☐ Collectibles/Novelties
- ☐ Antiques or Sewing Related notepads, figurines, etc.
- ☐ Costuming Supplies & Services
- ☐ Custom Materials/Services Please let us know what services or materials you offer, for instance, color matching, help lines, etc.

- ☐ Doll/Soft Toy Making Supplies
- ☐ Dyes/Paints
- ☐ Embroidery & Needlework Supplies
- ☐ Fabrics
  - ☐ Acrylic
  - ☐ Cashmere
  - ☐ Cotton
  - ☐ Hemp
  - ☐ Linen
  - ☐ Miscellaneous
  - ☐ Novelty Prints
  - ☐ Polyester
  - ☐ Rayon
  - ☐ Silk
  - ☐ Wool
  - Synthetic
  - ☐ Miscellaneous
- ☐ Feathers
- ☐ Hatmaking Supplies
- ☐ Laces & Lacemaking
- ☐ Leathers/Furs–Include Sequins, Rhinestones, Photo Transfers, Kimonos, etc.
- ☐ Outdoor Gear
- ☐ Patterns
  - ☐ Bridal & Special Occasion
  - ☐ Children & Infants
  - ☐ Costume

- ☐ Full Figure/Big & Tall
- ☐ Men's
- ☐ Project Patterns
- ☐ Women's
- ☐ Project Kits
- ☐ Quilting & Patchwork Supplies
- ☐ Sewing Machines
- ☐ Sewing Notions/Dressforms
- Various Accessories
- ☐ Silk Ribbon Embroidery
- ☐ Smocking & Heirloom Sewing Supplies
- ☐ Software & internet Adresses
- ☐ Snaps , Zippers & Other Closures
- ☐ Spinning Supplies & Raw Fibers
- ☐ Thread
- ☐ Travel, Tours & Retreats
- ☐ Trims, Cords & Tassels
- ☐ Upholstery Fabrics
- ☐ Videos & Other Media
- ☐ Weaving Supplies
- ☐ Yarn, Crochet & Knitting Supplies

- ☐ Other _____

Information Sheet for:
Books/Authors/Publishers/Bookstores

For those of you who have written a book, published a book, or carry related books or magazines in your store, to provide me with correct and complete information. If you need more space, please make copies as needed, or print the information directly from a computer system.

Please remember to provide all of the information requested, as this is the core of your book's information listing as my readers will see it. A listing providing complete information, as opposed to one without may be the deciding factor on whether to buy your book(s).

TITLE:

AUTHORS(S):

SUBJECT DESCRIPTION:

COST:

NUMBER OF PAGES: NUMBER OF ILLUSTRATIONS (b&w or color?):

OTHER PERTINENT INFORMATION (anything you feel is important that the reader know about this book):

TITLE:

AUTHORS(S):

SUBJECT DESCRIPTION:

COST:

NUMBER OF PAGES: NUMBER OF ILLUSTRATIONS (b&w or color?):

OTHER PERTINENT INFORMATION (anything you feel is important that the reader know about this book):

Registration Sheet

To receive your free update, please fill out these pages and return it to Oracle Publications. No photocopies will be accepted.

Name:

_____

Street Address::

_____

City, State, Zip:

_____

Country:

_____

Phone Number:

_____

The following questions are completely voluntary, and are not necessary for the registration of your copy of Sew Far Sew Good. We ask that you answer as many as possible, so that we may better serve your interests in the future.

Why did you purchase a copy of _Sew Far Sew Good_?

_____

_____

On a scale of 1-10, with ten being the highest, how would you rate _Sew Far Sew Good_ overall?

_____

How would you rate our sideline information?

_____

How would you rate our source information?

_____

What suggestions can you offer for improvement?

_____

_____

_____

_____

Do you own a computer?

_____

If Yes, do you have access to the internet?

_____

What hobbies do you and others in your home enjoy other than fiber and fabric arts?

❑ Cooking
❑ Gardening
❑ Athletics/Sports
❑ Collectibles or Antiques
❑ Pets and Animals

❑ Art, Painting, Drawing, or Sculpting
❑ Outdoor Sports, Hiking, Camping
❑ Automotive
❑ Travel

Do you own your own business?

_____

Do you work professionally with fabrics and fiber?

_____

What is your profession?

_____

Do you sew?

_____

Why does sewing appeal to you?

_____

_____

Do you make your own attire?

If No, why not?

❏ I Don't Have
   Enough Time
❏ Too Expensive
❏ I Can't Find The
   Right Fabrics

❏ I Don't Have the
   Right Equipment
❏ I Don't Have the
   Skills to Make a
   Professional Outfit.

Do you weave?

Why does weaving appeal to you?

Do you knit?

Why does knitting appeal to you?

Approximately how much do you spend per month on your fabric/fiber arts?

Do you attend consumer shows for sewing and fiber crafts?

What would you like to see more of in your update of _Sew Far Sew Good_?

If you had the opportunity to share your favorite timesaving hint with thousands of fabric and fiber enthusiasts such as yourself, what would you suggest?

If we use this tip in the update of _Sew Far Sew Good_, how would you like your name to appear? For example: Tip provided by: Your Name, (sewing, weaving enthusiast, etc.).

You know that with this registration you will receive your 1997 update free, but if you provide us with five new names and phone numbers of companies that are not in this edition of _Sew Far Sew Good_, we will send you a 1998 update for free.

Please note, this offer will apply only to those with at least three original suggestions that have not been sent in by others–so hurry to be the first, and be as creative as you can!

Mail To:
ORACLE PUBLICATIONS
1226 Carroll Avenue
Ames, Iowa 50010